EMPIRE
Milan
Turin
Venice
Trieste
Zagreb
Genoa
CROATIA
SLAVONIA
Sava
VOJVODINA
Karlovci
Zemun
Una R.
R.
Otočac
Banja Luka
LIKA
BOSNIA
WALLACHIA
ITALY
Livorno
Florence
Zara
(Zadar)
Zvornik
Travnik
Belgrade
SERBIA
Bucharest
DALMATIA
Sarajevo
Drina R.
Kragujevac
Danube R.
BLACK SEA
Split
Adriatic Sea
HERCE-
GOVINA
ŽUPA
BULGARIA
Metković
Novi Pazar
Civitavecchia
Dubrovnik
Kosovo
Sofia
OTTOMAN
Rome
Prizren
Plovdiv
Skoplje
SEE DETAIL
MAP ABOVE
ALBANIA
Vardar R.
Constantinople (Istanbul)
Bosporus
Naples
MACEDONIA
Dardanelles
Aegean
EMPIRE
Athens
MOREA
Sea
MEDITERRANEAN
SEA
Scale of Miles
0
100
200
300
Vaughn Gray

Njegoš, Bishop Rade of Montenegro, is the greatest poet the Serbian language has known. *The Mountain Wreath,* the historical epic poem that is his masterpiece, invents as much as it confirms Montenegrin nationality. A man of action as well as bishop and literary artist, Njegoš ruled his country from the age of eighteen until the year of his death, 1851, at the age of thirty-seven. In this role he continued the struggle to maintain his country's hard-won independence.

Marked by physical beauty and singular sensibility, Njegoš embodied the very soul of his nation. It comes as no surprise that Djilas, a child of the fierce Montenegrin tradition of freedom as much as he is the product of the traditions of European Marxism, should have turned to the writing of Njegoš's life. As readers of *Land Without Justice* will recall, Njegoš lore was part of the air Djilas breathed as a boy. This massive and scholarly critical biography is an international literary event. Written by a man who has himself become a historical figure, Djilas's *Njegoš* belongs to the heroic tradition of prison literature.

NJEGOŠ

BY MILOVAN DJILAS

The New Class

Land Without Justice

Anatomy of a Moral

Conversations with Stalin

Montenegro

The Leper and Other Stories

Njegoš

PETAR II PETROVIĆ NJEGOŠ

NJEGOŠ

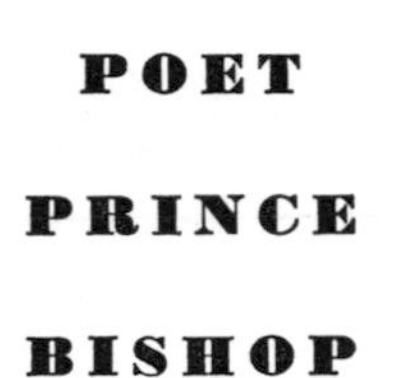

POET

PRINCE

BISHOP

by

MILOVAN DJILAS

Introduction and Translation by Michael B. Petrovich

Preface by William Jovanovich

Harcourt, Brace & World, Inc., New York

First edition
Library of Congress Catalog Card Number: 66–12915
Printed in the United States of America

ПОСВЕЋУЈЕМ ОВУ КЊИГУ
ВЛАДИМИРУ ЈОВАНОВИЋУ

Note on the Spelling and Pronunciation of Serbo-Croat Words and Names

s = s as in sink
š = sh as in shift
c = ts as in mats
č = ch as in charge
ć = similar to, but lighter than, č—as in arch
ž = j as in French *jour*
z = z as in zodiac
j = y as in yell
nj = ni as in minion
g = g as in go
dj = g as in George
lj = li as in million

Preface

On the publication in the United States of *Njegoš,* precisely four years will have passed since Milovan Djilas was returned to prison on April 7, 1962. He is still there, inside a stone-walled cell, suffering uncertain health and suffering, in the more complete sense, his most certain courage. Milovan Djilas is called the world's most famous prisoner, yet he has received, ironically, little attention and practically no help from the democratic peoples who value the instance and example of free thinking and individual dissent. There are still other ironies evoked by this publication. The present book, which may be considered Djilas's *magnum opus,* was written in jail during the period of his earlier arrest (1957 to 1961) under the communist regime in Yugoslavia that he himself helped to found. He will presumably not see this book in print, as indeed he has not seen two other books that were also written in jail and published since his rearrest, *Montenegro* (1963) and *The Leper* (1964). Not any of these books has appeared in his own language, nor is any likely to, although *Njegoš* is without doubt a great work of Serbo-Croatian literature.

The several penal terms of Milovan Djilas add up to thirteen years, of which he has endured eight. Unless he is pardoned, and should he live, he will remain in his cell another five years, until 1971, when he will be sixty years of age. Currently he is seen only by his wife and young son, whose visit is confined to a half hour once a month. He traverses the interminable days by reading and writing and is said now to be translating Milton's *Paradise Lost* from English into Serbian. How characteristic is this of his subtle, seeking mind may be seen in this book. Restating Milton is still another act that confirms, and reverberates, the comparison between Djilas and the great subject of this book, Petar II Petrović Njegoš of Montenegro, a comparison that Professor Petrovich skillfully draws in the Introduction that follows.

The central philosophical work by Njegoš is *The Ray of the Microcosm.* Like *Paradise Lost* it attempts to comprehend the unresolved struggle between good and evil that is told in the myth of Satan's rebellion against Heaven. This is the conflict within each man that by extension delineates the affairs of all men; and it runs, like the symbolic gold and black threads on the Montenegrin national headgear, through the lives and works of both Djilas and Njegoš. Knowing that good and evil are opposite but also complementary, always presenting a terrible choice between the short gain and the long truth, such knowing is a hard thing. It is a form of self-knowledge that has given pain to Milovan Djilas —the third color on the Montenegrin cap is red—but it has also sustained him. In his autobiography, *Land Without Justice,* the paradox of combining within oneself contradictory forces, of perceiving simultaneously both the dream and the reality, of living both within and without one's time, is expressed in terms that must be read against his present suffering. "A man can fight everything except his own times," he writes at one point, but then again, "The strongest are those who renounce their own times and become a living part of those yet to come. The strongest, and the rarest." In another context, the Yugoslav writer Ivo Andrić quotes a line from Njegoš that he says echoes like a sigh: "Woe to him who cares for you."

This book is the last of the manuscripts written by Milovan Djilas that I have had in my possession as his friend and publisher. I handed it to Professor Petrovich in 1962, and he has worked on it over a period of three years, not only translating Djilas's complex and oftentimes variable style but also verifying the sources that Djilas himself, because he had no access to references while in prison, had perforce to recall from memory. His translation is a work of superb scholarship, and it is more. Perhaps for Michael Petrovich as for me, both of us second-generation Serbs in America, there is a kind of inevitability in our connection with this work. By land, seven thousand miles distant from the sear, stony highlands of

Montenegro, but immeasurably distant in time, I grew to manhood on the plain beneath the highlands of Colorado. There, a few Montenegrins worked at will, yet like all Montenegrins they were somehow in exile, and it was from one of them, my father, who would sit evenings playing his gusle, that I first heard as a small child the lines of the epic poetry of Njegoš. It all seemed sad and lonely then, and it does now.

WILLIAM JOVANOVICH

Briarcliff Manor, New York
February 7, 1966

And all this vast array of things confus'd
Hath yet some rhythmic Harmony and Law.
—Njegoš, *The Mountain Wreath*

Introduction

by Michael B. Petrovich

This book is about Petar II Petrović Njegoš, Prince-Bishop of Montenegro from 1830 to 1851 and the greatest poet of the Serbian people.

It is about a man who is hardly known outside of Yugoslavia except to a few specialists. He ruled a minuscule land which was not even recognized as an independent state until over a quarter of a century after his death. Furthermore, Montenegro no longer existed after 1918 except as a province of Yugoslavia, one few tourists have ever visited or, for that matter, intend to visit. Though a ruler, he made little impression on European politics of his day and is not even mentioned in most history textbooks, even the thick ones. As for his poetry, it is practically impossible to appreciate its greatness except in the original language, and even translations are hard to come by.

All this would ordinarily not make for a very promising book. Indeed, the subject seems more suited to one of those dull dissertations about obscure figures whom some apprentice scholar is always grateful to dig up for the price of a doctorate. Worse yet, the book could be yet another attempt by a nationalist from a small, neglected country intent on proving to the world the worth of his culture and the greatness of his compatriots. However, despite its scholarship, this book is not an academic treatise, nor was it written especially for a non-Yugoslav public. Rather, it is an extraordinary book by an extraordinary author about an extraordinary ruler and poet of an extraordinary country. The reader deserves to know why.

To begin with the work itself, this is the first book in English or in any Western language about Njegoš. It is also the first major work in any language, including Serbo-Croatian, to treat Njegoš fully, in all his aspects—as ruler, poet, bishop, and man. This book is unusual further in that though it is a translation, it is being published as such before publication in its original language. Whether the original will ever be published is doubtful as long as the author continues to be in political disfavor in his own country, Yugoslavia. The work was completed in Sremska Mitrovica Penitentiary, between 1957 and 1959, and it thus joins the ranks of distinguished prison literature.

Many readers who pick up this book will probably do so not for its subject, but for its author. Milovan Djilas is undoubtedly the most famous political prisoner in the world today. Not since Leon Trotsky has any Communist given such a jolt to the Communist movement and its leaders. He is best known abroad as the author of the most important ideological treatise against the Communist party published since the end of the Second World War: *The New Class,* which was first published in this country in 1957. More recently, his book *Conversations with Stalin,* which appeared in 1962, only deepened the rift between himself and his erstwhile comrades.

Djilas's break with the Communist party was not like that of the intellectual converts of the thirties who lost their faith in "the god that failed." Many, like such well-known Western examples as Louis Fischer, Stephen Spender, and André Gide, were essentially "fellow-travelers"; even those who were formally party members, and all were not, never fully submitted their personalities to the party mold. Moreover, many of these ex-Communist literati—such as Arthur Koestler and Richard Wright—were never close to the mainsprings of party power. Djilas's experience is different. In many ways the Westerner he most parallels is Ignazio Silone, of Italy. Both came from poor mountain regions—Montenegro and the Abruzzi Apennines. Both became Communists in childhood: Silone was arrested at seventeen even before the Italian Communist party was founded, in 1921, while Diljas remembers declaring his adherence to Communism at the age of seven. Both wrote books and edited newspapers. Both worked in the underground, rose high in party circles, visited Moscow and suffered shocks of recognition. Both remained loyal to socialism after their break with Communism, and both had hopes of a socialist alternative to the Communist party—a "Third Front," as Silone called it.

Yet Djilas went farther than even Silone. He fought the German and Italian forces of occupation during the Second World War as a Partisan leader, and came to power with Tito. In his heyday Djilas was surely one of the four or five most influential Communist leaders in Yugoslavia. Unlike the fellow-travelers and the littérateurs, therefore, Djilas knew what it was to wield power after a successful revolution and to bear the responsibility for making the dream come true in the world of reality. When he denounced the Communist party to which he had given his whole life, he did it not in some non-Communist country, but in Yugoslavia itself, where he was subject to whatever penalties the Communist regime cared to inflict on him. And he has borne the consequences, not once, but repeatedly.

Though this book is about Njegoš, and not about Djilas, one cannot understand it fully without delving into the author's own experiences and motivations.

Djilas's quarrel with the Communist party of Yugoslavia first emerged in October 1953 when he began to publish a series of articles in the Communist daily *Borba (Struggle)*. At first, owing partly to Djilas's involved style of writing and partly to his reputation for orthodoxy, these articles did not arouse much attention. But then, as the series lengthened, they began to exert a cumulative effect. It became clear that here was blow after blow against the dictatorship of a bureaucratic Communist party machine. On December 20, 1953, he wrote, "Today no party or group, not even the working class itself, can claim to express the objective needs of the whole society. . . . The only possible answer is more democracy, more free discussion, freer elections." Though Djilas was rebuked, he shot back open replies at his most exalted critics.

The showdown came with an article Djilas published in the January 1954 issue of the Yugoslav Communist party's leading literary and political review, *Nova Misao (New Thought)*. It was a scathing satire of the high life of the Communist aristocracy, "those who own automobiles, travel in sleeping cars, buy their food and clothes in special stores and have become convinced that their exclusive right to these rare privileges is so natural and logical that only fools or the most hardened enemies could possibly question it." As though to emphasize the need for a new socialist humanism, Djilas chose to focus his story on a young woman, the wife of a Communist general, who had been ostracized by Communist high society because she was an actress. "Her profession is such," says one of these aristocratic Communists, "that she can only be a prostitute." Djilas was clearly referring to the troubles of a fellow-Montenegrin, General Peko Dapčević, and his actress wife. The article had an electrifying effect. The party hierarchy, no doubt urged on by their womenfolk, placed a ban on Djilas's further writing, and he was haled before a special plenary meeting of the Central Committee of the party on January 16 and 17, 1954. Tito himself presided on the first day. Djilas was rebuked by all, but simply told to mend his ways.

He did not. On the contrary, he later gave an interview to the Belgrade correspondent of the New York *Times* in which he denounced what he called attempts "to frighten the democratic elements in the party." Djilas's friend Vladimir Dedijer had given a similar interview to the London *Times*. Both men were brought to trial before a Belgrade district court to face charges under Article 118 of the new criminal code dealing with propaganda hostile to the state and the people. Djilas and Dedijer were given suspended sentences of eighteen months and six months respectively, subject to good behavior. Djilas was expelled from the Central Committee of the Communist party; soon thereafter he resigned from his two government posts, the Vice-Premiership and the Presidency of the Assembly.

Djilas found the terms intolerable. In December of 1956 he was brought before a Belgrade district court again, this time for statements concerning the Hungarian uprising which were deemed injurious to the best interests of the Yugoslav state. He was sentenced to three years' imprisonment, and was sent to the penitentiary at Sremska Mitrovica, some fifty miles from Belgrade. Ironically, this was the same prison in which he had spent three years—1933 to 1936—as a Communist prisoner of the royal Yugoslav government. Meanwhile he had completed the manuscripts of two books, which were sent to publishers in the United States. With the appearance of the first of these—*The New Class*—he was brought out of jail in October 1957 long enough to stand trial again. He was sentenced for "slandering Yugoslavia" and was returned to prison for another four years, twenty months of which he spent in solitary confinement.

Though *Life* Magazine had previously reprinted some of Djilas's earlier articles, the American and Western public first really began to take note of Djilas when *The New Class* appeared. No anti-Communist had ever written as devastating and telling an indictment of the Communist ideology. He argued that Communist dictatorship was more absolute than the most absolute monarchy, for it claimed a complete monopoly over truth, based on the infallibility of a science. "Beginning with the premise that they alone know the laws which govern society," he wrote, "Communists arrive at the oversimplified and unscientific conclusion that this alleged knowledge gives them the power and the exclusive right to change society and to control its activities. This is the major error of their system." The title of the book, *The New Class,* comes from Djilas's characterization of Communism as a form of state capitalism. "Ownership," he says, "is nothing other than the right of profit and control. If one defines class benefits by this right, the Communist states have seen, in the final analysis, the origin of a new form of ownership or of a new ruling and exploiting class"—namely, the Communist party. "As defined by Roman law," he wrote elsewhere in the book, "property constitutes the use, enjoyment, and disposition of material goods. The Communist political bureaucracy uses, enjoys, and disposes of nationalized property." Hence it is the new class of exploiters.

In January of 1961 Djilas was conditionally released from prison. Fifteen months later he was arrested once again, this time for the publication of his book *Conversations with Stalin.* A trial in May 1962 resulted in his being confined in Sremska Mitrovica Penitentiary again, this time for eight years and eight months.

During this time Djilas was engaged in that most arduous and difficult task a man can undertake: to take stock of himself. This reappraisal led him to seek out his own roots in the rocky soil of Montenegro. The fruit of this quest was his book *Land Without Justice,* which was published for the first time, in English, in 1958. Autobiographical in form, it was far more than that in content. In it Djilas described his life from his birth "on an unsettled afternoon at the beginning of spring in the year 1911" to his graduation from high school and the eve of his departure from Montenegro to enter the University of Belgrade. Actually, however, it was not Djilas who was the main subject of his autobiography; it was Montenegro, the blood-soaked soil that nourished his roots, the people from which he sprang, the rocky peaks to which he lifted his eyes, and the endless sky which led him to distant horizons.

Djilas devoted a second book to his homeland, *Montenegro,* published in 1963. This is a semifictional account of life in Montenegro in the period of the First World War. It was, for Djilas, a further step back into the past—toward Njegoš.

Montenegro is the smallest, both in size and in population, of the six constituent republics that make up Yugoslavia today. All of Yugoslavia is about the size of Wyoming. The territory of Montenegro is today less than five and a half per cent of the total area of Yugoslavia. Its population is around half a million. The name "Montenegro" came into the Western languages by way of Venetian Italian. It is a literal translation of the native name, Crna Gora, which means Black Mountain. The most widely accepted explanation for this name is that it came from the fact that the mountains of the region were once thickly covered with trees, that is, before the Venetians chopped down the trees for their ships and the goats ate the rest of the vegetation. At least, so the Montenegrins believe. In any event, the most conspicuous and awesome physical feature of Montenegro now is its bare limestone crags, some of which rise over eight thousand feet above the blue Adriatic. These form part of the Dinaric Range, which follows almost the entire coast of Yugoslavia. The Montenegrins have, too, the legend that when God created the earth, He had a lot of rocks left over, and so He simply dumped them down, and they landed in Montenegro. It is almost impossible to describe the utter bleakness and bareness of much of this rock-bound land, unless one is a Djilas. He writes:

> The land is one of utter destitution and forlorn silence. Its billowing crags engulf all that is alive and all that human hand has built and cultivated. Every sound is dashed against the jagged rocks, and every ray of light is ground into gravel. . . .
>
> It lacks the serenity of the desert or the spaciousness of the sea. It

has some of both—but the silence is stony and the spaciousness is overhead in the endless heavens.

It is plains and vales, terraced fields and stone huts—even more cramped and lost here than in the rest of the Karst. The trees are gnarled, stunted, choked in thickets, cut by man, exposed on bare limestone—neither oak, nor hornbeam, nor beech, but only dry grass, brittle, hardly green at all—a fantastic dream world.

To be sure, Montenegro has its river valleys and plains, but the greatness of Montenegro never lay in its lowlands. When the Ottoman Turks swept over the Balkans in the fourteenth century, conquering all in their path, it was to the highlands of Montenegro, then called Zeta, that many Serbs fled. There they took up the seminomadic shepherd way of life of the surrounding Albanian and Vlach cantons, or *katuni,* to use the local word, and reverted from their medieval civilization to a primitive patriarchal way of life. Though they were relatively protected from the Turks in their mountain fastnesses, the Montenegrins did not organize a state, at least not in any modern sense of the term. Their princes had all been killed or had gone over to the Turks as converts to Islam. What order there was resided in the tribes and clans. A kind of personal, patriarchal power was wielded by the clan chieftains, but there was no doubt that the ultimate authority lay in the people themselves, who made their wishes known in council and assembly meetings. The Westerner will find many similarities between this way of life and that of the Swiss cantons and the Scottish Highlands. However, perhaps the closest parallel is with Homeric Greece.

Eventually, the Montenegrins did develop a unique form of government. As time showed the need for a greater cohesiveness than was possible under a tribal and clan system, the freedom-loving Montenegrins avoided establishing a secular political authority that might impinge on the autonomy of their tribes. Hence it was by custom rather than fiat that a vague but real central authority was invested in the Orthodox bishop of Montenegro. Some writers with little understanding of the Montenegrin mentality or religion came to call Montenegro a theocracy because of this circumstance. This is a ludicrous error. The term "theocracy" fits Papal Rome, Calvin's Geneva, the Massachusetts Bay Colony of the Mathers, and Salt Lake City under Brigham Young far better than it does Montenegro under its Orthodox bishops. In Montenegro even the priests are anticlerical. The bishops had no power whatever to enforce their authority; they could only mediate and plead, acting as the conscience of the people. Early in the eighteenth century the succession of bishops came to reside in one family: the Petrović family of Njegoš. Since Orthodox bishops, unlike Orthodox parish priests, are celibate, the succession generally went from uncle to nephew. There was no constitution, no army, no police force, no regular taxes, no census, no schools, no borders until the middle of the eighteenth century, and some of these institutions did not exist until the middle of the nineteenth century.

And yet this handful of illiterate mountaineers in their rocky heights was invested with an importance and even greatness that far transcended its numbers and condition. Montenegro became the symbol of freedom in the Turkish-dominated Balkans. Here was a perpetually embattled warrior race defending its freedoms against the onslaughts of Islam. Montenegro was much more than a loose confederacy of tribes; it was a myth. This myth was assiduously kept alive, especially by the Orthodox church and by the oral tradition handed down from generation to generation by the guslars, or bards. To the sad hum of the gusle, a simple bowed instrument with a single strand of horsehair, these bards chanted in trochaic pentameter the great epics of the Serbian people. The greatest of these was the cycle surrounding the Battle of Kosovo, the Field of Blackbirds, at which the medieval Serbian kingdom fell to the Turks on June 28, 1389. There was not a Serb alive who had not heard the epic and who did not know that it was his sacred obligation to "avenge Kosovo" and to fight "for the honorable Cross and golden freedom." The Serbs of Montenegro came to look upon themselves as the last free remnant of their medieval kingdom. Each Montenegrin was born with the debt of Kosovo and the duty to fight as a man in defense of freedom. This was the heritage and the myth that even as distant an admirer as Alfred Lord Tennyson lauded in his sonnet "Montenegro."

> O smallest among peoples! rough rock-throne
> Of Freedom! Warriors beating back the swarm
> Of Turkish Islam for five hundred years,
> Great Tzernagora! never since thine own

Black ridges drew the cloud and brake the storm
Has breathed a race of mightier mountaineers.

This was the heritage to which Djilas was born. This was the heritage to which he returned once more in his biography of Njegoš.

At first it may seem strange indeed that a man like Djilas should write a book about Njegoš. A superficial comparison of the two men might lead to the conclusion that they had little in common except for the fact that both were Montenegrins—though that in itself would be something. Njegoš was a prince, and Djilas a revolutionary. Njegoš was an Orthodox bishop, and Djilas an atheist. Njegoš was an idealist in his philosophy, and Djilas is a disciple of dialectical materialism. Njegoš was a Romantic poet, and Djilas is most widely known for his turgid prose works on Marxist ideology. And yet it was precisely Milovan Djilas who has produced the most complete and rounded study of the many-faceted Njegoš. The answer to this apparent paradox is, of course, that the paradox *is* only apparent and not real. In actual fact, it is Djilas who comes the closest of anyone who has ever written about Njegoš to having shared both the variety and totality of Njegoš's experiences.

As political figures, both were rulers of men. True, Njegoš had the more exalted title, but it is not farfetched to claim that Djilas was no less powerful at the height of his career. More importantly, both men were revolutionaries who wielded power not for power's sake but in order to transform the societies over which they ruled. This is more obvious in the case of Djilas, who had devoted his life to achieving a socialist society in Yugoslavia. However, Njegoš also dedicated his life to the founding of a new order in Montenegro, an order in which the anarchy of the lawless tribes would be replaced by a modern state based on a central authority. It is no accident that Njegoš was the last of the prince-bishops of Montenegro, and that his successor found it possible to take over the state as a secular prince.

To accomplish their aims, both Njegoš and Djilas were ruthless at times toward their enemies, both foreign and domestic. Njegoš's foreign enemies were the Turks, Djilas's the Germans; Njegoš's domestic enemies were the recalcitrant tribal chieftains and unruly paladins, Djilas's were the bourgeois remnants of the old regime. The struggle was bitter and cruel. Djilas writes in his biography of Njegoš how this bishop, prince, and poet reacted when his men brought to him the head of his Turkish foe Smaïl Aga Čengić: "On receiving the proffered head of Smaïl Aga—washed and combed, as was the custom—he threw it into the air like an apple, and as he caught it he cried, 'So you, too, have come my way, poor Smaïl!' "

Another political comparison of note is the fact that both these men, proud Montenegrins that they were, were also conscious of being primarily Serbs, as well as Yugoslavs. Though each in his own way represented a Montenegro which had an identity of its own, nevertheless both saw Montenegrin history and especially Montenegrin destiny as only a part of the Serbian past and future. Moreover, both are genuine Yugoslavs, which is quite a distinction in a land where cultural and political enmities, especially between the Serbs and the Croats, have been and still are common and powerful. Njegoš went so far as to have printed on the flyleaf of one of his works that it was published in "Yugoslavia," a country which did not yet exist. Indeed, the very word had just been coined. As for Djilas, a significant incident took place during his trial before the Belgrade District Court in December 1956. Throughout the trial Djilas showed no particular emotion, until the chief judge described him as a Montenegrin. At this, Djilas leaped to his feet and cried, "I object. The statement should show that I am a Yugoslav."

Both men also suffered similar disappointments with Russia. It is hard to explain to outsiders just what Russia meant to the Montenegrins in their history. There is even a joke about it, of how Montenegrins used to boast "we and the Russians, a hundred million strong," when Montenegro was infinitely smaller than the smallest province of the vast Russian Empire. It was no joke, however, that in the eighteenth century Montenegro actually begged to be taken into the Russian Empire. So, too, it was the fondest hope of Djilas and his fellow-Communists to have Yugoslavia honored by becoming the next constituent republic of the Soviet Union. Like Djilas, who describes his disenchantment in *Conversations with Stalin,* Njegoš made several trips to Russia, and each time he suffered disappointment.

There are ideological similarities between Njegoš and Djilas, too. Formally, the former was an Orthodox bishop and the latter is a Marxist atheist. Yet both are heretics. Njegoš was tonsured to be a monk and consecrated bishop much against his will, as a mere youth who was the instrument of the ambitions of his clan. Not only was he not a priest by vocation, but he was unchurchly even by the standards of a pious layman. He rarely attended services except on a few holidays and when he needed to ordain priests. Indeed, in later years he hardly ever wore the robes of his office, but preferred to dress in the traditional costume of a Montenegrin chieftain. Yet Njegoš was a deeply religious man. And, in his own way, so is Djilas. The common source of their religious outlook is the folk religion of the Montenegrin people. Setting aside the dogma and rituals of the Orthodox church and the popular superstitions of Montenegrin folklore, and looking at the basic cosmogony of the Montenegrin people, it can be seen that it is essentially Manichaean, both in its dualism and in its asceticism. The Montenegrin religion sees as the central problem in the entire cosmos the struggle between the powers of light and darkness, God and Satan. The victory is not a foregone conclusion in this dialectic, because the two powers are equally matched. Man is caught between the two worlds, and is a part of both. The struggle is both outside himself and within himself, and that struggle is perpetual. Yet man must fight on the side of light and truth because there is in his nature the divine spark. This is the dominant theme of Njegoš's great work *The Ray of the Microcosm*. It is also the theme of all of Djilas's writings since his break with Communism. The last line of Djilas's *Njegoš* is this: "One must not give in to evil." And immediately following is the pathetic line in the manuscript: "In prison, in Sremska Mitrovica, 1957–1959." The struggle must go on, even in prison.

Even as writers Njegoš and Djilas share much. If Njegoš is the greatest writer of the Montenegrin people, then Djilas is certainly the second greatest. Though one wrote poetry and the other prose, both are poets, and both are profoundly influenced by the Serbian epic poetry of the guslars. No one can read *Land Without Justice* without feeling the essentially poetic qualities of this work, even in translation. Njegoš wrote three great works among many. The first was his *Ray of the Microcosm,* which some have compared with Milton's *Paradise Lost,* though the comparison rests largely on similarity of the subject matter—Satan's rebellion against God. Even greater is Njegoš's *Mountain Wreath,* which centers around a historic event in the late seventeenth century whose authenticity has never been proven—the massacre of the Islamic converts in their midst by the Christian Montenegrins. The third work is a historical drama entitled *Stephen the Small,* which tells of Montenegro in the late eighteenth century during the rule of a charlatan who posed as the rightful tsar of Russia, the husband of Catherine the Great. In all of these works the themes are those that also figure most prominently in Djilas's writings: the cosmic struggle between good and evil, both in the heavens and in little but great Montenegro, and the necessity for man to fight evil constantly and wherever he may encounter it, in the name of freedom.

It does not behoove a translator to complain about his task. As the Russian proverb warns, "People who fear wolves should not go into the woods." Still, the translator bears a responsibility not only toward his author, but toward his reader. Djilas's book compounds the problem of translating in that more than one author is involved, for it contains not only Djilas's prose, but also Njegoš's poetry. The reader deserves a word about both.

Djilas has an eccentric style which is notorious even beyond the borders of Yugoslavia. In his book *The Heretic: The Life and Times of Josip Broz-Tito,* Fitzroy Maclean, chief of the British Military Mission to Tito during the Second World War, comments on Djilas's "own turgid and confused style." Yet Djilas is a powerful writer, and, as the translator of his *Conversations with Stalin,* I can testify that he can be very clear indeed. It is all a matter of what he is writing about. Djilas's literary style, like his life, oscillates between Marx and Njegoš. His debt to both, as well as his inability to reconcile them, is reflected in the confusion of his prose. There is both the complexity of *Das Kapital* and the terseness of *The Mountain Wreath* in Djilas's style. Whoever would read Djilas in the original Serbo-Croatian must be prepared to encounter two challenges especially. On the one hand, he will have to fight his way through endless Germanic sentences bursting with involved clauses. On the other hand, he will often be caught unawares by brief phrase-like sentences whose meaning may be missed precisely because the substance of what might have filled whole paragraphs is suggested in but a few words. To make matters more difficult, Djilas is a real connoisseur of rare obscure and archaic expressions derived from a variety of sources, from Serbian epic poetry, Vuk Karadžić's *Lexicon* of 1851, the dialect of Montenegro, and Turkish and eighteenth-century Venetian words that were once a part of the Serbo-Croatian language. Djilas's prose also reflects the special terminology of philosophy and the jargon of modern Yugoslav literary criticism. Whatever may be the other faults of this translation, the reader may be sure of one thing: despite the translator's best efforts to be true to the original, the English, such as it is, is clearer than Djilas's Serbo-Croatian. Nevertheless, whether the reader is forced across Djilas's long suspension bridges or made to hop over half-submerged steppingstones, his journey has a charted direction, a variety of rich experiences along the way, and a rewarding destination.

Njegoš's poetry is another problem. Djilas quotes at length from Njegoš's three major works—*The Mountain Wreath, The Ray of the Microcosm,* and *Stephen the Small.* Personal inadequacy and practicality led me to rely on the best existing published English translations, though this was possible only in the case of the first two works. The standard English translation of *The Mountain Wreath,* and the only complete version in English, is that by James W. Wiles, *The Mountain Wreath of P. P. Nyegosh, Prince-Bishop of Montenegro 1830–1851* (London: George Allen and Unwin, Ltd., 1930). The first edition was published in February of that year, and a second edition in September of the same year. The translator had gone to Serbia in 1913, first as Reader in English at the University of Belgrade, then as head of the British and Foreign Bible Society for Southeastern Europe. As the leading Serbian authority on English languages and literature, Professor Vladeta Popović, remarked in his preface to Wiles's translation, "He has mastered the language and entered with real British sympathy into the soul of the people. His translation of Njegoš . . . is the result of long and patient work. Not least among its merits is its entire faithfulness to the meaning and spirit of the finest production of the greatest Serbian poet."

Djilas himself has other things to say about the possibility of translating *The Mountain Wreath.*

> Those who have analyzed translations of *The Mountain Wreath*—and it has been translated into nearly all the European languages—have shown that not one of these has succeeded even remotely in transmitting Njegoš's poetic expression and conceptual power. . . . They say that the best translations are the Swedish, because it was done by a poet, and the German, done by a person with expert knowledge of our traits and past, but that not even these are fully satisfactory.

One must say about Njegoš what is so often said about Dante, Shakespeare, Goethe, Pushkin: the poetry of each is the fullest expression and quintessence of the universal embodied in a particular culture. The universal is accessible to all men, but the form in which it is expressed is unique and impossible to recast in the mold of another time or place. Therefore let no reader judge Njegoš by Wiles's Victorian English translation, no matter how grateful the non-Yugoslav reader should be to Wiles. Njegoš has yet to find his Ciardi or Nabokov.

All excerpts from *The Ray of the Microcosm* have been taken from the English translation by Anica Savić-Rebac, which was published in Volume III of the *Harvard Slavic Studies* (1957), pages 151–200. She was Professor of Classics at the University of Belgrade, and died shortly before the publication of her translation. Describing it as "very free and perhaps idiosyncratic," the editor explains:

> It was not Mrs. Rebac's intention to give a close rendering of the diction and idiom of the original, but to present the philosophic content in a poetic form which she considered suitable. Her version is stylistically unlike Njegoš, but her faithful reproduction of Njegoš's ideas is a real *tour de force*.

I agree completely.

As for the excerpts from *Stephen the Small* and the lesser works of Njegoš cited by Djilas, the reader will have to content himself with my own translations.

Djilas probably did not mean to have his work regarded as a scholarly monograph in any strictly academic sense. Thus he did not invest it with the usual scholarly apparatus. (The footnotes have been supplied by me.) However, this work is based on a great deal of scholarship. Indeed, it synthesizes better than any other work both the traditional and the most recent research on Njegoš by specialists in history, literature, and philosophy. To give some indication of this, I have compiled a bibliography which lists the authors and works to which Djilas specifically refers in his text or which he probably consulted, judging by the context, in writing this book.

University of Wisconsin
January 1966

Contents

PREFACE BY WILLIAM JOVANOVICH ix
INTRODUCTION BY MICHAEL B. PETROVICH xiii
The Birthland 3
The Self-Taught Pupil 32
The Stripling Bishop 62
The Hermit of Cetinje 120
The Sovereign of Montenegro and the Highlands 154
The Poet of Serbian Cosmic Misfortune 261
The Ray of the Microcosm 266
The Mountain Wreath 310
The False Tsar Stephen the Small 373
Ideas and Realities 397
In Sickness 428
Death and Lastingness 453
GENEALOGICAL CHART 470
BIBLIOGRAPHY 471
INDEX 483

NJEGOŠ

THE BIRTHLAND

1.

ONE WOULD THINK that there was no more mystery about him, Njegoš. The facts are already known, at least the important ones.

But no one has the breath to fathom his depths and to bring to light the mystery. He himself was not able to do it.

Such as he is—with no mystery about him and yet unfathomable —Njegoš exerts the irresistible attraction of a man who, without himself quite knowing how or why, has grown one with his people and his land, and through them with the race of man and with the cosmos. As long as his people speak his tongue and fight for their survival, and without either they would have no existence, their every generation will revisit Njegoš's wellspring to garner strength and to gain knowledge of themselves by plumbing his, and their, mysterious depths.

He goes on being elusive. Just when was this greatest poet of the South Slavs and of the tragic fate of the Balkan peoples really born?

He knew exactly when, but he never left us a completely reliable date. Two years are accepted—either 1811 or 1813. It would not be a matter of great difference if it involved someone else. But the difference is made great by his own greatness. After all, was he seventeen or was he nineteen years old when he began to lay down the law in Montenegro and to bear the sorrows of the Serbs?

Njegoš thrice spoke of his birth. The first time it was to the Russian consul in Dubrovnik, Jeremija Gagić,* when he complained

* (1781–1859). Serbian merchant who became Secretary of the Governing Council during the First Serbian Uprising and served as its diplomatic envoy to

about how "that Kharkov postmaster Vučićević," whom the Russians had sent upon his accession to the throne—supposedly to assist him—had inveigled "three diamond crosses" away from him, supposedly to sell them for him, but who instead got himself married on the money, while he, Njegoš, being only "of eighteen years" at the time, had not known enough to get a receipt. It would follow that he was born in the year 1813. On January 20, 1850, he wrote to Knićanin,* "On Christmas I celebrated my thirty and eight years." Why he reckoned by Christmases it is difficult to divine, but this, too, would lead to the year 1813 were it not for the fact that in that same year, 1850, on August 18, he wrote to the same Knićanin, "Indeed I lack but some two months before I enter into the fortieth year of my life—which is a great deal in this life of travail." From this it would seem that he was born in the year 1811. To make matters worse, while the first two letters have been preserved, nothing remains of the third letter except this single sentence, which is cited by the reliable Andra Gavrilović, but for which he gives no source. That one lifted sentence, whose almost parenthetical outburst in the second half and whose preciseness are completely in the style of Njegoš, leads to the conclusion, along with some other facts, that Njegoš was born in the year 1811. It should be added that neither Njegoš nor anyone else disagrees about the day, but only about the year of his birth.

Some maintain that Njegoš gave out various birth dates as the need dictated: either to evoke pity for his youth or to appear more mature than he really was. For it is entirely true, and inevitably so, that the most tragic poet of our fate and the unhappiest figure in our history was accustomed to cry in despair even when he had no stomach for it and to boast even when there was nothing to boast

Austria and Russia. In 1811 he entered the Russian service, first with the Danubian Army and then, in 1813, with the Foreign Ministry. In 1815 he was assigned to the Russian consulate in Dubrovnik (Ragusa). He became Vice-Consul in 1825 and served till 1856. In 1850 he received a noble title as a reward for his long service.

* Stevan Petrović Knićanin (1807–55), prominent Serbian political and military leader who began his career under Prince Miloš Obrenović but joined the opposition as a Constitutionalist and supporter of Prince Alexander Karadjordjević. He led a group of Serbian volunteers during the 1848 Revolution in Austria.

about. After all, was not some of the rumbling against him based on the fact that he was too young to be installed on the bishop's throne? Was he himself not forced to plead his youth and to use it to gain support? Ever tearing himself apart, was he not forced to do likewise even with the date of his birth?

As to whether he knew when he was born—he knew.

Peasants have a good memory for death and birth. This is particularly so with Montenegrin peasants, who are still closely bound by ties of blood, especially where a male child is concerned. And there were people aplenty in Njegoš's family who could record and remember: a prudent and long-lived father, a bishop for an uncle, a literate older brother. Of course they remembered. They just did not write it down. Many more important things went unrecorded—both in the clan and in the land. For who could have suspected that the future Njegoš would be born in the house of Tomo Markov Petrović? They did not know him for what he was even after he had become someone. They remembered the birth of males—the bearers of weapons and procreators of the clan. And that was enough. The rest was up to the one who was born: he would be remembered for what he became.

Njegoš himself did not like to record everything. He made fun of his secretary, Ljuba Nenadović, for taking notes, even though at the time, in Italy in 1851, death was robbing him of strength and beauty before his very eyes. His unconcern for the things and doings of "this world" was as great as his belief in the permanence of those other, intangible, values. His whole being was oriented toward the untransitory, the eternal. He did not record the commonplaces of life, not even his own, and not even when these—birth and death—were hardly commonplace.

However, two men who were at his side, Medaković and Milaković, set down the same date of his birth: November 1, 1813. Milorad Medaković * was not an entirely truthful man; he was wont to have it his way, though he belonged less to himself than to the Russians. But he was at Njegoš's side when he sent the above date

* (1824–97). Serbian publicist and historian, born in Croatia, who served as Njegoš's secretary until the 1848 Revolution drew him back to Austria. In 1854 he returned to Montenegro as Prince Danilo's secretary and wrote several books on Montenegrin history and folklore.

to Stanko Vraz * in 1848. Dimitrije Milaković,† too, had been found for Njegoš as his secretary by Russian agents, Ivan Ivanović Vukotić and Gagić. He spent twenty years beside Njegoš, throughout his entire reign. Assiduous and withdrawn, more cunning than profound, he knew how to keep silence. After all, that was his métier. Thus when he put down the above date in 1856, he must have spoken truly: Njegoš's death had already set aside any reasons for concealing the date of his birth.

So it is with some cause that we have accepted the above date—which is according to the Julian calendar, as are all the other dates in this book.

2.

NJEGOŠ—RADIVOJE—WAS the second son, but it is not known whether he was the second child, of Tomo Markov Petrović and Ivana Proroković.

Tomo and Ivana were from Njeguši, but not from the same village and certainly from different clans. Insofar as is known, they had five children. The sons were Pero, Radivoje, and Joko. The daughters were Marija, who was married to the Serdar, or chieftain, of the Cuce, Andrija Pejović, and—as tradition has it—Stana, who married the brother of the Serdar of Rijeka, Filip Djurašković.

Njegoš was given the name of Radivoje at his christening. The historian Dušan Vuksan has discovered that in 1828 he signed himself Raphael. Vuksan maintains that Njegoš was put up to this by the eccentric Sima Milutinović-Sarajlija, who was residing in Cetinje at the time and who acted as a sort of tutor to Njegoš. Perhaps Sarajlija really fancied that according to some contrived interpretation Radivoje was a translation of the church name Raphael. However, that name does not appear again anywhere.

Njegoš never signed himself Radivoje, his real name and its

* (1810–51). Slovenian Romantic poet who later adopted the Serbo-Croatian language and became a leading supporter of the "Illyrian" movement for Yugoslav cultural and political unity.

† (d. 1858). Serbian littérateur and historian from Austria, who arrived in Montenegro in 1831 and served as secretary to both Njegoš and his successor, Prince Danilo. His most important work was a history of Montenegro (1856).

common form, but, rather, Radivoj. Someone, perhaps Sarajlija, must have told him that it was more correct and more beautiful. After his consecration as bishop he signed himself only by his monkish name, Petar, and his surname, Petrović: Bishop Petar Petrović. But the people never called him Bishop Petar, or remembered him as such. Rather, they took the short form of Radivoje—Rade—by which his kin called him. Hence—Bishop Rade. The people reserved the name Bishop Petar for his uncle. Njegoš also never used the Roman numeral II after the name Petar; this was added later, just as the Roman numeral I was placed after his uncle's name, to distinguish between the two.

Thus when we speak of the bishop and ruler, we say Bishop (*Vladika*) Rade, and when we speak of the poet, we say Njegoš.

No one knows exactly why he assumed the additional name Njegoš, and not Njeguš, the correct name of his clan and of his immediate home. This was probably something he adopted from his uncle Bishop Petar, who sometimes added Njegoš, and not Njeguš, to his surname, apparently to distinguish himself from the other Njeguši. Perhaps it was mostly because that was what the legendary founder of the clan—Vojvoda Njegoš—called himself, and because it was held that the Njeguš clan had migrated in the sixteenth century from the foot of Mount Njegoš in Hercegovina. Bishop Rade began to use the clan cognomen Njegoš regularly only from the time of his sojourn in Russia in 1833. Apparently the surname Petrović seemed too bare to him, too much like the common Russian patronymic, and thus to Russians he might appear to be without a surname. Petar Petrović—that sounded colorless and impersonal even had there not been a host of people with this name and patronymic in Russia. Only with the addition of Njegoš did the name sound right. Thus it was that Bishop Rade became and remained Njegoš. As for the other Njeguši—they could do as they pleased.

As in every clan, so among the Njeguši there persisted legends about their origins and progenitor. Apart from these legends, however, there is no proof of the existence of a Vojvoda Njegoš. As for the claim that the Njeguši immigrated in the second half of the fifteenth or beginning of the sixteenth century, it has been proven, on the contrary, that the Venetian archives refer to the Njeguši as early as 1435 as being in the place where they are now, four hundred households strong, as the historian Ilarion Ruvarac has established. The Czech historian Jireček * maintains that the appellation Njeguši is derived from a personal name: "Njeguši from Njeguš (the root meaning to tend, to cultivate, effort. Njegomir, Njegoslav, Njegovan, Njegota)." He points out that the name Njeguš—Niegusz—exists in Poland, and that it has been recorded among the Serbs as well, rather long ago—in Hercegovina in 1740, and elsewhere. Most probably the Njeguši had earlier called themselves Njegoši, and in time popular speech transformed the *o* into a *u*. In his *History of Montenegro,* Bishop Vasilije calls the Njeguši Njegoši. Be that as it may, the fact is that Bishop Rade adopted the older and already used form Njegoš, and not the form Njeguš used in popular speech.

It is not known when and how those Montenegrin clans originated which are mentioned as communities from the fourteenth century and before. Just because they are not mentioned by name from the time of the coming of the Slavs to the Balkans, beginning in the seventh century, does not mean that they must have originated later. The South Slavs immigrated into the Balkans in tribal units, which were later submerged and completely destroyed by the feudal society and state. If the Montenegrin tribes are not a conglomeration of immigrant Slavs and Illyrians, they are certainly much like the blood clan—the *fis*—of the Albanians, the oldest inhabitants of the Balkan Peninsula. It is hardly likely that the Njeguši were an exception; Njegoš's roots stretch through his clan into the mythological past of the Slavs and the Illyrians.

Like the other clans, the Njeguši were divided into blood groups—brotherhoods, or phratries. One of these was supposed to be the Herakovići, named after Herak or Erak, from which the smaller phratry of the Petrovići broke off. The other branch was the Rajičevići—after Rajić—and from these probably originated the Radonjići, called the Guvernadurovići because the governorship of Montenegro resided in their phratry.

The legend is clear, trim, and proud: from Vojvoda Njegoš derive all the Njeguši; from him or his offspring Herak or Erak come the Herakovići; and from them the Petrovići. The life of the clan and the brotherhood grows and branches out from the same

* Konstantin Josef Jireček (1854–1918). Specialized in the history of the Serbs and the Bulgars.

roots and from the same soil—the same blood from generation to generation through time out of mind.

In actual fact, not only is nothing really known about that Herak or Erak, but not even when and where the surname Petrović originated. Bishop Danilo (who reigned in the seventeenth and early eighteenth centuries) did not yet sign himself Petrović, but Šćepčević, and only once Njeguš. However, in the charter of Peter the Great, the Bishop's brother is called Petrović. Why was one brother called Petrović and the other Šćepčević? It would appear that both surnames derive from the father, grandfather, or some ancestor. It was Bishop Sava, who in 1735 succeeded Danilo to the bishop's throne, who first began to sign himself Petrović. From that time on all the Petrovići are certainly Petrovići.

Njegoš has no reliable family chronology, but he was born and he lived amid very vivid brotherhood and clan myths. In this respect he differed from other Montenegrin children only in that the bishops came from his immediate phratry—the Petrovići—while from the nearby and already rival phratry of Radonjići came most of the secular governors, the *guvernaduri*. There was still another difference at the time: the Njeguš tribe was one of those settlements from the Nahi (district) of Katuni, the mountain region around Mount Lovćen and to the north of it, which stoutly maintained that they had never paid tribute to the Turks "since Kosovo," but that they had preserved "the spark of Serbian freedom" in all its purity.

3.

Being a Njeguš, from the first glimmer of consciousness Njegoš belonged not only to a proud and militant clan, but also to that bastion of Montenegro and its freedom—the Nahi of Katuni.

The Nahi of Katuni was for Montenegro the same beacon that Šumadija was for Serbia and the Piedmont was for Italy. But it was also quite different from these. The Piedmont was a state, while Šumadija was a formation of free and nationalist peasants and merchants. The Nahi of Katuni was a collection of clans united solely by the struggle against the Turks, and then only somewhere from the seventeenth century on.

The clans of Katuni were certainly among the first to refuse, or, better to say, to persist in refusing, to submit to the Turks. What alone is certain is that they were the first to achieve a position in which they could finally offer resistance to the Turks. Other clans followed suit, mostly out of self-interest, in the struggle that the men of Katuni had already begun. Clan after clan had broken away before, then reverted to the Turks, and rebelled again. Just how and when this took place is known about many of them. However, once the men of Katuni broke away from the Turks—at the end of the seventeenth century—they were never to return to their sway. The same cannot be said about the clans of the other nahis—Crmnica, Rijeka, and Lješani—which comprise so-called Old Montenegro. Even under Bishop Petar their clans went their own ways and upheld their own interests. Against whom? There was no central authority—except the Church. Against the men of Katuni? Not really as much against them as against those aspirations which welled most mightily from their midst.

For their neighbors the clans of Katuni were like any other; they were to be regarded with a greater or lesser degree of hostility. But especially among themselves, in their own eyes, they were something special, even long before Njegoš.

They nurtured an inner spiritual implacability toward the Turks. They did not clash with the Turks solely for transient causes—high taxes or acts of violence. They were a different, opposite world—another conception of the world and of life. In their craggy heights, bleached by sun and storm and bereft of everything that a body needs, ceaseless struggle with the Turks was not only a way of life, but a cult. They not only believed in the myths of their religion and nationality; they lived by them.

One could cite, and we shall, a whole array of reasons why it was precisely the clans of Katuni which first finally broke away from the Turks, why it was among them that the myth crystallized into ideas and realities—into a program of action.

Certainly their position immediately next to the maritime provinces of the Venetian state, which was still great in experience and culture, served to turn the high and rocky wilderness of Katuni into an exposed Turkish gate which its inhabitants were to storm and to transform into a fortress and a nest of freedom. It is known that Venice kept the Montenegrin chieftains, and most frequently those of the clans of Katuni, in its pay; also, Bishop Danilo did not go only to Orthodox Russia to fortify his faith, but he went even more readily to the Doge to resolve Montenegrin troubles and needs.

The border with Venice, its influence, and the reliance it inspired certainly encouraged the Montenegrins to cleanse that bit of soil around Mount Lovćen of the Turks with their blood. Yet there had to be something else, and there was. There were the clans with a faith, a language, and myths all their own, an entity unto themselves, and as such always ready to resist foreign pressures and domination. One cannot imagine the growth of Montenegrin freedom without Venice's wars with Turkey, especially the Candian War at the end of the seventeenth century, in which the Montenegrins, too, played a lively role. Neither can it be comprehended without the vital forces of the clans and of their myths. The sources, the impulses of that struggle were more ancient and autochthonous—abiding within the clan as a living separate entity. The clan was Serbian in ethos and language, with its own myths and those of the nation.

One can find countless factors and explanations. But from Bishop Danilo's time, the men of Katuni and the Nahi of Katuni stood independent of the Turks, with the finality and purity of a myth—a myth transformed into an idea, action.

The great myths—a doomed Serbia, the flight of its nobility into the Montenegrin mountains after the fall of the empire at Kosovo, the duty to avenge Kosovo, Miloš Obilić's sacrifice, the irreconcilable struggle between Cross and Crescent, the Turks as an absolute evil pervading the entire Serbian nation—all these myths took on their sharpest and most implacable aspects here, among the men of Katuni. Here these sentiments went beyond and above all others. Obilić and Kosovo were not something that happened some time ago and far away, but they were here—in daily thoughts and feelings and life and struggle with the Turks. It was a struggle against extermination—for the survival of the clan—one in which faith and nationality, the Cross and freedom, were more perfectly merged than in any other province and anywhere else in the Balkans.

The men of Katuni and the Montenegrins of those times lived peculiarly in their myths. These were not only beliefs, but national history—its continuity, daily life. It is not important that their history was not like that, not actually so. What mattered was that they completely believed it to be such, and acted accordingly.

The men of Katuni, Montenegrins, were sharply defined in all things, and with finality.

Those were the beginnings, and they are always decisive.

But it was not only the myths, the ideas, that came to their highest expression there. Most of the folk epics—at least those Njegoš first heard and later collected—came from the Nahi of Katuni. Nothing reveals as clearly as they do the mentality of his immediate homeland. They string together events and thoughts, one after another—all very much alike—without embellishment, without color, stark and almost crude in their brittle monotony. It is not really poetry at all, just as the men of Katuni are ethnically neither a nation nor the kernel of a nation. But there is the basis for an imperceptible poetry, spare of fantasy and movements, a bare recounting, the carving out of vital and mythical truths, better to say, of vitally mythical truths.

One should look into the *Short History of Montenegro,* which was narrated by Njegoš's uncle Bishop Petar, a man of reliable intelligence and inexhaustible spiritual strength. Here are some fifteen pages of simple-minded legends which have no connection with historical science, but they embody the most final and most tangible truths for the people for whom he recounted them. One should read this work in order to understand just how deeply the legend and heritage of the national past lived in the being and reality of Montenegrins, and especially of the men of Katuni.

It was among the men of Katuni, more than anywhere else, that heroism was bound to become the highest virtue. Njegoš's cult of heroism was not fabricated, but borrowed—as was practically everything else of his—though refined and idealized. It is of a special kind—not only bravery in battle, but also humaneness and resistance to all evil; especially humaneness: to kill without torture, to raise weapons only against those who bear weapons, to take but not to steal, to forgive but never to ask for mercy. Marko Miljanov * called it *manliness*—and that is the most exact expression for it—

* (1833–1901). Renowned Montenegrin hero who led the Kuči clan against the Turks in 1862 and who distinguished himself in the War of 1876–78. He was also a writer who gained repute for his descriptions of Montenegrin life.

but Gesemann,* being unable to translate it, called it *humanitas heroica.* It is a contradiction: to kill and to be humane, to do evil while fighting evil. In Montenegro, in the Nahi of Katuni—and is it only there?—this was both logical and commonplace, reasonable and just: the struggle for survival, but based on ethical principles.

As a ruler a Montenegrin, by heritage a Serb, in ideology a Yugoslav, and in his ethics a universal man, Njegoš was to remain to the end a man of Katuni in his personal character, and especially in the finality and implacability of the truths that he uttered and that set him afire. His language, though interwoven with strands of other Montenegrin dialects, was that of the Katuni clans. So was his manner of expression, however personal. He, too, did not expend more words than he had to, and he recounted only what he could not resist telling.

The men of Katuni swear by God and their gusles, but they are not given to long prayers and chants. Nor can they be. Storytelling is like fighting. They tell tales aplenty, but these tales are also realities—"balm for the soul," with little of the imaginary. That is how they are in other things, too: reserved and withdrawn in their personal lives, poor in land and cattle, but not stingy, intolerant, or intemperate, rather, given to great ideas and to the struggle for their unrealizable realization.

4.

THE LAND IS one of utter destitution and forlorn silence. Its billowing crags engulf all that is alive and all that human hand has built and cultivated. Every sound is dashed against the jagged rocks, and every ray of light is ground into gravel.

The stranger is deceived by the aspect of the land. The Russian Captain Egor Kovalevsky, who came at Njegoš's request to look for precious metals, while his government sent him to collect intelligence on the side, made a note on the view from Lovćen: a sea of stone, and then, not without bitterness, he added, "For the Monte-

* Gerhard Gesemann. German scholar who in the 1920's and 1930's wrote studies of Montenegrin folk poetry, based on his recordings, and a book about the country, *Der Montenegrinische Mensch.*

negrins the road is everywhere," for there is really no road at all. Thus have said the English and others, down to this very day. For Pierre Loti this was a desert, a terrifying scene from the moon. In speaking of his region of the Kuči, Marko Miljanov blurted out just the right expression: *a crucified wilderness*. That is Montenegro, that is the Nahi of Katuni: a wilderness and a sea of stone, but one lifted high upon a confusion of peaks, gashed by canyons and gorges, and gouged by gaping precipices burrowing into stone cracked by heat and frost.

It lacks the serenity of the desert or the spaciousness of the sea. It has some of both—but the silence is stony and the spaciousness is overhead in the endless heavens.

It is plains and vales, terraced fields and stone huts—even more cramped and lost here than in the rest of the Karst. The trees are gnarled, stunted, choked in thickets, cut by man, exposed on bare limestone—neither oak, nor hornbeam, nor beech, but only dry grass, brittle, hardly green at all—a fantastic dream world. A painter of that region, Petar Lubarda, turned that stone into great art. And he found stone in everything—in the human form and beneath it, in that sky which is snagged on the crags and crests, and in the air charged with a violent storm waiting in ambush behind the clouds. Even here man has penetrated with his roads, fields, whitewashed walls. But all this, along with himself, soon gets lost. All is stone. Even all that is human is of stone. Man himself is made of it—without an ounce of fat, honed down by it all and with his sharp edge turned outward on the whole world. Every evil assails him, and he uses evil to ward off evil, on a soil where even the wild beast has no lair.

Once, perhaps not so very long ago—some two hundred or three hundred years past—the rock was covered by forest. It was certainly because of this forest that the whole region—and later the country as a whole—got the name of Montenegro, or Black Mountain, first recorded in the year 1435 in the treaty between the Despot Djuradj Branković * and Venice: "The Katuni of Montenegro." Jovan Erdeljanović † has shown through traditions and place names that the region once also had water. Humid groves lined the silver of the

* (1374–1456). Grandson of Prince Lazar, who was defeated at Kosovo by the Turks, and son of Vuk Branković. Became "Despot" or Prince of Serbia in 1427.
† (1874–1944). Serbian ethnologist who wrote on the clans of Montenegro.

streams: across the Plain of Cetinje there meandered the river that gave it its name; deer and mountain goats roamed the clearings and the heights. But the men multiplied. And the evils multiplied. In fighting the Turkish banc the clans also destroyed the forests and the meadows. Those same powers of sun, wind, and rain which once brought their bounties to the land now helped to bring it destruction. There remained the gashed, the ever-wounded stone, and handfuls of rubble on the hillsides in choked abysses. There remained the sand viper and the raven—and man, who survived in all this, sang new incantations and invented new charms, thought great thoughts, founded a state, and began to rally together a race which had been downtrodden and scattered over the Balkans.

How populated was the Nahi of Katuni when it inaugurated Montenegrin, Serbian, freedom? It is reckoned that in Njegoš's time Montenegro—all four nahis plus the numerous Piperi and Bjelopavlići clans—contained something over one hundred thousand souls, and that it was capable of sending twenty thousand soldiers into battle, inasmuch as everyone fought who could lift a rifle. The Nahi of Katuni could hardly have had over some twenty thousand souls—unlettered, without a municipal and administrative center, scattered over a space of barely one county, and isolated by the lack of roads, by ravines, clan hatred, superstition and misery, lawlessness and anarchy. This is where our national myth was crystallized, this is where our national history began.

As we said, the men of Katuni were not the first to rise up against the Turks. The clans of the Brda, the Highlands—the Nikšići, the Kuči, and others—were more warlike in the sixteenth and seventeenth centuries, and their irrepressible rebellions even splashed over into Old Serbia and the region of Užice. But the men of Katuni were the first to maintain their victory and to make the contest a final one. They were certainly always at odds with the Turks, or else they would not have declared the idea of final liberation and a war to the death. The ideas were few and the passion one, but everything about them was tough, keen, final. It was they who stamped the Montenegrin state and Montenegrin entity. Though Serbian to the core, the Nahi of Katuni alone was not to accept unification with Serbia in 1918 until the very end. It had made history too long by itself to permit others to make history for it.

History does not choose the easy way.

In the time of Njegoš, the Nahi of Katuni had not a single town, and not even a horse trail along which a caravan might travel without difficulty. It was Bishop Rade himself who was to lay such a road—from Cetinje to the Crnojevići River—and also establish the first hostel—at Krstac—to receive the traveler en route from the gentle coast into the skyward cliffs, into a state whose capital consisted of one monastery and three or four buildings, and whose government consisted of a monk and several shepherd chieftains. After Njegoš, at the very end of the century, Émile Vandervelde * visited the entire region and noted: Outside of the little town there is nowhere that one can find a decent lodging for the night in this wasteland, so similar to the desert on the moon, in which the woman is a family proletarian whose bare soles have been flattened by centuries of slavish animal drudgery. Even then—and there are such today—the houses were divided by a lattice—one half for the cattle, the other half for humans. A. A. Paton, an English historian, observed in the year 1846 that the houses in Njeguši were without windows or rooms—a single space. For all we know, the house in which Njegoš was born was no different. (The house exhibited today must have been renovated later.) The Senate building in Cetinje, the "Little Zion," which Bishop Petar had constructed, was partitioned by a wall, so that the senators, the government, entered on one side, while the horned cattle entered on the other. Njegoš was angry at the irrepressible Vuk Karadžić † for recording this. Njegoš's countrymen and contemporaries wore no underwear. A chieftain here and there might wear a shirt, which was saved and washed for feast days and for the fair in Kotor. Senator Stevan Perkov, one of the wisest and most important of Njegoš's advisers, went barefoot from Čevo to Cetinje—four hours across bare rocks—to protect his sandals from inclement weather and to be able to put them on, clean and dry, at the entrance. Such, too, was the food: lean, meager. Instead of bread, potatoes—brought from Russia by Bishop Petar; on rare occasions meat and cheese, with little or

* (1866–1938). Belgian statesman, Socialist leader, and political scientist.

† Vuk Stefanović Karadžić (1787–1864). Commonly known simply by his first name. Serbian ethnographer, grammarian, historian. Author of an epochal Serbian dictionary and supporter of the Serbian vernacular as a literary language. He visited Montenegro and wrote several studies concerning Montenegrin history and folklore.

no fruit and vegetables. When Vuk Karadžić came to Montenegro, at the beginning of Njegoš's reign, there were no pans, and what bread there was was baked in ashes. There were no trades. To be a tradesman was shameful, even long after Bishop Rade. The clothing was homespun and unadorned: gray goats' wool and white cloth with black drawstrings. In the houses the only illumination was from torches and splinters of pine and oak, used until everyone supped and was bedded down. Only in the churches and at graves were there oil lamps and little candles of soft wax, which were lighted only during prayers.

Nor was Njegoš's father rich. It is recorded that in 1824 he still owed a debt of seventeen years' standing, involving fourteen ducats, to a certain Marija Stanojević, of Kotor. The property mentioned in his will was certainly that of his eldest son, Pero, Njegoš's brother, who was very adept at trade, if not usury, and who got rich more quickly than any other Montenegrin.

Of Njegoš's uncles—Petar, Savo, and Stijepo by name—not one was rich, not even Petar, Bishop Petar. Thanks to Bishop Petar, who was as hard on others as on himself, not one of his kin—the Petrovići—was able to get rich. He lived an ascetic life and without any real power, as though he did not understand the power of money outside of military needs. Wars ruined him, especially the one in Kotor against the French. He spent both his own money and that of his monastery in that war, and neither Russia nor Austria was willing to give him a farthing of compensation, even though he had rendered them no little aid. Yet it was nothing new to spend the Church's money for freedom. A line of Bishop Danilo's has come down to us: "If we will sell our silver and gold things, we shall gather together an army and wage war on Albania and shed our blood for the sake of an unhappy and hungry people."

How could there have been any wealth when in many parts of Montenegro all trade was by barter? A little more land and cattle, a bit better food—that was wealth.

Everything was meager and spare, from day to day. There was honor and glory in fair measure—and nothing else.

5.

THE TRIBE AND the clan were already in dissolution, while the family had not yet sufficiently developed. The Russian historian Popov * observed: Only when the tribe lost political significance, and when the national assembly appeared side by side with it, was it possible for the conception of civic individuality to find expression. The individuality existed, but it was not a civic one, one responsible for its own actions, but, rather, one for whose actions the clan and even the entire tribe were responsible. The individual and the family were not yet legal entities. There was no law except tribal custom—for there was no real government outside of the tribes. Private property prevailed, but within the framework of clan ties and the tribal community. There was a mixture of several epochs: life was individual, thinking was tribal, and feelings were clannish.

The Montenegrin tribe was not like that of the American Indian or of the African Negro. Only the forests and pastures were held in common by the clan and the tribe, and these were constantly the cause of quarrels and strife with other tribes. Everything else belonged to the family as a collective unit, in the form of private property. Here the tribe was maintained as much, if not more, on the basis of hostility toward other tribes as through a tradition of blood kinship.

While some maintain that our tribes found their origin in cantonal shepherd communities, others cite blood ties. Cannot both the one and the other be true? Did not these tribes, already connected by blood ties, maintain themselves and expand under the conditions of a predominantly shepherd economy?

When the Turks came to Montenegro, they encountered tribes. In the other Serbian lands tribes had dissolved long before the Turkish invasion. Feudalism had been established in Montenegro as well, not only in the lowlands—in Zeta—but also in the highlands. The division into nobility and commoners took hold here, but in the mountains the tribes still held on, though as a territorial unit and not as a kinship community only.

* Aleksandr N. Popov, Russian author of several works published in the late 1840's on Montenegrin history and law, and a travel account.

It is not known for certain whether the Montenegrin tribes were the old Slavic kinship communities or new formations which were joined by alien clans—perhaps those of the aborigines—out of territorial or other necessity, and which in time accepted the myths and blood taboos of the dominant group. The belief in a common blood tie is stubborn and holds true without exception for all the tribes. But they also tell of the joining together of clans of various origins into one tribe. In such cases it is known which clans came from the outside.

Whichever way it was, the Turks found tribes in Montenegro, as well as in northern Albania. And it was these tribal collectives that came into conflict with the Turks.

There were similar territorial and kinship communities outside of Montenegro—in the mountains of Old Serbia and Macedonia. Some parts of Albania, and even the Morea (the Peloponnesus), especially in the mountainous regions, had some form of tribal organization whose autonomy was recognized by the Turks. Sometimes such communities even became independent. Like the Montenegrins under the Turks, they were usually obliged to go to war upon the Sultan's invitation and to pay him tribute, but in all else they were independent.

The Turks not only found tribes in Montenegro, but, as Professor Djurdjev * has proven, they even recognized them as separate entities.

Circumstances and the strength of the tribe dictated whether it was capable of taking further steps toward independence or whether the Turks would be successful in imposing serf relationships upon it, thus destroying it as an entity.

The tribes of Montenegro, especially of Katuni, had that strength—all the more so since they were of a different faith and tongue and way of life from the Turks, and because they had someone on whom to lean for support—on Venice—in an epoch of ever greater wars and other troubles which assailed the Turkish Empire.

The tribe resisted and rebelled as a unit. The Kuči, for example, did so many times. This was in keeping with their predominantly tribal consciousness. Still they could not persist alone in resisting the might of the Turkish state. It was most natural for them to look

* Branislav Djurdjev (b. 1908), Serbian historian who specializes in the Turkish period of Serbian history.

to ethnically and linguistically identical tribes for support. And indeed, in the course of the struggle there was formed a league of tribes which lasted up to the time of Bishop Rade, when that role was taken over by the state, since the tribes fell apart as soon as the rebellions and the wars were ended.

It was in the tribe, too, that the national consciousness developed and grew stronger, thanks primarily to the Church—the only surviving guardian of the tradition of the medieval Serbian state. It is important, perhaps even decisive, that this church had been autocephalous from the time of Saint Sava, as a Serbian church, and that it was coextensive with the Serbian nationality and the Serbian state. Only as such could it become the bearer of national consciousness and a state tradition. Religion and nationality became completely identified, all the more so as trade, rebellions, wars, and migrations integrated the Serbian population, and all the more easily inasmuch as the Moslems were aliens—whether as Turks or as the governing class of feudal lords and privileged free peasants. The resistance to exorbitant taxes and to serfdom was transformed into a religious and national movement.

The spark of resistance against the Turks never died out among the Montenegrin tribes and clans. It was they who fanned the spark into the fire of national resistance. The independence of internal tribal life was a condition for this. The destruction of that independence was later to be the condition for the formation of a Montenegrin state and for the metamorphosis of this resistance into a national struggle of the Serbs, and even the Yugoslavs, for liberation and unification.

The only thing that could destroy the Montenegrin tribes was extermination or internal dissolution. The Montenegrin tribes, or at least the majority of them, were not yet ripe for the latter at the time of the Turkish invasion. The tribe in Montenegro contained within itself, in its blood ties, inexhaustible powers and vital forces which one not nurtured by them can hardly suspect. In addition to these forces, here and there in little remote and isolated monasteries, there flickered the memory of the medieval Serbian state, feudal, but our own, which the inchoate and disintegrated feudal masses transformed into a myth and epic of ancient glory and hope.

It was a prefeudal form, the Montenegrin tribe, that encountered and survived the Turks. Its primeval strength and power, now inspired by a myth which emanated from the people and a concept of statehood propagated by the Church, expanded in ever greater circles to include individuals and movements beyond itself: the First and Second Insurrections in Serbia, Karadjordje, Hajduk Veljko, and Vuk Karadžić as well. This amalgam of tribal strength, the concept of the state, and the myth was greatest where the tribe had been best preserved, and where other conditions were also favorable—in Montenegro, among the tribes of Katuni, in Njeguši.

6.

As WAS so often the case with Serbian states, the tribe of Njeguši found itself on the crossroads between two worlds—West and East. As ever the Serbian people, so, too, the Njeguši found their own way. They made secure their way of life and molded our history. They were situated on a likely spot for this; besides, they were themselves resourceful and resolute. History favors the bold and the wise. It also seeks the line of least resistance. It only breaks through the weakest, most rickety gates. Here, around Lovćen, was the Turkish Empire's point of least resistance. The Njeguši found their own way—through strengthening the bishopric and inaugurating the governorship—in order to cut into a festering tumor. This was the doing of all the men of Katuni. They were fighting only for survival, but they began a new epoch in Serbian history.

True, there is no evidence that the Njeguši tribe excelled in any way over neighboring tribes. Yet they certainly enjoyed an advantage. For one thing, they were the closest to the Venetian towns on the Bay of Kotor—only some four or five hours away—and they were the farthest and the most remote from the centers of Turkish rule. It may thus be concluded that they were in the best position to break away, to get out into the world and to look farther. It was across their lands that trade and goods from the sea went into the interior of Montenegro, and with them gold and Venetian influence and the stream of a more civilized life.

In their struggle with the Turks the men of Katuni and the Njeguši not only depended on Venice for support, but they were frequently incited by Venice. Bishop Danilo writes to the Doge Bembo, "To the best of my abilities I shall serve and ever obey your most ill[ustrious] and most ex[alted] l[ordship]." This is the manner in which a weaker party holds converse with one that is stronger and more cultured. But Danilo was not fighting for himself, but for Montenegro—and he did not wish to serve the Turks. According to the historian Jovan Tomić, it was Venice that brought the Montenegrin tribes, and primarily the tribes of Katuni, into the Morean War on its side, and it was that war which brought a stronger unity to the tribes, and gave impetus to the role of Bishop Danilo, and, later, Bishop Vasilije, and especially Stephen the Small. It was certainly not mere chance that it was only after the Morean War—with the first real consolidation of the tribes—that the bishops began to come from the same tribe, the Njeguši, from the Petrović clan, and that it was this same tribe which also established the civil authority, with the governors coming from the Radonjić clan, upon the demand of Bishop Danilo's envoys—according to the historian Risto Dragičević—and by a decree of the Doge Cornaro in 1717 which was addressed to the men of Katuni and which gave them the right of electing a governor through communal and tribal delegates. If both the bishopric and the governorship came to reside in the Njeguši through Venice's support, this only shows that they—the Njeguši—had already distinguished themselves and had a place of pre-eminence among the other tribes, not only of Katuni, but also of Montenegro.

The Njeguši were themselves aware of their significance. Had they not ensured for themselves a continued succession to the bishopric and to the governorship? Bishop Vasilije, a successor to the first Petrović bishop—Bishop Danilo—praises the Njeguši in his *History of Montenegro* in terms even more glowing than the hyperboles he bestowed upon the other Montenegrins: "The district of Njegoš, in which is the town of Njegoš, where the chief Montenegrin lords and Officers reside." Bishop Vasilije did not do this entirely without reason. The Njeguši were indeed the most distinguished tribe. They were like all the other tribes in that they plundered others, defended their own, and avenged their dead. But they differed in keeping for themselves the two most important posts of joint rule. Vuk Karadžić has recorded that within each tribe as well the chieftaincy became hereditary, and that the elections were more in the nature of confirmations, inasmuch as the most powerful clan always stood behind the chieftain. But the bishop and the governor were not tribal chieftains. The bishop and the governor were elected at an assembly of Montenegro chieftains. And it was the Njeguši who first succeeded in having these joint rulers always come from their midst, thus making both positions quasi-hereditary. Though a tribe like any other, the Njeguši, primarily out of their own tribal interests, to be sure, became the strong hub of intertribal interests as well. Consequently nowhere was the idea of a common struggle for the liberation of the Serbs more determined.

Had the tribes of Montenegro disintegrated earlier, it is hardly likely that Montenegro would have been the first to wage the struggle for liberation from the Turks. At best it would have become liberated when Serbia was—and it might have become a state immediately without the special cult of heroism and certainly without Njegoš's poetry.

It was from the Njeguši tribe—from the commingling of tribal emotion and Serbian consciousness, from a feeling for myth and the mythical past as immediate reality—that Njegoš's poetry grew, just as his state was a link between the tribal order and the idea of the medieval state that the Church had nurtured and kept alive. When Njegoš called all the Serbs "a tribe, my tribe," he did this with a completeness of feeling that left no room for anything else, that knew of no other community but this blood kinship. It was this idea, plus folk poetry and state necessity, that elevated this tribal feeling into a passion and spread it throughout the entire nation.

Njegoš was a Serb, but a tribesman. It would be most exact to say that he was from the Nahi of Katuni, of the Njeguši, a Serb of the Petrović brotherhood—and especially this last.

For though a Njeguš by tradition, and to a degree in feeling, he could not, he was not able to, belong entirely to his tribe. Tribal willfulness and exclusiveness had already become a hindrance to the further struggle against the Turks and to the establishment of a central government.

7.

For all this, from his earliest childhood Njegoš had to be a Petrović in all things.

The sense of belongingness to a tribe was emotionally absorbed by the brotherhood. The tribe was more of a rational tie—involving pastures and battles. It was like a state—a community based upon an area and the interests of brotherhoods which tell, and believe, that they have the same ancestors. But in the very being and subconsciousness of the individual was the brotherhood, whatever its size or antiquity. Sins against it were unforgivable, while the sacrifices made for it were the sweetest and the most complete. The murder of a member of another brotherhood in the same tribe was settled by the tribe—through a peace settlement, making one member of the clan godfather to a member of the other, or through oblivion. A murder within the brotherhood, if such a monstrosity were ever to happen, had no way of being settled. The pain lasted until death and was remembered beyond it, though the shameful deed was never mentioned. The blood of the brotherhood was incalculably dear, the honor of its maidens peremptorily pure, its shame intolerable, and all it did just and true.

The tribe and its order had to be learned. The brotherhood was inbred, imbibed with one's mother's milk.

The family was only a particle, a unit of the clan. It was the warmest and dearest because it was the nearest, but its obligations and significance were those of the brotherhood.

Rade's father, Tomo Markov, already in his years, was a man of sound and deep wisdom and—what is rare—a very mournful man, overly sensitive to grief and misfortune. He made up epic poems in his head and chanted them to the tune of the gusle. But he was not especially distinguished. After all, it was not easy to step ahead of so many distinguished men among the Katuni and the Petrovići. Rade's mother, Ivana, on the other hand, was a hardhearted woman with an utterly insuperable sense for practical realities.

Rade liked his brothers. Pero was the older, Joko was much younger. But it is known that he reserved an exceptional brotherly love for his sister Marija.

There was one very special person in his family: his uncle Lazo Proroković, whose renown was known far and wide to all, let alone to his nephew. Medaković called him "a wild Montenegrin, huge, tall, with long mustachios, and ruddy face." There has remained a good sketch of him: bulging neck muscles, the entire face in little gnarls, the forehead as though chiseled in stone, the hair bristling —everything tense, savage, indefatigable. We find nothing of his in

Njegoš's refined features, except perhaps something of the moody violence, the turbulence of spirit. Lazo was a hajduk, a bandit, a great one for feasts and speechmaking and giving gifts, and a chieftain who demanded obedience and paid little heed to anyone. The long years he spent fettered in Kotor dungeons only steeled him to protect what was his own and to take for his own. Even Bishop Rade himself, severe ruler that he was, let Lazo Proroković alone, and not so much because he owed his uncle respect, but for fear of his cutting words. It was he whom Bishop Rade sent to represent him before an Austrian court. And when a treaty was made concerning that part of the border between Montenegro and Austria which touches the Njeguši, Lazo managed to join his sovereign in Kotor. While the negotiations were being conducted, Lazo interrupted him during the proceedings and defended what belonged to him with the keenness of a scimitar. The Bishop had agreed to return all booty. Lazo would not give in, but insisted: Finders keepers! The Bishop agreed to require passports of Montenegrins going to Kotor. Lazo would not give in: Our godfathers and friends are there, and who is going to go to Cetinje for a passport for every little thing? And so it was with everything else: "You make the border for Montenegro, but leave Njeguši to me, for I am their captain." Even in his way of life Lazo was different; he ran his household like a signior of the coast. In fact, all the Prorokovići were a special breed. Once, Njegoš ordered them to dress in their finest and then—and only he could think up something of the sort—he paraded them before the chieftains saying, "Behold how fair, O Montenegrins, are my uncle's kin!"

Little is known about the Petrovići of that time. That they were a bold and self-reliant brotherhood is evident from their exceptional role for over a century—from their whole line of bishops, and the number of their heroes, which the impartial folk epics never tired of tallying. They were to a man of swift mind, rather abrupt and wild nature, but stubborn will. Njegoš's bonds with his brotherhood must have been all the greater because of the role and significance of his forebears, and all the more so since they were the incarnation of a pledged goal, an idea, and a reality—Serbian freedom, the tradition of the medieval state, and daily bloodletting with the Turks.

It was not easy to be a Montenegrin, and especially not a man of Katuni. And it was hardest of all to be a Petrović. In those days chieftaincies were not yet distributed for money, and the Petrovići displayed none of that gluttony and ostentation and lordliness that came later under Prince Nikola. One was simply proud of being a Petrović then. And they really believed that no clan was equal to their own. But this had to be won by the sword and confirmed by decency. The Petrovići were wanting in neither, just as they were not averse to having their own way. This, too, Njegoš was to get from them.

But how did the boy Rade assimilate all this?

We know the environment and the atmosphere, but we know so little about his childhood. It has been handed down that he was big for his age; his clothes were too small for him and he was laughed at for it. Also that he learned to handle weapons from earliest childhood. But that was hardly anything special. What little Montenegrin shepherd boy was not adept at handling weapons? And who escaped wearing his brother's too-short hand-me-downs? There is not a word, not a reference to his childhood. And yet, what is known about Karadjordje's childhood? He herded swine, like all the other youngsters of Šumadija. And what is known about the childhood of Miloš, Garašanin, Pašić? All of our great men rose out of poverty and a hard life, out of peasant anonymity. So it was with Njegoš. Yet he inherited greater obligations than any of them.

As a Petrović he was born with obligations—clannish, Montenegrin, and Serbian.

The blood, the passions, and the aspirations of the clan merged with the great national ideas and age-old pledges in his uncle—in Bishop Petar. One could not observe this merger in Njegoš—he was so much of one piece.

This came from his father's sensitivity, his mother's sense, the will of his brotherhood, the liberty of Katuni, Montenegro's struggle against evil, the myths of Serbian history, the horizons and inspirations from books. But it came mostly from within himself: he was born to receive this, to fuse it all into poetry and a state, a cry and wisdom.

8.

ALL WHO EVER visited Montenegro in the time of Bishop Rade have confirmed the great piety of the Montenegrins. But hardly any of these visitors noted that this godliness did not have much to do with Christian dogma or even with church ritual. There was little of worship, and even less of dogma.

Vuk Vrčević once cited as evidence of their savagery the fact that one quarter of all Montenegrins were unbaptized—truly a wonder in a land where there was a surfeit of priests. But the fact he cited points to something else: to very powerful un-Christian beliefs in magic.

Indeed, among the Montenegrins of that time and later, the belief in devils, witches, spells and sorceries, werewolves, vampires, wizards and signs was emotionally stronger than the belief in Christian saints and their relics and powers. The saints were accepted from the teachings of the Church, but one experienced those mysterious forces directly—from caves and graves, or the neighbor woman's overgrown eyebrows. I remember reading in Jireček that every house in Montenegro has its own guardian spirit—a shade, which can be a man, a dog, a snake, or a hen. And the lakes, woods, and mountains have their shades, too. The saint in whom the Montenegrins believe most is a native one—Vasilije of Ostrog. They also esteem another—Bishop Petar. The former is involved in their entire life—public and private, civil and personal—while they believe that the latter worked miracles in his lifetime, that he possessed a special power. All the other saints are but abstractions—something learned and brought from church. The cult of the Mother of God, so widespread in the West, as well as the cult of Christ, so widespread in the East, are hardly noticeable here. Though a bishop and religious poet, in all his writings Njegoš did not mention the Mother of God, while he mentioned Christ only once, and then in a lyrical vein and more as "the mild, good teacher" than as God. As for the Holy Trinity, he makes no mention of it; the Montenegrins know nothing about it except what someone may have heard here or there from a priest.

Njegoš was generally uncongenial to dogma, while the Montenegrins were too primitive and too infected in earlier epochs not to be superstitious. Not only their superstitions, but even their Christian beliefs had the quality of magic. As for Njegoš, his lack of dogmatism, however personal, also reflected his milieu. So it was even with his uncle, Bishop Petar, a great ascetic and later a saint, but in whose numerous epistles one can hardly find any mention, and then only parenthetically, of Christ, the Mother of God, or a saint.

Yet Bishop Petar and Bishop Rade and the Montenegrins all had constantly on their lips the name of God—the one God, the Almighty and the Creator, who is in and acts on all things, the power and the law above all. Otherwise, the two bishops were rationalists—religious rationalists. They wished to introduce civil order into the land, and they were hindered by "old wives' tales," belief in magic and superstition. In his epistles to the Montenegrins Bishop Petar instructed and entreated them not to believe in such nonsense, while Bishop Rade poked fun at it in his works. Petar's understanding of God emanated from his faith and the Church, while Rade's was philosophical and poetic. But with both of them that understanding was, so to say, Montenegrin.

Alongside their belief in magic and superstition, the Montenegrins did believe in one God. They even expressed familiarity with him, in the thought that God's power was limitless, but it was here, in us. Lacking bells, some Montenegrins signaled the beginning of church services by firing rifles: Let our God hear us, one way or another. This magic and at the same time rational conception of God—magic in feeling and practice, and rational in consciousness—was very strong and shows profoundly and more completely than anything else the piety of the Montenegrins, and of the two bishops, Petar and Rade. Only, with them, and especially with the latter, this magical intimate relation with God became rational—more of a conception than a belief.

However, as soon as it was translated into practical life, especially in the struggle with the Turks, the Montenegrin faith showed to what degree there was something basically un-Christian, something even contrary to Christianity, in it. Anything that might impede this struggle disappeared from the Montenegrin religion, if indeed it was ever there. There is not a trace of nonresistance to evil. The Montenegrin can understand and can do everything except turn the other cheek. Montenegrins are the only

Christians who not only act out of revenge, but also believe in revenge as if it were the most consummate joy and the highest justice. Revenge is one's pride before men—a mystical dedication. One Montenegrin has said for them all: "Christianity was born in blood." It is a saying among them: "What we have not fought for we have not earned."

The Montenegrin God is a God of vengeance—not just that, but that above all else.

The fasts are strictly kept for the good of the soul, and the feasts are observed—especially the folk holidays, Christmas, the day of one's patron saint, and All Souls' Day. But there is little of prayers and processions, and what there is of these, the people do not put much store in. A Montenegrin once crossed himself while passing a garrison in Kotor, thinking that it was a church, and when this was pointed out to him, he replied calmly, "Well, the Devil has taken so many of my prayers, let him take this one, too!" Another Montenegrin, on buying an icon, did not wish to buy the one of his patron saint, Luke, because he was portrayed as barefoot and unimposing, and he preferred Saint George: "Give me that hero over there; and may Saint Luke forgive me as best he can!"

That faith and that God were also among the inherited obligations of the boy Rade—toward the cosmos and toward man. Having grown up quickly, he understood them all the sooner. And he was to join together all of these obligations toward his land, his people, and the brotherhood, through song, thought, and deed.

A handful of men stood fast in Katuni, and the blood of the Petrovići boiled—on a bare crag surrounded on all sides by a Montenegrin and Serbian world that was suppressed, divided, and bloody.

Only Lovćen stood above the darkness.

Lovćen's peak was close and unforbidding. On its gentle slopes the herds grazed mornings and evenings. From its heights one could see what the Njeguši could only feel: mingling of the sea breezes with the mountain air, the gentle and the sharp, the clash of two worlds. Here colors met and blended into one another like realities and hopes. The rock and the sea. Evil and good.

The sea that lapped one side of Montenegro was in the hands of the Latins, while the rock that melted into the Plain of Zeta was in the hands of the Turks. Between them rose the rough green-tinged wilderness of the Nahi of Katuni and the rest of Montenegro—embattled tribes and tributaries; all thinking the same thought, speaking the same word, and feeling the same pain in their breasts. Beyond Katuni, which lay at the foot of Lovćen, the chieftains of all the tribes had gone to the Turks and even now were flying their banners and taking their bribes to wage war on their own brethren and to fetter them in alien bonds. Everywhere darkness; only Lovćen blazed. Karadjordje had been driven from Serbia, while Njegoš's uncle Bishop Petar had been driven from the Littoral. The Serbian lands spread sight unseen, but even the skies above them were crowded with their misfortunes.

It was this land—Montenegro—small and troubled, across which Turkish and Latin cannon called out to one another, which bore the pledges of the whole Serbian race and universal greatness in its midst. It was a bad land, but a heroic one, accursed, but ours.

So it was. Such was life. This is what was handed down from one's ancestors—from the first to the last.

Bishop Danilo complained about his "accursed" and "senseless" people, about "this crazy country." "Consumed by many tribulations and by the fire in which we are burning in this land," his legs "rotting and putrid" from irons, wasting in cells through sleepless vigils, he observed that "it is enough that I am alive among this bad and unruly people."

And did not Rade's uncle Petar cry out that "in my old age I am fleeing from the violence of Cetinje." Blinded by his tears, he wailed that there was no more life for him in this wretchedness and that all were ready to scatter across the Turkish land, "some from hunger, and others from the wickedness and harassment of their brethren." He complained to the Njeguši and to the men of Katuni, "If I lived among the Turks I would not have to bear the travail which I suffer at the hands of the Montenegrins." And he complained of the sickness in his legs, and he begged and pleaded and implored enough to melt stone—but "none even turned to look," for "they loved evil and shame more than goodness and virtue." "If you could, you would even bring the Turks here!" And in his letters to the Montenegrins and Brdjani, or Highlanders, he began to sign himself simply as "still in vain your unfortunate benefactor." Painfully he bared before the Montenegrins his long life and long service: "Had I done this for any other people on earth, they would have been grateful and I would have lived among them in happiness and joy, and my name would have been held by them in eternal love, but among you my heart has shriveled from your misdeeds and my old age has become embittered so that I take joy in nothing."

This is how Danilo, too, wrote—and he signed himself: "With tears mingled with the words that I write, Bishop Danilo, mournful and sad, surrendering myself to death for the sake of Christ, that is to say, for the sake of the people."

That, too, was an inheritance—"to death for the sake of Christ, that is to say, for the sake of the people."

Rade did not know what they had written. But he understood, being immersed in it. This was bred into his uncle Petar and the Petrovići. This was sheer poetry—wailing over the fate of the land and people as over one's own.

There was much evil, and it was intolerable. There was also brilliance and greatness. But nowhere tranquillity or joy.

"For the sake of the people." One had to fight. It had to be so. Trouble and toil wherever one turned, as though man were conceived only for this.

And one had to learn. His uncle said so. He knew. He was Montenegro—wise, Serbian, and heroic. He was that Montenegro which was not evil, which wrestled with evil. He was the soul of the land, the head of the brotherhood, and the conscience of man.

Even if Rade had no desire or need for learning, it would have been his duty to obey the martyr—his uncle Petar.

THE SELF-TAUGHT PUPIL

1.

IT WAS LONG held to be a true account that Bishop Petar had brought his nephew Rade to the monastery at Cetinje in order to train him to become his successor.

However, this is not certain.

The Bishop had sent his nephew Mitar Stijepov to school in Russia after tonsuring him and appointing him archimandrite of the Monastery of Stanjevići. But Montenegrin youths sickened easily and died quickly on the cold and damp Russian steppes. This is what befell Mitar as well. As for Rade, Dragičević has established that they brought him to Cetinje in the beginning of 1825—the same year in which a third nephew, Djordjije Savov, had been named the Bishop's successor and sent to school in Russia. But Bishop Petar did not have any better luck with this nephew: Djordjije had no wish at all to be a monk, and got himself transferred into a military school in 1829.

Up to that point—up to the year 1829—Bishop Petar obviously could not have appointed Rade his successor. True, it is claimed that he made an effort on two occasions to send Rade to school in Russia, but that the Russians refused, on the basis of their experience with the other two nephews, and offered the excuse that it was better for him not to become accustomed to the luxuries he could not have in his own land. Neither in 1829 nor until his death did Bishop Petar specifically designate his successor.

From a strictly formal point of view, he did not have the right to do so: the bishops were elected and confirmed by the chieftains in assembly. Bishop Petar could only train a successor from among his kin and rely on circumstances that he would be confirmed.

This is what he actually did, and so it may be concluded with fair certainty, though there is no written evidence, that he might have gotten the idea in 1829 of making Rade his successor, especially since Rade had by that time practically finished his studies.

Bishop Petar made an effort to give all of his kin, including Rade, some sort of education. This does not mean that he had not taken note of Rade even before 1829. On January 20, 1827, he wrote to Gagić, certainly having in mind his lack of success with his previous heirs apparent, "I have still other nephews, especially one who spent a year and a half with the monk Josif Tropović at Topla; he can read a bit, and one can see that apparently he has a pleasant physiognomy and a good nature."

According to Dragičević and others, Rade remained in Cetinje from the beginning of 1825 to the middle of that year for his first schooling. In mid-1825 he was sent to the Bay of Kotor, to Tropović, where he remained until the end of 1826, for his second, and most regular, schooling. Sima Milutinović-Sarajlija arrived in Cetinje on September 25, 1827, and remained until 1831. He found Rade there when he arrived. During that time, but apparently for only one year—1828 with any regularity, Rade studied under Sarajlija—his third schooling.

Nevertheless, even in a literal sense, Njegoš was self-taught. His only teachers were autodidacts who taught him poorly and irregularly. Bishop Petar was himself an autodidact. This is how education was transmitted for centuries among these people—the self-taught taught the self-taught.

Rade also studied a bit during his first stay in Cetinje, in 1825, for he knew how to read by the time he went to Tropović.

But who could have been his teacher?

Not his uncle, who was old and too occupied.

A certain monk, Misail, is mentioned, as well as the Bishop's secretary Jakov Cek. But might it not have been Ivanchik, the Russian, also the Bishop's secretary? Svetislav Petrović maintains that his first teacher was Misail Cvetković-Bajkuš, of the upper Nišava Valley, whom rebellions against the Turks had brought to Cetinje and taken back again to his homeland—to the Monastery of the Mother of God. Bajkuš lived until 1888 and told this to the author Mita Rakić. There were many secretaries, and even more teachers —and so little time, and so few results.

Josif Tropović, priest in Topla, to whom Rade had been sent for schooling, was a nephew of the Archimandrite of Savina Monastery, Inokentije Dabović, and was born—according to Ljubomir Vlačić—in 1775, in the village of Presjeci, in the district of Herceg Novi. This means that he was past fifty when he accepted Rade as a pupil. The Bishop knew Tropović intimately as the result of his frequent sojourns and long military campaigns in Boka, the Bay of Kotor. Tropović also took in other children as pupils, and they had their board and lodging with him. Rade was in the hands of a literate man, but it was hardly a school. Indeed, Tropović himself had had no regular schooling, but had learned his letters in Savina Monastery. The pedantic and suspicious Austrian police have left us a record about Tropović: he knew some Italian, he was dignified and healthy, "of no great education, but he endeavors to conceal his lack of schooling and learning through his exemplary behavior." Also this: that he was avaricious, that he lent money at high interest rates, for which he was hated, though he was zealous as a priest. In politics he was circumspect and—the reports add—devoted to the Montenegrin Bishop, who ordained him.

Njegoš's first and only regular teacher, Tropović was a man who lacked broad horizons and knowledge. He looked upon his spiritual vocation as a trade and upon his teaching as a means to supplement his income, but he was a solid Serb and conscientious. The poet Njegoš could not have learned anything at all from him. But Rade did learn reading and writing, even though with Tropović one went only through the prayer book and the psalter, and maybe some sums.

Not even here did Rade remain as long as he should have—only a year and a half. Vrčević states that he matured too early and began to frequent the edges of town, and Tropović was afraid that the Bishop's nephew might become corrupted, and so sent him home before time. Be that as it may, Njegoš learned very little during this most regular schooling he ever had.

The first preserved example of Njegoš's writing is from the year 1828. As Isidora Sekulić observed, it reveals all "the misery and the greatness of Rade Petrović's education." He could write, and there is even verve in some of the lines, but truly, in his fifteenth year he was, as she put it, "all boy . . . complete illiteracy."

He was never to master punctuation and orthography. He would always be learning, from year to year, until his last breath, and his literacy and knowledge were constantly to grow. But he was to the last a self-taught man. His poetry reflected the self-taught man insufficiently taught. He was not able to conceal this in the civilized and learned world. To the very end his handwriting was to betray a mixture of the finest polish with a peasant laboriousness.

2.

WHILE STUDYING IN Boka, he imbibed an environment different from the Montenegrin. And he was always to yearn for it and to return to it, to his early youth and to his first new horizons.

Boka, the Bay of Kotor—that is where Montenegro treads into the sea. And yet it is not Montenegro. The language is the same, and the religion and the origin of many of its people. But different customs prevail there, another past and a different attitude toward the world and toward life.

Rock-hewn monsters stir about and quiver in the green and the gray and the violet, holding councils of war in the murky depths of the sea. Two elements—the sea and the mountain—confront each other in an eternal drama, exchanging blows and caresses. Where else is the rock so joyfully washed and the sea more childishly angry? The piedmont is nourished by the silt of the wasting limestone, while the peaks take breath in the salty air. The coast joins the mountains with endlessness. While the peaks are still covered with snowdrifts, all the coastland seethes with the vermilion and violet of blossomtime.

Here even the men are more serene and tranquil. Everything ebbs and flows, and we are here to last as long as we be, and not to remake the world and to catch storms in our caps. And the women are more diaphanous and shadowy, more curvaceous and feminine, each a mother and a sister and a female in one, without the sharp edges of Montenegrin women. Little towns face the high seas and lean their backs against the sheer crags. From time out of mind the men of the Bay tamed their mountain brethren and rejuvenated their own blood with theirs. Down here flourished the enduring pleasures and beauties of the Greeks, of the Romans, and of the Venetians; up there the tribes of the Illyrians, of the Albanians, and of the Montenegrins waged war with heaven and earth and with one another. The sea would be nothing without the coast; the man on the coast could exist without the Montenegrin, but without the man on the coast the Montenegrin would be reduced to savagery.

How much of the Bay rubbed off on Njegoš only he knew, if indeed this is at all possible for anyone to know. But those elusive hues, that barely perceptible fragrance, so different from the tart saps of Montenegro, that vibration of muffled undertones beneath the roaring of monsters and the hissing of hatred and steel—all this Njegoš might have gotten from the Bay. The Bay, the sea—yes, the sea, was to remain a constant, subdued, but ever-present motif of loveliness in his poetry. It was to appear in the poems he wrote on his travels, in the joyous visions, and in the deafening pounding of his blood as he sang the fate of a whole people in that awesome poem *The Mountain Wreath.*

The sea offered the only respite from the all-encompassing Turkish rule and from the limitless despair of the Balkans and of the Serbs, from the confines of Montenegro.

His uncle Bishop Petar, too, and, for that matter, all the Petrović bishops and later princes, yearned for the sea. Danilo erected the Monastery of Majine at the edge of the Plain of Budva, and there he was buried. Sava was buried in Stanjevići Monastery—actually in a foreign state, but within sight of the sea. Bishop Petar resided in Stanjevići for a while, until Russian love and Austrian force dislodged him. They were later to drive Njegoš away as well, and to chain him to the Montenegrin crag.

Njegoš's enthusiasm for Boka, for the sea, was not only political. He yearned for a link with the world and with more genteel and gracious living. This was a love beguiled by a new-found beauty. He was always to return to Boka, never relinquishing his first love, until his death. And even in his hour of death, he thought of the Bay, in the hope of finding there, if not a cure, then the soothing comfort of its serene expanse.

He spent nearly every summer there, at Prčanj, and hastened to the sea even in late fall. It was there, apparently caught by the intoxicating beauty of a woman of the coast, that he wrote his only preserved love poem, *The Night Gathers the Age,* that magical and elusive union of animal passions and terrors with a uniquely human, inexhaustible, and refined tenderness and regard in the throes of "a holy desire fulfilled"—the cosmic act of mating and love.

It was the Bay and its culture that gave Njegoš the polish, more apparent in his psyche and manner than in his creations, that served him in getting about in the world at large and in high society—and that gave form to his native elegance. The Bay opened a window for him beyond Montenegrin travail and Serbian bondage. Through it he gazed at the joys and beauties of the world. It enlightened, nurtured the poet and developed the human in him. It was the smile on a face stiff with pain and horror.

He also got something of all this from Tropović and his family, primarily from Tropović's wife, who, they say, had grown up in Venice. But the most important thing, not a learned attitude or manner, rather, an inner sense and content, he acquired and assimilated himself, being acutely observant and sensitive.

He did not, nor could he, receive any higher learning from Boka, let alone from Tropović. Nevertheless it was here that he first set foot in the infinite realm of learning and beauty, which he painfully sought all his life only to remain forever unsated—lacking in reading and even more lacking in learning.

This was just one of the woes with which he had to struggle to the end, relentlessly as in everything.

3.

THERE WAS SOMETHING else, which he could not have gotten from anyone in the Bay, but which he was to get in Cetinje, from his only real teacher—Sima Milutinović-Sarajlija.

Sarajlija showed up in Cetinje uninvited, led by the passions of adventure and poetry and, at the same time, deep patriotism.

He was neither the first nor the last stranger to be attracted by the blazing heroism and hidden power of Montenegro.

A gifted adventurer—Stephen the Small—had once wandered into this land from out of nowhere, and organized the first civil government.

There was something of the adventurer in the Petrović bishops as well—in every one of them, in one way or another. Danilo used to sign himself "War Lord of the Serbian Land." And just exactly what is a war lord? Neither a warrior nor a lord. And just what Serbian land that might be, even he did not rightly know, for Montenegro was but the hem of the garment. What a leap into the unknown was that rift of his with the Turks! Bishop Vasilije fabricated nobles and governorships in Montenegro, and styled himself "Exarch of the Serbian Throne"—when in fact there had been no trace of a throne for ages and he was but the bishop of a handful of Montenegrins and Primorci, or men of the Littoral. But that is how it had to be, that is what was needed in order to preserve and to renew the destroyed Serbian Empire. Not even Bishop Petar and Bishop Rade were free of these traits. Striving to rise out of darkness and obscurity, they, too, awarded themselves titles to which they had no right, titles that had yet to become real. Did they not themselves embody the ceaseless conflict between wish and possibility, the idea and the reality? Was not Njegoš's poetry itself the daring ascent of a shepherd boy from Njeguši among the great?

Sarajlija simply blew into the Montenegrin wilderness, fleeing before the Kotor police because of the irregularity of his documents. Through foul weather and over rocky crags, more dead than alive, he reached Cetinje with Schiller's poems in his bag and with a sash wound about his redingote—for among the Montenegrins only the women went about sashless. He was to captivate Bishop Petar from the first moment. "As soon as I laid eyes on him, he came into my heart," the old man wrote to Gagić, and added, "I do not know whether any other Serb would be willing to live in Montenegro."

The Bishop immediately took him in as a sort of secretary. Sima pushed himself forward and grasped for power. He was not only sent, but he went himself among the tribes to dispense justice and settle disputes. He took upon himself the education of the Bishop's nephew Rade. Then suddenly something came into his head and he disappeared into the mountains, shut himself up in a hut, and after several days returned with the tragedy *Obilić*. It was not by accident that this subject came to him precisely in Montenegro, where the cult of the hero Obilić was so widespread.

He had already been everywhere, had experienced everything, had seen many different forms of government—including those born of revolution and arising from the most primitive conditions. He was nurtured in rebellions and prisons, in political strife, intrigue, and espionage, and, being himself unstable, unpredictable, he was accustomed to quick upheavals. Bishop Petar was to have many trials and tribulations with him. Sima got the old man to sign unread letters which brought the latter into conflict with Prince Miloš of Serbia. Miloš, who recognized and had a regard for the genuine thing, was to pronounce a final judgment on Sima: "A young cloud-chaser whose nose scrapes the sky."

As soon as he arrived, Sarajlija began to think up schemes, to have ideas, to lay plans. How would it be, he proposed to the Bishop, if he went secretly into Serbia and proposed an alliance to Prince Miloš to attack the Turks? He was in the very eye of the Montenegrin storm which lay pent up in the stillness of the monastery waiting to break out at the death of the old Bishop.

Direct and provocative, Sarajlija hardly felt like a stranger. Nor was he regarded as such. They called him Čubro because of his little ears. Rade's cousin Stanko Stijepov, a man of penetrating wit and reckless heroism, once remarked, "What a good fellow this Čubro of ours is." Sima immediately took to this and began to sign himself "Čubro Goodfellow." It was as though his irrepressible nature had found a refuge for the first time, in a land in which—as he himself said—"every rifle is a cannon, every head anointed, every wish the general will, every home a castle, and every cliff a fortress."

He was a handsome man with a mighty frame, and this is not without importance in Montenegro. "A little above average height, a long fair face with strong features, a powerful chest, a broad back and well-developed muscles, a high and clear forehead," says Andra Gavrilović.

That is what his pictures also portray—masculine beauty, willfulness, energy.

He already enjoyed the fame of a poet, and his life was stormy even for those times of rebellions and revolutions.

He was born in 1791 in Sarajevo—hence his nickname Sarajlija. His mother was a famed Sarajevo beauty. His father was from the village of Rožanstvo, near Užice. From his birth his life was a constant adventure. It began with his family's flight from the plague and the Turks. Its zenith came during the Serbian insurrections, and it ended in the unmatched glory of a poet and in grandiose political plans.

A student at Karlovci, a sailor in Zemun, by 1808 he had become a clerk in the Council in Belgrade. He laid Dositej Obradović * to rest and fought in the guerrilla band of the mercenary soldier Zeko Buljubaša. It was in the blaze of the insurrection that his first poems were conceived. They were not revolutionary odes, however, but love songs. They came with his first great love—for the Turkish Fatima, who was tragically murdered. Then came Zemun, Pančevo, Arad, Vienna, Dalmatia, and then across Turkey, through Grahovo, then Sarajevo—not to forget his birthplace—and then the new uprisings of 1814 and 1815 in Serbia. In 1816 he was a gardener and a tutor in Vidin, then in chains for a year or two in a Turkish dungeon. Again in Serbia in 1818—but there was no rebellion this time, so down the Danube to Kishinev, to Russia. Here he remained, all too long, to write *The Serbian Maid.* He also sent reports to Prince Miloš's confidants concerning Karadjordje's followers in exile. This did not keep him later from turning against the Obrenović faction. Then Germany in 1825, where he enrolled in the University of Leipzig; but he did not tarry there. Instead, in 1826, he set out to be a clerk in Prince Miloš's employ. On arriving in Zemun, however, he turned about and went to Trieste, Kotor, and then Cetinje—led into Montenegrin chaos by a Serbian dream refined by fire and poetry, a dream that was to be his very life, a dream more wondrous than any of his poems.

Sarajlija remained in Cetinje over three years—until the spring of 1831. But he still did not have enough of Montenegro. He was to come another three times—to be sure, on secret, inexplicable, and perhaps even invented missions.

In 1836 he escorted Prince Miloš to Istanbul, only to find himself immediately thereafter in Prague, Vienna, and Budapest. He remained a while in Budapest and married there in 1838, in haste, of course—the proposal came a day after their first meeting—with a girl who swept him off his feet because she knew his verses by heart and interpreted them so well. In 1839 he was in Belgrade—deep in political intrigue. Again flight and wandering. In 1846

* (1742?–1811). Serbian classical writer and educator. Founder of modern Serbian literature. Commonly referred to by his first name alone.

he led a group of Serbian students to St. Petersburg, where they were to study.

He was himself enchanted by the magic of his life. Just before his death he said, "Were I born again, I would wish to relive my life."

He died suddenly—how else?—at the height of his strength and vigor, in 1847, in Belgrade, after a cup of coffee. Even if another environment and person were involved, this circumstance might have given rise to suspicions of poisoning. He was mourned by all, as the greatest Serbian poet, even in distant Montenegro, where his erstwhile pupil, Njegoš, dedicated to his ashes an ode which was lavish and unstinting in love and appreciation.

Sarajlija did not offer Rade any organized and systematic learning. In view of what he was, this was impossible. He himself did not know much, even though he studied whenever he could, on the wing, between battles, poems, and adventures.

He maintained that it was most important to give Rade a Spartan training—something the boy would have received anyway from the austere Montenegrin way of life. Sarajlija forced the lad to run barefoot over the rocks and to make his way through snowdrifts half naked and hungry. The teacher himself took part in these exercises, which must have been harder on the teacher than on the pupil, who was inured to rocks and deprivation from his birth on. Montenegrins frequently found them in comical situations, and they marveled and laughed at such learning. Sarajlija himself described how he got Rade to fire a pistol into his chest—after having secretly taken out the bullet—in order to test the teacher's boast that he was no less a hero than any Montenegrin.

This curious man knew a little about everything, and he introduced Rade to history, to philosophy, to poetry. They walked during lessons, like the Peripatetics in Athens. There was no schedule or program, but the teacher told tales, offered his companionship, and most of all encouraged the youth to read as much as he could. From that time on Rade was inseparable from his studies, though he never had the opportunity to devote himself entirely to them, for even a year or two.

Sarajlija's influence is evident in everything, especially in the beginning. Njegoš's first poems are allegorical, full of coined words and artificiality and contrived diction, all reminiscent of

Sarajlija's style. However, Sarajlija turned Njegoš to something else—cosmic themes and eternal laws. He was himself of that stamp. And when the teacher died, it was this that Njegoš stressed in heavy measured elegy full of pain and pensiveness:

> You first turned my gaze toward endless space,
> To reach for stars among the heavenly choirs.

That was the deepest and most direct influence. It was also the most obvious, though little noticed. One has only to compare Njegoš's *The Ray of the Microcosm* with Sarajlija's idealistic poetry. To be sure, Njegoš is his own man. But the similarities in conception are considerable, especially in what was most important—their views of the cosmos and of man's place in it.

It was Sarajlija who first began to unfold the mysteries of heaven for Njegoš. He first told him that the earth was dust and that man was a spark in the universe, that man's life and fate were but moments in the cosmic drama.

True, it was not difficult to lead Njegoš into this realm. The youth was already given to ideas, as is evident in his very first poems, where thought and feeling transform one another and become one. And his homeland, too, was at that moment turning with its whole being toward great ideas and laws.

For Njegoš was already a poet when he became Sarajlija's pupil. Unskilled and rustic, a beginner, but—a poet.

It is recalled that the lad Rade composed a humorous poem about a wedding in Čekliće, and that the old Bishop bellowed with laughter from his cell as he overheard him reciting it to the other boys. In those days marriages took place in which bride and groom had never seen one another, having been betrothed as babes in their cradles to further the interests of their clan and house. This led to some rather strange weddings. Something would happen at the wedding party—and a poem was born.

Sarajlija recounts that he recorded heroic epic poems which young Rade Tomov chanted. Such poems were sung by Bishop Petar, too, and by Rade's father. Folk poetry was an everyday affair in Rade's family.

That is important.

Njegoš was a poet, before Sarajlija and without him, even though only in the style of his environment. Sarajlija did not bring the poet to a turning point, much less arouse him, but he led him into unknown realms, showed him that there were verses other than the ten-syllable lines of the folk bards, and that there were subjects other than the taking of sheep from the Turks. He could offer as an example his own poetry, with all its freshness and variety.

Sarajlija attracted, encouraged, instructed. He spoke vividly and impressively. And he had something to say—especially about poetry.

All in all, he acted exactly as ordinary people imagine poets to act: he was absent-minded, impetuous, eccentric, full of surprises, and himself dazzled by everything taking place around him. That is also how he wrote: he would walk, walk, then quickly sit down and write, write. In this way he composed a great historical tragedy in a week's time. Words failed him, and he complained about the poverty of the Serbian language. No matter, he was to invent words. How he invented them! Words that were entirely alien to the language, and in the most impossible combinations.

He was a poet in all his being, though he was never sufficiently able to express all that was in him. And it was that personal charm which meant so much to Rade as a budding poet.

In his travels through Europe Sarajlija had met famous men and poets. It is known that in Germany he became acquainted with Herder, Krug, Gerhard, Jacob Grimm, Uhland, and even Goethe. The great Goethe, sensing that a different kind of literature and that a forgotten and new people heedless of sacrifices were emerging in the world arena, wrote two full pages in praise of Sima Milutinović-Sarajlija, the little bard of a great national poetry and of a no lesser revolution. And that meant much, for it was Sarajlija who turned Njegoš's gaze toward the great poetry of the world at large and toward a view of the world in the large.

Sarajlija's influences were obvious and numerous, though superficial: a more learned and less gifted poet tutoring a gifted youth.

Both as a poet and as a man Njegoš remained himself, and every eccentricity was alien to him. As early as 1831 he was to speak of "the giddy Milutinović," though he preserved a tender respect for him so complete that, while writing to him in 1846, he imitated his style. We find here a hint of the kind of pleasantry spontaneously evoked by persons who are dear and good, virtuous and brave, but also somewhat peculiar and not to be taken quite seriously.

Njegoš the personality, the poet, the ruler was of one piece. In each of his aspects he was an intact, integral whole. All these influences became diffused as they penetrated into his marrow.

Truly Sarajlija led him into all the realms of the spirit. Nevertheless Njegoš remained an autodidact. His real digging into books, for knowledge, came at a later time.

The Njegoš that Sarajlija shaped and stimulated had already ventured forth on his own, along his own path and to his own destinations. What Sarajlija gave him was a schooling beyond that of folk epics and folklore.

That was a great deal under those primitive conditions and for a completely unschooled youth. But it was also so little, for it was done in haste and without system. And not very decisive for a personality of such native powers.

4.

NJEGOŠ STUDIED LATER as well, ceaselessly and diligently—with his conscience as his only examiner. In this, too, he was left to himself.

His learning, that gained from books, has been measured and evaluated. It is known, in the main, what books he read and owned, though many have been lost, especially those with his marginal notes.

From his uncle he inherited a library of about five hundred books in foreign languages. They were generally good works, but selected without order or system. Njegoš himself bought books—in the beginning frequently and many—and he received many as gifts.

His library is sometimes called the National Library and sometimes the Cetinje Library; it was in fact the first library in the Montenegrin land. Many things had their beginning there. This was understandable, for he was the first Montenegrin ruler with real authority, and this gave rise to all the rest.

The majority of his books were in Russian. He had the greatest facility in Russian and knew it best. Perhaps it seemed to him in the beginning, as it does to every Serb who marvels at the linguistic similarity between Serbian and Russian, that he knew this language, so to speak, from birth. Prince Miloš used to say, "Make fun of Serbian and there you have Russian!" Njegoš used Russian fairly easily, though his knowledge of this language was neither deep nor precise. His Russian letters contain Serbian words, largely Russified, while his Serbian texts—even the most poetic ones—are invaded by Russian expressions, as though the speed of his thought did not give him time to find one of our words. What is more natural, he mixed Russian with Old Slavonic. It is not known either when he studied Russian or from whom. It was probably along the way—from many, including the Russian monk Ivanchik, who wormed his way into Bishop Petar's service as a ubiquitous secretary and who, like his predecessor, Deacon Alexis, was kept "for the sending of written secret matters to the Russian Empire." However, Njegoš probably learned most of his Russian in Russia itself, where he spent five months in 1833—which would have been enough for even a less gifted Slav.

Njegoš was not as well off with his other languages. According to some, he did not know Italian until 1833, although Nikola Banašević claims the contrary. We do not know how he learned Italian or from whom; most probably it came from his sojourns and travels along the coast and in Dalmatia, for at that time Italian was all too prevalent there, and was practically the only official language. He never wrote in this language, and there is no evidence that he ever read any belles-lettres in Italian.

In 1837 Njegoš undertook to gain a solid knowledge of French, and to that end he brought the Frenchman Antide Jome (Antid Žom or Jaume) from Trieste. He either built or designated a separate house for Jome and his wife, a very educated and beautiful woman from Ljubljana, but a woman of tender frame who was most unhappy in the wilds of Cetinje. Being under the constantly vigilant eye of the Russian government, Njegoš knew that the arrival in Cetinje of even a teacher of the French language would arouse suspicions, and so he made preliminary excuses to Russian representatives. However, the suspicions multiplied, thanks especially to Austrian instigation. Perhaps, too, Madame Jome's nostalgia became intolerable. It could also be that Njegoš came to feel that he had acquired all the French that he needed. At any rate, Jome went away after a year and half—to, of all places, Russia. Apparently he aroused suspicion only while in Cetinje.

Medaković states that Njegoš learned French in conversation.

Undoubtedly he used it—to read the newspapers, to converse, but not with that facility one might imagine from reading Nenadović's travel account. Nenadović was a romanticist and a patriot, in love with the Montenegrins, especially with that most Montenegrin Montenegrin of all—Bishop Rade. He did not wish to see anything but greatness and perfection. Being honest, he did not invent; he simply touched up the picture by not including everything. Therefore in his account Njegoš's French appears to be more perfect than it was.

Thus Njegoš had a reading and conversational knowledge of Russian, French, and Italian, but this knowledge was neither thorough nor excellent.

According to his own statement, he also began to study German. He did write in German to the Russian Ambassador in Vienna, but this was certainly the work of his secretary Milaković, who had received his schooling in Austria. (The letter contained the Bishop's request that the Tsar give his nephew Pavle an education in Russia. The Ambassador refused to transmit the request until it was written in Russian.) Njegoš did not really know German, though it is possible that he learned something of the language during his several stays in Vienna and while traveling through Austrian lands.

There has been preserved Njegoš's translation of one of Lamartine's poems. This translation was probably simply an exercise in the language. But Njegoš studied and translated that which interested him most intimately. Just as his translations from the Russian—the beginning of the *Tale of the Host of Igor* and the *Iliad* —were epic themes, so his translation of Lamartine's poem and excerpts from Hugo in his *Notebook* were meditative. Njegoš was Njegoš in everything: in all that he did, even in studies that he undertook as a matter of practical necessity, he sought and always found the profound and the imperishable.

He intended to study ancient Greek and Turkish. This was quite in keeping with him: the first for eternal truths, and the second for the daily struggle.

And what about the other sciences? Everything in bits and pieces—à la Njegoš.

He knew hardly anything of the exact sciences, though his unquenchable thirst for their truths led him to stories and to popularizations, as Banašević has shown by citing examples. He knew much of classical mythology as well as specific facts from Turkish history. In what he learned and remembered, Njegoš unswervingly traveled those paths to which his poetry led him—to the myths of the ancients, to allegorical and heroic themes, and, in the style of the poetry of that day, to history, for nationalistic motifs.

At first glance it appears strange, but there is no trace of the Bible in his studies—either the Old Testament or the New. Indeed, one is forced to ask whether this bishop and deeply religious man had ever read the Gospel except for those parts in the services. None of his writings contain Christian legends and myths. The myth in *The Ray of the Microcosm* is only externally Christian; in fact it is a heretical deviation from dogma. There is not a mention in his writings, or in all of Montenegro, for that matter, of Christian mercy and of nonresistance to evil. Like his compatriots, Njegoš belonged to a completely different tradition, but with no less passion and keenness than that of the greatest of the prophets and the rabble-rousers.

His knowledge of national history was evident and thorough. To be sure, it abounded in half-legends—scientific history was still in its infancy—but he knew them and profoundly discerned the truth and reality in them.

His acquaintance with popular traditions, proverbs, and customs is not to be attributed simply to his times and milieu. Broadly speaking, national history is involved here as well. True, this was not something he either learned or sought especially to remember. He grew up in it. But the knowledge he possessed of these things was such that it was almost child's play for him to distill it and to extract its essence. Njegoš possessed in abundance everything that the creativity of a people and an ancient and inexhaustible folk wisdom could offer.

His mind was receptive to everything, sometimes in the naïve manner of the primitive. He once came into possession of some sort of electric machine and delighted in confounding and angering his chieftains and dignitaries by giving them shocks. He received a microscope as a gift from the Governor of Dalmatia in Zara. The strange device caused him to marvel and to complain in a letter that no one in Cetinje knew how to put it together. Of what use was all this to him? This was the curiosity of a primitive and of an overgrown child; yet also of a sage yearning for knowledge and overwhelmed by the revealed mysteries of science.

These lines were already written when I received Njegoš's *Notebook*. It lends sharpness to the above picture. The *Notebook* is precious as evidence not only of the essence and evolution of Njegoš's philosophical thought, but also of his factual knowledge, of what he read and of what interested him. It confirms his most lively interest in ancient legends and in meditative cosmic poetry —with Hugo, Lamartine.

In his *Notebook* Njegoš included all sorts of observations dating from 1846 to 1850—the period of his maturity and after he had written *The Mountain Wreath*. This was when the unusual interested him most. Here we see revealed the self-taught man lacking in comprehensive and orderly learning. He is interested in the height and breadth of churches, in large diamonds, in legends about floods among various peoples, in the size of the Great Wall of China and its builders, in the bloody moon on the eve of a certain battle with the Persians, in Darius's mother, and in the balcony from which Napoleon reviewed a regatta. But the variety of these odd facts serves to reveal how unquenchable and universal was his curiosity.

There is a logic in this: he observes and notes precisely that which his exceptionally acute views have already led him to conclude—the brevity and evanescence of all that is human, the inscrutability of man's fate, the inevitability of evil and of the struggle against it. An autodidact gifted beyond all measure, he gained insights into truths and sought their confirmation on all sides. The *Notebook* proves that he read a great deal, observed even more widely, and reasoned most profoundly. Yet it is a fact that he was not well read, and still less learned. Isidora Sekulić rightly observed that he was a sage, but no intellectual.

Nevertheless, no matter how much weight we attach to the role of the conditions that shaped his personality, we must admit the importance of the personality itself. If by any chance Rade–Njegoš had not existed, or if something unforeseen had happened to him, there would have been no *Mountain Wreath* either, if for no reason other than the plain fact that there were no Montenegrins at that time other than himself who were sufficiently literate and well read to compose such poetry. "The spark from the flintstone had found its kindling."

The little from his teachers, a bit more from books, something from his travels and conversations, much from life—enriching, acquiring, polishing, all this is scattered and visible in his works. There is the autodidact's unrestrained quest for learning, notions and truths acquired from others. But above all, it came out of himself and his people. He was his own master and under no one's shadow. Only he was capable of expressing the truths and beauties that revealed themselves to him alone.

In essence he was like his character Teodosije Mrkojević in *Stephen the Small:*

> Self-taught am I, if aught I know;
> Reading words I studied books,
> I learned the world by reading men,
> Theology by reading stars.

5.

ONE PERSON INFLUENCED Njegoš to the core of his being. That was his uncle Bishop Petar. Through him were channeled the power of the clan, the human ethics and profound currents of the national history, and, incidentally, the evils of the day thereof. The great old man was the incarnation of all this—its distilled, purified essence, a bitter cry and a profound understanding.

All the students of Njegoš—from Lavrov to Isidora Sekulić—confirm this influence, though the data concerning it are almost nonexistent. Yet truly one can, like Isidora Sekulić, be quite categorical in this claim without any fear of effacing the originality of the personality of Bishop Rade-Njegoš.

Bishop Petar surpasses all previous figures in Montenegrin history except Bishop Danilo, about whom little is known, but who is unsurpassable because he was the beginning.

Bishop Petar's roots spread wide and burrowed deep. He excelled over everyone in his clan, and encompassed all that was Montenegrin. He was the most learned man in his land, as legislator and poet, cleric and military leader of the Montenegrin tribes.

It was with Bishop Danilo, however, that the Montenegrins began their history and the Petrovići their house. He was succeeded by two of his nephews—first Bishop Sava, and then Bishop Vasilije.

Bishop Sava was an impotent and myopic personality who would have found it hard to make his way even over well-trodden paths. But there were no well-trodden paths, nor could there be. Those were times that called either for endurance or for great leaps. Sava continued Danilo's ties with Venice, but he became dependent to the point of humbly taking an oath of fealty to Saint Mark. In a country where everything, even the flowers, can prick, he found the quiet of the monastery sweeter than all else, and instead of gathering troops and leading armies, he herded sheep by the thousand and oxen by the hundred.

Vasilije shunted him aside, for the country and the clan needed a leader, and ruled as his coadjutor. He made for Russia and began to set Montenegro on its feet. However great and bold he was in this pursuit, he was also a dreamer and a roamer. In his *History of Montenegro* he not only invented a country and a state, but he lived in that invention. He was one of those fantasts who can inspire great creations. What tradition says about him is essentially true: he pushed the Montenegrins into war with the Turks and then had to flee into the wide world. Having strained his own and Montenegro's strength, he died in Russia, unhappy and far away from his rocky crags and his shepherds, in whom he saw noble creatures, because that is what he wanted to turn them into.

After Vasilije, Sava was to come to the fore once more, with all his impotence, his simple-mindedness, and—with Venice. But the times always bring forth a personality which bears and expresses their essence. There came on the scene the pretender Stephen the Small: and with him, linked together, came resistance to Venice, severance from it, and, inside the country, the beginning of law and order. They say that this crackpot was a Dalmatian, perhaps a military deserter or worse, though he himself said, and the people believed, that he was the Russian Tsar Peter III. He took a liking to the Montenegrin land, seemingly intoxicated by its woe and heroism. He began to set it in order. Indeed, he was gravely wounded while setting a mine in the construction of a road that traversed the country. He had his throat slit by a hireling of the

Vizir of Scutari, in 1774, after seven years of struggle, deceit, perseverance, and progress.

Then came Sava again, now old and even more colorless and sour than before. After him the bishopric fell to his nephew, a man from another clan—Arsenije Plamenac, of Crmnica. But he, too, was soon to die, in 1784.

Petar was then only twenty-seven years old, and already an archimandrite. His whole life stood before him—unpredictable except for the many troubles ahead. He did not fear responsibility. Ceaseless sacrifice was a way of life with him, and a profound lesson for future generations. He was tall and well formed, white-skinned and dark-eyed. Foreign visitors noted that he was exceptionally handsome. His inner self was even more harmonious and fair, as though an evil thought had never cast its shadow over his ascetic and militant soul. His opponent, Napoleon's general Marmont, noted in his memoirs: "A man of great spirit and strong character."

However, that was not all there was to Bishop Petar, nor were instruction and the faith his only concern.

When Rade joined his uncle Bishop Petar, the greatest deeds in the life of the latter were already behind him—undying legends: long military campaigns against the French and two fateful battles with the Vizir of Scutari, Kara-Mahmud Pasha Bushati; and great projects, realities still not realized: the coalition with Serbia and the establishment of law in a land without justice.

There was the carnage in the Bay of Kotor and around Dubrovnik against the French, the successors of Venice's successors, the Austrians. The two campaigns—those of 1806–1807 and of 1812–1813, ended victoriously, but tragically: the lands that had been liberated by the blood of the Bishop's compatriots were again occupied by the Austrians, who succeeded the French. A wasteland remained wherever the Montenegrins had passed: partly they and partly the colonials, as well as the Russians and the French, razed and looted everything within reach. An even more devastating wasteland remained in the Montenegrin soul, in the consciousness of the Bishop: so much blood and suffering and desolation, and still Montenegrin land and Montenegrin people were to fall to the foreigner, with the acquiescence of brotherly

Orthodox and Slavic Russia at that. It was a bitter lesson—the kind that history is pleased to bestow generously upon the small and the oppressed.

This defeat in victory was hard not only on the Montenegrins and the people of Kotor, but also on the Bishop personally. Montenegro had thereby been deprived of an outlet to the sea, to the world, and its burgeoning strength was again bound in chains. The Bay of Kotor remained under alien rule, deprived even of those privileges its little towns and captains had enjoyed under Venice. Now it was simply one of many counties of a vast bureaucratic monarchy. The Bishop had wished to forestall the Great Powers by annexing the Bay of Kotor to Montenegro. In Montenegro itself the conditions were already ripe for the establishment of a government and a state. On October 29, 1813, the Bishop had created a Central Commission, half of whose members were from the Bay of Kotor and half from Montenegro, over which he presided and which was to administer and to unite both territories. That union of arms and culture, of warriors and literate men, was propitious for the creation of a state and a foundation for the realization of more final aims. Now, however, with the annexation of the Bay of Kotor by Austria, it was all over. The Bishop returned to the bleakness of Cetinje, and the Montenegrin tribes fell to feuding again. It was a great dream in a bloody, harsh reality, of which there had been so many before in the history of the Montenegrin people.

Nevertheless, these wars had not been in vain. They brought the name of Montenegro before Europe.

There had been some interest in Montenegro before the eighteenth century, but only among the Turks and the Venetians. The Russian historian Pavel Apolonovich Rovinsky remarks, according to François Lenormant, that there could have been no interest in Montenegro before the eighteenth century because to Catholic Europe Montenegro was a schismatic country. Nor had Montenegro's individuality come to the attention of the world before the eighteenth century. Not much was to be known about it even later. The Brockhaus Encyclopedia stated in 1827 that its capital was called Atinje and that it was inhabited by robbers—"a free robber people." Colonel Vialla de Sommière, who left valuable information concerning Bishop Petar, wrote that the Montenegrins spoke a

Greek dialect! It was Vuk Karadžić, in the time of Njegoš, who was the first to write a serious and conscientious book about Montenegro.

What usually happened was that whenever a foreign power decided to wage war on the Turks, it would remember the Montenegrin tribes and their mountains next to the sea, so convenient for the smuggling of weapons and for the raising of rebellions. And so it went, into the time of Bishop Rade, and even after him. However, from the eighteenth century, from Danilo on, the Montenegrins joined forces around their bishop and were not simply an object, but an active factor, at least in the play between Venice and Turkey. It was Peter the Great who, turning his face toward Europe and a future empire, was the first Russian tsar to take notice of Montenegro and the significance of its freedom amid the darkness of oppressed Orthodoxy. From that time onward, ties with Russia sometimes weakened, but they were never broken by either side.

The egress into the world, into Europe, began with Danilo. A new leap forward was made under Bishop Petar. Between them there was much building, mending, making ready, but also aimlessness and gaps. It was with Bishop Petar that Montenegro came on the scene, and it was to remain there for an entire century, unrecognized but also ineradicable.

Napoleon himself took an interest in Montenegro and in its ruler, while his generals prepared a campaign against it. In the settling of their mutual accounts, the Austrians, the English, the French, and, of course, the Orthodox Russians, all developed an ever-growing interest in it. It became involved in Great Power politicking—and in European public opinion. The name of Montenegro became known to the world, and poets, including Pushkin and Tennyson, sang its greatness. Under Bishop Petar it ceased being merely a rebellious agalik of the Pashalik of Scutari. Now Europe reluctantly recognized that this was not simply a plot of land which all the maps ignored. The Montenegrins, too, felt differently: it was no laughing matter to cut off the heads of almighty Bonaparte's generals—Delgos, for example—and to wage war shoulder to shoulder with the Russians and the English.

Blood shed in the cause of justice had not been spilled in vain this time: they gained nothing, but they became somebody.

6.

BUT BEFORE THE wars with Bonaparte there were to come battles with Kara-Mahmud Pasha Bushati, Vizir of Scutari, battles fateful for the internal development of Montenegro and the unification of the Montenegrin tribes.

If that plaster of Paris cast of Mahmud Pasha's head that they show in the museum in Cetinje is authentic, no one would discern in those spare, intelligent, rather ironic features that terrible foe of Montenegro and of Bishop Petar, the Vizir of Scutari, as he really was. Apparently nothing daunted this aristocrat of old, this vizir by inheritance and betrayer of his sultan. He could sense the restlessness among the Christians, all the way from Serbia, while the Montenegrin tribes, including those who had been pacified but yesterday, were rebelling constantly and refusing to pay the tribute and the taxes. This irrepressible and fearless warrior, who thought of taking the Morea and Macedonia for himself, must have regarded the rebellion of the Montenegrin tribes as the rankest lawlessness and the very existence of that monk in Cetinje as an outrage against the might of the empire and of himself. Montenegro had been the pashalik of his forebears, as he well knew, until it broke away completely under Bishop Danilo.

The Vizir's first campaign took place in June, 1785.

Bishop Petar was away on an ill-timed trip to Russia, during which the Vizir bribed many tribal chieftains and set the already feuding tribes at odds with one another even more than they had been. He then struck at the rebellious part of Montenegro, including the tribes of Katuni, burning everything, down to the hitching posts. He got to Cetinje without too much trouble and burned down what there was of the monastery, which had been rebuilt after two earlier demolitions. Unable to maintain himself for long in the wastes of Katuni—Cetinje had but one well—the headstrong Vizir turned back by the shortest route, paying no attention to the Venetian border, and leaving in his wake smoldering ruins and corpses as he proceeded through the lands of the Paštrovići.

Devastated, Montenegro still remained what it had been—a land of free and loose tribes.

This had been the third Turkish attack on Cetinje since the end of the seventeenth century, when it had become the hearth of Montenegrin freedom. For Mahmud Pasha it was his first visit. The second time only his head was to come.

The fruits of ten years of Bishop Petar's spiritual labors and travail, and the renewed restlessness of the once humble tribes, must have worried the Vizir. Old Montenegro was now more united than before the invasion.

Its tribes, gathered about their bishop, paid no tribute, elected their own chieftains, spawned and harbored bands of outlaws in their midst. In Montenegro both the tribes and the individual were free. Under the Turks, however, the individual had to give unto the Sultan at least, even when his tribe or province enjoyed some autonomy. Though the tribe might not, the individual always turned to Cetinje in the quest for freedom. The individual was not submerged by the Montenegrin tribe. On the contrary, one's individuality grew within it and sprang from it: the individual had something—land, house, weapons, spiritual kin, and friends.

It was from Cetinje that the tribes were called to mutiny and rebellion, and individuals to human freedom—for faith and fatherland. This was especially so under Bishop Petar, for whom these ideals were the very breath of life—timeless signposts in all kinds of weather.

Bishop and Vizir had always stood against one another—unswerving and unyielding in their aims. The day of reckoning had to come.

The first clashes erupted in the lands of the Piperi and the Bjelopavlići, who had broken away from the Vizir. Just as the Vizir knew that these two tribes would join Cetinje—free Montenegro—if he did not subdue them, so it was clear to the Bishop that they could not withstand the Vizir's might if he did not come to their aid with his Montenegrins from Old Montenegro. The Vizir sent a message to the Bishop warning him that he was not raising an army against Montenegro but against the Piperi and the Bjelopavlići: "I mean to set my fierce Albanians on them, God willing, and again I say to thee that whoever shall come to their aid, I shall strike at them as well with all my might." The Bishop paid no heed to the Vizir's message. He gathered together the tribal chieftains and entreated them not to betray their cause, but to go forth united into battle.

The first battle took place at Martinići, in Bjelopavlići country, on July 11, 1796. The Bishop led one half of the Montenegrin army, while the Guvernadur led the other half, as was the custom. The Turkish army was scattered, and the Vizir himself was wounded.

Even without that defeat it was clear to the Vizir that his main enemy was sitting in Cetinje. It became obvious to him that he must first deal with the Bishop if he would subdue the rebellious tribes and put a stop to further forays.

The folk epics say that Mahmud Pasha was embittered and stung by the defeat at Martinići. And indeed, hardly had his wound ceased throbbing when he raised another, still-greater, army—now against Old Montenegro itself. There were even French officers in his army, such were the lengths of the Vizir's determination and of young General Bonaparte's ambition. Again Bishop and Guvernadur led their armies into battle.

The Turkish army was put to rout at Krusi on September 22, 1796, and the Vizir himself lost his life. He was cut down by Bogdan Vukov, of Zalazi. Nothing is known about him. Yet it should be recorded, that his name might be remembered—for not many vizirs' heads were brought to Cetinje.

Not only did these victories widen the circle of free tribes and give rise to new resistance and hopes—all the way to Serbia and even Bosnia—but Montenegro finally freed itself from the pretensions of the vizirs of Scutari. Never again would they dare to wage war on Montenegro alone and with only their own, predominantly Albanian, armies. Montenegro's future battles were to be with the Porte, with the Sultan; as for the neighboring pashas and beys, there were the same massacres and raids as before, but no large-scale invasions. And so Montenegro became, and remained, a steadfast beacon amid a sea of slavery and despair.

Bishop Petar kept Montenegro on its guard against Austria as well, and even against Russia. He called upon the chieftains to unite in their resistance to Austrian pressure.

You will understand, I think, the evil that has been done when the Kaiser's soldiers began to arrest Montenegrins and to beat them with their rifles, men who, God knows, were guilty of no crime . . . so that they might drink their fill of Montenegrin blood and fill their jails and dungeons with Montenegrins. . . . Our brethren have been left dead and wounded, and their wives are held captive in the city . . . all of them beseech and implore me to write to you and to entreat the tribes of all four corners of the compass, in God's name . . . let none of you go to their market place or into the Kaiser's state.

Having learned once before that the Russians were given to vagueness and loss of memory when peace treaties were being signed, he did not join Russia against Turkey in 1828.

Montenegro became in fact independent.

But it was not Bishop Petar who created the government and the state. He could not have done so.

After the defeat of the Vizir of Scutari, Petar attempted to establish a court and a law code. They called his court the Kuluk (*corvée*)—a strange name, but one that expresses well the sense and the intentions of that first, and indeed every, government. The chieftains accepted the law because the Bishop compiled it. But they held neither to the court nor to the law, for they were still subject to the tribal courts and unwritten laws.

The times were not yet ripe, nor did the means exist for such ventures. But Petar made some attempts—which penetrated and stuck. He did all that was really possible: he finally freed the land and created the conditions necessary for the establishment of civil government. And the idea of that government was his. It grew and spread out of his very being and his work—out of his awful imprecations, out of the humiliations and the insults that were heaped upon him from all sides, out of the intrigues and plots to compromise his purity, and especially out of his identification of the Serbian idea with the irrepressible struggle of his tribes against the Turks.

For years, decades—he was bishop for fully forty-eight years—he went among the tribes, made peace, held court, and persuaded, counseled, preached, taught, and beseeched the Montenegrins "by Almighty God and the Venerable Cross and all the host of Heaven thrice and three times a thousand" to unite, to give up raiding and looting and fighting among themselves and seeking revenge, for before them stood great and sacred tasks.

That would have accounted for a long-suffering life even had it not been for the constant worry and fears over "poor Montenegro." He was held to be a saint even in his lifetime. But still they would not obey him. He was too much the bishop and too little the ruler to govern them by force and to wade in their blood.

Bishop Rade was of a different stripe. But he could not have done what had to be done and what he wished to do without the enormous labors that Bishop Petar completed before him. It was not simply that everyone must begin where someone else has left off. Bishop Petar cleared a path with the sword and with an idea so that Rade could immediately take up his task—the unification of the land under the authority of a state.

7.

RADE TOOK NO lessons from his uncle, the Bishop, yet he learned much from him—just by watching, listening. He learned especially from his uncle's life and experiences, and he grew up in his gentle and abiding light.

He learned how to make peace among the tribes and how to win over the chieftains. He gained sureness, and learned to be irreconcilable toward the Turks. He learned to be humane with humans. He learned what faith and nationality were.

Without even being conscious of it, he was to learn rhetoric and poetry from his uncle, too.

When he and Sarajlija were brought together by Bishop Petar, the latter was eighty years old. He was quite feeble. As with Danilo, so with him, too, it was his legs that first gave out. (Interestingly enough, Njegoš, too, was weak in the legs.) The old man lived in retirement—barely subsisting. He ate hardly a thing. A Russian monk would cook something or other in a pot, just enough to keep the fasting old man going. He was a tall, hulking skeleton, in which all had been extinguished except word and thought. The great ideas, the only ones—the Serbs, God—these still glowed and spoke. Concretely these ideas meant the unification of the Montenegrin tribes and the cultivation of heroism. Faith and fatherland. In the end, everything came down to these—to their glory and realization.

As may be seen in Bishop Petar's last letters, the stream of life was already passing him by. The history he had learned with the naïveté of a child as a myth was still fresh and untainted in his mind. Was not he like it?

Bishop Petar was not a poet, he did not write verses, though he did chant the folk epics. But he was a great orator. And true oratory is poetry—of the most direct kind. Vuk Karadžić observed that in the Montenegro of that time good orators were prized above all else. A chieftain who was not also an orator was not complete. Bishop Petar was the best orator of his time in his land. He generously paid his debt as a man to his nation.

All the Petrović bishops and rulers were gifted poets and visionaries. This, too, became an obligation to the land and to the idea.

From those few preserved writings of Bishop Danilo there emerges a full, most forthright expression and tragic identification of one's own destiny with duty, with the idea. When he wailed over himself, it was over the destiny of his land. His tears and his groans filled every space and every thought, as though there were nothing else. Bishop Sava was really neither a ruler nor a poet. Vasilije had an unrestrained fantasy; the world of reality and the world of imagination blended in him. His wild visions were like a refiner's fire, leaving nothing but the purity of the idea. Then came Bishop Petar. Then Bishop Rade-Njegoš. And then Prince Danilo, the impassive and violent Zeko. Though he spoke little and wrote even less, he always hit the mark and said exactly what needed to be said, and in the way in which it needed to be said. The last Petrović, Prince Nikola, also began as a poet, a gifted poet. But he subordinated his poetry more and more to his rule, and his gift waned as he served his own interests and those of his camarilla instead of serving the land and the idea. But it was never completely snuffed out. To the very end, in his old age, he was capable of expressing some great and true thought, though not always in writing. His ties with the land and with the idea slackened, became a matter of habit, though the habit never stopped; it lingered.

Bishop Petar had none of Njegoš's poetry, which was unique. Yet how much he did have!

There was the same manner of expression—here a picture, there a phrase—the same effervescence of the idea through just the right word. It will be said: Yes, but that poetry, that expressiveness of

Bishop Petar's, came from the people—from folk proverbs and folk songs, though in a rather more ordered, purer form. But, even with everything else, what was Njegoš but this? The ordering and the combination of words are different and express different meanings. Yet there is a similarity in the expression. Even in the tone there is that same tragic, rhapsodic, personal quality. Njegoš did not learn poetry from his uncle's letters, if he indeed knew of them at all. He did learn from his speech, that direct manner of expression—without involved descriptions, without comparisons, without a single excessive word. Bishop Petar must have been quite a poet in his daily speech—both by talent and by profession. Njegoš learned poetry from his clan—under his great uncle.

Of course, one ought to agree on what poetry is, and not risk missing the poetry in Bishop Petar's "epistles" and in Marko Miljanov. The epistles are not all poetry. Neither is Marko Miljanov. But how much poetry there is in the one and the other —a kind that is singular and therefore not always perceived!

New forms confront us: Bishop Petar experienced most fully that senseless and tragic discord among the tribes, just as Marko Miljanov was later to counter ugly, trivial reality with the moral, heroic side of our people. Neither of them aimed at poetry. The former wished to influence the tribes through his letters; the latter wished to save from oblivion the exploits of his comrades and compatriots. But it was poetry just the same. And with meaning, new ways of expression. The former linked his ideas with a still-unrealized ideal, while the latter linked an already-gained ideal with the reality, and thus rhetoric and ethics were turned into poetry.

Bishop Petar made speeches—and he had something to say, as, for example, in his letter to the Bjelopavlići:

> Behold it is twoscore years since you have thrown off from your necks the cruel yoke and chains of the Turks with the help of God and your Montenegrin brethren and my great efforts and expense. How long it is that I have been teaching, begging and imploring you to live in peace and in concord with one another, to labor for the sake of your own welfare and good name, to love your freedom and to fortify it, that you might never forget the cruel lot which your fathers and forefathers endured under Turkish tyranny and oppression. Today you no longer live off of Turkish leavings, you no longer pay the Turkish tribute,

nor tax, nor gifts, nor Turkish fines of any sort; you are not bound to quarter Turks in your houses, nor lick Turkish boots, nor run from village to village seeking honey and butter, hens and eggs and all the rest which the Turks demand, and they no longer sneer at you and command how you shall prepare this food or that; they no longer revile your faith and your law, they no longer call you the pig brood of sows, nor your women the sow brood of sows, and you no longer pay them fines because they have chipped their teeth on your bread; you no longer stable Turkish horses nor give them oats and hay; they no longer bind you at the thresholds of your houses and lead you away tied to the end of a rope, nor do they torture you in Turkish dungeons nor hang you in chains from the willows and gibbets, nor do they beat you with their canes, nor do they kick or slap you, they do not snatch your women from their husbands' sides nor bring dishonor upon your betrothed and unbetrothed girls. Your braids of hair do not stick through worn out caps, nor your elbows through unpatched shirts, but behold, today you wear silver breastplates and robes with ribbons and embroidered with silver and gold. You have pistols and knives of forged silver, sabers inlaid with sterling, fancy flintlocks and finely decked pouches; and behold, the fortified towers and Turkish domains of Spuž are in your hands; and behold your own precious will and freedom.

Here is a clear conscience toward the past, and a sure summons to the future—realities and ideals stripped to their purest expression.

Without knowing it, Rade, the great autodidact, had a teacher in all things, even in poetry.

His own man from the start, Bishop Rade-Njegoš yet certainly had somewhere to begin and someone to start from.

THE STRIPLING BISHOP

1.

EVERYONE EXPECTED THE death of the great old man, though he was not ailing. They said he himself knew that death was upon him.

He called upon the chieftains to assemble. The rest is conjecture —that he did so in order to designate a successor and to leave them his testament. It is known that there were other reasons aplenty for summoning an assembly: rebellions in Bosnia and Albania, and bad blood among the tribes. The Bishop did not live to tell them why he had summoned them.

It was late autumn, rainy as always in Cetinje, and the crag was pallid and dull as it thrust through the dense fog. On the morrow it would be Saint Luke's Day—October 19, 1830—and the chieftains were to gather in assembly. The Bishop had been feeling poorly the last few days, but it seemed no worse than usual even to him. The evening before, he went out into the monastery kitchen to warm himself. But he could not sit still. He returned to his cell. About seven in the evening he breathed his last. The light which had kept vigil to the last over the land and over its humanity was now extinguished.

Bishop Petar could write in good conscience, "I have spared neither effort nor property for the good of the people and for every good cause, rather have I dedicated my life and my soul to the benefit and the freedom of my fatherland."

Death has a way of surprising those left behind. The chieftains began to arrive without suspecting that they would assemble around the Bishop's bier the next day. The Petrovići, too, were caught by surprise.

The fact was that Bishop Petar did not have a successor. Not only had he failed to designate one, but there really was no suitable person. The successor had to be a monk and literate. The Petrovići were either illiterate or married, and of the two whom the Bishop had designated and sent to study in Russia, one was long dead and the other had stripped off his cassock to become an officer.

It was important for them all that Bishop Petar's successor be a Petrović. And it was a Montenegrin tradition which could not yet be circumvented that he had to be a monk. In government, in politics, it is inevitable that the form be almost as important as the content. The chieftains accepted the rule of a bishop, for this meant that they could keep their power and tribal independence. This is precisely why they would not have wished to have at their head a lay person, a prince, as in Serbia. The chieftains and the tribes were soon to consent, willy-nilly, that a monk—Bishop Rade—give and take away like a crowned prince. Now, however, assembled as they were around the dead Bishop Petar, it was obvious that they would agree only to the time-hallowed form, a monk, as a sign that the previous arrangement—the independence of the chieftains and the tribes—would be kept.

The Petrovići had still other difficulties, the kind that eat away and gnaw at one's insides. They could expect, and they did expect, a coup from within their own tribe, by the most closely related clan, the Guvernadurovići-Radonjići. If the successor were not to be a monk, the first place would then belong to them, for the most important secular leader of them all—the guvernadur—was by tradition of their clan, for almost as long as the bishopric had resided in the House of Petrović. The Petrovići could maintain their prestige only through a monk. And they had none. The Radonjići knew this, and they bided their time. A second misfortune of the Petrovići came closer to home—from their own midst. Not even they themselves were united. Savo Markov, the father of Djordjije —that unfrocked officer—opposed having the succession go to anyone but his son. Had not Djordjije been educated in Russia? Had not the Bishop designated him himself? And even if he was now an officer, in Russia, that was not important. He could become a monk once more and come here.

The quarrel among the Petrovići themselves broke through the walls of the monastery and into the clans.

The bishopric brought the clan no great benefit other than prestige. But the prestige meant a great deal—in arranging marriages, getting credit in trade, and in every other way. Besides, the bishop was only too happy to employ his own kin in the monastery. And now there was even the prospect that, if not now then perhaps the next day, the bishop's power would expand and establish itself even beyond the spiritual sphere of the Church. Who would occupy the bishop's throne was a matter of importance for the clan as a whole and for every house in it. Yet there was no successor. Many hearts grew cold at the thought of it. It was to tear the Petrovići apart, both as a whole and each man individually, giving rise to the most violent, the most irreconcilable passions and forces. The clan was crumbling, this most stable and most customary social unit. This offered especially good prospects to the Radonjići, and perhaps to some other powerful clan as well.

The trouble was that there was no time for waiting. The successor had to be confirmed the very next day, in order to end the confusion and to block the claims of others.

Around the Bishop's still-warm body there broke out a frenzied struggle over the succession. Hitherto concealed desires now became open demands. Every change in inherited power where the successor has not been previously designated is attended by such struggles. However, this was the first time for the Petrovići, and they were still unaccustomed, unused, to it.

Everything had to be done in a single night: designate a successor, appease the discontent and passions within the clan, win over the chieftains, and prepare for the burial of the great man.

The Petrovići managed to accomplish all of this, boldly and deftly, though not without sacrifice and compromise. Their clan was still a powerful entity in itself, united with other clans by their past and by countless bonds.

A most important fact should be made clear at this point, and that is that if Bishop Petar had had any thought of making Rade his successor, he had certainly never made this intention public.

There is no evidence that Rade had been prepared for the monkhood, for if such had been the case, the Bishop would have tonsured him himself. Moreover, the report has been recorded that Rade felt ill at ease at Cetinje, and that he had asked his uncle to permit him to go into business. The report has it also that the

Bishop said of Rade that he was a wise and brave fellow, and he added, "If only he had gone to Russia instead of Djordjije!" Still this does not prove that he intended to make Rade his successor. In actual fact, he could only designate him, propose him to the assembly of chieftains. But he had made no such move.

Bishop Petar was very sensible and extremely conscientious. Why had he not designated a successor?

True, the day after his death, at the assembly of chieftains at Velje Guvno around his coffin, there was read his testament, in which he designated Rade his successor. However, as is known today and as was suspected with reason even then, that testament was not written by the Bishop, but by Sarajlija. He signed not only his own name, as secretary, but also Bishop Petar's, though the latter was no less literate than he. That testament imitated the style and language of Bishop Petar, but this is not strange: Sarajlija had lived in Montenegro and had become a Montenegrin in his speech. Yet did not Sarajlija make a special effort on this occasion to imitate the Montenegrin speech of Bishop Petar as faithfully as possible?

Be that as it may, this designation of a successor, an untonsured youth of seventeen at that, was not consonant with the Bishop's way of doing things, for he strictly abided by the decisions of the assembly of chieftains and respected the customary principle of election, however much this might have been a pure formality. Besides, it also violated all hitherto established usages.

2.

THE CHIEFTAINS HAD reason to be astonished when they heard that Rade would succeed Bishop Petar.

As a matter of fact, Rade himself was surprised. His version is on record. It was not until the day after his uncle's death that he learned that he was to succeed him. His relatives simply summoned him to the monastery, dressed him in his uncle's cassock, and thrust a cross and staff in his hands. His cousin Stanko Stijepov, who was already a mature man, slapped him heartily on the back and shoved him outside, shouting at him to go and show himself to the chieftains and to the people as the successor and future bishop. The confused Rade was more propelled than escorted out. Then they came to kiss his hand, first his uncles and father—before whom he attempted to withdraw his hand out of embarrassment—and then the others.

After that there was held an assembly on Velje Guvno and the testament was read. There was an oppressive silence among the chieftains as the Archimandrite of Ostrog, Josif Pavičević, asked the assemblage if they accepted the testament. It was a silence that held a threat and a promise of mob action. It was then, according to a reliable account, that Filip Nikolin Djurašković, of Ceklin, Serdar of the Nahi of Rijeka, sprang forward and demanded to know if they accepted the testament, challenging anyone who rejected it to a duel. The chieftains shouted their assent, and Filip took out his long pistol and fired it in sign of rejoicing and confirmation. Others followed suit. With the firing of the guns the tension relaxed.

Serdar Filip was no ordinary chieftain. He came from a long line of serdars. We find one of his forebears, Serdar Janko, in *The Mountain Wreath,* as one of the more prominent chieftains in the time of Bishop Danilo. Filip was serdar in his own right—a renowned hero and a collaborator of Bishop Petar, famed for his berserk attacks on the Turks, for his sagacity, resoluteness, and forcefulness. He stood by Bishop Rade from the first, and there he was to remain, becoming his senator and helping him in everything, especially in putting down opposition and rebellions throughout Montenegro. He was to be beside him even in his dying hour. Filip had songs sung about him even in his lifetime, while Njegoš included him in *The Tower of the Djurišići,* extolling him as the greatest hero of Montenegro—in a time and place where every reproach and praise was measured out by the gram. Njegoš has sketched Filip in two or three portrayals: a slightly hunched warrior who never hesitated to strike a blow, a man made for hacking and hewing. That he was really like that is known from the tales recorded about him. He once cut down two Turks and captured a third, stuck the heads of the two on stakes, and bound the captive to a post in front of his house, a house more like a fortress ruled by a completely independent master, one whose strength and daring had no match in the country.

To have Serdar Filip on their side meant that the Petrovići could win over not only the Nahi of Rijeka but also the still-wavering chieftains. They might have known, and probably suspected, that Filip would stand by them—for the sister of the future sovereign was married to his brother, thus bringing together the two houses. He also had given lively support to the work of Bishop Petar. Is it possible that they had all planned to have him declare himself as he did?

It was clear that the Petrovići had their own following, their own party among the Montenegrins.

And there were other chieftains on their side.

One of these was certainly Stevan Perkov, from the powerful clan of the Vukotići in Čevo, who was to play a significant role later as Njegoš's senator and, just after Rade's acceptance as successor, in settling accounts with the Guvernadurovići. According to tradition, the first governor had been a Vukotić, but his son had sold the office to the Radonjići after the Venetians had poisoned his father. It is not important whether this is historically true. It was true for the Vukotići, and for the Montenegrins, because they believed it. They were a clan which could have had, and once did have, the governorship—and now they were for the testament, for the Petrovići. In a position to speak for Čevo and Bjelica, Stevan Perkov brought with him, if not all, then certainly a great part, of the Nahi of Katuni, the province of the most important and the most powerful opponent of the Radonjići-Guvernadurovići.

On the Petrović side there was also the Archimandrite of Ostrog, Josif, who brought with him the largest free tribe—the Bjelopavlići.

However, these were not the most important protagonists in the first act of this drama of Njegoš and the Montenegrin state.

A reliable tradition has been preserved that it was Stanko Stijepov Petrović who was the chief actor in the confirmation of Bishop Rade as the successor. He was the first to settle things among the Petrovići themselves, for he grasped the real significance of the moment: the struggle was between the Petrovići and the Radonjići, and the victory would go to that side which had the most presence of mind and first hit upon an acceptable solution. For the Montenegrins, for their chieftains, it was absolutely vital to have a bishop, even if only a potential one. The Radonjići could not come up with a bishop, for by tradition they never had any in their family. True, for the moment the Petrovići also did not have a bishop. But they had a presentable candidate. Stanko was the one who dressed Rade in his uncle's cassock (Archimandrite Josif was to tonsure him only a day later), who thrust him to the fore and pushed him into the fray. Tradition has it that Stanko was a hero of deep and quick intelligence. They say that Njegoš liked him better than his own brothers. His role in strengthening Rade's position later was also significant. Unselfish, he defended his clan and worked for it. But beneath it all was the thought of giving the country a sovereign and its first true government.

The second important actor was Sarajlija. He was an outlander, and it was never difficult to rouse up dissatisfaction against him on this score. But nobody could deny that he was a good Serb and that he meant much to the Serbian nation. Besides, he was literate, capable, and through his collaboration with the Bishop he had gained something of a reputation in Montenegro. He had a hand in everything, more than is realized. The testament was the work of his hand and the figment of his mind.

A third important actor was Prior Mojsije Zečević, of the Vasojevići—a tribe almost as large as all of independent Montenegro. True, they were not yet quite free, but they had been astir from time immemorial. His reputation was vast. Hero, sage, martyr, he was a living legend—a man whom a gun could not kill, and whose word alone opened coffers of treasure.

Mojsije worked in Turkish Montenegro to gather together the unruly forces of his tribe, and he held them together through guerrilla warfare and rebellions, through massacres and conversions, through ambushes, plots, bribes, and dungeons. He, too, was Bishop Petar's collaborator. His Vasojevići and the Lim Valley were an extension of free Montenegro into the hinterland of Serbia, connecting it with the regions then engaged in the struggle for liberation, for Montenegro's future as well. Those chieftains who did not understand this could at least feel it thanks to this monk who had taken upon himself every misfortune since Karadjordje's rebellion and who meant the Turks no good as he roused the tribes of the Has and Raška—all the way to Serbia.

He was a wondrous blend: monk, war lord, and legislator. He was on equal terms with the mighty beys of Plav and Gusinje—the Turkish lords of those two districts. It was he who united the chieftains and established a government and an administration apart from the Turkish. It was he who preserved the monasteries founded by the Nemanja dynasty, and who kept the Orthodox masses from becoming converted to Islam.

He came from an unliberated region. Yet the struggles and sufferings he and his land had gone through and which still faced them increased his reputation in a country winning its freedom. Besides, there was no defined dividing line between the free and the unfree tribes. One hardly took note of the borders between them; there were only different degrees and levels of servitude. It was but yesterday, in the year 1826, that the chieftains of Ceklin had gone to pay court to the Vizir in Scutari. The Kuči were considered to be subject to the Turks, yet they never paid them any tribute, and here and there they even fought against them. And what about Mojsije? In the heart of Turkish Montenegro, in the wilds of Gusinje, he burned down two towers and a fortress of Shaban Aga to avenge the razing of his own monastery.

The historian Ilija Jelić has established that the Vasojevići maintained their own self-rule even under the Turks and that "in the middle of the eighteenth century, in the time of Prince Mirčeta Rajić, they already had a developed legal system in nearly all the fields of jurisprudence and governed themselves by it." The claim is exaggerated, but not false. It was he who discovered that strange, precious, and wonderful law of the Vasojevići of those times, with its twelve articles, which forbade committing adultery with guests, which called for the castration of women-chasing clerics, which forbade witch-hunting, and which commanded "that all of the clans of the Vasojevići and the Serbs keep unconditional peace," "that mosques must not be built and the old ones must not be kept up," that "renegades must not be killed, but it is up to each clan to bring their own back into the faith of their forefathers." Furthermore, that law commanded: "whoever becomes converted to Islam today and accepts the false faith, let him be counted a Turk." Also this: "who does not come to help when the enemies strike at the border, let him have no part in the life of the tribe and let no one give him a maiden to marry"; "whoever steals from the Serbs and is caught, let him pay double and a meal for the peasants. If he is not caught, let him be cursed"; "whosoever steals from the Turks, good for him"; "whatever traitor informs the enemy of the counsels of the chieftains and the people, let him and all his kind perish without trace for all time and amen. Whoever goes over the heads of his chieftains to seek justice from the alien, let him be accounted guilty"; "whoever from this day hence goes to the vizir in Scutari . . . let him perish without trace." That law even includes the following: "God, and not Satan, has created woman, and so let it be for all time, amen. Who speaks to the contrary is accursed." How long that law remained and how it was enforced, nobody knows. It seems, however, that the Vasojevići compiled and accepted a law code before the men of Katuni had one at Cetinje. The men of that region were no less brave and knowledgeable than those around Lovćen, but the conditions under which they lived were less favorable. It is known that they raised great rebellions, from the time of the Crnojevići—before the Montenegrins had risen up under Danilo. And their banners were given to them by Karadjordje himself, whom they came out to meet when he penetrated all the way to Pešter.

All this stood behind Prior Mojsije, behind his stocky, bony frame and in back of that huge head of his, grown over with heaps of graying hair.

Mojsije was from the village of Vinicka, the prior of a monastery founded by the Nemanja dynasty—St. George's Pillars—and he was to remain at Bishop Rade's side to the end.

He was in his own region what the Bishop was in Montenegro, if not more.

And so it was that a teacher, a cousin, and a rebel, supported by a few chieftains, took hold of a youth and founded upon him something great—a state and a dynasty, for the further liberation of the Serbian people. It all happened by chance, and yet it turned out as though planned: the Serbian idea was represented by Sarajlija, free Montenegro by Stanko Stijepov, and the struggle against the Turks by Mojsije. Powerful factors stood behind that highhanded maneuver: the primacy of the Petrovići, the hope to influence the future sovereign, the desire to gain the support of the future bishop for new projects in one's own region. Great ideals meshed with petty and selfish schemes. There are no great decisions without this. The greatness lies in the decision itself.

Any wavering and dissatisfaction among the chieftains vanished with Filip's challenge. Yet everything was still up in the air and could take off in any direction. Two documents of ratification were signed the same day, one by the clergy, and the other by the lay chieftains, in which they swore to recognize Rade as successor. The Governor, Vuko Radonjić, protested. However, he, too, signed, though last.

An agreement was also concluded and an oath taken to keep the peace among themselves until Saint George's Day, for had it not been for this that the Bishop had called them together in the first place?

There exist two etchings, both probably the work of the same artist and done later, that record the two most important scenes: Serdar Filip's triumph and the general oath-taking to keep the peace. Both are devoid of distinction or beauty. But it is all there: the monastery and Josif and a tall youth in a cassock—Rade. And in the other picture, Bishop Petar's coffin with flintlocks stacked up over it—awesome and majestic, like so many sights in Montenegro. The Montenegrins had placed their death-dealing rifles over the body of their dead shepherd, at least until they lowered him into his grave.

They took an oath, and they signed it.

And no one kept any of it.

Radonjić was least disposed to recognize as his sovereign "that little snot of the Prorokovići"—that is how the opposing party began to refer to Rade.

Governor Vuko understood more clearly than anyone that the Petrovići wished to establish their supremacy. Everything had been designed to accomplish that end. The very manner—the haste, the surprise, the threat—and the person involved—a still-untonsured stripling—and, above all, a very suspicious testament—indicated not only that the Petrovići wanted the future bishop to be from their midst, but also that they desired possession of the civil, nonspiritual authority as well, though strictly speaking such an authority did not yet exist. Even had he not been governor, Vuko would have felt all this with full impact and bitterness, as a threat to one of the most fundamental bases of human and personal existence, perhaps the most essential next to the right of property.

3.

THE ATTENTION OF historians has perforce been directed to the Petrovići. Not much is known about the Guvernaduri. From all that is known, though, it is evident that the Radonjići were a renowned clan and that the governorship was not an empty title. Of course, the prestige of the bishop was greater. This is understandable, for inasmuch as there was no real central government, it was through the Church that the people and the tribes could be most effectively influenced, all the more so when the bishop was a strong personality. On the other hand, the position of the governor was rather shadowy. During the struggles with Mahmud Pasha it was equal to the bishop's. According to Rovinsky, the governor kept half of the seal and the bishop the other half, which would indicate that only those decrees were valid that had the agreement of both. The governors presided over the chieftains' assemblies. But so did Bishop Petar. In the beginning the governor had his seat in Kotor and was like any other Montenegrin chieftain, except that he was in the pay of the Venetian Republic. That the governorship was not merely a Venetian creature may be seen from the fact that it continued to exist even after the fall of Venice.

It is true that the bishopric was exclusively Montenegrin—an unbroken link with the country's past. But the Petrovići had held the bishopric hardly longer than the Radonjići had held the governorship. The latter possessed the governorship for a whole century. It had taken root.

Though not formally hereditary, the governorship became ensconced in the same family. This unhereditary inheritance was even more constant than the bishopric was in the Petrović family. This speaks for the strength of the Radonjić clan. It also indicates the need for a governor. Apparently some ties other than religion and warfare were required to make peace, establish borders, and regulate traffic among the tribes. One document proclaims: "We, the Montenegrin fatherland, all unanimously and by general consent will it and hereby confirm that the Montenegrin governorship shall remain eternally hereditary in the worthy house of the present Governor Jovan Radonjić . . . and if anyone, now or in the future, refuse to obey the Governor as the prime and supreme authority over the Montenegrin community, be he cleric or layman, let him be accounted a traitor to Montenegro!" Such was the decree of the Montenegrin Assembly of 1770, in the presence of Bishop Sava, and in the time of Stephen the Small. This was no unimportant matter, even though the governor did not become the "prime and supreme authority over the Montenegrin community."

Historical science owes the Radonjići and the governors justice and truth.

It is known that there were renowned governors. Petar I. Popović observes that in the year 1779 Governor Jovan Radonjić led a Montenegrin deputation to Vienna, one that included the future Bishop Petar. In 1784 the same Governor turned to Austria for help, and a year later headed an army, together with Serdar Ivan Petrović and Vojvoda Bogdan Vukotić, against Mahmud Pasha. According to Ljubomir A. Bakić, the Governor was designated to preside over that first court, the Kuluk.

It appears that until the time of Bishop Petar there were no significant quarrels between the governors and the bishops. But before Petar there were no important attempts—except possibly under Stephen the Small—to unite the tribes. The first serious quarrel—according to Dragičević—erupted in 1802, when the Montenegrins could not agree on a new governor, and were divided into the Bishop's party and the Radonjić party. Nevertheless a Radonjić was elected—Joko, the father of the last governor, Vuko.

The Radonjići became the most lordly family in Montenegro, with the right to maintain a residence in Njeguši. The women of their blood were famed beauties. They also had a vast network of friends, and their influence was widespread.

The Radonjić governors blazed many a trail, for the Petrovići and for all Montenegro. They were the ones who first conceived the authority of the state.

4.

ALL THOSE HASTY moves by the Petrovići to establish their dominion over Montenegro show that the theocratic form of government had really outlived its usefulness, and precisely in the time of the most bishoplike bishop of Montenegro—Petar. Vuk Karadžić observed this in a letter to Gagić. Yet no matter how much the Montenegrin consciousness sought a government, it was not ready to abolish rule by a bishop. The wisdom and boldness of Stanko Stijepov and the others lay in the fact that they preserved the outward shell—the bishop's miter—but filled it with a new content—the princely power. They respected the inherited form, which had already grown into a prejudice, in order to strengthen a new, real form—a government.

The haste continued even after Bishop Petar's burial—both in form and in content, both within and without. It was as though the very death of the venerable old man had come in good time.

Not a month after Rade's installation, a court found Governor Vuko guilty of treason. And, after receiving permission from the Vizir of Scutari, they had the Archbishop of Raška and Prizren, Ananija—a small man with a big beard, a good speaker and literate —come to Vranjina to install Rade as archimandrite on January 31, 1831.

To be sure, the first thing that had to be done was to get in touch with the Russians. Their attitude could well be decisive in a land where their influence was of long standing and enormous. As early as October 22 the newly installed successor wrote to Vučićević, a quasi minister of Bishop Petar's in St. Petersburg, calling for his help, for "the people are in distraught spirits, and my forces are too meager." On the same day he informed Gagić, in Dubrovnik, of the sorrow "which has befallen us in this unhappy land and into the farthest reaches of the fatherland," and how the Bishop had designated him "his God-fearing and wretched coadjutor and poor successor." One detects here an uncertainty that is not like the Petrovići, and a style that is not like Njegoš's. Sima, too, is signed as "secretary of the Mont[enegrin] peo[ple]." His touch is apparent in the official and all-too-Montenegrin manner of expression. The first "saving counsels" from the Russians were quick in arriving. They were sent by Gagić as early as October 30: "In your own house be neither like honey, lest they spread you thin, nor like venom, lest you poison them."

The young Rade was not prepared for any of this—not quite. He understood that everything he did he had to do as a member of his clan. But he knew little about governing. The government had not yet really been created. Perhaps, too, he was already burdened with sins and sinful thoughts and knew the delights against which the monk must wage a hard struggle. Inner crises were inevitable and obvious. "At the behest of the chieftains and the people, I was made an archimandrite on January 31, 1831, and they changed my name from Rade to Petar," he wrote to Vučićević. An archimandrite despite himself, he was all too aware of what was happening. He resolved to crush all resistance within himself and to set out on the road before him. Rovinsky observed, "Thus may be explained that dreadful quandary which the Bishop felt all his life as he vacillated between the monk and the secular ruler." This intelligent, lively, and complete man was forced from the start to preserve that shell by means of which the Petrovići could secure their power. For them, for the Petrovići, this was something quite natural, but to him it was something forced and unnatural. No matter how much he agonized, he was never completely to make the break and to become the bishop, though he was extremely conscientious in the duties the clan imposed upon him for his own sake—for Montenegro, for the Montenegrin poor.

How was it, why was it, that it had to be that way?

Any relevant economic and social data are lacking—if indeed they could explain it.

It is known that the problem of overpopulation was keenly felt: survival was impossible, given those conditions and methods of work. Under Bishop Petar and Rade, and before them, the Montenegrins migrated everywhere, mostly to Serbia and into the depths of the Bosnian forests. Even to Russia. But they came scurrying back from Russia, to escape becoming serfs. They went everywhere as workers, even to Istanbul, where they were prized for their honesty and reliability and because they had their own leaders.

Overpopulation was especially severe in the already liberated regions. After all, was it not also the struggle for their bare existence that drove the Montenegrins to wage war for the greatest ideals? Guerrilla warfare, the raiding of Turkish-held lands, was an important factor in the economy. This robber economy was typical of those Montenegrin tribes which were overpopulated. Plundering was a national and a religious obligation here—up to the time of Bishop Rade. Nearly all the Montenegrin heroic poems—including that most beautiful of all, about Vuk the Robber—have as their main motif the looting of cattle and sheep.

Overpopulation—and land hunger. The only way to get land was to take it away from the neighboring Moslems, the so-called Turks, and the Albanians, who themselves did not have enough. The struggle for Serbianism and for the faith was also a struggle for survival. This is not to belittle the greatness of the ideal. But it does make it inevitable, unavoidable.

There were also ever-deepening social differences, though classes as such had not yet been formed. The differences lay in the size of one's property and the number of heads of sheep, and hardly at all in social position or way of life, for they were all shepherds and tillers. Their conflict ran deeper with the outsiders—with those of the other faith, the Turks, outside the tribe. The privileged classes were among the Turks. Everything was determined by how much one was for the Turks, for the alien faith, for the agas and the beys, and how much one was against them. Within the tribe there were clashes and rifts over who would be chieftain. The chieftains might well have become the beginnings of a ruling class, but in that still-tribal society they never did.

And just who were the Turks? To begin with, they were not real Turks at all, but either Islamized men of Serbian blood and tongue or Albanians. Inasmuch as they identified themselves with the carriers of Islam, the authorities, and the feudal system, that is, with the Turks, the Montenegrins regarded them as such and called them that accordingly. Religion was identical with nationality, if not the Moslem, then certainly the Orthodox. That is to say that among the Moslems, the so-called Turks, there were many strains; but the Serbs were all Orthodox. This was so with the Orthodox both in reality and in their conception. Thus the battles the Montenegrins waged were not at all with the real Asian Turks, but with local Moslems and Albanians. On the one side were the Montenegrins of the "Serbian" faith, concentrated in the tribes; on the other side was the Moslem, "Turkish," faith, which had been diffused by various languages and nationalities.

All of this fighting was taking place along the distant periphery of the empire, in pashaliks that were almost independent of Istanbul.

The Albanians lived for themselves. They had their own accounts to settle, not only with the Montenegrins, but with the Vizir and with Istanbul. There were Serbian families, often whole clans, among the Moslems, and in Albania the Shqipetar tribes had become Moslem to obtain privileges, mostly to gain or to preserve free ownership of the land, and their ceaseless clashes with the Orthodox raia made them firmer adherents of the faith than were the real Turks. Both of them—Montenegrins and Moslems—were willful people and quick to evil and to heroism, plenteous in cruelty and filled with an astounding, astonishing nobility.

The Ottoman invasion had divided one and the same people and separated them into opposing camps. Time did not bring them together or bring them peace. The one side insisted on being the masters of themselves and believed in the resurrection of the ancient empire, while the other defended the new order, which they had accepted with their religion and which had brought them significant benefits as the sons of the true faith—at the expense of the former, to be sure. They identified their dominion with their adherence to Islam. They, too, clung to an extreme position: either to keep the Orthodox raia as raia or to lose everything—the faith and the land and the authority and the dominion—for Istanbul, with all its reforms and headaches, would not care about their destruction. In all their actions, views, and ways of life, both groups were engaged in a head-on conflict. The irreconcilable, unappeasable settling of accounts was to run its course for decades. Men were born in it and died in it.

Vojvoda Laza Bojović wrote to Bishop Petar in 1809:

When the fortress of Onogošt was besieged, there were two thousand families living around it, whom the malefactors of Nikšić scattered over all the parts of the earth. Behold you have them among you as well in every Montenegrin village and tribe, those who fled with their lives, but as for those that were killed and slaughtered, their number is unknown. Of the two thousand houses there, not even two hundred have been left whole, and what is worst of all, they subjected the naked poor to every kind of torture. . . . Every able-bodied man, every goodly youth and hero they killed. They took away all our horses and oxen, and our weapons, which defended us and them, and they plundered us completely, leaving nothing. . . . And all this we were willing to suffer, but they razed our churches, and they took wives away from their living husbands, and they stripped us bare and left us naked even as they reviled our faith and our law. . . . Of all the evil men that do live on this earth, none are as evil as they, for they pay no heed either to sultan or vizir, and they torment the sultan's raia, while they use the sultan's decrees for target practice.

Each side was bent on exterminating the other. The Turks could not wish this entirely, for then they would have no one whom to lord it over. The Montenegrins had to wish this if they wanted to survive. There was no space—no land or nationality—in which the two faiths could live side by side. "The gate is too narrow for two steeds."

The struggle the Montenegrins waged was different from that in Serbia, even though the traditions and the ideals were the same. Over there the raia rose up against the Janizaries—themselves rebels against the Sultan—and only as they gathered strength did they turn against Istanbul as well and fight against the alien. Over here, however, the half-free and internally independent tribes refused all submission to the Islamized agas and beys of the same blood and tongue, and only indirectly to the Sultan's vizir. Here the struggle took place within the same people, at their very roots; it involved Serbs and Serbian renegades who had become Turks. In Serbia the idea was to resurrect the Serbian state; here it was simply a matter of survival. There the Serbian nation fought; here the Serbian tribes. In Serbia class differentiation began to appear; here only the exceptional individual was distinguished from the rest. There vast and stubborn rebellions and huge battles took place; here there had been a ceaseless slaughter, but no battles for fifty or a hundred years at a time. Here hatred had reached the white-hot pitch of self-destruction, and every idea and conception had turned into naked passion.

It was this very kind of warfare, especially under Bishop Petar, that brought the tribes closer together and made them realize that their unification was necessary, indispensable. Something even more fateful was going on: liberation from Turkish rule strengthened and fortified the free peasant—the individual and the family, which had their own interests, distinct from the tribe's and the clan's, though not yet in conflict with them. This freeman wanted an end to everything that stood in the way of his further freedom. Freedom is insatiable and knows no limits. He wanted to buy and to sell, to get better farm animals and implements. How else was he to raise himself up? And all of this took freedom of movement. Horizons broadened and conceptions changed. The tribe and the clan were still necessary to him—they protected him from the Turks. But he also needed something else. The tribe was too narrow for him, especially since it put him, as its member, at odds with other tribes. He had to get out of the tribe. He spontaneously desired the establishment of some law and order which would hold for all the tribes and for all individuals. He could not turn to the Turks for this, for it was from them that he had wrested the land and the freedom he would lose under their law and order. Dependence upon the authority of the Church was the most natural, in the beginning. But that was a spiritual power. Force was necessary—against the ruffians and the outlaws.

It must not be forgotten that the Turkish invasion did not bring about the complete destruction of the old order, not even of the feudal state. The Serbian lords and their dominion and power had been crushed, but the Church remained—plundered, persecuted, oppressed, but not destroyed. The spirit of the old state survived. Tribe and Church began to build a new state—a fresh force and tradition. The Montenegrin tribes preserved many precepts of the medieval law—for example, bounties for catchers of thieves.

The liberated, free peasant found both tribe and Church wanting. Though still tied to them, he wished to use them as the most convenient vehicles to bring into being something new, something that would secure his freedom and even enlarge it. The struggles with the Turks, that merciless slaughter from father to son through hundreds of years, those long and frequent campaigns against the Turks, in which living bodies served as the "ramparts of Christendom," that ceaseless taking of slaves and destruction, rape and rapine—all this created not only heroes, but lawless and restless men who could not stop their banditry once peace and freedom came to their land. The tribe and the clan sheltered such men—for they were their kin. But discontent arose, within the tribe itself, for it is impossible to seek order for oneself without respecting it oneself.

The episcopal encyclicals and the chieftains' letters from the time of Bishop Petar, without exception, express this yearning for order against lawlessness and looting. Bishop Petar stated it fully and, certainly, most tragically: "I have no stake, and no rope, and no bayonets, nothing with which I can do anything save for what tongue I may have, and were it not for this, there would be bloodshed everywhere."

The ordinary man was beginning to demand security for his new-gained freedom. The stake and the rope—government. And a community that went beyond the tribe, in which one could move about freely, and finally—a state.

And since he really wanted these, he was soon to get them, in the only form possible, given the internal and external conditions, and one his mind was capable of grasping and accepting—a prince wearing a bishop's miter. A Petrović—out of a clan from which bishops traditionally came. Even if he were a mere stripling, something was bound to become of him.

The clan from which the governors came—the Radonjići—could have given a prince. But only a prince. And Montenegro did not want it. The independent tribes and the haughty chieftains did not want it. Nor would the ordinary man have understood it, for he was used to bishops. The most suitable solution was a prince in a cowl—a principality in a bishopric.

The governorship was a hindrance to such a prince and to such a government, to both the governor and his clan.

5.

As WE HAVE said, according to tribal tradition it began thus: Once there were two brothers, Herak and Rajić. From the former there sprang, in addition to other brotherhoods, the Petrovići—the bishops. From the latter came the Radonjići—the governors. The tradition ends with a bloody reckoning between them—brotherhoods belonging to the same clan—during, and over, the investiture of Rade Petrović Njegoš with power and the bishopric. Between the legend and the reality the hatred grew. It had come to such a pass that the Radonjići were angry if the wind brought them the smoke from Petrović chimneys.

Among the Petrovići the main personage in that reckoning was Stanko Stijepov. Rade was too young. Nor was Governor Vuko the principal among the Radonjići. He was dull and unenterprising. The chief person there was his brother, Djuzo Radonjić, intelligent, forceful, courageous, who had had some schooling abroad, had traveled a good deal, and traded in cattle, though he lived like a man of the people.

The first blow was struck at Vuko—the recalcitrant bearer of the governor's title. But everything was really aimed against Djuzo. Prior Rade could not keep from pouring this out in a letter to Gagić, written as early as January 12, 1831, in which he informed Gagić that Djuzo had arrived from Istanbul, and called him "a galley criminal and traitor to his fatherland . . . who spies for Aust[ria]."

Rovinsky is of the opinion that the Radonjići might have had a good chance if they had not been in league with Austria. Certainly the traditional and harmless ties of the bishops with Orthodox Russia could only have strengthened the lead of the Petrovići. The Radonjići themselves felt their weakness in not having sufficient support from Russia. Vuko even tried to establish ties with Consul Gagić. As for the Petrovići, they also sensed their opponents' weakness arising from their too great dependence on Austria. The Montenegrins were wary of Austria, not so much because it was Catholic, though because of this as well, but because it was a powerful neighbor.

The Radonjići certainly enjoyed an advantage in that they were the governors, and as long as the trend was in the direction of a central authority anyway, they were such an authority by tradition, even though on the downgrade. Yet even this advantage vanished, inasmuch as the Petrovići were able to offer a more acceptable, a more convenient form. The authority of the governor—to the chieftains this could only mean the loss of their own powers. The authority of the bishop could only mean this, too. But as men do whenever they can, the Montenegrin chieftains chose the lesser evil for themselves.

Even measuring by the standards of this time and place, which divide everything into the progressive and the reactionary and thereby impoverish both reality and thought, it cannot be concluded that the Petrovići represented some sort of progressive current. Certainly the bishops were more entrenched. The Petrovići accomplished the possible—which alone brings success in politics. The Radonjići hankered after something impractical

—a purely princely authority, something only Bishop Rade's successor, Prince Danilo, was able to realize. Having lost touch with reality, they also lost the future.

Yet did they betray their land and people?

What Vuko did after the agreement and the signature by which he sealed his own fate is not known. He expressed his dissatisfaction somehow. According to Rovinsky and Lazar Tomanović, he was summoned to Cetinje by November 17, 1830, and the chieftains—which ones and how, no one knows—sentenced him to death, after which Rade pardoned him, apparently to emphasize thus his own significance as sovereign. Vuko was charged, according to what emerges from later accounts, with having had a meeting in Kotor two days before, on November 15, with the Austrian general Tatz—allegedly to turn over Montenegro to Austria. This version persisted for a long time, even in serious studies, such as those by Tomanović and Lavrov.

Even if it were not for the obvious clumsiness of the charge—the fact that an act of treason is discovered and a trial held all in the space of two days' time—there exist three serious testimonials that belie the treason of Governor Vuko. The first was a statement by Stevan Perkov. He had always been in the forefront of the campaign to destroy the Radonjići, but naturally truthful and conscientious as he was, he told the equally truthful and conscientious Vrčević that he knew nothing of any such treason or meeting with Tatz. A second testimonial is in the Kotor archives. The officials of Kotor kept a vigilant watch over all outbreaks of trouble in Cetinje, about which they were informed by the spy Rucović, and whatever they found out they regularly sent on to the Governor of Dalmatia in Zara. These reports indicate that Austria accepted Rade's designation as an accomplished fact. True, the Governor had hopes that the Radonjići would win, but he advised the Austrian Minister at Kotor to bide his time. There is not a word about General Tatz and the meeting with him. Jevto M. Milović has only recently confirmed this. Being well informed about the internal squabbles of the Montenegrins, just two days following Rade's installation the Austrians presented their old claims to disputed territories. This might have been in support of the Radonjići. But that is all, and there is no evidence that the Radonjići supported Austria's claims.

A third testimonial is the popular conscience. Reacting by intuition, the people never accepted the charge of treason, except as an excuse to justify the fierce settling of accounts with the Radonjići. Not even Rade himself, who wrote to Gagić on November 22, immediately following the trial, mentioned the meeting with Tatz, but only that Vuko admitted having been in Kotor, and that he —Rade—would write the Russian Consul about the rest later. Today it is known that Vuko's statement was correct. And the cautious Gagić avoided having any ties with Radonjić: the Radonjići might have turned to Russia, but the Petrovići always had, from olden times.

Vuko's trial, which ended with a symbolical sentence, brought no benefit to the Petrovići. It might even have been interpreted as a sign of their indecision. The conflict remained unresolved, indeed all the more tangled and bitter. It appears that the intentions and resistance of the Radonjići became clearer and more final after Djuzo's return to Njeguši.

The second strike against the Radonjići was carefully prepared and hit its mark. On the very feast of Saint George—the patron saint of both the Petrovići and the Radonjići—Djuzo was murdered by Grujo Žutković, a man from a brotherhood close to the Radonjići. This took place neither by chance nor for personal motives. It must have stunned every Montenegrin, and especially the Radonjići, for it was a blow against all established moral and social norms: a man had been murdered by someone practically from his own brotherhood who desecrated his own and the victim's patron saint's day with bloodshed.

There is something in that first killing that sets its stamp on the entire further reign of Bishop Rade: the rending of primeval brotherhood and clan ties. The Petrovići, and Rade himself, apparently were not held back even by inherited and sacred injunctions when it was a matter of their power.

The Radonjići were dumbfounded, paralyzed. They groaned and invoked justice, honor, and tradition. But there was no will to resist.

The Petrovići gained confidence and reaped whatever was ripe. Soon after Djuzo's murder a regular little raid was organized against the Radonjići: five or six of them were killed in the mountains, their homes burned to their foundations, and the survivors with their families were driven out of Montenegro. Archimandrite Rade's letter of January, 1832, reveals that Governor Vuko and his brother Marko were put in chains in Cetinje, and the Radonjić family exiled to the Austrian Littoral.

There was as yet no prison in Montenegro. (The first one was to be established by Bishop Rade, in a little tower next to the monastery.) The Governor and his brother were locked up in the monastery fruit cellar, which had been dug out of the cliffside. Later the Governor, too, was driven out, and he soon died, in Kotor. All that remained of the suffering of the Radonjići and their broken power was the name that stuck to that fruit cellar —the *guvernadurovica.* And the people long remembered how cruelly the Radonjići had been treated—not as they deserved, but as it had to be.

The sentence of banishment, which the Montenegrin sovereigns were later to use frequently, was not as light as might seem today. The Montenegrin of those times was bound by his entire being to his brotherhood, his clan, his soil. To wrench him from these was tantamount to cutting all his natural ties, the veins that nourished him with strength and vitality. He could live without all this, but in terrible suffering, with an unquenchable yearning for the homeland. Even today such a punishment is regarded by some African tribes as the most terrible there is. In Montenegro, too, it sometimes lay heavier than a death sentence: many cases are known of Montenegrins who did not wish to flee, but remained to be shot in their land, with their brotherhood.

The punishment had been inflicted before—for incest and grave crimes. As it was applied to the Radonjići, however, it marked the transformation of tribal common law into civil law. Women and minors were also treated according to inherited custom—they were not touched. Nor were adult males killed if they were not personally guilty. The opponent was wrenched up by the roots, and the entire brotherhood was made to suffer. Yet account was taken of personal guilt. There was some kind of new, refined cruelty, but also some humanity.

The score with the Radonjići had been settled. But the disagreement went on, and even reached St. Petersburg, in a somewhat changed form. As late as 1839 Rade was to inform the Captain of Kotor that the Radonjići were preparing to kill either his brother or his nephew. The hatred and the denunciation were to last even longer, to the time of Prince Nikola, who would permit the Radonjići to return to Montenegro. But the fighting had stopped. By having crushed the Radonjići, the Petrovići took a fateful step—they cut themselves off from the clan and became a world unto themselves.

Young Rade's first step to power thus was an encounter with misfortune—the willfulness of the clan and the ambitions of the Radonjići. But the Petrovići, and he, were not able to shake off the misfortune. They had declared war on a legacy, and dipped their hands in the blood of brothers, for the sake of something new and great.

And can it be otherwise?

What was Rade's role in all this?

It sometimes seems that everything was happening without him. However, the documents show that he was a lively participant in it all, even if one accepts that his first letters were written by Sarajlija, and that both Sarajlija and the relatives took part in the decisions. Rade's cries for help to the Russians and to the Montenegrins in Russia, and the appeals to his youth, were not really his, and were a calculated attempt to evoke sympathy. He was to cry for help later as well—all his life. But how? Bitterly, proudly, as a man. There are certain errors in his letters to the Russians which he naïvely insisted on perpetrating—that Bishop Petar "thanks be to God . . . had time to write a testament to his people," and that his last words to his successor were "Pray to God and cling to Russia." Nevertheless one can feel Rade's personality here—Rade as a Petrović, but also Rade as himself. Though others influenced him, the manner was his—that of determination, forcefulness.

The tie with Sarajlija did not last long either. By January 6, 1831, Rade had informed Gagić that Sima "took certain liberties since the Metropolitan's demise" and took to his heels by way of the Bay of Kotor. In his letter of January 12 he was to go so far as to claim that Sima has "publicly proclaimed himself a traitor."

That conflict has not been explained to this very day. There is some conjecture that the quarrel was staged so that Sima could the more easily discover the intentions of the Radonjići, and of others—the Austrians, and perhaps the Russians as well. For the quarrel was neither deep nor final. That same year Sima was to come back to Montenegro, and Rade would assure Prince Miloš of his honesty. Pupil and teacher were to go on being close friends to the end. Probably the cause of the clash was precisely the one Rade stated: Sima had "taken liberties"—he tried to govern and to make the decisions. Neither the Petrovići nor Rade would permit this. They could make compromises, grant concessions, temporize and accommodate, but everything was done, both consciously and spontaneously, to accomplish their one aim. However, once Sima took himself away, along with his pretensions —and perhaps he left precisely because he perceived that nothing could come of his pretensions—passions subsided, the "traitor" became a friend once more, and relations returned to their real and normal state.

And so the third passion of Bishop Rade-Njegoš was conceived. For he had three of them: Serbianism, poetry, and power. He inherited the first in the struggle against the Turks. He was born with the second. The third he acquired. But they were inseparably woven together into his fiber from the beginning. The fighter, the poet, and the ruler were all one, just like his sense of hate, love, and duty. He had other passions as well—the hunt, women, sometimes gambling, and frequently traveling. He could suppress these, and deny them. But not those three. They burned within him—sometimes one with a greater intensity than the others, but none of them ever dying out. That was he.

6.

IN TURKEY—THAT Turkey next to Montenegro—there were great troubles: the vizirs were up in arms, and mutiny begot mutiny. Even now decisive battles were being waged between the Porte and the rebellious war lords.

Montenegro was internally disorganized; Rade's authority was not yet firm. Time was needed—and time waits for no man. Some strong support was essential to see things through. It could come, and did come, from only one place—from Russia.

That help appeared in a rather strange form—especially in the time of Stephen the Small—but it was significant and broad, both financial and political. In August, 1831, there came from Russia Ivan Ivanović Vukotić and his nephew Matija Vučićević. With them also arrived Dimitrije Milaković. Behind them stood the prestige and power of an Orthodox and Slavic state over whose endless territories the sun never set.

Russia was a religious and popular myth. It was also the only country to help the Montenegrins, from the time of Bishop Danilo and Peter the Great, when freedom gained its first foothold in Montenegro. It left them in the lurch more frequently than was necessary, and got them in trouble even when it had nothing much to gain by it. But it supported them in their resistance, took up their cause in Istanbul, and gave them financial support, though neither regularly nor much—a thousand gold pieces a year. Yet even that was some help—the only help. Hope in Russia was undying, and was not born simply of weakness. The ties with Russia were also spiritual, cultural, and as such all the more constant in the minds of primitive men who were simple, unlettered, and uninitiated in all the perfidies of international politics.

Russia's reputation was so great that Bishop Petar threatened the tribes and the Montenegrins in his every other letter with abandonment by their powerful protector to the north if they did not reform and come to their senses.

Such was Russia. As for Vukotić himself, he possessed none of its mystical and brilliant splendor. He was, above all, a Montenegrin—from the village of Golubovci, in Zeta, which was still under the Turks. He had left long ago to settle in Russia and became wealthy there after having come into an inheritance from a relative, Ivan Podgoričanin, the same one who is to be found in a folk epic. In Russia Ivan made his way up to the rank of a noncommissioned officer. He was already advanced in years, but love of homeland never left Ivan Vukotić. Bishop Petar carried on some affairs in Russia through him and his nephew. Having no family responsibilities, Ivan decided to use all his wealth for Montenegro.

The Russians sent Vukotić and his nephew to Montenegro on a mission whose aims were not clearly defined. Of little personal prestige, and finding himself in a difficult and tangled situation, Vukotić resorted to something not at all in keeping with his character: word got around that he was a general, and if he did not spread the report, he certainly did not deny it. And inasmuch as the Montenegrins were accustomed to receiving imperial "charters," on the occasion of his arrival in explanation of his mission, there was read a "false charter"—as Bishop Rade called it—with a seal, according to Nićifor Dučić, taken from a previous Russian imperial document of long ago. It is also not clear where Vukotić got that second surname of his—Ivanović. Milović claims that he assumed it in order to give weight to his alleged descent from Ivan Crnojević, and thus to his own princely pretensions. But it could be that the name was derived from that rich relative of his. Whatever may be the case, the surname was not his either.

The Petrovići and Rade knew all this very well. But their position was still not solid, and so they accepted these maneuvers of Vukotić's and the prestige they brought.

No matter how one evaluates the activity and the personality of Vukotić, he lacked neither seriousness nor intelligence, which is more than one can say for his nephew—a busybody and a nobody.

Not wasting a moment, Vukotić went to work and, thanks to his inflated reputation, began to organize a government—the governing Senate of Montenegro—and an authority—the Guard, or, as Bishop Rade explains it, the Police (*Polizia*). To be sure, it fell to Vukotić to preside over the Senate, while his nephew was given the vice-presidency. Milaković took over the post of secretary, which he was to hold even after Bishop Rade's death. The prominent chieftains were given a place in the Senate. Rade was left out—to be bishop, as though this could ever satisfy the strivings and ambitions of the Petrovići, in the light of their past and the still-undried blood they had shed in their own tribe.

If it was possible to get around Rade—who was quite young and not yet consecrated—one could not do so with the Petrovići. Vukotić had to bring the chieftains of their party into the Senate. As for a party of his own, he really had none, while he could hardly rely on the Governor's party, because of its Austrian leanings. Rade was not out. He was the future bishop and the future head of the Petrovići and of the land. The Senate was divided, from its very inception, into the newcomers—whom the natives needed because Russia stood behind them—and the natives—without whom the former could do nothing. Vukotić and the Russians—for the Montenegrins this was all the same as long as there was money to pay the senators and the Guard. Was it not this as well that made the Petrović party so accommodating? The incongruity of the roles played by Rade and Vukotić and the division within the Senate could only grow worse. The dualism between bishop and president of the Senate was all too reminiscent of the dualism between bishop and governor. And it was to heighten—until the final rupture, as with the Governor.

The whole previous struggle for power and the state was now transferred to the Senate and around it.

A *Current Journal* was also introduced, in which all the more important letters were recorded. A similar book existed in the Russian Consulate in Dubrovnik. Even the paper was the same. The Russian hand of the Serb Gagić may be detected in this. At any rate, a government had begun to operate, one with an administration and records.

Nićifor Dučić contended that the model for the Senate had been taken from Austria. Rovinsky traced it to Russia, while Vuksan claimed it had existed before, but as an irregular institution. There is indeed something Russian about the Montenegrin Senate, but something that could have come from any absolutist centralistic system. Despite the name and the similarity, it was a Montenegrin institution, conceived wisely and realistically: the clan chieftains headed by the one and only possible central figure—the bishop. The clan remained as an entity, and even had its man in the Senate, but in actual fact it was gradually losing its independence.

The Senate was created in January, 1832, by the action of an assembly which elected fifteen chieftains to be in it. No matter how significant this was, nevertheless the Petrovići had already finished the most vital job in scattering the Radonjići and hanging on to the episcopal throne. They could not have created the Senate —for that step the merit belongs to Vukotić—for they did not have the means in any event. The conflict with the Radonjići was not finished with the inauguration of the Senate; they were still in chains in Cetinje, and the Russians were certainly in a hurry to settle this murky affair. But the Petrovići were prepared for such a settlement. The letters of Archimandrite Rade—those written before Vukotić's arrival, apparently similar to those of Bishop Petar—bristle with a previously unknown toughness and sharpness, as though from an awareness that something new and great had to be done. He wrote to the men of Crmnica on July 15, 1831, "There are some dogs in Montenegro who would be glad not only to see us die, but all who cross themselves. . . . Some Montenegrins would sell for money [not only] a piece of God but of their soul and of their father and mother and brothers . . . and their most dear fatherland." And to the Banjani on July 28, 1831, "But rise up and castigate the evil, for, mark it well, the fetter will soon circle the necks of the evil men."

Gagić was not right in giving all the credit to Vukotić, though he may have done this as a matter of official duty. Those who denied him any merit whatever were still less in the right. True, he wished to take everything into his own hands and to place himself at the head of Montenegro. He even built himself a fine house in Cetinje—in which Bishop Rade was later to live, until he erected the Billiard. Yet he showed no signs of profligacy or lack of seriousness. He was a severe and willful man, but also reasonable and amiable. Vukotić introduced the punishment of flogging with rods, no doubt on the model of Russian serfdom. Such a punishment was unworthy of Montenegrins, who were reared in the freedoms of tribal life and rebellion. Bishop Rade was never to apply it, in deference to Montenegrin pride. But it was to reappear after him—for shameful misdeeds. Vukotić even wrote laws. In the beginning of 1833 his "Laws of the Fatherland" were adopted, but never executed. So it was with everything he did. It was full of stereotypes and incongruities, and yet there was something realistic and well intentioned about it all. It was the same with his government and administration.

Though it was directed against the willfulness of the clans and of individuals, the Senate in the beginning was also an expression of their will. Earlier that will had been expressed in irregular assemblies. Now the clans had their permanent representatives in the Montenegrin Senate. Bishop Rade himself, when he later began to place chieftains over the clans and to appoint senators, took care to have the most distinguished men from the clans in the Senate. Conceived as the highest tribunal, the Senate served, under those conditions, as the government, too. Its composition and the number of its members varied, as did its role, for—as Popov brings out—at times it betokened a compromise with the clans, and at times it was at odds with them. Under Bishop Rade it was to assume an advisory character. The senators were salaried from the very first, and their salaries rose in proportion to the decline of the Senate's significance. Still the Senate provided that form—and this was undoubtedly thanks to Vukotić—which facilitated the transition from clan heterogeneity to central government.

The institution of the Guard, on the other hand, was something new, or nearly so. It was established in all the districts and among all the clans, and it had—according to Bishop Rade's letter of December 6, 1831—one hundred and sixty-four members, who were paid and selected on the basis of courage and devotion. The Guard became both police and a court in the clans. Led by captains, it was at first almost completely independent of the clan chieftains. Its leaders (the title of "captain" actually came later, after 1837) were judges of the first instance, while the Senate was the higher court. Sekula Drljević brings out that Bishop Rade usually appointed the leaders of the clan as captains, and that there were several in each clan—apparently according to the need and the size of the territory. There had been field guards earlier whose job it was to keep watch over the meadows, pastures, and the like. Thus Drljević concludes that the "Guard was no public-law institution" but only a designation for the clan standard-bearer and field guards who served as the captain's helpers. Certainly this much is correct, namely, the tendency to turn the Guard into what it really came to be—a police and local court—on the basis of already existing institutions and forms.

The inauguration of taxes soon followed—in 1833. This was, and remained, the source of constant resistance, which was deeply ingrained in the people. Bishop Rade was not to yield on this point when he took power into his own hands. Certainly the sum itself was not involved—in 1834 the collected tax consisted of 14,227 florins—but the need to maintain order and to accustom the people to it.

A Senate and a government were being created while around Montenegro the Turkish Empire was shaking and crumbling. Meanwhile Rade prepared to go to Russia—to be consecrated bishop. He was learning something about government, and also about something else, which he had little desire to learn—liturgics. For this they got him a priest from the coast, a native of the Vojvodina, who therefore was sure to know the services well. After all, how was Rade to be consecrated bishop in Russia if he did not know the services? And so Rade diligently studied this, too. Without it he could not come to power. Along with the litanies he also wrote poems, his own and quite unecclesiastical. And he waged war on the Turks.

That is how it was with him in the beginning: on top of the inner crises and struggles came a duty—an inherited obligation which reached across centuries of human endurance—to bring oneself and one's world to expression.

7.

Bosnia and Albania were up in arms.

The causes of their rebellion were similar. And yet they also differed.

The canny Prince Miloš had already called the attention of Bishop Petar to the unrest in Bosnia, but the latter, being in advanced years, apparently gave it little notice.

The Bosnian mutinies against the Sultan's reforms, the *Tanzimat,* were hardly exceptional in the Turkish Empire of that day. In Istanbul itself, on July 2–3, 1826, a rebellion of the Janizaries broke out. Six thousand of them perished, while twenty thousand were exiled from the capital. In Bosnia, during the same year, the fuse was lighted with the announcement of an imperial decree on reforms. The resistance was headed by Husein Kapetan, of Gradačac, a man of considerable wit, enterprise, and honesty, and still-greater conservatism. Though he was humane toward his serfs, it never entered a corner of his mind that serfdom should be abolished. The unquelled mutiny was to flare up again in 1829: the Bosnian Moslems were of no mind to go to war against Russia for nothing. Mutinies and clashes broke out again in 1831, and this bey of an old, though hardly renowned, family, who by his own efforts came to be called the Dragon of Bosnia, was to prowl and fight from the Vardar to the Una, and to march on Istanbul, wounding and taking prisoner the Sultan's vizirs and pashas, burning the roofs over their heads and dispersing their armies, unwilling to have the Bosniaks ruled by the Turkuši—as the Bosnians called the real Turks, and defending the purity of

Islam in the hills and towns of Bosnia from the Caliph and Istanbul.

At the same time, there rose up in Scutari Mustafa Pasha Bushati, vizir by an inheritance then two centuries old. However, unlike Husein Kapetan, who was a selfless fanatic, Bushati was torpid and lacking in spirit, given to immobility, luxury, and a lordly existence. He sallied forth from Scutari reluctantly and simply waited for the Grand Vizir Reshid Pasha to take him prisoner, while Husein was truly like a dragon, scurrying from battle to battle and fighting until his last mounted warrior left him. Both the one and the other adhered to the true faith, as did the Grand Vizir. Husein was pure-hearted and loved his Bosnia for its looming hills and swift-running streams, its ways and its men, and cared nothing for the vizirate the rebellious beys had awarded him. As for Mustafa Pasha, his only concern was to keep intact his power and his privileges.

The Montenegrins had both respect and admiration for Husein Kapetan. It could be said about Mustafa Pasha, on the other hand, that he did everything possible not to deserve either.

The Montenegrins did not sit with folded hands. Archimandrite Rade, or, rather, Vukotić and the Senate, sent Husein Kapetan Mojsije Zečević, a man who knew what the bey was thinking even in his sleep. They also maintained good relations with Mustafa Pasha, and Archimandrite Rade encouraged him, saying, "Do not yield. The proof of heroes is in time of trouble!" Without asking Gagić, Rade promised the Pasha asylum in Montenegro if he became hard-pressed. Gagić was upset and reminded him that Russia was not only supporting the Porte, but also sending an army to the Sultan to save Istanbul from the rebels in Egypt, who were in league with Mustafa Pasha.

Archimandrite Rade, Vukotić, and the chieftains felt and knew that the Porte was now their main and most immediate adversary. Even under Bishop Petar they had more or less struck a balance with the forces of the neighboring pashas. The Bosnians of Husein Kapetan apparently suspected this and seemed to want greater and closer ties. After all, they were of the same blood and language and courage.

Prince Miloš acted more cautiously. He advised Cetinje to maintain good relations with Scutari, but he was against Husein

Kapetan, who was casting an eye on Jadar and Radjevina, in Serbia. The Pasha of Zvornik, Vidajić, Husein's enemy, was a close acquaintance of Miloš. Miloš sought to defend Rade before him as still a lad, and blamed Mojsije Zečević as a bandit out for loot. While Miloš supplied the Sultan's army with food, he would send the Montenegrins neither powder nor money. Rade held this against him—and never forgot. Miloš had no great ideas or ideals. These would only have gotten in his way. He was defending his princely title and, little by little, expanding tiny Serbia and putting it on its own feet. Whatever offered no prospects and was not tangible simply did not exist for him. It was precisely in this that his greatness lay, for he was a genius in his ability to assess the capacities of his people at any given moment. By not fighting and by helping the Sultan—neither zealously nor too much—Miloš was to extract three more Serbian districts from the Turks in their trouble.

Montenegro and Rade were different. Their meager strength seemed only to lead to greater enthusiasm and daring. "Better one day with a falcon than a hundred years with a crow." They were at extreme ends. Miloš did not find it shameful to be a crow for the sake of Serbdom and the princely title. Yet when he had to, he knew how to be a falcon as well. He justified himself to the Turks for maintaining relations with Montenegro, yet he also informed his deputation in Istanbul with great concern about the intentions of the Grand Vizir: "I fear Montenegro may perish, this only Serbian nest which has kept its freedom for so many hundreds of years even while all other parts of the Serbian people bear an alien yoke."

8.

MONTENEGRO WAS so inflamed by the thought of freedom that frequently, in doing what had to be done, it did not take stock of its resources.

The Moslems of Podgorica, Montenegro's enemies for centuries, were helping the Sultan's army against the rebels in Bosnia and Albania. Podgorica was the heart of Zeta—a gentle plain and the cradle of the Serbian medieval state. No Montenegrin could stand by and watch what the Moslems of Podgorica were doing while Montenegro stood alone.

At that time two Montenegrin attacks were directed against Podgorica.

The first took place in October, 1831—without Gagić's knowledge. Gagić was angry and issued warnings. And Rade learned how to bring off his first political trickery and dissimulation. He had to deceive his Russian patrons from beginning to end if he wished to do what he had to—fight against the Turks. And so he promised Gagić to heed his advice, made the Turks rude offers of peace, even as he wrote Husein Kapetan, "But we beg you as our dear friend to bear up like a hero and to be careful not to let that *sadrazam* [Grand Vizir] deceive you in anything." Vukotić also took part in this, intoxicated by this Montenegrin madness, as though he had not arrived from Russia but the day before with instructions to maintain peace with the Turks.

That first attack was not of large proportions. The second—in February, 1832, just after the inauguration of the Senate—was. Nor was Consul Gagić informed about this one by Rade and the Montenegrins, for they knew beforehand that he would have stopped them. Rade's subsequent explanations seem naïve: ". . . and a few Montenegrins went along the Zeta and there rescued from the hands of the Turks some Serbian priests and distinguished men whose lives the Turks were threatening." And that was all. Actually almost all of Montenegro had risen against Podgorica and Zeta. Generally, whenever he had to pretend and to pass over the truth—and this he had to do frequently—Rade did it transparently and awkwardly. He was not made for it. But when forced by unfortunate circumstances, he managed. This, too, was a weapon.

This attack was led by the young Archimandrite Rade and Ivan Vukotić—just as the governor and the bishop once used to divide the army between them. Vukotić took his part toward his native region, to the villages of Zeta, in order to get around Podgorica from the rear. Rade, with Mojsije, struck out from the Brda, encamped at Vizirov Most, crossed the Morača, and occupied Gorica Hill within sight of Podgorica itself, which at that time spread along the left bank of the Ribnica, where it flows into the Morača. The Montenegrins were being helped by the Hoti, an

Albanian clan whose co-operation the Montenegrin chieftains had been sent to obtain.

The attack was obviously prepared in advance. Yet, like the former one, this one ended in failure.

Podgorica was a walled city, though not particularly fortified. It certainly must have had a few antiquated cannon, for even smaller towns, such as Spuž and Žabljak, had them. It seems as though there were no imperial troops at all in Podgorica. But its citizens had something the Montenegrins did not: cavalry and order. The Montenegrins were able in defending themselves in the hills and in carrying out swift attacks. Here there could be neither the one nor the other. They had nothing for besieging a city—neither the organization nor the patience, to say nothing of experience or supplies. They were commanded by clan chieftains and were grouped by clans and brotherhoods. They had no training whatever. Even in later times they were to be grouped in this way—but the clan was to become a battalion. There was neither cavalry nor cannon. Moreover, like all mountaineers, they had a superstitious dread of cavalry, particularly in the plains, where they could be split and surrounded. The Montenegrins were not prepared at all for more complicated battles. Not even Bishop Petar had been able to take Onogšt-Nikšić when he wanted to lend Karadjordje a helping hand.

Furthermore, the attack was badly timed: the Grand Vizir had already subdued the Vizir of Scutari, Bushati, and possessed sufficient forces to have retaken Podgorica if the Montenegrins had succeeded in occupying it. The Montenegrin army must have felt insecure, seeing no prospect of any lasting success.

Even so, the immediate reasons for the failure are not quite clear. There had actually been no real battle. The first attrition took place among Vukotić's forces, which had surrounded some three hundred Turks in Golubovci. The Montenegrins had no food. It seems that the Hoti were the first to turn back. The tale has been preserved that some Montenegrin and Albanian chieftains, among them the Serdar of Rijeka, Filip Djurašković, and the priest Andrija Pejović, had received fat bribes from the Turks to disband their forces. There is no proof of this, while it is known that Bishop Rade remained on good terms with both of these men. Nevertheless there could have been, and there were, unreliable chieftains who were bound more to their clans than to the general cause, and who were accustomed to thinking of bribe-taking not as treason and shame, but as something clever of which one could boast. The district of Rijeka did in fact have lively commercial ties with the Moslems of Zeta. It seems that their men were indeed the first to withdraw, and this is probably how the story of the bribing of Serdar Filip got started.

On March 17 the Turks descended upon Zeta with their cavalry, rescued their people, and bore down on Vukotić, who had only fifty warriors left. Archimandrite Rade then led an attack on the Turks and thus relieved Vukotić sufficiently to permit him to withdraw. Then he himself drew back into the hills—"shamefully and disgracefully and needlessly," as Gagić complained to Dimitri Pavlovich Tatishchev, the Russian ambassador in Vienna. Vuksan relates that there were few dead, but many wounded.

This was Bishop Rade's first and only battle with the Turks. And that one was unsuccessful. Yet there was no Montenegrin alive who yearned as much to fight the Turks. This was but one —and the largest—of the gaps in his life between possibility and desire. This was the insurmountable difficulty of his uncle Bishop Petar, too, who once wrote, in Russian, "If only my abilities were commensurate with my desires." It was also one of the sources of Njegoš's poetry.

Though this campaign ended almost bloodlessly, for both sides, it had significant consequences. Embittered, the Grand Vizir Reshid Pasha prepared to attack Montenegro and to pacify that province, which he considered a part of his empire. His army looted and razed Montenegrin villages and would not let salt be taken out of Scutari, and he hanged and impaled all Montenegrins who fell into his clutches, taking the part of the Moslems of Spuž and Podgorica in every way. Perhaps out of fear for his own position, Gagić openly supported the Montenegrins and alerted the Russians. The foreign chanceries of the Great Powers began to stir. But the Russians were able to quiet Gagić down, especially since the Grand Vizir had to hurry off to Istanbul to rescue it from Mehemet Ali, of Egypt. Russian influence was powerful at the Porte in those days; a Russian army was fighting the rebels against the Sultan, and so the Podgorica incident was easily closed. But the Russians took the opportunity to tether the Montenegrins and the restless Archimandrite in order to spare them further trouble. It was largely for this that they sent Gagić to Montenegro. And so it was to be: whenever Bishop Rade lifted a hand against the Turks—whether in self-defense or to attack—the Russians would hold him back. He was not to dare even what he might have done. The only thing they could not restrain was his hatred, which grew more intense with the ceaseless border massacre and betrayal from within.

The Montenegrins and Rade were not frightened by the Grand Vizir and his strength. Rade wrote to him:

From the time the Serbian empire fell on the Field of Kosovo and was forced beneath the Turkish yoke, from that time to this day Montenegro has preserved both its independence and its religion . . . nor has it ever been willing to be subject to anyone. . . . And why do you call Montenegrins bandits and robbers? Is it because they defend their freedom and independence and because they know how to value and respect their religion? These are no bandits and robbers, but the faithful sons of their fatherland and true worshipers of God. . . . And if you attack us, we shall be forced to defend our freedom and our independence, which our sires also defended and for which many a one fell as a sacrifice. So, too, each one of us to a man will shed the last drop of his blood for our faith, freedom, and independence.

Though he was not first in the Senate, Rade was not without influence. He was the ruler, in the eyes of both the world and the Vizir. Through him spoke the striving of centuries of his people. He gave signs of being not only the future poet of *The Mountain Wreath,* but also a new and forceful ruler. From the very first the defiant notes to the Turks flowed effortlessly from his pen—thick and fast, powerful and from the depths.

Though he himself did not have the strength, he knew what had to be done and, still better, what should not be done. He announced to Gagić on November 1, 1831, before the Podgorica campaign, "I hereby inform you that the worthless and cowardly Pasha of Scutari has surrendered to the Grand Vizir." Mustafa Pasha intended to take refuge in Montenegro. He sent his harem and family by boat across Lake Scutari, but they no sooner touched shore than the Montenegrins made haste to plunder whatever they had. That could only have increased his fears—and he surrendered. He was dispatched to Istanbul and pardoned. Later he was to appear in Bosnia as a faceless official of the Sultan. With Mustafa's fall the Bushati family was forever deprived of the Vizirate of Scutari.

The last Bushati was the grandson of that Mahmud Pasha who fell heroically in battle against the Montenegrins. But the grandson inherited only the brutality, the easy, senseless kind at that. With Mahmud's head fell all the strength and courage of the Bushatis. He knew how to lose his head to save his face, while the grandson knew how to lose his face to save his head.

It was largely through centuries of struggle with the Bushatis that Montenegro became a concept and made a name for itself. Now that, too, was gone. Rade was not able to wrest Podgorica from the Sultan, but still through him Montenegro continued to rise and cleanse itself in blood. Through Rade-Njegoš it would achieve its greatest purity, in thought and sound, in the poeticized idea.

And when Montenegro was to fall, in the First World War, the descendants of Bishop Rade—King Nikola and his kin—were to leave their homeland as Mustafa Pasha left his: to save only their titles—without idea or conscience; just to save their heads—nameless and faceless—as though there had never been anything—neither battles nor poetry.

Poems were Rade's battles.

9.

HUSEIN KAPETAN WAS the final burst of brilliance, and an unforgettable one, of the Bosnian feudal lords and beys. It was with Husein that the beys would fall, and, soon after, their lands and power and their sway. After him the beys and dynasts of Bosnia began to sink slowly and ingloriously, to leave behind nothing of themselves but human sorrow, in songs of endless pain and beauty.

Husein gathered his armies with ease, but they dissolved even more easily. Though weaker at first, the Sultan's army was more united and tougher. It constantly chipped away Husein's forces, depriving him of his mighty beys and captains by either bribery or force. Husein's forces were unable to unite, for they consisted of feudal lords and their peasants, and the Sultan's pashas set them at odds with one another. Brave in battle, they were incapable of carrying on a long war without a clear program and a secure rear. Nor could Husein—that giant of a man—rise above his class and his time. At the head of the beys, with their servants and Moslem peasants, he could not win the war against the Sultan. The Orthodox and Catholic raia did not join him, nor was he able to do anything to win them over. True, Husein was to take the Serb Davidović for his adviser and the Franciscan Starčević for his scribe; even he saw that Bosnia was not only Moslem. But that was all. He did not dream of turning to the raia. It was as it had been in the fifteenth century, when the Turks advanced and the Bosnian kings and dukes perished because they were supported only by "men of substance." If the raia favored anyone but themselves, it was the Sultan, for he stood for some kind of order and for lower taxes, at least for the times. Mahmud Hamdi Pasha, who had been appointed vizir of Bosnia, advanced slowly but surely.

Still young—around thirty—Husein had become the leader of Bosnia, a province of the Sultan in which the old Slavic nobility had preserved itself by changing its religion. Bosnia enjoyed special privileges for guarding the empire against Christendom and for supplying the Porte for centuries with a fearless army of free mountaineers. Husein's father, Osman Kapetan, who was renowned for his strict justice, had been killed as an opponent of reform by the cold and cruel ascetic Djelal-ud-Din Pasha, Vizir of Travnik. There was the class of bold and proud nobles, and the class of free peasants—mountaineers and border provincials—who had accepted Islam in order to preserve their might and dominion. Istanbul had to come to grips with their willfulness and privileges. Old Bosnia had risen up and was to go down in blood.

Of medium height, Husein had a Georgian mother and thus had a fair complexion against which his big eyes seemed all the darker and sadder. He was to inject into Bosnia's resistance his personal bitterness and unhappiness. Yet he was a man who adhered to the justice of the Koran. He was also one of great bravery and pride. "My sword"—so he wrote to the Serbian Prince Miloš—"drew blood before yours was even fashioned."

Husein Kapetan fought his last battle on May 29, 1832, in the Plain of Sarajevo. His final hour was his bitterest. He was attacked from the rear by the beys of Hercegovina—his ancient rivals the reckless Ali Pasha Rizvanbegović, the irrepressible Smaïl Aga Čengić, and the wily Hasan Beg Resulbegović. Exhausted by defeat, Husein and his family crossed the Sava into Austria and settled in Osijek—amid infidels in an alien land. But death is sometimes the only solace for misfortune and humiliation. His funds vanished. The Austrian authorities pressed him. A handful of friends was threatened and demoralized. Meanwhile the Porte offered mercy—on condition that he never enter Bosnia. He sacrificed himself for his friends and family. After a touching farewell with his wife and little sons, he left for Istanbul at the close of 1832. He went the way of all penitents, even though he was not in fact pardoned. The Sultan was a *giaour,* but he was also a caliph of the true faith—Husein's faith. Everyone remains what he is in the end. Though Husein had rebelled against Istanbul, he did not wish to destroy the Turkish Empire. He languished, but not for long. A mysterious death took him in 1833. Soon after, an end was also put to the Vizirate of Travnik. It was transferred to Sarajevo, whose own municipal liberties were curtailed. Bowstring and rope for both raia and beys, until finally, in 1878, a new and alien power, Austria-Hungary, took over Bosnia and Hercegovina.

Montenegro and Rade continued to be confronted by a pasha in Scutari and the Sultan's officials, who kept replacing each other rapidly and just as rapidly made peace with the Montenegrins while continuing the same routine policy of hatred and revenge and inciting the surrounding Moslems and Albanians to raid Montenegro. Namik, then Ferik, then Hayil, then Hasan, then Rifat—clashes and massacres and ceaseless slaughter, until 1841, when Osman Pasha, of Skoplje, came, a man who knew nothing of peace and neighborliness and who was to inflict the greatest woes on Bishop Rade and evoke in him—in the letters Njegoš was to send him—the most sublime inspirations, those in *The Ray of the Microcosm* and even more in *The Mountain Wreath.*

To the other side of Rade—in Hercegovina—Ali Pasha Rizvanbegović was to remain in Mostar the whole time. In the beginning he was the fierce enemy of both Rade and Montenegro, as a pasha and a Turk, though of Slavic blood. In time, however, he was led by personal considerations to become a friend and blood brother of the Montenegrin Bishop. But not even on this side was Rade to have real peace or true friendship.

Osman Pasha Skopljak looked upon Montenegro as a part of his own imperial pashalik, which he could not suddenly take over with his army in one fell swoop because of the relations between the Porte and St. Petersburg. But with the Porte's indulgence, there was nothing to keep him from chipping it away piece by piece and from bearing down and eroding it from within.

Ali Pasha took pains to keep Montenegrin freedom from spreading into his own pashalik, which he had won in battle against Husein Kapetan. After all, he had his own plans and ambitions. Osman Pasha had none. He felt himself to be a pure Turk. In actual fact he was not, but a renegade from Hercegovina, the son of Suleiman Pasha, who had pacified rebellious Serbia in 1813. Ali Pasha took account of Hercegovina—at least of his pashalik. Osman Pasha took account only of his religion and of his Sultan.

Ali Pasha Rizvanbegović was from Stolac, and was therefore called Stočević. He was of a powerful old family. Jevto Dedijer relates that the Rizvanbegovići held themselves to be of Crnojević stock, of the rulers of Zeta and Montenegro. Ali Pasha both spoke and wrote in Serbian, in a rather antiquated way. He was pasha of Hercegovina and, though abandoned by the beys, he fought Husein Kapetan, and even began to arm the raia against the Sultan's rebels. Hard pressed by the insurgents, he shut himself up in his fortress at Stolac and there held out. He got rid of his own brother, Hadji Bey, for being a rebel, thereby earning the recognition and love of Istanbul. After the pacification of Bosnia he was ceremoniously welcomed and rewarded in Istanbul. It was then that he asked to have Hercegovina separated from Bosnia, and received the vizirate over it, which vanished with him when he, too, turned against Istanbul.

Even when Bishop Rade and Ali Pasha were at the height of their friendship—according to Nenadović as well as Rade—the Bishop regarded him as a most underhanded and heartless tyrant. Yet it was with such a man that Bishop Rade had to become a blood brother. Perhaps he secretly dreamed of restoring the destroyed Serbian Empire with his help. For this was always on Rade's mind, though Ali Pasha cared for practically nothing but the vizirate and the agalik.

Along a third front—by the sea—stood powerful, modern, cold, and unyielding Austria, by no means a friend of the youth and his rookery. It pressed, intrigued, threatened, and demanded what had not even belonged to Venice, whose heritage it had grabbed for itself without much trouble. It lay in wait and unerringly exploited every weakness.

The rebellions subsided, and with them Montenegrin hopes as well. The Grand Vizir and the Sultan's army went away. The pressure on Montenegro let up. For the moment it looked as if the evil had passed it by. Actually it had merely taken on a new form.

10.

SPRING, 1833.

The young Archimandrite finally set out for Russia.

Twice, in 1831 and in 1832, he had tried to be received in St. Petersburg; the Petrovići were in a hurry to have him consecrated. But Russia refused. It was to refuse to receive him many times later as well. It was still investigating what was going on, and was probably awaiting the results of Vukotić's mission. The first to make his appearance in Montenegro, in 1832, was Professor Alexander Reutz, supposedly in search of antiquities. He stayed in Cetinje four days, copied some old documents, and was ceremoniously escorted out again; the Montenegrins realized what was afoot. Reutz's report concerning Rade and Vukotić's decrees was favorable. Then came Consul Gagić, in June, 1832, and he was even more ceremoniously welcomed. Gagić was brought by a problem that worried both him and the Russians: the Montenegrins were feuding with the Turks while Rade was sending Gagić and the Russians letters telling them that he was just dying to maintain peace with the Turks. Russia was now friendly with the Turks and found it impossible to square its conscience—the protection of the Orthodox raia—with its *raisons d'état.* Montenegro was dragging it into embarrassing situations and constantly confronting it with aggravations. Gagić was also interested in Montenegro's administration.

The internal situation seems to have become stabilized. At the moment there were neither battles with the Turks nor serious raids. Certainly Rade must have learned the liturgy by then. Nothing stood in the way of his trip to Russia. An assembly of Montenegrin chieftains asked Russia to receive him and to consecrate him bishop. The Petrovići and the chieftains attached great significance to the trip, realizing that this was the way to end the dualism in the governing of the land.

He embarked at Kotor on June 7, 1833, for Vienna and St. Petersburg. This was Njegoš's first trip abroad. He went via the Bay of Kotor, Dalmatia, and Trieste, which he regarded as native lands under foreign rule.

In Dubrovnik he was met and escorted by Consul Gagić, while on the journey he was attended by his secretary Milaković.

Njegoš was to remain in close ties with both of them from the beginning to the end. They were to know everything about him, prying into his most secret corners. Both were inextricably entangled in his political activity, internal as well as foreign. Yet they left hardly a single note concerning the human, the creative side of Njegoš.

There was something similar about these two men—both in character and in manner of operation.

Jeremija Gagić, Russian consul in Dubrovnik, was a Serb from Gruža, near Kragujevac. As a child he had moved to Austria. He finished elementary school in Ruma, and took up commerce in Zemun. With the outbreak of the First Insurrection he crossed over into Serbia to become a scribe for the Administrative Council, where he belonged to the Russophile party. Even before the insurrection was quelled, he joined Milenko Stojković and Petar Todorović Dobrnjac, who were driven out of Serbia, and entered the Russian service, adopting Russian citizenship. In 1813 he was appointed vice-consul, and later consul, in Dubrovnik.

For forty years he was to supervise Montenegro from there.

In order to be someone in those times and in the eyes of a government that attached great importance to one's origins, Gagić requested the Russians to recognize his noble title. As proof he presented a coat of arms—a shield with a white cross and four torches—and a genealogical table going back to the year 1540. How important it still was at that time for one's reputation and advancement in the service, and especially in dealing with the Russians, may be seen from the fact that even Bishop Rade issued to some

Montenegrins patents of nobility. But an old Serbian coat of arms could not have been of much help to Gagić. He was a good civil servant and devoted to Russia—and that is what held him in the esteem of the Russian government. He was also not a bad Serb, though it was not always easy to reconcile this with the exigencies of his Russian service. But he managed to be at peace with himself—insofar as his position permitted.

A portrait of him probes more deeply than he might have wished: a noble major-domo, a merchant, and, most of all, what he really was—a diplomat. Also a family man who worried over salaries, honorariums, and career. Amiable, ingratiating, and retiring—both by nature and in his professional duties. There was nothing penetrating and creative about him.

Yet Gagić was not without intelligence and wit. The reports he gathered about Montenegro, about Bishop Rade, and about the chieftains were certainly verified with the conscientiousness one expects of a real career man. Of course, they contained neither imagination nor depth. But no one can deny their exactness. He had a flair for that kind of work. He even knew what was going on in Ali Pasha's apartments and what the Turks were thinking of doing about Montenegro, let alone what was happening in Cetinje, over which—both he and the Russians believed—he by right had some control.

He never understood Njegoš. Nor could he. Not because the latter was mysterious or complicated, but because he belonged to a different species and another world. When Njegoš sent him his *Ode to Liberty* for his opinion, Gagić was confused—perhaps for the first time—and replied somewhat vaguely, as every politician would reply to a poet: not bad, though the punctuation is not quite right.

But he understood Montenegro's situation and possibilities realistically, and sometimes profoundly. When Rade, then still a monk, complained about Austrian claims to Majine and Stanjevići and called them the fabrications of an aggressor, Gagić immediately—and correctly—began to doubt that Montenegro's rights were well founded, inasmuch as Austria was internationally recognized as Venice's heir. He knew what could and could not be done. Rade and the Montenegrins did not always know this—and did not wish to know it, for they were after something great and unrealistic.

Gagić understood them, and even approved inside himself, but he made them stick to the possible. Of course, the possible meant for him whatever mighty Russia did and planned. He developed an infallible sense, an instinct, for divining the intentions of the Russian government. He had frequent misunderstandings with the Montenegrins and with their Bishop. As far as he was concerned, all of this was simply a terrible headache—without end. For Rade, for the Montenegrins, his recommendations, reproaches, and prohibitions came from a lack of understanding and held them back. It was precisely in these misunderstandings that Gagić exhibited the greatest agility; he quickly passed over whatever was not essential to the policies he represented. At the time, Russian policies conflicted more frequently with Montenegrin wishes than with their possibilities. The Montenegrins were weak and unrecognized.

Gagić would always subordinate and sacrifice Montenegrin desires to Russian orders. This did not mean, however, that he did not love Serbdom and Montenegro. On the contrary, he worried over them constantly, though with a measured zeal.

The poet and the man Njegoš had no contact with him. With the nationalist Njegoš Gagić was in ideological agreement, though he was in frequent conflict with his decisions. He helped the ruler Njegoš a great deal. It was not that he saw farther, but he was in a position from which he was able to view the situation and to size it up. Their relations were disturbed, but not much or too often. Only once did they reach the breaking point. Generally these ruptures were mended by practical necessity.

Today Gagić is frequently done an injustice, because he did not understand what he could not understand—the depth of the Njegoš tragedy, which was not only a fateful national one, but also a personal one. But who did understand Njegoš during his lifetime?

All the same, Gagić was a good person to have around, and he was in a good spot.

As a Serb he was capable of feeling more deeply and directly the Montenegrin situation, and being in Dubrovnik, he was in a better position to observe and to get the feel of Turkish and Austrian politics. He was the guardian of Russian interests. But he always alerted the Russian government, and in good time, whenever danger threatened Montenegro. To be sure, his proximity also had its bad features: the Russians saw everything through his eyes, including the things that should have been kept from them. They interfered in everything, or in almost everything—usually impatiently and rudely. Knowing the land and the people better, Gagić managed to mitigate all this.

Rovinsky observed, "These Serbian gentlemen who were sent to Montenegro for Russian affairs, such as Gagić, or [Marko] Ivelić before him, turned out to be greater Russian patriots than the Russians, and more than the Russian government might have desired. This is why Bishop Petar I begged them to send a Russian official, a real Russian and not a Serb." It is always harder to deal with the servants than with their masters, especially if they are of the same blood.

But Gagić did not become completely Russified. He was, and remained, a Serb in the Russian service. He was less the tutor than the counselor, and gave more help than orders. He conscientiously carried out the duties his superiors entrusted to him. Yet he had a sense of moderation, and Njegoš found it easier to deal with him than with a real Russian or a Russified Serb: the former most frequently went from sentimental love to quarreling, while the latter would take power into his own hands in the name of the Russian Tsar.

Life does not conform to desires, least of all to those of civil servants. Gagić even overreached himself in his zeal, perceiving Montenegro's troubles and real situation. "Supposedly carrying out the government's aims," Rovinsky concluded, "he in fact went further than the government itself." Even so, whenever Gagić came to Montenegro, he never turned things upside down; he simply took a look, gave some advice, and returned as quickly as possible to the life of Dubrovnik.

Bishop Rade could always count on Gagić and his conscientiousness. If Gagić did not wish to hide anything from the Russians, Rade at least knew that he would not add anything either. If he frequently showed more concern for Russian interests than a real Russian would have, he was always the Serb. Gagić would not look at all so small and puny if he did not have such a giant as Bishop Rade standing next to him. Rade had to grapple with all of the difficulties of a still-backward and unrecognized state. Gagić helped him in this, if in nothing else. As a Russian official he furthered the

Montenegrin cause and, though of no great spirit or horizons, he lent impetus to Njegoš's upsurge from the depths of the past into the limitless future. It was not easy to work with Gagić, but somehow it seemed easier to live a troubled life with him than with somebody else.

Njegoš's relationship with his secretary Dimitrije Milaković was similar.

Milaković was a native of Mostar, born in 1805; he died suddenly and quite mysteriously in 1858. As a child he had fled with his brother from the plague in Dubrovnik. He was lame, which is probably why he devoted himself to learning. He attended a Gymnasium in Novi Sad and studied philosophy in Vienna, from where Ivan Vukotić had brought him along to Cetinje. He was educated, after a fashion, and had seen something of the world. He spent the entire year of 1836 in Russia, on a matter that might be regarded as official had it not taken so long, even by Russian standards of efficiency. Otherwise he was constantly in Cetinje and by Bishop Rade's side.

There was no person in Njegoš's entourage who was as close to him, or with him as long, and yet as unexemplary, as unremarkable, and therefore as puzzling.

Pale, weak, withdrawn, with a thin mustache, and peaked-looking, Milaković was a person who attracted notice in Cetinje only when he was needed for necessary official business or for his knowledge of foreign languages. As a personality he went unnoticed. He was not aware of the greatness and significance of his master; he left no information about him even though he knew absolutely everything and was a literate man, a highly literate man, who wrote grammars, and translated, and compiled a history of Montenegro—colorless, but not without value.

After his second trip to Russia, in 1837, when Russian pressure on Njegoš fell especially heavily and harshly, Bishop Rade took Milaković as his treasurer and personal secretary, which represented an advance over his previous clerical duties in the Senate. Many letters that are attributed to Njegoš—those insignificant and stylistically flavorless ones—were written by Milaković, and signed by Njegoš. Milaković's legible and impeccable handwriting is encountered everywhere—in the *Current Journal* and in all kinds of documents, but never anywhere in connection with the Bishop's poetic work, not even in letters of political significance—for they, too, were poetry for Njegoš.

Insofar as it is possible to delve into Milaković's personality, he seems to have meddled little in government, but was diligent in the conduct of administrative affairs. Indeed, real government administration in Montenegro began with him. He rarely went beyond its limits, and then unobtrusively and as a confidant. He made no decisions, but stood as a shadow behind Bishop Rade or his brother Pero and cousin Djordjije. There is no record of any friction between him and Bishop Rade. Milaković never had any conflicts with anyone. He played a significant cultural and administrative role in Cetinje, which would have assured him a modest place in the history of Montenegro even if he had not been at Njegoš's side.

He was to the core a civil servant, one whom circumstances forced to participate in many stormy events and to attend, without much understanding, the deeply moving drama of a creative genius.

He was openly oriented toward Russia, though one can only guess for the present—as long as the secret Russian archives remain unsearched—the extent of his ties with Russian officials. At that time it was still possible to be heart and soul for Russia as well as for one's own land; the appetite of the Russian government had not yet gone beyond the Danube and the Bosporus. Milaković was a Serbian patriot—but lukewarm and patient as in everything else.

Milaković could not have any influence over Njegoš. But he was of incalculable help in everyday matters. It was these that exhausted him the most and kept him from greater ventures. Milaković was a quiet, unobtrusive word of advice and a sure and trustworthy hand.

Njegoš's daily life would have been even more troublesome, if indeed his sufferings had any measure, had it not been for his secretary Milaković.

11.

THERE IS AN etching of Rade from that period: a youth in a cassock, still growing, lanky and bony, with a sparse mustache and a beard that barely shows. He is gazing vaguely—at youth, a new future. Rade was tense over his encounter with Trieste and Vienna—which were then centers of South Slavic culture. But he was most excited over his encounter with Russia, the mighty and all-embracing mother and protectress of the Slavs, to whom the Orthodox raia had long been looking for their liberation, and the bishops of Montenegro for deliverance from untold sorrows.

Rade carried with him a rather weighty collection of poetry, *A Voice from the Rocky Crag.* The title tells far more than the contents: the cry of a man on a rock. These were poems about the warfare of the Montenegrins against the Turks and about the battles of his uncle Bishop Petar. In the beginning Njegoš was transparent through and through, however much he cloaked himself in his self-taught learning and exoticism. Two motifs possessed him—the Montenegrin past and his uncle—and it was for these that he sat and wrote. So he was to do always.

The Austrian censors would not pass *A Voice from the Rocky Crag,* but since they had to have it translated to see what it was about, an Italian translation by an official named Petar Sentić has survived. The translation is quite bureaucratic and has preserved nothing but a literal transfer of the meaning. Professor Petar Kolendić has established that *A Voice from the Rocky Crag* is the original form of the *Ode to Liberty,* which Ljuba Nenadović published after Njegoš's death. It is the same work except that, having developed as a ruler in the meantime, Njegoš laid greater stress in the *Ode to Liberty* on the role of the dynasty of his uncle.

It was in the *Ode to Liberty,* that is, in *A Voice from the Rocky Crag,* that Njegoš abandoned the verse form of the folk bards, the guslars, and adopted the eight-syllable line. He also parted company with folk poetry in his imagery and manner of expression. He learned that poetry was not only what the people recited. Banašević concludes that Njegoš had already learned to manipulate his verses. Sarajlija's influences are quite noticeable—the coined words, the tension. There are other influences as well—Homer, whom he was reading at that time, and much Greek mythology. This was, of course, not fortuitous. Even later Njegoš was to see a great poet in Sarajlija—which he really was, given the poverty of our literature in those days. He also felt the similarity between classical Greece and Montenegro. Johann Georg Kohl reports that Njegoš specifically pointed this out to him. All of this entered unconcealed in those first efforts. That which might be considered original—and even here he was not the first—was his combining of the battles against the Turks and the French with a non-guslar verse form. Yet this combination did not engender great poetry. Njegoš was still learning, and though he had not found his mark, it is obvious that he understood that it was possible to treat the themes of folk poetry in another, nonfolk way.

The significance of the *Ode to Liberty*—not for literary history, but for Njegoš—lies precisely in the fact that through this first-born work he departed from his sources without cutting himself off from them. He had become a creator, though hardly a finished one. Later, in *The Mountain Wreath,* he was seemingly to return to the meter of the guslars, though only the event he described came from the folk; Njegoš's real subject was the tragic fate of Serbdom. Yet it was here that he was to lift this seeming folk poetry to a height that makes one lose one's breath at the wonder and the beauty of it. Let us grant the following theory as well—for even the most suitable theories are poor and do violence: in the *Ode to Liberty* Njegoš departed from the folk epics just as his rule departed from the earlier state of affairs. There were to be more of these departures later, far more visible and harmonious in their tendency.

Though it was poetry, the *Ode to Liberty* was not great poetry. Njegoš was least adept at occasional poetry. Not one of his odes—and he wrote a fair number of them—has deserved anyone's attention to this day, and justly so. And the *Ode to Liberty* is but an expanded ode—to the Montenegrins and to his uncle Petar. Russia was never to motivate his poetry, that real Njegoš poetry, nor were the Slavs—both factors in his politics. If they appeared at all, it was occasionally, in his odes, as something external and incapable of fusion with his foundations—a Serbianism that was myth and passion, and a religion that was philosophy and meditation. All of his other motifs were but derivatives of Serbianism and religion. Alien lands—Turkey and Venice—which we encounter as motifs provide but the reflections and contrasts of these two foundations.

It takes effort and the foreknowledge of the author's identity to discover in the *Ode to Liberty* the future Njegoš—especially the one who wrote *The Mountain Wreath*—despite a powerful image or expression here and there. It is even more difficult to detect him in his earlier improvised folk poems. All of this was an apprenticeship, like learning one's first words and sounds. The *Ode to Liberty* is a historical tale and not that incomparable passionate experiencing of the national past and poetic expression of that experience which were exclusively Njegoš's. Every so often it sounds a moving note, a mere harbinger of Njegoš's future symphony of a mythical Serbian history.

Njegoš was learning. He had not yet tasted all the bitterness. The tragic Serbian destiny had not yet become his own—his being.

The young Archimandrite was struck dumb by his first encounter with the men and blessings of high civilization. He was made ecstatic, on meeting renowned Serbs, by the hope that his name would also shine forth, thanks to the collection of poetry he had just completed. In Vienna Chancellor Metternich received him with a calculated rudeness—no doubt owing to Radonjić and the border difficulties with Austria, not to speak of his trip to Russia to be consecrated bishop. The Montenegrin bishops Danilo and Petar had done the same, but at least they were consecrated by Serbian hierarchs in the Austrian Empire.

But the omnipotent Metternich was not the only person in Vienna. There was also Vuk Karadžić, then and for a long time to come the most significant figure in Serbian cultural life. The details of their meeting are lacking. But the ties between Vuk and Njegoš were to remain unbroken from that time on. Vuk's strong impression on Njegoš was evident later, when the latter in fact adopted his orthography. Njegoš was also no everyday guest for thoughtful Vuk. Vuk wrote to Lukijan Mušicki * on August 22 that Rade was well read, that he praised the language of the people and regretted that Mušicki did not write more simply. These were the topics that had engaged an already experienced sage and a developing youth whose wisdom was a gift. Here was another Serbian hope in the offing whose very external appearance Vuk could not help but notice: "He is not yet a full twenty years, but he is larger and handsomer than a Viennese grenadier."

Njegoš was already a personality—still undeveloped, not fully formed, but whole. Vuk saw in him a most handsome grenadier,

* (1777–1837). A pseudo-classic Serbian poet and Orthodox bishop in Vojvodina.

but one who discusses poetry and language, politics and Serbdom with the wisdom of the mature and the experienced.

Njegoš had to ripen more rapidly, in everything.

12.

For a moment Njegoš's experiences in Russia confused him and went beyond his comprehension.

It was almost as though he was not in Russia at all, not even in St. Petersburg. He was in the heights of Russian society and in the brilliance of the imperial court. He was to come to Russia once again, not to be welcomed, but to be investigated and criticized. Not even then did he see much of anything, though his bitterness and self-assertiveness confirm that he did perceive the true face of official Russia.

He came upon the radiance of a St. Petersburg summer, the unconcealed splendor of the nobility, and a Russian hospitality that is inexhaustible even when it is official, a native cordiality combined with lavish honors and marks of grace.

Formally the Montenegrin Archimandrite was the guest of the Holy Synod; in actual fact, by the welcome and honors he received, he was the guest of the Russian Tsar and the imperial government.

The Tsar had decided to lend special significance to the consecration of the Montenegrin Archimandrite—to impress the world at large. Rade was received with the greatest cordiality—certainly with an eye to increasing his devotion to Russia. Besides this, by its struggle Montenegro has long been regarded a symbol of heroism and loyalty by the Russian public, especially in the Pan-Slavic circle to which the Tsar and leading elements were well disposed at the moment, all the more so inasmuch as they were carrying on a ruthless campaign at home against the so-called Westernizers—democrats and cosmopolites.

From his troubles and woes, his sandals and goats, a Montenegrin lad had been thrust into an imperial court whose oriental splendor was all the more dazzling because it cultivated the Western manner.

He arrived in St. Petersburg on July 20 and was quartered in the Monastery of St. Alexander Nevsky, an edifice that looked all the more huge because it was built in the old Russian style. It was situated at the southern end of the Nevsky Prospekt, a street that, if not the most beautiful in the world, certainly had the most beautiful name: both the street and the name could have come only from a Russian feeling for form and space plus a Western sense for planning. From the confines of Montenegro, in which even the sky is hemmed in, Njegoš found himself in a space whose vastness became comprehensible only because the creations of human hands encompassed it. The space the monastery encompassed was also vast: it accommodated twelve churches, the building of the Theological Seminary, the Theological Academy, the Metropolitan's palace, and several cemeteries with the graves of the great—Suvorov, Lomonosov, Karamzin. One could feel here, as nowhere else, a state and a people with a potential too great for even them to comprehend, with still-pent-up and unused forces.

Used to the clear outline of mountains, to the misery of stone hovels, and to the strictures of a rocky wilderness, Njegoš could not resist immediately reporting his excitement to Vuk:

> I barely remembered this morning that I promised to write you from St. Petersburg. The vastness of the city, the symmetry of its streets, the majesty of its buildings, and thousands of similar sights which are new to me are the cause of this tardiness of mine. Is it any wonder that I am tardy and find it hard to sit down and write when I hardly know if I am on earth, for I think that I have been lifted by the wings of Daedalus to observe from the air, as in a dream, the capital of a truly great tsar who is one with us in religion and race. . . . I am writing this to you this morning, half awake, from the Monastery of Alexander Nevsky, which is the name not only of the monastery but of all the surrounding buildings. . . . Every unbiased person who comes here must say and will say, "The Russian people are great, and the tsar of the Russian people is great. The omnipotent hand of the Creator has poured blessings on the tsar of Russia and on all his house. The omnipotent will of the Creator has raised Russia to such a height. The omnipotent hand of the Master has showered the rich gifts of enlightenment and philanthropy on its nobles."

For the first and only time youthful joy was to burst from Bishop Rade. It was a confused but only momentarily measureless wonderment, for Njegoš set a measure on everything human from the beginning and was conscious of immutable laws. It was at this very time that Morgunov painted that well-known and not very distinguished portrait of him. From the face there emanates a gentle, quiet joy which is unable to drown out the dark worry in the large eyes. The Bishop has a thin mustache which shows thicker at the ends, a hardly noticeable beard, and an oval face which shines amid the hair and shadows. All is dark—the cassock, the cowl, and the background, the shadows around a forehead too high and lofty not to overshadow the satisfied, rather plump, un-Njegoš face.

Where Njegoš went in St. Petersburg and what he saw is not known. Later he was to remember the pleasant excursions, the rides in liveried carriages drawn by four and perhaps six horses and shining with gold and lacquer. And he himself was dressed in everything new—in silks and brocades. Receptions, banquets, gatherings—there must have been all of these. A huge and complicated machine was set in motion, and all doors were opened. By August 2 the all-powerful Tsar received the Montenegrin shepherd in whom a new state was being conceived—this much the Tsar knew—and in whose poetry the centuries-old ancient striving of a people was to find its completion—this much only Rade sensed.

Tsar Nicholas I was a despot not only by ideology and by necessity, but by his entire frame. Herzen,* who knew the Tsar intimately, observed that he acted even toward his mistresses as if he was dispensing his favor. Not of great mind or spirit, Nicholas I was completely convinced of his vocation and believed in himself as the incarnation of the principle of absolute monarchy. By the time of Njegoš's sojourn he had already consolidated his absolute power: the Decembrists had been exiled and hanged, the Polish insurrection had been drowned in blood, Pushkin had been killed practically the day before—one did not dare oppose the Tsar's autocracy even with epigrams.

The youthful Rade did not see, nor could he see, the social structure of Russia under serfdom, rotting and in turmoil. What he saw was the Tsar and Russian might, the power and the glory of the nobility and the state. Only later, as the result of bitter personal experience—so it is always—was he to perceive the other, inner, real side of tsarist Russia.

* Aleksandr Ivanovich Herzen (1812–70). Liberal Russian publicist and social philosopher.

Like all despots, Nicholas I was fond of grand gestures and unforgettable sayings. Yet from the meeting between himself and Rade there have remained only Rade's words. When the tall, bony, gray-eyed Tsar found himself next to the youth, he remarked, "But you are even bigger than I am!"

"Only God is bigger than the Russian Tsar!" the Montenegrin lad replied neatly.

The Tsar had postponed his meeting with the Prussian King and Austrian Emperor to be able to attend, on August 6, the consecration of the nineteen-year-old Montenegrin as bishop, in the Cathedral of the Transfiguration of the Saviour. To be sure, all of officialdom was there. Rade had to have vestments specially made for him, for not even the Russian Church had any long enough to fit him. His breast gleamed with a cross of diamonds and a medallion—gifts from the Tsar. The ceremonious services were celebrated by the highest hierarchs of the Church. And there was the prayer—for the Tsar, the Tsaritsa, the Heir, the Synod, and for "the newly appointed Bishop Petar of the God-protected land of Montenegro and the Highlands."

The Tsar's grace was seemingly without limit. The stipend was increased: twelve thousand chervontsi would be sent to Montenegro with the Bishop, the yearly stipend was raised to twenty-six hundred chervontsi, and the Synod was giving five thousand rubles' worth of books and icons. Njegoš now had something with which to set his ideas in motion, ideas his acquaintance with the world at large had intensified and shaped.

Rade was received by the Minister for Foreign Affairs, the Ober-Procurator of the Holy Synod, and other dignitaries. He also received a substantial gift in money from Countess Orlova-Chesmenskaya. Some have chosen to suspect that a sentimental tie with Njegoš was involved. Actually the Countess was simply a God-fearing philanthropist.

All this imposed new duties.

In Montenegro Rade's elevation to the bishop's throne signaled a break that had finally penetrated the closed and immobile Russian administration and its crowned chief.

Meanwhile Rade Tomov became inseparably wedded to Serbian misfortunes—to Montenegrin woe and heroism.

13.

There came back to Montenegro with Bishop Rade a printing shop, and even a Russian printer. There came vestments and church books, and Njegoš's books with a secular content, too, which the authorities in Kotor attempted to bar; they worried for the soul of Montenegro as though it was their domain.

The young Bishop was caught up in dreams and enthusiasm: to organize, to liberate, to unify the land, to bring to it enlightenment and civilization. It seemed to him as though there were forces in his country he had not noticed before: Montenegro could and had to play the role to which it was destined by fate. He had to prepare it for this. Many of his intentions were to prove unrealistic. But Rade Tomov was not one to hesitate in the face of hardship. He did not balk at reality, for he knew that nothing human, if it was good for men, could perish; even if it did not bear fruit on the morrow, still it provided seed "for some far-distant generation."

With his return from Russia the old year—1833—ended.

Rade was bishop over Montenegro—elected and recognized.

Vukotić was ousted. The clashes and friction with him had begun earlier. Gagić had not failed to inform his government in good time. Old and sick, Vukotić was forced to go abroad. He was replaced by the very Senate he had created. The signal for this had, of course, come from Russia. Russia did not tolerate dual power even at home. Of course, the Bishop was young, and his government was not old—but one learns easily in power. The Russian potentates knew this better than anyone else. All that was left for Vukotić was to die—which he did after two or three years. He sensed it. He got himself entangled in intrigues—those of his nephew and Radonjić—like everyone ousted from power. Only now he was sad in his old age and as solicitous as a father when he wrote to Rade from Kotor, before the latter was to set out on his journey, "Forgive me for writing this, but my love and sacred obligation to the fatherland prompt me to remind you to maintain that regimen which I set in order and gradually to add to it, that each day it might be better." He also begged Rade to allow back the Governor's family—the innocent suffer though the Governor is no more. Vukotić knew well what it was to have and yet not to have a homeland.

But Rade had to go his own way. The bitter struggle he would have to wage in the name of great ideas would alter everything, even many of his good intentions.

Bishop Rade was not to convoke a single assembly of chieftains. He did not write a single article of any law, or pay attention to any already on the books, and yet he spent his entire life in a struggle for order. He was forced to do the possible while dreaming of something else, something higher. Yet such is the human lot—to be out of joint with the times, with reality. In Rade's case that was also the lot of a whole people, one which wanted what it could not have.

At the moment of his return from Russia, however, there were no such incongruities—or he did not see them. All was young and new and full of promise—he, the country, and his rule.

For this reason the difficulties and the disappointments did not seem so terrible. He did not realize that these not only came first, but would remain to the end. He was to drink the cup to its dregs.

The Austrian authorities took a lively interest in his journey to Russia. The Governor of Dalmatia transmitted to his minister his impressions of Rade's consecration: "The news of it has caused great joy throughout Montenegro." It was clear to the Austrians that this was not simply a matter of still another Serbian bishop—that was the least of it—but also of the conception of something new among the South Slavs, something unpleasant for the monarchy. Though they could not prevent the merrymaking of the wild and free Montenegrins, they were to do everything possible to prevent its spilling over into the Bay of Kotor or even farther. The Dalmatian Bishop Rajačić, who constantly bribed Montenegrin priests with Austrian money, received instructions from the authorities and obediently issued orders to his subordinate priests forbidding them to welcome the Bishop or to show him any honor, and requiring them to prevent him from holding services in their churches. The superior of Savina Monastery was to boast that he neither rang the bells nor clapped boards at the arrival of the Montenegrin Bishop, but locked the church in his face. And these were Serbs and clerics! Meanwhile Count Caboga, an Italian official in Kotor, even entertained the thought that Bishop Rade himself might perhaps be bribed with gifts.

The house of the merchant Conte Lumbardić, in which Njegoš was to stay again later whenever he passed through Kotor, was placed under surveillance. Confidential reports stated that Dafina, the Conte's daughter, who was married to the Montenegrin Serdar Sirović, was active in spreading the hope that the Montenegrins would liberate the Bay of Kotor.

There is also a report, unreliable but characteristic of that atmosphere, that Rade was being poisoned in Kotor and that he left for Cetinje a very sick man.

Spies, plots, betrayals—these awaited Rade and his enthusiastic plans, and would follow him to his grave.

It was with concern and an eager resolve that Rade set foot in the wilderness of Cetinje. It was winter, and the rocks angrily broke through drifts of snow six and even twelve feet deep. All was dumb and dead, and a man could be alone with himself—his thoughts fairly audible in the ghostly silence of the skies.

Bishop Rade-Njegoš was alone, and alone he would remain.

His personal drama had begun. It was not to be made turbulent by events, though his life and rule did not have a moment of calm. It was more of an inner drama.

How else could the drama of a nation unfold?

THE HERMIT OF CETINJE

1.

The Hermit of Cetinje is the title of a small collection of poems which Njegoš was to publish as soon as he had set up a printing shop in Cetinje. It was one of those strange titles of his which seemingly had no connection with the contents. The work consisted of odes and occasional poems, apparently written in Russia. Two of the poems—*A Montenegrin to Almighty God* and *A Montenegrin Captured by a Fairy*—are new and original in theme and expression. In them one can see for the first time and immediately recognize the future Njegoš. This was observed by Pavle Popović, while Isidora Sekulić wrote a separate study concerning these poems. Truly they are Njegoš in the bud.

Still nowhere in the entire collection is there any mention either of a wilderness or of a hermit. Upon his return from Russia into the rocky wasteland of Cetinje, Njegoš felt like a hermit and so hit upon this title, as though to say: thus sings a hermit. But behind this there is also a deeper meaning, as there usually is with him. Though no wilderness is mentioned, it is sensed, particularly in those two poems, in their presentation of another spiritual world—of God and the national past. These two themes contain that passionate and complete immersion of the hermit which would be a part of Njegoš to the end.

Some students maintain that Njegoš wrote these two poems while on his journey. Even if this is so, the entire inner structure—in both word and thought—arises from a profound loneliness and preoccupation with the mystery of man and the Serbian people. For the first time, and at the very outset, Njegoš expresses his own

—and man's—identity, kinship, consanguinity with God, through the union of the light of the human mind and soul with the power of the divine light. At the same time he tells us of the unhappy fate of the Serbian people—with a verse that might have come out of *The Mountain Wreath.*

First about God:

> I have hope that aught of Thine
> Also in my soul doth shine;
> Though uncertain, I take pride
> Something in me doth abide
> Which, however small it be,
> Yet can be like unto Thee.
> From the brilliance of Thy pyre
> Every smallest spark of fire
> Which is scattered forth in flight
> Through the darkness of the night
> Falls back in that fiery sea
> From which it first came to be.

Then about the people:

> Great Nemanja's son in blood
> Took his right in raging flood,
> Throne and goddess, in the surge.
> Serbia's court in God's curse lay,
> In the gloom no roundelay
> The fairies sang, but mournful dirge.

Isidora Sekulić concludes, "Characteristically for the later Njegoš, both of these verses are poems of the narrative type, a kind of religious ode. . . . Here one already perceives the poet of original scenes and visions which always contain—and this is certainly Njegoš!—a spiritual element, and it is precisely this which lends force to the element of imagination!"

Both of Njegoš's motifs, the myths of God and Serbdom, would receive greater emphasis later—the former in *The Ray of the Microcosm* and the latter in *The Mountain Wreath,* but they would never be separated. They made their appearance at the very inception of his creativity—in a man young and bereft of all, in the loneliness of Cetinje—as weighty duty and primeval urge.

In the wilderness Njegoš was at first in constant conflict with its desolation: he built buildings, established a school, and went frequently to the Littoral, to which he was drawn by a yearning for comfort and beauty, but duty always drove him back. He was condemned to the wilderness and to fight with it. He was young, and yet was not permitted to be. He was a ruler, but consecrated a bishop. He took joy in the "delights" of the coast and yet was chained to the rock of Cetinje and a stony loneliness. His fight with the wilderness also encompassed his struggle with the clans and with the Turks—for a secure and decent life.

But the wilderness would not yield. There are deserts everywhere, and the thinking creative man cannot escape them; rather, he discovers them in the struggle with life.

Bishop Rade traveled frequently—always in the fall, to escape the winter, when the wilderness of Cetinje pressed heavy, like some supernal evil and malediction. He was to try to escape on the eve of his death. But there was no escape. And to what purpose? The wilderness and wasteland are everywhere. One must fight. That way it seems as though they are disappearing, or perhaps they even become attractive.

If it were not for wastelands, for the wasteland of Cetinje, what would become of men, of Bishop Rade, of Njegoš?

What can the young Bishop feel as he climbs to something that might be a throne? What does this richly endowed lad with still-untried strength think about? A wilderness. Not desolation, but a wilderness, something every Montenegrin, particularly one from Katuni, can feel, even though not as sublimely, deeply, or as poetically. The stony silence of winter, with the winds hissing and swishing like serpents, and no help from anywhere. Here appears this man with his awareness that his personal fate and that of his people are but a part of an omnipotence which fills infinity, which holds sway over day and night, light and darkness, good and evil, and plays with the suns as though they were apples.

Njegoš and the Montenegrins never spoke of the wilderness. Yet its stamp was on all they had—on his poetic imagination and their reluctant acquaintance with every grief.

This was not an ascetic wilderness, though it had some of that as well. It was simply a lack of all the joys of life which marked the stone monastery leaning against a cliff, with two or at most three houses around it, on a little plain shrouded in white. There was also a lack of men to whom Njegoš could speak of the thoughts and desires that sprang from him so forcefully. He was condemned to keep all this to himself and to tell it only to himself—in poetry.

He was not an ascetic who sought, who yearned for, the wilderness. He lived in it because it was his duty—out of necessity. True, it had some life—an existence. But both those men and that life, like his episcopal calling, were in conflict with him. His wants were too novel and his strivings too far-reaching for them.

Njegoš did not surrender himself to the wilderness. He fought it even while in its midst. That was duty. That was how Bishop Danilo saw it as he tried to conquer it: "This land used to be twice as bare, and not a cock crowed in it, and there was then not even a Tsar Peter or a Bishop Danilo to be reviled for everything and to be blamed for all that went wrong."

The wilderness and duty went together. Especially in so bare, so utterly bare a land.

The wilderness imperceptibly cleansed Njegoš's thought, forcing it to stand by itself. In loneliness his emotions seethed and exhausted him, only to rise as a pure cry into the heights.

That title—*The Hermit of Cetinje*—did not correspond to the content of the poems. It did to the circumstance and the stance of the poet. It was not only the contrast with the mundane luxuries of Vienna and St. Petersburg that produced that title. There was something deeper. It was the song of a wilderness that did not wish to be what it was.

The wilderness is an evil.

What good could possibly come of it?

2.

IN THOSE DAYS the Plain of Cetinje was a bare little patch—hardly an hour in length and half an hour in breadth—framed by a rock rim and completely lying on rock. What little water accumulated in the springtime was swallowed up by underground streams. How often a plow was stopped by a rock in the sandy soil, and a scythe struck sparks as it hissed through the withered grass! The plain got its name from the Cetina River, which once flowed through the plain, when there was still a forest there, and even now it wells up in the fall and remains till spring. Bishop Petar built a mill on it. From the Cetina, and from the Plain of Cetinje, came Cetinje's name.

But there was no Cetinje as yet. That which is called Cetinje today was then called the Dale of Lovćen. The name Cetinje existed then, but it referred to the plain, and perhaps also to the monastery and the meadows and pastures which surrounded it. However, the plot on which the monastery itself had been built was called Čipur, which, they say, comes from a Greek word supposedly meaning a garden, a place good for vegetables.

In the summer the place is arid and the air is dry, yet beneath the topsoil it is damp; the rough, porous rock holds the water, and it makes its way up through invisible cracks and pores and into the sand, the walls, and the clothing. The heat blows down from the crags, while the plain shimmers in the torrid air. But the nights are cool and clear—to the very stars.

There were no cottages in the Plain of Cetinje, but there were some along the rim—both on top and on its lower edge. They were low stone huts which hugged the rock in scattered clusters. In the beginning of the sixteenth century the whole Plain of Cetinje contained seventy households. Thanks to burning, killing, flight, slaughter, and decimation, this was not even to double by Njegoš's time.

Cetinje was the monastery and a couple of buildings—and nothing else. As for those few buildings next to the monastery, one was built by Bishop Petar and housed the senators; a second belonged to Ivan Vukotić; while a third was an inn Bishop Rade's brother Pero, together with a certain Jabučanin, built in 1832. Thus trade and government—Pero and Rade—began in the wilderness on a bare rock. In the midst of the plain there was a little church, believed to have been built by shepherds in the fifteenth century. After Njegoš's death a new one was built by someone on its site, so that all that remained was its name—the Church of the Vlahs.

Toward the end of Bishop Rade's reign, Cetinje had a hundred and twenty souls, including its guards, who accounted for almost half that number. At the beginning of his reign, however, there were two or three servants, two or three clerics, Milaković, and a handful of senators who would stay a few days and then hurry away to conduct their public duties or to return home.

Messengers, spies, and letter carriers came frequently. Others came to seek justice, to offer up prayers, or to beg favors. These generally spent the night at the monastery's expense.

Njegoš's day was spent in conducting business with the senators, in correspondence, or in dealing with messengers. He also liked to go riding—he was a good horseman—or to hunt—he was an excellent shot. In those years he conducted services frequently in church; later he was to neglect this completely. At this time, too, he went more frequently among the people—to hold court, to make peace, to give courage.

His correspondence with Kotor shows how his time was mostly spent: always tussling with the troubles of the Montenegrins. Sometimes it seems, as one reads this correspondence, as though he and the Senate were nothing but intermediaries between the district captains of Kotor and the Montenegrins. Whenever a Montenegrin had a complaint against Kotor, or Kotor against Montenegro, it went before the Bishop: "six oxen unjustly seized"; "Jovan . . . charges Captain Anton Radimir, who owes him 80 Thal[er]s"; "do me the favor of permitting the priests of Ostrog to carry on their work throughout the Littoral"; "it will be five and twenty years since Djuro Petrović, the Serdar of Njeguši, pawned his silver dagger to Ivo Djovanin . . . and asks to have it returned, and he will give him the money"; "that the stolen lock and bell be returned"; "concerning the murder of Joka Krstov Kosjerača"; "the men of Špilja are letting their cattle roam on the lands of the Zalažani . . . and are harrying them. . . . The Zalažani are forced to fight"; "owe 43 Thalers since 1831 for a dried mutton"; "the same Krstina told me in spiritual confession that she had been taken against her will"; "that his sister Mara . . . is being ill-used and beaten by her brothers-in-law"; "innocent Montenegrin men and women are suffering at the hands of Imperial and Royal soldiers in Kotor"; "served well . . . but became sick and could not carry out his duties, for which cause Knez Djuro dismissed him and promised . . . to pay him off"; "the dog of one of these soldiers slaughtered three goats . . . belonging to Jovetić of Crnica"; "the Dapčevići of Ljubotinja have a feud with Andrija Radovije Nobile of the Paštrovići over a head . . . if possible, that they be reconciled"; "his in-laws are doing injury to his mother's people"; "Andrija Pejović, Serdar of the Cuce, did not treacherously entice

Marko Mršulja of Grblji into his house, nor did he . . . take from him by force 10 Thalers and a saber"; "I cannot settle such old debts because many of said debtors cannot be found, and the debt is so old that it can hardly be settled at all"; "on behalf of the maid Dafina, whom some Stijepo Franićević has by violent means deflowered, or better to say, ravished"; "that Pero Stankov Palamida appear before this court"; "Mare . . . is divorced and unattached, and is free to marry another"; "took from him his silver rifle"; "swore by God's justice that he robbed the church at Muštici . . . was unjustly cast in a dungeon all this time. . . ." And so it went, day in and day out, until his death. Sometimes there were several of these in a single day. People came to him to complain of their troubles, and the Bishop wrote to Kotor. Not all of these letters, which give so valuable a picture of life in that time and place, have been preserved. Professor Kolendić once told me that a Yugoslav district official in Kotor wanted to get rid of some files, and so gave a pile of papers, including several of Njegoš's letters, to fishwives. Especially noticeable in these letters is the general search for justice before a court, which is all the more pronounced as the individual emerges from the dissolution of the clan. The sovereign Bishop was not to be free for a moment from these daily cares. Indeed, his rule consisted chiefly of just that.

On the other hand there were also daily troubles with the Turks, but of a different kind—clashes, armed encounters, conspiracies, and rebellions.

Montenegro was developing into a state through the daily conduct of administrative and political affairs with Austria. Even the border between them was to be settled. Turkey, however, did not yet recognize that state. No one paid any attention to its daily troubles; the centuries-old struggle between two religions, two worlds, went on. The border there was measured by the length of one's saber.

There was still another kind of correspondence with Austria—the verbal defense of a people's historic rights and the right to exist, though the correspondence concerning daily troubles was more frequent. Rade's correspondence with Turkey is full of history—of the myths which fire the blood and inflame the mind.

As for Russia, the correspondence with it was of a special kind—not of daily cares, as with Kotor, or a historic settling of accounts, as with Scutari, but of self-justification and a shallow gratitude—no more.

It was under such conditions, in the wilderness of Cetinje, that Njegoš had to carry on, to think the greatest thoughts and to write the most refined poetry—and to rule a state.

It was all a jumble. On the very eve of the day on which he was to proclaim an encyclical to the Montenegrins declaring Bishop Petar a saint, he had to request the intervention of the Captain of Kotor to have a stolen mule returned to one of his subjects. So, too, he was to write poetry in the midst of worldly and political turmoil.

Actuality and myth, dreams and reality, duties and ideas, were all of one piece with Njegoš.

3.

THERE BEGAN A long, complicated, and unfathomed period—and with respect to his personal life, an unfathomable period—in Njegoš's career. Dr. Ljubomir Durković-Jakšić, the best expert on Njegoš's bibliography and circumstances of his life, maintains that the journey to Russia in 1833 was the turning point in Njegoš's life and work.

Indeed, upon his return from Russia, Njegoš not only took all power into his hands, but realized that to keep it was his first and greatest duty. And with those two previously cited poems he also revealed himself to be a poet.

As a ruler he was to have still another serious turning point—if we can so call the progress and maturation of a man for whom all was from the beginning an integral whole. Upon his return from Russia in 1837, he was to assert his independence of his protectors in St. Petersburg and to rid himself of any illusions about their supposedly disinterested help as people of the same religion and race. With this Bishop Rade came of age and attained maturity as a ruler.

But the poet remained silent, almost completely, for ten whole years—until 1844, when he wrote the poem *Thought* and, according to Medaković, perhaps that single love poem of his ever found, the charming *The Night Gathers the Age*. True, in 1834 Njegoš did publish *The Flow of Turkish Ire.* But these are poems in the folk style—neither better nor worse than the poems of the Montenegrin bards, except for two or three rather forceful images and novel expressions. The rest are odes, unpoetic as usual, with a few haphazard and vague improvisations, and three or four mediocre and worthless poems on abstract moral themes.

Throughout that whole period Njegoš wrote only two noteworthy poems: *Ode to the Sun Written on a Moonless Night,* published in 1837, and *Dirge or Sad Memorial on the Death of My Ten-Year-Old Nephew Pavle Petrović Njegoš,* which was most probably written in 1842.

The first poem is reminiscent of *A Montenegrin to Almighty God,* though it is not its superior either in style or in inspiration. Its basic idea—the sun, light as the source of divine power—is more developed and formed. Most significant of all, it is in this poem that one finds the inception of the basic theme of *The Ray of the Microcosm*—Satan's rebellion against God. He sings to the sun:

> The race of man without thee would resemble
> Those rebellious spirits in the heavens
> Who did think to topple from His throne
> The King of Heaven and of all creation.

The second poem is a broken, and therefore all the more painful, cry for a nephew, the son of his brother Pero, who died as a child in a distant land. Bishop Rade had sent him to St. Petersburg for his schooling, evidently with the intention of designating him his heir. Uneven both in worth and in composition, it is a tangle of commonplaces with the most sublime emotions, of the most trite realities with the most tragic conceptions. One also finds in it some of Njegoš's later motifs on life as phantasmagoria, and the cup of poison. This poem is valuable as a personal and as a poetic testimonial. It reveals how hard it came to Njegoš to be a hermit pledged to monkhood. From it also emerges that specific characteristic of Njegoš's to transform an objective motif and element into an intimate lyrical experience and to transform a personal theme into an all-human and cosmic drama. That was to be developed later, in *The Ray of the Microcosm,* as a religious motif, and in *The Mountain Wreath,* as a national motif. In general, the poem is moving in those places where it expresses the deep and heavy sorrow of a man who is prevented by an unreasonable vow from exercising a right that is inseparable from his nature, to multiply and thus to extend his being through eternity.

Taken more broadly, this poem belongs to the later peak period of Njegoš's creativity, which begins in the year 1844 or just before it.

There exists still another poem—*Who Is That on Yon High Mountain?*—which Dušan Vuksan discovered among some files for the year 1833. However, in theme and expression it obviously belongs to a later time—in or around 1844. As in *The Ray of the Microcosm* and elsewhere, Njegoš sees the poet here as "a son of nature," and also as "a little creator closest to the Divinity," who

> Over every other living creature
> Is the nearest to the great Creator,
> Bearing unto Him the closest kinship,
> For he, too, can bring worlds into being
> Through ideas which on high go soaring
> As the mighty Father did create them,
> Quickened by the power of His utterance.

The idea of poetry as creation identical with God's is met expressly here for the first time and is, in fact, the development of that previous thought concerning man's kinship with God. This poem, too, is a prelude to *The Ray of the Microcosm,* even in its verse form and expression. Chronologically it is probably not far removed from it either.

If, then, we sum up all that Njegoš expressed in poetry during those ten years or so, the result is almost a complete silence—except for some twenty little poems which are in the folk style, occasional pieces, or didactic verses.

What was happening to him during that time?

The ruler was developing meanwhile and was very active. But the poet kept still.

Something was invisibly seething deep inside the poet who was so occupied with his public duties as a ruler. Though Njegoš did not separate his duty from his poetry, neither did he place the one above the other.

Today it is not difficult to perceive the later Njegoš in the earlier. Yet even if the later had never been, the earlier would have found a place in literary histories, at least the thicker ones. But that was still not Njegoš—that something which was as much wisdom as poetry, and, above all, the poeticized myth of a people.

It was after 1843 that Njegoš's real, consummate poetry was suddenly to burst forth. The ruler was by then sitting firm and had made himself independent in every respect. First to appear was his poem *Thought*—a prelude to *The Ray of the Microcosm,* to its philosophical underpinnings. Medaković relates that in that same year, in Prčanj, where Njegoš went bathing, he flirted with a pretty neighbor woman and, in a manner typical of him, that is, by subjecting a direct experience to a metaphysical transfiguration, he wrote a love sonnet on that occasion. If we bear in mind that only one of his poems of that kind has been found, *The Night Gathers the Age,* it may be concluded that this is the poem meant in Medaković's account. Though exceptional in theme, *The Night Gathers the Age* also belongs to Njegoš's meditative and metaphysical lyricism, as do *The Ray of the Microcosm* and significant parts of *The Mountain Wreath.* In any event, it confirms the poet's rapid ascent.

After *The Night Gathers the Age* and *Thought* in 1844, within the space of two or two-and-a-half years—from 1844 to 1847—Njegoš was to pour out his three great poems: *The Ray of the Microcosm, The Mountain Wreath,* and *The False Tsar Stephen the Small.* After that he was to grow silent again—until his very death. True, he wrote *The House of Aleksići* and *The Tower of the Djurišići* after that, but these poems were in the style of the bards and more significant as broadsides at the enemy than as poetry. He was also to write a few occasional poems. Strictly speaking, these include the poems written during his tour of Italy.

But Njegoš had already said all that he had to say in his great poems.

We do not know if he regarded his occasional poetry merely as a part of his political and other daily activity. No one will know what else he had in him to say. He was cut down at the height of his powers. One thing is sure: Njegoš wrote poetry when he had something to say and when he had to say it.

Bishop Rade's rule began with a sharpening of relations—both foreign and domestic. The border with Austria was not settled, and the Turks still regarded Montenegro as part of the Pashalik of

Scutari. Internally, a still-insecure central government faced the self-willed clans.

Was there not also a whetting of the poet as well? Njegoš had yet to rise above a still-living, pervasive, and powerful folk poetry.

Njegoš was not afraid to be silent.

Poetry was his sacred calling, a "sacrosanct vocation," and he dedicated himself to it as such.

Njegoš was also not afraid of oblivion.

He regarded his obligations to society as a tragic but higher calling, subject to an absolute law which a man is bound to fulfill, just as he had to fulfill the creative obligations of the poet.

That is what he did.

4.

BEHIND NJEGOŠ's activity, both as a ruler and as a poet, stood the wilderness. Even his personal life abided in it.

When he returned from Russia, it seemed as if he did not know what to take hold of first in the enthusiasm of new ideas and plans.

He hurriedly set up a printing shop—small and poor, but a weapon for thought and enlightenment.

There was considerable effort involved—to transport the paper, the machines, and the type from St. Petersburg to the Montenegrin crags, where not even bridle paths existed, and where no human creature, save himself and his secretary, had any interest in books, and where the literate clergy could be counted on one's fingers. Even long after, the sale of books in Montenegro was to amount to only one per four thousand souls, and of this number Njegoš alone bought a third of the books, while the rest were bought by the unanimously illiterate chieftains, no doubt thanks to his influence and to the suspicion that the books might come in handy for future generations.

In this printing establishment Njegoš printed his poems *The Hermit of Cetinje* and *The Flow of Turkish Ire,* and also Sarajlija's *The Montenegrin Pride,* Vuk Karadžić's *Proverbs,* the almanac *Mourning Dove,* a primer, and all sorts of other things.

Njegoš's printing press operated without the archaic letter known as the "hard sign"; in other words, it adhered to Vuk's orthography. Illiterate Prince Miloš was to resent Njegoš's abandonment of the unhappy hard sign, over which, at that time, the Serbs were waging furious intellectual and, to be sure, political battles with each other.

Everything printed in Cetinje was in Vuk Karadžić's language. Njegoš, too, was a disciple of Vuk in the beginning. When, later, he was angry over the printing of *The False Tsar Stephen the Small* according to the new orthography, and when he refused to give Vuk his blessing for his translation of the New Testament, this was, as he himself expressly stresses, for political reasons. After all, why should he, poor and powerless as he was, aggravate the difficulty of his situation over this and multiply the multitude of his enemies? He supported Vuk's language reform and was a follower of Vuk in practice—in language and in deed—leaving the waging of the struggle to those who were more directly concerned. His printing press was also Vukovian. Small, wretched. On a rock, and born in poverty, but—the first of its kind among the Serbs.

The original idea of establishing the printing press was not Njegoš's. But, as in so many other things, he was the first to realize it.

The first schools and printing press had sprouted in the unrestrained imagination of Bishop Vasilije. But inasmuch as they were quite impracticable, he sent Montenegrin children away to be schooled in Russia, where most of them died.

Who else after him but the great enlightener Dositej Obradović would have thought of founding a school and a printing press on the only free patch of Serbian soil—in Montenegro? Bishop Petar had neither the means nor the need to establish schools; he taught some Montenegrin lads as much as he could, while circumstances pushed Dositej in another direction—into Serbia and the First Insurrection—to realize the same idea on a broader and more solid basis.

There was some schooling to be had in the monasteries—in Cetinje, at Ostrog, in Morača. But it was Bishop Rade who founded the first real school—if indeed it may be called a school.

This, too, was a feat in that wilderness, in the backwardness of Montenegro.

That school looks strange today, but it suited the conditions and the needs of the time. Bishop Rade selected for it boys from the better families. He thereby fulfilled a pressing need of the state: the need for literate and reliable men for his government. The pupils, all of them grown lads, were given scholarships that provided room and board, and lived at the expense—one can already use the expression—of the state, though actually at the Bishop's expense, for it amounted to the same thing, especially when it came to financial matters. In the school there was all too much disorder and lack of discipline. A pupil would leave for days on end, often to join a guerrilla band, and it became a kind of unwritten rule that a severed Turkish head was accepted as an excuse for one's absence. These pupils were also, to be sure, armed warriors. And yet they were learning to read and to write.

Does not just such a school prove how great was the impetus behind its establishment?

Njegoš's printing press subsequently closed down, for reasons still not clear, and the type was melted into bullets during the time of Prince Danilo's wars with the Turks. But the schools did not close; they increased and multiplied—down to this very day—from that first school founded by Njegoš.

Bishop Rade did not begin his rule in Montenegro with only naked force and taxation, but with a school and a printing press, and with roads and wayside inns.

He tried then—and only that once—to put a stop to the practice of cutting off Turkish heads. Some Bjelopavlići once presented him with some heads, and he returned them to the Turks, as much out of a desire to pacify them as out of humanitarianism. "As we, as well as the rest of mankind, observe how you carry out your frequent attacks, our heart has not found satisfaction in this unhappy occupation." He wrote this on April 27, 1834, under the still-fresh impress of Russian and other opinion, which looked upon head-hunting as a barbarous custom. He was still young and wanted to transform Montenegro into a corner of civilized Europe. However, he was soon to encourage head-hunting—to maintain the martial ardor of the Montenegrins.

He clearly understood that the light of learning and culture was needed to penetrate the darkness of the Montenegrin wilderness. But there was something else. The willfulness of the rampant clans and of individuals had to be suppressed by force.

He immediately began to mete out punishments. But how, with

what power? Probably with the help of the group of youths around him and of the Guard. There was no hesitation about what had to be done; however, as is always the case when something new is being tried, he had to get the feel of things and to contrive how to get them done.

On leaving again for Russia, he proclaimed and ordered, on November 12, 1836, "whichever Montenegrin or man of the Highlands is found to be making trouble, he shall be punished more severely than if I were here, for he shall have shown himself to be a public agitator and the destroyer of his own fatherland."

In Russia itself he explained to the officer Rakeyev, "Before I assumed the position of Montenegrin ruler and bishop, Montenegro presented a sorry spectacle of internecine and every other kind of disorder: the strong pillaged the weak, clan fought against clan, there was no peace anywhere, and the right of might was triumphant. I put an end to that savagery, established peace and tranquillity, and provided security for life and property. . . . In order to carry out such changes in the administration and government of a people which was not given to order, it was impossible to get along without punishment, and those who evaded it sold themselves to the Turks and to Austria."

He exaggerated the account of his success. He did so to justify to the Russians the aid he was receiving from them.

Yet he was undeniably aware of the depth of the transformation and of the need for the severe measures he had to employ to carry it out. The adversary could choose only between complete submission or treason.

Such were the first years of his rule—when there was as yet no regular state power.

He had not yet created his own bodyguard, with their plumed hats. What kind of guard, then, did he have? It was formed hastily, of men nurtured in their brotherhoods, unlettered, without uniforms. If these guardsmen obeyed at all, it was only not to lose their pay. They hid and protected their own kinsmen. The Bishop had to go personally to collect taxes. "I was not able till now to reply to your four much-esteemed letters," he excused himself to Gagić on March 1, 1834, "because I was among the Bjelopavlići collecting the annual tax from the people—a Thaler per house, and succeeded well in this, although with great trouble." He spent days and months collecting taxes, going from village to village and house to house, cajoling, threatening, fining.

Everything was out of joint, untried, unfamiliar, unresolved.

Bishop Rade did not yet resort to shooting Montenegrins.

The clans still kept to themselves. Their chieftains—the serdar in the district, the leader and standard-bearer in the clan, the knez in the brotherhood or community—were still hereditary, and the Bishop merely confirmed them. These chieftains were not paid, but they were recognized, deeply rooted, and had arisen from campaigns against the Turks and against rivals. Their power resided side by side with the Bishop's. Every so often, either because of taxes or because of fines, tempers would flare up and fire the passions and sensitivity of whole clans.

Vuk Karadžić arrived in Montenegro in the fall of 1834. Infirm, he descended to the Bay of Kotor to winter there, and returned in the spring of 1835. He noted concerning the taxes, no doubt having in mind that "great trouble" of which the Bishop had spoken, that Bishop Rade had not succeeded in establishing taxation in Montenegro. Evidently some places adhered to custom—sometimes they paid, and sometimes they rebelled. The Bishop had to give gifts in order to win over the distinguished men. The Montenegrins were so eager for bounty, as Vuk pointed out, "that even a man of means exposed his very life to obvious danger simply to pillage some trifle."

The Montenegrins wore fezzes and long hair—to their shoulders—but shaved the front of their skulls. The monks wore both turbans and fezzes, and could not be distinguished from Turks. There were many parish priests, and these were dressed no differently from the rest. The priesthood was, as a rule, hereditary. The priests were without any schooling. Being illiterate, they learned the more important prayers by rote, and that was that. Blood revenge was in everyone's blood. For the Turks there was nothing but the blade. In the Bay of Kotor looting and murders were daily affairs. Vuk observed, "In Montenegro there are traces of every form of government, and yet this is perhaps the only society of men in Europe which has no government in the true meaning of that word."

It was in such a place that Bishop Rade laid the anchor of his ship of state—with no trained men, with no experience, "without mite or farthing."

Yet he had to make haste.

The cause, Serbdom, could not wait.

5.

ON TOP OF the unresolved boundary question with Austria and the unsettled domestic situation, relations with Scutari and Mostar became increasingly acute. "I am hemmed in on all sides!" the Bishop exploded in a letter.

The Turks of Spuž and Podgorica and Hercegovina were constantly harassing the Montenegrins. And what was Bishop Rade to do? Look on silently—just to keep the Russians from getting angry—while the Turks garnered heads in Montenegro to exhibit on the walls of their towns and receive bounties for them? That would have meant alienation from his own people and from the sacred struggle. It would also have been contrary to his very being. He did not forget, and dared not forget, that his vocation was war, and not peace, with the Turks. When he sent back the Bjelopavlić heads to the Turks, he warned them not to be deceived: "What measure you mete out to us, in like measure shall we give back to you." Whenever he did work for peace, it was all in vain—the Turks themselves provoked clashes. "But all their [Turkish] promises were but a net with which they sought to trap Montenegrins all the more easily to drink their fill of blood," he explained to Gagić. "I have not failed to recommend to the Montenegrins that they abstain from seeking revenge as much as they can," he told the same Gagić in self-justification. That appendage "as much as they can" is characteristic, both of Bishop Rade and of Montenegrin-Turkish relations. He would not, could not, ask the Montenegrins not to avenge themselves on the Turks—else they would not have been Montenegrins. What would have become of the Serbian struggle and cause if the Montenegrins had ceased to fight in that arena of ceaseless strife? The Turks would have subjected them and wiped them out! The reality was different from the one the Russians would have wished. The state and independence could only be wrested from the Turks.

In the midst of peace negotiations, the Turks of Podgorica cut down some twenty Cuce shepherds and stole their sheep. Who could stop the Montenegrins? Bishop Rade hinted revenge to Gagić: "It is hard for the Montenegrins to endure the loss of twenty of their brethren, especially while their heads are dangling from the walls of Scutari's citadel." Only after revenge had been taken did Bishop Rade remember to give Gagić an explanation, for he informed Gagić of the matter on March 12, 1835, after the Montenegrins had already attacked Žabljak and taken it from the Turks on March 11. The attack had been long in the planning, and Njegoš would certainly have known about it—even if its leader, Kenjo Stankov Janković, had not been close to the Bishop and to Cetinje.

Bishop Rade's problem was that if he did not restrain the Montenegrins, the Russians would draw the conclusion that he had no control over them and that his government was ineffective. From the beginning he was caught between two fires: he was driven by duty and the highest obligation to an evil thing—to be insincere toward those he least wished to offend, the Russians. An extremely delicate diplomacy and an underhanded struggle on all sides were inevitable.

The attack on Žabljak was not only characteristic of Montenegrin-Turkish relations in those days, but it was also a significant event in Bishop Rade's reign.

Kenjo Stankov and about ten companions climbed up the wall of the little fortress during the night and took it after killing the guards. The story is told that a Montenegrin servant girl measured the height of the wall by permitting a ball of yarn to unravel, as if by accident, down the wall. Kenjo made posts according to the length of yarn she broke off and thus surprised the guard. Though Kenjo's ruse to take the citadel succeeded—in a way that would have been worthy of song even in a land not caught in the passion of war—the town below remained in the hands of the Turks, despite determined efforts by the Montenegrins to take it.

Two Bjelopavlići—Vido and Mirčeta—had undertaken a similar venture before that. They penetrated the citadel at Spuž and brought back two cannon which—according to a folk song—the Turks had captured from the Montenegrins.

These were no great battles. But they were inspiring exploits.

The cannon were brought from Spuž to Cetinje, and Njegoš inscribed verses on them to heroism and to the heroes.

Hafis Pasha, Vizir of Scutari, did not observe civility in a letter of his. He regarded the Montenegrins as raia and shamelessly sought to win over the Bishop. Rade replied in kind, not forgetting to inform the Russians, "you now seek to have from us that for which we have paid with our blood for centuries and for which we have fought and bled since the fall of our empire, that which could be bought with nothing but blood and which truly shall not be sold except for blood." Another step toward *The Mountain Wreath.*

Relations with the Vizir of Mostar, Ali Pasha Stočević, took the same course. Montenegro had broken away from the Pashalik of Scutari. The clans of Hercegovina—the Grahovljani, Drobnjaci, Župljani, and others—were now breaking away from the Pashalik of Bosnia. The Rovčani, hidden away in their gorges, had already broken away—no one even knows when—and so had the Morača, under Vojvoda Mino Radović—though only the upper part. The Upper Morača was being settled by the Uskoks—malcontents who had fled from the beys of Hercegovina. Tied to their homeland and brotherhoods, they kept stealing back to wreak vengeance on their former landlords, and to plunder even the raia. The Vizir did not have to think it over: what was past was past, but if one more clan broke away, others would follow. He strove desperately and savagely not to give up a foot of the Sultan's land—his land.

The men of Grahovo, the neighbors of the Katunjani, were especially active in this ancient, yet always new, ceaseless and irreconcilable struggle. Grahovo was important to the Turks. It jutted into Hercegovina, which was at least outwardly still submissive. The war lord of Grahovo, Jakov Daković, refused to pay the agas the remaining two parts of the tribute money; a third part his father was already bearing to Cetinje. "We shall pay you neither a para nor a dinar of tribute," he wrote to Ali Pasha. "We are not the Sultan's raia, nor do we recognize the Sultan's authority, but we are the men of the Bishop of Montenegro, who is our sovereign."

There was nothing to be gained by negotiation in that quarter. The Bishop had just concluded an understanding with the Turks of Hercegovina, and had not even reached Cetinje, when the news came of a massacre in Župa. "Such is a peace with the Turks of

Hercegovina!" he cried out to Gagić, not without reproach. He did likewise in a letter of March 1, 1834, after having just returned from Russia, at a time when he really wished to please the Russian government.

As a sovereign he was not to the taste of the Russians. But he was to the Montenegrins. He kept peace with the Turks because he had to. He also established order, though it was not to the liking of all the Montenegrins, and this, too, because he had to.

Njegoš was becoming that which he was and which was required of him by the course of the national struggle and Serbian history—and by a law that stands above all, one in which he believed and which he bore within himself.

6.

TRULY THERE IS no need to seek more convincing proof that Bishop Rade encountered internal difficulties immediately upon his return from Russia than the fact that he proclaimed his uncle, Bishop Petar, a saint.

Bishop Rade accomplished this on the fourth anniversary of his uncle's death, on October 18, 1834. The manner in which he did it—by a proclamation to the people, and in such haste—provoked dissatisfaction in higher ecclesiastical circles, especially in Russia, and ridicule among enlightened men.

Still insecure, Bishop Rade wished to lean for support on his uncle's mystical influence, which was rapidly growing stronger through folk legends. In his proclamation, Bishop Rade did not hide the fact that internal political reasons had prompted this act: "whichever Montenegrin will fail to maintain concord, peace, and unity, Saint Petar will pursue him in the other world and in this world as well."

The proclamation of the new saint created a great stir. The authorities in Kotor worriedly informed their superiors that their people were swarming to Cetinje to give offerings. Vuk noted the same thing. The Bishop of Dalmatia had to forbid his priests to go to Cetinje. Bishop Rade wrote to Turkey and Hercegovina for contributions which the Turks prevented without even hiding behind religious motives, as did the Dalmatian Bishop, but openly proclaimed their fear of such an influence on the raia.

And yet it was not just political necessity that inspired Bishop Rade to that act, but a religious impulse as well. For there is an obvious difference between the Njegoš of that period and the later Njegoš. He was religious later, too, sincerely and deeply so, but in a different way. Now he believed that God and the saints, including his uncle, were judges in the daily affairs of men, while later he saw God as a universal law by which all creation was governed and new worlds sprang out of chaos, as the light of reason which broke and dispelled demonic darkness. And while the cult of the new saint, his uncle, struck ever-deeper roots in the masses of the people, Njegoš, the very person who had canonized him, was to neglect it more and more as his own role as a ruler and his views changed. The evolution of his authority was reflected in his manner of living and outlook, and conversely. Vuk has recorded that in those days the Bishop wore a cassock and "dressed as befitted a monk to whose order he belonged, only his vestments were of better cloth." In 1850, when Djuko Srdanović, a kind of majordomo, a butler, for the Bishop, said to him as they came out of St. Peter's in Rome that Cetinje's Saint Petar was as influential with God as was Rome's, Njegoš laughed heartily, saying, "That's just what I think, Djuko." In that scene, described by Nenadović, there are all sorts of things: Djuko's primitive and national pride, and the resentment of poverty against such splendor, with the hope that at least in heaven there was justice for all; but there is also the fine irony of the sage—Njegoš, who had long since learned to distinguish between mystical and rational faith, metaphysics and religion.

Being of one piece, he found a contradiction in everything and was in constant conflict with everything. But the poet in him prevailed over the monk, the ruler prevailed over the bishop, the enlightener over folk superstition. This took both time and effort. A small, a very small land needed to be transformed; not destroyed but preserved. A tempest in a teapot is as much a tempest for those who live in the pot as one on the sea. Such was Bishop Rade's task in those years. He set aside the incidental and went to the heart of things, both as a poet and as a ruler. Beneath the black cassock quickened a youth and a ruler, one who was breaking through mystical faith to a philosophical outlook, and through folk myths to poetic inspiration.

What did he experience, and how did these imperatives make themselves known to him?

There were intrigues, accusations, and some reports even point to plots on his life, while a reliable tradition among the Petrovići tells how he was fired upon while among the Bjelopavlići. In 1835 there arrived from Russia his cousin Djordjije, a Russian officer. Rovinsky relates how plans fell through to hand over military power to him, a new kind of power, more tangible than that of the governorship. Meanwhile the Radonjići were gathering signatures among the people on complaints to Russia. Gagić substantiated the complaints. They charged the Bishop with squandering Russian money and enriching the Petrovići with it. It is true that in 1836 he built a new and beautiful house in Njeguši—they say, that he might have a place to celebrate his sister's wedding. His brother Pero was a merchant and was no doubt already a man of means. To just what uses the Russian aid was being put, and whether by any chance it was being spent for powder and lead—which the Russians had expressly forbidden—this was to be gone into much later, and in a very offensive fashion.

This hurt Njegoš deeply. He was in confusion. His whole inherited world was tottering within him. He escaped in frequent hunts; also in diversions in the Littoral—in gambling with officers and amusing himself with women of easy virtue.

But this was of short duration and on the surface. He was one of those who emerges from crises stronger and more confident in himself and in his vocation.

7.

HE SUFFERED TWO especially grave and severe blows in 1836. They struck at his whole being—one hit the still-insecure ruler, the other the would-be loyal kinsman: rebellions broke out in Crmnica and the Nahi of Rijeka, in Ceklin, while at Grahovo some Petrovići lost their lives.

These rebellions have remained unexplained, but taxes were certainly the main cause. There had been a drought, and, of course, a lean year. Yet it was not those who had fared the worst—the men of Katuni—who rebelled, but those who still had a little something.

The discontent arose not only from hunger, but from something deeper. It was put down by Stanko Stijepov and Djordjije—apparently thanks more to cunning than force.

The central government was still weak and liable at any moment to become shattered by clan strife. Bishop Rade wrote missives as his uncle did, though he resorted less and less to entreaty and increasingly to commands. The rebellions were an affront to his rule and reputation—especially before the Russians, who were still sanctifying his government with gold and the Tsar's blessing.

It was hard on the young ruler, whose best intentions confronted such resistance, and even harder on the Petrovići, because of their losses at Grahovo.

The reports on the number of Petrovići dead vary from nine to twelve. There are also disparities in the accounts of the event.

Vuk Vrčević's account is probably not quite exact—that the Petrovići lost their lives after having become drunk at the wedding of the Bishop's brother Pero—for the latter had been married earlier. Rather, it has been established that it was precisely at that time that Vojvoda Jakov Daković refused to pay Grahovo's tribute to Ali Pasha. The Vizir's army struck at Grahovo on August 6, scattered or enslaved the inhabitants, and burned down everything. Jakov and a few comrades ensconced themselves in a cavern before which a tower had been erected. The Montenegrins then set out to relieve him, but not in great numbers—according to Bishop Rade, "up to three hundred warriors." They rescued Jakov. But then the Turks surrounded the Montenegrins, or at least a group of them, and cut down about forty of them at Čelikov Potok, among them some Petrovići. According to the account, this was accomplished by a swift maneuver of the cavalry of Smaïl Aga Čengić, lord of Gacko, renowned for his heroism and fortitude not only in Bosnia and Hercegovina but throughout the whole empire. Among those cut down was Stanko Stijepov's son Stevan and the Bishop's brother Joko, who was affectionately called Piljo, a youngster of fifteen. The Turks exhibited Joko's head as a significant trophy, according to one account, in the fortress of Trebinje; according to another, in the fortress of Mostar.

The men of Grahovo were in a desperate situation: there was hardly any help whatever from Montenegro, the Austrians would not accept them, and their kin were scattered in flight. Finally

Jakov and the chieftains succeeded, through Smaïl Aga, in gaining the mercy of Ali Pasha, who excoriated them and allowed them to return to smoking ruins, but only on condition that they pay the tribute to an emissary of his from Nikšić, Muy Aga Mušović. They say that Bishop Rade demanded of Jakov that he wipe out Mušović and his retinue, but Jakov rejected this as a breach of faith and for fear of bringing more grief upon an already ruined people.

It was a heavy setback, both for the Petrovići and for the Bishop's efforts to wrest Grahovo from Turkey. There even arose a provocative poem among the people:

On Grahovo's wide and spacious plain
Of Petrović men full nine were slain
By Čengijić Aga's gleaming sword,
To the shame of Montenegro's lord.

Njegoš bore the misfortune without a groan, though never dreaming of forgoing revenge. After all, he, too, was a Montenegrin —and the most Montenegrin of them all. As much as he mourned over his kinsmen, he mourned even more over the taking of their heads by the enemy. The pain and the affront, the loss of prestige and hatred for the Turks, all fused together. But not a sign of the pain: he informed Gagić of the massacre without even mentioning the Petrovići. As for Ali Pasha, Njegoš wrote to him with a caustic taunt, to hide his own pain and anguish, that he just happened to hear that as a result of the incident he "had thus become a clerk"—that is, vizir—and that "among those Montenegrins there were several striplings of my house, among whom two died who were only fifteen years old . . . whom thou didst smite by stealth and by stealth didst steal away . . . but know full well that no one yet has gained glory at Montenegro's cost."

In Russia the complaints against him fell on fertile soil. He was blamed for the disaster at Grahovo. Being without money, he sent Milaković to Russia in the hope of getting, if not what had been pledged, then at least what he had spent to stir up the Montenegrins against the Turks—in defiance of Russian orders. Gagić, too, turned against him. Bishop Rade was aware—though he himself resorted to uncharacteristic and, for him, impermissible countercharges against his opponents—that the crux of the matter was not this or that point in the accusations, but who was to rule

Montenegro and how. Upon the return of the Governor's brother Marko to Montenegro, Njegoš wrote, on May 13, 1836, to Gagić, who had supported his return, "You know, gracious Sir, that there are evil and sinister men who can incite people to rebellion and who are a danger even to firmly established governments, let alone among a free people, which has never been used to having the reins of government held over it." How much there is in those words! Above all, the consciousness that it was his duty to place "the reins of government" over "a free people." How, what for? Even earlier he had felt Serbian misfortunes as his very own. Now, in this same protest to Gagić, he identified himself with the sorrows of his land: "The evil which is done to my fatherland is an evil done to me."

Bishop Rade did not waver in what had to be done. As for what he had to impart—he sang the unhappy fate of the Serbs.

In Majine he stroked a youthful mustache before a mirror and sang to himself:

> Fair-haired head, where shalt thou fall?
> Mustache black, where shalt thou pall—
> In Scutari or Travnik?

Here is a bitter pride without measure.

8.

HE HAD TO go to Russia again—to defend himself against the accusations, in order not to lose the aid. The chieftains urged him to go as soon as possible. Not even the Petrovići were convinced that the tax and the other measures were a good thing. Misfortune had also shaken them. His own uncle entreated him, on taking leave of him, not to impose taxes on the Montenegrins. He took Djordjije along, not at all by chance, and left in his own place Archimandrite Josif Pavičević, and a written order which he proclaimed to the people. He did not inform Gagić when he embarked, in November, 1836, for Russia. Bishop Rade sometimes defended himself poorly and unconvincingly, but also bravely and proudly.

In Vienna this time Metternich received him rather more cordially and noted: "spiritually and physically developed; has little respect for the principles of religion and monarchy and is not firm in them; given to liberal, revolutionary ideas; to be placed under surveillance."

From Vienna Bishop Rade sent the Russian government an angry memorandum in which he demanded an increase in aid and the annexation of the Plain of Zeta to Montenegro—or else the Montenegrins would move out, and he with them. The Russians rejected it entirely, and he had to wait long for them to approve his journey to St. Petersburg. He toyed with the idea of going to France, but Metternich refused to issue him a passport. Why Metternich did this is not hard to divine; he had quite enough of democratic and nationalistic ferment without the Bishop of Montenegro. But what did the Bishop want with France? To seek aid? Or maybe to get away from it all? That was hardly likely. Perhaps someone advised him to turn to France. But was it necessary to convince freedom-loving France? And France was that under Louis Philippe, by comparison with Russia and Austria.

The relations between Russia's administrations and Montenegro's bishops were never to the liking of the one side or the other.

The bishops and Montenegro sought ties with Orthodox and Slavic Russia for spiritual reasons and even more out of material necessity and political weakness. But the tsarist government only seemingly pursued a Slavic policy. Actually it oppressed its own non-Russian Slavs. Absolutist and based on serfdom, it did not understand the South Slavs, who had shaken off Turkish feudalism and were yearning for their own national states, any more than it understood the Poles, whose religion and nationality it was suppressing. The reason the conflict between the South Slavs and Russia did not take on the Polish form of resistance was simply that the tsarist government did not reach that far. Nevertheless friction inevitably appeared at every stage of their independence, whether it was Serbia, Montenegro, or Bulgaria that was involved.

Bishop Danilo was the first to turn to Russia, by making contact with Peter the Great and getting aid from him. Though his ties with Russia were spiritual, his ties with Venice were livelier and firmer—dictated as they were by daily material needs. His very residence, Majine, where he spent most of his time, belonged to

Venice. Thus he maintained a certain equilibrium—looking to the East in spirit, and to the West for his livelihood—and in this dichotomy he formed an integral whole and garnered the independence of the clans which gathered about him. The manner and the forces were new. Yet Saint Sava had done the same in the thirteenth century, when he detached the Church from Rome and the state from Byzantium. Danilo had to pay the price for this dichotomy of ideas and interests, a dichotomy no one to our day has been able to escape and which bears within itself both our difficulties and our peculiarities. There has been preserved an inscription from his time, in a chronicle: "In the year 1711 Mihailo Miloradovich came to Montenegro from Tsar Peter in Moscow bearing charters for Bishop Danilo and the Montenegrins, to the great misfortune of the Monastery and of Montenegro . . . [for Vizir Kiuprili in 1714] razed Montenegro and destroyed the church and the Monastery."

Bishop Sava also went to Russia, to beg Empress Elizabeth Petrovna for aid. But he depended too much on Venice. Bishop Vasilije eased him out precisely in order to turn the country more to Russia and to restore equilibrium. He sent Elizabeth petitions begging her to become Duchess of Montenegro and to accept Montenegro as a protectorate. He was in Russia three times, and finally left his bones there—abandoned, in disfavor, disappointed.

Bishop Petar had the greatest troubles with Russia. Prince Golitsyn refused to give him a passport to go to Russia for his consecration. Prince Potëmkin drove him out of Russia without a passport. At the last minute Catherine the Great wished to make up for Potëmkin's action, but Bishop Petar refused to return, vowing that his foot would never again tread on Russian soil. Of course he kept his vow. Russian emissaries, who suspected him of having sold out to the French because he had not given in to them, tried to entice him into boarding a Russian vessel in Kotor and to ship him off to Russia, probably to Siberia. The Russian emissary Mazurevsky * conducted an investigation of the Bishop's secretary Dolci † because of his connections with the French. That Dolci maintained some ties is true. But was it with Bishop Petar's knowl-

* Aleksandr Josifovich Mazurevsky, Russian consul in Kotor from 1804.

† Francesco Dolci de Visković (1742–1805), Catholic priest in Perast and Dubrovnik, vicar in Vienna and St. Petersburg.

edge? Dolci was strangled in Stanjevići. In 1804 the Russian Holy Synod distributed a declaration through Montenegro against Bishop Petar. A Montenegrin assembly had to defend its leader, and wrote to Tsar Alexander that their Bishop "has never been under the authority of the Russian Synod, but only under His Imperial Majesty's patronage, which was a moral one at that."

Bishop Rade knew of these relations. But he knew even better that without Russia, without its moral and material support, his measures to transform the Montenegrin clans into a state would be not only difficult, but virtually impossible.

A Russian, Rovinsky, has written with surprising objectivity about Montenegrin-Russian relations, without regard for the interests of his own government. He concluded that it was the pretensions of Venice and Turkey that turned Montenegro to Russia. That is true. Having nowhere to turn in the terrible struggle for the survival of their people, the leading spirits of Montenegro turned to the past, to their mythical origins—to the ancient homeland of the Slavs—all the more readily because it was not only Slavic but Orthodox, and because it was not only a Great Power but an increasingly powerful factor as a counter-Turkish and counter-Austrian force.

From the time of Bishop Danilo Russia had been a troublesome support, but the only one. The ties with it were rooted deeper and farther, as were its failures to comprehend our woes and circumstances. As always when a myth is in the making, disappointments and shocks were inevitable for those who held this myth to be necessary and the only way. So must it be—until human sacrifices and efforts concede to reality, or until a new myth is created.

For Bishop Rade, too, Russia was a profound, mythical emotion. But also a reality. He could not have divorced himself from it even if he had so wished—not even the Petrovići would have followed him, let alone his Orthodox people. But that move of his in France's direction reveals that the pressure of Orthodox Russia and the inherited Russian myth were beginning to wane within him. Seemingly everything was to go on being as it had been: the Russian Popov was to take joy, in 1842, in finding the Emperor's picture on the Bishop's desk. Nevertheless around the year 1837 the essence of Montenegrin-Russian relations changed, at least insofar as they became clearer, unsentimental. Bishop Rade was becoming spiritually independent; he was realistically basing his relations on political and material interests. One had to conduct politics with everyone, in pursuit of one's own interests and prospects. This is the lesson he learned from his relations with Russia and the message he left after him.

Yet he had to experience it all himself.

Russian misconceptions regarding Montenegro's circumstances and relations were daily, and quite petty. And inasmuch as the Russian government was dispensing financial aid, all of this took place at the price of Montenegro's and Njegoš's humiliation. Upon the Bishop's return from Russia in 1837, the Russian government began to send wheat to Kotor as aid to the hungry. The Bishop held that it would be more reasonable and beneficial to sell a part of the wheat there and to use that money to buy the same amount, if not more, in Zeta instead of transporting the cargo across the pathless crags. But the news reached Russia that its wheat was being sold, and the Bishop wore himself out trying to convince Gagić, and through him the Russians, of the true state of affairs and the reasonableness of his action.

As with all aid, Russian aid was generosity to the Russians, and to us—humiliation. But we were too weak and too poor to subsist and survive on our own. Bishop Rade was to cry out over that aid, to Vrčević, "Whoever gives with one hand what is not his due holds you by the pigtail with the other." The aid did not, nor could it, strengthen the spiritual, ideal aspect of their mutual relations, but, rather, deteriorated them.

It is not at all by chance that Russia was never Njegoš's poetic inspiration, though he was a poet of myths who transformed into pure lyrical expression everything that he touched. He does not mention Russia in *The Mountain Wreath,* though an emissary of Peter the Great, Colonel Mikhail Miloradovich, visited Bishop Danilo. In *Stephen the Small* the Tsar's emissary Yuri Vladimirovich Dolgorukov is neither particularly intelligent nor important. What Njegoš left concerning the Russians were the folk poems of his youth and the forced semiofficial odes of a ruler who had to beg for money and support.

Prince Danilo, Bishop Rade's successor and a marvel of energy, was to take a step in practice that his predecessor took in spirit:

he was to set out for Paris to seek the aid and support of Emperor Napoleon III.

Even after the year 1837 Njegoš wrote greetings to the Tsar and to Russian dignitaries, but without any feeling or enthusiasm—with a false pathos.

Something snapped in his attitude toward Russia, and as he did with everything controversial, he placed his relations with Russia on the razor's edge when he wrote to Nesselrode, on February 26, 1837, "If you deprive me of the right to punish evil troublemakers, I shall not be able to go on being Bishop of Montenegro. My spirit cannot endure anarchy, and that extreme—I shudder to report—seems imminent to me." Everything is lightning clear: either he was to be master in his own land, or else let the Russians do the best they could. Conscious of his role, he became in essence, within himself, independent toward Russia as well.

It should not be lost from sight that he wrote the above words from Pskov, which he reached on the way to St. Petersburg and where he was detained by order of the Russian government until his case was examined. He in fact found himself under a kind of house arrest, being kept in Pskov and Velikie Luki four long months, until the end of May, when Gagić's reports from Cetinje arrived. It was then and there that Bishop Rade finally took a firm stand toward Russia and everything became clear to him.

Gagić arrived in Cetinje during March. His reports were unfavorable to Bishop Rade's person, though they supported his government. Surely this overly punctilious official did not lie, but neither did he understand. "His only pastime is hunting and the writing of verses," Gagić reported concerning Bishop Rade, and added, "and he plays at cards with Austrian officers." At the end of 1837 he wrote in greater detail, "The Montenegrin Bishop is a hothead. . . . He was never meant to be a bishop but a good grenadier, and they speak of him as a young, bold, lawless man made dissolute by the reading of depraved books and thus dangerous both to himself and to the Montenegrins!"

It was natural that certain inherited usages and moral conceptions should have snapped in the young Bishop as he was being transformed into a sovereign, a prince. But what was the poet in him to do but write verses? And what was the man hungry for learning to do but read and read, those very books that seemed depraved to Gagić and to the Russians? Njegoš had already seen that the Montenegrins did not defer to the cloth. Without a state there could be no Serbdom, and the state could be created only by the sword and agility.

The Russians would finally accept that fact. However, they could never make peace with Rade's unmonkish behavior. According to one account, even during his exile in Pskov he acted too freely for the Russians—by going on rides with noble ladies. The top Russian officials must have been enraged—and not only those in the Church. No wonder! Accustomed as they were to reading confidential reports, they accepted as unexaggerated everything that was in them. They were a closed circle, a world to themselves, so that everything that did not conform to their pattern and ways seemed wrong and unnatural. Yet, for the sake of their influence in the Balkans, they were willing to accept the Bishop as he was.

Bishop Rade had already formed an outlook of his own.

It is from this period that we have that well-known portrait of him, by Giuseppe Tominz, probably made in Trieste on his return from Russia. Except for the photograph taken by Anastas Jovanović in Vienna in 1847, this is the most exact portrayal of him, though from a time when neither his face nor his poetry was yet marked by painful thoughts. In this picture Njegoš appears in a costly silk episcopal vestment with a cowl on his head. Despite the romantic feel, everything is exact down to the most trifling detail. The Bishop is sitting in pensive attitude, with his right arm propped up on a table on which there is some sort of picture or mirror. His wide sleeve is turned back to reveal a fine hand and wrist against the shining silken foam. The face is oval, with gentle shadings and light ruddiness. The hair reveals a scar on the left side, they say from the blow of a mule when he was small. It went far but did not quite break the arc of the eyebrow, which turned down abruptly at the end. The eyes are big and dark, the same color as the thin curling mustache and still-thin, sparse beard. Njegoš had a fair complexion and almost completely black eyes and hair. In the portrait that blackness contrasted well with the white-and-ruddy face. Nor did the painter conceal the slight tendency of the nose to veer to the right—for which the people had a saying: "God did not make even Bishop Rade perfect." This is the portrait of a poet, an artist, or a noble officer given to spiritual problems; of the bishop there is only the vestment. The face is full and filled with a mighty, though restrained, strength. The mouth is noticeably, openly sensuous. Here was a not-too-pious young man enshrouded in a monk's luxurious black cassock decorated with a cross and medallion of pure gold and jewels, who had already developed into a ruler and an artist.

It is step by step from being to becoming.

9.

HAVING KEPT HIM far too long in Pskov and in Velikie Luki, the Russians kept Njegoš in St. Petersburg hardly a month. This time everything was different—the opposite of what it had been during his first stay in Russia.

The Tsar received him on this occasion as well. Yet he did not fail to reproach him for his intended trip to Paris. The Bishop later recalled that he replied with silence. Upon his departure, in a letter to the Tsar, he was to justify his intention by his desperation. To be sure, there certainly was desperation in this, but also the new thought and awareness that the world did not begin and end in any one country, even Mother Russia. Bishop Rade never lost heart. There always remained in him an unshakable base and a fiber that did not snap no matter how taut.

His messages from Russia to his household and to the Petrovići are touching. "I, the Bishop, greet all. Be of good cheer and in good health," he wrote encouragingly to his father, in a letter of Stanko Stijepov's—the latter being by his side in those decisive days. A bit later he wrote to the Senate and the Guard. "We herewith inform you that we have, thank God, arrived safely in St. Petersburg."

Relations with Russia reduced themselves to the realities; the age of romantic, mythical relations with Russia was forever gone.

The Russians substantially increased Rade's allowance to nine thousand ducats a year.

He changed, too. The youth matured, and bishop turned into ruler.

On his way back, in Trieste, he engaged the Frenchman Jome and took him along to Cetinje to teach him French. Though he was not to open windows to the West in his politics, being weak and poor, still he was to do so with respect to his own cultural elevation and way of life.

He was escorted back by Russian Lieutenant Colonel Jakov Ozeretskovsky, who had been instructed to take stock of the situation in Montenegro. The Bishop was concerned, not only as a Montenegrin but as a ruler, that this man should receive as good a welcome as possible. The terrible poverty behind all this is touching. The Bishop wrote from Warsaw on July 18, 1837, to his confidant Radovan Mrčarica, a Piper:

> As soon as you receive this letter, you will write to Vido of the Bjelopavlići to find three or four youths who are pleasing to look at and each of whom is to have two silver-handled pistols and a knife and white kerchiefs. Write to Tolicin that Todor Mušikin of the Piperi also choose same, who shall be dressed and armed in the same manner . . . for there is coming a distinguished man, and I shall be glad to have him see them. . . . And do not let anyone know of this. And see to it that you whitewash your houses, let everything be proper and clean. . . . And have them whitewash those chambers at Stanjevići, those two, I mean, and have them replace the glass in the windows if any is broken.

Montenegrin protocol had begun.

That year, upon his return from Russia, there is the first mention of the Bishop's bodyguard. Special caps were designed for them—according to some, with a feather in each, from which they got their name, *perjanici,* from *pero* (feather); others say the caps bore the initial of the district from which each man came. This was a kind of uniform. The guardsmen were chosen for their courage and birth. And for their reckless obedience. Rovinsky noted, "The Montenegrin people have preserved to the present the memory of them as powerful, ruthless and merciless men against whom no resistance was possible."

Ozeretskovsky became intimate with the Bishop with a broad Russian heartiness. Montenegro charmed people with its simplicity and heroism, and especially with its twenty-four-year-old ruler. And Ozeretskovsky was a real Russian.

But who was that Radovan Mrčarica, called Radovan Piper, to whom the Bishop had turned to have arrangements made for Ozeretskovsky's welcome? Bishop Rade's most trusted person. He is mentioned then for the first time, but he was to be involved in many, if not all, of the secret and nefarious matters that inevitably go with rulers and politics. He had no title, was seemingly an ordinary guardsman. But he bore and guarded the Bishop's most secret intentions and decisions.

The Bishop was in a hurry to get home, to Montenegro. In Trieste he saw Dositej Obradović's works, which had been printed in Serbia, and sent Prince Miloš a sharp letter against those "evil and depraved works." These were the vestiges of the past in him and the result of Russian influences. Never again would he scold Dositej. Indeed, he would himself take the path Dositej blazed in the name of reason and science. Actually he had already set foot on that path.

The wilderness was again before him, indestructible. It was in the men, in objects—in everything. A man no sooner masters one task than another challenge faces him.

Day by day the time doth flow,
And every day brings its own woe.

And what wild changes! Something unchangeable was always changing. Indestructible matter, unalterable laws were always appearing in a new form, a new way. And everyone has his own dream, his own passion, to shape—at least this is what he believes. This is man's transient fate in his permanent existence in eternity. Of the wilderness, flux, and desire for change there is never any end.

In Montenegro this meant effort upon effort to make men humans, to oust the Turks, and to clear the paths to the good and to freedom. Bishop Rade carried this out with concern and conscientiousness, convinced that this was laid upon him by the laws that govern the universe and mankind.

He kept constantly conquering wilderness after wilderness. Perhaps that is precisely why he was never for a moment to leave the wilderness.

Montenegro had gained a sovereign.

THE SOVEREIGN OF MONTENEGRO AND THE HIGHLANDS

1.

OUTWARD APPEARANCES ARE sometimes more important than content. A new content cannot really be expressed except by way of a new form. And the latter has to be created.

Nothing is except as it appears, and thus it can never manifest itself exactly and completely.

Nor could Bishop Rade establish his new government in the old dress. He shed his bishop's cassock.

He was more prince than bishop when he greeted the Saxon King Friedrich August on his visit to Montenegro in 1838.

Bishop Rade overestimated the political significance of this visit, perhaps because it served his purpose to call attention to Montenegro's independence and to external, ceremonial trappings of his government and state.

The King was attracted to travel by a hobbyist's passion—he collected rare flora. He was accompanied by the Italian botanist Bartolomeo Biasoletto, who described the King's journey through Montenegro—from Kotor to Cetinje and then to Budva. The King himself made some notes in his own diary.

At first Bishop Rade thought of going down to Kotor to greet the King there. Once upon a time that is just what he would have done, but he remembered that he was the sovereign of an independent land and that it did not behoove him to greet his guest on the soil of a foreign state. He therefore met the King at the village of Mirac—on his own border.

The primitive character of the welcome could hardly be

avoided, especially since the Bishop obviously wished to give it a Montenegrin heroic-epic stamp.

They dined at Njeguši—on roast lamb which a Montenegrin had deftly hacked into pieces with his dagger and which was, everyone observed, very tasty. On the way to Cetinje, in the hills, bands of Montenegrins welcomed them with the firing of rifles. They arrived in Cetinje at dusk, dead tired, to the volleying of cannon; the Montenegrin capital was greeting a foreign ruler for the first time.

Bishop Rade showed the King the sword and head of Mahmud Pasha. (Both have since disappeared.) The Pasha's head, dried and wrapped in a turban, was kept in an oaken box, as a great relic. The King presented the Bishop with a diamond ring. Captain Friedrich Orešković, an Austrian spy who had worked his way to Njegoš and been assigned, not fortuitously, to the King's retinue, talked the Bishop into dressing in his ceremonial vestments when he visited the King the next day. It was all rather grotesque inasmuch as the Bishop was forced to move from room to room, for the King was lodged in the monastery, which was the Bishop's residence. Apparently Rade readily agreed to anything that would contribute to the ceremonial air of a ruler.

Yet all this did not touch Njegoš the poet and the Montenegrin. He remained what he was. Not only did he greet the King with a poem, printed on his own press, but, what was even more remarkable, he hardly concealed the ennui he felt as he escorted the King to the border again: the King turned off every once in a while to gather grasses while Njegoš waited silently, but once he blurted out, as though to himself, that there was grass of all kinds in Montenegro, but nobody had ever bothered to gather any of it.

The German press printed all kinds of nonsense about that visit, exaggerating the King's mad daring in venturing among head-hunters, and portraying Bishop Rade as a savage chieftain who fell on his knees before the King. This made Njegoš angry, and he sent corrections—in vain. And he thought to himself: A mad King! And here we are, beset by Turkish attacks and slaughter among ourselves.

The King's visit confirmed how right the Bishop was in wishing, immediately after his return from Russia, to build the castle, or the new palace, as they at first called what later came to be known as the Billiard. The first two names never stuck, but gave way to the Billiard—after the central room on the second floor, which contained a billiard table. That room was used as a kind of salon and would have attracted the most attention anyway, even if it had had no billiards to suggest the luxury and entertainment of a court. There guests could always find diversion, and there the chieftains spent many an evening with their sovereign.

Work on the Billiard began as soon as Bishop Rade returned from Russia. It is not known who made the plans for this gloomy patchwork of a castle, a garrison, and an office building, which it really was. Today, located as it is in town, the Billiard does not give the air of being as ponderous and as mournful as it was when it was first built—on an empty field below a bare crag.

The Bishop consulted with Ozeretskovsky as to where the foundation of the building should be laid. They hit upon locating it in the middle of Dolac, but the Bishop changed that—to bring it closer to the monastery, with which the Russian agreed—for they had to conserve land, the greatest scarcity in those parts.

The Bishop took an active part in everything that had to do with the building, for he was eager to have it finished as soon as possible. By the autumn of 1837 the materials were all there, and in 1838 the building was capped by a roof, made of lead, but the interior was not finished. The Bishop installed every institution there—the Senate and the bodyguard, his own and the national kitchen, the library and Milaković, and himself as the ruler of an ancient but lawless land.

The Billiard was about two hundred and thirty-seven and a half feet long, and its width was eighteen feet without the wings, about forty-four feet with the wings. Surrounded by a stone wall with little round towers at the corners, it was constructed simply—a corridor on one side, and rooms on the other. It was both solid and full of symmetry. It contained twenty-five rooms—eleven on the ground floor and fourteen on the second floor. Hence Prince Danilo's bodyguard used to say when they had to beat anyone, "Lay on as many blows as there are rooms in the Billiard."

The Bishop installed himself, and withdrew into the southern corner of the building. That wing contained the armory—the Bishop's salon with weapons on the wall. Behind this room one entered the bedroom, in which the Bishop ordinarily also worked, especially at night. The windows of that corner room looked out upon Mount Lovćen, and from them one could see the monastery and the unfinished tower over it, the Tablja. Bishop Rade had also built the tower, though when he saw that it was unsuitable for a fortress, he had had stakes set into it on which to stick Turkish heads—which had previously been done on the walls of the monastery. As he wrote, meditated, and created, Njegoš had before his eyes all that he needed to have—enemy heads, Mount Lovćen, and an ancient house of worship.

There was nothing comfortable about this pile—more a fortress than a palace—by which the government buttressed itself and in which Njegoš immured himself. The Bishop was no ascetic; the ruler had to be a sacrifice to the state. He reserved only two out-of-the-way rooms for what little he had of a private life, and even these were not separated from the rest.

He was also to build other dwellings—for his brother Pero and for Novica Cerović. But these were men with families. Bishop Rade could not have a personal life. His place was, to the last, here, in the Billiard, in the fortress, "keeping watch," Medaković says. Keeping watch over everything—the country, the government, Serbianism. And poetry.

Luxuries of one kind or another found their way into the Billiard—a bit of European furniture, porcelain and silver, French wines, coffee, and fine victuals. Yet all of this was used sparingly, and saved for distinguished visitors.

The Bishop brought to it something of himself and of Montenegro. The pictures in his rooms were official—such as that of the Russian Tsar—or souvenirs—such as the one of Friedrich August. But there were also those associated with the cause—Karadjordje—or affinity—Pushkin and Byron. The weapons on the wall were not just those taken from the Turks, but also Austrian ones, captured during an encounter on Paštrovići Hill, in July, 1838. The Bishop never failed to point out that the muzzles of the rifles were twisted in the struggle between the Montenegrins and the Turks during the battle on the Salkovina. He liked, collected, and made gifts of beautiful weapons.

The authority of the state was expressed in other ways as well. The seal—the seal was especially important. Bishop Rade took his from the fifteenth century, from the Crnojevići—the last sovereigns of Serbian blood who ruled over this land at the time. The seal displayed a double-headed eagle whose folded wings made him look more like a falcon. Bishop Rade also introduced the first decoration, the Obilić Medal, which lasted as long as the Montenegrin state. They say that at first he wished to inaugurate a medal portraying Nikac of Rovin, an eighteenth-century hero who, like Obilić, came supposedly to surrender himself, along with forty volunteers, to the pasha, then killed him in his own tent and, despite being covered with wounds, managed to break through the encircling Turks with five or six of his comrades and to make his escape. However, Stevan Perkov, whom the Bishop fondly called Zvizdo, reminded him that Nikac was a clan hero. Rade then adopted Obilić—who was uncontroversial and the purest mythical figure of the Serbs. The distance from Nikac to Obilić is not great; Montenegrin heroism lived in the myth of Kosovo. But the distance between the one medal and the other signaled the creation not only of a state, but of a dynasty.

Since he was creating a state, Rade wished to coin his own money—the gold perun. He even made a mold. But he did not have a gram of gold, or a press. Poverty and inadequate means were the bridgeless gaps of his intentions.

Forms of address were also changed. The Montenegrins addressed Rade's uncle as "Holy Bishop." They began by calling Rade just "Bishop," and were to end by calling him "Sire"—including his father and brothers. And foreigners, too, gradually changed the form of address from "Bishop" to "Sire," and even styled him "Autocrat" and "His Highness." Djordjije was given the title of "Illustrious Prince."

When Bishop Rade was informed, in 1845, that the Russian Holy Synod had awarded him the title of "Metropolitan," he thanked the Tsar, being aware that he had received it for political reasons. Nevertheless that appointment was to have no influence whatever on his unepiscopal bearing; he had set out on his own path long since. He never signed himself "Metropolitan," but, out of habit, simply "Bishop," though in actual fact he was "Sovereign of Montenegro and of the Highlands." The Highlands comprised the seven clans of northern Montenegro, all of whom had not yet been really united with it.

The Bishop's dress changed, too. The fez disappeared—from

both his head and the heads of the Montenegrins. But the first to go was the cassock, in 1838. No one ever saw him in one after that date. He gradually went over to the national costume—which none of his predecessors had ever worn. The cap which today is known as Montenegrin he took from the Bay of Kotor—from Risan. He had his costume made of broadcloth richly decorated with gold thread. Such was the origin of the Montenegrin costume.

The poet expresses the nation; the ruler changes the face of the earth.

2.

IN ALL OF this—in the style of the Billiard, in the seal, the empty testimonials of noble ancestry, the titles, the proctocol and dress —there was something feudal. Those helmets on Danilo's head in *The Mountain Wreath* and on the Obilić Medal were part of Njegoš's fabricated heraldry. In 1846, while in Vienna, Njegoš still wore a fez. The fez remained for so long a part of the national costume partly because of the popular belief that it had originally been a Serbian cap which the Moslems then adopted. It was in Vienna that he was struck by the idea that it was high time to get rid of the thing.

Bishop Rade introduced feudal paraphernalia of state and office in the search for ties with the historic and mythical past. Yet there were other more immediate reasons: whenever a peasant wants to raise himself above other peasants, he always does it in the style of a noble landlord.

Bishop Rade was not troubled by the fact that the surrounding pashas and beys were feudal lords nearly as much as by the fact that they were Turks. To be sure, in practice this attitude necessarily led him to wage a struggle against feudalism. But that is not how it looked to him. He thought of it primarily as a religious and national struggle. Orthodoxy and Serbianism, and later Yugoslavism, were with him essentially antifeudalism. His paraphernalia were semifeudal because they stood for a restoration —the resurrection of Serbian state independence. With us nationalism and capitalism were the work of princes—Bishop Rade, Miloš Obrenović, and others—while in other lands the princes were actually the ones who stood in the way of these forces. These Serbian princes arose from a predominantly peasant struggle against an alien, Turkish, feudalism. In our peasant backwardness they had to have a feudal outlook and look back to a mythical past, though in actual fact they stood for something else.

The clan chieftains at least tried to look like nobles. They could not become such at the time, but they felt like bluebloods and aristocrats. The new government—the Bishop's—nourished that feeling. Everything resembled a tardy medievalism, even though the Middle Ages were long since past. Today this does not look quite so strange, for it is known—especially after the research of Professor Djurdjev—that Montenegro had its own native Orthodox landlords under the Turks. What makes this case exceptional is that neither domestic nor Turkish feudalism did away with the clan, but, rather, conserved it. An autochthonous clan life went on in Montenegro and in northern Albania under both the Serbian landlords and the Turkish beys. Bishop Rade's feudal trappings were not all that new, even if we dismiss their connection with the ancient Serbian state. Nor were they simply a mere device. Rather, they represented a government over peasants who had just recently pulled free from the Turkish beys. When Njegoš distributed feudal titles, which was not often—in 1840 he "conferred the rank of vojvoda" on Serbia's Prince Alexander—this was no mere amiable ingratiation, but the fruit of a delayed, feudal mentality. Consequently it had to be naïve and unrealistic.

It was a society made up predominantly of peasants who had emerged from feudalism very late and still thought and felt in feudal ways. It was also a form of government that the neighboring absolutist states, especially tsarist Russia, found more acceptable than any other form.

We appeared to be, and had to appear to be, what we were not.

Even Njegoš's poetry had something of the feudal, perhaps aristocratic, about it. It, too, grew out of a peasantry which was freeing itself from feudalism and had not yet embraced capitalist relations. Serbia was decidedly ahead of Montenegro, and yet it could produce a folk bard such as Filip Višnjić. Socially lagging behind Serbia, Montenegro was precisely for this reason closer to the ancient sources and could produce poetry, through Njegoš, which could more authentically express the people and how they saw their own destiny. But like the government that was increasing peasant proprietors and free trade under the aspect of feudalism, so this poetry was using the myths of the feudal and prefeudal past to disclose other realities and truths.

Everything else was similarly in flux—concealing and revealing itself in new shapes.

Upon his return from Russia, Bishop Rade set and increased the salaries of the senators and others. Soon they were to attempt to raise their salaries by their own efforts—by imposing fines. By preserving the clan titles and personal dignity of the chieftains, he in fact made them into his own servitors. He began to appoint chieftains over families which had never had any with such a title before. Any assembly of chieftains was pointless in such circumstances, for it would have been merely a gathering of appointed and paid officials. The last was convened in 1837, to permit Gagić to investigate the charges against the Bishop. After that their convocation depended entirely on the Bishop—and he did not wish to convene them. Once significant, such assemblies could now only create confusion by trying to exercise rights unsupported by any real power. In Serbia similar assemblies developed in time into a parliament. Here this was impossible. The only factors were the sovereign and the chieftains, and they were half-shepherds.

The Bishop went to church less and less. If he was forced to fulfill some office as head of the Church, he did so hastily and reluctantly. Every priest has to be individually ordained. Bishop Rade did it in batches. Once he gathered some sixty of them and ordained them at a single sweep. His dean, a man from the Littoral, reminded him that this was contrary to canon law, but he dismissed it, saying, "Here, I am the highest church law." The Bishop was replaced by the Prince. That he did not also replace the cowl with the crown only shows that he could not leap over his times except in spirit and could not transcend the realities and forms that suited those times. Though the Montenegrins might have been willing to accept a sovereign, they were not willing to lose a bishop. And only the bishop was able to become the sovereign.

Bishop Rade attributed so much significance to his own external image and that of his government that it all seemed to come spontaneously from him. His movements and bearing passed from a natural dignity to decorum. Frequently, and with obvious relish, he had himself painted in ever-finer clothes. His retinue was more and more finely outfitted. It was very important to him to have foreign newspapers write about himself and Montenegro. Yet he was too intelligent to fall victim to these inevitable but transitory features. No one ever observed in him the pomposity, the disdain, or the lordly superiority and arrogance of the *arriviste*. He was obviously above all this spiritually, and interested in something more profound and, for him, more real. Yet he did not treat the glitter of government—which was at once both lackluster and too brilliant in the poverty of Montenegro—as though it were something imposed and to be despised. It was clear to him that there could be no government without external splendor, and he himself devised and discovered its most suitable shapes and forms.

If the splendor was not his aim, it was because the government was not his aim either. For him the government was the materialization of an idea, a vehicle for a cause. This is why, no matter how crude it was in some ways, his rule had not only a primitive simplicity about it but also a certain spiritual purity. When writing to the Turks he signed himself "Russian Cavalier"—to impress them, but also to let them know that behind him stood mighty Russia. Yet he did that only in his letters to them. He made use of government and its forms only insofar as he had need of them, whether for daily needs or to further the idea. Just as much as he needed—that is the extent to which he organized and used the authority of the state. The first sovereign, he was not yet the first prince. The form was not for its own sake. Though he held power, he did not love it. That is because he was Njegoš, a thought and a passion made flesh, an idea without any false glitter.

It was the misfortune of this sovereign that he was also born a poet. Yet would he have attained those poetic heights had he not become a sovereign?

3.

EVEN IF THE creation of a state did not entail the drawing of frontiers, Njegoš would have been forced to this by Austria and Russia. There was some talk about it with Metternich in Vienna in 1837, and certainly in St. Petersburg. His government at home and Russia abroad drove the Bishop to define borders with Turkey. Mostly at the behest of the Russians, he was to try to establish tolerable relations with the Turks. Yet the determination of that border was not only not in his interest, but was also impossible. The neighboring clans and raia were on the move, so that no one knew under whose authority they were. Besides, Turkey did not even recognize Montenegro.

Negotiations concerning the border with Austria proceeded without serious difficulties until the matter came up of the frontier between Crmnica and the Paštrovići. The Venetian-Turkish frontier was taken as the basis for delimitation. But between Crmnica and the Paštrovići—the latter were an autonomous community under Venice—there was confusion over the state border and the clan border, and this was frequently a matter in dispute. And so a dispute among clans became an international one, and even resulted in a serious armed clash which delayed an agreement until July, 1841.

Especially sensitive was the question of the two monasteries—in Majine and Stanjevići—which Austria claimed were on its territory, that is, on territory formerly belonging to Venice, whose internationally recognized successor it was. The monastery at Majine was built and occupied by Bishop Danilo. Bishop Petar stayed there frequently, until the Bay of Kotor finally fell to Austria. Bishop Sava held Majine to be unhealthy and retired into the heights, to Stanjevići, where he erected a monastery in which he lived and died. Bishop Rade visited both monasteries often. He was in Majine in the spring of 1836, to supervise work in the fields and repairs while Vrčević copied his *Ode to Liberty.* Before he established his court at Cetinje, the Bishop liked to take his guests to Stanjevići—into the airy heights, toward the limitless azure horizons. And so, personal and family sentiments intertwined with religious, state, and national interests. What was most important of all, the loss of the one monastery especially meant cutting Montenegro off from the sea, something Austria stubbornly attempted to do, with foresight.

Both monasteries were rather run-down—as happens with things whose ownership is not sure. It was indisputable that Majine lay on former Venetian territory. True, according to a tradition which the Montenegrins firmly believed, Majine and the region around it had been taken from the Turks by the Montenegrins, for Venice was not able to fight over it, or perhaps not interested. However, one could not regard as reliable Austrian claims that Stanjevići, too, had belonged to Venice. Here might played a greater role than right.

Austria had, in fact, raised the border question in the time of Bishop Petar. But he was unyielding. Rejecting any deals concerning the monasteries, he wrote to the Austrian authorities, "Cover those bare rocks with gold and you will still not be able to buy me off. What we have gained by the sword we shall not give up without the sword, though we wade in blood to our knees. . . . The people will not permit the rending of a garment bought with blood, as you are accustomed to doing with our other brethren who suffer under the whip of your arbitrary rule."

Yet Bishop Rade had to accept an agreement under Russia's added pressure to make him establish the limits of his realm at least toward Austria. As for egress to the sea, Austria would not permit it—with or without Majine and Stanjevići.

He agreed on October 12, 1837, without many qualms, to sell the monastery at Majine and its lands to Austria for seventeen thousand florins sterling. He gained the support of the Montenegrin chieftains for this decision, while Lavrov emphasizes that the Russian diplomats also had their fingers in this agreement. However, Njegoš would not leave Bishop Danilo's bones in an alien land; he brought them to Cetinje. They say that before the burial he kissed the skull of the progenitor of the state and the cause.

That particular transaction did not meet with any serious discontent inasmuch as Majine was deep inside Austrian territory —in the Plain of Budva, next to the sea. But the sale of Stanjevići —for the same sum, to which Bishop Rade agreed only on May 6, 1839—became a source of dissatisfaction and reproach, even in later generations and on the part of persons who were not partisan in their judgments. Not only opponents, but his closest kin—including his cousin Djordjije—as well as such historians as the Russian Lavrov and the Serb Dučić, held this step against the Bishop. He himself felt the unpopularity of his action and hastened to justify it at least to Gagić. He wrote in his letter of

May 8, 1839, "Inasmuch as all the buildings at Stanjevići had already fallen in disrepair, so that it was necessary either to spend a good deal of money to repair them or to allow them to fall to ruin . . . I judged it best to sell Stanjevići, which my predecessor and uncle Saint Petar acknowledged in writing, at the time Caboga came to Cetinje, as lying within the Austrian border—and to use the money thus gained for the benefit of the people in times of necessity, rather than to spend it on some needless building which brings no benefit."

It did, indeed, seem wrong—at least at first sight—to sell Montenegrin land and one's inherited patrimony. But, in actual fact, Bishop Rade acted both wisely and honorably. Perceiving that Austria would not relinquish the region around Kotor, to which it buttressed its right with both force and documents, and inasmuch as any settling of a border without this region was out of the question, Bishop Rade agreed to a sacrifice. The sale of the monastery signified the denial of ecclesiastical jurisdiction in the Littoral. But it also meant the settlement of frontier relations with an enemy whose threat was not immediate and whose recognition of Montenegro's sovereignty would have a great influence on the attitude of others, especially Turkey. Contemporaries saw in this the surrender of even that little bit which had been gained in blood. Those who came later judged out of national egoism. Neither the former nor the latter were caught in the fire that roasted the Bishop: he had to establish a government, and this could not be done without settling the border. He knew that his decision ran counter to desires and customs. Though it was the least convenient, this was neither his first nor his largest sale of state and church property. But he saw the situation and, needing money, he finally gave in.

What would have happened had he not agreed?

Austria would have secured the border it held to be its own by force of arms, as it had done before, and would have accomplished this all the more easily because Montenegro could not have counted in this case on any real support from Russia.

The further progress and realization of the Serbian idea was impossible without a state, and this could not be secured either externally or internally without establishing regular relations with Austria. Led by the idea of a state, Bishop Rade hardened his heart and risked both loss and shame. He was certain that for liberation and unification nothing was too dear or sacred. He did not spend the money he got for the monasteries, though they were no less the property of the Petrovići than of Montenegro. Rather, he deposited every last para, together with other sums, in a Russian bank and left it all to the state and the people.

Even though reality and ideology can never be reconciled, a clear conscience is always a sure defense before the future.

4.

THE RENUNCIATION OF the monasteries raised moral qualms; the delineation of the border, especially between Crmnica and the Paštrovići, involved practical matters, such as pastures, water, and right of way. Even had he so wished, the Bishop could not have ignored the needs and desires of the Crmnica clan, which was powerful and strong-willed beyond all others. By the same token, there were difficulties on the Austrian side because of strategic considerations, which were not at all artfully concealed behind the demands of the Paštrović clan.

Being friendly to Austria at the time, Russia insisted that the question of the border with Austria be settled. To this end, with Austria's acquiescence, the Russians sent an official, named Chevkin, in the summer of 1839, who acted more as a representative for Montenegro than as an intermediary between it and the Austrian government. But this did not put an end to the tugging and squabbling either, so that the border settlement was not completed until July, 1841.

By this act the Montenegrin state regularized its relations with a neighboring empire and received *de facto* recognition, even though at a high price. Metternich sent its Sovereign a gift in the name of the Austrian ruler—a diamond pectoral cross—and the Russian Tsar sent him a high decoration—the Anna Cross, First Class. Nor did Gagić fail to mark the change: thereafter he never addressed Bishop Rade as a spiritual leader.

Relations with Austria became more normal, but Austria was a cool neighbor. Relations between Austria and Montenegro were to remain that way to the end. Austria tolerated the accommodation, but resisted every serious strengthening of the new state. Montenegro was bound to respect, but not to like, its too powerful neighbor, which, moreover, held in subjection so many people of our blood and tongue.

There was to be an abundance of incidents and clashes—the people were not used to state borders. Bishop Rade proposed setting up a special local court—a kind of border commission—"for the Austrian tribunals move too slowly for these precipitous parts." But that was not accepted. Nor was there a discussion of the question of property that Montenegrin subjects possessed in the Bay of Kotor. Murders, looting, and raids continued to be frequent, along with the disputes created between people artificially divided.

In his relations with Austria, Bishop Rade clung to two principles—the equality of states and justice. For justice he had to wage a ceaseless struggle. For equality he could only wish. Thus unless the Austrians offered sure proof, he refused to punish Montenegrins. He openly served notice on the Austrian authorities: "In the event that your soldiers should offend any Montenegrins, and the latter attack them under God's justice, I have no right to punish the Montenegrins, for they will be defending their honor, inasmuch as it is the custom in Montenegro: whosoever shall unjustly offend a Montenegrin, if the latter does not repay him in kind for the injury to his honor, he thereby becomes an object of ridicule among his own people."

Bishop Rade had no illusions about the fairness of Austria's courts, or any enthusiasm for its excellent bureaucratic system. The order for which he yearned was not based on the rule of officials; it was one that would mete out justice according to the ancient code of human morality. He wrote to Gagić in June, 1838, angrily and mockingly, concerning a clash on Paštrovići Hill, "The Austrian army burned down around 60 . . . stables in Crmnica . . . when nobody was guarding them . . . who would have said that even the good Austrians are capable of such a thing!" He wrote more severely and with a finer irony to the Austrians themselves, on August 21, 1841, "As for your saying that you had not expected this to happen, in view of the fact that the Austrian government has tendered me and the Montenegrins every possible consideration, we thank God that we are in the middle of the 19th century. And if we are shown any small consideration, it comes from an enlightened empire which sacredly observes the delicate laws of European enlightenment."

As it happens in politics and in international relations, the tensions and misunderstandings increased because of other differences as well—economic, nationalistic, cultural, and even those involving moral and personal traits. The Bishop sent Austrian noblemen, high officials, gifts of weapons and horses captured from the Turks, as a sign of especial esteem. It is not difficult to imagine what these people thought of these trophies of a warfare they regarded as plain looting. They carefully surrounded the Bishop with spies. This was normal for them, while he was horrified.

Relations were also complicated by the replacing of captains in Kotor, which was a point of daily friction with Cetinje. At the beginning of Rade's rule that post had been assigned to Gabriel Ivačić. The latter quickly grasped the situation and sought to settle all disputes reasonably. However, despite the Bishop's efforts, he was transferred in 1845. They soon brought him back briefly —after 1848—for his successors, especially the quick-tempered and ruthless Eduard Griez de Ronse, were overzealous in poisoning relations with Cetinje.

The last commander in Kotor during the Bishop's lifetime was the insensitive and picayunish Paolo Rešetar—the Ragusan Serb Reszetar—who had no consideration even for Njegoš's sickness and dying. He was the father of Milan Rešetar—the most conscientious and diligent commentator on *The Mountain Wreath.*

It happens that sons suffer for and make good sins for which their fathers' consciences did not even hurt.

5.

Relations with Turkey, with the neighboring pashas, were to remain a welter of irreconcilable desires and clashes. Inasmuch as it was not to Turkey's benefit to recognize Montenegro's independence in any way, that country could hardly desire to establish a border in a territory teeming with the rebellions of kindred clans. It was in the very struggle against Turkey that Montenegro was, in fact, becoming a state. Only in that struggle was it able to complete itself and to expand to its natural borders—to include neighboring clans.

For the weakened empire Montenegro had become a source of trouble and Great Power intervention. The Porte strove at all cost to prevent the expansion and recognition of Montenegro, for that would have aroused the raia and the demands of the other nationalities. Yet it was forced to appear tolerant and accommodating before Europe. For this reason the Porte tried, especially in the time of Bishop Rade, to keep its own hands as clean as possible while at the same time encouraging the neighboring pashas to put pressure on Montenegro.

There was no difference in the policies of Mostar and Scutari until the forties.

After the failure of Bushati's rebellion, the vizirs of Scutari differed from one another only in their zeal to see who could serve Istanbul best. Faceless and dull, they replaced one another in quick succession—until Osman Pasha Skopljak, who was also a servant of Istanbul, but one who was enterprising, stubborn, crafty, cruel, and with a distinct personality of his own. In the struggle with Montenegro he upheld not only the privileges of the feudal landlords and of Istanbul, but also the right of the faithful to lord it over infidels.

The Vizir of Mostar, Ali Pasha Rizvanbegović, was not a servant of Istanbul, but a powerful and deeply rooted aristocrat whose personal interests happened to coincide with those of the central government during the Gradaščević Rebellion. Istanbul regarded his behavior during that critical moment as proof of his fidelity, while he thereby asserted his separateness from Bosnia. That separation was to remain to the end, and both the one side and the other were aware of it, despite the compromises they made. However, it was not until their differences began to come out into the open that Bishop Rade was able to enter their play. Until then he was to have a harder time with Ali Pasha than with the Pasha of Scutari. Ali Pasha cared little about defending the faith, and the empire even less; he was rather more concerned about defending the power of the beys, but what concerned him most of all was his vizirate over Hercegovina.

Just as the Vizir of Mostar began to tussle with Istanbul and to show the smiling side of his face to Bishop Rade, the implacable Osman Pasha came on the scene in Scutari. If the Bishop did not get a true friend in Ali Pasha, he certainly found an irreconcilable enemy in Osman Pasha.

On his way from Russia by way of Vienna, Bishop Rade had agreed, certainly with prompting by the Russians, to meet with the Turkish envoy Ferik Ahmet Pasha. Something of the kind had heretofore been quite unthinkable for the Montenegrin mentality and his own. One could negotiate with the Turks only about how both sides would survive between two battles in the unceasing mortal struggle. Now, for various reasons and purposes, both sides were looking for a way to give the world at large the impression that they cared for peace. The results of the talks between the Bishop and Ferik Ahmet Pasha were without any significance. True, the Bishop was later able to throw these supposed negotiations in the faces of the neighboring pashas in his protests: Your Sultan is for peace, but you do not obey him. That was all.

In his conflict with Austria, Bishop Rade was faced with a modern European power with which one was at peace when there was no war. As a Great Power with a Slavic majority under an aristocratic German center, Austria was wont to look with suspicion and apprehension upon the growth of any new state in the Balkans, even a non-Slavic one, as long as it was not subservient to it. Still Austria tolerated it and even helped this growth when its interests dictated. Austria was neither the traditional nor the mortal enemy of Montenegro. Besides, the Bishop wished to form his state on the European model.

There was no love lost on Austria. But for Turkey there could be only hatred.

Toward Turkey Montenegro existed and took shape as an opposite world. Here there could be neither peace nor armistice.

6.

THERE WERE, and there remained, two principal unresolved questions in the relations with Ali Pasha: Grahovo and the Uskoks. There was much negotiating and correspondence over them, even three treaties, but mostly raids, battles, and sweet words. There was no real solution.

Grahovo was free in that it elected its own chieftains and sent its share of tribute money to Cetinje. It had not yet torn itself completely away from its feudal dependence, for it also still paid dues to the beys, albeit irregularly. As everywhere else, it was the hills that resisted most stubbornly. Rovinsky states, "One must also observe that the people of Grahovo, particularly those who settled the Plain of Grahovo, were not distinguished for their steadfastness or faithfulness, either toward their vojvoda or toward Montenegro, and consequently it was easy for the Turks to collect the tribute."

Bishop Rade could not renounce Grahovo, for that would have meant renouncing the further struggle, and even that which was his inheritance. He defended his rights before Gagić thus:

> Neither is Grahovo Turkish today, nor was it theirs over 100 years ago, but Montenegro's. . . . It is true that they used to pay the Turks something, but that came from certain lands and pastures which they held around the town of Klobuk. I never forbade them to do this, nor do I forbid them to pay it now. . . . There are also other Montenegrin clans now paying for Austrian lands here and there, but they do not thereby cease to be Montenegrin clans. . . . And the Montenegrins always judged them. . . . But what belongs to us, that we do not easily relinquish, just as no one else gives up what is his, for if we began to give in, then our small race would disappear among its many-numbered enemies.

His meeting in Vienna with the Turkish envoy had dealt chiefly with Grahovo. Immediately upon his return, he began negotiations with Ali Pasha. He also began building a fortress on Humac, which commanded the Plain of Grahovo. Gagić was angry over that fortress and appealed to the Russian Ambassador in Vienna, Tatishchev, in a complaint against the Bishop, "who spurns all my warnings and friendly advice, and governs with the passion of a native Montenegrin." Ali Pasha understood the Bishop well, else he would not have lied when he said that he could "not imagine the purpose of the Bishop's fortress at Grahovo."

Bishop Rade was not concerned about a piece of land, but about survival. He did not get a clear title to Grahovo, but neither did he lose it.

Something similar took place regarding the question of the Uskoks.

Refugees from Hercegovina who had settled along the upper Morača, the Uskoks constantly harassed the Turks with their raiding parties. Captain E. N. Kovalevsky, the Russian geologist and geographer who had come to Montenegro at the request of the Montenegrins to search for ores, especially for gold in the Zlatica River, on account of its name (*zlato* means *gold*), has left in his conscientiously written and lively book an impressive and moving description of the Morača, that is, of life under the constant tension of warfare. He observed that no bishop of Cetinje, certainly neither Petar nor Rade, had visited these people, who had spent ten or fifteen years fending off Turkish campaigns and in raiding, neither sufficiently strong to repulse the Turks nor willing to submit to them. This trembling between destruction and survival must have been all the more awful for the Uskoks inasmuch as they were refugees who maintained ties with their homeland by way of the hajduks and occupied lands the Turks regarded unconditionally as their own.

Ali Pasha's demands went beyond the prevention of Uskok raids. He required the Bishop to drive the Uskoks away from their newly built hearths. Ali Pasha knew that the Uskok lands would never be his as long as these were inhabited by such unruly people. But the Bishop also knew that they would sooner or later be his for the very same reason.

The Turks had every right to demand that the raids cease. But it was the Bishop's duty to defend and protect the Uskoks and his people.

Turkish rights and his duty were made even less reconcilable by this affair—as though they could ever be reconciled!

7.

ALTHOUGH HE WAS not able every time to gauge his forces down to the last—a man of ideals cannot always do this—Bishop Rade was aware that he did not possess enough strength of his own to wage war on the Turks, even if the Russians should permit it. On the other hand, neither could he establish peace and stable borders with the surrounding pashas. The peace, which was settled at the behest of St. Petersburg and Istanbul, was broken by both sides before the signatures on the treaties were dry. Actually there was no war in the usual sense anyway, but a state of rebellion—the reckoning between two viewpoints, two ways of life.

In any event, no peace treaty was ever to be concluded with Scutari. The first peace treaty with Hercegovina was concluded at Cetinje on October 20, 1838, and then largely owing to the efforts of the Vizir of Travnik, Vegi Mehmed Pasha, who came forward in the name of the Porte and sent his men to the Bishop and to Ali Pasha. The treaty confirmed the existing state of affairs, with the addition of solemn pledges by both sides to keep the peace. The refugees from Grahovo were amnestied and allowed to return to their homes, on condition that they paid imposts as before. "At the same time eternal peace is hereby concluded between the independent territory of Montenegro on the one hand and the Pashalik of Bosnia and Hercegovina on the other, that is, beginning with the top of Kom Kučki to Dragalji." Even if what the people of Grahovo were supposed to pay was not in dispute, the border itself was not defined clearly—merely from Kom to Dragalji, without any specifics!

The paper and the words were, and remained, without significance. What was significant was that the Turks had to negotiate and to conclude a treaty with "the independent territory of Montenegro"—the first time these words were uttered in Turkish-Montenegrin relations.

No one observed the peace treaty. Still the Porte was obviously dissatisfied, believing that too much had been given to Montenegro.

It was not more than two months before Ali Pasha grossly violated the treaty.

The Bishop's confidant Radovan Piper, the Vojvoda of Grahovo, Jakov Daković, priest Šćepan Kovačević, and three men of Grahovo had been sent to the Vizir in Travnik. Not suspecting anything, Radovan Piper induced the chiefs of Grahovo to strike out by way of Mostar on the way back. The Pasha detained the chiefs and cast them in irons.

Ali Pasha's act was all the more grave in that the chiefs were going openly from one vizir into the recently pacified territory of another. The Pasha kept them in a dungeon from December, 1838, until April, 1839, when they were released as the result of numerous interventions and complaints, probably from Istanbul. Several men of Grahovo who risked a raid to liberate their Vojvoda were impaled on stakes.

Thus was the treaty violated.

They say that Vojvoda Jakov commented at the time, "My head may come to Mostar once again, but my foot never." Yet uncertainty is the only certain thing in a warrior's life. Vojvoda Jakov soon had to go to Mostar again, to beg the Pasha for the hostages who had taken his place in prison. Later, when Jakov and priest Šćepan visited the Bishop, he advised them not to provoke clashes, but he added, "From now on we shall act differently with the Turks."

So it was, despite the later friendship with Ali Pasha.

Relations grew even more tangled under ever-increasing tension and more and more raids. Ali Pasha "breathed evil"—this is what Njegoš felt about him as he paid him twenty ducats for every Uskok head exhibited in the serai of Mostar, while Bishop Rade in turn held up his own end by presenting silver-inlaid pistols to the Montenegrins and the Hercegovinians for Turkish heads placed on stakes on the Tablja.

These relations persisted until 1842, when "the savage and deceitful vizir"—as Bishop Rade described him—was forced for reasons of his own to seek support where he least expected it—in Montenegro—while Njegoš found a friend where he least wanted one—in Ali Pasha.

Everyone was to remain what he was.

It would seem that the essentials of human and social existence can only be destroyed, but not transformed—for in being transformed they in fact cease being what they were.

There is a saying, "The winter is so cold that the cat and mouse are sleeping together."

Worlds not only destroy one another, they also coexist.

8.

THE FRIENDSHIP BETWEEN the Bishop and Ali Pasha was brought on by a notable event. It strained relations between them to the point of war, yet it also caused them to draw closer together in the hope of surviving side by side.

In addition to Ali Pasha there were two other distinguished Turkish governors in Hercegovina: Hasan Beg Resulbegović, in Trebinje, and Smaïl Aga Čengić, in Gacko. While Hasan Beg was known for his cleverness, Smaïl Aga was renowned for his daring and his heroism.

Smaïl Aga was of a powerful family, but one apparently not noble before they adopted Islam. According to some, the Čengići were real Turks, but it is more probable that they were of Slavic blood. Smaïl Aga so distinguished himself in the Sultan's wars and in the suppression of peasant and landlord mutinies that the Sultan appointed him his *kapidjibasha,* and as *muselim* he had under his jurisdiction Gacko and Taslica (present-day Kolašin, and Plevlje), a region larger than the Montenegro of that time. His ties and influence reached Istanbul. He also carried on correspondence with Prince Miloš, largely through Jovan Mićić, a leader in Užice with whom he had family ties. His daughter was married to Osman Pasha Skopljak, who as Vizir of Scutari gave so much trouble to Bishop Rade. Bishop Rade wrote concerning Smaïl Aga, "This notable person was greater and meant more in these parts than any of the vizirs."

All the tales told about Smaïl Aga seem to confirm that he was not hard on the raia, at least not as hard as the rest, though he never gave in to them either. Many anecdotes have been recorded about him; some have never been set down in writing but have been transmitted down to our day.

He excited the popular imagination even during his lifetime, because he knew how to treat his serfs with a gentlemanly cordiality. Between conflicts he was friendly with Šujo Karadžić, the renowned rebel of the Drobnjaci, who eventually got to Karadjordje's Serbia. This Šujo used to shut himself up with his kin in a cave above his house and from there make war and peace with the Turks. They say Smaïl Aga rather feared the Black Dog—as he called Šujo, half endearingly, because of his dark complexion. And indeed, Šujo came close to killing him several times. Once the two of them were riding alone—the Aga ahead and Šujo behind him. Šujo was overcome by his old urge; he unslung his rifle and pointed it at the Aga's back. But the gun misfired. The Aga heard the familiar click of the cock, but before he could turn around, the hajduk had slung his rifle over his shoulder.

"You wished to kill me just now, you Black Dog, but your rifle didn't fire," said Smaïl Aga.

But Šujo swore it was not so, "God forbid such a thought," he protested. "I was playing with my buckle and it just seemed like it to you."

Smaïl Aga was a personality born out of an epic milieu, but one opposite the Montenegrin.

Living in a turbulent time, from battle to battle, he placed his hope in force and fortune. His manor, in the midst of fields and meadows, would have reflected more the rich and powerful landlord than the bellicose war lord were it not for the tower beside it. With no splendor or lordliness, the manor seemed to have just recently sprung up out of an epic peasant simplicity. Smaïl Aga was still involved with small farmers, holding them in his grasp, and yet intervening in their troubles with an inherited and familiar justice. In his time the relationship between lord and serf, though intolerable, had something natural about it. The next generation was to be quite different. Ded Aga was lordly arrogance, while Rustem Beg was a bully who made life miserable for his raia by pestering his women serfs and trampling upon their honor.

The idea of killing Smaïl Aga cropped up in various places. It was inspired by both the personality of Smaïl Aga and his role in Hercegovina toward Montenegro. It seems, however, that the idea came to mind first and most forcefully to Bishop Rade and to Vojvoda Jakov Daković; those fallen Petrovići and the troubles of the people of Grahovo must have provided a good leavening for it. Jakov's son, Vojvoda Anto, tells in his memoirs that, after the disaster of the Montenegrins and the Petrovići at Grahovo in 1836, Bishop Rade had sent his brother-in-law, Andrija Pejović, with fifty of the Cuce clan to order Jakov, and to help him murder Hasan Beg, Smaïl Aga, or Muy Aga Mušović, Captain of Nikšić, who was then collecting the tribute in Grahovo. The Bishop had given orders, says Anto, to kill Jakov if he failed to obey, for the Bishop blamed Jakov for the disaster. Jakov was caught in a quandary: he had just made peace with the Turks, and if he killed any Turks now, two thousand souls in Grahovo would suffer; if he did not, the Montenegrins would kill him. He had ostensibly agreed, but later he made the excuse that neither Hasan Beg nor Smaïl Aga ever entered Grahovo. That did not mean that Jakov was against the murder of Smaïl Aga. He did not want to do it at the wrong time and in his Grahovo. The grapevine had it that it was actually Jakov who suggested the murder of Smaïl Aga as the only revenge worthy of the Petrovići.

Four years flowed by, but no opportunity presented itself to strike a heavy blow at the Turks and to avenge the Petrovići. Not until 1840.

A part of the Drobnjaci, headed by Novica Cerović, rebelled and refused to pay the tribute. One could with certainty expect Smaïl Aga to come to Drobnjak to quell the raia.

New faces joined the plot, but the chief person remained Novica Cerović, already known as a rebel from a very ancient and leading Drobnjak brotherhood. The Turks had killed his father, the priest Milutin, by violating a safe-conduct at Taslica. Priest Milutin had been blood brother to Stanko Stijepov Petrović, who had played such a prominent part in the installation of the young Rade as bishop. And when Stevan Perkov and Pero Tomov, the Bishop's brother, went to the Morača to establish a court, a seat of authority, they became acquainted with Novica, who happened to be there by chance, and put their heads together. The ties between Cetinje and the Drobnjaci went all the way back to Bishop Petar —somewhat the same as with Grahovo. Novica told Vrčević that Bishop Rade had written to him personally to kill Smaïl Aga.

It was hard for a distinguished personality to exist in those days. But the personality counted for more because the Turks did not have a developed political mechanism. To kill Smaïl Aga would be like winning a great battle.

A family's desire for revenge, reasons of state, and the discontent of the raia all became tangled in a single knot.

The fruit was ripe for the picking.

9.

THOUGH SMAÏL AGA was eager to pacify the Drobnjaci, he was not alarmed. This was hardly the first time serfs had rebelled against the size of the tribute, nothing new either to the Aga or to the Drobnjaci. Consequently Smaïl Aga did not muster a larger army. He was escorted by some hundred or so horsemen and foot soldiers, and was joined by as many Turks from Nikšić under Büyükbasha Ahmet Bauk. Ahmet was a notorious tyrant. It was said: "Where Bauk goes, there are woes." He did not leave in peace even the women of his own religion; he was finally killed by a Moslem wedding party when he attacked the bride.

Smaïl Aga encountered no resistance whatever in the villages. The peasants and elders came out to meet him, complained about the taxes, and feted him and his company. They promised to pay the tribute, and some even brought it. Šujo Karadžić came to meet the Aga along the way and remained with him the whole time, to be at his side and to serve him. Novica Cerović was the only one among the more notable Drobnjaci not to come before the Aga. He was the ringleader of the mutiny. He would not humble himself in his Tušina, which neighbored on the already free Upper Morača and the Uskoks.

On September 22, 1840, Smaïl Aga came to Mljetičak, a little plateau on the way to Jezeri, beneath Mount Durmitor, from which one had an unobstructed view of the looming heights of the Morača and the green hills of Lola and Krnovo. Smaïl Aga apparently enjoyed the beautiful sight, and he made camp there. Beneath him spread the humbled Drobnjaci and farther up the valley lay defiant Tušina. To proclaim his presence in the heights, he shot two or three rounds from a cannon he was taking with him for appearances, and in case he should encounter any resistance from a tower.

According to the accounts, Šujo Karadžić was with him, along with some kin and lads from the Drobnjaci who were attending the Turks. One of the Turks, or one of those lads, entered the nearest house to ask for some sour milk for the Aga. In that very house lived a kinswoman of Novica's who had married there. When she was reproached for not adding fresh cream to the milk, she replied angrily, "Let the Aga wait until tomorrow, and he'll get plenty!"

No one paid particular attention to the woman's words. And so Smaïl Aga spent the night there.

It was as though Smaïl Aga suspected that his head was in peril. The story has come down, and has been set down in writing, that the priest Golović actually told him so, but that Smaïl Aga had him beaten for it, charging him with lying, as he had done the year before and caused the Aga to turn back. Despite the beating, the priest continued to walk alongside the Aga's horse. When the Aga expressed angry surprise at this, he replied, "Mother beats, mother pets." The account tells of Šujo, on the other hand, that he sat with the Aga in his tent long into the night. He was a good bard, and Smaïl Aga liked the gusle and epic poems—even the ones in which the Serbs were victorious—and so he asked Šujo to chant him some. But that night he was in a bad humor, and when Šujo began to chant a poem in which the Serbs won—for he either knew no other or did not care to chant it—the Aga cut him short, saying, "What's the use, when you don't know any in which the Turks win." They also say that he reassured Bauk, who was apprehensive about an Uskok raid, by saying, "I myself can take on a hundred of them, and you another hundred."

The Aga was obviously taking courage in order to dispel his dark suspicions. Here he had traversed all Drobnjak and had come within sight of the Uskoks, and not a sign of Novica. He had no choice but to go back in shame or strike at Tušina with what forces he had.

According to the plan, Novica was to muster as much of an army as he could and strike at the Aga at night by surprise, while Šujo was to draw him on. It seems that the old hajduk Šujo did his work well. Šujo's very presence pacified the Aga and his retinue. Meanwhile Šujo's lads did a good job of hobbling the horses, especially the Aga's, to render them useless in an attack. However, Novica had trouble in assembling a force. The Drobnjaci were afraid. Besides, he had to work secretly. He got together a few Moračani and Uskoks, a few kinsmen and other Drobnjaci—only three hundred rifles in all. This motley company was late in forming, and day was already dawning by the time they reached Mljetičak, a small wood next to Smaïl Aga's camp. There was even talk of their turning back, but Novica was adamant—come what may. Decisions were hard for him, but once he decided, he never turned back.

The morning mist helped the attackers to surprise Smaïl Aga's camp with their firing. Smaïl Aga was already up and drinking his coffee. He cried out and rushed from his tent. Confusion overtook the camp. "My horse!" the Aga shouted. But the horses were not on hand, and besides, they were hobbled. Misfortunes never come singly. At that moment a bullet struck the Aga mortally. As soon as they saw the Aga fall, his confused retinue took to their heels down the slope from which they had come. The encouraged attackers would not let them go, but kept hunting them down the whole day long. Bauk got away with his men and reached the road to Nikšić. About forty Turks lost their lives. Mirko Aleksić was the first to get to the Aga, and he cut off his head.

In Cetinje Bishop Rade received the tidings of Smaïl Aga's death from the monk Makarije, known as Šumadinac. He had wandered into Montenegro from somewhere in Serbia and was serving at the time in Bijela Monastery, in Drobnjak. They say that the Bishop went out to the rim of the Plain of Cetinje to welcome Novica and his company. On receiving the proffered head of Smaïl Aga—washed and combed, as was the custom—he threw it into the air like an apple, and as he caught it he cried, "So you, too, have come my way, poor Smaïl!"

It was a handsome head. Smaïl Aga had been of medium height, but of powerful frame, dark-haired and with a large head adorned with the thick graying mustache of a man of fifty.

This time the Tablja was richly and notably bedecked.

A priest's wife, fearing that something might happen to her son in Gacko, dug up Smaïl Aga's body, stuffed it into a sack, and brought the load to his kin.

The initial Turkish reaction was wild fury. The Turks waylaid that unfortunate messenger-monk on his way back from Cetinje to Krnovo and cut him to pieces at Oštra Kosa. Smaïl Aga's brother, Ali Aga, the elder of Taslica, cut down a traveler from Serbia and six Drobnjaci who were passing by.

Ali Pasha soon sent an army on its way to punish the Drobnjaci. It devastated and razed villages and killed some seventy Drobnjaci. The Bjelopavlići, who came to their aid, suffered no better fate. Support from Old Montenegro was weak. Bishop Rade reckoned the Turkish losses at twice those of the Montenegrins, but that was probably an exaggeration. The defeated side generally takes comfort in the enemy's losses.

Smaïl Aga's death did not lead to the liberation of the Drobnjaci, but it did bring their most active part into a fight to the finish with the Turks. Smaïl Aga's death shattered the Turkish might. It was not in vain that Bishop Rade said, when the murder of Smaïl Aga's son Rustem Beg was proposed, "Hit the snake on the head, not on the tail!" The Bishop's influence rose in the unliberated regions.

As for Novica Cerović, who could not go back to the Drobnjaci, Bishop Rade made him a senator and his closest adviser. Next to Stevan Perkov and Mojsije Zečević, he was the most renowned and most interesting personality in the Bishop's entourage. The make-up of the Bishop's intimate circle of collaborators was not haphazard. Stevan came from the heart of free Montenegro, while Mojsije and Novica were from regions still fighting for their freedom. The Bishop granted Novica the title of ban—to him and him alone in Montenegro. He hit on the title from epic poetry or history and thus distinguished Novica from the other chieftains. The Bishop also built him a house in Cetinje. He took Novica along on trips and spent many an evening with this master teller of tales.

There was still another person who rejoiced, secretly, at Smaïl Aga's death—Ali Pasha, in Mostar. Along with Resulbegović, Smaïl Aga had been Ali Pasha's most serious competitor, all the more dangerous inasmuch as the Pasha had already begun to part ways with Istanbul and to take more account of himself than of the Porte's orders.

Novica Cerović used to tell that Resulbegović and Smaïl Aga wrote to Prince Miloš asking him to intervene with the Sultan against Ali Pasha, but whether intentionally or by error, and most probably through an intentional error, Miloš sent their letter to Ali Pasha, while he sent them the one he addressed to the Pasha. Novica related that the headstrong Smaïl Aga once said to him, "If it were not for that Pasha of Stolac, I would reach Cetinje from one evening to the next and beard that monk of yours."

There is rather more reliable proof that Ali Pasha could hardly wait for Smaïl Aga's death, if indeed he had not been implicated in it. He avenged Smaïl Aga's death only on the Drobnjaci, whom, as the Sultan's raia, he had to pacify in any event. In his later relations with Bishop Rade, which became lively and intimate, he never reproached him for Smaïl Aga's death. Moreover, by October 26 of the same year—a month after Smaïl Aga's death—a treaty was concluded between Ali Pasha and Bishop Rade. The treaty was not kept—no more than the rest, for that matter. Yet it was at that very time that it had been concluded.

Smaïl Aga's death embittered both Gagić and the Russians, as well as the Porte and foreigners, who wrote much that was not so, but who unerringly perceived that all the signs pointed to Cetinje. A veritable furor ensued. Bishop Rade had anticipated something of the sort and, in informing Gagić of the event on October 4, he not only passed over his own part in silence, but he also intimated that Smaïl Aga had been gathering an army to strike at the Morača. "I bring this to your attention lest anyone else tell your Ministry something else," the Bishop added.

However, neither the Russians nor the Turks were able to undertake any serious action.

Bishop Rade could rest easy, at least for the moment—as an avenged kinsman, as a Serb, and as a ruler.

10.

THE DEATH OF Smaïl Aga provided the theme for a famous poem by the Croatian poet Ivan Mažuranić. His characters and their roles are different, and he has his geography confused. But, of course, that is without importance. The poem, with all its variety and harmony, merely makes use of Montenegro as a motif.

Despite this, in the last quarter of the nineteenth century there was a controversy over who its author was—Mažuranić or Njegoš.

It all started with Nenadović. In his *Letters from Italy* he reported that on two occasions Njegoš recited the lines "The eagle makes his nest . . ." and "One can see on him . . ." both of which are in Mažuranić's *Death of Smaïl Aga Čengić*. Njegoš also told him that he had written a poem about Čengić, but that someone had run off with it, and he had no copy. Nenadović had a way of embroidering truths, or, rather, he did not wish to look at their bad and ugly side. It was not that he told untruths. Unfortunately, he had taken notes on his meeting with Njegoš in 1851 in Italy, and wrote them up in his *Letters from Italy* some fifteen years later. His report was seized upon by a penetrating logician—Ljubomir Nedić—for such are the kind that make the most trouble when they set out to prove something senseless. A literary dispute soon turned into an ardent and even more senseless Serbo-Croatian row.

It cannot be doubted that Mažuranić is the author of *Death of Smaïl Aga Čengić*. Sensible people have always maintained this.

Yet there is no serious reason to doubt Nenadović. It is possible that Njegoš, too, had written a poem about the death of Smaïl Aga. The verses by Mažuranić that Njegoš reportedly recited resemble those in epic poetry, and users of the folk ten-syllable line, among whom was Njegoš, memorize them easily. Mažuranić's poem had been published three years before Nenadović's meeting with Njegoš. Since Njegoš received everything of importance published in our lands, it is very likely that he was familiar with Mažuranić's work. There is even some very reliable testimony concerning this: Novica Cerović recounted that Bishop Rade once told him that someone had put him in a poem about the death of Smaïl Aga and made him out to be a renegade Turk—which jibes with Mažuranić's poem. Novica was not much offended at this: "Let them write whatever they please, the truth is known."

There is no trace in Njegoš's poetry of this event, which was so important to him and to his rule. All that has survived are some accounts and notes about Novica Cerović, but these are hardly of the same value as Njegoš's poetry and ethics.

Novica was to encounter Smaïl Aga once again. It was during the War of 1876. The Montenegrins had occupied Gacko, and Prince Nikola and his suite, which included Novica, found themselves at Smaïl Aga's grave. The Czech journalist Josef Holeček described the scene, with rather less Slavophile embellishment than he was wont to do. They had the inscription on the Aga's marker interpreted for them. When they heard the part in which the mangy dog and son of a bitch Novica Cerović was cursed to the ninth generation, the chieftains wished to destroy the grave. But Novica would not permit it. "That was not written by Smaïl Aga," he explained, "but by his kin. Soon I, too, shall be in heaven and will find Smaïl Aga there, and he will come up to me, shake my hand, and say, 'I have waited for thee, murderer from the earthly vale, where I hated thee, but here I love thee.' "

Novica also left these words behind: "What is life? Struggle. When God gave me life, he made me a fighter. . . . Whatever is human has error, falsehood. . . . The beaten man is no longer my enemy." And Nenadović recorded Novica's reasoning: "If there were fewer of us heroes, and more wise men, we would have fared better at Kosovo." Marko Miljanov made a similar comment: "The hero leads the wise man's horse."

Novica lived long and told much. Unfortunately, little of it was left in writing. When he killed Smaïl Aga he was in his prime—just past thirty, young but mature. Of medium height, large head, and with a carelessly dangling mustache, the expression of a solicitous host, and a forehead wrinkled more with thought than care, he was neither boastful nor proud about killing Smaïl Aga, capturing Turkish citadels, or meting out justice to Montenegrins. He was merely carrying out tasks assigned to him, as other men plow, build houses, or do something else. Heroism and manliness, life and struggle, were all identical to him. He was no teller of tales, but poetic and wise sayings flowed unceasingly from him. He talked even in his sleep. They would have to wake him up for fear something unseemly might slip from such a man.

The killing of Smaïl Aga was a bold act which personal passions and dark interests cannot overshadow. It was one of those events that become turning points and set off whole chains of occurrences. By it Bishop Rade risked a Turkish invasion and loss of Russian support, while Novica risked death and the destruction of his clan. Such decisions require great moral strength—the kind that springs from a passionate idea turned into a living fire.

The people felt instinctively the significance of that event, preserved it in the depths of their memory, and rewarded its participants according to their merits: the Bishop's wise decision, Aleksić's naked courage, Novica's risking all save honor on the cast of a die.

Everything human is fleeting. But it is also indestructible—being transmitted to new generations in a different form.

Wisdom does not die, even when it goes unrecorded.

11.

THE KILLING OF Smaïl Aga gave courage to the raia near and far and sealed the friendship between Ali Pasha and Bishop Rade. In spite of subsequent quarrels and fierce raids, as was normal between Turks and Montenegrins, the two men expressed a constant desire for co-operation.

In Bosnia the antireform movement revived, secretly aided by Ali Pasha, who felt threatened in his almost independent pashalik.

Bishop Rade intervened in a discreet and deft manner in these Turkish affairs. The ceaseless and just struggle for freedom was also fated to become part of this sinister play for power and domination.

Raids by the bands of both sides did not cease. Neither did the negotiations between the Bishop and Ali Pasha. In the spring of 1841 a meeting of the chieftains of Hercegovina and Montenegro took place; however, no treaty was concluded. That same year the Porte's commissioner Selim Bey arrived; his task was to establish the border with Dalmatia, but, in consultation with Gagić, he took it upon himself to mediate between the Bishop and Ali Pasha. The Bishop made a trip to Dubrovnik. He reached an agreement with Selim Bey, but Ali Pasha would not accept it.

And so it continued until the summer of 1842.

Since 1835 the people of Grahovo had generally been at peace with the Turks. But relations grew tense again. Gagić informed the Bishop that the Vizir was raising an army against Grahovo. The Bishop went to Grahovo. On July 12 the leaders of both sides met and concluded an armistice until September 23. However, the problems were insoluble. An unequal struggle was in the offing. Both sides made preparations even as they negotiated. It was the Pasha who finally proposed to the Bishop that the two of them meet. The Bishop accepted and underscored his wish "to confirm our personal friendship."

The Pasha's kinsman Hadji Ali Bey worked especially zealously to have that meeting take place. He wrote to the Bishop, "If dear God so order and judge . . . we shall establish a firm peace and trust so that the wretched poor will not suffer." Ali Pasha also wrote, affixing thereto a black seal, "I am content with what God has apportioned unto me, his servant Ali." Here was talk of the poor and appeals to God's mercy, and, behind it all, concern over one's power and rule. Ali Pasha was also worried about his prestige; he had to make sure beforehand of the success of the meeting, "to keep the Turks and Germans from scoffing."

Ali was determined to press for an agreement.

The Bishop was able to sense a new undercurrent among the leading Islamic families. Even before the negotiations with Ali Pasha, Mehmed Spahi Lekić, magistrate in Podgorica and a leading enemy of the Montenegrins, desired a relaxation of tension with Montenegro and sent the Bishop confidants who told him what could not be set down in writing, that Ali Pasha was in the same predicament. Could not something serious come of that secret resistance to Istanbul by the Pasha?

Bishop Rade, who also guarded his own prestige, would not agree to have the meeting at Metković, on the grounds that his way was "blocked . . . nor can I find a suitable vessel to take me there."

Nevertheless, in this play for prestige, the Pasha proved to be the more experienced. The Bishop arrived in Dubrovnik on August 31, 1842. He liked to visit "that most beautiful city," even though he regarded it as "everybody's flunky." This time he had to wait for the Pasha, who pleaded ill-health and bad weather and did not arrive till September 8.

In view of the fact that the negotiations were taking place on their territory, the Austrian authorities advanced the condition that their representatives attend the discussion. Gagić also joined in, on the pretext of having come to greet Ali Pasha. The Russian Popov happened to be in Dubrovnik at the time. After the meeting he continued on his way to Montenegro with the Bishop. In his book he recorded interesting and reliable details about that trip, including the meeting in Dubrovnik. There are other reports as well. Professor Kolendić has extracted some quite vivid and important details from the archives of Dubrovnik.

The Bishop and the Vizir had met to outmaneuver and outsmart one another. They parted as friends and remained such.

There are no worlds between which politics, that is, the struggle for life, is not capable of destroying bridges—or of building them.

12.

Both the Bishop and the Vizir were eager to vaunt their power and distinctions before one another, as well as before the Austrians. They lent all the more importance to the external splendor of their meeting insofar as both suspected that nothing substantially new would come of the treaty.

The Bishop brought along his cousin Djordjije, Secretary Milaković, Joko Petrović, Novica Cerović, the octogenarian priest

Ivo Radović—a worthy of Bishop Petar's time—four more chieftains, and Filip Vuković—an unknown who is mentioned as being his adjutant. The Bishop's retinue was dressed and armed as impressively as possible. The suite of "His Majesty," as the Vizir's subordinates addressed him, numbered thirty ghavazes, fifty Albanians, and numerous officials. Hasan Beg Resulbegović, Kadi of Mostar and commander of Nikšić, joined them with his own retinue and guards.

The Vizir's splendor won the day, even had it not been for an incident that laid bare to the skin all of Montenegrin primitiveness and poverty. As Professor Kolendić tells it, on the basis of the archives of Dubrovnik, many Turks and Montenegrins stood, as a kind of guard of honor, before the building in which the Vizir and the Bishop were conducting their parley. At one point the Vizir emerged and began to broadcast coins by the fistful. The Montenegrin chieftains rushed into the melee to scramble for the aspers. In that one moment they toppled over the whole dignity of government the Bishop had taken such pains to create, and the very men who should have represented it brought it to derision.

The Vizir was in ceremonial dress and wore a medal of diamonds. A stout man, he would have moved about with difficulty even had he not been lame. He was already past sixty, but he looked older—racked as he was by aching bones and dissipated by pleasures. By his youthful suppleness, tall stature, and good looks, the Bishop was his very opposite. While the Vizir's conspicuous wealth aroused wonder, all admired the handsomeness and inborn dignity of the Montenegrin Bishop, who moved with ease and whose head, capped by a small fez encircled by a white band, shone with a transcendent beauty.

Everything proceeded decorously and without any difficulties.

The conversations began on September 9 and lasted three days. Djordjije and Resulbegović held meetings separately as well, as did the Vizir and the Bishop. They even became blood brothers in a moment of high emotion. Vrčević's version is that the Vizir, fond of plum brandy, was tipsy, and the Bishop could not spurn his proposal that they become blood brothers. That is probably what happened, for they never addressed each other as blood brothers after that in their letters, despite their friendliness and cordiality.

The treaty they signed does not confirm this intimacy. The chief questions—Grahovo and the Uskoks—remained unresolved. It affirmed the desire of both parties for peace and their determination to suppress plundering bands and to pursue the guilty by establishing border guards. Nothing more.

But what had Ali Pasha and the Bishop agreed upon beyond the treaty? That they made a firm compact with one another may be seen from one of the Bishop's letters soon after: "And know that whosoever shall be a transgressor against thee and the enemy of thy land, we shall be his foes even as thou art. Let all the world see that men met in Dubrovnik who do not value their heads above their honestly given word. And know truly that after our meeting in Dubrovnik, thou hast no greater friend than myself, either Turk or Christian."

There was nothing haphazard about Bishop Rade. He was not lavish with words, for they always carried weight with him. Something really significant must have transpired between himself and Ali Pasha in Dubrovnik. Between Montenegro and Hercegovina feuds continued to crop up. After all, they were Turks and Montenegrins. In a land where plundering and killing were a passion and a profession, that vice could not be curtailed at once. Montenegrin hajduks came in search of loot all the way to Belgrade and Sarajevo, while the Kuči went as far as Plovdiv, let alone into the neighboring region. Nevertheless such raids no longer created quarrels between Bishop Rade and Ali Pasha or set armies on the march.

Bishop Rade knew that he would have trouble with the Montenegrins if he forbade them their raids into Hercegovina. Raiding parties, which engaged also in sheep rustling, were a branch of the local economy, and one of the most profitable at that. However, he took determined action in this matter. Immediately following the meeting at Dubrovnik he issued a proclamation to the Montenegrins in which he informed them of the newly established amity and sternly warned them: "Know ye well that whosoever does any mischief at the border of the Vizir of Hercegovina is committing a deed against me and that there is no place for such a one in my land."

In his efforts to regulate relations with Ali Pasha, the Bishop concluded a new treaty with him on October 28, 1843, which was signed by Milaković, as the Bishop's plenipotentiary, and Osman Aga, of Zvornik, as the Vizir's plenipotentiary. This treaty was rather more concrete in that it specified in detail to whom the people of Grahovo were to pay tribute and how much. The Montenegrins agreed to raze their fortress at Humac, but the Vizir was to pay eight thousand ducats—a sum that was obviously too large —as compensation for what it had cost. Border guards were agreed upon. Medaković cites that the Vizir even agreed to help pay for the Montenegrin guards, at two thousand ducats per year. It seems that he actually paid out that sum the first year, though it is hardly likely that it was spent for this purpose, since it is not even known whether these guards actually existed.

This treaty, too, was preceded by an event similar to the killing of Smaïl Aga.

Blood and gold sealed the friendship between Ali Pasha and Bishop Rade.

How can it be otherwise when good and evil make common cause?

13.

IMMEDIATELY AFTER THE meeting in Dubrovnik, the Bishop and the Vizir began a series of consultations through their confidants, without any written confirmation. The letters do not give any clear picture of what went on. However, it was obvious that the two men were dreaming up something that only they and their confidants knew anything about. The Bishop wrote a reply to the Vizir, on April 17, 1843, stating that he agreed to a meeting between them on Saint Peter's Day, and added, "I, too, cannot and will not be at the second, be sure of this, as I have written thee before and have said in oral messages through my messengers."

Information is lacking. I would say that these secret communications between Ali Pasha and Bishop Rade had begun even before the meeting in Dubrovnik. Moreover, it would seem that Smaïl Aga's death confirmed rather than inaugurated their relations.

The negotiations over a proposed meeting between Ali Pasha and the Bishop and the exchange of confidants continued—Radovan Piper for the Bishop, and Mustai Bey Hajrović for the

Vizir. In his letter of June 11, 1843, the Bishop mentioned their secret "dealings" and insisted on their earliest completion. He stated that he had had a long talk about this with Hajro—this is how he called Mustai Bey—and added that the Vizir did not have to take the trouble to come to a meeting since everything could be settled without him, as Hajro would tell him. Soon after that the Bishop called for a meeting on Saint Elijah's Day and advised the Vizir to "Tell those men whom thou hast named in thy letter to come to Nikšić and to me in Ostrog the same day that I shall arrive in Ostrog, so that we do not wait for one another and that we might settle this matter."

Those men were chieftains from Hercegovina.

They arrived in Nikšić at the appointed time. Among them were the Vizir's son, Mustai Bey, and Hasan Beg Resulbegović. But the Vizir's son became ill before their departure for Ostrog, and Resulbegović, who apparently suspected foul play, refused to go.

The accounts and the documents do not quite agree on the number of chieftains who went to the meeting, or on the course of events. The Englishman John Gardner Wilkinson, who was there a year later, reported that there were twenty-two Turks, while Lazar Tomanović reported that there were nine. Possibly the discrepancy arose because Wilkinson also counted the servants, which Tomanović might have ignored, since the Montenegrins would have remembered only the chieftains and their fate. Bishop Rade reported in a letter to Gagić that the Turks bickered with him five days before setting out from Nikšić to Ostrog. He stated that he did not wish to receive them or to meet with them. But why, then, had he asked them and waited so long for them? All this would confirm the version, which I heard from my father, that they arrived in Ostrog, in front of the house where Bishop Rade was staying, and that the latter put his head out the window when the Turks greeted him in God's name, and replied, "God be with your coming, and God be with your going." Vrčević has recorded that when his guards asked him what they should do about the newly arrived Turks, the Bishop replied, "Beat the turds!"

It is certain that the chieftains of Hercegovina returned from Ostrog without having spoken a word with the Bishop. At Bašine Vode a Montenegrin ambush killed nine of them, according to

Wilkinson, and according to Tomanović six. Among them was Ali Pasha's confidant Hajrović—either by mistake or as an inconvenient witness. The killed included mainly men from Stolac and Nikšić, who were known as having scant respect for Ali Pasha. According to the accounts it would seem that the Turks came across a second ambush party, which they deceived by their cries that Montenegro and Hercegovina had united. It is remembered that when he heard of the killing, Resulbegović said, "Wise is the Mother that bore me, f— her mother!"

The slaughter of the chieftains sent to the parley remains a fact. Yet it is also true that Ali Pasha and the Bishop never mentioned this slaughter in their correspondence, and soon after that they concluded a treaty. As for Stevan Djeknin, who led the ambush, not a hair of his head was harmed.

Nevertheless the Bishop and the Vizir set their armies on the march. Bishop Rade even told Gagić of battles that in fact never took place. In the supposed clash between fifteen thousand Moslems and forty-five hundred Montenegrins the losses were too insignificant to be of any account.

Popular tradition was reliable: it neither forgot nor forgave Bishop Rade for that.

That both Bishop and Vizir secretly knew of the plans to wipe out the chieftains of Hercegovina became clear as soon as the deed took place. Gagić protested bitterly to the Bishop, unable to accept his truly naïve excuse that the Montenegrins had killed the Turks in a rage on hearing that the latter had planned to murder their Sovereign.

Historians, both the nationalists and the dynasts, were glad to leave this event in darkness, while the foreign ones were horrified. Wilkinson even tells the story of a priest, Stevo, a refugee from Hercegovina. Ali Pasha allegedly wished to talk the priest into poisoning the Bishop. However, when the priest and the Pasha could not agree on the sum, the Pasha betrayed the priest to the Bishop, and the latter had him hanged. Whether true or not, and whether one agrees or disagrees in one's appraisal of the Bishop's deed, this story certainly shows in what dark and tangled circumstances the Montenegrin Sovereign had to act.

Glad at every Turkish misfortune, he could only rejoice that history was repeating itself in reverse: once upon a time it had been the Serbian magnates who exterminated one another with Turkish help and thus paved the way for the Osmanli, and now, in their decline, the latter were betraying one another into the hands of rebellious Christians.

Bishop Rade correctly saw Istanbul as the main enemy. There was no national feeling in Ali Pasha, but there was some sort of vague Hercegovinian feeling, though that of a feudal lord. This was not very much for Bishop Rade, who burned with the national idea, but he was not inclined to underestimate it either, from the standpoint of practical politics.

If his relations with Russia and Austria were an example of a refined and farsighted diplomacy, his relations with Ali Pasha confirm his perspicacity in practical politics.

Bishop Rade always regarded and called Ali Pasha a cruel tyrant. And with reason. The Vizir's ghavaz—the commander of his bodyguard—Ibro Pijulija, was a most infamous criminal. He raped, bludgeoned, and impaled, often out of a maniac passion, according to Vrčević, "willfully killing twice as many men, especially those who opposed his assaults on women and girls." The Vizir's Büyükbasha—the commander of the militia—Murat Borčanin, once was quartered in the house of the Gacko elder Rade Božović. The militiamen who were guests in the house went after the women. Rade and his son killed them and fled, for which the Vizir dispatched an army and forced the men of Grahovo to surrender the pair.

On the other hand, being in a weak position, the Bishop regarded Ali Pasha as a truly valuable and real ally. In vain were the Bishop's hopes that the Serb in Ali Pasha might awaken. But there was realism in his view of Ali Pasha as an increasingly dissatisfied feudal lord.

An indifference toward the means he chose came quite naturally to Ali Pasha. It arose from the nature of the thing he was fighting for—naked power and unlimited dominion. With his pure ideal and weak strength, Bishop Rade had to grasp at means not to his liking.

In Cetinje a new word was beginning to make the rounds—*politics*. The sagacious Stevan Perkov translated this unknown word into the language he understood—as *axle grease*.

14.

Bishop Rade remained true to Ali Pasha to the end. But while he was occupied with his army in Hercegovina, in the supposed conflict with Ali Pasha, the Vizir of Scutari, Osman Pasha, carried out a well-conceived assault on Montenegro from the other side. Did Ali Pasha, sly as he was, know about this? Be that as it may, he did withdraw his army when the Bishop was forced to send his to the other side—and thus kept faith with his blood brother.

The Vizir of Scutari brought over his army by land and by water on the night of September 15–16, 1843, and attacked the island of Vranjina and Lesendro Rock, which rose out of the middle of the lake, blocking the exit at the Crnojevići River and commanding the exit from the Crmnica River.

Vranjina is a double-humped hill in Lake Scutari with a fishing village and a monastery—the see of a medieval metropolitanate. Lesendro, some fifty yards wide and a hundred or so yards long, is near Vranjina, with a fortress, which Osman Pasha later built —a warship anchored in the stagnant green water to prevent attacks from the streams surrounding the wide lake and their estuaries.

The army reached Vranjina by treading the shallows, while the little tower at Lesendro was attacked by boats armed with cannon and manned by a crew of twenty-six. Lesendro fell on September 17 and Vranjina on the 18th.

The Bishop described this attack to Gagić in detail and with incontestable accuracy.

He was obviously taken by surprise and at first was comforted that the Vizir's success would not endanger the fishing catch, inasmuch as most of the pockets where fish were caught lay either in the estuary of the Crnojević River or along the Crmnica shore.

The Bishop immediately had his army block the exits from Vranjina and Žabljak toward the Crnojević River and the Nahi of Lješani. However, the Turks had no intention of striking at Montenegro. For two whole months the Bishop maneuvered his troops in an attempt to drive the Turks from Vranjina and Lesendro. He had no ships; his only two cannon were old and the cannon balls were smaller than the bore of the cannon and could not reach the Turkish positions.

It was here that some English tourists, Mr. and Mrs. Charles Lamb, found Bishop Rade. Lamb left a graphic description of the Montenegrin Sovereign and the martial air that clung that November to the forbidding rock mountains and muddy gray water. Some forty Turkish tents were strewn over the heights of Vranjina—the leader's with a red banner. Turkish cannon were pounding away from the tower on Lesendro, breaking the murky calm of autumn sadness over the waters and the hills.

The Turks attempted a breakthrough at Dodoš, but, encountering stiff resistance, they dug in on the islands and began to fortify them.

Osman Pasha could truly be pleased. Had he waged war on Montenegro itself and reached Cetinje, this would have inflicted less damage—for he could not have long maintained himself in Cetinje, if for no reason other than his inability to assure a supply line in the midst of the embattled tribes, while the town itself had only a single well. By having seized Vranjina and Lesendro, he cut off the defiles into the Plain of Zeta and had Montenegro by the throat. The Turks could always claim that the islands were theirs anyway—there was as yet no set boundary—and that they had to occupy the islands to make themselves secure from Montenegrin attacks and piratic raids, which were numberless. They thus cut off Montenegro's trade with Scutari and Podgorica, which used the water route as the cheapest and most natural way. Without that trade—the sale of animals and fish and the purchase of salt—the Montenegrins could hardly survive.

Having closed Montenegro's windows, the Vizir simultaneously opened himself a door into it. He could exert daily pressure on the two neighboring Nahis—Crmnica and Lješani—by interfering with fishing, farming, and traffic, and by bribing the fearful and the weak-kneed, of whom there must have been a goodly number in the midst of a still-unknit nation which was divided into feuding clans and almost devoid of any state organization.

The Bishop was right in belittling the military significance of that venture: "They don't dare stick their noses out any farther, let alone penetrate deeper," he wrote Gagić on December 3 of the same year. The Bishop soon perceived that it was not Osman

Pasha's aim to march through Montenegro—the Porte would not have permitted it, because of relations with Russia—but to seize a vantage point from which he could throttle and poison Montenegro.

One bare hill and one rock could hardly have served this purpose better, and admittedly only a malicious man who had carefully sized up Montenegro's situation and potential was capable of choosing precisely them. Protected by water and fortified, out of danger, the Turks could sit there without concern and probe Montenegro at will, immune even from the reproaches of diplomats over their attacks, for the attacks were no longer necessary. The investiture of these islands made it possible for the Turks to play such a two-faced game, thanks to their interference in Montenegrin affairs through the Montenegrins themselves.

In many ways they overestimated their position, especially with regard to the moral resistance of the Montenegrins. Though they knew with reason that there would be Montenegrins who would succumb to their blandishments, not even they, conquerors with centuries of experience, could perceive that Montenegro was filled with men forged in the heat of battle, whose ethic no higher force or convenience could any longer pacify or compromise.

The Bishop informed Gagić, on November 19, 1843, that the Turks told some Montenegrin chieftains at a meeting that he—Bishop Rade—would gain a position similar to that held by Prince Miloš if he reached an agreement with the Porte and recognized its sovereignty. Any such idea was not only far from the Bishop's mind but incomprehensible to him. That which Prince Miloš had obtained through negotiation with the Turks was only a step toward independence. Even before that, in 1839, the Bishop wrote in a reply to Hasan Pasha, "That which thou dost write in this screeve, that I sit here thanks to the Sultan's pleasure, is most amusing for me to hear, for thou knowest well that I sit here at no one's pleasure but that of this people, which did never begrudge shedding their blood for their land." Serbia had become strong enough to make compromises. For Montenegro this meant ruin and going back to a vassal status. Its main strength was spiritual, and precisely for this reason it could, and had to, be irreconcilable.

The Turks ran into this irreconcilability of the Bishop and the Montenegrins from the start. Spurned, they then undertook the tried tactic of applying pressure and sowing dissension. Vranjina and Lesendro were transformed into Turkish fortresses in Montenegro to which disaffected clan leaders could turn for support.

A web was slowly spun about these islands by European diplomacy. In addition to the Russians and the Austrians, the English and the French also mixed in. They all reached an agreement concerning a commission in Scutari which would investigate the quarrel. Out of generous intentions and ignorance, the French mentioned that the Bishop ought to go to Istanbul. But Britain, ever solicitous to maintain a balance, supported the Turks—until Gladstone. Nothing came of the matter.

The Bishop soon sensed the danger and the weakness of his own position. He had scant hope of Russian intervention. He hurried off to Vienna, embarking on a ship at Kotor on January 2, 1844. Metternich received him cordially, even invited him to dinner. From Vienna the Bishop implored the Russian Tsar for help—and the latter did indeed concern himself. The Bishop turned to all sides, and everyone promised help—but in vain. He hastened back, again with one thought, to depend on his own forces. From Trieste he went off to Venice for four days, to order war matériel. In Dubrovnik he engaged shipbuilders. Austria put a stop to this. It also blocked the delivery of the munitions; Austria's good intentions did not include Montenegrin cannon.

As the Bishop's efforts proved more and more ineffective, his bitterness grew beyond measure. A saying remained among the people: "He burned like the Bishop over Lesendro." And truly he burned—and burned himself out.

Man's fate can revolve and crash over a rock as easily as over anything else.

15.

In Osman Pasha Bishop Rade found an opponent who inflamed all his passions and those of the Montenegrins and who strained their emotions to the breaking point.

That clash would transform the aspirations of Njegoš and of the Montenegrins into a spiritual cry. Njegoš's words would lose all immediate sense and meaning and would become, rather, a mystical lay of the martyred past of a people and its leader during a time of ultimate exertion to deliver themselves from a cruel and inhuman reality.

Feeling and thought merged into one, as did past and present. It was as though nothing remained but a painful spiritual continuum. It was misfortune, in the shape of Osman Pasha, which gave that final thrust that launched Bishop Rade into the starry heights. This was the blow that released the lightning pent up by daily cares. An Osmanli forged by a Turkish heritage and a bloody reality, imbued with the "savage strain and thirst for blood in the wicked Turk"—this was Osman Pasha. He was the incarnation of all the evil, that cosmic evil, which had come in the fullness of time to afflict our people and disrupt our history.

Bishop Rade tried all that he knew and was able to do in dealing with Osman Pasha, but to no avail. This relationship dragged on for a long time, for years, until 1849, and the Bishop's death.

It began as a military encounter, a political contest, and a game of wits, but after Lesendro it became a disease with the Montenegrins and Njegoš. It turned into a hatred that lost touch with the immediate reality and became the passionate impulse of men cursed with suffering and doomed to struggle for bare existence.

When nothing else helped, Njegoš tried to awaken the sense of nationalism in Osman Pasha. The Vizir did not deny that he was a Bosnian, a Serb, and replied to the Bishop, in December, 1844 (signing himself "in peace the peaceful Osman Mashar Pasha of Skopie"), "You write that we are birds of the same nest, and I know that we are of one blood, our sires and we, and I am very glad that we are friends and shall be all the more so inasmuch as we are of one blood, and so beforehand I am all the more glad."

That "one blood" was for Osman Pasha but a weapon in the political struggle, while for Bishop Rade it stood for the survival of an idea, a heritage, and a future.

With Ali Pasha Bishop Rade did not invoke their common national origin. Rather, they became friends out of political necessity. Nor did Ali Pasha show any sign of establishing or conducting his relations with the Montenegrin Sovereign on the basis of their common origin. He was the Islamic lord of Hercegovina—"my state"—mutual interests brought him closer with a neighbor, and that was that; let anyone think and feel as he pleased. With

Osman Pasha it was another matter. Cetinje and Scutari clashed in the realm of practical politics. Involved here was not simply the private dealings of a neighboring Montenegrin bishop and an Islamic lord, but behind Osman Pasha stood the Porte—the rule of a conqueror and the Islamic idea. Osman Pasha was not simply the master of a province. Such had been the Bushatis and even Ali Pasha. But he was the servant of his Sultan, the Caliph of Islam, even while being aware that he was of our blood and tongue. He was the instrument of an idea and a rule mortally opposed to the Bishop's idea and rule. Moreover, he served and governed in Albania, an alien region—against the people of his own blood and tongue.

What nationality and the national idea were for Njegoš, Islam and Istanbul's overlordship were for Osman Pasha. In vain did the Bishop cry out to him, "The Albanians are a quite different people though they are now under thy command, but thou art our kinsman, even though of a different religion. And thou canst be proud of the glorious freedom of the Montenegrins, if not in this savage spot then at least in the great and enlightened world, for they are of one blood and one race with thee." But Osman Pasha was deaf to this. What was nationality compared with religion, and Serbianism compared with service to Islam! If the Bishop was committed to his ideas through his family as well as his personal fate, so was Osman Pasha: his father, Suleiman Pasha, had quelled the uprisings of both lords and peasants, hanged the raia in batches among the Drobnjaks, and rose to be the commander of the Sultan's army against the greatest rebellion in the Balkans—Karadjordje's, in Serbia. One could also sense in Osman Pasha an intense personal hatred for the Montenegrins and the Bishop. He smarted at their murder of Smaïl Aga Čengić, the father of his wife.

Yet all this paled before the clash of ideas and the metamorphosis of worlds. Osman Pasha was to exclaim to the Bishop, in a moment when anger overcame his wile, "I am a Turk, and thou art a *giaour,* and we cannot agree." The Bishop had even heavier broadsides to hurl at him, from his own positions.

Between these worlds of absolute ideas it did not occur to the contenders to choose their weapons, as long as these served their end—the extermination of the other side.

In 1846 the Pasha enticed the Bishop to a meeting in a seductively honeyed manner: "I am older, I could be your father, we must make peace for the sake of our people, why shouldst thou think evil?" But the Bishop would not put his head in that noose. At the same time, the Pasha bribed a Montenegrin to light a keg of powder beneath a corner of the Bishop's room. The Englishman Wilkinson spent the night along the Crnojevići River at the inn of a widow whose husband had been hanged for attempting to poison the Bishop while his servant. The Bishop, in turn, selected a certain Gigoje Belomov and sent him to Scutari, in the guise of a fugitive, to kill the Pasha. Gigoje got all the way to the Pasha, as his servant, and then lost the courage to risk killing the Pasha, and so fled home again. There has remained a saying about cowardly failure: "He went like Gigoje to Scutari." In 1846 some eighty-five Montenegrins went by sea to seek work in Istanbul. Montenegrins were well known there as faithful and good workers, especially as gatekeepers and bodyguards. The ship ran aground in bad weather and the Turkish authorities passed them on to one another until they reached Scutari. There Osman Pasha cast them into a dungeon, and the Montenegrin Sovereign sent appeals out on all sides for three months, until he was finally able to get them released from the hunger and filth of a Turkish jail.

The Vizir knew neither measure nor bounds in the mischief he concocted. It came to him naturally. He incited the clans, bribed the chieftains, closed markets, sent raiding parties, and provoked rebellions in Montenegro. The Vizir was always capable of conjuring up new tricks, new troubles; the Bishop was not. But the Montenegrins became ever more implacable and inflamed with the cause. Their desire for peace was overcome by hatred and by their readiness to take up arms. The conflict between the Bishop's ideas and his capabilities—his weakness—erupted in the most tragic cries of human and national desperation, which he directed at Osman Pasha himself, his protagonist and archfoe:

Thou sayest that we cleanse our hearts and use every good means to bring harmony to our borders. My heart is ever pure and clean before men, but with those who are inhuman a man must deal inhumanly, for there is no other way, even if he so wished. . . .

Thou sayest that I always seek something. And what is it that I seek, and with whom would I seek it? When Bayazid (called Ilderim) conquered Bosnia and when the savage Asiatic hordes destroyed our small but heroic empire, then did my forebears and certain other select families who were not killed by the Turks leave their fatherland and take refuge in these mountains. I am alone and bereft. Think, where are my brethren, the glorious and renowned princes and dukes of our empire? Where is Crnojević (Bushati)? Where is Obren Knežević (Mahmutbegović)? Where is Kulinović? Where is Skopljak? Where is Vidajić? Where is Filipović? Where is Gradičević? Where is Stočević? Where is Ljubović? Where is Čengić? And where are many others? Where are the lords and the flower of our nation that we might together seek our fatherland and our glory, that we might be all one? With them might I then seek something great.

God alone knoweth when they shall recall their glory and how long these brethren of mine shall remain strangers to their own brothers and call themselves Asiatics, and how long they will do the work of others while forgetting both themselves and their own. From that unhappy day when the Asian rent asunder our empire, against whom has this handful of mountaineers fought for the general honor and in the name of our people? All against our own native brethren turned Turk. Brother beats brother, brother cuts down brother, the ruins of our empire have curdled our blood. Here is our common misfortune! It was this misfortune and hatred among brothers which has done more than any alien force to turn our heroic race into the hirelings and minions of strangers, even as thou art a hireling. Hapless Montenegro was almost strangled by this division in our people, but it survived. . . . I would like above all things on earth to see concord among brethren in whom the same blood courses, whom the same milk has nourished, and the same cradle lulled. As for myself and this handful of people, I seek no greater honor than we already have in the great and more enlightened world, and yet something more is to be wished for, as our food is bloody and our honor bare. I would wish to have been born later, for then would I behold my brethren cognizant of themselves and their kin, declaring unto the world that they are the worthy grandsons and progeny of the ancient knights of our people. When this word shall be spoken, then shall blessings come upon our race. Then shall the names of the Montenegrin, Bosnian, and other knights of the Serbian people be venerated as sacred talismans to be borne in our breasts.

I hear that thou dost call the Montenegrins hajduks. That name bears not a whit of shame. . . .

It is true that some Montenegrins are murderers, plunderers, and cheats, but they have been made so by the unbridled and savage Turkish violence as well as by heroic necessity. Think, my dear compatriot, how many people have been crowded into these mountains and enclosed practically on all sides. When it is at all a good year, one can get along fairly well, but when a year comes along such as last year, then it brings a living torment. Last year I took refuge for several months in Vienna and in Venice just to keep from seeing this torment with my own eyes and because I am of such a sad heart that I would give away all I had, though I have certainly very little left for myself. When thou dost speak to me as my Bosnian brother, then I am thy brother, thy friend. But when thou speakest as a stranger, as an Asiatic, as the enemy of our race and name, then this goes against me and would go against every honorably thinking man. I know that thou shalt say on receiving this letter: "Of what all doth this man not write and dream?" Yet I hope that our progeny will, at some time, put a worthy price on the patriotic thoughts and letter of a bishop who is regarded by all today as a white crow.

At the same time he also cried out to his friend Vuk, in a letter of November 1, 1847:

God and I alone know my position. A hellish hatred is spreading. The devils of old feared the Cross, and those of today fear freedom. Were a man as constant as he should be, I would be its most zealous hostage, but at times the bloody and hard struggle overwhelms me, and I curse the hour when this spark rose up from the ashes of Dušan's greatness and into these mountains of ours. Why did it too not die where the Serbian hearth was smothered, but it sped up the mountain and glows and brings upon itself the thunderbolts of malice and envy. . . . An ill wind is my constant fellow-traveler, and there is no refuge for me save the grave. . . . O fate, fate, why art thou so stern toward me? I am thy great martyr.

There remained only faithfulness to the cause—the very one he cursed because of the horror into which it cast both him and his land. He did not forget, in his letter to Vuk, to add about the spark of freedom, "God help me, I am the greatest sinner on earth when I think aught against it—for it alone separates us from the other animals."

Cosmic evil became domestic. Or perhaps it is the other way around: only one's own evil is cosmic.

Yet man can conquer evil. It is his duty to fight evil.

16.

The Sovereign of Montenegro and the poet Njegoš was from the start wholly dedicated to the cause, to the fulfillment of his vocation as ruler and poet as the highest duty. If he underwent any evolution in this, it was in the direction of absolute resistance to evil, toward reason and enlightenment, toward an implacable national struggle, and toward the state as its instrument. Powerless to bring these ideas to fruition, the ruler accepted them as a tragic personal obligation, and the poet transfigured them into a supreme consuming passion.

Such was the man and the ruler.

Such also was Montenegro.

The one attended the other. The realization of hallowed ideals could not take place without the unification of the people, and this could not take place without a state. The Turks perceived this and instigated clan ambitions and unruliness.

Bishop Rade was forced, and later was willing, to wage a relentless struggle with the Montenegrins and to deal with them mercilessly.

Njegoš's domestic policy was, in fact, a ceaseless civil war, but of a special kind. He least of all wished for such a war. Yet he could not turn back from his intentions and ideals either as a ruler, as a Serb, or as a man.

If he wished to fight the Turks—and he was forced to under the circumstances—he had to unite the clans under his authority and curtail a willfulness that did not stop even at collaborating with the Turks. This could not be accomplished without putting an end to the violent acts being committed by individuals who were protected by their brotherhoods and clans. The weaker brotherhoods and their members were exposed to the most senseless and brutal attacks. They say that seventeen of the Begovići, the sons of one mother, formed a band and not only raided Turkish territory, but also took what they could from Montenegrin villages. Bishop Rade had to deliver the people from this tribulation. In the end, after he, and the Turks, were through with them, only one of the brothers survived, enough to keep the family name from being extinguished.

Rovinsky observed that the masses were with the Bishop, but

passive. It was, indeed, largely a clash between an absolute monarch and the ambitions of long-established chieftains. The people were active in the struggle against the Turks, but aloof in the settling of accounts between the Bishop and the chieftains. They were still bound to their clans and chieftains by ties of blood, yet realizing that unless the chieftains were sacrificed, the struggle against the Turks could not be a successful one. The people wavered and vacillated from side to side. The *koljenovići*—the incipient clan aristocracy—were against Bishop Rade to a man. It was a clash between two principles—the state and the clan. The former stood for order and a nation, and against chaos and treason; the latter stood for clan freedoms against the arbitrary actions of an impersonal central authority—the Senate, the Guard, the captains.

In addition to resistance by the chieftains came also that by free individuals, nurtured in clan independence and in the struggle against the Turks. The Bishop upheld the struggle against the Turks, but he inevitably came into conflict with those who fought for their own aims and would not submit to him, that is, to the general interests of the Montenegrin state. The Bishop had to humble not only the traditional chieftains, but also the headstrong heroes and brave adventurers. He could cajole and bargain with the chieftains and make them his own, but he had to kill the unruly paladins, for with them no agreement was possible. The chieftains were brought to submission during his reign, but inasmuch as the paladins—men such as Marko Miljanov and Jole Piletić—were born out of the struggle against the Turks and came to the forefront of their clans during such, they were to continue their resistance even into the reign of Prince Nikola. The chieftains grew out of the clans as a social institution, while the paladins arose out of a militant anti-Turkish and antifeudal society. Sometimes they were the same men, and then the conflict became most complicated and difficult. As the clans merged into a national community, the chieftains became the privileged servitors of the prince. But the heroes could not be transformed into anything. They stood for something that went beyond Montenegro—for Serbdom and Yugoslavism—and yet their mentality was that of the clan, even Marko Miljanov's.

As he struggled with the clan heroes, Bishop Rade had to uphold heroism as the highest ethical virtue.

One must be precise: the Bishop in fact came, and had to come, into conflict with the traditional clan type of hero, but not with the hero in general, that is, the kind who placed the struggle against the Turk above all else, including his own clan. The hero he suppressed differed little, under the conditions of an incipient civil existence, from the willful bandit who looted and killed not only the Turks but also frequently his compatriots from other kinship groups. Such rampant boldness presented a serious obstacle to the state, even where it expressed itself only against the Turks, for it was necessary to wage a united Montenegrin, Serbian policy against them. Were not wildcat raids a serious obstacle to the regularization of relations with Ali Pasha? Njegoš did not suppress the heroes in general, but did suppress the paladins of a certain social environment—the clan—and of a certain type—the clansman.

After all, everything occurs in a concrete situation. Every struggle is directed against concrete forms and for concrete forms. Bishop Rade was to preserve and develop heroism as an ideal, and out of his struggle for a centralized government a new type of hero was to be born, one whose thoughts were turned to Cetinje and Serbdom, yet stirred by passions still tied to the clan.

To be sure, much happened differently from what Bishop Rade wished. This was only natural. If men see clearly the form they must destroy, not even to Njegoš was it given to foresee infallibly what would come later.

Bishop Rade wanted the Montenegrin to be a free citizen, and he actually turned out to be an undeveloped citizen and the discontented subject of an absolute monarch. Heroism in the face of the outsider would remain, even strengthen and spread. In the Great War of 1876, not one Montenegrin surrendered to the Turks. But inside, in the face of despotic power, the courage of the citizen failed. Medaković noted that Montenegrins were heroes, but cowardly before a stern government. Actually, the Montenegrin was never a citizen. There are no citizens in the clan. Here the personality is neither free nor enslaved, but internally bound to inherited custom, rules, and conditions of life, while it is energetic and free toward the outside world. The most marked individuals remained free even toward the central government. But the mass of clansmen would not be transformed into free citizens, but into humbled and humble subjects.

The root of national heroism lay in the clan. But there was no soil here for the cultivation of the citizen. The latter can come only out of the ruins of absolutism.

What took place was the end of feudalism and of the foreign yoke—a mighty step toward human freedom, but in an unexpected form—that of oppression.

An absolute monarch and a stratum of privileged chieftains on the one side, and free peasants on the land on the other side—this was the end result of what Bishop Rade began. That peasant was not yet a citizen, just as the ruler had not yet accustomed himself to not being a feudal lord. With the appearance of trade and the crafts, after the cities were taken from the Turks in the Great War, the citizen was to awaken in the clansman, and the feudal lord was to die in the ruler, or, rather, to become senseless and absurd.

Doing what he could, Bishop Rade brought about something he did not wish.

The struggle Bishop Rade began his successor, Prince Danilo, was to heighten to a senseless pitch, trampling upon all established forms, in order to prepare the country for war—and to buttress his own power. "I'll kill him," he said about a certain hero, "were he as great as Mount Lovćen, if he does not obey." His brother, Vojvoda Mirko, the father of Prince Nikola, led a punitive campaign against the Kuči in 1856 to make them pay their taxes and surrender those chieftains who dallied with Scutari. Marko Miljanov recorded the details of that campaign with a natural, and thus all the more horrifying, simplicity. Here is one scene: "The heads of the men and children which were cut off were gathered together in the priest Luka's apiary and were placed on stakes around the beehives so that Vojvoda Mirko could look them over and see how many there were. They say there were 243 of them, of which there were barely 17 of soldiers able to go into battle against the Turks, while the rest were all of old men, the infirm, and children."

It was Bishop Rade who introduced the Montenegrins to spying and secret murders, mostly by ambush, those inevitable fellow-travelers of every absolutist government. But there is no known case or mention of violence against women and girls. Prince Danilo took revenge by burning, by exiling whole families, by punitive campaigns such as the one against the Kuči, and by marrying off the women of living husbands to other men. His fall was more probably the result of personal vengeance than a political plot.

Bishop Rade's violence was still callow and almost entirely motivated by his ideals. He respected Montenegrin and human sensibilities. Power and ideals had not yet merged into one with him. Though an absolute monarch, he was also a warrior. His successor, Prince Danilo, also a renowned ruler by virtue of his struggle for independence and for the unification of the land, was to trample upon all sensibilities and to identify himself with the state and his own power with the cause.

Freedom, too, appears in a concrete form, that is, limited by conditions—and appears as un-freedom to those who must go farther.

17.

Bishop Rade had to wrestle with the peculiar Montenegrin mentality, as he did in the case of the heroes, in such a way as not to break it in bending, but to purge and develop it.

That mountaineer swagger and quick temper, that Montenegrin self-indulgent pride and personal touchiness, as well as resistance to order and discipline, were all to the good as long as the struggle against the Turks did not also require a denial of personal and clan contumacy or autonomy.

Bishop Rade wished to preserve the Montenegrin as he was, and yet rule him according to his own will. He once told a Scotsman in Split, "Do you know where there is the greatest freedom? In Montenegro, whose keys I hold."

A Montenegrin once said, "I would like best of all to be turned into stone on Lovćen's peak, so that the whole world could just look at me."

How was one to reconcile keys with freedom, and such a Montenegrin with an absolute master?

This was a contradiction, but what is not?

All of Bishop Rade's work, the whole integrity of his personality, lies in a maze of contradictions and in an inability to make peace with reality. So it is with every man. But not everyone is Bishop Rade—with that spiritual depth and sensitivity.

Bishop Rade acted here with an instinctive and statesmanlike care, though he was at odds with extremes which welled from the very Montenegrin psyche.

One can speak of this psyche in Njegoš's time without much danger of committing errors that every sociological generalization contains, inasmuch as the Montenegrins were almost undifferentiated, while their state of mind was largely prefeudal and primitive. Although there were as yet no distinct classes in Montenegro, the dissolution of the clan, along with its corresponding morality and outlook, had long since been in progress. The Turkish invasion had but slowed it down and evoked its extremes, thus lending sharpness to the Montenegrin features.

In that mentality there is no moderation or anything of the ordinary. In it one can see, as perhaps nowhere else, the human. Here heroism rubs shoulders with cowardice, altruism with avarice, self-sacrifice with bribe-taking. The Austrian general Thomas Brady knew well in 1798 "that one can accomplish most with Montenegrins through gifts and money," and yet it was at that very time that they were recklessly throwing away their lives in acts of heroism against the Turks and the French.

Here the sky touches the earth. Here one can see in man the lowest vices and the highest virtues. Here the earth produces little, but its fruits are among the sweetest and the bitterest.

Sometimes these extremes meet in the same individual, but usually the men remain pure types—either of the highest idealism or of the lowest selfishness. As for their susceptibility to bribe-taking and yet their unconcern for all that is material, there is a saying: "Every Montenegrin is capable of spending a king's ransom." And their women are shrewish yet affectionate, irascible but faithful, household slaves who sing, "O radiant sun, I am fairer than thou." Montenegro does not like, it cannot stand, mediocrity.

"These mountains brook no rules."

They contain a special breed of violent mountaineer. Jovan Cvijić was able to make these generalizations:

> In the main and in most cases very destructive. . . . Such people can be revolutionary in the realm of thought or more frequently bring about events which bear with them great, profitable, and fruitful consequences. They sense the direction of a social current and raise a hue and cry over an idea or a movement which captures the masses. Such a violent type was Karadjordje and many leaders of the First and Second

Insurrections. Such were the men of old Montenegro, impetuous heroes of great will and indefatigable energy, who think and act honorably, generously, "out of manliness." . . . An ever tense touchiness over honor, pride, face, reputation, which can lead to malice, envy, spite and malevolence. . . . Passion is rarely seen, mainly feelings. . . . It was largely these violent types who coined those winged words and slogans which enthuse and sweep up the Dinaric man. They have too much confidence . . . and not enough foresight.

Bishop Rade was the quintessence of such a violent type, and at the same time he was forced to curtail and to check those who were like himself—to bring order among them. To do it he tore apart himself and the land and the Montenegrins, and they tore him into bits, and still nothing gave way. There remained a saying: "Montenegro is tough, like Bishop Rade."

He bore this hard, relentless land within himself, though filled to overflowing with its bitterness. "Our climate," he wrote to Count Wendel V. Lilienberg, Governor of Dalmatia, on October 29, 1838, "is severe not only in itself but in what it produces." It produced also men. Many are of a mean and violent bent—and these are the most conspicuous. They will join the Turks, not from necessity, but for spite. "Some are led by money, and others by lawlessness and a mean streak, to become renegades and vagabonds," he complained to Balerini, the Austrian consul in Scutari, on May 15, 1845. "That is just the way it is," the Montenegrins agreed with Vuk, "you are right, but we are a bad and unfortunate people, and we love evil more than good." "To rejoice over evil as over one's own brother"—the Montenegrins say about themselves. And this, too: "They rejoice more at the misfortune of others than in their own fortune."

They are a ragged and poor lot who are capable of the most exalted exploits and the darkest misdeeds. Some are proud of their heroic poverty: "The bare man leaps higher." Others will trample everything underfoot in order to grasp power and wealth. The purest spirituality and the coarsest avarice exist side by side and clash. It is the extremes that stamp a country and form its visage. Here one can truly say: "The greatest distance is that between the human and the inhuman."

The clan was dissolving, and the state was still being formed.

All the old bonds which had once restrained the evil side of man were breaking. The Bishop broke them himself.

Raids and skirmishes, not only with the Turks, had entered the blood and had become a way of life. Marko Miljanov recounts:

> Pressed by the pangs of hunger, the Kuči were eager for battle, and even if there was no cause for fighting, they would find one, just for the sake of plunder. . . . The people believed that God and Christ were sending them the tsar's army to bring arms and glory, as the spring brought them food. The Kuči called any great army the tsar's and rejoiced at its coming, while they called the smaller neighboring armies of the Turks the Barelegs, for there was little to take from them! . . . The Kuči would say to one another, "If there is nothing else to be done, it is better for your soul to knock down the branch of a Turkish oak than to fast on Fridays or Wednesdays. . . ." The Kuči is so beset by the devil that if he has not fought with Turks for a time, his whole body will itch to fight.

The Bishop had serious trouble over incursions not only into Hercegovina but even into Austria—long after he had signed the treaty fixing the boundary. In March, 1848, he wrote to his Njeguši, "I write you to no avail, to no avail send I commands unto you to cease committing evil and mean acts against the Emperor's subjects; but I see that which I had hoped not to see, that ye do not even turn your heads at my command." This was in reference to a raid on Dobrota, led by his uncle Lazo Proroković, at a time when the Austrian government was in the turmoil of revolution.

The foreign difficulties into which its own subjects embroiled the new state were a daily occurrence. It was even worse on the domestic scene. Sir A. Henry Layard conscientiously noted three hundred to six hundred murders every year. The lawlessness went so far that trees were cut down even in the Bishop's own woods, and it was as much out of personal consideration as legality that he threatened the Vukčevići and the Globari, "As for thee, Captain Simeon, who dost wish to plunder and cut down the sovereign's woods by force, perhaps thou dost not have enough of trees." Marko Miljanov has recorded what the people had to say about Bishop Petar: Petar was made a saint by the woes and troubles the Montenegrins caused him, for even as he did good to the people, they returned it with evil.

Bishop Rade was to cry out in even greater pain than his predecessors, "O unhappy, accursed and lawless land!" In his letter of March 20, 1848, he drew the following lesson from his reign: "One may expect anything from such a people. Woe unto him who is their ruler. This is the saddest fate in the world."

Yet he had a boundless love for that land and its people—not only out of duty to them, but because they were what they were. It was possible here to be the man—to fight for the highest human and national ideals.

Bishop Rade was in conflict with Montenegro, in order to preserve and to develop that heroic, manly—and he would have said, divine—side of it.

Though men cannot exist without evil, they must fight against it.

18.

EVERYTHING WAS IN such flux and disarray that there could be neither law nor real courts under Bishop Rade. Law was established only under Prince Danilo, in 1855, and even he did not adhere to it.

Still that does not mean that lawlessness reigned in the land. Within each clan there was order and justice. Under Prince Nikola, Professor Valtazar Bogišić compiled a criminal code that was a marvel of wisdom and beauty of form and expression; he did not fabricate anything, but constructed both his code and its terminology on the basis of the customary law. What conflicts there were occurred between the clans, or between them and the central authorities, or between the latter and individuals.

Montenegro was without courts and laws. But the Montenegrins knew justice and fairness, just as every human society does. The quest for justice in Montenegro was all the more striking and simple in that it could be realized in the midst of lawlessness.

Under Bishop Rade justice was meted out according to conditions and the customary law.

There was no judiciary as a separate institution. The executive and the judicial overlapped: the captains judged the petty cases, and the Senate the more serious crimes. Being an ordained cleric, the Bishop could not participate in the deliberations of the Senate when the death sentence was involved. Yet he approved such sentences and ordered many executions. There is no record of the sentences, nor were there real trials: the deed was known or became so, the guilty party was jailed, the sentence was handed down even without his presence, and immediately carried out.

Kovalevsky states that three crimes were punishable by death: murder, insult to the Bishop, and treason. There were death sentences for other crimes as well—grand larceny and rape—but for the first three crimes almost without exception. These were, in fact, political crimes, even murder, since it took place most frequently as the result of a blood feud, or could give rise to such, and feuding was the most widespread and most stubborn expression of clan insubordination. The state, that is, the central authority—Bishop Rade—took upon itself, and had to do so, the right of vengeance hitherto exercised by the clan, and in its most extreme form—a head for a head, as the clan law decreed.

Disobedience cropped up most frequently in two forms: the nonpayment of taxes and the blood feud. The first was resistance to the state as such; the second was an inherited custom. Taxes were the Bishop's fight with living, while feuds were his fight with the past, with the customs of the Montenegrins. While taxes could cause clans to rise up and the people to mutiny, the clans accepted as a higher cause the executions with which the central government sought to end feuding. The blood feuds with their killings indirectly hurt the state and its order by giving rise to conflicts between the clans.

To levy taxes meant to elicit recognition of the state as the highest power, to establish the state in and over the life of the nation.

The eradication of blood feuds went deeper and further than is ordinarily thought. To take over the right of avenging a murder meant, in fact, to prevail over the clan internally by taking away its prerogative to stand behind a fellow-clansman.

As a deep and, so to say, instinctive phenomenon, the blood feud was bound up with the esteem and vanity of the chieftains. It also became an instrument of Turkish machinations against Montenegro and Bishop Rade, not only in that it caused conflict and dissension among the brotherhoods and clans, but because the murderer could escape unpunished into Turkey and carry out his attacks of vengeance from there. Such fugitives were frequently to be found in Turkish bands.

Though entangled with the chieftains' ambitions, the spontaneous resistance of kinship groups gave way before the central government. The clan community was dissolving as a society, but the clansman still felt, still breathed as he did a thousand years earlier, if indeed not as he did in the primeval beginnings of human society.

Moving dramas took place. Many murderers in blood feuds, especially under Prince Danilo and Prince Nikola, did not wish to flee, but surrendered to the authorities and calmly awaited their execution, because they were unable to leave their homeland and because they had already found balm for their hearts in blood.

The Montenegrins submitted with the most profound sorrow to their Sovereign's unwritten laws; so it had to be if they wished to become free of the Turks and live under new conditions. But their clan chieftains did not. To some of them, chieftaincies meant everything—their life and their repute—and they had no wish to have their position confirmed by their Sovereign, for this would mean the loss of an authority and power they had inherited and derived from the clan.

Bishop Rade was ruthless, with reason, toward the resistance of the clan chieftains, who did not balk even at seeking the support of the Turks in order to preserve their inherited privileges. His conscience was clear because he had taken upon himself the punishment of murders and all crimes. He carried this out with a mechanical exactitude and implacability. This is, after all, the attribute and the *raison d'être* of every government and state. Yet, being himself a man from a clan and a brotherhood, he found it hard to endure the resistance he encountered in his suppression of blood feuds.

True, there is not a trace of this in Njegoš's works and letters. Of all the Montenegrin customs, only peacemaking between clans is not treated in *The Mountain Wreath.* Peacemaking is referred to only in relations between Montenegrins and renegade Turks. *The Mountain Wreath* is a poetic work based on an idea, and very consistently so. Njegoš did not wish to give prominence to something against which he was struggling—the blood feud—by depicting the scene of a truce. Yet one can feel throughout *The Mountain Wreath* the horror of an impending slaughter among the clans. Bishop Danilo speaks of it. Bishop Rade, too, spoke frequently of disunity and dissension among the clans, and even more frequently of human, that is, of Montenegrin, foolishness.

Thus Bishop Rade found himself in conflict with a deeply rooted custom—the blood feud—with which he dealt without mercy, but openly, and with the clan chieftains, whom he had to outsmart, to bribe, while even he was amazed at their faithlessness.

It was extremely difficult to choose one's means, as always when force does not take over in the name of law or is unable to hold its own. The means became confused, and so was the resistance of the chieftains, with the blood feud and with the willfulness of the hajduks and bandits. Bishop Rade himself played several roles at once: as a ruler who had to establish and maintain a government, as the inspired prisoner of a great idea, and as educator and reformer. The national struggle against the Turks was being transformed into a religious war, though it was far removed from any religious fanaticism. Similarly the resistance and disobedience of the chieftains and the clans were being transformed into a civil war, though it was in the name of peace and order—of a special kind, to be sure. "Wherever two brothers sat around a hearth," states Marko Miljanov, "the dissension divided many so that one went to Cetinje and the other to Scutari." It cannot be otherwise wherever an idea asserts itself as something exclusive and unconditional—and this is how it was, and had to be, in the Montenegrin struggle against the Turks, precisely because it was a war for bare survival. Under such conditions all means seemed justified if they were effective. The conditions and one's role determine the means, and at times these were contrary to the Bishop's own inherited conceptions.

Wholly devoted to the idea, Bishop Rade could not choose his means. That was an evil thing. And he did evil things. For him, too, the end justified the means.

Marko Miljanov was a clansman, and perhaps the last of that kind. He was perhaps the greatest Montenegrin hero who ever lived. He cut down over eighty Turks. He is undoubtedly our most ethical, most integral personality. "Ethical beauty and wise heroism is the feeling for justice and mercy," as Sima Matavulj * put it. Like every revolutionary after the revolution is finished, Miljanov

* (1852–1908). Dalmatian writer and educator who taught in Montenegro and was tutor to Prince Danilo.

turned against the despotism of Prince Nikola, but he did not forget the violent acts of Bishop Rade either. True to the popular notions of justice and freedom, he recorded, "The people have kept count that Bishop Rade killed 83 select men of the Highlanders, the Montenegrins, and the Littoral." They were neither murderers nor traitors. They were not "select," but simply men who would not submit to the Sovereign's will for one reason or another. At his behest his guards—so it is told—killed the renowned hero Petar Kršikapa because he would not hand over a flintlock taken from the body of Smaïl Aga. What did a monk in Cetinje want with a weapon, and one a hajduk had won in battle at that? But the Sovereign must be obeyed, else he is no sovereign, and he asked for the weapon of such an eminent leader so that he might preserve it in his, the state's, armory. A certain priest, Tomo of Zeta, which was then under the Turks, uttered a harsh word about Bishop Rade. He was enticed to Cetinje, thrown into a dungeon, and killed. There is even a letter of the Bishop's which reveals that the priest Jovo Plamenac was jailed for talking too much.

These were not the only cases.

There was in Bishop Rade also something of the Renaissance princes, for whom all was fair as long as it served their ends.

Who was capable, while burning with the idea, of choosing means, which in reality differed from those that served the idea?

Evil knows no measure, even when it is aimed against evil.

19.

Bishop Rade's domestic efforts were accompanied by the zealous interference of the Turks, on a tiny patch of soil considerable parts of which were not even wholly free, so that at times the clans recognized his authority, and sometimes they did not, depending on the circumstances and interests involved. Refusal to obey the Turks exposed a clan to invasion and devastation, and Bishop Rade's Cetinje was rarely able to come to its aid. Yet this is precisely what Bishop Rade demanded—in the name of a cause that also infused the clans. The force that sustained the Bishop and that he unleashed—liberation from the Turks through a national monarch—was so irresistible that the Bishop's arm reached far even in fomenting rebellions. He found everywhere prominent personalities who were willing to take the risk and to incite mutinies. Moreover, that same arm was also capable of removing opponents outside the limits of his actual power. Nor was there any lack of men who were engaged in either defending the momentary interests of the clan or following a contrary path.

It also happened, of course, that they deceived the Bishop, realizing how much he insisted on refusing obedience to the Turks. It is reliably recorded that the Bishop refused to receive Miljan Vukov, later the renowned vojvoda of the Vasojevići, when he came to Cetinje for the first time, with the intention of wresting his clan away from Turkish suzerainty. "You people of the Highlands," said the Bishop, "promise to break away merely to get money out of me." Only after Miljan brought him Šehović Pasha's head did the Bishop believe him and embrace him. They say that a certain senator said a word on that rare occasion, the kind that is always welcome and remembered in Montenegro: "Never to this day have my eyes seen two prettier heads—Miljan's living and Šehović's dead."

It happened, too, that the chieftains of still-unaffiliated clans would come to Cetinje and reach a sincere agreement with the Bishop, only to find on coming home to their clans that either this was not to their liking or else conditions had changed. Sooner or later they became turncoats. Marko Miljanov recorded such an agreement, between the Vojvoda of the Kuči and Bishop Rade:

After this Bishop Rade decided to unite the Kuči with Montenegro. He said to Vukić Popov, "Why dost thou not bring the Kuči to unite them with Montenegro, that we might fight the Turks together?"

Vukić replied, "The Kuči next to Albania cannot get around all the Highlands and Montenegro to get even salt from Kotor, let alone all else that they need. Let us rather strike at Podgorica: thou with Montenegro on your side, and I with Kuči from my side, and when we take Podgorica, then will I bring thee the Kuči to unite them with Montenegro with thee as our ruler."

Stanko Stijepov, the father of Prince Danilo, who is well remembered by the people of Montenegro and the Highlands, foresaw as a wise man that nothing could come of all this. He spoke to Vukić Popov and to Bishop Rade: "Thou Vukić, let our Rade be, and this union with him and the attack on Podgorica. What wilt thou with Podgorica? Even if ye take it, the Turks will take it back again, for ye cannot hold it! If the Turkish tsar sent but all the gypsies in his realm, they could take it from you. If he sent but all the men in his realm called Muyo and Ali against you, they could take not only Podgorica but all of Montenegro, if they really tried. Rather, thou Vukić, dig into those rocks of thine and guard those few Kuči from being scattered by the Turks, and let Rade guard this speck of Montenegro, and if ever the Turkish tsardom shall turn elsewhere and be weakened by other tsars, then let us open up our eyes and work for unity, but do not, as Saint Petar did, deceive yourselves with a hope where there is none. He wished to unite the Kuči with Montenegro, and could not even hold court in Cetinje, for the people of Cetinje oft did break the roof tiles over his very head and all he could do was to weep. I can see by him and by you that even were a good opportunity to present itself, ye would have trouble enough to take advantage of it for Serbdom, let alone now when ye have no opportunity at all.

Stanko Stijepov was one who faced realities and weighed possibilities. He even regarded Karadjordje as an adventurer. Vukić Popov, a wise ruler and an indomitable hero, also finally faced up to the impossibility. Yet it cannot be said that Bishop Rade saw things unrealistically either. To him reality was the idea shaped by the sufferings and endeavors of centuries. He invested reality with it, used it to break reality and to change it, and at times even forced reality, as unyielding as it was, to resemble the idea. For Bishop Rade the possible was not that which was coming into being, but that which was yet to come. This was a different conception of reality from that of Stanko Stijepov—one that struck out into the distant future. Bishop Rade blazed paths across the reality of our dark centuries precisely because he neither accommodated himself to it nor submitted to it. A given reality was for him a means, an instrument that could be put to use for the idea. He got rid of Vukić Popov, too, because, being cognizant only of the immediate possibilities, the latter refused to obey him and to rise against the Turks. The uncorrupted Marko Miljanov revealed, "He was killed by kinsmen and blood brothers all, men who had received money from Bishop Rade."

With the help of Mojsije Zečević, Bishop Rade also got rid of another still-more-renowned and important leader—Nikola Consul, that is, Knez Nikola of the Vasojevići.

Nikola was a Milošević, and of the brotherhood of the Radonjići, from the Lijeva River. While still a child he went out into the world, received a schooling, and served in Russia as an engineer. Then he went to Serbia and Turkey, and finally made his way to Novi Pazar as an English consul—hence the nickname by which he is remembered. He had to flee from Novi Pazar because of the Turks, and reached Paris, where he established ties with the Polish émigrés around Prince Czartoryski. He then returned to his own Vasojević clan. He had already come to know Bishop Rade during an earlier trip to Montenegro. On arriving in his homeland, he took over the government of his clan, which was up in arms but not yet liberated, with the undoubted aim of creating a state independent of Cetinje. This aim coincided with Polish plans, which were, as usual, brilliantly conceived and quite unreal, to penetrate Poland by way of the Balkans and to incite the population against both Russia and Turkey. To be sure, these plans were not made without English and French connivance.

Like all of our famous pretenders, Nikola Consul was a spinner of dreams and given to fabricating his own royal lineage. He, too, was led by the passionate idea of nationalism, a dark urge for power, and his own weakness—a compulsion to explain and to justify all of this and himself through fabrications. In an article published in Paris, he claimed, along with certain correct statements, that the inhabitants of his "Holmia"—the "Slavo-Ostrogoths"—were distinct from the Serbs. Yet he had a clear conception of a centralized government—much like Bishop Rade's—and a government that would, of course, be independent of the Turks. As such, he was a danger both to the extension of the Bishop's authority and to the influence of Prior Mojsije in the clan. Besides, he was a fierce opponent of the Russians—as is frequently the case with those schooled in Russia.

He was invited to a parley in Cetinje, but never arrived. He was waylaid in Zagarač and killed, on May 30, 1844. Tradition has it that he was murdered by the three Toroman brothers from Njeguši. What Bishop Rade wrote Sarajlija about this killing was both untrue and malicious. Consul's wife, a Russian woman, erected a monument to her husband at the place of his death, but Prince Danilo ordered it to be destroyed and the grave leveled, so that no trace might remain of the crime and of the man who, while wandering about the world, dreamed ceaselessly of the liberation of his homeland under a rule separate from Cetinje's.

The murder of Nikola Consul gained a widespread notoriety and lingered in the popular memory as something vile. The story behind it also shows why Adam Mickiewicz attacked Bishop Rade in his lectures in Paris. Even after Nikola Consul's death, the Poles continued with their fantastic plans to use our lands as steppingstones to their unhappy homeland. They established ties with Ilija Garašanin, and it is claimed that they even tried to win over Bishop Rade, but the latter, being dependent because of his weakness, had to stick to Russia.

Knez Nikola was indeed a daring and dangerous dreamer. What would have become of Montenegro, divided as it was, had it been split into two states? What could it have accomplished in the struggle for liberation without despotic Russia? Even so, Nikola Consul was renowned for the grandeur and the boldness of his project.

With Nikola Consul's death vanished all attempts to detach the Vasojevići. Still this great and dynamic clan always felt itself to be something special—Serbs, regardless of the Montenegrin government.

Wholly given to the idea, Bishop Rade, who had to grasp at all sorts of measures, was bound to clash with reality. Indeed, Montenegro appeared to him to be an endless rough sea of trouble. Inside, there was the resistance of the chieftains and the contumacious clans, defiance and a lack of understanding among those who were closest to him. Outside, the Turks ruled over a shattered Serbdom while myopic, despotic Russia and a selfish Europe looked on. Everything, except the pale flame of the idea, was steeped in evil and given to evil. The state, a government, was indeed the only means to counter this evil and to give the idea broad horizons.

There was no measure to the courage, the determination, and the farsightedness of this ruler. "I look every trouble in the eye," he wrote Knićanin on January 20, 1850, at the end of his reign.

This is how he saw things from the first day he assumed his inheritance. On October 22, 1830, three days after being installed on the bishop's throne, he wrote of "this unfortunate land and home of every excess." As the ruler gained strength and the sage came to know himself, the troubles increased, for the struggle became sharper. "Were Montenegro beautiful, it would not be called Black Mountain but the land of milk and honey. . . . Eden itself, had a similar fate befallen it, would have become filled with evil and poisoned with evil. . . . Montenegro is driven by an evil destiny, and I who am its son cannot utter its name without feeling horror. . . . But it is a chip of the ruins of our empire . . . a nest of martial pride, where . . . all sacrifice themselves willingly, but to keep pure the honor of their sires."

Born in evil and out of evil, Bishop Rade knew that he himself could not be free of evil, but he never succumbed to evil entirely. And as often happens, in order to justify his ways and means, he formulated an appropriate ethical philosophy:

To do evil fighting evil,
In this there can be no evil.

Only men who are conscious of their limitless moral strength and entirely dedicated to a cause can say this.

As is rarely the case, this philosophy was neither shallow nor contrived exclusively to satisfy material needs.

It can happen that immediate necessity gives rise to ideas which far transcend it.

20.

THERE WERE TWO serious rebellions against Bishop Rade's rule —those among the Piperi and in Crmnica. They emanated from something more than the disaffection of the chieftains or Turkish intrigues, though these provided the leaven and set their course. Both flared up in late 1846 and lasted into the spring of 1847—apparently for the same reasons, though it has never been confirmed that their instigators were in league with one another.

The repercussions of these rebellions shook the other clans. The discontent grew out of conditions and circumstances that went deep and were common to all the clans. In fact, the participants only confirmed this precisely by offering such various and sundry excuses. The imposition of a government and a state was putting an end to the independence and internal freedom of the clans. There were indirect causes as well—the hunger and the poverty, Osman Pasha's intrigues, occasionally the Bishop's own mishandling, and often the highhandedness of other Petrovići and of those around them. Moreover, personal passions and unfulfilled desires rose to the surface. It could not be otherwise when all was ripe for one world—the power of the state—to take the place of another—the liberties of the clans.

The rebellions broke out while the Bishop was absent from Montenegro. That does not mean, however, that they would not have taken place even had he been there.

In the fall of 1846 the Bishop set out for Vienna, for two reasons: to continue from there to St. Petersburg in the hope of obtaining the return of Vranjina and Lesendro, and to publish *The Mountain Wreath* in Vienna.

He had sensed the discontent in the country earlier, especially in 1845; there is a hint of this in his letters. In January, 1846, he informed Gagić that he had come into possession of ten banners which the Vizir of Scutari had distributed among the Montenegrin clans. Acceptance of such banners was a symbolic sign of their willingness "to rise up against their government and to make common cause with the Turks." The Bishop knew better than anyone else that there could be no lasting peace between the Montenegrin clans and the Turks. Their entire way of life, thinking, and feeling had long ago taken a direction contrary to that of the Turks. "Stupid Turkish politics!" he added in the same letter. "Even were they able to overthrow the Montenegrin government, which they are not, what would they gain thereby except another lot of Montenegrins." He knew well and sensed that the clans had irretrievably entered the stream of a Serbian nation, for he was both the product of that movement and its standard-bearer. It was on this, on the irreconcilability of the clans with the Turkish order, that the Bishop had, spontaneously as much as consciously, based his policy.

Yet it was not clear to him, nor could it be, to what lengths the malcontents in the clans would go to make common cause with the Turks, for transient reasons, against him and his efforts. The rebellions did indeed astonish and shake him. Reasonably sure that the harvest would not be reaped by the Turks, still the Bishop had not anticipated the necessity of fighting for every kernel with his own reapers.

The goal of national liberation, which directed the current of life ever more unremittingly and drew our people to their destiny, had to traverse a path not only thorny but mired with the personal selfishness of those who were supposed to achieve it. Bishop Rade believed with reason in the power of pure ideas, though he did not know that they are the products of the human spirit under determined conditions, of the unremitting upsurge and victory of new forms of human life. Although he understood that, in the struggle for national liberation, he had to make use of the sordid means that were imposed on him, still he was appalled at the shortsightedness and selfishness and, one can say, the lack of idealism of those who had to be liberated, those whose inherited sacred duty was to struggle for the cause. He knew that he had to quell the rebellions, but they were a heavy burden to bear.

The year 1846 was a dry year. The following year was inevitably a lean one. In July the Bishop wrote, "This year there has been a drought such as the present generation cannot remember. The fields have not even yielded seed enough, and the whole population is without wheat. This is worse than the plague. The Pasha of Scutari is promising, in the name of his government, to every Montenegrin a gift of enough wheat to tide him over for this year, if only the Montenegrin will publicly declare himself against his government." Maksim Šobajić recorded the following recollection: "There were lean years. . . . We were full only in the fall. . . . Through the winter we ate chiefly cornmeal mush, and in the spring boiled cabbage and milk, and even that rarely. It was in the infamous and shameful year 1847 that the Montenegrins and the Highlanders went to the Pasha of Scutari to sell themselves for bread. The Pasha gave them food, money, and clothing." The Pasha also gave the clan leaders silver-mounted weapons, and inasmuch as the Turkish army was adopting new uniforms at the time, there were old uniforms aplenty for the naked Montenegrins.

The role of the Vizir of Scutari, Osman Pasha, was neither slight nor lacking in skill. He did not even ask the clans to pay the imperial tribute, nor did he appoint chieftains, but merely required their secession from Cetinje. By forgoing the tribute he impressed the masses, and by permitting the free choice of chieftains he impressed the powerful brotherhoods. Cetinje had nothing with which to counter this save the Serbian Idea.

For a moment it seemed that everything that had been accomplished since Bishop Danilo's time, and before him, would go tumbling down the abyss. Bishop Rade appeared to be repeating the experience of our medieval rulers. King Stevan Tomašević had written to Pope Pius II, "The Turks have constructed several fortresses in my realm and are showing favor to the peasants, promising that every one of them who falls away shall be free. The simple peasant mind does not understand the trickery and believes that this freedom will last forever. It is easily possible that the people, led astray by this deceit, will forsake me if they do not perceive that I am strengthened by thine authority. Nor will the nobles hold out long in their cities, if they are abandoned by the peasants." Bishop Rade did not know of these words from the fifteenth century, but he knew of the tragic fate of our rulers and our state. He was now experiencing their fate as his own curse.

All of these were good reasons, and the Bishop used them to justify both himself and the rebellions. Yet these were not among the most profound and hidden real reasons—those having to do with the dissatisfaction of the clans over the regime the Bishop had forced upon them. These reasons the Bishop passed over in silence, while Gagić did not comprehend them. The latter reproached the Bishop for going to Vienna to deposit money in an Austrian bank while letting his people go hungry and permitting vizirs to show them more charity than their own sovereign.

In actual fact, the clans which had rebelled were not among the poorest or the hungriest. Crmnica is fertile and always yields something, even during the cruelest drought. It was those who were most irreconcilable in the struggle for their liberties who rebelled—the Martinići and the Bjelopavlići, whom Njegoš himself had once reproached for their zeal against the Turks. The rebels also included renowned heroes, even chieftains from the Bishop's closest entourage—Captain of the Guard Markiša Plamenac, of Crmnica, and Senator Todor Mušikin Božović, of the Piperi.

The conflict between an ascendant absolute monarchy and a declining clan order, which had festered before, now was transformed by conditions into an open contest which found its leaders among the least likely.

Worlds do not take on new shapes except through the destruction of the old forms.

Man is free within the forms in which he lives, and yet their slave.

21.

The Bishop set out on his journey in September, 1846, and by October he received a report from Djordje Srdić, the Clerk of the Senate, that "the Highlands have been seduced by Turkish bribery." Turkish bribery had penetrated openly even into Old Montenegro—in Komani and the Nahi of Lješani. The Bishop's brother Pero, who usually replaced him as president of the Senate, informed him that there was great hunger among the people,

> while the Pasha of Scutari is again handing out bribes and gifts, only whereas till now he used to give caftans and baubles, he has now begun to present pairs of small silver rifles, like the two he gave Jovan Mušikin, or the small silver rifle and knife from Peć which he gave to Petar of Ravni Laz, and a third which he likewise gave to their comrade. These three stole away to Scutari on Christmas itself, and after they returned, other Piperi and Martinići also went. All the Piperi, except Božo Bešina with his brothers, the Mitrović brothers, and Vule Nikolin, agreed to wipe out the house of Piletić, and we are sore pressed, Sire, to find a way to save the Piletići. The men of Ceklin also intended to go to Scutari, but as soon as we heard of this, we brought them to Cetinje and had them bound. Crmnica has also become restless, and several men from the Lim went to Scutari, led by Marko Božović, but when we got wind of it, all of us, including those men of Crmnica who are loyal to the cause, hurried over there and so some of the Lim houses were burned down. There were some men of Crmnica, though, including even chieftains, who took the side of the evildoers and defended them, and they almost came to blows with the men of the court. . . . There are some six hundred souls from among the Piperi and Kuči slaves who are in Scutari being fed by the Vizir, and whom he is using to entice our people, and nothing can be done about it. . . . We do not hear a thing from anyone about the Nahi of Katuni, that anyone there is saying a thing or acting up, even though they are in greater need than all the rest.

This conflict and treason were of long standing. Even Bishop Danilo threatened "those who are in league with the Turks." Bishop Petar cursed such men and drove them away from him like lepers. Bishop Rade had to crush them to have it be as Danilo wrote: "In our somber crags may there be neither renegade nor Turk."

These were the days when Njegoš was making final corrections in *The Mountain Wreath* in Vienna—rendering the bitter expressions bitterer and the grandiose scenes even grander, sharpening his ideas and quickening his cries.

It is difficult to conjecture just why Markiša Plamenac, the Bishop's favorite, fled to the Vizir—after Pero's letter—and rose against his own sovereign. Pero and Markiša had never liked one another. Medaković tells that when the Bishop heard in Vienna about Markiša's disaffection, he ordered his arrest, and then recalled the order and bade them wait until he came. Medaković cited as the direct reason for the conflict the marriage of Pero's daughter with the son of the priest Jovo Plamenac, which would have deprived Markiša of the clan captaincy, since that title would fall to the future son-in-law of the Petrovići.

Perhaps it was so.

Yet behind the personal motives stood the irrepressible habits and passions of the men of Crmnica and the powerful Plamenac brotherhood. The Crmnica clan had been dissatisfied with the border with Austria that the Bishop had negotiated. Violent and self-reliant, they had rebelled against Cetinje before, in 1839. Being rather well off, they were not as dependent on the aid that the rest of Montenegro was receiving from Russia through Cetinje. From their cultivated lowlands, they looked upon the men of Katuni as boors and beggars. Father Jovo Plamenac had been arrested in 1839, according to the Bishop, for speaking too openly, and according to others, for wishing to incline Crmnica toward Austria. This arrest of Father Jovo created such a stir in Dubrovnik and Zara that the Bishop had to let him go.

Being unable to reduce the Plamenac brotherhood, the Petrovići then sought to befriend one of their branches and thus divide them. The Plamenac brotherhood was one of the most powerful in Montenegro, and would remain so as long as the Montenegrin state lasted. Many renowned men bore its name. To cite only a few—two Montenegrin bishops were of their blood, while Sava Plamenac had been a kind of minister for foreign affairs under Bishop Petar and had dealings with St. Petersburg, Karadjordje, and Prince Miloš. They were the only Montenegrin brotherhood which could and dared to vie with the Petrovići. That not only Turkish intrigues were involved, but a tangled skein of clan discontent, and family and personal ambitions, may be seen from the way in which the skein was later untangled: only the ringleaders were punished, while Markiša's nephew, Father Ilija Plamenac, who carried the banner before the armies of the Vizir and of Markiša during the mutiny, was later to become Minister of War to Prince Nikola. Once having defeated the Plamenac brotherhood, the Petrovići decided to make peace with them and to grant them concessions.

The eruption and inflaming of passions did not await Bishop Rade's return. He certainly made haste. He stopped in Venice just long enough to see the city and to collect some documents. The Russians hurried him as well, by not approving his journey to St. Petersburg—for the second time—with the excuse, and perhaps it was the real reason after all, that he ought to get home as soon as possible.

Fearing Pero's vengeance, Markiša fled to Scutari. Up to that point his cause appeared pure—resistance to arbitrary force. But from then on, it became pure treason. A mighty hero and chieftain and a proud member of his brotherhood, Markiša was not strong enough to endure the loss of his power and that of his brotherhood, and so he allied himself with the Vizir and bound his own fate and that of his brotherhood with the Vizir's plans of conquest. He incited the lowlands of Crmnica to rebellion. Scutari stood behind that venture, for as soon as the rebellion began to peter out, the Vizir hastened to Markiša's aid and sent an army to the lowlands of Crmnica. From a rebellious clansman and a malcontent in the brotherhood, Markiša Plamenac was thus turned into the instrument of Turkish designs.

The invasion by the Turkish army, whose path in Crmnica had been opened by Markiša's rebellion, took place the very day after the Bishop landed in Kotor—on March 26, 1847.

It was a bitter welcome for the Sovereign. Nevertheless the ever-faithful men of Katuni gave him an enthusiastic Montenegrin welcome. Military fanfare and volleys accompanied his every step to Cetinje.

The indirect causes of the rebellion were no longer of any significance. What mattered now was Montenegro's survival as an independent country with Bishop Rade as its sovereign.

Not wasting any time, the Bishop called together the men of Katuni. Others joined them as well. Under Djordjije's command he sent them against the Turks and the men of Crmnica. The Bishop himself did not take part in the campaign. The battle took place on April 10. Brave, battle-wise Djordjije hit hard, even though he had been wounded in the leg at the very start. Outflanked, the Turks withdrew, while the rebels scattered. Apparently the losses were not great. The Bishop informed Gagić, "A few houses were burned down in the village of Boljevići." Without this there can be no warfare.

Only now was it clear how significant Vranjina and Lesendro really were, as bases from which the enemy could easily make forays and in which he could take refuge. According to tradition, Markiša, too, fled to Lesendro after the defeat, and talked the Vizir into fortifying the little rock island of Grmožur, which was even closer to the entrance to Crmnica. Construction work actually continued throughout 1847. This compelled Bishop Rade to erect a tower at Besac, opposite Grmožur, overlooking Virpazar, in order to guard the entrance to Crmnica.

Tomanović reports the tale that Markiša repented and sent the Bishop a message offering to take the island from within, with the Plamenac and Strugar men who had fled to Lesendro. It seems that the Bishop agreed, but on November 4, 1847, Markiša was fatally shot by a youth from Krnjic, probably on orders from Cetinje. The Bishop rewarded the avenger with the Obilić Medal, the first he awarded. The Turks later caught Markiša's murderer—Krnjic was in Turkish territory—and hanged him in Scutari. Reports from that time have it that Markiša, while dying, asked his kinsmen to bury him in Montenegro, next to the church in Boljevići, where his ancestors were also buried. But he remained in Turkey; there was no room in Montenegro for his bones either. It was with some reason that the Montenegrins came to fear that there was no escape from Bishop Rade's hand.

Bishop Rade's letters show that there was unrest in Crmnica even after the rebellion had been quelled. But any real resistance was crushed and the disaffection faded away as the fugitives returned and surrendered.

There is barely any record of the Piperi rebellion. It is known that two brothers, and it would seem also the son of Senator Todor

Mušikin, of the powerful and renowned Božović brotherhood, went to Scutari, and then incited the majority of their clan, the Piperi, to refuse obedience to Cetinje.

If the rebellion in Crmnica, in the neighborhood of Cetinje, struck at the very heart of the Bishop's realm, the rebellion of the Piperi threatened his flanks. The Piperi closed off the roads from Podgorica to the clans of the Highlands, and having allied themselves with the Vizir, they opened the roads to the Turks. Internally this rebellion was weaker than the one in Crmnica. Moreover, it appears that a battle never took place between the Bishop's army and the mutineers, but that the latter merely simmered down.

It is known that the Bishop enticed Todor Mušikin and his brothers to Cetinje and had all three of them shot. It has not been established that Todor had instigated his brothers to go to Scutari, though it appears certain that he defended them in Cetinje after that. In any event, it was not the uncertainty of Todor's guilt that left nearly as much of a bad feeling as the fact that he had been killed through a violated pledge. As they were led to be executed, Todor and one brother shouted, "May our death bring fortune to Montenegro and the Bishop!" The third brother uttered a curse. The execution, by "musketing"—as it was known in Montenegro—was sometimes carried out by fellow-clansmen of the victims—to avoid blood feuds. However, the clan and the people generally looked askance at such executioners, and so the job became the regular work of the guards. The execution took place next to the Vlah Church, on the present Obilić Field. The criminal would stand unblindfolded but with tied hands some twenty-five paces in front of ten guardsmen. Attendance at executions was open to anyone, and relatives usually carried the dead man away. At the command "fire" the guardsmen would shoot. At that moment the criminal was permitted to run, and was pardoned if the first volley did not kill him, though no one remembered that anyone had ever escaped such a volley unscathed, though some survived it. The first shots did not kill Todor Mušikin, and since it was not the custom to finish off the criminal, the guards were afraid that he would survive, so one of them slit his throat with a razor.

After the ruthless settling of scores came generous pardons. This immoderation, both in the settling of accounts and in pardoning, was typical of Bishop Rade, as indeed of all revolutionaries with exalted, extreme ideologies. Consistent with this was an inevitable moral condemnation. Bishop Rade, as a poet of a people who still expressed everything in poetry, was to do this through the epic poem *The Tower of the Djurišići*. Probably the short allegorical poem *The Eagle and the Swine* refers to the same events, but it, too, is without much depth of feeling or expression and suffers from too many obvious allusions. Though written after *The Mountain Wreath,* they have nothing in common with it. In *The Tower of the Djurišići* Bishop Rade tells of the Crmnica rebellion and lists the traitors—for posterity—bitterly dubbing Markiša a "Turkish captain" and describing Todor as "a goodly hero, but no face." The poem is interesting as a document of the Bishop's struggle.

It was the Sovereign who wrote these. The poet of myths and of the national past transformed into lyricism, Njegoš was not a great poet when treating immediate events (is there any such great poet?), especially those events in which he was an active participant. Such poems were but his pastimes.

All poetry is inspired in some way by the reality of its times. Yet the reality of poetry is not the reality of the events themselves.

22.

THE YEAR 1847 was drawing to a close. The Montenegrin rebellions had been quelled or were on the wane, and Osman Pasha, too, was letting up; the boundary lines at Scutari were becoming stable. Bishop Rade had firmly established himself as a sovereign. *The Ray of the Microcosm* and *The Mountain Wreath* were in print, and he was writing *Stephen the Small.* And thus the poet was completing his labors.

Bishop Rade-Njegoš was thirty-four years old. His personality was mature and distinct in every aspect.

A saying lingered among the people: "As fair as Bishop Rade." Whoever knew him and has left any description of his appearance—and this was done by many, both Serbs and foreigners—was astonished at his proud and striking comeliness. Their descriptions and impressions agree with one another, as well as with the numerous portraits of Njegoš.

It was as though the tragic graces of our people found their expression and culmination in his form.

The view is not correct that he was unduly tall. It was exactly as the people said and as Vuk recorded it: He was taller by a head than any Montenegrin—and the Montenegrins are among the tallest people in Europe. This would correspond with the report by Wilkinson, who, in addition to noting various Montenegrin curiosities, did not fail to measure Bishop Rade: six feet, six inches. Stratimirović's claim that the Bishop was seven feet ten inches tall cannot be taken as reliable, not only because Wilkinson generally lends the impression of greater exactitude, but because his report corresponds with the observations of many—that he was taller by a head than people of average height. Nobody remembered, or dared, to measure Njegoš's skeleton. The armchair at Cetinje, which is held to be his because its legs were lengthened, would have originally been too low even for a man shorter than he, while in its altered form it might be too high, depending on one's legs and how one sat. There is no reason to make a giant out of Njegoš. He was tall enough to be unusual and fair enough to be exceptional.

Height often overshadows beauty. However, because Njegoš was proportionately built, it only enhanced his handsomeness.

On the other hand, few noted that his body was particularly strong. Medaković called him, rather vaguely and immoderately, "that powerful man." There is an account by Blažo Radović, a man of great physical strength, of how the Bishop easily threw him to the ground in a match, and how he, Blažo, cried out, "I'm as angry at the Bishop as a rabbit at a mountain." However, this is not reliable, and was told much later, when Njegoš had already become a myth. Besides, it would be difficult to find a youth who would dare best his sovereign in a wrestling match. Bishop Rade did not compete with other Montenegrins in jumping or rock-throwing, which measure both strength and agility. It is known that his limbs were not strong and that his chest was somewhat sunken—a sign of his susceptibility to tuberculosis. His legs were long and well fashioned. His arms were even more handsome. Yet, being a Montenegrin and very much a man, he felt embarrassed about his small feminine hands and fingers, which caused him to wear black leather gloves most of the time.

From his broad and straight shoulders there rose a rather elongated neck, crowned by a longish head. The face had a smooth complexion and full features. Njegoš's high forehead went more into breadth, as though to emphasize his intellectuality. Gentle and pensive-looking, his inwardly absorbed expression caught the eye. Those who knew him more intimately also spoke of a certain nuance of violence and severity: beneath those heavy-hanging eyelids fiery eyes flashed forth against a pale and gentle skin. Medaković recorded that Bishop Rade was given to bouts of anger which, once they took over, were long in passing, and during which a vein at his temple would swell out the whole time. His calm, restrained face was framed by a beard which he kept clipped, thus increasing his nonclerical appearance. Similarly, his hair was rather long, but not as long as the Montenegrins wore it at that time. Rather, it was shortened at the neck, in a style of his own.

Everything about him was curved, rounded out, and tempered. He was neither fat nor bony, but was more flesh and veins than bones and sinews—a fine frame and subtle contours.

Njegoš had himself painted frequently, perhaps from a desire to make known his unusual and lordly comeliness, of which he was as conscious as he was of his poetic gift, though his concern to please and to impress might have sprung as much from moral superiority and the requirements of a ruler as from native dignity of bearing and expression. In all these pictures one may observe not only the romantic artistic manner of the times, but also the desire of a primitive and unrecognized ruler to display his very real and imposing handsomeness. No one notes that he was a dandy or extravagant.

Durković-Jakšić has established that the portrait of Bishop Danilo in *The Mountain Wreath,* as well as the features of Obilić on the medal that bears his name are of Njegoš himself. He felt in his whole physical being an intimate bond with our mythical past and with his clan. His bearing was natural, but it was that of a dynast who was carrying history forward and a creator who felt his own exceptional spiritual strength.

The upper part of his body swayed slightly as he walked, giving him the appearance of a majestic calm and conscious cultivation. He frequently slid his hand into his sash—a sign of self-restraint and pensiveness. This is how he was in conversation, though he was not much given to talk. An attentive listener, he chose his words and spoke sparingly. Violent and unabated forces lay hidden in him which broke out in decisive moments and in acts of creation. He bore himself as though he had been born to rule—as indeed he had been—and the fire within him was known only to himself. Ali Pasha once blurted out, "That veritable lord of Kosovo!" And Imbro Tkalac * recalled, "He was indisputably the most handsome man I have ever seen in my life: a radiant figure with a frame perfectly proportioned in all its parts, a classically beautiful face and a serious though deep and mild expression, with feminine small gentle hands, and yet a husky voice which even exceeded his great and proud stature."

Despite the imperfection of the photographs of that vintage, the Viennese one of 1851 by Anastas Jovanović, which shows Njegoš in his armchair, has preserved most faithfully his features and expression. Externally that photograph differs from the portrait done in 1847 in the very same pose and dress only in that Njegoš is wearing a glove on his left hand. The inward difference is incomparably greater: a slightly raised left eyebrow expresses the pent-up energy, the heavy-laden eyelids shelter an unquenchable fire. Though captivating, the eyes are mysterious and penetrating. Njegoš is not sitting back, but is at the edge of the chair, as though he were about to leave. He was not having his picture taken, but they were taking his picture. Calm and energy, the suffering of a man who could not be broken.

Njegoš's beauty was indestructible.

Always different, it remained what it was to the end.

23.

Bishop Rade's way of life differed hardly at all from his physical and spiritual likeness, and even less from his social role.

He was not too immoderate in food and in drink, or in dress, if we take into account the fact that he had to keep up appearances as a ruler, though we need not believe Medaković when he says that Njegoš wore patched robes.

During the first years of his reign he gave himself over to hunting. Montenegro is poor in game, except for the ducks and fish of Lake Scutari, where he could not go because of danger from the

* Imbro Ignjatijević-Tkalac (1824–1912), Croatian publicist and journalist, author of several works on Serbian history.

Turks. There were, however, foxes and rabbits and partridges, apprehensive and sly. Perhaps this is the origin of that description of Montenegrin women in *The Mountain Wreath* as skittish partridges. Later he evidently abandoned the hunt. The cult of horses and riding was not widespread in Montenegro; the roads were suitable only for pack animals. As ruler, the Bishop had to see to it that he had good horses. Yet he liked them, too, and, being a good horseman, he enjoyed going out for a gallop. Because he was rather heavy, and the Montenegrin roads were so steep, he always had to take along an extra steed. His love for weapons was even greater, though he rarely carried any.

No one remembers ever having heard our greatest poet sing—not even to the tune of the gusle, which he sometimes played. He never chanted in church, not even the Lord's Prayer or the Creed. He did not care much for prayers and praying but he did like to listen to good church chanting and that of the guslars. Sometimes, in the morning, he would chant verses from epic poetry, most frequently the poem about Nikac of Rovin. His voice was deep and strong. It is not known what kind of ear he had, but probably he was as deficient in this as are most Montenegrins. In his writings he mentioned music only as an expression of cosmic harmony. Yet he had a very developed inner musical sense, a feeling for poetic rhythm and the sound of words. In this his ear was infallible and naturally keen. He possessed an inborn sense for harmonious ideal beauty.

Njegoš enjoyed storytelling very much—"the soul's delight." During the evenings, while Little Zion—the old Senate building—was still in use, the chieftains would sit on stools or on the stones around the fire. When the Bishop came, a stone bench was placed next to the wall, over it was thrown a hide, and then the stories were spun, yarn after yarn, each man striving to outdo the other. These long bouts of storytelling, which usually treated the mythical historical past, battles remembered and fought, and comical incidents, made for polished diction, precise language, and the neat turn of phrase. Love of storytelling is, after all, a trait of Montenegrin life, almost a kind of compensation for the poverty and the lack of entertainment for the mind. Prior Teodosije says in *Stephen the Small:*

Though there is no place for living,
There is place for storytelling.
Stories are the soul's delight. . . .

There is something personal, something of Njegoš in this. Bishop Rade told stories only rarely, but he delighted in listening and getting ideas.

When the Billiard was built, the evening gatherings and the storytelling did not stop, but were transferred to it. The Billiard was not made for telling tales. It was too formal and office-like, and cluttered with furniture. The chieftains spontaneously sought a fire, and so both they and the Bishop crowded into the kitchen, for without a fire there could be no real storytelling; it relaxed the body and quickened the mind. Everyone knew that the Bishop enjoyed a good story, and so care was taken not to interrupt the tale but to let it unfold itself—like life.

The Sovereign's ordinary days would have been much too monotonous had they not been interrupted by troubles with the Turks, with foreign states, and—by the Montenegrins. He arose early, and after having dressed while chanting a bit of a folk epic, he sat in a wrought-iron chair, the work of a Cetinje gypsy called Lazo, and lighted up a short pipe. He had there a small breakfast—something light. Then he began work: holding court, correspondence, meetings. At noon he ate a single course with a little glass of plum brandy and a bit of wine mixed with water. Then back to work. Around five o'clock came a fuller meal, and then a walk. The Bishop would tire of his pipe, and in the afternoons he smoked cigarettes made of a strong tobacco from Lješani. Evenings were for the gatherings in the kitchen. He had newspapers or books read to him then, too. This was hard on the chieftains, for they wanted to tell stories. Yet the Bishop did not wish to miss any important news or new idea. On noticing the predicament of those around him, he would finally order the reading to stop. The evening was then spent in unquenchable storytelling. The neighbors would come—for the stories and to hear a word from the Bishop. The Bishop would be served coffee. Coffee was also made for the chieftains, but the cook cheated them—either he stole a bit of the coffee or he was sparing. In any event, he added just enough coffee to the pot for the smell. If anyone noticed at all, he pretended not to. If the weather was warm, they would sit in the Bishop's dining room. There were two tables there. One was the Bishop's writing table. He dined at the other—alone, with his intimates, or with guests. There were three benches and three chairs. If the Bishop had something to write, they would light the candles, which would be snuffed out immediately after; one economized a great deal in this palace. Before the party broke up, a guardsman brought brandy and rubbed the Bishop's feet with it.

Bishop Rade was not much of a night bird. Yet at times he worked deep into the night—writing or reading. However much he enjoyed storytelling, he also yearned to be alone with a book or a pen in silence. His deacon Djurašković told that he would peek through the door and the Bishop would be sitting and reading; then after a good long while, an hour or two, he would peek again, and the Bishop would still be sitting and reading, by the feeble light of a candle, reading, reading, reading.

The last light to be snuffed out in the stillness of Cetinje was that in Bishop Rade's room.

A German, Ludwig August Frankl, observed another, darker, aspect of this life, typical of the court of a poor and primitive despot. Even if we take into account that his description reflects his personal animus over his poor welcome and the arrogance of a man from a superior civilization, not to say race, his observations are so concrete that the conscientious reader can scarcely doubt them. His impressions were published in the *Allgemeine Zeitung* of March 18 and 19, 1840. Soon after, on May 27, there was published a correction, sent from Budva. Cetinje read what was written about it and reacted insofar as it could or dared. Ritter Frankl depicted, in an undoubtedly derisive vein, the stuffy atmosphere in the small, rustic court of a parvenu: the monarch-bishop and his secretary were asked about every little thing. Tony, innkeeper and cook, a deserter from Austria, waited for Milaković to whisper in his ear an order to serve coffee to the guests. Very frequent whispering, suspicious winking, and pursing of lips. Spying, brutality, and the false etiquette of primitives. And behind, the Tablja, with its Turkish heads on stakes—a pincushion.

And that was Cetinje—the court of Bishop Rade. A *Ritter* did not wish to understand, or could not, that such was the other side of every court and of every dynasty, only it was more noticeable here inasmuch as it was all still in the making.

There was no peace and tranquillity in Cetinje. It teemed with daily visitors. The poor came seeking bread and justice in God's name, agents brought news of rebellions and campaigns, monks begged alms for religious establishments which were destroyed or would be destroyed, charlatans of all kinds promised uprisings and enemy heads. Plots were concocted, betrayals and murders were paid for, hajduks received bounties for heads.

Cetinje was the spawning ground of mutinies and revolts.

Everything was as it had to be. Good and evil, which men cannot do without, are human qualities and categories.

24.

ALONG WITH POWER and its responsibilities, poetry and its insights, Njegoš also developed a sense of proportion and beauty.

He constantly probed and studied. He even learned to swim, much too late—in 1844 and almost at the cost of drowning. Yet this did not bother him at all, and he continued to take delight in sea and sun, each for itself, but best of all the two joined together. Colors and forms never escaped him, though he was not a descriptive poet. He had little to say about landscapes, and even less about love. Yearning for peace, he was never to find it. He himself was restless and unappeasable.

He traveled, investigated, observed, wrote and composed, wrestled and fought—always with some idea, some aim in mind.

Bishop Rade's especially developed taste for travel reveals his refined, intellectual, insatiable spiritual hunger. He was in Vienna five times—each time on business. He traversed Italy while gravely sick, yet more as a tourist than as an invalid. Just before his death, in the beginning of 1851, he concluded, "It is a shame to complain about traveling. Who has not traveled has not lived, he does not know what the world is nor the world's variety. The world is a book which has to be studied to learn what the world is about. The world is a comic stage on which men appear in various and sundry masks."

His taste for beauty, even for pleasure, came to involve his daily life, in its every detail—from the binding of books and choice of vignettes to beautiful furniture and elegant clothes, down to china and champagne. To be sure, this was proper for a ruler who sought to acquaint himself and his state with the comforts of civilization. Yet one can perceive his personal stamp on all of this. His conception of the world was permeated with a passion for physical beauty. But he cultivated his love for the beautiful. The primitive in him, which was never eradicated, he did not even try to eradicate. After all, he had no reason to. The primitivism he inherited lay in simplicity and not in boorishness. In actual fact, he possessed a native sense of beauty which he gradually developed and refined, shaping it in the manner of European intellectuals, the greatest spirits at that, while remaining a Montenegrin—with his gusle and flintlock next to his engravings and Dante.

Bishop Rade enjoyed the relaxation of gay society. Traveling to Trieste on board the *Stürmer,* he took delight in the sea, and in the city itself he discovered among the beauties of life the "gracious Flora" Fabri-Brettini, or Fitz-James, a dancer in the theater, who

> By her zephyr-like movements,
> Her enchanting eyes,
> Could change even hell into paradise.

He liked to jest, though he was no jester. He never confided in others, as though he was able to reveal his depths only to himself. Yet he hastened to grasp every extended hand. He felt childish joy when his greatest enemy, Osman Pasha, sent him some fezzes as a present. A good man, he was not kind. He had men shot and hanged and broke faith—with infidels—yet he could not look at "The Laocoön" in Rome owing to the horror of the visions it evoked in him. He never abandoned himself to amusements and entertainment.

This is how he was before the ruins of the Colosseum and before Michelangelo and Raphael, before the might of Vesuvius, and in his own deathbed. He took joy, felt wonder, observed, remembered, and noted. But he never lost himself in anything. A part of him was ever alien to the sensual, to "the things of this world." His sights and visions always led him into a private world all his own: for him the *Stürmer* bobbed on the waves like the mind from subject to subject, while that little dancing plaything could evoke in him the vision of paradise and hell.

It would be too little to say that he was absent in his thoughts from the sensual world; he lived and felt joy, yet at the same time he pondered all of this. Njegoš had a world of his own which was inaccessible to others. More precisely, he instantly formed his own judgments concerning everything that happened or that he thought about; there was nothing that did not cause him to meditate and to build himself another world as a pendant to this sensual one. This was not because of his religious philosophy, which holds that the body is the temporary prison of the soul; rather, he was a being who never took part in anything without the most complete conscious intellectual involvement and passionate enthusiasm. He ceaselessly sought the hidden thought in everything, including his own spirit and actions.

Such a Njegoš was and had to be a profoundly lonely being. Fewer anecdotes have come down about him than about any other Petrović ruler. In his entire correspondence there is not a person to whom he revealed himself, if only for a moment. Not that he was insincere or did not yearn for companionship or was indifferent to cultivating friendships. It was just that a part of him and of his world was accessible only to himself. He lived his own intimate, ultimate life in that world. His life was tragic in everything. But the tragedy was in himself, in the nature of his being—in the burden of his spirit, in the presence of his thoughts and meditations about everything around him.

Such were he and his world.

Moreover, his sense of beauty and order in life was founded on his inner life, on his conception that everything good and beautiful tends toward harmony and submission to eternal laws.

Bishop Rade committed many offenses—none of which are forgiven or forgotten. Yet he is the most moral individual in our history, and we would say in any other history, when we take into consideration the circumstances with which he had to struggle.

Certainly the murder of Nikola Consul was a breach of faith and an evil thing, yet Njegoš neither could nor dared permit the weakening of his still-unestablished state and unliberated land. And the massacre of the Hercegovinian chieftains was also an evil thing, but they themselves did not hold to their word. The hajduk Kršikapa should not have been murdered, nor should Todor Mušikin have been lured to his death, but the Sovereign was to be obeyed and the fraternization with Scutari had to be stopped.

In the heat of battle—a battle for life and death—Bishop Rade outdid himself. Yet he never did anything merely for his own sake. He devoted himself completely to his duties and calling, which were for him the imperatives of absolute laws and cosmic strivings for the good and for order. He made an effort not to violate the inherited moral order and to preserve and to elevate the hero in the Montenegrin and his sense of human dignity.

It is a matter of record that Njegoš possessed physical courage. In the battles for Vranjina and Lesendro he was almost struck down by Turkish bullets. He evidently regarded courage, too, as his obligation in the battle for order and the good. He was angry at his nephew Stevan Perović-Cuco, for writing poetry, though he himself was utterly devoted to poetry as the highest obligation and understood it as such. Yet there was a deeper significance to this: he was angry at his nephew for dallying with poetry while neglecting his education.

Njegoš's justice was inexorable, but it was completely founded upon an idea that made it steadfast and selfless.

For him honor was not a mountaineer's self-esteem, but a higher law. "Life without honor is like body without soul," he exclaimed over the loss of Vranjina and Lesendro.

After all, the idea of nationalism, in whose name he in fact committed all his misdeeds, also emanated from the absolute rule of law that governed the cosmos.

It is not a matter of justifying him, for nothing that happened can be justified, but of comprehending him. Neither evil nor good can be weighed with exactitude, for no one can know beforehand how much of the one or the other is needed to hold one's own, to gain the victory. But Bishop Rade's scales were more delicate than anyone else's, for they were wielded by a moral character led by an inner necessity.

In the very midst of the nineteenth century he had to wage a struggle to wrest his land from the Middle Ages, an alien medievalism at that, and to bring it into the society of European states. One had to give up everything for Serbdom, in order to make it beyond price. He was a ruler and a man who lived in a cruel time and in a lawless land, but he never trod upon traditional popular justice or the human conscience in himself, in his own cosmic, rational, and enlightened order.

He never lost his balance, least of all his sense of ethics, which remained, to the end, ever vigilant, always on duty.

His activity was not cut short in any of its aspects. The ethical line was perhaps the straightest and the most evident, from the very start of his activity, in the *Ode to Liberty:*

> Every man is born and dies but once.
> Everything doth perish saving honor,
> This lives on through everlasting ages.
> Life eternal marks the honored grave;
> A life of shame leads to eternal death.

Perhaps it may not be so, but this, too, is an aspect of human existence, not the most convenient one, but the most manly.

25.

It is safe to conclude that this man of passion and enthusiasm never surrendered to any passion but that of the spirit.

Though love is the most complete, and perhaps therefore the most joyous, expression and reflection of life, including, to be sure, the life of a man, Bishop Rade never gave himself up to it as such, and not only because he was a monk. He never paid much attention to it. For him love was a duality—a sensuous passion to which he succumbed like others, but also the fulfillment of an eternal law. This is what made it complete for him, a sacred obligation. One may conclude indirectly, from his personality and his outlook, that he was too much the man of duty to neglect it for the passions of love. Too full of life to miss tasting the delights of love, he was at the same time too spiritual and ethical to play with love. No one knows of any woman, and there probably was none, whom he might have loved with a life-or-death intensity.

Njegoš's love life was carefully hidden, yet also diligently investigated after him.

He himself—the Bishop, the Sovereign—concealed it. The Petrovići also concealed it. In the poem *The Night Gathers the Age,* which King Nikola's daughter presented to the Cetinje Museum, someone's hand had made changes in the hope of creating the impression that the love act had nothing to do with the author of the poem—Bishop Rade. The concealment was owing also to an ill-conceived patriotism, a false morality, and the reputation of the Church. On the other hand, those who investigated the matter did so out of various motives—frivolous curiosity seekers or the opponents of the Petrovići, who hoped to find ammunition. To be sure, there were also those who wished, by uncovering that side of Njegoš's life as well, to get a more complete picture of his personality.

Nothing has been disclosed that was not known anyway, but if anything of any little significance has been hidden, there ought to be new evidence about it in the recently opened archives in Zadar.

It was hardly a secret even in the Bishop's lifetime that he did not avoid female companionship and that he was least disposed to observe canon law in this respect. This much has been transmitted. This is confirmed by the facts—and by his poetry, in which there are, however rare, powerful erotic passions.

Yet there is not a trace of any great moving loves. I maintain that there were no such loves in his life, nor could there have been. To Njegoš a woman could not have meant much more than an affair of passion, however much he might have wished it to be otherwise.

A youth tonsured against his will and a bishop transfigured into a ruler, and a handsome male besides—he sought women, though, to be sure, not many of them were indifferent toward him. Yet he was a Montenegrin of his times. To those men there was apparently no love or passion outside the marriage bed, while the cult of the sweetheart did not yet exist. There was even no marked cult of the mother. Among the men of the clans, where the dominant position of the husband and the male was almost absolute, love of women was something rather shameful. There were no suicides for love, while murders over women were in fact affairs of honor—over a seduced sister or the violation of one's womenfolk. Only the cult of the sister was something powerful and elevated; the sister was a bond between her own family and another and the guardian of the blood community. The love of a sister was a pure and unselfish bond which kept watch over the brotherhood. In

Montenegro a mother was but a mother, but a sister was born into the brotherhood and drew life from its unceasing breath.

This was Njegoš's most subtle, most moving motif: Batrić's sister kills herself over her brother, for only she—a sister—can love unto death in Montenegro. Another motif, that from *The Night Gathers the Age,* is passion, almost plain copulation, "something primevally human and primitively male, from mythical times and from the age of the poetry of sexual intercourse," Isidora Sekulić concluded. I would say that there was something Montenegrin about it—passion, but not love in the Romeo, Werther, or any other sense in which sexual intercourse does not also represent an irresistible submission to the impenetrable mainsprings of existence. A third and most significant motif—the Miljonić bride from the dream of Vuk Mandušić—is similar to the second, though more refined, more distilled—the mad passion of a berserk hero. Mandušić's passion is so powerful that it loses all corporeality and is transformed into pure painful yearning for a woman—the Milonjić bride, who is almost an incorporeal being of idealized beauty.

In sum, the image of womankind is the sister, and love is passion.

Montenegrin epic poetry of the bards also has hardly a trace of love motifs. In it women are captured like any cattle. Here and there some heroic mother or tenderhearted sister appears but for a twinkling—and that is all.

On the other hand, the lyrical verse sung by Montenegrin women is full of the most subtle tenderness, purged of color and sound to the point of transcendence. Love pours itself out in this poetry, while passion takes cover in it. What the Montenegrin woman yearned for as a woman she strove to attain as a poetess.

But Njegoš was a man.

He was a man of fabled male beauty and the sovereign of a peculiar breed which was but emerging from a mythical past and still living in heroic legendry. On top of everything, he had charm—rather primitive and thus all the more attractive. Three Englishwomen dressed in men's clothing made their appearance in Cetinje. The inexorable and ubiquitous Stevan Perkov was bound to say that things had come to a pretty pass when women were dressing like men. But the Bishop put it another way, also in Montenegrin fashion: "This is the first time I have seen three doves in falcons' feathers." Milica Stojadinović was neither ugly nor a beauty, but as a poetess she was significant as the first Serbian woman of that calling in that time. She was narrow-minded and condemned Njegoš's South Slavic breadth. Yet he had an attractive and well-considered word for her, when he met her in Vienna: "I am a poet, she is a poetess. Were I not a bishop, Montenegro would now have a princess."

Truly, as bishop and ruler he had to guard against everything that his enemies could use against him. He dared not enter into any liaison with a woman that he could not break off at any moment. But this restraint of the ruler and of the imposed cassock only fired him on in his quest for women. Passion, the quenching of passion—such were his loves. Here, too, he was what he was and had to be—caught between wish and possibility, duty and desire. In his ideas and obligations in life there was no place for woman except as a natural, though delightful, necessity.

"The passions are a magnet. Only through them does this world become pleasant. . . . The passions are the terrestrial spirit. . . . Could my moral self triumph over my physical self, I would be in the order of angels and would look upon man and the world as they really are," he wrote in his *Notebook,* by which he meant to say: The earth is a nest of evil which becomes pleasant for us through passion, and were man able to free himself of all that was earthly, and especially of the terrestrial spirit—passion—he would become a bodiless spirit—an idea. Thus all that is earthly and human would become clear to him—"as they really are." Matter could not be pleasant if it did not have its own spirit—the passions, which are the magnets that draw us to what is earthly. It is through the passions that we find, and must find, enjoyment, for the moral self is not stronger than they, though it belongs to a higher, spiritually pure sphere.

With Njegoš there was no inconsistency. His passions were a submission to necessity and not irrational hedonism. This is why they were all the deeper and more violent in their intensity.

Though profound intellectual dramas, his loves, his passions, manifested themselves in short-lived erotic affairs.

Life in Cetinje was cramped and under the surveillance of a patriarchal milieu to such a degree that he would run off after women, usually to the coast, with a wolfish hunger. The Austrian authorities, who watched his every move, reported even the times he found himself in gay company, usually with officers who would be joined by women. Professor Kolendić has read reports of this kind in the Zadar archives and has given an account of them; they involve women who sought and sold pleasures. He could well have had such experiences, and did—in Vienna, in Trieste. Perhaps even in Montenegro—with great caution, for his guards protected him from his enemies, while the Montenegrins would have been sensitive about this, even had a bishop and the honor of their own women not been involved. After all, Bishop Rade guarded the reputation of others as he did his own.

To be sure, time, curiosity, and malice have woven tales that do not merit belief, not because they are ugly, but because they are not credible. Djordje Stratimirović noted rather loosely upon the arrival of the sick Njegoš from Italy in Vienna, "He is quite weakened, from a grave illness as well as from a great love." If he had at least said "love affairs," one might believe him, though Njegoš's sojourns in Italian cities were brief and, being taken up with sightseeing and courtesy calls, hardly suited to love affairs. True, he was accompanied by faithful men who would have been quite capable of hushing up his weaknesses. But he was a sick man, undergoing a cure as a matter of duty and devoting himself to his last passion before dying—seeing the sights. Where in all this was there the occasion for a great love? The story has been handed down that the scar which ran across his left eyebrow was from the scythe of a miller whose daughter the impassioned Sovereign wished to take by force. Bishop Rade was not like that. He himself wrote the Captain of Kotor demanding that the authorities force an adulterer to marry a dishonored girl. "Such a transgression," he wrote, "is more blameworthy in Montenegro than murder." And even had he been what he was not, which miller would have dared lift a hand against him?

The Petrovići and Bishop Rade had enemies who saw evil even in the good that they did. They grasped at trifles, embellishing, twisting, and inflating them so as to make it appear as though everything that was wrong emanated from the contaminated and perverse bloodline of the Petrovići. As if the tales concerning the dissolute life of King Nikola's sons were not enough, they had to invent baseless stories about their father as well. A certain priest, Tomo Davidović, from the Littoral, was in Bishop Rade's service.

He enjoyed the favor of his Sovereign, who sent his son to school in Russia. Father Tomo was strangled in Cetinje. The story was spread that he committed suicide. It was also bruited about that he had been discovered to be an Austrian spy, which is most probable. The Captain of Kotor, Griez, who was in Cetinje while Father Tomo languished in prison, reported that he had been caught stealing and that he had intended to kill the Bishop—obviously Cetinje's version. Be that as it may, the enemies proclaimed that the Petrovići had strangled Father Tomo, who had been charged with drowning the Bishop's bastards, in order to keep him from telling. An addendum has it that the priest's son thereupon drowned the Bishop's nephew in Russia. Actually the latter died of a lung disease. That Bishop Rade might have entrusted something of the sort to a priest from the Littoral is nonsense! There were also stories about an illegitimate son of Bishop Rade. They even gave him a name. Such were the titillating inventions and salacious fabrications of the enemies; the concrete facts tell us nothing new.

But why go on?

Nothing human was alien to Bishop Rade.

"Some have counseled me not to set eyes on the female sex," he wrote in his illness, "whereas a man can hardly help casting a glance at a beautiful creature, even from his deathbed."

The poet intoned:

When I see the pretty charmer,
I embrace her as God wills it
And beneath my tent I take her
To fulfil a hallowed yearning.

One way or another, love is the bond between a fleeting life and eternity.

26.

FOREIGNERS REPROACHED Bishop Rade for cruelty because of the taking of heads. They did not comprehend our sufferings and passions, or Montenegro.

They should have understood, first of all, that Montenegrin-Turkish relations were totally irreconcilable, even after death.

They should have comprehended the tragic impotence of Montenegro against its inescapable task of restoring the destroyed Serbian Empire. Here was a living myth in a ceaseless contest with death. They should have understood the customs that became a part of the blood and the very nature of the Montenegrin. How much there was that they should have understood! They should have known that the Montenegro of this world was a world in itself, and yet one as human as every other.

To be sure, the foreigners observed what was in plain view, the outer appearance—the heads lined up on the Tablja above the monastery and the Bishop's palace. The heads exuded a sickening acrid stench, and as the flesh and bones rotted away, the dogs dragged them all over Cetinje. Wilkinson told Ali Pasha that this custom ought to be stopped, but the latter excused himself on the grounds that Bishop Rade refused to do so. Bishop Rade replied similarly that the Turks would not.

The foreigners would not understand that the taking of heads was proof of heroism and victory.

It is not known where this custom could have come from if not from the Turks. It was as old as the feud with them. It was not to be discontinued even under Prince Danilo, though they did not then exhibit the heads, but turned the Tablja into a belltower. They threw the heads into a ditch behind the monastery and kept a careful tally of them. The cutting off of heads was to be maintained into the beginning of Prince Nikola's reign. It was only during the Great War, in the year 1876, that he forbade the beheading of prisoners and the taking of heads. Nevertheless the soldiers secretly cut off noses and ears and brought these to boast before their comrades. There were cases of this even during the First World War.

Head-hunting had been inherited in the struggle against the Turks, and only with that struggle's passing did it cease to exist.

The severed head was the greatest pride and joy of the Montenegrin. He regarded the taking of heads as the most exalted act and spiritual solace—having been nurtured in mythical history and in the naked struggle for life. He did not feel any hatred for the cut-off head, the hatred he was bound to feel for it in its live state, but only esteem and solicitude. He washed it, salted it, combed it. After all, it was a human head and the badge of his own highest merit. The Montenegrins did not exhibit the heads to terrify their enemies, as the Turks were wont to do, but as signs of public acclaim and recognition. The number of heads one took was remembered, handed down, and marked on gravestones. The expression was frequently heard, even from Bishop Rade himself: such and such a number of heads were taken. These were the fruits of glory and of valor. When new weapons were being distributed in Ljubostinje and the men were told that only those who promised to cut off Turkish heads could have them, there was a real run on the weapons. Maidens were proud to be courted by head-hunters. Head-hunting entered into the most profound and intimate aspects of life.

Bishop Rade knew that head-hunting was not a pretty custom in Europe's eyes and that it hurt Montenegro's reputation. He was aware that this custom had to be stopped. He not only did not praise it in *The Mountain Wreath* or in his other works, but did not even mention it. He always used the excuse before foreigners that even the cultured French cut off heads. But that was not the same thing: in France this was a method of execution, while in Montenegro it was an act of heroism which the supreme authorities encouraged. That was the point. In the kind of struggle the Montenegrins had to wage, head-hunting was an inducement. This is what Bishop Rade also emphasized.

That which seemed like savagery to the foreigner was for the Montenegrin the poetry of warfare.

After all, it was not easy to come by a head. Just as it was regarded as an honor and fortune to take a head, so it was held to be shameful to permit such a thing to happen to one's own. The fiercest fighting arose around a corpse or a wounded man, not simply to drag him to safety, but to keep him from being decapitated. One had to brave a raging fire of opposition, within reach of enemy scimitars. Inasmuch as prisoners were beheaded to a man, few permitted themselves to be taken prisoner.

In time, especially after the government began to hand out bounties, head-hunting, like every pursuit, became a business. Abuses set in. Ali Pasha was brought the heads of corpses from graveyards, even from the bodies of Moslems, just for the money. Similar things went on in Cetinje. Yet the head of a distinguished man or a renowned hero continued to be prized to the very end. Once, during a certain battle, the Montenegrins who were pursuing some beys shouted to their comrades, who were chasing after ordinary soldiers, "Let the small ones go, let's cut down men!"

The taking of heads was a kind of ritual, the most solemn act in the life of a Montenegrin. It, too, belongs in the conceptual framework of the struggle, and as its motivational, emotive element at that. When a Turk once begged a Montenegrin not to cut off his head, the latter replied, "Whatever else thou dost ask, I shall do for thee, but this I cannot." So it was: he could not. A power stronger than benevolence kept him from it. Stevan Perkov saw it this way: "Had Adam cut off the heads of a couple or so angels, God would never have chased him out of paradise, for he would have seen that he had created a hero and not a good-for-nothing."

Bishop Rade was wise not to forbid the taking of heads. The struggle with the Turks was still a fact of life—not just a war between states, but a war of rancor and extermination.

Njegoš was the poet of massacres in which the cutting off of heads was a sacred and heroic act.

The ruler could not bypass the poet, or the civilized European the Montenegrin.

What gave inspiration brought victory that much closer.

27.

OUR OWN PEOPLE—AND precisely because they were our own—unjustly accused Bishop Rade of stinginess.

The Montenegrin Sovereign had no personal fortune, and the monastery revenues were insignificant—from the fishing on Lake Scutari and from some mills and a bit of land. There was no real state treasury, not even after 1837, when he appointed Milaković and inaugurated a kind of bookkeeping system. He purchased an iron safe in which he kept money that he did not deposit in banks. He covered current expenses either with Russian aid or with tax revenues; he obtained the former at the cost of humiliation and the latter at the price of fierce resistance. Every expenditure of any importance was subject to Russian review as well as to local criticism.

Even had he not been very conscientious, Bishop Rade would have been forced to handle his money with extreme parsimony.

His state was not as yet something abstract and inscrutable for the common man. It was naked power and not a bureaucratic state. Its leaders were the very chieftains with whom these same peasants quarreled over boundaries and landmarks and fought over pastures. Now these chieftains were gathering taxes, just like the Turks, and using them to pay salaries to their neighbors to judge their fellow-villagers, thus replacing the clan courts which had taken only fines. Everything was in plain sight, everything the authorities did was direct and completely in vew of the hungry and embittered subjects.

Russian supervision was not as direct, but it was offensive and perilous, inasmuch as the Russians could at any moment cut off the aid on which the government and much else depended.

There was no free spending, nor could there be. But there was theft and misappropriation. Was it not always possible for those who resold Russian grain to retain something for themselves out of any difference in the price?

There was no distinction, either in theory or in practice, between public property and the Sovereign's private property. But in this respect Bishop Rade was hardly an exception; it marks all feudal, Oriental, and even contemporary despotisms. Nevertheless, thanks to him alone, one knew under him better than under any absolute ruler just what was his and what was the state's. After his death he left a considerable sum—considerable as a personal fortune, though hardly much as a state treasury—about a half-million francs of that time. Where did he get all that money? A significant part of it came from the sale of monasteries and from monastic alms, as well as from that tower at Humac for which Ali Pasha had paid. The Bishop left the interest from that sum to his closest of kin as their income for life, while he left the principal to the Montenegrin state. This was conscientiousness in the extreme; after all, he had invested much effort in gaining that money, and it was certainly not right to abandon his parents and sisters. Yet he knew that, strictly speaking, that money did not belong to him, but to the people, to the state, and that he was merely leaving it to its rightful owners.

There were also political reasons, profound and noble, that compelled Bishop Rade to strict parsimony. Dušan Vuksan recounts that Bishop Rade intended to collect a sum large enough so that the interest from it might equal the Russian aid, and thus free him from the latter. He lent money, even on a mortgage—as in the case of a certain Elisabeth Graf in Vienna. He even sold his pectoral cross. It should not be believed that he did this in order to feed his people, as Bishop Petar had indeed done. Such a sum would have been too small to feed Montenegro. Besides, he never gave any of the rest of his money for food. Apparently he simply needed the money, or perhaps it occurred to him that the cross was dead capital. At any rate, the story about spending the money for food is a fabrication. He was indeed stingy with his money. The Austrian authorities, too, noted that he was tight with money—but never for his own benefit.

Bishop Rade was quick to perceive that in politics money sometimes played a greater role than force. Many great Montenegrin plans and his own failed through penury. Poverty dogged his every step. He wished to become independent of the Russians. He once said to Vrčević, "Who gives you money with one hand holds you by the pigtail with the other." He had to be closefisted—for the sake of his country and for its freedom.

Our rulers of that day, like all powerful men, were surrounded by men each of whom was convinced that he was not rewarded according to his deserts. Some held this opinion with reason, while others without any reason. There is no sure measure in such matters, for it all depends on the concrete circumstances and political needs. The Bishop refused many—and this provoked resentment and tales about his stinginess. Yet he did carry his parsimony to great lengths. To be sure, he was wise to refuse Sarajlija the money he wanted to build a brewery, for this was nothing but one of Sarajlija's pipe dreams. Nevertheless, he should have remembered his teacher. Nenadović reports that the Montenegrin Sovereign gave no tips while in Italy, using as his excuse that there were needier people in Cetinje. He avoided expensive rooms, and he did not buy rarities. There was also some pretty shabby avarice. Parsimony, like profligacy, has no limits. It has been recorded that, on being asked for money to finance a rather uncertain rebellion in Turkey, he replied, "And what if the rebellion should fail? The money will be gone."

He stretched himself in spending only as much as he had to, and only where necessary. If ever he went too far, it was in parsimony and never in profligacy. He was a good host and was generous in giving gifts—but he knew to whom and when it was necessary.

It was clear to him that every penny spent was taken from the mouths of Montenegrins, and he acted accordingly.

He was not really a miser.

Yet miserly rulers are better than the other kind.

28.

NJEGOŠ'S POETIC WORKS remained practically unrecognized and unnoticed by our littérateurs for a whole thirty years, until Svetislav Vulović.* Yet the injustice done to Bishop Rade as a ruler lasted even longer, till the end of the nineteenth century, the time of Rovinsky and Tomanović, and in some respects down to the present day.

In the popular memory that reign was regarded, like Njegoš's poetry, with a compulsive certainty, as something brutal but unavoidable which ruthlessly destroyed the bonds of blood relations, but which also boldly did away with the general insecurity—and thus as something more good than bad. Such a view was in keeping with the sense of popular justice as well as with the outlook of a clansman who had accepted the authority of a state government as a vital national necessity, though spiritually he had not yet made it a part of himself.

The unfavorable judgment of Bishop Rade's reign arose from an erroneous and superficial view precisely because it was made according to the standards of a time in which the extension of the national frontier, in the only possible way, to be sure—through war and battles with the Turks—was the order of the day and seemingly the most important thing. Such a view rested on a policy of so-called national unity. Bishop Rade did not engage in a single great battle, nor did he manage to enlarge his country; he even lost something—Vranjina and Lesendro—of the poor little patch that he had. This view also could hold that by his premature dynastic ambitions, which in turn caused him to adopt severe measures, he had divided the Montenegrins and set them against one another.

* (1847–98). A literary historian and critic, and professor at Belgrade University.

Victorious battles and conquered territories are only one aspect, and never the most important one, of any reign; besides, sometimes it is necessary to divide a people in order to release new social currents and to prepare the way for more significant and decisive victories. That is exactly what Bishop Rade did, and all that he could have done. What would Napoleon have been without the rationalists and the revolution? At best a good artillery colonel.

Like everything else, a state cannot find expression except in a concrete and specific form—through a certain form of government—though it may at the same time be the expression of the immanent tendency of human societies to band together in order to expand and further the conditions necessary to their survival. Even before the Petrovići and aside from the bishops, the Montenegrin clans had made significant attempts to unite under one government. The feudal lord Vujo Raičev, of Ljubotina, had been a kind of all-Montenegrin prince in the beginning of the seventeenth century. Even under the Turks up to the year 1628, the Montenegrin clans possessed a certain political identity as a separate sandjak with a significant number of *filuriciye,* or free peasants. Enserfment and the abolition of autonomy through annexation by the Sandjak of Scutari, in the first half of the seventeenth century, aroused widespread and lively resistance and a banding together with the purpose of forming their own government, a state of their own. In 1613 the Vizir of Scutari had to recruit an army in the seven sandjaks of Albania, and among the Montenegrins as well, to put down the rebellious Bjelopavlići and Piperi. The clans of Nikšić joined in the resistance with those of Katuni at the end of the seventeenth century, but were unable to preserve their independence. At the same time, if not before, the Kuči managed to unite about themselves the Orthodox population all the way to Sjenica. The rebellion in which the Montenegrins broke away from Turkey and turned to Venice as an autonomous dependency did not take place under Bishop Danilo, but before him, under Bishop Vissarion. Vissarion found it useful to record that the Montenegrins "of their own good will . . . did escape the Turkish hand and join Venice." In the realization that his own efforts were but a link, Danilo wrote, "This is neither the first beginning nor the final end." The elders of Raška held an assembly in Nova Varoš in the middle of the eighteenth century and tried to gain the help of the Russian Empress.

And in the beginning of the nineteenth century the farsighted and perspicacious Prior Gagović, of Piva Monastery, like the Montenegrin bishops, gathered together the neighboring clans and made a journey via Serbia to Russia.

The national state emerged from struggles, from fits and starts without number, but it was Bishop Rade who found the manner and form in which it was achieved—through supplanting the self-government of the clans with the power of the prince. That was a revolutionary act of far-reaching consequences, and it is in the discovery and realization of a particular form of rule that the Bishop's greatness lay, as is the case with every great statesman.

To be sure, such a feat required great spiritual and moral exertions, especially on the part of one who was himself a clansman. Yet Bishop Rade never for a moment lost conviction in his aim—in the idea.

Without that difficult task it is impossible to imagine the later victories and accomplishments of Prince Danilo and of King Nikola. This is not only because every human activity within a given civilization is linked to previous activities, even those it negates, but because Danilo and Nikola could not even have begun, let alone waged, their long and unequal struggles had they not inherited a centralized princely rule and the political unity of the Montenegrin clans. During Omer Pasha's invasion, one year after the Bishop's death, the Montenegrin clans would have fallen apart, and some might have gone over to the Turks against Cetinje, as was frequently the case in pre-Njegoš times, had it not been for Bishop Rade's achievements, which were hard on both himself and the Montenegrins.

Danilo and Nikola were also significant rulers.

Danilo—"Little Rabbit," as the people secretly dubbed him because of his small stature and green bulging eyes—completed the consolidation of the government with a brutality inconceivable even to the Montenegrins of those times. His penchant for violence derived not only from reasons of state but at times from personal caprice. He was the state. And he paid with his head for an act of arbitrariness and lust for revenge. Bishop Rade also issued harsh orders, but they were never degrading. Danilo swore and threatened: "Be careful what you are saying. Stop bleating, for if I come out there, stone will not rest on stone." He always carried out his threats. He fell like a thunderbolt upon Montenegro and ground into ashes all personal and clan resistance. As such he was a ruler of unfailing enterprise and industry. The entire Montenegrin past and psyche and all of his uncle's ideas were compressed in his deeds. He did not hesitate to part with Russia and to wage war on Turkey. He did not balk at massacring the helpless and at cutting off the most distinguished heads for the slightest opposition. He subordinated all to his authority, and subordinated this in turn to the struggle against the Turks. It was a reign of terror such as not even Montenegro had known. As a result, clan resistance was never again to be a serious problem; the idea of the state had been driven into the brain and flesh of the Montenegrins. They did not hate him; an authority such as his was inevitable and beneficial. As a matter of fact, they admired him. Yet there was no one in heroic Montenegro who did not fear him. He showed Europe and the world by his deeds—his victories and the establishment of order—that the Montenegrin state was a fact which could no longer be ignored. He remained great because of the keenness of his swinging blade—and because he perished before his arbitrary rule clashed with reality and became senseless.

His successor and nephew Nikola was a prudent ruler, and yet one not lacking in boldness or even in caprice. He was witty, loquacious, and possessed an unusually keen memory and comprehension. He knew most Montenegrins on sight, and, what is more significant, he had an unerring feel for the mentality not only of individual Montenegrins, but also of clans and brotherhoods and even families, and he certainly made use of it in his political maneuvers. He was wise in his craftiness and deliberate in his despotism. It was not only his fresh blood but his diplomatic agility which made him a father-in-law in Europe's most distinguished courts. He made an effort to shed as little blood as possible and killed off his political enemies by the silent treatment—he forbade anyone to visit them, he surrounded them with terror and intrigue, and forced them to quit Montenegro. Until the end of the century, when his rule clashed with new national and social relations—with Serbia's role as a Piedmont and with the advent of capitalism—and became unadorned and senseless brute force, he was in fact the most attractive figure on our national and cultural scene. He, too, was a poet. Laza Kostić, a great poet despite his exaggerated bizarreness, ranked him above Njegoš, obviously in a moment of romantic and somewhat sycophantic enthusiasm, but also because of his Westernized failure to grasp *The Mountain Wreath.* Actually, Nikola was a poet of no great talent, and his poetry was as much an educational and enlightening pendant to his rule as it was an inspiration. Yet even as a poet he blazed trails in an illiterate environment which had ceased to belong to the folk epic and which had not yet become something else—though he was jealous of true poetry, especially that of Bishop Rade, which gave him no peace as it commanded increasing admiration for its soaring heights. Nikola gained stature, both for himself and for Montenegro and the Balkans, by means of a great and significant war—that of 1875–1878—after which he won formal political independence at the Congress of Berlin in 1878, and proclaimed himself king in 1910. He enlarged Montenegro beyond its natural and ethnic borders and brought its education and economy a significant measure of progress. But he fell into an even greater war—the First World War. As always, the fall was more final than the rise. The latter half of his reign was marked by personal despotism which became an aim in itself and by the orgies of the camarilla of a primitive and beggarly court which tarnished the luster and prudence of the ruler's own past. As it is with all who carry over a form of government from one era into another, it was Nikola's misfortune that he lived too long, or, rather, that he reigned too long, and thus almost shattered the image of the most attractive and most significant political figure of our romantic period. It was his own loss as well as a loss to Serbdom and Montenegro.

Danilo and Nikola were both the fruits of Bishop Rade's labors.

If Bishop Petar was the culmination of episcopal, that is, theocratic rule over the clans, Rade was the beginning of civil rule. He thus broke the continuity of Montenegrin history. I would also say, moreover, that he broke Montenegro as well, specifically the Montenegrin way of life, of thinking and feeling. He did it, to be sure, by uniting the clans into a civil union and by giving this union a poetic and intellectual identity through his formulation of what it was to be a Montenegrin. With him Montenegro, its clans —for that is what Montenegro really was—reached its apex, but it also began to be transformed into something else and to lose itself in the larger political and national union. Of course, he was not aware of these consequences, nor could he have been. No one could. It is impossible to foresee the shape of realities inasmuch as they do not depend on our will alone. Yet that does not diminish his real greatness. All later currents have their source in him. A human community—class, nation, or people, group or caste—will accept any form of government that permits them to expand the opportunities for existence, all the more so if that form is the only possible one. Conversely, they will destroy all that stands in the way of their individual or collective survival.

Having brought out that Bishop Rade did create the only possible form of government, and not a state as such, we must also add that he did not found the Petrović dynasty, though he was in fact its first, uncrowned, prince. The historian Ilarion Ruvarac, who had reason to be exasperated by the inaccuracies and fabrications of Montenegrin histories, concluded formalistically that the Petrović dynasty began with Danilo's coronation in 1852. No, even here Bishop Rade created a break in something that had begun with Bishop Danilo: he first inaugurated the right of succession by inheritance—confirming this by his Testament in his own handwriting.

Still Ruvarac was right to connect the beginning of Montenegrin political history with Bishop Danilo. The Montenegro from the times of the Crnojevići and before them was not Montenegro, but vassal medieval Zeta. The very name Montenegro, which Ivan Crnojević was the first to use, referred to a region and to a feudal holding, and not to a state. All that transpired from the time of the Crnojevići to Danilo was slavery and struggle. It was not until the time of Bishop Danilo that Montenegro became the independent spark of a new Serbdom, and more than that—a mentality and a frame of mind recognized as something separate, a world within a world. Thus began its history, just like every other history.

Bishop Rade was a turning point in a modern age. He was this not only politically and socially, but in every other respect. With him and through him our ecclesiastical and folk culture came to an end and a new civil and individual culture began. It was with him and with Prince Miloš that we, as a people and as a state, actively entered the world arena. And Njegoš's poetic image of our people taking their place among the nations found fulfillment and became a universal imperative. Everything that is ours has its turning point in him and emanates from him. Even our moral concepts took a turn with him. Matavulj observed that until Bishop Rade and Prince Danilo "united the clans with bonds of iron into a nation" nothing was shameful—neither to steal nor to murder—as long as it was outside one's clan. Bishop Rade did not create it, but a bourgeois society in Montenegro in fact begins with him, albeit as something peculiar and in its incipient, peasant form.

The peasants, who under him became free of the clans and the chieftains, who resembled feudal lords but were in fact his servitors, brought Montenegro independence in the course of several wars.

Yet with independence and the acquisition and development of the first cities, there also began a decline of Njegoš's Montenegro. This found its first expression in the moral revulsion of the resistance leaders—Marko Miljanov, Jole Piletić, and Perko Pavlović—against the despotism of the prince and of his kin, and then in the discontent of the peasants caught in a market economy, and was finally embodied in the demands of the intellectuals for a parliamentary government and unification with Serbia.

Having attained its spiritual zenith in Bishop Rade and being broken to statehood under him, Montenegro—the land of myth and manliness—also began in fact to disappear with him.

It is not easy to be at a turning point, much less to break others and to be that breach oneself. If he felt the difficulties more deeply than others, Bishop Rade also had the strength to face them.

A task begun is a battle won—even if with the arms of successors.

No one has ever created a new world without destroying his own.

29.

NOTHING CAME EASY to Bishop Rade.

There was such hate and heroism with which to counter the Turks that they were the least of his worries. It was the Russians, his protectors, whom he should not have had to guard against, who occasionally confronted him with most unpleasant surprises. With Austria there was a concealed hatred which took on the guise of a cold amity. Thanks to the Russians, he neither could nor dared worsen relations with this mighty neighboring empire, a circumstance the experienced Austrian administration exploited at every turn.

Around him gathered all kinds of men, tossed by the times on free and unpacified Montenegro in search of a haven. The conditions were such that the domestic adventurer had not yet degenerated into a charlatan. Free-lancers came from the outside. Patriotic and wild Cetinje attracted our great spirits and curious foreigners, and also vagabonds and adventurers who were spoiling for a fight and eager for glory and easy pickings. A certain Joakim Djaković came fleeing from Austria for having counterfeited paper money. In Montenegro there was nothing to counterfeit, and so the Bishop engaged him to design and mold letters for the first Montenegrin primer. There are all kinds of stories about fugitives who sprang up as patriots and then just as quickly disappeared.

Seething with causes and taut with tensions, Cetinje was the target of plots, trickery, and espionage. And it was with all this that the Montenegrin Sovereign had to contend daily.

Thanks to the very false amity to which the Bishop was bound, the Austrian authorities were particularly successful in spying on him. It was important for Austria to keep track of Russia's moves in Cetinje. The Austrians were especially vigilant with regard to ties with Serbia; they surmised that something great and fateful was in the offing for the old multinational monarchy. The Austrians resorted to everything, and Bishop Rade was simply surrounded by Austrian informers. They got hold of his letters, messages, and even intimate political thoughts. Thus some valuable testimony came to be recorded, as well as a portrayal of the tangled and ominous atmosphere in which the Bishop had to live and work.

Today it is held that, in this respect, the craftiest spy of all was Captain Orešković, who wormed his way into the Bishop's favor by posing as a good Yugoslav. He obtained books for him, performed little favors, and offered his services as intermediary in the correspondence with Vuk Karadžić. This Yugoslav friend was not only a calculating spy, but he detested the Montenegrin Sovereign from the depths of his poisoned Austrophile soul and urged his own government to invade Montenegro. He not only detected the Bishop's granite steadfastness as a Montenegrin, but he also sensed the strength of his Yugoslavism, and even the uncertainty of his Christian faith. He recorded a piece of information that, though simplified and misrepresented, as a spy would, is a valuable clue to Njegoš's conception of things: that Bishop Rade was prepared to believe even in the sun if only he had something to gain from it.

Father Jakov Popović, of Kotor, who corresponded with Vuk and sent him reports concerning Bishop Rade with details that today are precious, was also an ordinary Austrian spy. Even the physician Golgi, who was sent to him from Kotor in 1838 when his leg began to pain him, gathered information on the side for the Austrian authorities.

Pressure from the neighboring Great Power was so great, and the yearning for power so irresistible, though the power was barely embryonic, that even Djordjije maintained close relations with the Austrian authorities, accepted their petty favors in Kotor, and told them things that were not for telling. Pero, too, the Bishop's own brother and deputy, sent roast meat to the Austrian officials in Kotor, by way of his wife, along with little notes in which he reported confidential or supposedly confidential items. Though still heroic in conception, the primitive milieu of the Montenegrin court was already corrupted by lust for power and intrigue.

Bishop Rade did not know about all of this, but he suspected as much. He knew only too well that one cannot shout on every mountaintop—and so he kept his counsels to himself. He frequently complained that he was "surrounded by spies." No sooner was one plot discovered than another was hatched, while betrayal followed upon betrayal.

The supporters of Austria were to make their presence felt at the Montenegrin court to the end, coming out into the open as the country fell under the blows of Austria in the First World War.

Bishop Rade surmised and observed to what lengths the struggle for power could go. "Better to reign in hell than serve in heaven," says Milton's Satan, and Njegoš holds the same. But he knew, too, that without authority there was no law and order among men—or freedom for Montenegro and for Serbdom.

He remained concerned for his people though he was angry at them. He elevated his participation in the suffering and misfortune of his people and subjects to the height of an ethical imperative. His uncle Bishop Petar used to say, "Whenever a Montenegrin house gets holes in its roof, it seems as though the water drips down my own neck." And he himself was to say, "Whenever a Serb groans, I, too, feel the pain."

He went to extremes in everything—both in his anger and in his cares for the land and the people. The solicitous head of household gave advice and talked of the chances of rain, while the merciless Sovereign threatened the people of Kotor, foreign subjects but men of our blood, who were about to go over to the Italians: "That ye cease your mischief . . . If, however, ye will not heed me, know that I shall bid you good morrow with my Montenegrins and that I shall be harder on you than the Turks, and ye know that I do not jest."

He cared for all that was Montenegrin or Yugoslav. To be sure, most of all for the idea. He tried to intervene with the Russian government to save a single lone Montenegrin who had been converted to Islam in Istanbul. At the very end of his life, a sick man, he wrote to Garašanin, "I fear that after me all those troubles which came before me will return to Montenegro and that eternal misfortune may be the lot of this little people, unschooled but warlike and mighty in spirit and in heart." A few days before his death he asked the Captain of Kotor to see to it that some citizens of Kotor returned a debt of cattle to Djuro Martinović.

He was a despot. But it was a young despotism, which arose out of the people and their terrible struggle. Everything about it was still intimate, like a family affair. The most brutal squaring of accounts took place, as among kinfolk and out of personal scores. Regard for honor and Montenegrin pride was an absolute rule with him. He was easily accessible, and one could say everything to him. When Prince Danilo once asked Stevan Perkov in what way his own heroes differed from those of Njegoš's time, the latter replied, "They spoke their thoughts freely to the Sovereign, while these shrug their shoulders as soon as the Prince asks them something important."

Bishop Rade felt the demonic lust for power, but it never conquered him. His power was still a means and not an end. He tried to weigh his every act on the scales of an impersonal and absolute justice.

Isidora Sekulić knew of no poet—and she knew many and thoroughly—who used the word *folly* as much. That is true—about his poetry. As a ruler, his pendant to that word was the word *evil*. These words are involved in everything that had to do with him. They emerge from his conception of the world and of human destiny, including, of course, his own. These are the inverted expression of faith in reason and in a higher necessity, in the duty to struggle against evil.

The Sovereign wrestled ceaselessly with evil and ignorance.

The poet snatched moments when under the greatest pressure to give expression to what he experienced and endured as man and ruler. *The Ray of the Microcosm* was written soon after the loss of Lesendro, *The Mountain Wreath* in the heat of domestic betrayals, and *Stephen the Small* while he was beating down mutiny with his other hand and ridding himself of rebels. His years of greatest political tensions were also those of his greatest creativity. For nearly ten years—from 1837—Bishop Rade consolidated his authority and state to ready it for the final struggle, and during all this time the poet matured within him—ripe for the greatest beauties. The tension was not apparent, yet within the space of three or four years—from 1844 to 1848—his whole being unabatedly poured forth all his talents. It was during his fierce struggle to preserve the authority which he had spent years to establish that his poetic truths poured forth and flowed.

The ruler and the poet were two in one. To write poetry, to dispense justice to the Montenegrins, to wage war on the Turks, to play a game of wits with the Austrians, and to outwit the Russians—all were but different aspects of a single activity, different sides to the same personality. He regarded both poetry and ruling a duty—a higher calling. Truly his rule was both an epic and a bitter lyric.

A personality devoid of Njegoš's conceptual profundity and uninspired by the inscrutable depths of the national past could never have dared to engage in such radical enterprises as a ruler. Even were such a man to be found, only a poet was capable of expressing the terrible struggle the ruler had to wage. The ruler inspired the poet, and the poet heartened the ruler.

Bishop Rade came and went, like his times. His real life is preserved in his art—in his poetry. Yet insofar as our previous tragic existence was broken by him and across his back, this is the cry and wail of his poetry.

Life is not a poem. But poetry is life.

THE POET OF SERBIAN COSMIC MISFORTUNE:

THE RAY OF THE MICROCOSM, THE MOUNTAIN WREATH, STEPHEN THE SMALL

ANY STUDY MUST disengage the ruler from the poet. It must also distinguish Njegoš's poetical works from one another; once created, each work of art comprises a world in itself, and only an analysis applied to it specifically is able to re-create it.

Although they differ in theme and treatment, Njegoš's three major works—*The Ray of the Microcosm, The Mountain Wreath,* and *The False Tsar Stephen the Small*—lead into one another and even develop one out of the other. It is possible to observe a deeper connection here: *The Ray of the Microcosm* is Njegoš's broadest canvas of the world—a cosmic drama that will appear in *The Mountain Wreath* as the Serbian destiny within the frame of Montenegrin events, only to end in *Stephen the Small* in, so to speak, the everyday reality of Montenegro. This is how it looks in the round. And this is the actual shape of Njegoš's conceptual and emotive progression and development.

Moreover, these works are so close to one another chronologically that this alone would render their substantive separation artificial, though there might well be an objective reason for such a separation—in Njegoš himself: *The Mountain Wreath* looms so high and embraces such breadth that the other two can be nothing but overshadowed by it. Yet there is no separation, and certainly no subordination, with Njegoš. This is something others have perpetrated out of political and ideological motives, by using him as a front. To tell the truth, I myself am not guiltless in this. As the exigencies of the moment caused me to grasp at one aspect or another of Njegoš, it happened that the whole Njegoš became forgotten and that *The Ray of the Microcosm* and *Stephen the Small* were slighted. Today such is most frequently the fate of *The Ray of the Microcosm* because of its predominantly religious character. In the past this was the case with *Stephen the Small* inasmuch as it was overshadowed as a national drama by *The Mountain Wreath.*

The consequences of setting Njegoš against Njegoš and of using him as a prop did not, of course, affect his works. Artistic creation is impervious to calumny or even to perversion. Yet the magnetic power and fateful meaning of this poetry have been and still are so great, and the controversy in this arena so fierce and extreme, that the tendency to exploit Njegoš did not lessen with time but, rather, increased, changing only its form and motivations. Moreover, there is little hope that any generation of our tongue will ever be able to judge Njegoš's poetry dispassionately and to grasp it in all its purity, inasmuch as it speaks of our own existence.

As long as we are on this subject, it must be emphasized that such expressions as *fate, existence, destiny,* and the like are very diverse in meaning and require some definition on my part. If we abstract certain qualities from something that, in a given moment, appears existential in relation to art, science, and level of knowledge—and this is both possible and inevitable in the philosophy of art—then these qualities will appear to the human consciousness as the essence of that something or, to speak the language of art, as its destiny, fate, or, in the language of science, as the mode and condition of its existence. Of course, essences do not exist. Everything may be presented as an essence in one aspect or another. Yet even if essences really do not exist, the very necessity of living and thinking—of living by thinking, within the limits set by the level of learning and our own vital personal and social needs and passions—condemns us to accept as the essence of every form those aspects we can grasp and formulate as philosophy or express emotively through works of art. Matter, the world, things, exist independently of ourselves, but we are capable of comprehending only moments, fragments, and certain of the laws of their existence. Art records the rhythms and the visions of our existence in the world and, to be sure, in society, and our emotional relation to it. Science unfolds the accessible and finite laws of matter. Religions try to bring man closer irrationally and to subordinate him to those laws which are obviously inaccessible and immutable, and to which laws he is already subject. Philosophy, somewhere between science and religion, generalizes essences, that is, what things appear to be in any given moment, and which from a practical standpoint constitute the truth, as actuality, for a certain group of men at a given time.

In the life of our people, particularly during their long slavery under the Turks, certain traits manifested themselves in the mode of their existence and in a way of thought which seemed to Njegoš to be, as they in fact were in his times, realities, destiny and truth. Yet Njegoš was too perceptive and sensitive not to surmise that nothing occurs outside the rest of the universe, that in the final analysis the same laws hold good for everything and everybody. The Serbian destiny, and Njegoš's own, did not unfold in an indifferent cosmos, or under a different set of laws; it was only a concrete aspect of cosmic and universal human encounters. That destiny is fulfilled daily, under concrete circumstances, determined by absolute laws and shaped by concrete conditions. That is, after all, the arch shared by every great thinker and poet—the connection between the abstract and the concrete, the discovery of laws in forms.

The separation of Njegoš's works—and we are speaking here of the three poems cited above—inevitably shatters and mangles his poetry, inasmuch as that poetry forms an indivisible part of his thought, his conception of the world and of the human and national destiny in it, and is nothing but the poetic, lyrical expression of that thought, that conception. To do such a thing means simply to reveal one's own troubled conscience and disability. There exists not only Njegoš's head—*The Mountain Wreath*—but his limbs—the philosophical flights in *The Ray of the Microcosm* —and the experiences of life in *Stephen the Small*. To be sure, *The Mountain Wreath* embraces and sublimates all of Njegoš's aspects, including those that predominate in *The Ray of the Microcosm* and in *Stephen the Small*, but it is more difficult to grasp and to comprehend without the motivations and inspirations of the other two.

This is how the matter stands from the formalistic point of view as well: *The Ray of the Microcosm* is a pure poem, *The Mountain*

Wreath a poetic drama, while *Stephen the Small* could be called a Montenegrin social drama, even a comedy. As they proceeded from the abstract to the concrete, Njegoš's thought and experience flowed uninterruptedly into their corresponding poetic forms.

To be sure, Njegoš had no previous intention of linking his views and experiences and presenting them in three different parts —the general, the national, and the immediate. All this flowed from him spontaneously, in due course, as it matured, and he put it to paper, very rapidly and without much polishing. Yet it is the same man, the same thought and experience in motion, endowed with perception and form. Moreover, he was a genius: he encompassed our national destiny and rendered it into poetry, as a profound and, I would say, a universal sage as well as a warrior. The whole took shape in the various aspects of each of his three mentioned works, first in one way and then in another. Of course, Njegoš's personal fate and the unequal struggle of the Montenegrins and the Serbian misfortune at Kosovo all merge in their tragic themes to provide his basic inspiration, but never outside or contrary to the laws that govern the cosmos and the destiny of mankind. Inasmuch as we are dealing with works of poetry, what is essential here is not whether Njegoš's conception of these laws was correct, but with what intensity he experienced and expressed this conception, and with him this was related to our national misfortune, and, it should be said, to his own.

It is possible to enjoy *The Mountain Wreath* on its own. Yet a more complete understanding of both Njegoš and *The Mountain Wreath* requires insight into *The Ray* and *Stephen the Small.* The road from *The Ray of the Microcosm* had to lead to *The Mountain Wreath.* Yet without *Stephen the Small,* despite the fact that it is inferior as poetry, that road would not be completed—in the immediate reality of Montenegrin life.

Njegoš arrived at the destination he had chosen—from the abstraction of *The Ray of the Microcosm* to the national myth of *The Mountain Wreath* and to Montenegrin concretions in *Stephen the Small*—from a little shepherd Petrović on a bare rocky plain caught between Austrian snare and Turkish sword, to the sovereign of an independent state. Not for a moment, not by a hairsbreadth was that journey broken. It is the most complete and most moving in our history—thought, verse, and deed in one.

Njegoš expressed our destiny; he embodied our destiny—and this happened only once.

Were we to dissect him, we would be dissecting ourselves. Perhaps that is the way it is—everybody dissects himself.

THE RAY OF THE MICROCOSM

1.

OTHERS HAVE ALREADY established the sources of *The Ray of the Microcosm* and have indicated Njegoš's debt to other poets.

It was long held—even by such serious critics as Svetislav Vulović, Pëtr Alekseevich Lavrov, Jaša Prodanović, Milan Rešetar, and even Jovan Skerlić—that *The Ray of the Microcosm* could not be regarded as an original poem because it leaned so heavily on foreign influences, especially Milton's *Paradise Lost.* This initial impression is all the more damaging inasmuch as Njegoš's poem is both narrower in scope and lacking in Milton's rich imagery as well as in the power of his dogmatic dialectic. As soon as one begins to delve into the essence of both the one poem and the other, there come to view the differences between them and Njegoš's originality in all essentials. This is especially the case with respect to those other influences which are less significant than that of Milton.

Dušan Stojanović, who has made the most detailed comparison of *The Ray of the Microcosm* and *Paradise Lost,* has confirmed the already established fact of Njegoš's originality, not only poetic but also thematic. Such is also the case with respect to the composition and the action of the six cantos, along with the "Dedication" to Sima Milutinović-Sarajlija, which comprises a philosophical introduction to the poem. In 2,210 lines—compared to Milton's 10,300—Njegoš presents the journey of his soul through the heavens and its remembrance of Satan's rebellion in which Adam participated as one of the discontented angels, as well as the defeat and the fall of the rebels. Milton's poem includes only the rebellion, developed in much greater detail, and Adam's earthly transgression.

Proceeding from a different standpoint, Njegoš's religion, Bishop Nikolaj Velimirović was the first to defend the originality of Njegoš's poem.

The German scholar Alois Schmaus went further in that defense, making comparisons with other influences as well. He arrived at the proper conclusion that Njegoš differed from Milton in something fundamental: Milton's Adam violates God's commandments as the first man, while Njegoš's Adam is a fallen angel who had existed in heaven, but who, because of his participation in Satan's rebellion, was cast upon the earth to atone for his transgression. In this Njegoš is far from any Western influence, and Schmaus has traced its roots to the East—to Plato and to those earliest Christian teachings which were still under the influence of the Greek Idealist philosophy.

Isidora Sekulić has confirmed the poetic-philosophical independence of *The Ray of the Microcosm.*

The influences on *The Ray* are manifold and varied: influences on its subject matter and action, on its religious-philosophical views, and, finally, on the sources from which they sprang. This third element—the sources—has remained the least investigated, while one may say that the first two have been definitively established.

The subject of *The Ray of the Microcosm* is the myth of man's first sin. This is also the subject of *Paradise Lost,* as well as of many other poems and legends. Milton's most obvious influence on *The Ray* is not so much the principal subject; as already stated, Njegoš's Adam is a fallen angel while Milton adheres to the Bible with a Puritanical purism. Especially reminiscent of Milton is Satan's rebellion against God's omnipotence—a dramatic element in both poems—but the influence is more a matter of the action itself rather than the motifs. Yet the very way Njegoš goes about uncovering the secrets of the heavens—a guardian archangel leads his soul to heaven as a divine spark—obviously reflects Dante's influence: the poet of *The Divine Comedy* is also led through the other worlds—though by Virgil and Beatrice.

The investigation of similarities in the action took still other directions and also arrived at convincing and interesting results. Thus Radivoje Vrhovac and Nikola Banašević have pointed to the heavenly visions and to Satan's rebellions in the old church writers and in the Apocrypha. It is worth recalling that copies of these were to be found in Montenegrin churches of the time.

Veselin Čajkanović and Sofrić were successful in recording folk tales about how God had created men with wings, that is, like the angels. There is a Montenegrin fable about the evil Tsar Dukljan —the Montenegrin name for Diocletian—who had enslaved men and rebelled against God, defeating even his blessed servants. According to that tale, Dukljan, like Njegoš's Satan, was immortal, and only God was capable of finally curbing him—by placing him in fetters. The tale does not indicate whether Dukljan's evil kingdom has existed ever since the beginning of man or from the moment of his first sin, though it clearly deals with the primeval life of man. Even if this fable might have been an influence on Njegoš, his motifs of evil and the kingdom of darkness are more clearly defined and more profound, harking back to the primeval cosmic struggle between light and darkness.

The influences on *The Ray of the Microcosm,* then, came from various quarters—from books and from religious and folk tales.

These influences serve further to reveal another of Njegoš's characteristic features: he borrowed the action in all of his poems, and then transformed and expressed it in his own manner. A poet of vast imagination when it came to imagery and vision, he did not like to invent plots, but always proceeded from existing motifs, developing these in conformity with his own views and inspirations.

Nor is the case any different regarding his views and conceptions. Their roots, too, are elsewhere, despite all the originality with which they are developed and carried out.

Njegoš's fruits drew their sap from various roots and from great depths, as is the case with every real creator.

2.

RESEARCH SCHOLARS HAVE experienced special trouble in ferreting out the source of the idea of pre-existence—the belief that, before the first sin, man lived in heaven. And then Schmaus solved that, too.

One of the most important philosophical problems in the Middle Ages was that of so-called theodicy, which converges on the question: Why does God, who is absolutely good and just, permit man to sin?

The explanations of the Church proceed from the Biblical myth: despite God's prohibition, Adam ate of the fruit of the tree of knowledge, for which he was driven from paradise. No matter how deeply this legend has penetrated the destiny of man, and regardless of the fact that it has become part of Christian dogma, Njegoš departed from it and adopted the conception of pre-existence, of man's original life in heaven. We find this idea in Origen, the most significant religious thinker in the beginning of the third century; he tried to explain the stories of the Bible as allegories and to reconcile Christianity with Platonism. We find various aspects of this conception among the Gnostics as well, and also among various medieval sects, including our own Bogomils, and especially clearly among the French Albigenses, who regarded the soul as a fallen angel whose punishment was to be shackled in the body.

The church councils condemned Origen, as they did so many others, for a teaching that one of our bishops—who was hardly a church dogmatist and still less a bishop—accepted as the explanation of man's misfortune. Conscious of the incongruity of his position and his view of the Church's teachings, Njegoš rather unaccountably, in the sixth and last canto of *The Ray of the Microcosm,* threw in the Christian myth of Adam's life in paradise and ended the canto with a short and moving hymn to Christ, all of which has no connection either with the action or with the conception of the remaining text.

We find the teaching of pre-existence in Klopstock * as well, while the idea of light and darkness, of good and evil as antagonists, which lies at the base of Njegoš's conception of the world, is to be found in almost all the religions of the East, including Christianity, and is especially developed in Zarathustra and in Manichaeism. Having *The Ray of the Microcosm* and Njegoš in mind, I, too, have discovered a whole series of models of that kind. This will be the experience of everyone who reads anything about the Eastern religions or the medieval mystics—and so there is little to be gained by citing sources. It might almost be said that pre-existence and the struggle between light and darkness are the common ground of the Eastern religions and the medieval mystics.

The teaching of pre-existence was not original even with Origen. It may be found, in somewhat less clear form, in Plato—in his

* Friedrich Gottlieb Klopstock (1724–1803), German poet.

Orphic myths—as well as in various Eastern cults, by way of which it penetrated ancient Greece. Banašević discovered a simple but significant fact: in Njegoš's library there was a Russian translation of Dumont d'Urville's voyages, which describe the Eastern teaching of pre-existence and the belief that the visible world was created as a punishment for man. If the former—pre-existence—is the basic motif in *The Ray of the Microcosm,* then the latter—the material world as a punishment for man—is one of Njegoš's philosophical and religious postulates.

We should be clear about one thing: Njegoš had no intimate knowledge of the many models and sources that have been ascribed to him—the cabala, the Gnostics, and perhaps even Origen—except insofar as they came from the most general histories, which he owned and was fond of reading. A direct tie with Plato seems to be not only probable but proven. Like every autodidact, Njegoš eagerly sought and easily found the support of the greatest authorities. In "the divine Plato" he found confirmation of his most general and most essential views, as well as of certain details. For example, like the Greek philosopher, so Njegoš, too, though less clearly, has ideas living an independent existence in the heavens.

Many things came to Njegoš by way of cultural crosscurrents and legends. Indeed, with him it is more a case of incorporating and blending like views and inspirations than of copying and imitation. Such a course is quite natural for every creator. Goethe himself pointed out that he made generous use of the motifs and views of others, only to develop them in his own manner, while there is not a single work of Shakespeare the roots of which are not to be found elsewhere.

Surprisingly few studies have been devoted to Njegoš's native inspirations.

Svetozar Matić has shown that Njegoš's teacher Sarajlija had an interest in cosmic themes. Njegoš himself stated, in verse, that Sarajlija first led him into the problems of heaven, and he dedicated *The Ray of the Microcosm* to none other than Sarajlija. Let us observe in passing that Matija Ban also recorded Njegoš's severe but just opinion of Sarajlija's poetry, to wit: a completely uneven poet, but one with frequent, wonderfully powerful flights of imagination. It was left to a Czech, Julius Heidenreich, to make a comparison between the cosmic motifs and visions of Sarajlija and Njegoš. The similarities are great, astonishing. Like Njegoš, Sarajlija regards the soul as "a spark of God" which flies heavenward and glorifies God. In his *Mazda,* too, celestial visions are glorified and God brings new worlds into being. Obviously Njegoš's first cosmic motifs originate with Sarajlija. Nor is it any different concerning, so to speak, the terrestrial problems. Njegoš was not alone in the poetic comprehension and presentation of our national history; there were others, and Sarajlija in particular. Both the cosmic and the national themes of Sarajlija are apparent in Njegoš's early poems—in *A Montenegrin to Almighty God, A Montenegrin Captured by a Fairy,* and others. Schmaus emphasizes that Njegoš could have got certain ideas from still other contemporary native writers—Jovan Subotić, for example—as well as from the native press. The *Srbski narodni list (Serbian National Journal),* to which Njegoš contributed, published philosophical teachings, including the following: "Man is fundamentally by nature also an entire divine or spiritual little world (a microcosm)," while "God [is] the spirit of the world, distributed everywhere from a center, the source of all life, like unto light, and by nature tantamount to truth."

Besides these contemporary and readily available sources, there were other, more remote but also more substantial, native influences—the Montenegrin and Serbian reality, to which the historical mythical past belongs. To be sure, the link with such influences is usually the easiest to accept and the hardest to prove. These influences are of two kinds: the spiritual climate—conceptions and beliefs—and the immediate reality—its reflections and transformations in Njegoš's spirit.

Nothing great is conceived at once and without a connection with something else. Everything is constructed on the basis of existing relations, forms, ideas, forces, and their configurations, inter-relations, syntheses. This holds true especially for a conceptual work of art. *Faust* was developed from a medieval myth, while it was long disputed whether the *Iliad* was a collection of folk poems or an original epic which brought these together. Nor can Plato's philosophy be divorced from religious and poetic myths, while Kant had reason to regard himself as Locke's disciple, and Marx as Hegel's disciple. The new is new by virtue of being a transformation and development of the old.

In *The Mountain Wreath* the very subject matter brings into relief and renders obvious its native ideas and realities. However, *The Ray of the Microcosm* is a different matter: here many folk conceptions and beliefs have receded, while any attempt to discover Montenegrin and Serbian realities in the celestial and intellectual spheres can only lead to superficial and forced schematization.

Nevertheless there are some things to which we can turn. First there is that Montenegrin religiosity—the belief in an omnipotent God without a developed cult of Christ or the Mother of God and without the Holy Spirit. This we find also in *The Ray of the Microcosm,* though, to be sure, in a more elevated, more finished form and presented so harmoniously that one might speak of its tendency to turn into a philosophical religious system. Together with their belief in demonic powers and the miracles of local saints, for the Montenegrins—as well as for Njegoš—God is abstract, involved in all that is human and secular, not as a physical force, but as a mysterious power which is immanent in all creation. The Creator of all things both visible and invisible is also this for Njegoš, but elevated to a general lawgiver and poetic, artistic Creator. This difference is understandable: the still-animist Montenegrin conceived of God as an omnipresent and immediate reality, while Njegoš was already an abstract thinker who was trying to explain the world in its entirety and its laws. Even in the Montenegrin view the cited conception of God is the more abstract while the conception of demonic forces is predominantly animistic. Furthermore, although Montenegrin beliefs lack any specific idea that the world and man are governed by primeval forces of good and evil, or light and darkness, matter and spirit, still one can positively derive from these beliefs the idea that man's actions are subject to the omnipresent powers of evil and to an omnipresent God and his angels and saints. Finally, even if there is no specific Montenegrin belief in a God of light, we have it in John's epistles and elsewhere in Christian teachings. Njegoš drew on popular and other beliefs—thoroughly and to the end. And from these influences was woven the poetic and the philosophical texture of *The Ray of the Microcosm.*

One can find reliable sources and proofs for these conclusions in the renowned Marko Miljanov—after Njegoš the most famous

Montenegrin and Montenegrin writer. Though younger than Njegoš, Marko Miljanov was closer to the people by virtue of his lack of learning, and thus he expressed more directly and in less altered form what he found among the people. He states explicitly that man is governed by higher powers of good and evil: "This is not permitted by nature, this is not permitted by the blood which contains some divine force which rules over man's good will and bad." Putting quotations aside, Miljanov is lost in admiration for the good, for humanity and reason as the higher imperatives over man.

As long as we are speaking of external sources, it should be mentioned that there is proof of the connection between Lamartine's and Hugo's views on the one hand and Njegoš's on the other. In his *Notebook* Njegoš inscribed a multitude of verses by both these poets, and exclusively those dealing with cosmic themes. Yet this is more a case of the similarity of ideas, which both Hugo and Lamartine got from the East and from the Middle Ages.

The Ray of the Microcosm is a strange and complicated blend of local life and color, to be sure, quite modified, with Western influences on the action, and Eastern influences on the ideas. Yet Njegoš's cosmos is Montenegrin—a conception that binds the rock and evil with infinity and the absolute laws of good. Especially his are the expression, the vision, and the imagery. Isidora Sekulić concluded concerning *The Ray of the Microcosm,* "Nowhere in his work did he betray the necessity of having to venture beyond himself and his own native region and art for the essence of his thought, poetry, and language."

3.

THE INQUIRY INTO many even more direct ties between *The Ray of the Microcosm* and the realities of both Montenegro's and Njegoš's actual existence is not without foundation.

All the more prominent students of the question agree on one thing: the bitterness and travail that were the Sovereign's lot drove the poet to seek explanations in the cosmic order and in universal laws. Njegoš was too wise, and, besides, too proud a Montenegrin, to seek solace in anything or from anyone. Yet his struggle with the clans and the Turks did not occur as simply his personal fate: it was abstracted into a conflict between good—order—and evil—chaos. To clip the wings of evil, of evil men, and of lawlessness—this was the order of the day, not only for Bishop Rade, but for the ordinary Montenegrin. The poet had to extract poetic images and philosophical abstractions from this encounter, and he did. I do not wish to imply that art is but a reflection of reality. But it is a re-creation, a creation of something from reality or fantasy, that is, from fantasized reality or concrete fantasy. *Nescio quid.*

Njegoš is no abstract Western logician, or a scholastic dogmatist, but a sage spawned in the myths of Serbian tribal lore. He also has something of the Church and of the Middle Ages in his imagery and décor, and even in his viewpoints—as in the external form, after all, of his reign. But his reaction is for the most part direct, primitive, and as such a distilled quintessence of reality, of his own experiences and views. His God in *The Ray of the Microcosm* has much of the medieval monarch—like Bishop Rade himself—while his angels appear as vassals. It is these recastings of Montenegrin realities that first catch the eye. Satan is borrowed, even as to his appearance, from ecclesiastical and other mythology, but his figure and power and willfulness all point to a discontented clan chieftain.

This is so only if we oversimplify. Yet if we do precisely this, we shall then perceive how much truth there is in it. Njegoš's God is, above all, a creator, that is, a poet. He is "caught up in the poetry of creation," for his very creation is poetry—an artistic act. Njegoš was far from playing God. Nevertheless he maintained that man was bound to God in "kinship." This kinship was something real: the soul, reason—these were the light of God in man. Thus man, too, possessed something of the highest creative power. Njegoš never ceased to speak of his own "kinship" with God. The divine light overcame chaos in the cosmos, while human reason had a similar effect, being of the selfsame light. Njegoš felt that the order he had established in Montenegro was the fulfillment of God's commandment. The realities of Montenegro's and Njegoš's existence, though not only these, were simply transposed to the heavens and placed under the aspect of eternity. It was not without reason that Pero Slijepčević recognized certain patriarchal Montenegrin traits in God and Satan: he saw Satan as some chieftain who did not demand all the power for himself, but was willing to share authority with God, as long as he was independent in his own heaven—the clan. This is another trait that distinguishes Njegoš's Satan from the one found in myths and in literature. To be sure, neither Satan nor God, nor anything else in *The Ray of the Microcosm,* can be reduced to just that, not even essentially. Satan is the celestial image of man's terrestrial misfortune. Yet his attitude, expression, coloration are Montenegrin.

Even celestial social relations, if we may call them so, were reflections of Montenegrin society: there was a multitude of equal gods until a mysterious event sent their kingdoms crashing, and God, one of those gods, took unto himself the power of creation and the ordering of the universe—the cosmos. It is indeed on behalf of the old order, the former gods, and the autonomous heavens that Satan rebels.

Hear how God and Satan portray themselves and the state of affairs in heaven, between an absolute celestial ruler and discontented celestial chieftains.

God says:

> The laws of general order are my pledge,
> They are the life of nature. If all worlds
> Began to overthrow them and destroy,
> My powerful hand should arm itself with wrath,
> And crush them into shapeless fragments, throw them
> Into the yawning chasm of gloom, and then
> I should call up new worlds from the abyss,
> And crown them on their bright celestial paths.

And Satan speaks of

> The former fate of heaven's lofty spheres,
> And how the haughty sovereign of the skies
> Had seized omnipotence and then begun
> To dominate the overwhelming space.
> . . . .
> In ancient times th' entire space was sown
> With radiant spheres; no spot of gloom appeared,
> And every sphere resembled then our heaven
> In breadth and brightness: they were equal all.
> On every sphere there was a throne erected,
> As high as now is heaven's highest throne:

On every throne there sat a crowned prince—
But suddenly a terrible event
Destroyed the greatness of primeval heavens:
All worlds through all the boundless spaces trembled
And shook with a disastrous destiny.
. . . .
Then all the gods were hurled from their thrones,
And all the worlds, precipitated, rushed,
And with a roaring thunder all were flung
Upon the altar of the sovereign gloom.
The terror of this spectacle no brain
Imagines. Hurrying to their giant grave
The orbs there broke each other in their flight
And fell in fragments huge into the gulf.
In everlasting ruin all had sunk.
One single world outlived the storm unhurt,
Protected by an eyeless destiny:
Thereon the throne is rising of my foe.
. . . .
The new celestial master now created
Small worlds, and filled them with inhabitants
So weak that all should humble subjects be.
. . . .
I ask to share the might with him in heaven,
And raise the fallen worlds from the abyss,
To give to nature back her ancient law,
That everyone should reign with power supreme
As only lord and master o'er his heaven.

Most impressive of all is the reflection of the struggle between the Montenegrins and the Turks in the struggle between God's angels and Satan's rebels—a parallel that has been perceived by many and that strikes one at first glance.

Reality is one of the elements of a work of art.

Njegoš created his own world from that of reality.

Marked by its time and milieu, a work of art is a fragment, an instant snatched from the absolute, from eternity—at once universal and beyond time.

4.

NJEGOŠ WAS DEEPLY religious, not so much by inheritance, much less by way of mystical rapture, as out of the knowledge that man's destiny is determined by some higher order. This was the religion of the sage, and it came from penetrating into the mysteries of man and the universe. It is not essential here whether that knowledge was scientifically correct or what form it took—in this case a religious form—but whether it was sincere and in what measure it admits us into the mysteries, or at least brings us emotionally closer to them. It neither tries nor is able by its very unscientific nature to solve any mystery.

Njegoš had no need of a God to pray to. He turned to him as to the ultimate mystery and explanation of the secular order and of man's fate. Like the great Idealist philosophers, Njegoš, too, wished to discover the essence of being and the ultimate truths.

That the cosmos, in all of its least parts, is governed by immutable laws is something about which all serious thinkers agree, regardless of their school. Nor is it a matter of dispute whether man can know those laws one way or another. Differences of opinion arise from the approach to those laws: some regard them as determinative and independent of matter, while others maintain that they are the qualities of matter and modes of its existence. These differences entail still others: either man perceives absolute truths because these laws are accessible to him independently, or, on the contrary, man perceives only relative truths inasmuch as he can arrive at these laws only by way of matter, to which he himself is bound in subjection according to the degree of his knowledge and technical proficiency.

Social factors are, of course, not the least among those that form a thinker. Nor should even personal inclinations be discounted if we would know what elusive skein of circumstances turned Njegoš to philosophy, whether it was philosophy that impelled him to seek to explain the world or whether the need to explain the world drew him to philosophy.

There was no single motivation—either of inheritance, duty, or social circumstance—that could have forced Njegoš to take another course. On the contrary, everything drove him toward idealism and religion—his reading, his personal inclinations, inasmuch as he was an individual who was both sensitive and exceptionally rational. He was a rationalist pure and simple, though not of any philosophical school, but, rather, in his manner of thinking and acting —all so logical and reasoned out—and especially in his faith in reason and its absolute divine power and divine quality. As such, Njegoš was bold and unwilling to be stopped by a mystery and to admit his impotence, whether in the act or in the consciousness. He knew that he was not able, that it was not given to him, to unveil the ultimate mystery, but he never reconciled himself to this. He constantly probed and plumbed. Perhaps this was really getting at the mystery after all. "Why was I not there to see when the clouds of endless night were first pierced by that light whose particles fall on our earth and bestow eternal life on every flower and fruit?" This was Njegoš, this was what he asked in his *Notebook*. The very question reveals the force of the turbulence within him, and also the depth of his contemplation and thought.

That there is no ultimate cause, that there is nothing beyond matter or anything that occurs except by its own immanent laws —such a view also requires courage and depth. All the more so inasmuch as this view places upon man, whose brain has the capacity to comprehend the law, the full responsibility for man's fate.

But Njegoš did not belong to that trend, which does not mean that he was not of the greatest and, if one might say so, most definitive spiritual thinkers.

How comical it is to reproach Njegoš for not having adhered to a school which had just come to the fore. It is even more stupid to hold that the school to which he adhered was in itself worthless and absurd. For it is not important by which method and through what form we have arrived at an artistic, that is, a relative philosophical truth, but whether it is really that. Let us add in passing: to maintain that one view is always and everywhere unconditionally correct—and I happen to belong to the materialistic—is not a whit wiser, more freedom-loving, or more just than to maintain that one's religion is the only true one and therefore the only permissible one. Also this: any given view has behind it not just the aspirations of some social force, though these undoubtedly exist, but much else besides, and each view entails its own method —whether logical or empirical—and its own inclination—whether toward the cosmos or toward man. Man is neither a puppet manipulated by objective conditions nor wax on which the objective world with its laws makes its impressions. He is a creative being—a living, thinking piece of the cosmos who perpetually renews himself together with his nature and his society.

Njegoš does not expound on the external world, as though he did not experience it, or on man taken separately, but on man in the cosmos—the relationship between man and the world, that is to say, man and absolute laws. To put it most succinctly and essentially: Njegoš was oriented toward man, to be sure, not toward man in general, but toward man whose soul behaves in accordance with absolute law, inasmuch as the law itself, the spirit of reason, is a divine light and a part of Almighty God himself.

Though of this world, Njegoš was to remain oriented to the end toward philosophy and the cosmos. He drove this point home in his *Notebook* with a moving picture: "A man alone on a high mountain, in the moonless night, beholds the gladsome movement of the heavenly bodies, and of the silver waves playing on the sea, while he stands lost and silent on the mountain."

A Christian by heritage and a bishop by virtue of his duty as a ruler, a primitive who reacts to the higher powers as toward an immediate reality, a rationalist both by social role and inclination, Njegoš was not a theologian, much less an ecclesiastic, and least of all a mystic. There is no mention of a single church writer or theologian, though he must have known at least the greatest ones, while in that most essential question—the origin and cause of the first sin—he consciously departed from the teachings of the Church. He combated superstition among the people, and regarded enlightenment and education as his own and the nation's highest duty, if not as something divine—the spread of the divine light of reason and order among men. Njegoš made no mention of paradise and hell. Apparently he did not put much stock in them, and he probably did not even believe in them. God was a being of light without any kind of mystique. To be sure, God's acts were enigmatic in that they were beyond the ken of mortals, but they were not mysteries; rather, they were laws and under the law.

Njegoš was simply a sage in the style of the ancients, though one of ours, in whom philosophical thought and religious belief had not yet been separated. He believed because he knew. He had attained the perception and, I would say, the feeling that there are laws by which all things act, even God himself. And he knows, perceives, because there is in him something of that supreme, divine power—reason, light, spirit.

5.

NJEGOŠ MUST HAVE toiled and struggled long to clarify and to reconcile all those premonitions and perceptions he bore inside himself from the beginning. He began his poetic labors with two motifs—God and nationality, that is, the faith and Serbdom—which would have been simply traditional, inherited, had he not treated them in a novel way of his own. Both the motifs and their treatment were the harbingers of later ideas and interpretations which matured within him through the years, only to appear in an instant as inseparable and complete entities in *The Ray of the Microcosm* and *The Mountain Wreath.* Struggle and evil seethed all about him, and he, too, burned in them. Struggle and evil were also visible in nature—especially in the bare Montenegrin wilderness, and he also found them described in books. There was enough of this in the Greek poets and philosophers, including the greatest among them—Aristotle and Anacreon—and the Greeks were his favorite reading from the beginning. Banašević records that Njegoš's library included Buffon's *Histoire naturelle,* which describes the struggle in nature very graphically and in detail. There is some of this in the church books as well—in the *Hexameron* of Basil the Great and in Ambrose of Milan, whom he must have read while preparing for his consecration as bishop. All of this corresponded with what a less perceptive man might have observed, even had he not been a Montenegrin of that time who was struggling to preserve his bare existence and his name. He had to struggle fiercely himself—for a bare rock. All of this came together and was synthesized in his head in the wilderness of Cetinje.

Struggle and merciless extermination are laws to which everything on earth is obviously subject. But is this all of nature? And is all of man in this? No, this is not all of nature, much less all of man, but only the other side. Are not nature and man enveloped in sunshine, in light—a divine light—and decked in all the iridescence of beauty and gladness? Struggle and evil are the other side of nature.

These are questions and answers which Nikolaj Velimirović uncovered in Njegoš.

Njegoš took joy in the obverse side of nature as a pantheist, but he was horrified by its reverse side as a poet of the apocalypse. It was this reverse side that he saw most frequently and most deeply.

For all must struggle "against want," against rampant force. To live, to exist, is to struggle. "Self-preservation is a condition of life." So it is on earth. But in the cosmos, in the heavens? It is no different there. There, too, light and darkness reign and strive with one another. The struggle is there as well. So say the Biblical legends and the folk tales, and also the greatest poets and sages. Struggle is universal. That on earth is but a reflection of the cosmic one —a cosmic law in a microcosm. Man, too, must struggle, like every creature—fiercely and ruthlessly. How else was he to survive in a world of struggle and evil? Yet in addition to that "rampant force" he also has a mind that reasons and seeks to rise above the animal, the material, and the terrestrial—toward the light and heaven, toward something that is pure order and law.

> Rapidity and cunning he was given
> To be himself a worthy member of
> This mad and maddening throng and fair on earth:
> The pillars and foundations of his will
> Are on the pinions of inconstancy:
> Desire, the instigator and blind teacher
> Of dreadful passions, envy, malice, fear,
> Th' inheritance of hell, abases man,
> And deeper does he sink than meanest beasts
> —Whilst reason equals him to the immortals.

Life on earth is tragic—all struggle, pain, and misfortune:

> Our earth, the mother of so many millions,
> Yet cannot crown one single son with bliss.

The joys that life and nature offer are limitless, yet man ceaselessly chases after a fortune he can never capture.

> The more to glory's summit he ascends,
> The more he grows the foe of happiness.

Why is it so with man, on earth, and whence the contradiction and struggle in the cosmos? If the world and all things are subject to some order, some law, whence then all the darkness and evil, whence the tragic elusiveness of happiness on earth?

The Biblical explanations, which trace man's misfortune and anxiety to the sin of the first man, Adam, could not satisfy Njegoš. Adam disobeyed God's commandment by eating of the fruit of the tree of knowledge, whereby he was deprived of the original bliss of not being able to distinguish between good and evil. Such a myth might satisfy a Christian were he not also a ruler who was bringing enlightenment and justice to his land, and a thinker, unschooled and primitive, who in the nineteenth century, when science and philosophy and technology were quite developed, had to search for rational and, above all, uncontradictory explanations. For how was one to reconcile God as the supreme good and reason with unreason and evil on earth? How was one to reconcile man as a divine, rational creature of higher powers with his evil and folly? If the earth was a haven for every evil and sin—as indeed it is—how then could it have been paradise for the first man? If Adam violated one single commandment on earth, whence all the struggle and turmoil in the entire cosmos? Whence, finally, the conflict within man—between his incorporeal thought and unlimited power and a poor body subject to all manner of affliction?

As soon as such questions are posed—and Njegoš was driven to posing them by his social environment as well as by his personal fate and inclination, and also by their timeliness in our church and folk culture of that epoch—their answer must be sought by plumbing the absolute laws that govern both the earth and man, in other words, by linking oneself with the cosmos, by seeking one's fate in the cosmic. A religious man, such as Njegoš was, spontaneously sought the keys of man's fate in the traditional conceptions of heaven—in God as a supreme sovereign and in the destinies of heaven. Yet at the same time, as a rationalist of the nineteenth century, he tried to arrive at answers that were as logical and as reasonable as possible. He was spontaneously given to the mythological explanation, for he was a religious man from a backward environment, but also to an explanation that was more metaphysical than Christian, for he was a sovereign and a rationalist, one who was well read for his time and milieu, but most of all because he was a poet and sage of his people.

Njegoš transferred man's original sin to a far anterior time, and from earth to heaven, making it a part of a primeval cosmic conflict. He obviously borrowed his basic idea, that prior to his fall on earth man existed in heaven, for this idea offered an answer to his search and desire to find an ultimate explanation in absolute laws and in the very origins of matter itself, that is, of the cosmos. This idea became vested in religious dress, for its creator was religious, and thereby found a bond with already known poetic and philosophical thought. In this he found a source in folk legends, in kindred philosophers—above all in Plato—and even in the church fathers, especially in such independent and profound religious spirits as Origen, who wrote, "God, who himself is pure spirit, created all spirits originally in the same perfection and granted them free will to do good through their works. Those who remained faithful to God, the angels, preserved that perfection, while many who were too heedless to adhere to God in their free will more or less fell away from him. It was as punishment for this blameworthy rebellion that God cast them down. The worst among them became demons, while the less evil became human souls. The latter were punished by being enclosed in matter which, from the sinful fall, took on its crudely sensuous character." The most important part of this for Njegoš was the fact that the idea and myth of man as a fallen angel resolved the contradiction between the reality of earthly misfortunes and faith in God's mercy and justice: man had been temporarily punished through incarnation and driven to dwell upon the earth, but his divine quality—his mind, a soul which shows his unearthly origin—was not destroyed in him. God—absolute law and pure spirit—is good and just despite the existence of evil; he condemned man only to a temporary sojourn in the body and in transgression.

Njegoš's conception of the soul was made consonant with the teaching on pre-existence and light.

According to Christian doctrine, the soul is immortal—divine, radiant. Being immortal, it then must have existed in some other form before it was imprisoned in the human body. Every nondogmatic religious and idealistic view that accepts the immortality of the soul is logically and spontaneously drawn to the doctrine of pre-existence. Plato arrived at this, and so did the bold Origen in his effort to reconcile Christian and Biblical myths with Greek philosophy.

Njegoš believed similarly that the celestial spirits—the angels, which with him are principles, though he did not work this out or make it clear—were of the same light-bearing fabric as God, albeit without his creative and perceptive powers. Man—a fallen angel—is through his soul a light-bearing creation of God. The people of Montenegro also pictured the soul as a wisp of mist which leaves the body in the hour of death and returns to heaven—to light, to infinity and eternity.

Incidentally, from this came both the title and the theme of the work itself—*The Ray of the Microcosm*—that is, the light of a small world—earth, man's soul on earth, in sum, the fate of the human soul, man.

Consistent in everything, Njegoš never abandoned this conception, which, however original, was also held by the people, by Plato, and by others. Upon falling gravely ill, and sensing the nearness of death, he wrote to Dr. Marinković on August 10, 1850:

> During my illness I have also thought of death, and this thought did not pain me at all. My idea flew boldly between heaven and the tomb, and I conceived of death thus: either it is a peaceful eternal slumber such as I experienced before birth, or it is an easy voyage from one world into another to be numbered among the immortal hosts in eternal bliss. I felt not the slightest fear, for a hellish spirit is not within me, and I do not picture God as a Nero or Mohammed II, but rather in all his majesty, as a most magnanimous spirit who is most merciful unto his creatures. I imagined man's soul as a kind of mysterious focus which, on becoming separated from the body, sends up a flashing ray to kindle the deathless flame of our life and blessedness in the heavens.

Though it came first, the idea of man's pre-existence was not Njegoš's most significant attempt to reconcile secular evil with God's goodness. This was, one could say, his theological explanation. In actual fact, Njegoš used pre-existence to search out something deeper, an explanation for the existence of good and evil, light and darkness, spirit and matter, order and chaos, and the unending struggle between them. Pre-existence and the first sin, that is, man's angelic life and his fall on earth because of participation in Satan's rebellion—these are poetic visions and religious motivations of still another, and ultimate, set of opposites: light—darkness; good—evil. To these he subsumed his depiction of the cosmos and its history.

Again there were many sources from which Njegoš could have borrowed this theory of light—from the Bible, from Christianity, from folk tales. G. Lovrich noted this motif in his critique of Alberto Fortis. The myth of the struggle between darkness and light, the god of good and the god of evil, is among the oldest myths of mankind. It is encountered in one form or another in all human societies. Indeed, it is the first integral image of the world to be formed in the mind of man, older even, and simpler, than that of Thales. It is the simplest explanation for the relentless struggle among men and living creatures in general. Inasmuch as light is good, then God is light—and conversely. God is also the bearer of order—and light is order. Njegoš, too, links light with God, as an antithesis to darkness and evil, though in his own way.

It was not only intellectual consistency and a consistent religiosity that forced Njegoš to look upon man as an angel which had been expelled from heaven for having violated a higher law and which was "temporarily" bound to the body—to a lump which is decaying and forcing man into evil in order to maintain itself. Njegoš wished to explain evil on earth, and, we might extrapolate, evil in Montenegro as well, the most dreadful form of evil, from which he also sought deliverance. This is what drove him relentlessly to light and darkness, seeking philosophical answers, of course, in conformity with his religious and other views. The reality—evil and darkness—lashed his indomitable spirit into seeking an explanation.

As in everything else, the outcome was something other than one would desire: neither a complete philosophy nor a definitive explanation, but a moving and passionate poetic quest for answers to the greatest and most basic insoluble mysteries—the poetry that links man with the cosmos and the human destiny with a cosmic one.

6.

As one might expect, Njegoš's depiction of the cosmos is a medieval one—Dantean and ecclesiastically Ptolemaic: with six movable and six immovable heavens, and God in the center—the source of light. Beyond the heavens is darkness and chaos.

Njegoš could have known, and probably did, about the dominant astronomical theories of that time—those of Newton and Kant-Laplace. One can see in the *Notebook* that he took a lively interest in the discoveries made in that field, while *The Ray of the Microcosm* reveals that modern views were not unknown to him: his cosmos is spherical in shape. But his religious feeling and poetic vision corresponded more nearly to another cosmos—an ancient or feudal and a semimythical one. Ancient Greece fascinated him, with its drama and poetry and heroic contests. His was not only a social and intellectual affinity for ancient Greece, but also his cosmogony was derived from ancient and medieval times.

Yet in his conception of the cosmos there was something else—that primeval view of the world as a duality of light and darkness. Njegoš's conception of the cosmos, and of everything else, cannot be separated from his conception of light.

He maintained the simple but very logical view that by following a ray of light, one could finally reach the center of the cosmos, that is, the source of light. This is how his journey in *The Ray* begins. He speaks of this expressly in the *Notebook:* "Were I able to ascend from the earth along the Morning Star's rays, I could arrive at the source of the rays, but how is a mortal to be as light as a ray!" This shows that he, too, pictured the cosmos as being round, as well as that he believed in its radiant divine center.

In accordance with this was his notion that light becomes increasingly thicker as one penetrates more deeply toward its source: "The closer you are to heaven, the finer becomes the mesh of the fiery screen and the more pleasing becomes the spiritual nourishment." The absolute light, there in the center, is God, absolute spirit and pure spiritual bliss.

Let us add, incidentally, that those "philosophical" reports by the spy Orešković were not entirely without foundation.

Njegoš was truly not far removed from deifying light as something identical with God as spirit, creator, artist. Moreover, Njegoš was moving unremittingly and swiftly in that direction, though he did not go the whole way but remained within traditional Christianity. His philosophy is closest to idealistic pantheism. That this is so may be seen in *Stephen the Small,* his last work of any significance, which, in a certain place, has the Montenegrins praying, not to God, but to the rising sun. These verses rise to a pitch of pagan awe before the natural elements and reveal in him new horizons and visions as he links man—Montenegrin heroes—with the cosmos and its laws and forces:

> Before the rising sun two thousand knights do bow.
> Kissing Mother Earth they pray for tranquil peace.
> . . . .
> The sun receives their prayer, earth pledges them a
> glorious grave. . . .

His heresy went deeper and did not end with his acceptance of pre-existence instead of the Biblical first sin. Even though Njegoš did not get to construct a philosophical system, or, more exactly, a new emotive religious view of the world and its absolute laws, he had already departed so far from the Church and from Christianity that he probably would have broken with them had he not been prevented by his duties as a ruler and national leader, which he regarded as a higher calling. Besides, though he was definite about everything, Njegoš was hasty in nothing, least of all in his views and inspirations; he presented and fashioned nothing until it had ripened. Being a man of integrity, he could not abandon his moral obligations for the sake of his views or subordinate them to his poetic inspiration. His ethics and personal morality also developed and grew out of his views and experiences.

There is in *The Mountain Wreath,* and elsewhere, more than a single place whose entire poetic beauty is revealed only if we know Njegoš's conception of the cosmos and of light as being divine, as a poetically creative force. His Mićunović says that the Montenegrin warriors are

> . . . noble sacrifices
> Who pass from fields of battle
> Into the blissful realm of poetry,
> As the little dewdrops of light
> Rise to heaven in gladsome rays.

On the surface the image is a simple one, but it has a complex and deep meaning: to fall on the field of battle in defense of a just cause means to rise into the realm of poetry—into light and immortality. Only in this sense does the image gain all its graphic beauty. Njegoš's secret and inexhaustible talent lies precisely in presenting ideas through images, thus linking reality with absolute laws through another, poetic aspect. No matter how profound, his views would actually lose their ever-fascinating attraction were they not translated into poetry, into lyricism. Because of this his religion also, regardless of its archaic quality, or perhaps because of it, and especially his metaphysic, insofar as it may be separated from the former, do not lose but constantly gain in their attraction. It is, above all, poetry and an inspiration, and therefore a profound view.

In the center of the cosmos, Njegoš's God is like the Church's creator. Yet Njegoš's God creates constantly as he gives life to ever-new worlds which he has raised out of darkness and chaos, where confusion and lifelessness reign. The heavens, then, are ultimate and in ceaseless expansion, and immeasurable; only God is capable of knowing their limits. The struggle between God-light and Chaos-darkness is an image, but it also represents the state of the universe. Heaven widens through God's creativity, which is an artistic, poetic act. At first glance this is not a significant departure from the Church's teaching that God creates through his word. But Njegoš's God is an artist. He does not create out of nothing; rather, he fashions and infuses with beauty dead, inchoate matter. His heaven is dynamic—the encounter of light with darkness—and spreads as its light wrests worlds from chaos, bringing them into order and harmony. One day the light shall prevail. Then, as he himself says, God shall rest. His work shall be done, and there shall ensue absolute harmony, light, order. I point out in passing that it does not require much effort to perceive that here we have in the main Njegoš's own variety of religion, his faith in the final victory of good over evil, in other words, a belief in the perfectibility and power of that other, spiritual nature of man.

Njegoš's God, then, is not identical with the supreme law, but acts according to it, inasmuch as he comprehends it. This is confirmed by Njegoš's history of the cosmos, which is certainly borrowed from some myth: There were once many heavens whose sovereigns were gods on an equal footing, until, by an elemental blind chance, they were broken up and cast into chaos, leaving only the kingdom of the one God. The dominion of that God is identical with light, that is, with the struggle of light against darkness and chaos. This God does not renew the old heavens, but expands his own radiant realm.

With this cosmic drama the human drama became involved. More precisely, the former was the backdrop for the latter. In the cosmos in which light and darkness—God and Chaos—struggle, the archangel Satan rose in rebellion, gaining on his side the angel Adam. Njegoš does not say whether Satan is the representative or the ally of Chaos, but he is the destroyer of that order which the omnipotent and sovereign God imposes on the worlds he wrests from darkness. Actually, Satan represents an order different from God's. He stands for evil as an active force; in Chaos there reigns a stagnation which is disorder only in relation to that which God-light-goodness creates out of the kingdom of darkness. Being an archangel, Satan is immortal, eternal, and so is the angel-man Adam, that is, his soul.

Cosmos-light against darkness, God against Satan, and good against evil. This is Njegoš's cosmos. This struggle will come to an end. Goodness and light shall finally prevail. But men are subject to this struggle as long as they are invested with their corporeal nature, as long as they are men. Njegoš's cosmos is an arena for the struggle between good and evil and where it is man's tragic lot to be torn between the eternal and the transient within himself.

Men frequently construct worlds in the light of their own needs and conceptions. Whatever might be true and beautiful in this ordinarily does not lie in the world itself, but in the idea that led them to create it and in the image with which they expressed it.

7.

THOUGH MANY VISTAS open up on all sides in *The Ray of the Microcosm,* there are also many inconsistencies and deficiencies. The undeveloped motivations of Satan and God present a special obstacle to the final formulation of Njegoš's ideas.

Nikolaj Velimirović, himself a bishop with an independent religious outlook, concluded the following: With the victory of light-God, evil will disappear and Satan will be forgiven. Njegoš indeed states expressly that evil, which he regards as inevitable on earth as long as man's spirit is bound in the flesh, will be destroyed and mankind will thus return to its original bodiless heavenly state.

Yet there is another, more important, aspect of this question.

In his fundamental outlook and vision Njegoš remained a Christian. He believed in the final victory of good, light, God over evil, darkness, Satan. Both as a ruler who was carrying on the age-old struggle of his people and as an individual whose every last atom was engaged in that struggle, he believed, he had to believe, in the triumph of good. Still, side by side with that traditional Njegoš there emerges another from the struggle against evil, one who went farther and deeper, though, to be sure, he never became separated from the other Njegoš but tried to win him over and accommodate him to himself and to his own development. For it never occurred to Njegoš to deny Christianity, but, rather, he tried to reconcile it with his views.

If we strip Njegoš's thought of religiosity and all other accretions and elements, we are led to the conclusion that evil, darkness, Satan are inherently immortal and that they will last as long as goodness, light, God himself and his creative action against Chaos. Evil on earth, among men, and in Montenegro, too, is of cosmic origin, arising out of the conflict between God and Satan. Earthly struggles thus have their setting in a higher conflict, that between the darkness of Chaos and the light of Order. All in this world is under the stamp of an absolute law which governs both God and Satan, good and evil.

Njegoš did not say expressly that evil, darkness, chaos lie in the very nature of the cosmos and in everything within it, as do goodness, light, and order. But this follows from his conception of the cosmos as well as from the conclusions he made on the basis of his own personal experience. He had barely conceived this unuttered idea, but it lies at the heart of his outlook and sentiments. What he expressed in essence was this: On earth, among men, evil is as much a necessity as good, and this is so according to a higher law which is allegorically expressed in the rebellion of Satan and Adam against God.

In regarding evil and the struggle against it as absolutes, as long, at least, as men are men, Njegoš departed from the Church. Even his Christ, "armed with the weapons of justice and the arrows of sacred enlightenment," is sent on earth "to wipe out malice and tyranny."

Just as the roots of Njegoš's pessimism lie in the necessity for the existence of evil, so his militancy springs from the inevitability of the struggle against it. Njegoš's revenge is "a hallowed beverage blessed by God" and he baptizes Moslem renegades "by water or blood." For life on earth is an absolute misfortune and evil, but it is given to man to fight against them and to prevail over them. These imperatives, drawn from a mythical past, pervade his entire thought and his nearly every poetic image. Though struck by the absoluteness of evil, Njegoš nevertheless calls all to battle against it.

Many of his visions and impulses originate with the Church, but his conclusions and, it need hardly be said, his artistic forms go far beyond this and, like everything essential with Njegoš, belong exclusively to him.

Njegoš's conception of evil continues to be uninvestigated and unassessed, even though it seems to me to be of the greatest significance to his work as a whole.

Brana Petronijević was the first to approach Njegoš's philosophy as an expert. He concluded that if Njegoš did indeed hold that darkness must reign side by side with light, this was a brilliant conception. Isidora Sekulić took a further step in that direction in revealing the metaphysical, cosmic character of Njegoš's evil, but not even she stated it categorically. Truly it cannot be expressly said that Njegoš regarded anything of the sort as a cosmic absolute law.

The heart of Njegoš's conception lies incontrovertibly in the idea that darkness will appear side by side with light, that is, chaos will appear side by side with order and goodness as long as God's creative activity lasts, for it is inherent in the very removal of this duality. The absence of this conclusion in Petronijević can be explained only by his excessive conscientiousness and by his lack of historical and other data, including Njegoš's correspondence. Isidora Sekulić might have gone farther, but she was concerned primarily with the poetic side of Njegoš's works.

In the final analysis, one may also conclude the following: Njegoš holds that evil and good on earth are a necessity, which proceeds from man's very duality—the existence of his soul, immortal light and goodness, in a mortal body subject to evil. Njegoš had indeed arrived at precisely that "brilliant conception," and there are many reasons he did not express it outright—his circumstances, a lack of philosophical training, and, above all, the fact that the idea had not matured within him and, despite its boldness, had not yet disengaged itself from the whole of his views and obligations. Though but the germ of an idea, it was truly a brilliant one.

This dual conception of the world, that is, this acceptance of the necessity of good and evil, was consonant with Njegoš's conception of God as absolute spirit and with the duality of spirit and matter.

Njegoš's God is pure spirit, whom he regards as the source of light and order. In this identification of God with light—a kind of pantheosizing of God—Njegoš went even further in *The Mountain Wreath, Stephen the Small,* and in his *Notebook.* On the other hand, he also went further in depicting him as the agent of absolute laws.

Njegoš's God is unbegotten; he exists of himself. All that is spiritual—the angels, man's soul—is but an emanation, a part of the absolute spirit which is God. But matter, too, is uncreated and exists of itself. Njegoš's God does not create matter; it exists from the beginning—at first in a perfect world, and then cast in chaos, from which God the creator-poet draws it forth and constructs it into suns and new heavens. There is an observation in the *Notebook* that expresses this quite clearly: "The fiercest hurricanes cannot cause a particle of the earthly globe to disappear." The indestructibility and self-existence of matter is explicit in Njegoš, and the above citation only confirms that Njegoš's philosophical thought moved beyond *The Ray of the Microcosm,* though in the same direction.

Spirit and matter, then, are two fundamental and discrete substances. By itself matter is dead; spirit gives it form and motion. It is also the opposite of spirit, but not absolutely so, not in conflict with it, but only as the subject of the spirit's creation of harmonious worlds from its formlessness. The spirit which is God acts on matter according to the highest law, which is not beyond him and over him but in himself, immanent in him, though not identical with him.

Lifeless and passive, matter is not an absolute evil, an evil in itself. Only the earth is evil, evil is on earth—because of man's tragic destiny. There universal strife and insatiable desire reign. There is evil in man because his body has imprisoned his immortal soul. And evil will last on earth as long as these bonds endure. The earth will not be destroyed, for it cannot be; rather, the souls of men will return to their source, while the earth will return to the aimless wandering from which it was summoned as man's temporary penitentiary, that is, it will finally be made a part of the harmony of light.

The absolute duality of the universe does not signify the inevitability of evil. I do not think that Schmaus was right when he concluded from Njegoš that matter is in itself evil. Njegoš's matter is passive, while evil with him is an active force, the violation of higher laws. Njegos's dualism—spirit-matter—is an image of the world, but it is not necessarily the cause of evil. Given life by the spirit, Njegoš's matter radiates with beauty and joy. Njegoš's evil is not absolute, neither cosmic nor earthly evil. The latter springs from another duality: divine spirit and the human body. For if darkness and light are inevitable in the cosmos until light triumphs, then evil on earth can exist only until the spirit frees itself from its bodily prison. Only on earth is the spirit fettered in the body. Though fundamentally cosmic, evil is predominantly an earthly phenomenon, linked with man and with his existence.

In these, and other, views of Njegoš I do not find a trace of the modern philosophers—Bacon or Hume, Leibniz or Spinoza, Kant or Hegel; even though he could have had knowledge of them and must have known something about them, there is no evidence of his interest in this respect. The fact that his heaven is as ultimate as Kant's does not indicate any connection between them, for their bases and starting points are different. Njegoš could not have had any contact with modern philosophy, for he proceeded from inspirations and myths and, of course, his own personal experiences, and not from the attainments of scholarship.

Njegoš's conceptions are nothing new in the history of philosophy and the history of religion. Their power lies in their graphic expression and in the wealth of imagery in depicting evil. It is not by chance that Satan, the bearer of the principle of evil, is the most developed figure, the most graphic idea, in *The Ray of the Microcosm.*

Yet Njegoš's conception of evil—evil on earth—has a certain logic which makes it novel. Though he was not definite about what motivates the cosmos, he was in defining earthly, human evil. I know of no one who was as deeply and irrevocably convinced of the inevitability of evil in men.

Regardless of their form and motivation, Njegoš's views, like every intellectual creation, have a deeper and true meaning: throughout his existence man has encountered evil in man and must fight against it.

8.

EVEN THE MOST superficial analysis would suffice to show that Njegoš actually derived the idea of the inevitability of evil, that is, the cosmic, metaphysical character of evil, from the tragic destiny of the Serbian people, from their mythical history, whose ultimate expression was in Montenegro itself. The catastrophe of Kosovo and our tragic fate were preordained by our sins, the sins of our magnates, in accordance with the supreme law. Indeed, only after the general propositions in *The Ray of the Microcosm* concerning cosmic law and world destiny begin to be translated and graphically expressed—through the prism of contemporary problems and the personal tragedy of Bishop Rade in our own national drama—does Njegoš's thought gain its keenest edge and most profound depth, and his poetry a rarefied epic lyricism and spirituality. The first chorus in *The Mountain Wreath* is one of the most exalted and, in this respect, one of the most characteristic of his achievements:

> Our God hath poured His wrath upon the Serbs,
> For deadly sins withdrawn His favour from us:
> Our Rulers trampled underfoot all law,
> With bloody hatred fought each other down,
> Tore from fraternal brows the living eyes;
> Authority and Law they cast aside,
> Instead chose folly as their rule and guide!
> And those who served our kings became untrue,
> Crimson they bathed themselves in kingly blood!
> Our noblemen—God's Curse be on their souls—

Did tear and rend the Kingdom into pieces,
And wasted wantonly our people's power.
The Serbian magnates—may their name rot out!
They scatter'd broadcast Discord's evil seed,
And poisoned thus the life-springs of our race

And then that most chilling and awful curse of Serdar Vukota's, pronounced over his own land—Montenegro:

O Land, thou art accurst, and fallest all to ruin!
Most dread and horrible thy name is now to me!
O Land, if I some knightly son may have,
In youth's first blush thou takest him from me;
Or if perchance I have some valiant, dear-lov'd brother,
He too is snatch'd away before his time;
Or if were mine some lovely bride—
A bride more sweet than any wreath of flowers—
She too would victim fall to thy fell scythe.
My land, I see thee delug'd in our blood,
Now thou art nothing more in very truth
Than heaps of bones and mouldering tombs,
Whereon our brave, determin'd youth
Holds solemn festival with War and Death!
O Kosovo, thou Field of ever-tragic name,
No heavier doom had Sodom in her flame!

Here are the true roots of Njegoš's evil—Montenegro and the Serbian fate, and, of course, the terrible struggle Bishop Rade had to wage. The Serbian misfortune, Montenegro's woe were conceived in the cosmos. The cosmic drama is reflected and refracted in our own.

There are our own syntheses. Other peoples and lands, made of different stuff, synthesize otherwise. Only a land so choked with every evil—Montenegro—and a people with so tragic a fate as the Serbs could synthesize out of themselves, through poetry, such a thesis—to link their daily and historic fate with the cosmos.

To be sure, this thought is still inchoate in *The Ray of the Microcosm*. But it has its inception here. In *The Mountain Wreath* the proposition of the inevitability of evil on earth and of man's highest obligation to fight against it merely reverted to its source—the Serbian misfortune—though with a still-deeper insight and in another light. Without recognizing this circuitous path of

Njegoš's thought and inspiration, one cannot explain, or feel, the beauty and the meaning of his poetry. Only in this roundabout way—from earth to heaven and back again to Montenegro and the Serbian past—could Njegoš attain those awesome poetic heights. The linking of our destiny with eternal laws and the cosmic tragedy is, of course, just one of the ways—one specifically ours, Njegoš's—to render that destiny and that poetry universal, without which there is no real art.

Yet what is this evil, to whose inevitability ultimately the very destiny of our people is subject?

There is no express, direct answer to this question in Njegoš.

But he does offer an idea, seemingly thrown in haphazardly: Satan and Adam possess free will. Prvulović concluded with reason that in Njegoš the ultimate cause of original sin, as well as of other things, resides precisely in free will. The cause of original sin is obviously not in the realm of darkness—Chaos—inasmuch as it existed before all creation, but lies in the freedom of the spirit —man's spirit, which can also choose evil. Aroused by passions, Satan—and man as well—does just that. In this Njegoš fundamentally upholds, or concurs with, the teaching of the Church.

However, while this might lead us to the root of evil, it still does not explain it. It seems to me that Njegoš's premonitions followed their course to the end and that he maintained that the origin of evil had to be sought in the existence of the realm of darkness—Chaos—and not merely in Satan's disobedience, from which only man's misfortunes directly sprang. For if light and darkness, order and chaos, are a priori and absolute entities—and according to Njegoš they are—then evil and good should also belong to such a monad and proceed from it. Yet such a conclusion would lead Njegoš too far—to deny that God is the bearer of order and light, inasmuch as God himself would then be subject to the struggle between the primeval entities of light and darkness. Njegoš's God is truly nothing less than the supreme and omnipotent executor of the law. But as to that very law, and even the ultimate cause of evil, whose consequence would also include free will—all this was left undefined.

In any event, Njegoš's evil is manifested in the violation of absolute laws, that is, the order on whose foundation God Almighty has established them. So it is in heaven. On earth evil consists of violating inherited, traditionally accepted ethical principles. Njegoš does not speak of them, but they are understood with him; the people, men, have lived by them from time immemorial. It is also understood that these principles are nothing less than the supreme laws brought down to men, laws men are bound to live by precisely because they bear within themselves the spirit, just as they must commit evil for the very reason that they are corporeal and as such susceptible to sin. To this violation of established eternal moral norms, Njegoš obviously added the violation of the civil order as well. "I am the enemy of inhuman anarchy and disorder," he wrote in 1848, and many other times.

Obviously he left both the ultimate causes of evil and evil itself undefined.

So it was also with the Serbian destiny: Njegoš held that it was tragic because "our Rulers" trampled underfoot moral, that is, absolute laws. But he did not explain why they had to act in this manner.

Something nagged at Njegoš, something took shape in him—something he spoke about only when he had to, himself aware that he was doing so at the behest of a higher law: "The ants, which have been called into being by the Creator, build their artful ant heaps, and the bees their magnificent palaces. And I, as the handiwork of the wise Creator, should uphold this general harmony." So he wrote to Sarajlija about *The Ray*. This is borne out by his other manuscripts, though the manuscript of *The Ray of the Microcosm* has unfortunately not been preserved; all were written as though with a single stroke. Everywhere one feels this same sureness of thought. He wrote his own Testament with additions and corrections and left it that way, and though he made many corrections in *The Mountain Wreath,* he did that, too, with a single stroke.

Everything is done under necessity and out of it.

The beautiful and the true are not ultimate by virtue of the discovery of an ultimate cause—for that does not exist—but through the molding and formulation of what exists. And they are accessible.

9.

THOUGH HE WAS consistent in his religious philosophy, Njegoš never got around to developing it into an idealistic system. Thus it is understandable that his ethical and theoretical conceptions likewise remained undefined, and without these there can be no real philosophy. Yet precisely because his views were integrated and tended toward formulation into a system, it is possible to deduce certain things from them, especially from his ethic, which was most highly developed of all with Njegoš, inasmuch as he based it, as he did so many other things, on already existing elements, and because it required the least philosophical learning.

Njegoš's ethical views are founded on a conception of duty as something given to a human being a priori. He would say that it was given to man with his rational, divine quality. Even Njegoš's God creates worlds and establishes order according to some inner duty. He himself says:

> I am the only one who can create,
> . . . .
> And if my sacred duty I deserted,
> The reign of darkness should remain for all
> Eternity. . . .

To create and maintain order, to spread light in the heavens, and to struggle against evil on earth—these are but the same supreme sacred duty, to which God is subject there, and man here. Such an ethical outlook is obviously one aspect of his conception of the world and of man's fate and role in it, and both the personal and the objective circumstances that influenced such a formulation are evident. Man is duty bound by a higher law, a sacred law, to struggle against evil. This duty is imposed upon him by that other, spiritual side of man's nature which makes him "in quality" identical with God.

This principle, like Njegoš's other views, is revealed in all its clarity and plastic beauty only when it is applied to the realities of earthly, and especially to our national, existence. According to some higher dispensation, under which man has to sin, he must—he even has the right to—do evil. Bound by a "slight but firm bond" to the earth, as Bishop Danilo puts it in *The Mountain Wreath,* man gives in easily to force and money, to violence and bribery, in the hope of survival, so that "fear for life besmirches honor often." But man's spirit, fortified by the feeling of honor which makes men strong in spirit, heroes aware of their higher calling, resists fear and surrender to bodily, earthly necessities, and it turns man back to his moral and spiritual essence. Evil —violence and willfulness—is a general law which governs all living creatures. "Nature herself doth ever furnish arms" to all living things, but as a rational being, man also has duties. If man has the right to do evil, it is his duty to struggle against evil. Njegoš does grant evil its right in principle, inasmuch as it, too, is in nature and given by a higher law. Evil reigns in nature, and most of all on earth. The world is "a frame of hellish discord," universal warfare. Yet all this, this chaos, is not fortuitous.

> And all this vast array of things confus'd
> Hath yet some rhythmic Harmony and Law:

it is stated in *The Mountain Wreath.* Still there is, by the highest dispensation and man's quality, the obligation to struggle against that right to evil.

> As Wolf doth on the Sheep impose his might,
> So tyrant lords it over feebler fellow;
> But foot to place upon the Tyrant's neck,
> . . . .
> This of all human duties is most sacred!

To be sure, in his view of the conflict between right and duty, Njegoš does not see right and duty in the juridical sense; rather, he sees the first as a natural quality, a kind of right to survival, while he sees the second as the highest calling. Thus Njegoš's ethic follows from his dual image of the world and the basic conflict that reigns in the cosmos. The world is in itself a conflict, expressed in terms of ethics: a conflict between right, that is, the imperative of existence, and duty, that is, the imperative of order. In *The Ray of the Microcosm* this conflict is conceived in the heavens; in *The Mountain Wreath* it is brought down to the reality of Montenegrin life:

Nature herself doth ever furnish arms—
Defense against a force that may break loose;
Arms to supply a lack, arms to resist attack;

. . . .

This world of ours awakes the human will,
And duty is not done apart from thought;
Nor can our life proceed without defense.

Though this holds true for Njegoš in general, it is most applicable to his ethic, which was developed and harmonized with his other views. It springs from the images and conceptions of the people, especially the idea of Montenegrin manliness. To the people manliness means adherence to established moral standards in the face of everything else—despite life's misfortunes and necessities. For Njegoš it meant acting in accordance with the supreme law of reason.

Njegoš's conviction passes over into a metaphysical conception: man is man also by virtue of a spirit which holds to a higher moral order. That is what humanity really is—a departure from the unconcern and unreason of animals. It is ethics that makes a man a man, something different from other living creatures. The cosmic extremes are our own human ones. It is obvious that in this regard Njegoš relies on the folk view. Vojvoda Miljan Vukov, Njegoš's somewhat younger contemporary, was wont to say: God laughed twice—the first time when they wished to make a man into a brute, and the second time when they wished to make a brute into a man.

This is how it stands, too, with Njegoš's stress on heroism as the greatest virtue—something he developed out of a popular principle into a universal one. Only through courage is it possible to conquer evil. "Heroism is king over all evil." It is an aspect, a concrete form of that immanent obligation of man—to struggle against evil. Heroism speaks with eternity and immortality.

It is likewise possible, though with somewhat greater difficulty and risk, to trace the bases of Njegoš's epistemology.

From these bases it follows that man's spiritual powers are fettered by the body and by the earth, and that he has no possibility of knowing ultimate truths as long as he exists in this state.

To be sure, Njegoš does not deny the possibility of a growing cognition of the world: he himself established schools and spread enlightenment. Moreover, in accordance with his basic outlook, he declared:

> Ah, ignorance is a dreadful prison,
> Enlightenment the Creator's dear child.

It is not only possible for man to penetrate into the mysteries of nature, but it is given to him to do so through his intellect, his spiritual side.

In his ode *Thought,* Njegos says:

> And thou dost also give to man the might
> To cast his light into the depths of spaces,
> To unfold with his own mortal eyes
> All God's wonders. . . .

Thus man must learn, just as he must struggle. Knowledge and the struggle against evil are two aspects of one and the same necessity to which man is subject, two sides of his highest and most essential quality.

Cast upon the earth from unknown space and chained by inscrutable forces to an evil with which he is engaged in ceaseless struggle through his mind, which gradually and unceasingly delves into mysteries it will never fully uncover, Njegoš's man feels his existence as a muddled dream before his return to eternity. Through his mind, thought, spirit, soul, man senses that he is something special and higher. Through them he also perceives a higher order—absolute laws that only confirm his relationship and subjection to them. They lead him to remember that once he belonged to them entirely and had knowledge of ultimate things before he appeared in his body.

For what is man?

The encounter with eternal law of a transient unstable mold of matter, an irreplaceable substance in a temporary shell. He is this always and in all that he does—in his sacrifice for an idea or for good, as well as in his mating, by which he carries out a sacred act that is sweeter and dearer than life itself. Of mysterious origin and fate, in constant discontent, in turmoil and rebellion against necessity, and in pursuit of an unattainable happiness and inscrutable ultimate laws, however powerful in his perception, man always remains the greatest mystery to man. His short life—his "span on earth"—his uncertain fate and imperfect knowledge spring from some confusion and chaos—a "derangement" man is constantly resolving and mastering without ever attaining his goal or tranquillity. Man creates, he makes his way as best he can through nature, but time and destructive earthly forces take their toll of his every act. Creativity is immanent in man. It is his quality, and it is godlike in that thought brings about its own order in the material world. Yet man's creations, which he must produce, are ephemeral, even though his creative potential is unlimited, like God's. For all that man creates he does within matter and with it, and it is this that irresistible forces constantly destroy and change. Creation is the other aspect of man's struggle against evil—the shaping of matter in the midst of turmoil and struggle. Thought creates by its very cognition, by directing man's actions. Njegoš's poetry is as much an apotheosis of the human spirit and its power as it is a cry over man's earthly limitations and evanescence.

Both God's creativity and man's are a poetic, artistic act. Creation is poetry.

But what does Njegoš mean by this? What is poetry for him?

Njegoš's outlook does not seem unusual, especially today, though it is in accord with his other conceptions.

As with all great bards of societies bound by myths and by blood, with him, too, meditation and inspiration, thought and image, merged and flowed into one another. His philosophy and his poetry are inseparable, as are spirit and creation in his outlook. For him poetry is identical with cognition, and the latter with poetry. The God who knows ultimate laws is also a poet through his creativity. It is no different with the earthly poet. Poetry is ideation, endowing the existing state of the world with greater order, raising from "the muddy earth," from matter, the "germs of a heavenly life"—order. Creation and cognition are identical with poetry.

I am a lover of poetry [he wrote to Ludwig August Frankl * seven days before his death]. It occupied me much. Ah, divine poetry, mysterious spark! I could never understand: is it a spark of the immortal fire, or is it some raging fancy—the offspring of our confining clime? From a

* (1810–94). Austrian poet and philanthropist, professor of aesthetics in Conservatory of Vienna Musikverein. Established first Jewish school in Jerusalem.

wordly vantage point I see it as a gusty squall, but when a man rises above himself, then he sees the wretchedness of man, and when he is a poet, he can say that he is the surveyor of the universe. The poet is the shout of a mortal from our windswept mountain, the poet is a cry in the wilderness; he dreams of immortality, calls after it and plunges in pursuit of it. He sees the great page of the book of life spread before him, and reads in it of the Creator's wonders, which intoxicate him like the most delectable drink. Through the power of imagination he raises from the muddy earth the germs of a heavenly life, and deifies the corruptible.

Vuko Pavičević observes that with Njegoš the highest form of perception is poetic perception. It is also identical with reason. Poetic perception is identical with creation—the quality of reason. It seems to me that Njegoš's identification of the poetic creative act with creation and with the mind is one of the most profound and most original thoughts he or anyone could have.

Here is how he expresses it in *The Ray of the Microcosm:*

> Th' Almighty whispers sacred mysteries
> Here only to a poet's burning soul.
> All wonders of the sky and of the heavens,
> That flourish, bursting forth in sacred rays,
> Or worlds or minds, all mortal or immortal,
> And beauty's spell—what is it all, compared
> To the begetter of all poesy?
> The poet's calling is a sacred one,
> Heaven's breath is in his voice, the glorious ray
> His leader through the darkness, in his speech
> A shade of the Creator's majesty.

The Sovereign of Montenegro and the Highlands truly believed that by his poetry he was establishing order in a lawless land. Whoever knows anything whatever about the role that poetry played in the intellectual and emotional maturation and social integration of the Montenegrins will agree without any hesitation that the poet did not deceive himself and that his poetry accomplished more in real life than all his coercive measures as a sovereign.

To perceive is to create.

10.

MAN IS FATED to live in a world of implacable and irreconcilable contradictions.

> All trials and ills of every kind
> Are to man dowry in this world.

Forced to struggle against indestructible evil, which springs from his very nature, with unlimited intellectual powers and yet prevented from knowing ultimate truths, man lives out his days in an irresistible quest for complete—and unattainable—happiness. For he himself is an irreconcilable contradiction—crucified between spirit and flesh, desire and possibility, ideal and reality.

> No one is happy, and no one content;
> No one hath quiet, and no one hath calm.

The flow and mingling of inexhaustible somber bitterness and radiant delight—such is man's existence. For man must ceaselessly make order. He exists only in a constant compromise and contest with evil and in the struggle against it. Man's life is a "mortal sad harmony." In his destiny there is no change, no progress, no matter what instruments he has invented, given the changeless laws to which he is subject, even though he constantly gains more insight into them—without ever apprehending them. Man builds, penetrates, creates, and learns. He must do so in order to survive physically and spiritually and socially. But his nature and his destiny remain unchanged. Only the laws remain—ever the same and impenetrable. There remains evil and the struggle against it. Though it constantly changes shape, there is something in the spirit and in things which remains unchanging and beyond reach. Man himself is but a form of an unalterable human existence—a moment of suffering and creation, joy and slumber in eternity.

> And cup of gall for honey equally doth call,
> That so, the mixture one may easier drink.

For life is neither good nor bad; it is existence compelled by necessity and duty. There are moments—and there were so many of them in Njegoš's life—when misfortune and bitterness and frenzy strike with such mighty overpowering waves that it seems as though they will drown out every spark of joy and reason. But man will not give in; he must fight, for he might possibly win.

> O'er all this curious mixture of a world
> There yet doth reign one overarching Mind
> Which shall not suffer ill to dominate.

The artistic creator, the fighting man, does not give in. He wrestles and constantly wins for his people some part of the border between two contending worlds.

While dying—a bare skeleton which contained but a breath of spirit—Njegoš declared, "Over my narrow patch the tyrant thunder ever rolls, and, lo, my little land is covered with the darkness of savagery. For the wholesome thinking man there is neither sorrow nor joy on earth, for all human delights are mixed with gall, and all sorrows have some recompense. When his time comes, man is as ready to sweetly weep as he is to sing."

Neither a too easy joy nor a senseless despair.

"While praising the past and desiring a better future, men poison the present."

Such is life.

11.

In *The Ray of the Microcosm* Njegoš's thought just began to engage in great themes. In it poetry and philosophy, thought and inspiration, are frequently and noticeably divorced. One feels a cleavage, too, between the law and man's fate, between the existence of a man or nation and the cosmos. All of this will come out in the end and merge into one in *The Mountain Wreath.* Likewise, the action in *The Ray of the Microcosm* is undeveloped, deficient. It reveals many and strong influences and accretions from without, despite the fact that it also contains an original idea and conception as well as exceptionally impassioned, imaginative poetry.

There are other even more important faults—in both its expression and its language. Be that as it may, *The Ray of the Microcosm* is both a perceptive composition and a great beginning for a poet.

Especially in his language, Njegoš started with our own cultural heritage—both of the people and of the Church.

Njegoš's language in *The Ray of the Microcosm* is popular, but with numerous unintentional borrowings from Church Slavonic and Russian. There is significantly less of this in *The Mountain Wreath* and in *Stephen the Small;* Njegoš's language became increasingly purified along with his thought. Still, strangely enough, that ecclesiastical and Russian terminology in *The Ray of the Microcosm* does not sound unnatural; the very theme and atmosphere call for the archaic. Those Church Slavonic expressions even help to evoke an atmosphere of ascetic visions and ancient myths. Njegoš also faced difficulties in that many expressions were still totally lacking in the language of Vuk Karadžić. In having cast aside the Church Slavonic language completely—so it goes with us whenever anything needs to be changed—Vuk thereby also destroyed a developed terminology. Church Slavonic had been the vehicle for intellectual expression for the educated men among us, such as they were, throughout several centuries. Even Sarajlija, who was Njegoš's teacher at the time the latter was writing *The Ray of the Microcosm,* wrote in the popular style, but made up for its deficiencies with rich borrowings from Church Slavonic diction. In general, Njegoš was no linguistic purist, but the atmosphere of *The Ray of the Microcosm* led him on, and thus he borrowed too many expressions from the Russian and Church Slavonic, if indeed he ever differentiated between the two.

Still it is in *The Ray of the Microcosm* that one feels, so to speak, the full power of our popular tongue in the realm of meditative and cosmic themes, precisely where the language of the Church might have seemed more appropriate. In *The Ray of the Microcosm* a still-unaccepted popular language sounded a new note—an echo from heights once thought to be the province solely of the Church and clergy. This went unnoticed. Nor did anyone at that time notice that a novel, independent, and heretical thinker had invaded the sacred precincts of church doctrine with the language of the shepherd and the blind bard. *The Ray of the Microcosm* did not contribute much to Vuk's victory. But its language does reveal the boldness and depth, for its day, of Njegoš's endeavor. Perhaps one might say that Njegoš did not know Church Slavonic well, even had he wished to express himself in it. This is true. Yet his greatness lies in the fact that he used a new vehicle, the popular tongue, to sally forth into old domains. The poet—and only in the popular tongue could one be such—easily prevailed over the churchman in Njegoš. Branko Radičević was more important to Vuk's victory, but it was Njegoš whose use of the popular language was the most profound. In this respect he owed much to his uncle, and to the Montenegrin clergy—unlearned men who were close to the people. Yet even in his language he was primarily led by a creative drive. Only a truly great poet of the Serbian tongue could have done this at that time.

The decasyllabic line—the verse form of the folk epic—chosen by Njegoš for *The Ray of the Microcosm* is not quite that of the folk epics, and particularly not that of non-Montenegrin Serbian poems. It is not as stately and does not lend itself as much to the narrative form. Nor is it quite like that in *The Mountain Wreath,* for it contains fewer of those monosyllabic words that break up the line and make it easier to recite. In *The Ray of the Microcosm* the verse hums along more, without those bursts of sound and imagery. The decasyllabic line in *The Ray of the Microcosm* is used for the last time, and for the first time, to its fullest extent, to relate popular and church legends, as a drama and a philosophy.

Before that time, Njegoš had not made use of the ten-syllable line. In *The Night Gathers the Age,* in *Thought,* and elsewhere he picked various verse forms, but never the ten-syllable line. It would seem that he chose that form for *The Ray of the Microcosm* for practical reasons, if one may put it that way, as much as for profound ones: he had the ten-syllable meter in his blood, in his ear, from the cradle, and could use it almost as easily as conversational speech. Every other verse form would have caused him difficulties in writing a poem that, though long in the creation, had to be written in one breath.

In language and verse form *The Ray of the Microcosm* is a beginning, but a great one.

Nothing can be great apart from the manner in which it is expressed.

12.

GREAT THOUGH undeveloped, *The Ray of the Microcosm* also brought to the fore Njegoš's diction: a simplicity, nonpreciousness, a directness based on conceptual clarity which exerts a moving effect because everything, even the most profound and the most subtle, is expressed spontaneously and without a profusion of words. It is here, more, perhaps, than in any other way, that *The Ray of the Microcosm* revealed an original and great poet—Njegoš.

This is not occasional verse or the poetry of fleeting emotions. It has no psychological, or any other, nuances. It even lacks dramatic and theatrical conflicts. It is poetry without descriptiveness, almost devoid of adjectives. Its attributive adjectives are there not so much for the sake of description or the action as they are surrogate nouns whose function is to reinforce the meanings of nouns.

The language and the verse are popular, but, forced to express new ideas and passions, they have been reshaped and transfigured. An extraordinary poet, who contemplates with passion and whose thoughts are pure passion, also devises a new expression—speech and not description, image and not narration. The most abstract thoughts, ideas, become tangible, solid, and white hot with his diction.

The Serbian misfortune was transformed by *The Ray of the Microcosm* into a cosmic and a universal one—into the idea of the struggle between good and evil—revealing its plastic expressiveness in God and Satan and their encounters. Yet not even Satan—the most vivid of all the characters—is portrayed through descriptions, or even images, but through the passion and sure power of his principles. Convinced in his own cause, and overweening and impregnable in his pride, he defiantly casts his shadow over the entire cosmos, resolved to suffer being cast into the depths of hell rather than submit to the sovereign Lord. He is truly the boldest, and the most democratic, Satan in world literature. Such a Satan —pure principle—is of the very warp and woof of the finality of Njegoš's own attitude. It is in Satan that we find the real Njegoš, the one of *The Mountain Wreath,* who has transformed myths and ideas into passion, into a passionate subjectivity. In Satan we also see that Njegoš is largely the poet of monologues and dialogues. With him it is not men, but principles, which clash, and these are dramas of ideas and not of human beings—though ideas concretized into passions, images, and visions, all in two or three words.

Medaković states that Njegoš liked *The Ray of the Microcosm* more than any of his works. This is not unlikely. Everyone likes turning points, and *The Ray of the Microcosm* is precisely this in Njegoš's poetry. It paved the way and gave a start to that consummate poetry, complete in every detail—*The Mountain Wreath.*

The Ray of the Microcosm must have been for Njegoš a terrible spiritual and intellectual drama, one he himself had to experience in order to explain the world to himself, only to give it fullest expression in *The Mountain Wreath.* In *The Ray of the Microcosm* he also explained himself to himself.

One of the most definitive aspects of existence, whether of a nation, an individual, or of any human society, is the capacity to create a new world and to make it the possession of all men.

THE MOUNTAIN WREATH

1.

THE SUBJECT OF *The Mountain Wreath* is a massacre of the Turkish renegades in Montenegro at the end of the eighteenth century. The event has never been historically proven. Yet the entire action revolves about it, along with the portrayal of customs, beliefs, and scenes of daily life, so numerous that they seemed to Rešetar to comprise the main part of *The Mountain Wreath*. The massacre provides the conflict between the Montenegrins and the Turks and its resolution, while behind it echo centuries of woe and the struggle of the Serbian people. Moreover, the massacre is a real expression, a reflection of the fundamental cosmic struggle and the laws of that struggle which hold relentless sway over the world and men. The concrete events are Montenegrin, the backdrop and the cause are Serbian, but in everything and over everything are the absolute laws.

But did the massacre actually ever happen?

The first to ask this question—which was heretical from the prevailing point of view—was the courageous Ilarion Ruvarac. He proved that such an event, at least as described in *The Mountain Wreath* and in the Montenegrin histories of that time, had never taken place. He established more particularly that Bishop Danilo's record of that event was a falsification, as was the bell at Cetinje they claim was Danilo's. Being pitilessly conscientious and of a cynical, sharp wit, he exposed the Montenegrin fables that some wished to palm off as historical facts—either for dynastic reasons or out of Montenegrin vanity, or, as I suspect, out of an atavistic mythological feeling.

Ruvarac ushered in a revision of all historical knowledge concerning Montenegro, destroying legend after legend with no less passion than had those who fabricated them.

Montenegro remained under the Turks from the middle of the fifteenth century to the end of the seventeenth. In 1688 the Montenegrins raised a rebellion and joined with Venice in the Morean War. The bishop at the time was not Danilo Petrović, but Vissarion Bajica, so that even if a massacre had taken place, it would have been under the latter. Of especial importance is the fact that Bishop Vasilije, who could easily have remembered any such massacre, does not mention it in his *History of Montenegro,* though he does not forget to include incomparably less significant clashes. Montenegrin tradition has preserved nothing of a massacre as an event; rather, it became a part of tradition later, mainly from *The Mountain Wreath.* Ruvarac surmised that the massacre was of recent fabrication—in the thirties of the nineteenth century. There was indeed no previous mention of it in a single factual document. It would follow, then, that the massacre was the handiwork of Bishop Petar. There is no need to maintain that he invented it. He probably heard something of the sort, or deduced it, and inasmuch as he was given to imagining—to reliving the past as historical reality—he thought up the massacre. From Bishop Petar, Sarajlija and others took up the myth, while Njegoš got it from Sarajlija and family tradition—his own uncle's telling. Especially interesting is the fact that the massacre is not mentioned in Njegoš's earlier poem *Ode to Liberty,* which deals with a string of less significant events and in which he has much to say about Bishop Danilo. The verses that speak of Bishop Danilo's expulsion of the Turks obviously describe the struggle as a process rather than as an event. The massacre came to a head and emerged in Njegoš's spirit because it was something specific—an expression of all the basic Montenegrin and Serbian national and human aspirations of that time.

Apart from historical fact, I find two other serious reasons to believe the massacre never took place.

Neither in the tradition nor in the mores of the Montenegrins is there any trace of the killing of women and children or the extermination of people of another religion or nationality. There was forcible reconversion to Christianity: Miljan Vukov had some Islamized families among the Vasojevići baptized as late as the second half of the nineteenth century. But there was no extermination, no memory of it.

Moreover, it could not have taken place because the Turkish renegades belonged to Montenegrin brotherhoods, and the blood tie was still stronger than any other. The reception of Islam did not yet mean a complete separation from the brotherhood and the clan. All those Moslem Ljuce, Mikići, Mušovići, Lekići, and Pelevići were Montenegrins who intermarried and visited with their Christian clan brothers, and died for one another. Even had the Orthodox brotherhoods been willing to condone a struggle against their own kin, and their expulsion from the clan, it is difficult to believe that they would have agreed to their extermination.

The reception of Islam did not automatically lead to an emotional alienation from the clan, but only an ideological one. What was involved was less the conversion to another faith than the acquisition of privileges, for the Moslems were not serfs (raia); rather, they paid a tax only to the Sultan, they had a right to a steed and weapons, and they were exempt from many imposts. It meant belonging to the ruling class and not simply to a world religion.

The Turks themselves, by the way, very rarely resorted to forcible conversion to Islam, and even then it depended on the political situation—the defense of the empire in border regions or as a measure against discontented serfs. The Turks were tolerant of other religions, for these also represented the lower social orders on which their feudal system mainly rested. Mohammed did not found only a new religion and a new state, but also a new privileged class, a new civilization.

In breaking up and crushing our lands, the Turks did not abolish the feudal property and all the privileges of our feudal lords immediately and everywhere, but only their power—which passed over largely into the hands of Ottoman Turks. Gradually, all feudal privileges were transferred to the Moslems, albeit in a different form. Serbian spahis, or feudal landlords, still existed at the beginning of the seventeenth century, but by the eighteenth century there was not a trace of them. All privileges, especially those concerning the land, passed over in time to the Moslems. Therefore not only the restoration of our ancient state but any movement against feudalism had to take the form of resistance to an alien creed, Islam, particularly inasmuch as the people of that time were generally religious in their ideology. And as the Turks were the leading and ruling caste among the Moslems, a Moslem was identified with a Turk even when he was of our nationality and language. On the other hand, Orthodoxy was regarded among us as corresponding with Serbdom, and even with belonging to a certain class—the raia. The destruction of Turkish rule was tantamount to pushing back Islam, ending serfdom, and restoring the ancient, now national and civil, state.

All these contradictions were heightened by one—the religious. And there were so many of them, and they were so final, that they could be resolved only by severing them, by pushing back the one religion or the other, that is, by wiping one out within the ranks of one's own people.

Very tolerant of other religions, the Montenegrins had to be intolerant toward the Moslems because this meant resistance to the privileges of an alien nation as well. They were especially forced to be intolerant toward the Moslems in their own midst, those who had become converted in order to gain privileges over their poor kinsmen and to impose an alien yoke upon them. Here was "the adder in our breast" which poisoned our own people and stood in the way of the restoration of the destroyed kingdom, which our mentality identified with the liberties of the peasantry and of the nation.

The massacre was long in the making, with all the forces and circumstances that led to the liberation and creation of our own state. It was a social and a spiritual event—even if it never happened. It signified the first step in putting an end to the pro-Turkish leanings and tendencies of the clan chieftains in their resistance to the central government.

There had been Turkish renegades in Montenegro, on the very Plain of Cetinje. Records have survived that attest to this, as well as Moslem names. Yet from the time of Bishop Danilo there is no longer any mention of Turkish renegades. They vanished—having been wiped out in various ways around the time of Danilo's installation. As for the resistance of the clan chieftains, which only benefited the Turkish renegades and the Turks, while the removal of the Turkish renegades meant the beginning, the resurrection, of Serbian freedom, Njegoš experienced this in actuality, and with special keenness, at the very time he was conceiving and writing *The Mountain Wreath.* Dynastic reasons also led him to the massacre as a subject—the chance to play up Bishop Danilo and his crucial role, for it was from his time on that Montenegro was truly independent and had its beginnings as a state. The massacre was for him a symbol of what was so desired and what had to be—a Serbian state, with a dynasty of its own. Sarajlija, too, took note of the significance of the massacre: the fifth act of his *Pride of the Montenegrins* is devoted to it, and has Bishop Danilo as its central character. It was also clear to Njegoš that the massacre marked an end and a beginning: the title he had originally given to *The Mountain Wreath* was "The Rising Spark."

Pavle Popović states that the massacre was a turning point in the history of Montenegro. In the struggle against the Turks it was certainly that in a spiritual sense.

Had it taken place, the massacre would have been something less than the First Serbian Insurrection, from both the political and the national point of view. Even though it did not take place, it meant much more to the Montenegrin spirit—the breaking of a bond.

An event can exert influence even though it never occurred.

2.

MONTENEGRIN ORAL TRADITIONS have one certain peculiarity among many: the events and persons they treat of have been confirmed by historical research, though, to be sure, there are some divergences in time and place. This is true of even the oldest among them—the one about the conversion to Islam of Staniša, the son of Ivan Crnojević, and the derivation of the vizirs of Scutari from his line. He was not really called Staniša, but Stefan, and he did not get to rule the Vilayet of Scutari, but Montenegro, for he signed himself as "Lord of the Sandjak of Montenegro, the Littoral, and all the land of Dioclea."

Though the massacre has no place in tradition, its protagonists, whom Njegoš included in *The Mountain Wreath,* have been confirmed with an astonishing accuracy by later historians, especially Vuksan and Dragičević.

The only exception is Vuk Mandušić, about whom tradition has kept a stubborn silence. Not even his surname exists in Montenegro. He obviously is not to be identified with the Dalmatian of the same name. Nevertheless one reference to him, as well as to Knez Rogan, has been found: he is mentioned by Zaharija Orfelin, who was not far removed from him in time, so that his existence may accordingly be regarded as confirmed. That last scene in *The Mountain Wreath*—where Mandušić mourns over his broken sword —Njegoš took, so Dragičević thinks, from his own times, probably the Battle of the Salkovina, from which he kept a broken rifle.

Yet there is one important event from the time of Bishop Danilo —the Battle of Carev Laz—which is not mentioned in *The Mountain Wreath* despite the fact that folk tradition and poetry, as well as the convincing evidence offered by Vuksan, all attest to its occurrence. It was fought against Tahir Pasha Bushati, not, as some say, with Ahmet Pasha and the main Turkish force.

This battle would have had to take place after the massacre, as a consequence of it. Njegoš could not very well have included it in *The Mountain Wreath,* since his subject was the massacre itself. As a matter of fact, Njegoš does not treat famous events at all in *The Mountain Wreath;* even the massacre is presented obliquely. Such treatment indicates two things: he was mainly concerned with presenting the confrontation between the Montenegrins and the Turkish renegades, the Turks, which came to a head in the massacre, and in so doing, he was extremely conscientious and careful to avoid using anything that could not have been founded on tradition or on documents. This was his procedure generally, even in *The False Tsar Stephen the Small,* where he doctored the facts here and there out of dynastic considerations, but never actually changed the facts or his own principles.

The account of a Montenegrin uprising at the end of the eighteenth century came down in a different version before Njegoš. This version described a protracted seething which from time to time produced powerful eruptions. Danilo's episcopacy was obviously a turning point—both for Montenegro and for the Petrovići. It is perfectly natural, after all, that the process of Montenegro's liberation, begun in the time of Bishop Danilo, and before him, in the course of which the Turkish renegades disappeared, should have spontaneously merged in the mental image of a single event— the massacre. For there is very little difference between an event and a process, where both are founded on tradition, and it must be kept in mind that the Turkish renegades were in fact expelled. I maintain that the massacre actually took place, though in much smaller proportions and significance, for even if we do not find it in tradition, this does not mean that Njegoš and his uncle and Sarajlija did not encounter it. The tradition, as it is presented in *The Mountain Wreath,* is too precise to permit the thought that Njegoš simply invented it—for he was not given to invention. Nor did Bishop Petar make up the massacre; he, too, as usual, accepted the tradition as a fact. Ruvarac was right only in that he denounced such facts as being unhistorical, as indeed they were. Njegoš must have seen in the tradition concerning a massacre a meaning that was even deeper and more far-reaching than ordinary events, even great ones. The event, or the process, had evidently been already transformed into a legend when Njegoš took it up, connected it with Bishop Danilo, who was truly a pivotal figure, and placed it on a broader all-Montenegrin and Serbian plane, in the light of an ideological significance it had already assumed by that time in his own mind.

A poet who experienced myths as reality—for this is what they really were in their hidden meaning, compressed realities and truths —had to take for his motif an event that was decisive for him both as a ruler and as a Serb.

In Serbia, for example, the idea of the extermination of the Turks and Turkish renegades was not as developed or as sharp: there were hardly any renegades there, and they were not to be found in the villages anyway, in a Serbian milieu, but were concentrated in fortified cities. In Montenegro the idea of extermination was bound to be more vehement and persistent because the Turks, the renegades, lived in their very midst. The hatred against the Turkish renegades, which was powerful even before, must have assumed extremes of intolerance in Njegoš's time, when the restoration of the state and final liberation from the Turks were set as immediate goals. The "domestic evil"—the Turkish renegades and those who held with the Turks—was a hindrance to both the one and the other. The massacre stood for a hatred that was not petty and everyday, but something that welled up from vital deep-seated impulses heightened to the level of an absolute and unalloyed ideal.

Višnjić's *Rebellion Against the Dahis* was also composed under the aspect of eternal laws—mystical, heavenly. But its motivation lies in the necessities of life, even in economics—the raia could no longer endure the taxes and the attacks on their faith and honor. In Njegoš's massacre there are no material motivations, at least none that are compelling. From the very first verse it is motivated by an ideal, one that is implacable, ultimate, irrevocable.

Viewed from a dogmatically humanistic standpoint, the massacre seems identical with the St. Bartholomew's Day massacre of the Huguenots—the extermination of human beings because they are of another religion. Yet nothing could be further from the truth. If something of the sort really happened, it was not only a national and class conflict in a religious guise, but also the struggle of a people for physical and spiritual survival. When Njegoš says that all were slaughtered who did not accept baptism, he is expressing something beyond a religious quarrel—the defense of the Serbian name and existence, man's duty to fight against evil and tyranny. For Njegoš, and for the Montenegrins, the massacre was the product of a long process and a clash of laws under which men are vital, independent, but subordinated forces. The massacre is a necessity and not just a settling of old scores with an enemy. The massacre is a misfortune and an evil. Before it took place, Bishop Danilo did everything to avert it, but by its inevitability it became the most sacred obligation. It was the defense of a nation against being destroyed by its own alienated children in the name of another creed and a foreign rule which appeared to Njegoš and to the Montenegrins as injustice and tyranny, which it really was. Certainly it was defense against evil through evil. Njegoš himself passionately stresses this. But it is also the only way to save oneself from it. For the Montenegrins the preservation of their name and ideal had become identical with bare physical survival. Retribution thus became a most sublime experience, a cosmic propitiation. "Who gains revenge gains holiness," say the Montenegrins. "The wounds of Kosovo no longer give him pain," Njegoš adds.

I would say that Njegoš's motif of the massacre has its roots not only in our centuries-old slavery under the Turks and the concrete conditions that obtained in the Montenegro of that particular period, but also in the time before the Turkish invasion, in our legends concerning the discord among the magnates, in eastern and old Slavic myths concerning the irreconcilability of light and darkness which our tribes brought with them from their endless swamps and great rivers—from the Pripet, the Dnieper, the Don—and which are to be found in the magnificent Russian poem of the twelfth century *The Tale of the Host of Igor*. Njegoš did not know about all this, though he did translate *The Tale of the Host of Igor*. But he sensed the mythical theme of irreconcilability with evil in the concrete case of the Turks and the Turkish renegades. After all, it was not just with the Turks that we as a people faced the question of being or not being; that question only assumed its sharpest form under the Turks. This had been going on ever since we were conscious of our existence—from the time we became distinct from the numberless Slavic masses and migrated to the Balkans to be ourselves and in our own world. It is this to which Njegoš gave expression. With what great travail were our medieval states established! Here we were in the Balkans from the sixth or seventh century, while our first states were founded only in the eleventh and twelfth centuries, after several centuries of darkness and agony in a struggle for survival. And even after we established those states, they stood on the edge of disaster, constantly reeling under the blows of Byzantium, Venice, the Crusaders, and barbarian invasion out of the east. Did not Nemanja have to wipe out the Bogomils? What drove Saint Sava to break away from both Catholicism and the Patriarchate of Constantinople? The Turks were elsewhere as well, yet nowhere did relations between themselves and the Christian raia flare up so violently in the realm of idea and reality. It was as though some fateful catastrophe cast us on the watershed between East and West—into the hills and into want, to fight for pure ideals, for bare survival. All this the Turkish invasion reduced to naked extremity. The massacre, the struggle for "honor and name," was a part of our history since its inception—so Njegoš saw it—to culminate with our emergence into modern times, with the creation of the states of Serbia and Montenegro.

Njegoš's *Mountain Wreath* is the quintessence, the poetic configuration of that destiny and that mortally bitter experience. This is not a humanistic poem in the accepted sense, nor is Njegoš an ordinary humanist. Neither before Njegoš nor after him was there, among our people, nor could there be, any forgiveness for evil and tyranny and dishonor. We have had only one humanistic thinker in the West European sense of that term—Dositej Obradović—and even he, a Westerner, remained misunderstood and without successors, as someone great and useful, but not really one of us. For we had constantly to grapple with the most terrible evil, in the struggle for survival, in the hope of extricating ourselves out of "misery and devastation," as Constantine the Philosopher described our situation in the fifteenth century, and which the Turkish invasion transformed into a cause and our calling. Njegoš's humanism, and ours—the mastery over evil through evil—is dark and bloody, but it was the only possible kind—and will be, it seems, until the Balkans are shunted to one side as though by some tremor and cease to be an arena for opposing worlds.

Njegoš's massacre was not the first among us, or in the world, and it will hardly be the last. Massacres take place and will always take place when no other means are left save naked force to realize aims, whether these be ostensibly for the preservation of one's own world or for the conquest of another. But Njegoš's massacre was the first, or at least among the very rare, to be a poetic and even a humanistic motif, one in which the very deed is magnified. What is new is the light he casts on this deed, the demonstration of its inevitability and justice, and, above all, its poetic expression. Njegoš was the first to experience passionately and to give expression to a massacre as an aspect of human destiny, as a higher ordinance. Herein lies its originality and its greatness.

Njegoš saw the massacre portrayed by tradition as a turning point, as a part of our destiny, our existence, and that of mankind in general.

Evil does not exist simply as such, but as something that can be escaped from.

3.

NJEGOŠ PROCEEDED thus: he presented the situation and described the advent of the fateful event—the massacre. The event itself is relegated to the background as something incidental which the participants merely tell about. Once done, it is a thing of glory—an apotheosis. Its grandeur had already made itself felt, as it was being prepared. Its importance does not lie in itself but precisely in that preparation—in the heightening of the crisis. The essence of the massacre is in the very inevitableness of the crisis, the cause, and not the event itself. The event is but the denouement, the final act. Moreover, in that act there is no longer that passionate hatred, that outpouring of implacability and bitterness from verse to verse to the point of frenzy, rampage. What happened had to happen, and then a calm, solemn, and aching peace—the "sad mortal harmony"—and Danilo's consolation of Mandušić—that his heroism would endure even without his sword—comes over the settling of scores.

Njegoš encompassed the massacre in one stroke and in all of its aspects. It was clear to him that what mattered was not any single event but the setting and the development of the final crisis.

The Mountain Wreath is divided into three parts.

The first part consists of the Whitsuntide assembly at Lovćen, and is very short, only one hundred and ninety-seven lines. This serves as an introduction to the action. There is the great monologue of Bishop Danilo—a grandiose vision of the invasion and the fall of kingdoms, and soul-stirring meditations, and a cry of loneliness and helplessness. Immediately thereafter come the encouraging words of Mićunović and the carrying of the crosses to Mount Lovćen, accompanied by a heavenly portent—the crossing of two flashes of lightning over Montenegro—and an earthly one—the appearance of the cuckoos, Lazar's daughters, and the release of the captured partridges.

The second part includes the assembly on the Feast of the Nativity of the Blessed Virgin Mary at Cetinje, though not the actual assembly but the disputes and events surrounding it. It begins with a chorus in the form of a kolo, a circle dance, the voice of the people, a stirring cry out of the depths of the past, evoking images of historic disasters and misfortunes as well as of the shameful present. This longest part of *The Mountain Wreath* ends with an oath—not to forsake one another in the fateful encounter that will surely come. The scenes and the characters and the motivations constantly change, but all—the folk customs and scenes of daily life—point to the final reckoning. Njegoš seeks out the inner logic of the action. At first glance, far from having any inner connection, and even more removed from the leitmotif of the massacre, scenes and dialogues follow one after the other: the indecisive counsels, the quarrel with the Turkish renegades, the reply to the Vizir, the

Mandušić love episode, the relating of dreams, the return of Vojvoda Draško and his depiction of Venice so as to vaunt Montenegrin wholesomeness and eminence, soothsaying with the shoulder blades of sheep, the wedding feast, the mourning women, the episode with the unlearned priest, the scene with the alleged witch who is the Vizir's hireling, the appearance of Abbot Stefan with his justification of the massacre as the highest law, and finally the decision—the oath. Behind every detail allusions flit and challenges flare as the somber cries of the chorus range across the backdrop of Montenegrin history—from Kosovo through the Crnojevići and the famous battles before the massacre. The hatred is justified and drawn taut in preparation for the reckoning. The action moves evenly and logically as it establishes the motivation and develops the basic motif until it brings us to the inexorable—to the massacre as the only way to unravel the skein of circumstances and to fulfill all Montenegrin desires.

The third part is another short one—three hundred and eighty-two verses. It tells of the extermination of the Turkish renegades, district by district, first of all, to be sure, in Katuni on the very eve of Christmas, and then in Rijeka, in Crmnica, and finally in Lješani, all through Mandušić's report and the vignette concerning his broken sword. Here, too, comes the Abbot's memorial service for those who have fallen in battle for liberty and his renewed justification of the massacre—this time by laws that obtain on earth, in nature. There are no violent scenes, as though there never existed that unendurable hatred, that contest of evil with the Turks and Turkish renegades, and the fearful entreaties and positive assurances. There is only the peace of Christmas and then its celebration in triumph, a great hero—Mandušić—but one who is as tender as a child, who tells of the fierce battle and is inconsolably sad over his broken sword, as he was earlier over his mad and sinful love for the Miljonić daughter-in-law, and who is consoled when the leader of the Montenegrin clans, Bishop Danilo, presents him with a sword. The massacre is done, everything is over, once and for all, with the sundering of all ties of kinship, of humanity, with the fateful extermination of the enemy within, and now the struggle will continue to final victory. Peace and blessings have descended over the unfortunate land, the state has been restored and freedom has been resurrected, and two different causes and worlds have finally been sharply defined. There stands ahead a laborious life of creative toil, under clear skies and with an inner satisfaction.

It is impossible to determine the degree to which Njegoš pursued this conceptual inner unity of the action, and to what degree it came spontaneously out of his creative fire. It is more probable that he carefully and gradually developed the inspiration and the idea, which were with him one and indivisible, while keeping in view the internal thread of the action, animating it purely with his poetic enthusiasm and imagery.

Wholly a man of ideas, he was this in a distinctive way of his own—through enthusiasm and passion. He was not generally the poet of daily life, but of great historic movements, panoramas of thought. He painted everything with two or three strokes, in one or two colors. With him the spontaneous was indistinguishable from the premeditated. He wrote poetry, especially in *The Mountain Wreath,* effortlessly, the way a good reaper reaps or a good marksman unerringly hits the mark. Permit me these oversimplified comparisons. He breathes with a poet's thought. Spontaneity and sensitivity, like the imperceptible hum of a bell which sounds even when it is not being rung, are given to him. But he is able to move and to marshal these gifts, and at the right time. He is a poet with a fine sense of proportion, sparing of words, with the barest possible expression for everything.

The Mountain Wreath is created with feeling and intellect—with passion.

Is not all true creation a spontaneous ordering, an inspired conceptualization?

4.

It has long been a mystery just why Njegoš presented this bloody renascence of a people and the birth of a world in the form of a drama.

Even Njegoš's educated contemporaries noted, long before Vulović, that *The Mountain Wreath* was not a drama. Matija Ban reported, after a conversation with him, that Njegoš also recognized this, and that he even agreed to make changes and turn it into a drama. Luckily he did not do this. Ban tells that Njegoš regarded

The Mountain Wreath as his best work, which agrees with Nenadović's report. Though Njegoš was not sure about the degree to which *The Mountain Wreath* was a drama, still he was aware of its worth.

Vulović concluded that *The Mountain Wreath* was a dramatic epic, or, rather, an epic drama. Pavle Popović thought much the same, and he criticized Njegoš for its lack of action and inept development. Slijepčević regarded *The Mountain Wreath* as a drama of a primitive Montenegrin milieu in which experiences were still collective and epic, and the same ideals were held by all; the entire people figured in that drama, and it resembled more a medieval production or Aeschylus than a modern drama. The characters make themselves felt, but they are not there to participate in a personal drama. According to Slijepčević, they are there to converse, to take counsel together in a manner typical of a society which has not yet been socially and intellectually differentiated, one psychically earlier than the ancient Greek—a pre-Sophoclean presentation. Pavle Popović demonstrated that its characters did exist, and so did Radovan Zogović; without denying this, Risto Kovijanić noted nevertheless that though the verses of *The Mountain Wreath* are easily remembered, one usually forgets which characters spoke them. Slijepčević's view corresponds with the conclusion of Milivoje Pavlović that *The Mountain Wreath* is a drama, but an incomplete one, like the early Greek ones—the *Persians* of Sophocles, for example. Popović also stresses that Njegoš owed more to the Greeks than to Sarajlija. Skerlić exclaimed testily, "It is, in fact, a unique work, a work such as only great spirits are capable of creating and which elude narrow limits and the arbitrary formulas of mediocrity." Yet *The Mountain Wreath* reminded him, too, of the dramas of antiquity. Isidora Sekulić went further in her claim that *The Mountain Wreath* was a dramatic poem. Zogović also calls it a poem, while affirming its dramatic character.

These disagreements arise mainly from the unusualness, the originality, of the work itself, which is not easy to grasp at first glance.

Njegoš obviously had the ancient Greeks as a model. He found in Sarajlija both the motif of the massacre and the verse form, and even some of his images remind one of Sarajlija. Yet in regard to

Sarajlija, these are similarities rather than emulation. Insofar as Njegoš looked to anyone for a model, it was to the ancient Greek dramatists. He was led to them by his inclination for Greek mythology. He had begun to translate the *Iliad* from the Russian, and in the decasyllabic line. Ancient Greece attracted him even more directly; through its greatest spirits, it also was turned to the world of ideas, and it, too, like Montenegro, lived in myth and heroism. Njegoš read the Greek dramas. They were found in his library, one with his notes in the margins. After all, the kolos in *The Mountain Wreath* and in *Stephen the Small*—though our own native folk dance and song—were obviously modeled on the choruses of Greek drama. But the similarities with Greek drama are not essential. In its expression *The Mountain Wreath* has more of our folk poetry than of Greek drama in it; indeed, it has the feeling of a long folk epic, though it is no closer to folk epic than it is to drama.

The Mountain Wreath is neither an epic nor a drama, but a dramatic poem—an original form which corresponded to the motifs and the ideas Njegoš wished to express.

The Ray of the Microcosm is pure poetry. But there the situation is far removed from immediate reality; it is simplified, almost reduced to just two principles—evil and good—and to their protagonists—God and Satan. The plot is quite simple—a rebellion and a defeat. *The Mountain Wreath* is a much more complex work. Earthly affairs are more tangled: the struggle of the Montenegrin clans with the Turks (and Njegoš was careful not to forget either), their consolidation, and the beginnings of the state and dynasty amid a scattered and disunited Serbdom. *The Mountain Wreath* also had to be a gallery of customs, mores, beliefs, in order to be convincing. It has more of a foundation. Njegoš could have chosen to express himself in an epic poem. But here he would have lost himself in description, in something not for him, for his forte was narration, the materialization of ideas through characters, scenes, and expressions. Nor is drama suitable for this, for action and characters are crucial to drama. It is a matter of record what practical end Njegoš had in mind in writing *The Mountain Wreath:* he wished to offer the Montenegrins a work that would inspire them to battle and unity, one, then, that would put forward certain ideas, in a comprehensible form, through the portrayal of customs and characters out of clan tradition.

The Mountain Wreath could be neither drama nor epic, even though it had in it something of each.

Though Njegoš's starting point was Montenegrin reality, even Montenegrin needs, he wished to produce a work that would, so to say, express the Montenegrin soul, the very spirit and destiny of Serbdom, by linking this reality with eternal laws. The epic is unsuitable for something of this kind. How could he have presented his ideas? Who would have voiced them? And in a drama, how could he have brought out our mythical past? Who would have expressed those cries of an entire people?

Having before his eyes both Greek drama and our folk poetry—being drawn to the former by his reading and intellectual inclinations and to the latter by his poetic heritage and the spiritual life of his place and time—he carried out a compression of forms that was unique to himself—combining the domestic with the foreign, Miltonian epic with local legendry, the abstract with the real, and in this case Greek drama with our folk poetry. This compression was not mechanical, but spontaneous, unforced, creative, arising out of the subject itself through inspiration. Moreover, what we have is not a combination but a different form, corresponding to what was, what had to be expressed, for without that expression it would not have been what it was.

The Mountain Wreath is not a play turning on a single event, but a poem about it.

Because this event stood for ideas that were decisive and crucial for him and for Serbdom, and it involved real people, Njegoš embodied those ideas in the main participants. His characters have human personal traits—Mandušić with his secret and illicit love, Bishop Danilo with not a little tragedy of the skeptical intellectual. Yet all of them are, above all, and for the greater part, animate ideas.

Ideas lend the heroes of *The Mountain Wreath* their most distinctive and sharpest profile: through Bishop Danilo speaks the nation's history; through Mićunović, implacability and, by that very token, heroism, the idea of retribution; Abbot Stefan is wisdom, absolute law incarnate; Batrić's sister is a cry of the brotherhood in Serbian misfortune; and so on down the line. There are, of course, persons who might be called folk characters—the priest Mićo, who represents the ignorance of our clergy; Vojvoda Draško, who is folk wisdom and simplicity; the fun-loving Knez Rogan; Knez Janko, who is so bitter against the Turks that he cannot stand the smell of them.

The Turkish renegades, too, are incarnate ideas: Mustaj Kadi is delectable wile and hedonism; Skender Aga is fearful and crafty appeasement; the Vizir, via his letter, confidence in the omnipotence of force and in the faith of the Prophet. Such, too, is their world and their outlook—filled with pleasure and power. Through the words of one of them, Mustaj Kadi, and his description of Istanbul, Njegoš has again given us one of the most exalted odes to pleasure and delight. Yet even here beauty is idealized:

> O Stamboul; thou delight of Earth!
> Thou honey's Cup, Thou Mount of sugared pleasures!
> Thou sparkling bath of life and light,
> Where in sherbet bathe the fairies!
> O Stamboul, Palace of the Prophet!
> Thou sacred source of strength and might,
> . . . .
> How many hundred times in days of youth,
> Fresh from my sleep I've stepped toward the dawn,
> Thy sea of light all wond'ringly to greet—
> Reflected there thy visage fair,
> Fairer than sun or moon or morn—
> In silver mirror there to greet the sky,
> And all thy towers and minarets sharp pointed;
> To hear uprise into the azure blue,
> At break of day in all the peace of Dawn,
> A thousand, thousand holy voices,
> Proclaiming to high heaven, "Allah alone is great,"
> And upon all the Earth Mahomet's name and dower . . .

And on the other side, Serdar Vukota—Montenegro beshadowed by the disaster at Kosovo, with poverty and sacrifice as our lot:

> O Land, thou art accurst and fallest all to ruin!
> Most dread and horrible thy name is now to me!
> O Land, if I some knightly son may have,
> In youth's first blush thou takest him from me;
> Or if perchance I have some valiant, dear-lov'd brother,
> He too is snatch'd away before his time;
> Or if were mine some lovely bride—

A bride more sweet than any wreath of flowers—
She too would victim fall to thy fell scythe.
My Land, I see thee delug'd in our blood!
O Kosovo, Thou Field of ever-tragic name,
No heavier doom had Sodom in her flame!

Yet Njegoš did not merely present bare ideas. For him they were realities, the most essential and the most final at that. Thus he materialized those ideas, wove them into the flesh and blood of men and into the fabric of reality. Having been given substance, they could be expressed only concretely, through scenes from life and especially through individuals and their impassioned monologues. And conversely, the very Montenegrin chieftains and conditions would have been empty and mere husks had they not been filled with impassioned and conceptualized ideas.

If we carry this analysis further, we shall discover how Njegoš's method was not only refined but also precise. In *The Mountain Wreath* the men of Katuni—Mićunović is a Katunjanin—are the most resolute, while the men of Crmnica are near Scutari and thus vacillating, and make a show of swearing loyalty—as in the case of Knez Nikola, who is from Crmnica. Despite the fact that the characters are generally Montenegrin and Serbian, they may be recognized also as the representatives of specific clans and districts.

Njegoš did not fabricate anything, not even ideas: Obilić and Kosovo, the encounter of Christianity and Serbdom with Islam and the Turks—these were vital, these held out survival. These were the ideas that Njegoš brought to their ultimate expression in vivid utterance and imagery.

Everything fell together and developed as though by itself.

And throughout, in everything, was the idea—the idea of the massacre. Every action seems to take place only as a link with, a portent of, that other drama, the inner one, the real drama—Njegoš's own.

Yet the poem does not lose its dramatic quality for all this. Slijepčević discovered several dramas in it: the one of Serbdom, against the background of the struggle involving all living things on earth, and light and darkness in the cosmos; then the personal drama of Bishop Danilo—a sovereign who was compelled by a cause to sanction the massacre of his own people; and then the drama of Montenegro—the extermination of brethren turned Turk. Still other dramatic elements could be found here, especially in situations such as the cockfight, during which the Montenegrins root for the smaller and the Turks for the bigger cock. Here is but a vignette in the tension between two worlds. And the lament of Batrić's sister is pure pain and poetry, but it is also an appeal to the entire national past and a curse upon the unworthy, wretched reality of the present.

It has been observed that the historical color of *The Mountain Wreath* is weak, though its subtitle purported it to be "An Historical Event at the End of the Eighteenth Century." Such a criticism is correct only from the external and formalistic point of view. If, however, we do not look upon the past as a mere series of facts but as the experiencing and the expression of an atmosphere, an essence, the myth of bygone happenings—and an artist cannot do otherwise—then *The Mountain Wreath* has something more than historical color, for it has captured a feeling for the past—and in verse, in all its expressiveness.

It seems in the poem as if there were no past or measurement of time. Here the past lives in a present idea, as a part of living memory. It is as though the Crnojević princes lived but yesterday. After all, the men of Njegoš's time also boasted of their pastures and mills, and the disaster at Kosovo even now beclouds Montenegro. It was observed long ago that Njegoš's wise and cautious diplomatic correspondence and exchanges with Osman Pasha were of the same stuff as *The Mountain Wreath*. Past and present live side by side and merge into one with Njegoš, and it is in *The Mountain Wreath* that he carried out this fusion most completely.

There was, to be sure, also a personal reason, if one may so call it, that drove Njegoš to give his poem the form of a drama: he was truly a great master of dialogue.

Thus the lack of a dramatic quality in *The Mountain Wreath* is only seemingly so. On the face of it his characters seem at times to be holding aimless conversations with one another, and even with themselves. But this, too, is the dramatization of an idea—the delaying of the massacre, and that crossfire of scenes and thoughts, serves only to delineate and to clarify the basic ideas. Thus though one is constantly caught unawares by some unexpected thought or new image, all is in harmony with the development of the real drama—the drama of the idea. The thread throughout is never lost, but unravels: the massacre is advanced by passionate appeals and wise counsels, a dialectical give-and-take, and scenes from the life of the people. A wedding party is no mere wedding party, but a contest with the Turks. And so it all mounts and builds up until the resolution—the massacre.

To be sure, Njegoš had no intimate and detailed knowledge of dramatic art and especially of stagecraft. It was good fortune that he followed his own bent in *The Mountain Wreath,* pursuing his own inspiration and idea instead of what he had half learned from books and the advice of others. How much he himself felt *The Mountain Wreath* to be a poem may be seen from the fact that he did not divide it into acts and scenes as in the case of *Stephen the Small.*

Njegoš composed in the manner best suited to him, the one he found most natural.

One could easily impose a dramatic form on folk poetry if one wished to express certain ideas, not fanciful ones, but those that live in artistic reality. Greek tragedy is the tragedy of ideas, while our folk poetry is the mythical past brought to life. Njegoš bore within himself both the idea and the myth from the very beginning and found them both in his reading and in his environment. In *The Mountain Wreath* he started out with something that was already there and developed it.

This undramatic drama of a people and an idea, this lyrical discourse on epic themes, has always attracted and always will attract men of the theater, despite the fact that its presentation on the stage overshadows its essence and greatest beauties. The first attempt at a theatrical presentation was in 1851 in Risan, in a private home, inasmuch as the Austrian authorities apparently would not permit a public performance. After this, numerous other attempts were made, some of them successful. But the power of *The Mountain Wreath* is not in its drama, but in its recitation of inspired ideas. Slijepčević insisted that *The Mountain Wreath* could be performed only as a festival piece, while Isidora Sekulić suggested an oratorio. It seems to me that both are right, but only on condition that a great composer with a sense of theater undertake the task.

In this case the drama does not lie so much in what is happening, but in how it is told. It does not present the personal conflict nearly as much as the movement of a whole people.

Goethe discovered a general law in the development of new forms out of existing ones.

In some ways the artist does act like nature.

5.

NJEGOŠ'S VERSE was also one of the products of his gift for synthesis and enlargement.

On the face of it, his verse was derived from epic folk poetry—the ten-syllable line with the caesura after the fourth syllable.

Relying on the folk epic and mode of expression, but creating in his own right, Njegoš did likewise with his verse. He found it, encountered it, in the folk poetry of the guslar, especially in its Montenegrin variety, as well as in Sarajlija, and then developed it further and quickened it.

It was a historian, Vladimir Ćorović, who definitively explained Njegoš's verse.

In the decasyllabic line of folk poetry, almost without exception the ninth syllable, that is, the first syllable of the fifth foot, is either a long accented syllable or an unaccented one, as in the following cases:

> I shall take thee now for mine own darling . . .
> To the tsar thou shalt give salutation. . . .

This is natural: the chanter lets his voice drop on the ninth syllable in order to take breath for the next verse he must sing. In the folk decasyllabic line trochaic meters predominate over the dactylic. In the poem *Banović Strahinja* the ratio between them is, according to Ćorović, 74 : 26, and this is approximately the same with the other poems of the guslars. Besides, the folk poem as a rule has neither imagery nor Leonine verse.

With Njegoš it is different: in his verse the ninth syllable is most frequently accented—and this is a basic distinctive feature of his verse. His decasyllabic line is meant to be spoken, recited.

Characteristic of Njegoš also is his preponderant use of accented words of one syllable, which lend the meter a recitative rhythm and break up the monotony of the guslar's decasyllabic singsong.

Njegoš had a very fine and keen understanding of the difference between the popular meter and his own. In *The Mountain Wreath,* because it is the people who speak there, he wrote each kolo in the popular decasyllabic verse, as he did his poems *The Tower of the Djurišići* and *The House of the Aleksići,* both of which were obviously meant to be chanted to the gusle.

As long as we are on this subject, it should be noted that the people do not use the ten-syllable line for the kolo, but the eight-syllable line—and such are the kolos in *Stephen the Small.* Njegoš, however, wrote his kolos in *The Mountain Wreath* in the ten-syllable line, the popular one at that, for a deeper and finer reason: through them speaks the national past, and so it was most natural for their rhythm to be that of the guslars' poems, virtually all of which tell of the mythical past. The Serbian gusle and the guslars' poems are, after all, quite old; there is mention made of our guslars at Polish courts at the beginning of the fifteenth century. It is probable that we came to the Balkans with the gusle, and Njegoš knew this and felt it. As for *Stephen the Small,* this is a kind of Montenegrin social drama and the kolos in it thus correspond to those in real life.

In his verse Njegoš attained rare finesses and harmonies. The rhythm, tone, diction, expression are all in accord with the theme, with the thoughts—with the idea.

Even the order of words is often different with Njegoš from what it is in folk poetry, but always with the intent of gaining in recitative quality, flexibility of line.

In Njegoš there are also rhyme and Leonine verse, though rather rarely, particularly in *The Mountain Wreath,* and, as a rule, wherever they contribute to an epigrammatic economy of expression.

Thus Njegoš did not invent his verse, but developed an already existing form into his own. In this verse form he found, he forged an instrument for his epic and lyric, or his ideational and epic, motifs. His dactyl has more relief than the popular, and that stress on the ninth syllable, which feels so empty and unnatural in the Montenegrin decasyllabic line, lifts Njegoš's line and gives it a recitative quality.

It is interesting that Njegoš's verse in *Stephen the Small* does not have that measure of melodiousness and—if I may put it so—fieriness *The Mountain Wreath* has. In the former the verse tends to approach prose speech: its dactylic forms are more frequent, but less prominent. Both in conception and in execution *Stephen the Small* is more of a social drama than it is an epic poem, and thus such a verse form is more suitable to it—insofar as any verse form can be.

Njegoš's inner sense of hearing was developed and in harmony with all the rest of him. It was enough to set one element in motion to make all the rest move about and function accordingly.

One should realize that Njegoš heard his own verses differently from the way we hear them today. The sound they had for him was conveyed in the speech of Katuni: only two accents—a short very sharp one and a second very gentle and arched one. Thus its recitative quality was much more heightened than what we hear today in Njegoš's verse, as are both the militancy and the gentleness. The contrasts are clearer, sharper. His was a flexible, supple verse with a keen edge and full of nuances—chiseled. It was a transition from recitative to melodic speech. The speech is concise, measured, but rhythmic and melodious.

A sensitive poetic being such as Njegoš was could easily discern that that recitative verse of folk poetry and of Sarajlija would be the most suitable for expressing the tragic drama of the past and of struggle—through dialogues and monologues. *The Mountain Wreath* is precisely that kind of dramatic presentation, and that verse form is its distinction, though we also find it in *The Ray of the Microcosm,* in *Stephen the Small,* and elsewhere in somewhat less consistent and developed form.

The Mountain Wreath is a tragic recitative—of flashes and clashes, of flying sparks and slashing thrusts. Ideas as clear and as immutable as the bare rock sound with a melody of their own in which every beat, every note is sharply distinct from every other—just as every detail in a picture is a picture in itself. There are also transitions and soft shades, but sharpness and definition predominate—and it is mainly these that make for the harmony.

Njegoš looked upon verse as but the other aspect of an idea—a form in which a theme, a thought, an inner impulse is expressed. His ten-syllable line was best suited for his lyrical, personally experienced epic themes, which, being such, were not for chanting, but recitation.

On the other hand, the dedication of *The Mountain Wreath*—"To the Ashes of the Father of Serbia"—Karadjordje—was written in a sixteen-syllable line, which best suited its solemn elegiac tone, its condemnation of an evil conceived in a primeval past and in earthly conflicts and resolved over the headless corpse of the most resolute leader of our greatest insurrection—one of the darkest and most shameful of all Serbian misfortunes.

No one has ever been able to chant Njegoš's ten-syllable line, nor shall they ever; for no one except Njegoš has ever felt its closeness to reality, to the ideas and myths of our past and of our life. Such a verse form required one to bear these realities within oneself, to live in them, to identify oneself with them.

Human sound is human thought.

6.

NJEGOŠ'S LANGUAGE was that of the people, with all the peculiarities of the Montenegrin dialect, especially those of the district of Katuni. Nevertheless one frequently encounters Russian and Church Slavonic expressions in that language, though with increasing rarity as Njegoš matured and departed from occasional and even religious themes.

In *The Mountain Wreath,* as a rule, the Russian and Church Slavonic words are to be found only in the meditative and religious places. In *Stephen the Small* there are even fewer of these, and for the same reason.

A young and gifted philologist, the late Danilo Vušović, devoted a special study to the grammatical and syntactical peculiarities of Njegoš's language. As for that other aspect of his language, its expressiveness, only Isidora Sekulić has written anything substantial about it, and with a truly refined acumen. Many aspects of Njegoš's language—the historic, ethnographic, psychological—have remained uninvestigated. Many words had a different meaning in Njegoš's time, while the charm of his syntheses lies hidden in his language—in his all-encompassment, expressiveness and precision, or, as Isidora Sekulić put it, "not the language of the dictionary and of style, but verbal sinew and muscle, a musculature which, with each verse, represents marble statues of various saints, martyrs, victors." How little there remains of Njegoš once his language is taken away is best seen from those letters of his whose translations in a foreign language have been preserved. When these are translated back into Serbian, they are no longer his, but, at best, the letters of some wise ruler.

This infallibly precise and keen language is made especially graphic by the speech of Katuni, that is, the old Montenegrin dialect Njegoš used. No other dialect, especially not the one we call today our literary language, could have transmitted the atmosphere of that locale, of those events, and of the past. It is this dialect that forcefully directs our attention to the fact that this cosmic and Serbian drama is being enacted in a rocky land which is so small that not even a dead man has room to stretch out his legs—as Marko Miljanov once said of Montenegro. It lends a special rhythm, lilting and clear-cut, and a keenness to the theme itself. These dialects abound in terse expressions which tolerate no blurring or smudging of an image or a thought.

Yet Njegoš did not pursue local color, nor did he burden his text with it. He did not distinguish a local expression from those out of the general storehouse of the Serbian language. The old Montenegrin speech differs from the Hercegovinian—the basis of our literary language—in accent but not in vocabulary. There are no bizarre and strange words in Njegoš; what is new about them is the place and manner of their use.

Though popular and old Montenegrin, Njegoš's language is his own in its expressiveness. With him, words—in contexts and meanings other than those in the popular tongue and folk poetry—assumed a different plasticity and power. By changing the position of a word from its usual place and putting it in a new relationship, he thereby altered its inner meaning as well. These Montenegrin expressions in our language not only create atmosphere and lend realism to abstractions, but they in fact quicken and sharpen meanings and put finishing touches on images. Even when taken by themselves, many of these words mean something deeper. They are the very breath of our past and a delineation of our present. In this respect Njegoš went after most refined and subtle distinctions.

Njegoš's language broke loose from the popular tongue and departed from it, just as his subjects and thoughts rose above it. Nothing reveals as much as his language the totality and fullness of his ties with the destiny and being of our people. It was through his poetry that these became manifest, embodied. It is not enough to say that Njegoš's ties and development were expressed in his language, for they had their very being in it.

Isidora Sekulić declared, "*The Mountain Wreath* is, perhaps from the first to the last word . . . line by line, the native essence, the definitive expression of a language which is powerful, though little known to the world."

7.

As WITH the folk bard, so with Njegoš—especially in *The Mountain Wreath*—his leitmotif is the tragic destiny that overtook the Serbian people at the Battle of Kosovo. Yet the difference between them is immediately apparent: with Njegoš Kosovo as an event hardly exists, but its tragedy permeates every act, every thought, and the national being; it is felt from verse to verse throughout the entire work as a fateful misfortune imposed on the Serbs from on high. For the folk bard Kosovo is a turning point and as such a fateful event. He had God force Prince Lazar to choose between the heavenly and the earthly kingdom. With Njegoš, too, Kosovo is the height of misfortune, but neither the beginning nor the end, rather, the constant destiny of the Serbs. With the folk bard higher powers—God and the saints—act directly and simply; with Njegoš supreme and immutable laws are at work under which our misfortune was conceived long before Kosovo, because our magnates departed from the higher eternal order. It follows, according to him, that our people are ordained to misfortune and tragedy, defeats, internecine slaughter and betrayal, but also to great feats of heroism and sacrifice. Ivo Andrić has written:

> All who were born in those mountains came into the world with the reflection of the blood of Kosovo in their glance. . . . Njegoš is the prototype of the Kosovo warrior. Both as a poet and as a ruler, and as a man, he is obviously the personification of the struggle at Kosovo, the defeat and the indomitable hope. He is, as someone has said, the "Jeremiah of Kosovo" and at the same time an active, responsible fighter for "the lifting of the curse" and the realization of Obilić's idea. . . . Yet the tradition of Kosovo is not only in the realm of thought and poetry. . . . For Njegoš it is life itself. It is as much the

subject of his active and circumspect diplomatic correspondence as it is the subject of his principal poetic work.

I would add: Kosovo is for him a world, though not entire, and the main element in his world outlook, though in a recast form. Misfortune and evil are our lot, as well as the struggle against them. Kosovo is in our very being.

His lament over the misfortune of Kosovo is inconsolable because it is over the inevitable, and it is compelling because it is expressed in the concrete terms of Montenegrin reality. He linked this Montenegrin reality with the Serbian destiny; indeed, he manifested the latter in the former. Our national existence is permeated with our primeval calamity; it was our own leaders who opened the gates of our woe to an alien faith and rule. Our unhappy people drag and shake off their chains, but always alone and weak, disunited and irresolute. Kosovo, condemnation to misfortune—this is for Njegoš our attribute, our essence.

He finds our essence also in heroism, and in treachery as the obverse of heroism. The symbols of the one and the other are in Kosovo, with Njegoš as with the folk bard: Miloš Obilić, who sacrificed himself in order to slay the Turkish sultan and cleanse his honor and that of his people; and Vuk Branković, the traitor, who withdrew his army from the Battle of Kosovo at the crucial hour. Yet his Obilić, like his heroism, is not the same as the popular image. With the people Obilić is the greatest hero; with Njegoš he is a mythical being, a demigod, a principle. It was Obilić whom the Turkish renegades and traitors in this world would have to face in the other. Marko the King's Son, the favorite and most complete figure in popular Serbian poetry, is a minor figure in Montenegro, for he, too, was a "Turkish courtier"—actually a vassal. Marko is an entity full of human faults and virtues; Obilić is without contradictions—pure idea, ethical transport—and as such was bound to grow into a Montenegrin ideal. In *The Mountain Wreath* Njegoš links his absolute heroism with eternal law, with immortal light:

In proud repose the puissant Leader lies:
There from his veins did spurt his noble blood,
Where he so proudly trod a while before,
His breast possess'd by one sole dread intent,
As he did press his way through Asia's hordes,

> He swallow'd them with his great eyes of fire
> Where he so proudly trod a while before,
> Seeking his hallow'd tomb and life immortal,
> Scorning alike the failures of small men,
> And all that false and senseless company.

Vuk Branković, too, is a principle with Njegoš, though not as developed and definite. He is evil because he betrayed the fatherland, the highest ethical laws.

Both Obilić and Branković, as opposites, heroism and treachery, are linked with Kosovo and find their origin in the Serbian misfortune.

Njegoš obviously looked upon heroism as our special trait—our essence. It was certainly the most prominent Montenegrin characteristic of that time. In Montenegro, unlike other nations, heroism was a cult, and a Montenegrin was a hero for the sake of heroism—heroism as a virtue, as a principle. Njegoš's heroism is the bright side of the misfortune of Kosovo—the negation of evil, the highest ethical principle, and our national distinction.

The opposite of heroism and Obilić, treachery and Branković, are that other, evil side of ours. Yet there is hardly any treachery in *The Mountain Wreath;* except for a frightened old woman, not a single Montenegrin character is a traitor. *The Mountain Wreath* is an ideological work, even a political one, and the Montenegrins, in whose midst the spark of Kosovo, of freedom, was nurtured, had to remain pure. Yet this does not mean that *The Mountain Wreath* and the Montenegrins do not also have that traitorous, evil side to them: there are the Turkish renegades and those nameless Montenegrins who consort with them. The hatred expressed for them in *The Mountain Wreath* knows neither measure nor limit. They are an evil nurtured in one's own breast. Our betrayal is portrayed obliquely in *The Mountain Wreath*—through men of our blood who have adopted an alien faith. Yet they are the very reason the chasm between them—the Turkish renegades and the fighters for freedom—has become unbridgeable. For this is the ultimate treason—the acceptance of an alien faith, way of life, and even language, that is, those delights and Turkish expressions that are characteristic of our Moslems, and which Njegoš emphasizes.

Njegoš did not know a single personality, nor actually was there one, who could serve as Obilić's counterpart in his time except

Karadjordje, just as there was no event similar to the massacre except for the First Serbian Insurrection. Njegoš felt this kinship, and very intimately so. He made quite a search for Karadjordje's sword, which had come into the possession of a certain Jovan, a smith in Zemun, only to disappear completely, while under Karadjordje's portrait he wrote verses about the fire which "burns the memory of his [Karadjordje's] name in Serbian breasts." Thus it is not by chance that Njegoš dedicated *The Mountain Wreath* to Karadjordje. He thereby linked the past struggles of Montenegro with those in Serbia, and the past with present myth.

It was long believed that those dotted-line interruptions in the dedication referred to Prince Miloš and his crime—the murder of Karadjordje. This confusion was caused by the biased Medaković. Pero Šoć finally presented documentary proof that nothing more was involved than a poetic pause, which was customary in Njegoš's time. Is it worth mentioning another error—that the dedication had originally been addressed to Prince Miloš? It could have referred only to Karadjordje, and so it was dedicated to him. It contains certain allusions to the murderers and slanderers—"Upon thy shining grave let Envy outpour spite." But the dedication itself—a passionate, heavy, and somber encomium—in the very spirit of *The Mountain Wreath* must have been meant for the leader and the resurrection of a cursed Serbdom. Karadjordje had been foully murdered at Prince Miloš's behest—a heroic sacrifice. He was for Njegoš something similar to Obilić, though he was less myth and perfection—"the tyrant's scourge," the champion against darkness and brute force, a sacrifice to the highest duty, as though Obilić had descended among the Serbs, tragic in his immortality, the incarnation of Serbia's evil destiny.

Yet these are only a few essentials of Njegoš, though the most significant and prominent ones. Also essential to him are those fine nuances of expression, of his thought, in his delineation of popular types and the characteristics of the life of the people. Here is a description of the Plain of Čevo: "bloody field of human slaughter" which has "grown drunk with human blood"; or that Ruža, wed to a bad husband, whom a character mentions only in passing, but through whom Njegoš depicts an attitude and one of our customs—the marriage of a girl against her will—and with a powerful image at that: the imprisonment of a fairy in a tower. All of these are essences of Njegoš. He seemingly cannot write without them. From behind every verse, from every word there emerges some idea endowed with life—an essence.

Njegoš was not the first to recognize our traits and destinies, in the only form in which they could have appeared real at that time. All of this, as we have already pointed out, is to be found in folk poetry and in other writers. But it was Njegoš who lifted our essences and made them universal. He drew them out of our past and immediate present as ideas and expressed them in the vivid language of poetry.

But Kosovo and Serbia's misfortune, like evil, are but one side of Njegoš's poetry and thought. He seeks to bridge the inherited misfortune. The stress on evil and condemnation are only the obverse side of the tension created by the effort of men and a nation to escape them. The absolute laws of good and light do battle in our history and present against their adversaries—evil, darkness:

> The Crescent and the Cross, great Symbols twain,
> Do no advantage gain save in a world of slain!
> It is our lot to sail this crimson stream,
> Toss'd here and there upon Life's labouring ship,
>
> . . . .
>
> Let come those things men thought could never be. . . .

The Mountain Wreath is the poem of that struggle—of those things men thought could never be, a relentless effort to emerge from darkness through courage, to restore the fallen kingdom. "Let come those things men thought could never be." "Nowhere in the poetry of the whole world nor in the destiny of nations have I found a more terrible battle cry," Ivo Andrić once exclaimed. "Yet without that suicidal absurdity, without that stubborn negation of reality and the obvious, no action would be possible, or any thought of any action against evil." The struggle in *The Mountain Wreath* is resolved in the end—the good triumphs, being the essence, if not the very aim, of life and of the world.

It was out of that resolution of the struggle that Njegoš drew the title of his poem—*The Mountain Wreath.* "The Upward Spark" or "The Rising Spark," which were the titles he first conceived, told only one side of what went on and what he wished to express—the massacre as a turning point and a beginning. But the blessedness of sacrifice for the cause—Kosovo—was lost in these titles. The word *wreath* accomplished all of that. And much else besides. There is more than one sense to the title of the poem. It, too, is one of Njegoš's syntheses. *Mountain* indicates not only high places, but something exalted, while *Wreath* indicates both a garland and a crown—a crown of glory for mountaineers, an anthology of their life, and also the glory and the idea. The title has a festive and rousing ring, as M. Pavlović has already observed, but it is also encompassing. The poets of national myths of that time chose titles that were too direct and hence banal—*Lazarica, Miloš Obilić, The Serbian Maid.* Njegoš did not go after the bare idea even in his title, but sought a vivid image: *The Mountain Wreath* encompasses all aspects of the work.

Njegoš's essences, and for that matter his realities, are real because they are poetry.

For art is action.

8.

I HAVE PREVIOUSLY pointed out that the characters in *The Mountain Wreath* are embodied ideas. Yet they are not merely this. With Njegoš ideas are not bare, but vitalized. These characters are individualized as human beings as well, with their own stance, tone, outlook, and clan membership. They are integral entities, completely in harmony with what they are primarily and essentially—ideas. There are only two characters with any significant inner conflicts—Bishop Danilo and Vuk Mandušić. The former is, above all, caught in a clash of ideas and moral obligations, while the amorous passion of the latter is tragic and unrealizable because it conflicts with moral standards—he is in love with his *kuma,* a member of his godfather's family, and this spiritual kinship is a most sacred thing in Montenegro.

Bishop Danilo is, to be sure, the most developed and most complex character. It is not difficult to discern that through him speaks the poet himself; his fears, doubts, uncertainties, and resolutions are also Njegoš's.

Many have compared the vacillation of Bishop Danilo with Hamlet's. Any similarity between them, however, is only external.

There is no proof that Njegoš had even read Shakespeare, though this is not to be excluded. However boundless and illimitable, Shakespeare was, above all, the poet of human passions. Njegoš's characters seem to have no passions. What they say is passionate, and so is the way in which it is expressed, but they themselves are not. Still Shakespeare belongs to the Renaissance in all its prodigal wealth and splendor and to a country, under a great ruler, which was striding forward to world empire and a new civilization. Njegoš was born of toil and trouble, of shepherds and cantons which still chanted the poetry of myth and felt collectively and traded their blood for every morsel of existence. Of course, neither Shakespeare nor Njegoš are just that, nor do the differences between them arise purely from the circumstances of each.

So it is with their heroes: Hamlet is a refined intellectual skeptic who feels revulsion at the evil and senselessness in the world and who has transformed that awareness into his own personal misfortune and absolute suffering. His tragedy has its origin in the duty he must fulfill—to avenge his father—and in a world that deserves no effort or sacrifice.

Our own Bishop Danilo experiences something Hamlet-like with respect to earthly evil and disorder. But his pain arises predominantly from a national misfortune, and his doubts and vacillation come from the necessity of exterminating his own converted brethren for the sake of inherited ideals and the liberation of his own people. He also feels *Weltschmerz* but, like everything else, this, too, is filtered through Serbian and Balkan destiny. Absolute law speaks through Bishop Danilo as well, but through Serbian misfortune, while his personal obligations and encounters are in fact national. To be more exact, he assumes national duties as the highest ethical obligations, and being exposed and forced to carry them out through the massacre of his own people, he experiences personal suffering and misfortune. Standing at the head—"on the mountain height"—he "sees more" and has a greater duty, and hence his personal misfortune is greater. Yet he must carry out his obligation—through a new evil and a new misfortune:

> While pondering o'er this council for today,
> Hot horror burns within my soul:
> Shall brother brother ever thus war down;
> Shall not such strife so bloody and so long

Destroy the very seed within the womb!
O cursed day!—may God blot out thy light—
That thou didst bring me forth upon the world!
Last year a hundred times I cursed the hour
Those Turks did fail to make an end of me,
Lest I should falsify my people's hope.

There is nothing of Hamlet here. Yet the features are profound and original in their contours.

Even his contemporaries reproached Njegoš for Bishop Danilo's vacillation. Had he by any mischance heeded them, instead of a Danilo we would have gotten still another resolute and wise Mićunović, but we would have lost the broader Serbian, Balkan, and cosmic motivation behind the massacre, presented through his personal destiny as his own misfortune. Without Bishop Danilo, and, of course, Abbot Stefan, the massacre itself would be something of a cruel and senseless slaughter. Were Bishop Danilo not torn by doubt and constantly raising questions, were he not to feel personally the misfortunes into which his land had to plunge, he would be a lifeless and conventional stereotype out of folk poetry and myth, the kind with which our romantic poetry especially abounds.

Bishop Danilo later becomes resolute and is transformed in his summons to the massacre:

Strike for the Cross! strike for heroic name!
Whoe'er girds on his shining arms
. . . .
Hunt we the leper now from out our fold;
Let chanted be some terror-bringing song;
Let the true altar rise on bloodstained stone!

But this summons was even previously motivated by the highest national necessities. More than that, if one could make comparisons, Danilo wailed and wails over the inevitability of the massacre —the inevitability of evil—over those who must be punished. His tragedy lies actually in his being driven to fulfill a higher, absolute necessity involving his brethren turned Turk—a misfortune because of the inevitability of evil in the world, in Serbdom, in Montenegro. Bound by his position in the nation and by his personal conviction that he must carry out the sentence, Danilo is at the same time in conflict with it—with the will of the course of history, with absolute laws. He is crucified between his calling and ethical principles—between the worlds of good and evil. He is unusual precisely in that he does not submit to absolute law until the end, and he is great as a human being because he does not surrender completely to misfortune. While fulfilling his duty and his calling, he is unhappy precisely for this reason—caught in the conflict between the human and the eternal.

Bishop Danilo remains such to the end, even after having decided in favor of the reckoning, the massacre. He constantly seeks a way out, for solutions that would be ethically justified and would not cast Serbdom into new misfortunes. But life, reality, does not offer such possibilities. One must "plunge into the river of blood." He turns to God in a marvelous and moving prayer—to him "who wheel'st the planets in their orbit bright" and who has endowed with meaning and the power of life "Both . . . proud lion and . . . the little ant," asking him to "send cheering light on Montenegro's Mount" and to spare it the "dread thunder and the lightning's bale." He justified the human weaknesses of the Turkish renegades:

> But what is Man? In truth a feeble creature!
>
> . . . .
>
> E'en to chill lip of Age is honey sweet,
> And how much sweeter unto Youth's warm taste!

He has hopes of turning them back—"Sweeter to find the lost than ne'er to lose at all"—that Montenegro will make requital for its loss, that his soul would become tranquil "as some fair morn in vernal Spring," that the light from Lazar's Crown would shine on him, and that Miloš Obilić would return. But all is in vain; the inevitable must be accomplished and the decision rests in his duality—in the antithesis between one's knowledge of the law and one's ethical resistance to fulfilling it. There is no inner peace, and cannot be. Bishop Danilo remains great and tragic to the end.

In portraying Danilo as such—contradictory and tragic—Njegoš was not as interested in depicting a character and a personal destiny as he was in a conception and an idea. Once having presented him in accordance with this conception and thus having brought the Serbian drama into focus as a cosmic one, he practically forgot him.

After verse 789, the end of his invocation to God, Danilo appears again to read the Vizir's letter and his reply to it, and then there is a whole series of scenes and dialogues until verse 2056—the scene with the illiterate priest—when he must appear as the only literate person, as one who is "very deep in books," to confirm the non-existence of witches. Bishop Danilo plays no more of a part than is required by the course and logic of the action, but after that invocation to God, in which he is given the fullest expression, there are no more of his monologues. Moreover, his role of justifying the massacre—which he carries out largely in the name of national history—is taken over by Abbot Stefan, who lays primary stress on the highest universal laws. So it always is with Njegoš: the characters take their turn and disappear, while the idea, the conception, of the poem remains, develops, and grows stronger.

Bishop Danilo is sublimated suffering, disturbed intellect, and indefatigable duty. Finding himself at a crucial hour at the head of a country and people, he is the personal expression of the Serbian destiny. Had Njegoš not established that tie between the personal and the general, the national tragedy in Danilo would have remained without passion or any personal motivation. The idea and feeling would not have fused into pure intellectual pain. The personal-national tragedy thus received a concrete, dramatic form. It unfolds as Danilo is reaching his decision regarding the massacre, when consciousness of duty and the necessity of the reckoning have become inescapable, at a time when the powers of the people are still few and dormant, and when the decision itself will bring with it new woes—"Shall brother brother ever thus war down." The Bishop yields to necessity and duty, but conscious that in our very national essence there is a shadow of evil, "imperfection" and incompleteness. He is unhappy in a world and in a race into whose destiny he was born. There is not a sound or a chord that does not tremble with pain and unhappiness, but also with reason and necessity.

> But what can I! What helper is me nigh?
> We have but few strong arms; our strength is small;
> We are as wisps of straw tossed on the wind;
> As orphan'd sad, forsaken of the world,
> I see my people sleep a deadly sleep,
> No parent's hand to wipe away my tears;

God's heaven is shut above my head,
Giving no answer to my cries and prayers.
This world is now become a hell,
And men but demons in disguise.
Oh, dark, dark Day! Oh, outlook ever black!
My fearing folk held ever underfoot!
Sure I have seen thy woe and all thine ill,
Yet 'gainst the worst I now must set my will!

A pain without measure arises from the consciousness, but for this very reason it is not desperate. It is the consciousness—reason and light—which imposes the struggle against evil and darkness, while his people and his destiny and the past call for an uprising against the Turkish renegades and the Turks. The misfortune and the necessity inspire Danilo to his endeavors while reality reminds him of his duty and decision. He has doubts of absolute happiness and poses the question in terms of those very absolute laws, yet at the same time he thunders out curses and calls upon the distant centuries to vengeance and extermination. Danilo is tragic and a skeptic, but an optimist in the fulfillment of duty. He will bear the terrible burden of the massacre in peace and serenity. Danilo's, that is, Njegoš's, pessimism arises out of the incompleteness, the imperfection of all that is of this world—for men are forced to act in the ways of this world even when they are carrying out absolute law. Yet in carrying out necessity, the absolute law, he is resolute and an optimist. Like Njegoš, Danilo is a tragic warrior, for he knows that in the inevitable struggle there is evil and imperfection. He looks and sees beyond the need and task of the moment and wails over the losses and misfortunes the massacre itself will bring with it, even as the absolute law is being carried out.

Out of the consciousness of the necessity of the struggle and the reckoning with evil there also grows, despite any doubts, his militancy against the concrete aspect of the evil—the Turkish renegades. For if absolute law makes evil and misfortune inevitable, then the struggle against them is also inevitable.

Personal, national, and cosmic, present, history, and laws—these are Bishop Danilo all of a piece. He is complete and inscrutable, like all ultimate, original works and types in art. Through Bishop Danilo Njegoš expressed his own views, the Serbian destiny, and the Montenegrin reality—to be sure, in a special way, in a new form, a new expression. By this fusion an aspect of human destiny was revealed—the inevitability of the conflict between consciousness and duty.

But the deed is in the fusion, the unity.

9.

BISHOP DANILO is Njegoš—of one piece and in all of his aspects.

Yet the intellectual, cosmic side of Njegoš, which he displayed in *The Ray of the Microcosm,* is further developed and made optimistic, despite earthly strife and disorder, in another figure—in Abbot Stefan. So, too, his other aspects and views and feelings will manifest themselves in one or another character in *The Mountain Wreath.*

Abbot Stefan himself, though a less complex personality than Danilo, is created in the same simple and perfect mold.

He appears, and not at all by chance, at the very end of the assembly of the Virgin's Nativity, when the Montenegrins have already resolved to engage in a holocaust with the Turkish renegades. What has come before are the kolos in which the national past and present reality have been evoked, the quarrels with the Turks, the lamenting women, and the correspondence with the Vizir. All that remains is the oath. Yet before that comes the ultimate motivation—the supreme law. This will be presented, this will be expressed, by Abbot Stefan.

A blind octogenarian who has been to all four corners of the earth, Abbot Stefan has little of the earthly in his external features. He himself says that his soul is about to be released from the bonds of his body. As such, he most completely expresses the absolute law and the inevitability of its execution. There is much of the earthly in Bishop Danilo—a popular leader, something of a sovereign. Abbot Stefan seems as though he sojourned but a while in Montenegro in the course of his preaching and serving a hard supreme justice. His attitude toward the world and toward life is more profound and universal: he sees the radiance and the beauty, the face of nature and not just internecine destruction, as does Danilo. He is less national than Danilo—hardly at all. A churchman, he is religious—like Njegoš—for deeper reasons, from an awareness, a perception of the laws and their immutability and necessity. Something greater speaks through him, something deeper and more lasting in human existence (and in ours because it is human) than the national idea or duty.

Njegoš was acquainted with the role of the Church in our resistance to the Turks. In the name of religion and for its own special reasons, it strengthened the feeling of special identity among our people and preserved within itself the tradition of our medieval state. But Njegoš also knew that the Church had already played its role and that new forces—the monarchy and a free peasantry—would take over the role of creating, or what was for him the restoration of, a national state.

Though national, Njegoš was not nationalistic, particularly not in the modern, bourgeois sense. His nationalism was devotion to the people and their language, or, more exactly, to the people's struggle for and right to an existence and identity. The Serbian people have endured and survived despite all tribulations and their own transgressions, and their very existence was for Njegoš proof of a higher law and an absolute will. The Church was but one of the ways by which our people resisted and endured. Still Njegoš saw something higher in this, though he was unchurchly and convinced, with reason, that the Church was not capable of restoring the state: it was through the Church that the higher law spoke and made itself manifest over so many centuries of our struggle for spiritual and physical survival.

There is something medieval in such an outlook. But Njegoš's profundity and poetic peerlessness lie precisely in his ability to link the Middle Ages and our still-more-ancient myths with modern times and to affirm the existence of our people in terms of absolute law, that is, as something independent of a given form or time.

Only the Church, a churchman, could have affirmed this existence, inasmuch as the Church has been the most enduring aspect of our life. Besides, the Church is the representative of religion, which for Njegoš is practically identical with eternal laws. Yet though the Church was the most enduring aspect of our national life, it could not express that extratemporal existence of the Serbian people as an ecclesiastical Orthodox dogma, for the Church hardly explains all higher laws. This is possible only through another viewpoint, through the philosophical perception of the absolute laws governing human and Serbian destiny. In Abbot Stefan, Njegoš linked the one with the other—Church and philosophy—and in a natural and masterful manner.

Like Bishop Danilo—and, for that matter, like Njegoš himself —Abbot Stefan is not churchly in outlook, though he maintains a tie, however shaky and vague, with it and its dogma. He adheres to the ceremonial and canons, but lays no stress on them and gives them the significance only of symbolism and custom. The Abbot comes closer to absolute law, whose incarnation he is himself, precisely because he is on the verge of losing all his bodily strength. He has come to know the law through a most rich and bitter experience, but also because his spirit finally prevailed over his body. Again like Bishop Danilo, he, too, sees misfortune and evil everywhere. Yet that does not disturb his gentle serenity—a serenity born of the knowledge of ultimate truths, those under which all is settled and made right. His pure wisdom emanates from neither senseless despair nor irrational joy, but from an acquaintance with life and the human destiny as such—"For come what may, I am not unprepared!"

Njegoš fashioned Abbot Stefan with care and without the slightest inconsistency. To a degree, he contrasts him with Bishop Danilo, who is preoccupied with national misfortunes. While Danilo weeps on hearing of the massacre, the Abbot laughs because his soul—which Njegoš holds to be man's highest essence—"sings." The Abbot seems to say that evil and good each come in their turn, for so it goes in this world, but the massacre fulfilled the supreme law, and this should only give cause for rejoicing.

The Abbot is a piece of eternity made alive, personal. He is human wisdom as such, purified of all else and brought into our Montenegrin reality in a churchly guise, in order to justify and to bring on the final reckoning. Such are his first words, his first entrance on the Montenegrin scene:

> How many a twinkling light have I fir'd up,
> On altar of our Church—the Right Believing!
> And as a blind old man I come to you
> To brighten still, so much as in me lies,
> These holy fires of yours upon your altar,
> Upon the altar of your Church and Honor

He then immediately turns—in a long and exalted monologue—to the experience he has gained in a long life of travel, service to the Church, and meditation over the fall of Orthodoxy before Islam, all of which confirms and reveals absolute laws—those of *The Ray of the Microcosm,* but here made more concrete and definite: a rational force justifies its existence only if it struggles for higher principles, if it "doth merit name of Honor." For what is man —"Small creature he, and by the Earth deceiv'd"? Yet it is his to be a man—a rational force, that is, a force against evil in a concrete reality, to which the Abbot addresses himself and the Montenegrins around him:

> O generation mine, created to be sung!
> From age to age shall muses vie
> To bring thee wreaths that cannot die;
> What ye by deeds proclaim shall poets teach,
> In songs that shall be sung down deathless years.

Precisely because of that deathless eternity, whose laws he has come to know, the Abbot does not falter before the final reckoning among brethren:

> It is your lot and call to bear the Cross,
> Alike to strive with brethren and with strangers.
> The thorny crown is sharp, sweet after be the fruit!
> Except by way of death was never resurrection.
> . . . .
> There die glorious death, since die once thou must!

The Abbot's experience is personal and he himself is a concrete personality in all his spirituality—a boundless serenity, with a touch of humor and wit and a perfect calm in the knowledge that sorrow and joy walk hand in hand. The sage elder also makes his physical presence felt: he counts his beads as though plucking at bits of eternity, and he is blind—"For oft impedeth sight both speech and mind." He calmly waits for his departure into the realm of spirits, and meanwhile unswervingly summons to the fulfillment of the law. He does not even invoke Miloš and Kosovo —for the Serbian destiny, too, is subject to the law. He pays no attention to the canons in the decisive moment, but administers communion without confession and places on his own soul the sins of the perpetrators.

Abbot Stefan is the idea brought to its ultimate and as such made concrete, incarnate. The world is in Montenegro as Montenegro is in it; the eternal and the immutable in the ephemeral and the concrete.

10.

VUK MIĆUNOVIĆ is a most remarkable figure, Serbian, though, of course, in Montenegrin and even Katuni dress. He is cast in a consistent and simple mold, as most of Njegoš's characters are. He has Obilić and Serbdom constantly before his eyes, but he speaks the language of Montenegro—heroism and absolute irreconcilability not only with the Turks and the Turkish renegades, but with those Montenegrins who consort with them. Any wavering with respect to the Turks is certain to provoke his reaction. For him there is no room for anything Turkish, and every inch of him seethes with a noble hatred and sacred vengeance.

He is more than all this: he is the principle of heroism, not in the abstract, to be sure, but in concrete action—against the Turks. He is true to this principle, to himself, in every moment—as when he remembers to ask Vojvoda Draško whether the Venetians chant to the gusle, when he points out that Montenegrins who befriend Turks are more repugnant to him than Turks, and when he picks fights with the Turkish renegades and sends the Vizir a cartridge as a defiant reply to his threats. Mićunović is against soothsaying and telling of fortunes, at least he says he is, and his heroism is conscious, rational, though it emanates from his entire being. Except for the Bishop and the Abbot, who present the broader motivations behind the massacre, he is the main popular figure —straight out of the Nahi of Katuni. He justifies the reckoning and the final solution by invoking the ethical principle that is most immediate to the environment from which he has sprung—heroism. For him heroism is the condition of Serbian, Montenegrin victory. And of something more than that—human survival in a world of frenzied struggle. Mićunović justifies even banditry as being moral—against bandits. It is also interesting that the word *massacre* first comes from his lips. And the first dialogue in *The Mountain Wreath* is between him and Bishop Danilo—an encounter between a more universal and Serbian outlook under cosmic laws and a Montenegrin Serbianism shaped by the conditions of this world. Only a figure of absolute heroic and Serbian purity, such as Mićunović, is able to caution Bishop Danilo not to "sink beneath the waves of all our woe." And only a figure who is the incarnation of struggle—both the Serbian and the human—is able to remind Bishop Danilo of his duty. He sees about him youths whose chests are bursting with chivalry—the holy incense of the hero. But he also sees something more—the natural law that teaches the Montenegrin to fight, just as wolf cubs learn in play to sharpen their teeth on each other's throats, and the falcon fledglings learn with their first feathers to demolish their nests and, shrieking with joy, carry off the straws into the skies.

> In all these things a lesson is to find!
>
> . . . .
>
> And to this struggle no end shall ever be,
> Until the Turk has disappeared—or we!
>
> . . . .
>
> When Fortune smiles 'tis easy to be good;
> Adversity is e'er the hero's school!

Mićunović is Montenegro—as a reality and as a principle.

And it is he, Vuk Mićunović, such as Njegoš created him, who shows perhaps most completely how spontaneously the creator of *The Mountain Wreath* sought after the idea: pure, complete, and formidable, shining with courage like burnished steel. Mićunović is not even mentioned in the massacre itself; his part is finished as soon as he has spoken for the idea. Or perhaps Njegoš adhered to tradition, according to which it was the Martinović brothers whose lot it was to play the principal role in the massacre. One way or another, even this shows that Njegoš was not interested in heroes and in their destiny, but in them and in the massacre as ideas.

Njegoš's Mićunović is an example of how a work adopted by the people—and such is the case with *The Mountain Wreath*—itself creates a myth. It has been maintained, with reason, that Nikac of Rovin was the greatest Montenegrin hero. Perhaps Njegoš could not use him because he belonged to a time following that of the events in *The Mountain Wreath*. But he did not overlook Nikac's father, Vuk Tomanović, though only as an incidental and sketchy figure. Perhaps there was a tradition that Mićunović was the most distinguished hero of Danilo's time, and so Njegoš attributed to him the appropriate qualities. One way or another, *The Mountain Wreath* turned Mićunović into a mythical figure—the perfect model of Montenegrin heroism, accepted as such even today.

He, too, is personalized in the Njegoš manner—in attitude, tone, idealism, and, above all, in language. Mićunović's language is made up of cutting, hard words which get to the heart of the matter and leave no room for ambiguity. This is what makes him, as an idea, a living being and a Montenegrin reality.

Another graphically defined hero is Vuk Mandušić, but he is of a different sort. While Mićunović's heroism and stance proceed from the deepest consciousness, Mandušić's are—if one may put it so—more instinctive, impulsive, and born of passion. Njegoš liked symmetry in everything, and without a hero of flesh and blood such as Mandušić, *The Mountain Wreath* would have been too horrible in its unrelieved solemnity. Mandušić takes joy in fighting for itself. Dark and powerful forces rage within him. He whips his sister-in-law to rid her of evil spirits—the Devil—and he falls insanely in love with a woman to whose family he is bound in spiritual kinship through a godfather. Yet even in him Njegoš has struck a balance—to keep his passion from undoing his heroism. Though driven by passions, Mandušić will not exceed the limits beyond which he would besmirch the purity of his heroism, and, sensitive beyond all measure, he will weep over his "shorn" sword. All made of passions and vivid hues, he will have his place in the massacre, in the slaughter and the daring, and he will play in it, if not the most significant role, then certainly the most heroic.

Mandušić reveals how carefully and with what infallible consistency Njegoš treated his characters and pursued the ideas in his poem. Mandušić is from his first to his last word pure impulse, mad heroism. *The Mountain Wreath* begins with a confrontation between Mićunović and Bishop Danilo—heroism and intellect—and it ends with a conversation between Bishop Danilo and Mandušić, who is bloodied and with broken breastplate, still smelling of powder and carnage. Mandušić bewails more the loss of his sword than the dead, and the Bishop consoles him by presenting him with a new weapon for new combats. Perhaps there is nothing symbolical about this, but it certainly reveals the inner logic and harmony of *The Mountain Wreath:* from visions and ideas everything moves irresistibly toward reality and ends in it—with a real-life hero and Bishop Danilo as a ruler.

One cannot know to what degree Njegoš modeled the heroes of *The Mountain Wreath* on his contemporaries, or who they were, but it is deemed reliable that Vojvoda Draško was modeled on the Bishop's chamberlain and butler Djuko Srdanović, who accompanied him on his last voyage, to Italy, and who, according to Ljuba Nenadović's notes, actually contributed the witty observations of a primitive concerning the decadence and extremes of a superannuated European civilization. There is indeed much similarity between Djuko's observations and Draško's, and that same wittiness which forms the link between the primitive's lack of comprehension and the justified scorn a natural man feels for the perversities of civilization. Yet while in Nenadović's Djuko the resistance to the unnatural and the artificial does not predominate, with Njegoš's Draško this is precisely the main thing.

Vojvoda Draško is a well-rounded, unintentional wit who merely pretends that he does not understand, though without any mischievousness. He sets off a concrete set of opposites—Montenegrin heroism and Venetian guile, primitive and natural Montenegro and civilized and artificial Venice. Yet he is something more than this—a world that lives in a natural primeval order in conflict with the pampered and spoiled world of luxury and lordliness, conflict and exploitation. There is in the vitality of Vojvoda Draško, and he is perhaps the most vital character in *The Mountain Wreath,* also something of Njegoš's philosophy—that concerning evil and the struggle against it. For what is Draško's Venice like? Violent, soft-living, and perfidious, sunken in riches and dissipation, which makes our men into galley slaves, chops off the heads of its own doges, and holds its own citizens to obedience through terror.

He concludes from the Venetian reality—from the fear of spies and dungeons in which no person "would tie his dog down there!"—that the Venetians have transgressed the higher laws, "that such men must have gravely sinned, and therefore shall their Kingdom fall,—fall into hands not so defil'd." Seen historically, Draško's picture of Venice is, of course, incorrect and quite one-sided. He saw the dark side of a magnificent civilization, a city born out of the sea which gave more to the world than whole nations have, and which aroused the human spirit to its highest potential. Draško saw that evil side of Venice which lay heavy on our own people. But he saw in this its violation of moral universal laws, and thus its inescapable destruction. In Draško we find the germ of another, if not fairer and more moral, civilization—for there are no such—then at least another kind.

Outwardly simple, Draško represents our heroism and our wisdom in the face of the civilized Western world. By his speech and attitude, and especially through those little remarks and asides of his, he leaves a vivid impression, perhaps more so than any of Njegoš's heroes. He is the image of Djuko Srdanović, lumbering and deliberate, a big-headed Montenegrin with rough features, a keen expression about his eyes and a smile hiding behind his whiskers.

Draško is our popular type, but a principle as well as flesh and blood with a point of view.

Draško is both humorous and heroic, serious and natural in his outlook.

Njegoš was reflective in struggle and in passion and in humor.

Ideas do not exist outside of human minds, yet only through them can the reality be perceived.

11.

NJEGOŠ CREATED the likenesses of the Turkish renegades and their world, such as he saw it and imagined it, out of the same cloth and in the same manner. They, too, are materialized ideas.

Mustaj Kadi is the most rounded and best-defined character among the Turkish renegades.

He is intoxicated and carried away by beauties and delights, and also by the faith of the Prophet. Wily, wise, and pliant, he is as firm and militant in what is basic to him—loyalty to Islam—as any Montenegrin is in his views. To be sure, he expresses himself in his own language, which abounds in sweet and soft words. He also has his own stance, not only of a crafty simulated appeasement, but of a world by itself.

Njegoš lifted Mustaj Kadi above the image the Montenegrins had of him—an "artful fox," "full of foulest cunning." Bogdan Djurašković's curse on Mustaj Kadi—"By Montenegrin gun let him be shot!"—will be carried out by his own hand, in keeping with Njegoš's view of immutable fate. Yet the poet has given life to the leader of the Turkish renegades, Mustaj Kadi, and has elevated him to a symbol. In contrast with Montenegrin austerity and sacrifice for the cause, he represents the joys of life which should endure even after death. That world of Mustaj Kadi's, his outlook, is also an idea—a reality in itself. In confronting him with the Montenegrin outlook, Njegoš did not make him shallow and reduce him to a vulgar seeker after material comfort, but raised him to the level of a principle. Moreover, Njegoš does not deny either the worth or the beauty of that world of Mustaj Kadi's but merely confronts it with the Montenegrin world, thus showing that in that set of circumstances, in Montenegro, they cannot live together if one of them wishes to survive.

There are other Turkish renegades who are vividly portrayed, though only in two or three strokes: Ferat Začir, conciliatory and tolerant in the defense of his faith; Hadji Ali Medović, a kadi, or judge, resolute though inclined to make peace; and the implacable Skender Aga, the counterpart to Mićunović, and likewise in the name of laws that govern the earth, in the real world: "Each several folk hath its peculiar faith." One can form a picture even of the Vizir, through his letter—a force which is conscious of itself and unalterably opposed to Montenegrin objectives.

The Turks, the Turkish renegades, in *The Mountain Wreath* are more conciliatory than the Montenegrins. Their ideas are limited and secular, and even when they dream of the life hereafter, they are bound to the joys of this life as an ideal. Seeing them in this light, Njegoš did not portray them in unrelieved black, but in the full vividness of their views, outlook, and expression. It is not essential here whether they were like this in reality, and to what degree they are true types, but what is vital is how real they were in the poet's imagination and in what measure he was successful in presenting them as such. In this respect Njegoš made no difference in the way he imagined or treated Montenegrins and Turkish renegades. In all that emerged from his mind and that was quickened by his imagination, he was consistent to the last. For this very reason, though he was passionate as a poet, Njegoš could not be anything but dispassionate in this regard.

There is this, too: if the world of reality cannot be perceived except through ideas and images of it, then ideas and art are real, each in their own way, of course, only insofar as they become a real world of their own.

12.

NJEGOŠ's only female characters are in *The Mountain Wreath,* and even here they are incidental.

In Montenegrin public life women played an even lesser role than in *The Mountain Wreath,* though it may be disputed whether they received the role there that they played in actual life in general.

In *The Mountain Wreath* Njegoš portrayed six female characters, five of whom, as Matavulj observed, are typical representatives of Montenegrin life—ideas in Njegoš's sense. The old woman —the sixth type—who tells fortunes on behalf of the Turks, is not Montenegrin, for she is from Bar. In introducing women into his poem, Njegoš obviously guarded Montenegrin purity; there are no Montenegrin traitors even among the women. These female types do not appear and do not speak directly, except for the Batrić sister, but through the accounts of others. There is Ruža, the wife of Kasan, a beauty who leaves a bad husband, runs after a Turkish renegade, and loses her life tragically in her transgression. The Montenegrins mourn her and do not condemn her, as they did in life, for the brotherhood accepted an unfaithful woman if there was a good reason for it. There is Mandušić's sister-in-law, who is an insane woman. There is the Miljonić daughter-in-law, with whom Vuk Mandušić has fallen in love, and who is made alive through his telling of a dream, the perfection of womanly beauty and tenderness. Ljuba, the wife of Radun, is a warrior who loads the men's rifles in battle and urges them on. And finally there is Batrić's sister herself. Matavulj concluded, "Before us are love, sin, a lost mind, a beauty as perfect as it is tragic, a sister's love in the highest degree, and a woman hero. . . . These five types of women have lived for centuries in the steep and glorious Montenegrin crags, and they have entered into the eternity of the Serbian artistic realm . . . into which the immortal Bishop brought them."

Though *The Mountain Wreath* is a poem of animated ideas, Njegoš was careful not to depart from reality in anything, especially in social relations. As in Montenegrin life, so in his work no woman appears in public except for the Batrić sister, who is a mourner. Any other appearance before men was considered improper. Lamentation and mourning are exclusively female functions and sacred duties. The men also mourn, keen, and wail in Montenegro, but briefly, in prose or in epic style, and only on approaching the house of the deceased. Female mourning, on the other hand, is a poetic improvisation. Good mourners are known and valued. A mourner will think beforehand of what she will say, and improvise usually during particularly moving moments, by her wail lifting her sorrow to the pitch of oblivion and frenzy. The mourner speaks for the brotherhood, either that of the dead man or a friendly one; she expresses the eternal remembrance and love of those who remain. A mourner will use interchangeably the eight-syllable and four-syllable line—the first being appropriate to a sad chanting, and the second to a recital of moving images and dreadful visions. For a myth-immersed society which sees death and dead men as but a different aspect of existence, there is nothing more moving than a real lament that will link the facts of the life of the deceased with the visions of irrevocable disappearance.

Yet in bringing on the scene, in *The Mountain Wreath,* lamenting women and the Batrić sister as a mourner, Njegoš's aim, as in other cases, was not simply to give a faithful portrayal of Montenegrin life; rather, he thereby expressed some other and even more crucial typical elements. That mourner is a sister—an altogether special concept and relationship in Montenegro—and she laments not only in the name of the brotherhood and her own love, but through her speaks the land and a people engaged in a massacre.

Njegoš took the Montenegrin cult of the sister as it was and transformed it, as he did the rest, into a principle and a poetic inspiration. His tenderness for sisters is well known. In a letter of August 18, 1836, to the Commander in Kotor, he points out, as he complains how the brothers-in-law of his niece Stana wish to despoil her, "A Montenegrin holds it to be a great shame and insult if anyone offend a sister, even by a single word." The purest and most spiritual love known in Montenegro is for a sister. It was a sister that Njegoš had give voice to the greatest pain of the brotherhood, as well as a country's curse. Both the one and the other are typical for Montenegro. A real lament always deals with the general misfortune and the struggle against the enemy.

In the lament of the Batrić sister Njegoš linked a personal tragedy with a common destiny, in an image and expression of incomparable pathos and vividness. Many laments have been collected and published, some of them quite beautiful, but none lifts itself to the heights of the Batrić sister's lament, just as folk poetry, even when it is better than second-rate, cannot be compared with *The Mountain Wreath.*

The motif itself of Batrić's death—his torture and slaying after the Turks violated their pledge—was taken by Njegoš from a folk epic, one rich in dramatic moments but in which a sister is not even mentioned. Njegoš created the Batrić sister, distilled her from Montenegrin reality and his imagination.

The grief of a sister is absolute, and only death can assuage it. Alive as direct sorrow and despair, she is also a sister as a principle.

That grief is expressed here in a new way—in images, visions, and words that differ from the folk dirges in their refinement, in a certain abstract purity, and yet they are concrete and living and taken from daily happenings. How much this sister has to say to her brother! Her words of affection range from the tenderest and warmest to the most exalted and proudest, appalling and moving images mingled with curses and a summons to battle and the massacre. Not in all of Njegoš's poetry, or in Serbian poetry, is there a poem that begins on such a high note from the very start and then rises without once faltering as unadulterated grief and pure love.

Through the Batrić sister Njegoš gave expression to one of the most beautiful elements, and perhaps the most beautiful, in our patriarchal and clan life—a sister's love—lifting it at the same time into a mythical summons of a nation to sacrifice and a reckoning. Yet all the abstract beauty of this limitless and tangible pain is revealed only when one realizes the significance to the Montenegrin mentality of those images and expressions of death, sorrow, and misfortune the sister employs. One must bear in mind the moment of her lamentation in order to understand the whole fateful significance of her dirge.

The sister begins by asking her brother-falcon whither he has flown from so noble a flock—his comrades in battle and in arms, and his brotherhood. Immediately thereafter she blurts out the cruel and just reproach: "Didst thou not know the faithless Turk?" From verse to verse, from comma to comma, this is fused into personal and general sorrow and an unrequitable pledge, only to end in a curse of the land and its chieftains, one all the more terrible since their inaction closes off all outlets for this absolute sorrow and misfortune:

> Forgiveness o'er thy deadly wounds, Batrić belov'd!
> The whelming woes of our whole race—Not pardon'd these!
> Our land falls under Islam's yoke!
> Oh, judgement-stroke!
> Our chiefs have now all heart of stone,—
> Let death come to their home!

The voice of the brotherhood and of a sister, the Batrić sister, is Montenegro—afflicted, wounded, and injured, angered and shaken to the core. The sister is presented as a concrete being only insofar as it is necessary not to lose touch with this living pain. The Montenegrin land also weeps and is exalted by its daughters above the ceaseless human slaughter and destruction.

The Batrić sister affords a model—the only one of its kind—of Njegoš's female poetry. For it is forgotten, or else not noticed, that Njegoš, *The Mountain Wreath,* is the most sonorous male poetry, in the sense in which Vuk Karadžić divided folk poetry—according to who sings about what. There is a deeper reason for this division according to the different ways in which men and women experience and express what they feel—one of the essential divisions of labor in a clan and feudal society. Even after Njegoš this dualism was very marked in Montenegro. Subordinated in society, though not nearly as much in the home and in intimate life, with definite and most difficult duties, women expressed themselves in poetry and embroidery and succeeded in manifesting the most delicate and repressed feelings. Unlike the poetry of the guslar, Montenegrin female poetry is all of nuance and suggestion, of ethereal substance. It had its own language and own mode of expression. Only it had such tender expressions as "sight of my eyes," "my lost hope," "my rose." A man's expression is different—hard, final. This would correspond to the view that the world of ideas is predominantly masculine—if such a division can be made—and the world of feeling is feminine.

The Mountain Wreath is the zenith and the extreme limit of such male poetry, and the Batrić sister in it, of female poetry. This is, of course, only one side of *The Mountain Wreath* and the sister, for Njegoš not only went farther, but in all directions. Yet this side of Njegoš exists, too, especially in *The Mountain Wreath,* and it reflects a premythical, even pre-ethnic inspiration and division into female and male.

The male narrative in *The Mountain Wreath* has its own special tone and expression, and a special content. Likewise, the sister's dirge is something above and beyond idea and myth. It is the personal poetic expression of the collective.

Such, too, are the kolos.

In these the people sing of the past, or the past sings through the people—in mythical narration it is all the same. In it the past, the people, prescribe inexorable duties. This expression of poeticized ideas is identical with pure poetry. The hoary past and irrevocable oaths sound out with the admonition and the curse of the vast faceless masses of the people. Images and visions, oaths and obligations require no re-enforcement, nor do they permit any ambiguity. It is all one—the color, the sound, and the thought—and all is there, waiting only to become deed.

Pavle Popović was struck by the fact that the kolos proceed in the same chronological order as the events they narrate. And Rešetar noticed that Njegoš introduced that order only in the final draft of *The Mountain Wreath.*

The kolos were wisely and spontaneously inserted as key points, to remind one in decisive moments, and to point to the basic idea—the massacre. These accounts of woes and battles gone by, that expression of primeval tribulations and striving, have only an ideational tie with the action in *The Mountain Wreath,* and thus the closest ties. The final kolo glorifies the already accomplished massacre, but as though it were leading up to it and as though the entire course of history since Kosovo, and before, were fulfilled thereby.

Through the kolos Njegoš brought in the people, that is, mythical history. What is more natural for a poem whose basic theme is an event that is crucial in the life of the people than to bring out that people directly to express themselves and to remind their leaders of their duty? And what would be more logical for a struggle that is tied with the past and with a poet of myths than to have the past sing through the people?

The kolos sing of the past as though it were still alive—and indeed it is in the Montenegrin outlook and struggle. The images are direct and the expression fresh despite the tone of antiquity. They offer several links: between history and nation, present and past, people and idea. All are exalted, solemn intonations, and their language is the most select. In them there is no uncertainty over the idea, or unclarity of expression—in this poem of limpid and boundless mountain beauties.

If the sister is a cry of reality as idea, the kolos are an evocation of the past as idea—a mythical love and mythical history, the personality and the people.

A Frenchman once wittily observed that the novelist is a historian of the present, and the historian a novelist of the past. Njegoš's poetry, *The Mountain Wreath,* is a link between past and present, directed toward the future. This is how he saw and expressed the Montenegro of that time.

Is there not something of human destiny here? And is not art alone capable of expressing that trinity of mankind, man's existence in time?

13.

DRAMATIC and with all the amplitude of a poem of ideas, *The Mountain Wreath* is also a work of great scenes. To be sure, these are not theatrical; rather, they are the encounters, crystallizations, and animations of profound and rare thoughts.

Such are, more or less, all the scenes that depict the life of the people, above all, those scenes in which they confront the Turks. Each time a conflict of ideas is stretched to the snapping point,

Njegoš simply cuts short the scene, the situation, and goes on to something new, having said what he wished to say and once the inevitable has taken place.

The Montenegrins invite the Turkish renegades to an assembly on the Feast of the Nativity of the Virgin, supposedly to make peace, but in fact to see where they stand with respect to one another and to try to return them to the true faith. For Danilo has made his decision even before this, and the kolo sings of the betrayal of Siniša. When the Turkish renegades arrive, the discussion with them becomes increasingly ominous. The impetuous Mandušić casts an admiring eye on Arslan Aga's turban, and the latter offers it to him—on condition that Mandušić act as his son's sponsor. Mandušić refuses out of hand, for he does not consider it possible to be a real godfather to a Turk, and he does not wish to be a mere "stand-by" witness. There is some of Njegoš's humor in that scene—somewhat marked, as though some higher beings were amused and smiling at it all. But even here there is a total clash of principles: to reject spiritual kinship was a great sin, and it is known that a form of this kinship, known as the "tonsure," existed between Montenegrins and the Turkish renegades. Mandušić's rejection says all that has been left unsaid, and Njegoš ends the discussion and the scene with a description in prose: "A great uproar between Turks and Montenegrins; the wiser intervene to prevent slaughter. Then all are silent." And in that ominous silence there ensues a kolo which glorifies recent Montenegrin battles and the hajduk Bajo Pivljanin. Only following this does a new scene take place—a new and still-more-bitter confrontation: a letter arrives from the Vizir—power and resplendence—and there is a reply by Bishop Danilo—defiance and resistance. Aspersions and charges follow, to the point of an open challenge flung at the Vizir's messengers and the repugnance the Montenegrins display for the very smell of the Turkish renegades. Night ensues and peace descends over the hostile and sleeping camps. The time comes for something that transcends evil and disputation—Mandušić's love dream. But the morning is more foreboding than the day before. The Montenegrins relate their dreams—clear omens and summons to a final reckoning with the Turkish renegades. And when these accounts have reached their positive peak, Njegoš cuts them short: "The Turks all go away in file; sad and angry."

The conversation continues anew, but the subject and the tone shift.

That is how scenes are handled in *The Mountain Wreath.*

In sum, all the great scenes in *The Mountain Wreath* are, without exception, those in which ideas become white-hot and are cast into molten characters and images. And just as Njegoš's heroes are symbols rather than flesh and bones, so, too, his scenes are confrontations of idealized and poeticized worlds rather than theater.

It is almost impossible to take out the scenes without breaking, without disrupting, the mounting dramatic tension of the plot. On the surface only loosely connected, the scenes flow along logically and naturally with the uninterrupted lyrical ascent of this epic and reflective poem. It may be said that the scenes that are most vital for the course of the plot are precisely those that are the most eloquent and the loftiest from the standpoint of the poetic conceptualization of ideas, namely: Danilo's monologue and the first kolo, the Vizir's letter and reply, the sister, the Abbot's monologue, and the closing scene with Mandušić.

Nevertheless it would be wrong to assume that whatever lies between these high points—both those mentioned above and still others—is there just to prepare the way and to lead there. Both the high points and all that is between them are gradients of one and the same ever-developing plot. It is because of this, and because *The Mountain Wreath* is not a drama, that excerpts from it affect one with an undiminished force, as though they had not been extracted from an integral whole.

Njegoš has hardly any descriptions. He most frequently employed images to express that about which he felt most sensitively, myths and ideas. It is in this that his distinction as an expressive poet lies, and also in his ability to express himself concisely, tersely, in the manner of an aphorism, which M. Pavlović had reason to call Njegoš's gnomic style.

Even when he describes and narrates, Njegoš does this through ideographic images and in an extremely compact style. Mandušić's dream, which has no direct connection with the massacre, is entirely made up of a few simple, chosen images, without going into any detail and without being drawn out. And these images of the nocturnal encounter of an irrepressible hero with feminine beauty relate and bring out the essence of the idea of the moving and unearthly beauty of the Miljonić daughter-in-law and of Mandušić's sinful and primitive male love. It is night, and a fire blazes in the middle of the camp. The moon is shining in the sky, and the daughter-in-law goes out to the fire to mourn her husband's brother in quiet solitude and to comb her hair, which her father-in-law would not permit her to cut in mourning, for he prized her fair tresses more than his own son—and thus violated a time-honored custom for the sake of her beauty. A lock of hair falls over the daughter-in-law's breast as she sings a lament for her husband's brother. There is a terse description of her physical beauty: her eyes light with fire, and her forehead is like the moon —the only radiance in the darkness of boundless space. Her beauty is first alluded to abstractly—on her account her guardians violate custom—and then concretely—the comparison of her eyes and forehead with the fire and the moon. And that is all. There are no details about the features of the daughter-in-law. To go into detail would indeed destroy this harmony of the fire and the night, the moonlight and feminine beauty, and the daughter-in-law's eloquence. And so Mandušić weeps. Not as much over her lament as over her unattainable beauty:

> This girl's laments, they tore my heart;
> Her glowing eyes my spirit fired;
> Clear as the moonlight shone her brow;
> I wept—shed tears just like a child!

Immediately after these verses comes the end, with Njegoš's usual abruptness, but he does not fail to express the idea and the image of unutterable beauty and the measureless pain of love. This, too, is expressed, of course, in the simple folk style, and yet in an insuperable image and thought:

> How blest is Andrija so to leave the world,
> When eyes so glorious thus weep o'er him,
> When lips so lovely thus do mourn him.

The essence is always there, and the directness of expression—whether a description or an event is involved, the fate of worlds or the destiny of nations. After all, with Njegoš there is nothing without ideas, nor ideas that are not tangible, expressive reality.

Man first exists, to be sure, but he is also a creator. His thought is creative, and his work is the expression of all his powers.

14.

NJEGOŠ achieved this expression through those same elements from which his entire work took shape, and, of course, through his exceptional and manifold talent. Sprung from folk wisdom and a national and ethnic outlook, he very soon rose beyond all of that and crossed over the border of what Rastko Petrović called mythical narrative. Encompassing and expressing several centuries of our known and even more unknown existence, he had to resort to a more concise mode of expression, one even more aphoristic than the popular. Had he used proverbs and popular stereotypes to express his mature ideas and situations, he would still have been a remarkable sage. But he went further, for he was more than a sage; his proverb was the image—his was a wisdom recast into imagery. For he was a poet, a poet above all, though his poetry was inseparable from his other gifts.

The poet of such a breed was bound to interlace his own thought and expression with popular allusions, sayings, proverbs, saws. Someone once made a wicked attempt to omit from *The Mountain Wreath* all that Njegoš had borrowed. Practically nothing was left, at least nothing of any great worth. And still Njegoš was not a composite of popular forms and expressions. He transformed these folk elements, brought them into a new context, expressed them differently with the help of added ingredients and greater depth and nuance. He in fact made use of the folk element to express realities only a personality of genius could grasp. Take Bishop Danilo's reply to the Vizir. Here is Njegoš's own vivid expressiveness with generous borrowings from the people. But the tone is different—pure and solemn defiance such as does not exist in that measure in folk poetry. The salutation to the Vizir by the Bishop and the people is horribly calm and defiant, and though uttered in popular terms, was never said quite like that by the people:

> This hard nut is fruit that giveth wonder:
> Thou crack'st it not, except thou crack thy teeth.

In a folk proverb the tooth would crack on the hard walnut. The folk would say *walnut;* Njegoš uses "fruit that giveth wonder," which prompts the thought that the Vizir must have got himself into a very uncommon match with a very special people against whose defiance he will shatter his forces. That allusion, that saying, gains full impact when one realizes the occasion on which it was uttered, and who uttered it—the Bishop, at the conclusion of a barren parley with the Turkish renegades. There ensues a series of illustrated epigrams, ever more provocative and harking back to ancient lore and experience, until the culmination is reached in a not very covert insult and charge:

> A mind all wild with virulent desire
> Becometh well wild hog, but not a man!
> Along his path who maketh might his Right—
> Rise stenches of inhuman cruelty.

This image contains an ulterior and brutal allusion: the Turks and the Vizir are compared with animals, moreover with savage beasts which their religion regards as impure. To escape vulgarity and yet remain true to his aphoristic mode of expression, he made only an allusion, and thus strengthened the essence of what he wished to depict—the ruthless and ugly cruelty of the Turks. The letter piles up further provocative allusions until it reaches a high point, and then suddenly it ends with the personal experience of the Bishop, described in popular terms, but tersely and with a touch of humor: tradition has it that the Bishop had once been captured by the Turks but was released for ransom, hence:

> I have essayed descent upon your rope!
> And, truth to tell, I was most like to choke;
> Friends at a distance since are we;
> Into my head some wisdom have put ye!

In sum, Njegoš developed proverbial expression into his own style. Besides, a folk bard relates his view of the world, as well as of the national past, mainly through description and narration, and in a sprawling and hardly systematic way. With Njegoš all of this is different: he speaks with a concise idiom, and narrates but rarely and briefly, and then in his own language.

One would expect Njegoš to use the folk style above all in his scenes of popular life, and yet it is precisely in these that we see Njegoš's originality revealed in every way, and the incomparable, incompatible difference between him and the folk bard.

Njegoš drew those scenes from two sources: from life and from history, myths.

The defense of the faith and the taking of vows are popular customs. There is a record of an oath of vast proportions taken, at Bishop Petar's behest, by an assembly of Montenegrin chieftains in the year 1799. They vowed to shed their blood for their faith, to defend their fatherland and freedom, to curse the traitor and to forbid him entry into the assemblies of the land: "may he be without honor and decency, may he with his kin remain in shame and dishonor down through the ages as befits a traitor to his faith and law and a blasphemer against the name of God and the hangman of our entire people." There are curses in our folk poetry, awful and unforgettable in their expression, especially the one on the eve of the Battle of Kosovo. But Njegoš's curse in *The Mountain Wreath* has surpassed any of these. The language and the concepts in it are also of the folk, of myth, but their meaning and expression have been heightened and brought to the ultimate range of possibility—in a single sweep of ever-deeper and more vivid colors:

> Who basely shall betray our leaders,
> Let each created thing to him be stone!
> May mighty God by His great power
> Change all the seed placed in his fields to stone,
> Change, too, the forming babe in womb to stone,
>
> . . . .
>
> Let ne'er within his room a rifle more be slung,
> Nor any man of all his house e'er die on honour's field!
> For manly head his kin shall vainly yearn!
>
> . . . .
>
> No Christian hope for him! a dog's creed be for him!
> Let blood be pourèd out in place of wine
>   Upon his Yuletide log!
> Let all the joy and pleasance of his Slava Day
>   In grief consume away!
> Let him eat not of lamb, but his own kin
>   Upon his festal day!
>
> . . . .
>
> Behind his stiff, cold body, and behind
> The corpses of his kinsfolk, may there follow
> Mourners untrue and hearts all insincere,
> Telling their lies alway!

Here not only the people and their fate find expression, but also a new and different view, one of even greater finality: everything of the traitor's is turned to stone, and over him and all that is his there remains after him a lie. We, the people, with our customs and destinies, are here, but there is also a concrete and relentless advance toward the massacre, expressed in such a way that there is nothing anyone could add to it.

There are in *The Mountain Wreath* individual sketches from the life of the folk which are not directed toward the massacre—for example, Mandušić's dream. But these exist to hold together the basic poetic and conceptual fabric. Even if something may not be essential to the massacre as an event, it is still a part of life, of Montenegro, which is first and foremost in *The Mountain Wreath.* The most beautiful and most striking parts are, after all, those that deal with Montenegro—Njegoš's quintessence.

There is something else that especially sets off *The Mountain Wreath* from folk poetry and at the same time constitutes its most particular and highest distinction. That is the lyrical character of this epic poem, its lyrical mode of expression and feeling. Goethe regarded Greek tragedy as the highest form of poetry—the fusion of the lyrical with the epic. *The Mountain Wreath* is precisely that kind of lyrical-epic fusion. It was not for nothing that Njegoš turned to the Greeks, and particularly to their tragedy. Njegoš experienced a personal and inspired sense of duty as a ruler and to his nation's past, which was so intertwined with the present. Indeed, the very survival of the national idea and of his land was at stake. Under such circumstances his own survival as a poet was also involved: he could find expression only in personally experiencing and expressing the Serbian destiny and the present itself, else all would simply be a repetition of folk poetry.

Every detail, every cry and image in *The Mountain Wreath,* is imbued with his blood and charged with his feeling. The Serbian destiny is expressed as his own. The lyrical expression, the subjective perception of the idea, and the personal involvement in every detail—these constitute the distinctiveness and the highest and most moving beauty of this thematically epic poem.

All of the fearful horror betwixt life and death, actuality and dream, all that real and rock-bound world of causes, myths and scenes of tragic heroism, the identification of all that with one's own destiny, all the antiquity and the immediacy—these Njegoš experienced in a personal way through his own passion, expression, and language. It is he, Bishop Rade, who wails over Kosovo and Montenegro's woe. It is he who makes the mountains shudder with the lament of the Batrić sister and who appears behind the sage serenity of Abbot Stefan.

The Mountain Wreath is also Njegoš's personal drama.

Njegoš is there in *The Mountain Wreath* in his entirety: the concerned ruler of a lawless land and the troubled sage of *The Ray of the Microcosm,* the man who assumes every national misfortune as his very own and every duty as an inalienable heritage. He is aware even in his sleep that the fate of the land and the people is upon his shoulders and that he is himself a participant in the Serbian and the cosmic drama.

Njegoš does not even know why anything around him should not be a part of him, nor does he know of anything occurring that he also should not experience.

A passionately personal, subjective feeling, whose validity is preserved through mind and reason, the lyrical treatment of an epic theme—these comprise the Njegoš amalgam that has produced the most fateful poetry and most impassioned truth. Folk poetry knows no such fusion and empathy.

Nowhere does Njegoš even momentarily depart from his ethnic base. Yet it is also true that he attained heights that, by the very nature of his collective expression, the folk bard could neither reach nor behold.

It looks as though it is popular and ethnic—but it is not. It has new beauties and polish, more acute thoughts.

A personality may stand for the people, but not the people for a personality.

15.

The Mountain Wreath concerns itself with a particular subject and a particular phase—the massacre and the establishment of a Serbian state. Montenegro itself was a particular case; it, too, brought into focus several centuries of our existence at a decisive hour and through a decisive act. Myths, sayings, customs, and a terrible national and cosmic drama intertwine and emerge in the same images and expressions. That is a special language, a special world, expressed in a special manner, with a multiplicity of elements whose omission would render difficult, if not impossible, the comprehension of the whole.

The Mountain Wreath is incomparable. Isidora Sekulić suggested that it was possible only to recast it.

Those who have analyzed translations of *The Mountain Wreath* —and it has been translated into nearly all the European languages —have shown that not one of these has succeeded even remotely in transmitting Njegoš's poetic expression and conceptual power. Mladen Leskovac has done a devastating critique on the translations of *The Mountain Wreath*. They say that the best translations are the Swedish, because it was done by a poet, and the German, done by a person with expert knowledge of our traits and past, but that not even these are fully satisfactory.

The special qualities of our way of life and of Njegoš's diction, at times of Montenegro itself, and, of course, of the poet himself —who is reflective and inspired to the highest degree—are possible to transmit only if the other language and even the destiny of the other people contain at least similar concepts and imagery.

Take, for example, the very common word *blood*. In Njegoš it does not simply denote a sticky red liquid and life and misfortune, but the very essence of man's survival and the bond with his brotherhood and people. This is the kind of blood on which Turks and evil men feed, the blood that has a fatal power and force, the blood that will come out of their ears—the blood one cannot translate without entering into Njegoš's thought and imagery, or unless there are corresponding expressions and concepts among the people into whose language one is translating. Or take the expression "destroy the seed in the bride," which means not only complete extermination, but the extermination of a friendly brotherhood, and at the same time with the accent on the horrible past of Turkish invasions and internecine slaughter. The image of destruction is such that one can only diminish it, if indeed one is able to find an expression that corresponds to the destruction of seed in a bride's womb. Or take the expression "To him Kosovo's Field no pain shall yield," referring to the one who took part in the battle of Kameni against the Turks, whereby the sweetness of revenge and the resplendence of present heroism is expressed, as well as a past of bottomless despair. The line "So passed the Serbian Cap and Name away" does not mean simply defeat, but a defeat that extends back into the entire past, through the existence of the Serbs.

The Mountain Wreath is replete with such peculiarities of our life and destiny.

This poem requires a commentary that will be different from Rešetar's, one that will explain the meaning and diction as well, and not only the facts, one that will plumb its beauties, and the characters themselves, and ourselves. To put it most accurately, what is needed is an up-to-date commentary, for time and new modes of existence inevitably alienate us from Njegoš, and his beauties become ever more absolute and impenetrable.

To interpret is also to quicken.

16.

NJEGOŠ's educated contemporaries did not comprehend the beauties and the significance of *The Mountain Wreath*. It seems that the main cause for this lack of comprehension lay in the fact that Njegoš's poem somehow seemed too common. They themselves were just emerging from folk poetry and national myths. They were not able, nor was it possible for them, to distinguish between the essence of *The Mountain Wreath* and the commonplace, between myth and actuality.

Time has had its effect, as it always does in the case of anything new and great. That which once seemed common and ordinary in *The Mountain Wreath* came to be seen as the poeticizing of our individuality, our, so to say, extratemporal and extraspatial existence. The destiny of our people became manifest and found expression in the purest poetry. Yet the efforts of many were necessary and indispensable in order to reveal all the beauties of *The Mountain Wreath* and the fact that it was somewhat loftier and deeper than the unlearned and unsophisticated contemporary naturally took it to be, that it transcended folk poetry and legendary and folk wisdom.

Still many new efforts will be needed to uncover the beauties and the meaning of *The Mountain Wreath.* For that poem is somewhat like life itself—a ceaseless being and becoming. It calls for delving into the truths and beauties of one's own existence as well as those of humanity and of the cosmos. *The Mountain Wreath* extends beyond the existence of our people. In it is recounted all the suffering, all the spiritual beauty, of our life here in the Balkans, all the bloodshed, woe, and misfortune, as well as the inextinguishable quest for the good and light.

The Mountain Wreath shall be, and must be, constantly rediscovered and re-experienced, in ever-new ways, as long as the Serbian nation and tongue shall exist. It will move and inspire anew each succeeding generation and every person who enters into its beauties and essence.

The Mountain Wreath is a poem that has never been excelled in our literature, nor can it be, as a conceptual synthesis and poetic expression of our destiny: the Serbian destiny under absolute laws, human resistance to cosmic evil, the lyrical expression of a national drama—our people in song.

In *The Mountain Wreath* and through it the Serbian people became conscious of themselves and declared themselves to the world. That people will continue to affirm itself in new ways, but *The Mountain Wreath* shall ever remain the expression of our own destiny.

The Serbian people live inextricably in Njegoš and *The Mountain Wreath;* Njegoš and *The Mountain Wreath* will outlive even the Serbian people.

A work of art endures beyond those to whom its existence belongs, for in it is also the human destiny.

To express oneself—this, too, is to endure.

THE FALSE TSAR STEPHEN THE SMALL

1.

Overshadowed by *The Mountain Wreath* and *The Ray of the Microcosm, The False Tsar Stephen the Small* has been largely ignored, though the wonderful poetry with which Njegoš amply endowed it has not gone completely unnoticed. There have been several reasons for this unjustified neglect. *The Mountain Wreath* occupied a central place, especially because of its ideological content, for our people were still struggling for their national survival. For the same reason, even *The Ray of the Microcosm* was shunted aside, though to a lesser degree, inasmuch as its metaphysical themes did impel and motivate national aspirations. The needs of the time deflected attention from *Stephen the Small.* An attempt at a Montenegrin social drama, it did not concern itself much either with nationalism or with religion and philosophy.

The only study of any significance about *Stephen the Small* is that written by Isidora Sekulić, in her sensitive and studious work about Njegoš. She characterized *Stephen the Small* as "a kind of social drama," "a specifically Slavic comedy which is not very happy, and more of a dramatic poem than a comedy, one in which there is incomparably more poetry than plot," for "the Bishop did not have a talent for drama, nor did he have a feeling for the stage." She concluded, "If we reduce the matter to a portrayal of Montenegrin life, then *Stephen the Small* emerges as a supplement to *The Mountain Wreath.* In *The Mountain Wreath* Montenegrin life was depicted in the lofty poetry of chivalry. In *Stephen the Small* Montenegrin life is portrayed without pathos, but with realism and a practical everyday psychology." Despite its being an oversimplification, this view seems to me to be correct.

The subject must simply have occurred to Njegoš. It, too, was out of the Montenegrin past, though not so remote a past that it could not be remembered in his own time.

Stephen the Small ruled over Montenegro—though this is not quite the way to put it—from 1767 to 1774, so that Njegoš's uncle Bishop Petar, who was a young monk in Stephen's time, remembered well the pretender who had usurped the reins of government from his uncle Bishop Sava.

Pretenders were a phenomenon quite typical for Montenegro and still thriving in Njegoš's time. A people who lived in myth, devoid of a central authority or of educated men, totally dedicated to a fateful cause, was bound to be inclined to accept everyone and everything that contributed to its struggle and its dreams. Prince Nikola Vasojević, whom Bishop Rade had removed, was a pretender. Bishop Petar had his hands full with the self-styled Count Vujić, a man from the Vojvodina who twice came to Montenegro, on behalf of one Great Power or another, to set off a rebellion of Christians in Turkey and whose aim was nothing less than the restoration of the Serbian Empire. In 1792 Bishop Petar even promised this Vujić twelve hundred Montenegrins as mercenaries, while in 1795 the chieftains elected him Protector of Montenegro! In 1819 there appeared in Montenegro a certain monk, a fool-in-Christ called Avvakum, who went from clan to clan posing as God's messenger and calling the people to war against the Turks, so that Bishop Petar had to send out circulars against him in order to bring his "ignorant and foolish people" to reason. Matavulj describes a pretender known as the Duke of Medun, a fraud without ideas or ideals, at a time when the institution of Montenegrin pretenders was already in decline, in the seventies of the past century. Matavulj even advanced the spiteful but not entirely incorrect observation of a stranger that there is in every Montenegrin a bit of that fraudulent Duke—the tendency to exalt one's own person with glory borrowed from the clan or from Serbdom, but always within the framework of already existing legends, hopes, and prejudices.

Even when they did not originate in Montenegro itself, pretenders found fertile soil in a Montenegro caught between myth and the concrete exigencies of the struggle against the Turks. As in *The Mountain Wreath,* so here Njegoš considered it his mission as an enlightened ruler to instruct his unenlightened and credulous people. In Njegoš's time the acceptance of pretenders was an especially harmful feature of Montenegrin life. It also hurt him as a ruler who had to organize all forces toward liberation from the Turks. The example of Stephen the Small, whom the Montenegrins accepted with open arms as the murdered Russian Tsar Peter III, was instructive in every respect.

Here, too, in taking for his subject the affair of Stephen the Small, Njegoš was consistent: he thereby turned to an important element in Montenegrin life, another essence. However important they were, his educational and civic motives were in fact incidental. The basic impulse came from the inspiration of a poetic imagination. More correctly, both were there, and other motivations as well, since with Njegoš the elements with which he created and with which he himself was created cannot be isolated—except in an abstract analysis.

Everything can be essential in a work of art, provided, of course, that the artist is capable of creating the work.

2.

YET NJEGOŠ had the most profound reasons for taking up the subject of Stephen the Small.

The appearance and rise of this impostor are important because they signaled the first practical attempt to create a civil government in Montenegro. That attempt brought down on Montenegro a Turkish and Venetian campaign, which served only to point up the significance of both his personality and his work. Njegoš perceived this significance in Stephen and the positive side of his role, though he condemned him from an ethical, and from a dynastic, standpoint: "Stephen the Small was a fraud and a vagabond," he begins in his Preface, "but in calling himself the Tsar of Russia he inaugurated an important epoch in Montenegro and the surrounding territory." In the work itself Njegoš emphasizes Stephen's role in establishing order, and, even more, the significance of the encounters with the Turks and Venetians brought on by his coming on the scene. Njegoš perceived Stephen's ambivalence: a fraud, yet a sensible one who spoke wisely and gave counsel beneficial both for the people and for the cause of Serbian liberation. Being a ruler and dynast and enlightener, Njegoš not only condemned the first, but stressed the second—the creative, positive side, if not so much of Stephen's personality, then of all the elements he brought into being and that were connected with him.

The work begins with a vision by Serdar Vukale that now, with the appearance of the Russian Tsar in Montenegro, there will ensue the restoration of the Serbian Empire and its glory—a vision distinctly Njegoš's of the past brought to life:

> Rejoice, ye ashes of the Nemanjići,
> Nemanjići and Grebljanovići,
> For once more your diadems shall glisten
> As the sun which shines in eastern heaven.
> And your unfurled banners now shall flutter
> O'er the ruins of your once great cities,
> Now shall streams of blood come coursing onward
> With the impure blood of Hagar's offspring
> To wash out the stain on Serbian honor.
> Open, then, ye sepulchers of knighthood,
> . . . .
> Join together, thunderbolts and earthquakes,
> Give the Serbian land another visage.

Stephen the Small is one of those significant signposts in Montenegrin history to which the rule and ambitions of Bishop Rade were tied—the creation of a civil government in the struggle against the Turks. Njegoš himself felt this, but he felt even more the necessity of warning against frauds and impostors to whom the people succumbed, all the more willingly because they were intoxicated by their hatred for the Turks and by their desire for freedom. If one delves carefully into the reasons why the Montenegrins in *Stephen the Small* acclaimed a sham tsar so easily and with such alacrity, it will become clear that there is something here that goes deeper than credulity, namely, the conviction that the clans would thereby gain a standard-bearer who would lead them into battle—in other words, a central authority. The priest Andrija sums it up thus:

> Whoever he may be, I do not know him,
> . . . .
> But the people took him for the emperor,

They did give him honor and they feared him,
And the people spun about this title,
Spun about him just as we desired,
As the earth spins round about a drunkard;
And through him we kept our folk united

. . . .

Losing Stephen we have suffered greatly;
Now shall Montenegrins run unbridled,
Wont to do whatever is their pleasure;
Then there shall be no one to keep tally
Who doth drink the wine and who will pay it;
Then compared with our domestic troubles
Turkish evil shall seem like a wedding;

. . . .

In a lawless land have we been nurtured,
May the common plague now take all of us,
Oh, if times of yore would but return!

The massacre was for Njegoš a break, a turning point in Serbian and in Montenegrin history. The time of Stephen the Small, which was closer and more concrete, signified a further impetus in the direction indicated by the massacre, especially in the realization of the means—the unification of the clans through a civil government—through which alone their pledged ideals could be finally achieved. It was so in fact. From the massacre on, there was no occurrence in Montenegrin history that was more important than the events of the time of Stephen the Small, and particularly those most directly connected with his person. The fruits of the massacre were reaped in Stephen's time. And inasmuch as Stephen is a sequel to the massacre, so, too, *Stephen the Small* is a sequel to *The Mountain Wreath,* albeit in a different manner, under different circumstances.

It was the very course of their lives and their history that aroused and drove the Montenegrins to accept Stephen. Njegoš perceived this with an infallibility that was instinctive, even had his own personal fate not forced him to recognize it. For this reason he clearly distinguishes in his work between Stephen's mendacity and popular credulity on the one hand and Stephen's actual role and the substantial need of the people—for the creation of a government that could carry on the struggle against the Turks. Moreover, Njegoš justifies the former with another argument: the Montenegrins are credulous because they are imbued with their ideals, and thus Stephen is not an ordinary fraud inasmuch as he acts in response to the people's needs in carrying out those compelling needs. He does not simply usurp power, but he establishes order to further the struggle against the Turks. He does not just give reasons, which the simple people find convincing, why he supposedly had to quit the Russian imperial throne, but he directs at the Montenegrins the most impassioned calls to action against the Turks. These calls inflame and intoxicate, for they express the essence and the meaning of the Montenegrin past and present.

History and reality directed Njegoš to Stephen the Small; personal considerations merged with the general.

A man primarily constructs his own world, but only, of course, as circumstances and possibilities permit.

3.

Truly Stephen the Small and his times were enticingly colorful, and especially so to a poet such as Njegoš to the extent that they exhibited most completely the Montenegrin character, way of life, and mentality. Heroism and credulity, as well as a practical wisdom —reflected by Abbot Teodosije—all of which have always been present in Montenegro, played an especially conspicuous and important role in Montenegro in Stephen's time. Not only the ideals of state and nation, but also Montenegrin peculiarities and Montenegrin life in all its tension and striving—these marked Stephen's time. And this is just what Njegoš wished to depict.

That period and its representative, Stephen, comprising so many colorful contrasts, attracted the poet who was himself marked by the attributes of a Montenegrin sage and a creative ruler.

Except for rare instances, Njegoš did not depart from national history in his inspirations. Moreover, it may be said that it was in history—in its individual periods—that he sought and found the confirmation of his ideas and the substantiation of his inspirations. Even *The Ray of the Microcosm* is, in the final analysis, a transposition of the national destiny. The time of Stephen the Small was too close to him to be converted into myth, yet still distant enough to be on the edge of myth. While adhering to tradition, as he did in *The Mountain Wreath,* Njegoš still had to base his action on verified facts. The very meaning of that epoch—the attempt to create a civil authority—led him to concrete historical fact and to a comparison with his own role. He himself points out that he made use of both tradition and documents from the Venetian archives, and concludes that in his poem there is nothing that has been invented.

To tell the truth, it must be said that this reliance on documents was not thorough, and yet it was conscientious enough to preserve the author from distorting historical factualness and to enable him to divorce his subject sufficiently from mere tradition to make it credible. Professor Kolendić has established that Njegoš sojourned in Venice from February 13 to March 15, 1847, during which time certain documents were made available to him from the archives, some of which he used in *Stephen the Small.* Kolendić concluded, "The copying was neither as exhaustive as the Bishop thought it was, nor was it systematic." Without Njegoš knowing it, the Austrian authorities engaged in much letter writing before approval was granted to permit copies of documents to be made for the Montenegrin Bishop. They were rather apprehensive that he might make use of a document in support of his claims against Austria and Turkey. Njegoš was helped in this project in 1848 by Niccolò Tommaseo, who was himself suspected by the authorities to be one of the leaders of the democratic and anti-Austrian movement in Venetia. Njegoš obtained two hundred and twenty extracts—the charters of our rulers in Latin and the reports of the governors of Kotor from the sixteenth to the end of the eighteenth century. Not one of these extracts has been preserved, so that it is impossible to determine what in the poem was based on tradition and what on documents.

That Njegoš was not entirely led by the historical evidence—and there was no need for him to be—is best seen by the fact that the role he assigned to Teodosije Mrkojević (or Mrković), the most developed and thus most significant character in the poem, is contrary to the role he played in real life. As Jovan Tomić has established, Teodosije was one of Stephen's chief helpers, whereas in *Stephen the Small* he stands at the head of his enemies. It is also true that this same Teodosije Mrkojević was later the trusted supporter of Bishop Petar, and so Njegoš, who must have known this about him, pitted him against the impostor Stephen the Small. This is not to exclude the possibility that Njegoš may have found out something about Teodosije's co-operation with Stephen, for at one point he has the two of them becoming reconciled, on the insistence of the chieftains, for the sake of harmony among the people. Though Teodosije's role in the work does not agree with the archives, in essence—and this was the important thing for Njegoš—even that character is fairly true to what he actually stood for and did in real life: in the time of both Stephen the Small and Bishop Petar, both in the poem and in actual fact, he stood for the national cause. In portraying him as Stephen's antagonist in the poem, which was not factual, Njegoš had him act thus not on behalf of any clan or anarchy and lawlessness, but in the name of reason and truth.

Despite the extreme scarcity of published documents and analyses, it may be concluded that Njegoš's Stephen the Small and the historical one are close. Though an upholder of his own dynasty, Njegoš approached the personality of Stephen with extreme conscientiousness. This does not prove that he understood the full importance of this strange figure. Njegoš had a tendency to overstress the ethical element, that is, Stephen's fraudulent side, and thereby to overshadow and ignore his altruism and capability. After all, Stephen was maimed and lost one eye setting mines to carve out roads in the Montenegrin wilderness, and he finally had his throat slit by a hireling of the Vizir of Scutari. Njegoš's Stephen is more wily than enterprising and more the product of chance than of his own initiative. This was essentially the Stephen handed down to Njegoš by oral tradition—the lore of the brotherhood, still biased and not yet faded into myth. The Petrovići of Njegoš's time must have been bitter about the pretender who had deprived one of their blood—Bishop Sava—of all power, and even locked him up and took away his sheep. Yet one cannot accuse Njegoš of bias or inaccuracy. In the poem Stephen's personality is ambiguous, split, while as a historical figure he was portrayed with substantial fidelity as the founder of a civil government. Njegoš's bias in favor of his own dynasty shows less in the way in which he belittles Stephen than by the forced manner in which he includes his uncle Petar in the poem. One thing is true, however: Njegoš did not portray Stephen fully, to the end, nor did he make him the figure that Stephen deserved by virtue of his qualities and his role.

Nowhere in the poem does Njegoš give prominence to the Petrovići, while his Bishop Sava is historically accurate—irresolute, vague, characteristically colorless. Though a dynast, Njegoš does not overvalue and vaunt his kin in the face of the facts. He does not exaggerate even when treating his uncle Petar, who was an archdeacon in Stephen's time: Petar plays no active role in the drama, as he did not in the actual events. Rather, Njegoš has others foretell his future fame as they marvel at his horsemanship.

Njegoš did not tamper with historical fact in violation of his own conscience. He would not have done it even had he not been conscious of having to answer to history.

After all, when all else is lacking, conscience is a fair criterion of truth.

4.

In his effort to approximate reality and to adhere to the facts, whether gained from archives or from a still-fresh tradition, as a poet, Njegoš exposed himself to a whole series of problems. He passed from myth to a reality that time had stripped of the superfluous and reduced to the essential. This is what the poet had to work with and what he had to re-create within himself. Thus Njegoš departed from ideas as such—though ultimately realities were for him only the concrete aspect of ideas. The subject itself —a not too remote set of events directly connected with the rule of his uncle Petar—compelled him to deal with facts. And his very inclination to continue with his narration of Montenegrin history, begun in *The Mountain Wreath,* and to instruct the Montenegrins, impelled him to select the motif of Stephen the Small. I maintain, however, that there was something deeper involved: every artist expresses himself in a manner that cannot be repeated, and Njegoš could not say anything essentially new along the same lines as *The Mountain Wreath.* The massacre is a single and unique event in Montenegrin history. No one can say what Njegoš might have created had he lived longer, though it seems a warranted guess that he would have continued along the path he had taken in *Stephen the Small* by going on into the time of Bishop Petar, which was also so significant for Montenegro. Starting out with cosmic problems in *The Ray of the Microcosm,* Njegoš inevitably went on to realities—first to Montenegrin history in its mythical conception, and then further still. One way or another, he had to change his subject, and thus also his style of expression.

It must be admitted that the poet did not come even close to solving the problems posed by the subject of Stephen the Small, as he had in *The Mountain Wreath,* even though *The False Tsar Stephen the Small* is a significant work. In short, one can feel that Njegoš tussled with certain problems in *Stephen the Small,* some of which he resolved completely, others only halfway, while in *The Mountain Wreath* everything fell into place, already worked out long before. After *The Mountain Wreath* Njegoš did not advance; rather, he declined. It should be borne in mind that the poems *The House of the Aleksići* and *The Tower of the Djurišići* refer to events taking place during his own reign, that they were written long after *Stephen the Small,* and that they are hardly different from average Montenegrin guslar poems. One may therefore conclude that Njegoš's powers as a poet declined as his subjects came closer to his reign, to the actualities of his own epoch. Born in myth, he was truly and above all a poet of reality transformed into myth. And the time of Stephen the Small was still more reality than myth.

As a result, Njegoš had to proceed differently with respect to both his expression and his composition.

A prosaic, almost narrative, tone is more pronounced in *Stephen the Small* than in *The Mountain Wreath,* where it hardly exists at all. Those clusters of short words and images which are bursting with fullness, those unexpected turns of thought and flashes of anger and pain—of all this there is very little in *Stephen the Small.* At first glance it has the same verse form as the recitatives in *The Mountain Wreath,* but both its tone and its commonplace words make it more like prose narrative. This is also in keeping with Njegoš's theme: *Stephen the Small* is more a poem about actuality—the kind that has not been distilled into an idea —than is *The Mountain Wreath.* This is most essential in explaining its weaknesses and in perceiving that which is truly novel about it among Njegoš's works—that it is a social drama.

Both in appearance and in composition *Stephen the Small* is more of a drama than is *The Mountain Wreath.* It is, in fact, a Montenegrin social comedy, but an exceedingly serious and tragic one, with many tears and much heroic pathos. And inasmuch as Njegoš was not a dramatist, by either craft or talent, and since the subject of Stephen, despite its strong comical elements, is too bound up with the very serious and bloody reality of Montenegro, the result was something that was neither drama nor comedy.

Njegoš was naturally drawn by his propensity for mythical reality and the poeticizing of myth, that is, by the dramatic poem, while his subject and its reality pulled in the direction of drama, of comedy. The subject also led him to prose and description. Stephen the Small is a transitional work, perhaps like the very period of Stephen the Small—a transition from myth and poetry toward prose and everyday realities. Njegoš himself never quite made that transition, nor was he given the time to make it. Others were to do it after him. *Stephen the Small* is still great poetry, especially through that quality that makes *The Mountain Wreath* unexcelled—the lyrical expression of myths, essences.

Njegoš wrote *Stephen the Small* before he resolved the manifold contradictions into which he was bound to fall once he decided to move in the direction of immediate reality. Yet since it dealt with a strong personality of irreducible completeness, it remained, with all its deficiencies and irresolutions, a lyrical rendering of epic themes, by a poet of myths and ideas. *The Mountain Wreath* is full of contradictions, but they have been synthesized. In *Stephen the Small* there has remained a fair amount that is deficient, unsynthesized, but also much that is the work of a great poet, one who sets out even if he does not always get there.

Though a drama in outward form, *Stephen the Small* is in fact a dramatic poem. Its actual internal drama, however, is incomparably inferior to that in *The Mountain Wreath.*

Not even in *Stephen the Small* was Njegoš able to divest himself of his own essence. The poem rises and gains dramatic impact to the degree to which Njegoš succeeded in transforming reality into idea, and idea into poetry, but it never develops into a social play—whether drama or comedy.

How anything is expressed has something to do with how it is understood and experienced.

5.

TRUE TO HIS INTENTION and inspiration—to express in poetry the crucial moments of Montenegrin history and to expound certain ideas—Njegoš sought to get at some essences in *Stephen the Small*. In view of the subject and the period that he chose, these were bound to include the traits peculiar to the Montenegrin mentality. The subject itself—the Montenegrins allowing themselves out of noble impulses to be deceived by an impostor—contained and revealed the peculiarities of that mentality. The proximity of the time, of that Montenegrin reality, only heightened those peculiarities and practically compelled this poet of ideas to bring them to light. Thus *Stephen the Small* is a poem of Montenegrin mores. It is not that alone, of course, but this is the most important thing about it. This holds true not only for the poem as a whole, but also for its most significant pages and its most elaborately constructed scenes. The characters, too, are essentially more Montenegrin than Serbian. Likewise, as a poem about heroism, it is more specifically Montenegrin than pan-Serbian. There are no characters in *Stephen the Small* that express the essence of myth and idea such as Bishop Danilo and Abbot Stefan in *The Mountain Wreath*. It has no Mićunović or Mandušić. Few of the folk customs and scenes from daily life that it portrays contribute to the idea. On the other hand, it does include more types from everyday Montenegrin life than does *The Mountain Wreath*. *Stephen the Small* is a work of great dialogues in which animated, living ideas contend with each other in a specifically Montenegrin mentality and setting.

So it is also with respect to Njegoš's metaphysical views.

It was precisely in *Stephen the Small* that Njegoš, a poet of ideas, that is, of essences, and brought closer to an immediate reality, developed to their fullest extent his views on evil. From the cosmic and metaphysical necessity of evil in *The Ray of the Microcosm,* Njegoš descended, by way of a doomed Serbdom in *The Mountain Wreath,* to evil as it was in an immediate reality—the bloody struggle of the Montenegrins with the Turks and with one another. The motivations behind the evil in *The Ray of the Microcosm* are basically the same in *Stephen the Small*. Only the approach to evil is more concrete in the latter; the evil is a fact of everyday Montenegrin life. Bishop Sava claims that a victory over the Turks, word of which has just arrived, confirms that God himself is watching over Montenegro, this bloody nest, and Vojvoda Drago comments that out of evil and misfortune are born good and joy, for life itself is so ordered:

> Fortune is the offspring of misfortune,
> Wailing is the mother of gay ditty.
> . . . .
> He who would desire to live forever
> In this world would only be a martyr.

Vojvoda Drago continues: Beset on all sides by everyone, the Montenegrins must fight and plunder, for that is their way of life. Moreover, Njegoš enters here into the purely economic motivation of the Montenegrin resistance: the Montenegrins were not merchants or artisans, for there were no prerequisites for this: the enemy destroyed what few crops they had, and so they had to be what they were—warriors for freedom:

> Say what would become of Montenegrins,
> Hemmed in as they are by fiend and devil,
> If by awful sacrifice and bloodshed
> They lived not e'en as their days were numbered.
> For they carry on no kind of commerce—
> They know naught of it and have none of it;
> Their most fertile fields and all their lowlands
> Are the prey of the oppressor's forces,
> Which destroy their grain and hay, their harvest;
> Neither have they any skill as craftsmen.
> If one gives the matter any thinking,
> How can a Montenegrin change his being
> And still truly be a Montenegrin?
> All in vain, if we were burning candle,
> Still we never could be any other
> Toward the foe of our true faith and freedom.
> Let us rather strike the foe of freedom,
> While there still is breath in any of us,
> Who shall die, in glory shall he perish;
> Who remains, he shall abide in glory;
> For to God of all the dearest off'ring
> Is the blood that gushes from a tyrant.

This also reveals the direction of the evolution of Njegoš's religion: Njegoš's God, who was a warrior even in *The Ray of the Microcosm,* has now grown into a passionate avenger.

Inasmuch as evil is the only given quantity, it is vain and senseless to try to bend before it. The only reasonable thing, from both a practical and a metaphysical point of view, is to struggle against it. One should always expect evil, and it is with evil that evil is vanquished. This is also the thinking of Marko Miljanov: "For Turkish evil—evil return"; "an insatiable force deserves no humanity." That is how it is here in Montenegro, and it is probably no different in more distant lands. This is what Teodosije Mrkojević wishes to explain to the Russian emissary Prince Dolgorukov, who maintained that the Montenegrins did not give much thought to things, but lived carelessly as "the sons of nature":

> Prince, I think, with thoughts my head is bursting,
> Thoughts which have inflicted on me troubles
> Twenty times greater than heavy labors.
> . . . .
> In a tight spot one is forced to ponder,
> Though these thoughts of ours from yours may differ.
> Your thoughts go from good to something better,
> And if by mischance you lose this better,
> Then your good has been changed into evil,
> Which is all a funny way of thinking.
> I give thought to evil made still worse,
> I endure the bad, I shun the worse.

Teodosije is not thinking here of metaphysical evil, or at least not primarily of that, but of the cares and misfortunes of life, somewhat like that Montenegrin woman who wailed, "Woe is me, even were I someone else, things would still go badly for me!" In part, this evil is the consequence of earlier historical misfortunes. Serdar Jovo says:

> Emperors and governors have perished,
> Perished as if struck by living lightning,
> On all sides the Serbians have perished,
> Perished both in body and in spirit,
> Neither house nor highway has been left us,
> But we are beset by every torment,
> 'Tis through evil and terrible vengeance
> That we cling to life in these our mountains.

The more Njegoš approached daily life, the more he understood evil as a practical Montenegrin, Serb, and, I would say, human reality. Moreover, this caused him to overlook the tie between this evil and the cosmic one; the action in *Stephen the Small* is not nearly as much subject to higher laws as that in *The Mountain Wreath*. Yet he does not completely forget these higher laws even in *Stephen the Small*. Perhaps it is this that leads him to a new great thought: that although justified, the struggle for freedom is a great evil, because it has been provoked by another evil.

Involved in human conflict, Njegoš's God, who had never been gracious, is angry and almost malevolent in *Stephen the Small,* though, to be sure, in the struggle against evil: the blood of tyrants is his most pleasing sacrifice. Yet inasmuch as there are practically no metaphysical motivations in *Stephen the Small,* Njegoš's God is embroiled in human affairs, He is more mundane, like everything else in the poem.

It was in *Stephen the Small* that Njegoš formulated most completely the principle according to which the commission of evil in defense against evil is not evil.

It was in *Stephen the Small* that Njegoš had to work it out, for here he was forced to deal with the facts of life, with evil appearing in a concrete—Montenegrin—form. Njegoš does not place this evil in the context of higher laws, but he implies that the evil is in confrontation with a higher good and with justice, though he has left these sketchy and only hints at them. The evil in *Stephen the Small* covers the Montenegrins as well, with some justification and, if we may so put it, justice. Their greatest virtue—heroism, courage—is also evil, the resistance to evil with evil.

In *Stephen the Small* Njegoš's views on evil finally crystallized; they are based on the immediate reality that surrounded him rather than on myths, or on his reading. But this reality was linked to myth and still lived in it and with it.

It was in *Stephen the Small,* too, that Njegoš rounded out his picture of Montenegrin heroism. This Montenegrin heroism is rather more concrete than that under the aspect of higher laws. Here Njegoš displays its various sides in several ways, through the lips of Montenegrin heroes, and especially through the non-Montenegrins: Patriarch Brkić, Dolgorukov, and Stephen, and even the Turks. A whole two acts—the second and the fifth—are predominantly about this, directly or indirectly. The theme of heroism is conveyed throughout the entire poem and establishes itself as its dominant motif—as it is in the Montenegrin reality. With the help of the Venetians, the Turks have waged war on the Montenegrins because of Stephen. Hard pressed, the Montenegrins send to the pashas as negotiators Teodosije Mrkojević and two old men, inasmuch as old men—as Teodosije himself puts it—are of lesser worth in Montenegro than anywhere else and so will not be too great a loss if the Turks slay them. Yet what kind of negotiating is this? Outsmarting, disputation, and, finally, a quarrel. The entire fifth act—a dialogue among the Turks in Scutari—is predominantly there to bring in and to justify Montenegrin heroism. The idea of heroic pride is skillfully and loftily treated in *Stephen the Small* against a portrayal of the harsh Montenegrin reality.

The Mountain Wreath is also a dithyramb to heroism, especially to its Montenegrin variety. But the treatment there is different. In *Stephen the Small,* heroism, like everything else, is presented more in its outward form, as a slice of life, reality. In *The Mountain Wreath* essences, ideas, and myths actually act, whereas in *Stephen the Small* they are merely displayed, described.

Stephen the Small is more of a Montenegrin poem—if one takes into account the realities rather than ideas as distilled and sublimated reality, whereas *The Mountain Wreath* is a poem about the Serbian essence in Montenegrin form.

Therefore *Stephen the Small* not only magnifies the virtues, but also stresses the vices of the Montenegrins. Montenegro is not just heroism, but also the "bellow of a foolish people," and Njegoš stresses, in his own merciless, unmitigated way, the Montenegrin weakness for taking bribes.

> Men are quick to lick the hand with money,
> While they pay no heed to one that's empty.

Stephen the Small is a portrayal through opposite and extreme types of the Montenegrin mentality and of its contradictions. Also exhibited—often with bias—are Montenegrin political and social relations. Internal quarrels are offered as the main reason for Turkish successes. In *The Mountain Wreath* these quarrels were spoken of distantly, in allusions, while the Turkish renegades were treated as the main obstacle to liberation. In *Stephen the Small* clan feuds are treated as everyday occurrences and in all their nakedness. The priest Andrija says:

> Then compared with our domestic troubles
> Turkish evil shall seem like a wedding.

The Turks openly count on these troubles.

In *Stephen the Small* we see also the political problems that beset Njegoš the ruler.

Is it not precisely because it deals with a reality not quite transposed into poetry that *Stephen the Small* holds a lesser place than *The Mountain Wreath* as poetry?

And, for the same reason, are not the ideas in it—of good and evil—inferior both as truth and as poetry?

At their best, ideas have value outside of their temporal, spatial, and other limits as one of the aspects of universal human destiny. Reality, which is different everywhere, has an absolute value, but only in itself.

6.

THOUGH THEY still represent ideas, most of the characters in *Stephen the Small* are taken straight out of a recent and living Montenegrin reality. And they also betray the irresoluble nature of that contradiction to which Njegoš succumbed by taking a Montenegrin subject from real life: many characters were left unfinished, and the most colorless and sketchiest among them are precisely those taken from real life—mere reproductions of actuality.

The most finished character is Teodosije Mrkojević, who is in no way inferior to the greatest figures in *The Mountain Wreath.*

Teodosije is reminiscent of Abbot Stefan, but only at first glance. Like the Abbot, he, too, is sheer wisdom and sheer experience expressed in poetry. In his own self-aware and sage serenity, Teodosije, too, is quick and conclusive in his answers. He infallibly knows the measure of everything. In negotiating with the Turks he consciously risks his life rather than surrender his principles. His mind is omnipresent and always working. He has merciless insight, and there is no appeal from his judgments.

Njegoš's Teodosije, like Abbot Stefan, is a paean to the human mind and wisdom—to the divine light in man. But whereas Abbot Stefan is the incarnation of that wisdom, in Teodosije the wisdom has been brought down to earth, wrung out of Montenegrin realities. Therein lies the difference: Abbot Stefan is the embodiment of a cosmic, Christian, and universal human wisdom, while Teodosije reflects all of these in a Montenegrin and Serbian way.

Teodosije also links himself with absolute laws, but he is, above all, the experience of a centuries-old suffering and resistance, that which has taken shape in heroic endurance and Montenegrin tribulation.

Not one of Njegoš's characters has been elaborated in such detail and with such lively responses to everyday challenges. Yet even such as he is, he, too, is a symbol—of stored-up, ineradicable experience which resists things as they are. He is Montenegro—positive, reasoning, and, as such, unsubmissive to evil.

Teodosije sustains the play and is its central character. The subject, the plot, revolves around Stephen, but Teodosije is the most active, the most completely drawn, and the most developed figure.

The most poetic passages come from Teodosije's lips—as the expression and images of the primeval consciousness of man and of the nation. It would be quite accurate to say that Teodosije's intelligence and wisdom provide the foundation of both the drama and its ideas. Here is the triumph of intelligence—made animate in a personality and made concrete in a Montenegrin setting—set against stupidity and evil.

Though he is all of a piece, Teodosije is not presented in one or even two colors, but in countless hues—like wisdom itself. He is witty to the point of sarcasm, serene and unperturbed to the point of oblivion and nonchalance, mild to the point of forgiveness, and ingratiating to the point of sacrifice. Whenever he opens his mouth, he utters truths wrung from a past and present life spent in evil on this crag, Montenegro, whose man he is, one saved from ignorance by his intelligence, and one who has broken free from evil to hold out on the heights of heroism and humanity.

Teodosije is sufficiently strong to make up for all the Montenegrin stupidity around Stephen. And he is sufficiently profound and vivid to guard the poem from being monotonous and schematized. It is his monologues and disquisitions that bring *Stephen the Small* to the heights of *The Mountain Wreath,* as its sequel in the practical realities of Montenegrin life. Through him Njegoš has revealed still a new aspect of his talent—the ability to draw and to carve out types, that is, ideas, from the immediate reality just as he did from the mythical past. Moreover, this gift—the ability to transform myth and idea into poetry and to mold it into a figure—became further developed in him, only this time in the context of a nonmythical reality. With Teodosije, Njegoš rounded out and fully demonstrated his already boundless potential.

Like every poet, Njegoš depicted his contemporaries in the heroes of his poems. Yet there are even fewer facts to sustain this point for *Stephen the Small* than for *The Mountain Wreath*. Who could Teodosije have been? Who could he not have been! Even in Njegoš's time, Montenegro abounded in integrated personalities, embodied ideas. There is in Teodosije something of the venturesome sagacity of Novica Cerović, of the wise courage of Stevan Perkov, and the bold wisdom of Abbot Mojsije Zečević—perhaps most of all the last.

Teodosije is also our fulfillment, our formation through struggle and want—the wisdom gained from life and by living.

7.

NJEGOŠ lifted Stephen to the level of an idea, though only through one side of him. An impostor who skillfully makes out in all circumstances, he is sagacious and sensible, even moral in that aspect of him that is basic—in his historic role. His love for Montenegro, expressed not only in hatred for the Turks and Venetians, but through his efforts to establish order, is not beclouded for a moment or subordinated to his personal interests.

Contradictory both in his person and in his role, Stephen is also like this in Njegoš. Yet it is for this very reason that he remained unfinished, rudimentary, in his tragic complexity and significance. Njegoš's talent did not extend to irreconcilable contradictions which did not lend themselves to synthesis, whereas Stephen was a personality which had to remain split, if only because of the role he played.

Yet the great poet appreciated the historic enigma and uncommon luster of this tragic pretender who was driven on the road of deception by his perception of certain truths—the need for a central government, and the impossibility of his achieving one, because he was not a Montenegrin. It was as though he was foreordained to be the sacrificial victim of this and still other contradictions. This is why he is irresolute and fearful wherever he is involved, but sensible and determined when it comes to the fate of the people, for he is as touched as a child by the misfortunes of the Serbs. This is no common impostor, but one who sensed the course of history and subordinated to it his own personal destiny.

We have, then, a moving personal and historical drama, but one not worked out and brought to completion precisely with respect to those elements that make it what it is—the brilliant conception of a brilliant poet who had no gift for drama or for the incongruous and the discrete.

Still there is in *Stephen the Small* one character—Prince Dolgorukov—who is a mere schema, devoid of poetic animation, and as such quite exceptional in Njegoš. One could almost say that Dolgorukov is a bare fact, that is, one not abstracted into an idea, an essence. Yet as schematized, unpoeticized, and impersonal as he is, he turns out to be the typical representative of a great empire: fairly overbearing and ostentatiously magnanimous, too overly conscious of the power of the state he represents to have any feeling for Montenegrin needs and realities. If Njegoš wished to portray the type, the image of a Russian emissary, then he indeed succeeded, though in a manner more photographic than artistic.

The poetic truth about Dolgorukov—insofar as it is only this—is prosaic and gray, like the person himself. Herein lies its verisimilitude and its significance. It sheds no less light on the intimate relations between the ruler—Bishop Rade—and Russia than between the poet and the hero of his poem. It is in *Stephen the Small* that Njegoš speaks for the first and only time in his great poems of Russia and of the Russians, without betraying or subverting the poetic or historic truth even by a hair for the sake of any political interests of the moment. There is in *Stephen the Small* glorification of Russia, but only as a great state, and it is largely the Turks who do this in giving vent to their envy of the power of another. As for Dolgorukov, an inane bureaucrat devoid of blood or soul, thought or substance, from his very first step in Montenegro he finds himself in conflict with high-strung, defiant, enterprising, and spirited mountaineers. The people and the chieftains set themselves against Dolgorukov and use force to free Stephen, whom he has imprisoned. Though this act stems from the enthusiasm an ignorant people has generated for Stephen, their reproach to Dolgorukov for the way Russia has got the Montenegrins into its wars against the Turks and then left them in the lurch when peace was concluded is both intelligent and true.

As the image of a cold, empty, and senseless power—an image too exact and real not to be political and not to come of political experience—Dolgorukov is set off against the Montenegrins, who are prepared to face all evil, but who are also ready to sacrifice themselves for the most abstract ideals. This conflict, which holds some possibilities for a dramatic situation such as we have with Stephen, remained unresolved, undeveloped. Too faithful to historic truths and accounts, Njegoš was not able to express them to their ultimate, for they were not also myths. And while he wrote the fawning letters of a beggar to the Russian Tsar and to his magnates, at the same time, in *Stephen the Small,* he referred almost contemptuously to the Tsar's puffed-up and arrogant emissary: "There is a great outcry among the people; the people stream in a mass, break down the door of the cell and release Stephen. There is great joy among the people over their liberation of Stephen. Prince Dolgorukov, who is very angered at the Montenegrins, remains for several days in Montenegro, until he brings the Montenegrins into conflict with the Turks, and then, being provoked over this and many other things, as are the Montenegrins against him, he practically flees from Cetinje."

Though the ruler had to dissimulate and keep silent, the poet remained ever true, faithful to his inspiration and perception. The poet thus does honor to the ruler and the man. Yet at times, as in the case of Dolgorukov, and even Stephen, precisely because he was so conscientious in his adherence to the facts, the poet braked his own impetus and suppressed any development of the drama, though its inner momentum spontaneously tended to propel it beyond the limits of reality and to turn it into a work of art. For Njegoš this was obviously a problem of conscience and conscientiousness. He could not express anything poetically of which he was himself not convinced. Had he not accepted myths as truths —which they really were as transformed, compressed reality—his greatest poetry would hardly have been possible.

Both in his poetry and in his approach to poetry, Njegoš remained, above all else, a moral being.

Brought to reality in *Stephen the Small,* he drew from it a series of characters and types which do not appear in *The Mountain Wreath.* Among these is a special type, one which did exist among our Moslems but which was all the more conspicuous by its rarity: Mula Hasan, learned and just, with an oriental serenity and our own intelligent and limitless courage. Pasha Šuvalija is a new type as well—a Turk who keeps his word, a man of definite noble attributes.

These are Turks such as they really were in their world, in reality, and not as the Montenegrins imagined them to be. Njegoš was obviously trying to present a social drama.

The characters in *Stephen the Small* possess hardly any heroic pathos. They are wanting not only as poeticized ideas but as passionate human beings of flesh and blood. When they have any passion, they are like the characters in *The Mountain Wreath,* and when they are something else, they are but the germ of something nascent and undeveloped.

Even the kolos in *Stephen the Small* do not correspond to those in *The Mountain Wreath* in form; as poetry they are undistinguished and down to the level of a description of reality rather than being myth that sings.

Myth is not deed. But if deed is not also myth, it is no deed.

8.

Stephen the Small has neither the kind nor the degree of inner tension that marks *The Mountain Wreath.* What it has are largely long and skillfully conducted dialogues in which Montenegrin traits and essences are displayed. All of them are disputations—between the Montenegrins themselves, the Montenegrins and the Turks, the Montenegrins and Dolgorukov, and finally among the Turks themselves. The play contains less stage action than does *The Mountain Wreath.*

Yet in the pursuit of his basic conception—to present the Montenegrin mentality and to exalt Montenegrin heroism—Njegoš remained consistent, and in this respect the poem mounts and the idea grows in intensity to the end. In this, and only in this, does it have any of the dramatic quality one finds in the depiction of the Serbian destiny in *The Mountain Wreath.* This drama is expressed in an ever-wiser wisdom and ever-more-heroic heroism. There is something of this same kind of drama in the characters, too, and not only in what they express and relate. This proves that *Stephen the Small* is basically a depiction of Montenegro, and that Njegoš is a poet of ideas, essences, even when dealing with everyday matters.

Stephen the Small is not on the same high level as *The Mountain Wreath,* and its ideas are not on a par with those in *The Mountain Wreath*—for the one deals with destiny, and the other with daily life. Yet taken as a portrayal, as the essence of that daily life, *Stephen the Small* is a work of significant poetic and intellectual worth.

Here, too, are truths—the truths of Montenegrin life—expressed in a picturesque and compressed manner, directly and tersely. That narration through images and aphorisms—most often through pithy imagery—is also presented here in a consummate way and with a choice poetic diction which is, not at all by chance, even purer as folk language than that in *The Mountain Wreath.*

Yet *Stephen the Small* is in significant measure a lyrical work—and that is its greatest failing in comparison with *The Mountain Wreath.* It does contain epic themes as well, but its principal theme is social and comic. And what is most important of all, the actual feeling and the telling are epic, and even narrative. There could be none of that lyrical and epic, mythical and descriptive tie because of the subject itself and the manner in which Njegoš approached it.

In that which makes Njegoš great, *Stephen the Small* is a work of high and still-unappraised value. Here, ideas, essences, myths ring out with a pure sound and shine true as soon as Njegoš touches them.

Stephen the Small is poeticized Montenegro—the one the world knows even apart from Serbian myths. It is a myth in itself. Its reality is mythical—that Montenegro about which the British statesman Gladstone wrote inspired passages: "That is a people which, when tribute is demanded of it, offers stones instead. . . . Montenegro . . . we can freely say, shall not perish. Neither the Russian nor the Austrian eagle shall build its nest in its lofty heights."

In *Stephen the Small* Montenegro is presented as Montenegro, in *The Mountain Wreath* as Serbdom, and in *The Ray of the Microcosm* as a world of its own amid other worlds. Even without Njegoš, it was, and would be, something special. Yet with him it also became poetry through which it has gained survival in time and space. That survival would not be complete without *Stephen the Small*—without its immediate reality.

Reality outlives itself in works of art and the spirit.

IDEAS AND REALITIES

1.

THE 1848 REVOLUTION, which ended feudalism and dealt a blow to absolute monarchy, took Bishop Rade by surprise when it happened, even though he had been intellectually prepared for it.

The revolution took others also by surprise. A revolution always comes as something of a surprise, even for those who carry it out. Vienna, Venice, and Budapest, let alone Belgrade and Zagreb, did not expect with certainty those revolutionary eruptions that spread from Paris, the spiritual center of the revolution. So exceptional in the life of nations and social systems, a revolution as an event is but another, inevitable, way of resolving irresoluble relationships. Whatever the revolutionaries are able to foresee and to undertake beforehand is not the revolution itself, for the revolution also involves the manner of execution; all that is merely the setting of the course and getting organized. In Montenegro there was nothing to organize, nor was Bishop Rade a revolutionary in the modern sense. Montenegro was too removed from the capitals of Europe in every way—by its way of life, its practical problems and living traditions, and even in its way of thinking and feeling.

The Bishop kept up with the foreign press. Yet a good part of it, especially the official press, reported the revolutionary events incompletely and tardily. Bound to the crags of Lovćen, embroiled in the troubles of Montenegro (he had just suppressed the Crmnica rebellion), and being engaged in poetry (he had just completed *Stephen the Small*), he was able neither to devote much attention to the revolution nor to understand it until it appeared unbidden at his very doorstep. And even when it was in full swing, he did not nurture for it any of those special, almost mystical, inclinations that are so frequent among artists who look upon revolutionary outbreaks as events bound to free men and nations of all evils forever. He was carrying out a revolution of his own in his small country, though from above. And inasmuch as this revolution brought, in fact, the establishment of order rather than something destructive, he did not look upon what he was doing as a revolution, but as a ruler's obligation and a necessity for Montenegro. He was not at all opposed to, or far removed from, the liberal ideas of that day, but these were far too remote from the Montenegrin reality, and therefore from him. He could not judge the revolution other than through the prism of Montenegrin and Serbian interests, that is, in the light of what it had to contribute to the liberation and the unification of the Serbs, and of the Yugoslavs. Being cut off and removed from the rest of the world by its peculiarities, Montenegro was not touched internally by the revolution. Yet insofar as the revolution disturbed European relations, and thus Montenegro's external position, Bishop Rade took his own stand accordingly. He determined his attitude toward the revolution on a practical basis, taking as his starting point its concrete effect on the national liberation of the Serbs. This means that he judged the revolution according to the prospects it offered for the realization of his ideas concerning the national liberation, ideas that were neither his alone nor exclusively political, but the vital necessity of all the South Slavs. He looked at it soberly, without any prejudices. Intellectually it did not surprise him; its aims were quite clear to him.

Njegoš's political ideas were derived from his view of the world, and mostly from that inherited semimythical conception of Serbdom and its destinies which he had expressed poetically. His Teodosije declares that as long as the Turks are in Europe, there will be no end to Montenegrin hatred of them and struggle against them. This is also Njegoš's pledge and program.

To be sure, his ideas also adapted themselves to the realities of the times, but they remained basically the same, inasmuch as they were never realized, that is, they were not yet to triumph. No matter how much they changed, these ideas never developed into a modern, bourgeois nationalism. Njegoš's policy was national—Serbian and Yugoslav; it was based on Montenegrin conditions, of course, but it looked to the restoration of an independent Serbian state and liberation from Turkish rule, and not to a capitalist order. Independently of his will and his consciousness, that policy led to capitalism, a capitalism that came late and thus never had the strength necessary to take root among us, much less to solve the problems of our economic and social development under modern conditions. For him the important thing was liberation from the Turks—and in this he was right, since that was the most vital problem both for Montenegro and for Serbdom as a whole. As to how this liberation was going to be accomplished, with the help of what forces, and to what kind of order it would lead—all this was for him incidental. This distinction between what Njegoš wanted and knew and was able to do and what it would all lead to is quite important, for it explains his view of the revolution, not as an occurrence that was either absolutely good or absolutely evil—for there are no such—but as one that could momentarily contribute to Serbian survival, which meant in actual fact to the struggle against the Turks. This distinction also shows how much-later nationalists were wrong, especially those in most recent times, in appropriating Njegoš as exclusively theirs. For their nationalism has become identical, in both theory and practice, not only with the forms of their undeveloped capitalism, but also with the correspondingly absolute monopoly of the ideas and the power of the capitalists. Njegoš's Serbianism, on the other hand, was derived from the existence of the Serbian people throughout several stages of social development, I would say from the very time of their inception as a civil and a spiritual identity. The nationalists are no different in this from others, and did only what they had to do; everyone regards his own ideas and way of life as best. But Njegoš and the Serbian people have existed and shall exist without them and despite them, as they did through other forms of government, property, and ideas.

Thus Njegoš approached revolution from a broader and deeper point of view—unburdened by bourgeois nationalist ideas and property interests.

But he had to approach it from the standpoint of his immediate political aims and prospects, too.

While he was a sage of vast breadth who derived his ideas from unfathomable sources, Njegoš also had to be a ruler and a practical politician. Moreover, he did not separate the one from the other, much less set them at odds with each other.

After all, ideas are at their truest and most realizable when they are the most unselfish and altruistic.

2.

THOUGH THE REVOLUTION was not even noticed in Montenegro, it did sweep over Dalmatia and Kotor—which were Austrian, and, earlier, Venetian, provinces.

At the very height of the revolution, the Montenegrins pillaged the village of Dobrota, next to Kotor. That raid went beyond such customary raids, and it must have been particularly troublesome for Bishop Rade because the Montenegrin raiding party was led by his uncle Lazo Proroković, Captain of Njeguši and a frontier commander. It was supposed to have been a kind of revenge for an attack by Austrian soldiers on some shepherds from the village of Zalaz. Lazo first tried to raze the fortress of Trojica, and when he could not harm a stone of it, he attacked these Austrian subjects, who were people of his own blood and tongue. The Austrian authorities connected this Montenegrin incursion with the spreading of the revolutionary movement from Italy, though the only connection there was simply that the Montenegrins took advantage of the confusion and the impotence of the Austrians. The Austrian authorities took the raid on Dobrota to be the Bishop's step toward annexing the Bay of Kotor to Montenegro. But this was not true, no matter how much Njegoš, like all the bishops and sovereigns of Montenegro, might have yearned to do so. Bishop Rade regarded the revolutionary events carefully and soberly, conscious of the futility of an attempt that would have got him into trouble with Russia and embroiled him in unforeseeable conflicts with Austria. He consistently followed the Serbian and Yugoslav line, but he never went beyond the limits of the possible. The Montenegrins had raided Dobrota without the Bishop's approval. It was the same with a later attack on Kotor, when the Montenegrins howled over Kotor one whole night in 1848 while the citizens turned their roof tops into battle stations and cannon from the citadel boomed all night to dispel the fright of the garrison and the citizenry.

In Dalmatia, as well as in the Bay of Kotor area, there was a movement among our people for annexation by the newly formed Venetian Republic, which came to be led by Daniele Manin and Niccolò Tommaseo, a prominent Italian poet from Zara, who had a previous close acquaintance with Njegoš. This movement in Dalmatia did not arise so much from traditional ties with Venice, which had lorded it over our Adriatic coast and fought over it with the Turks for some three or four centuries. Our people had no reason to mourn for Venice. But the peasants yearned to be rid of all serf obligations, which the revolution in Venice promised them, while the city inhabitants desired the freedoms it proclaimed.

As impotent as they were there, the Austrian authorities were even more paralyzed by the movement in Austria, in Vienna itself, and thus unable effectively to counter the pro-Italian sentiment in Dalmatia. Besides this pro-Italian sentiment, however, there appeared in the Bay of Kotor pro-Montenegrin and pro-Croatian currents, while the peasant movement, which had begun as early as the spring of 1848, bore a predominantly class character.

A peasant rebellion broke out in Grabalj. Enserfed, and yet next door to the free Montenegrins, Grabalj had rebelled both under Venice and under the French, and it has been noted that it raised rebellions even back in the times of the Crnojevići.

At this time the Captain in Kotor was Eduard Griez de Ronse, an incapable man, and a harsh and suspicious one, as though made to order to increase discontent in restless times and to confirm the historic truth that a system in dissolution brings to the fore its worst types. To Grabalj's protest against feudal dues, in an atmosphere of general unrest, Gruyet replied with an expedition of soldiers from the Kotor garrison. Apart from the fact that the soldiers were practically all Dalmatians—Serbs and Croats who felt the same troubles at home that oppressed Grabalj—the force was too weak to put down the inhabitants of Grabalj and the Montenegrins who sprang to their aid. The troops were repulsed on September 27, and they shamefully fled back to Kotor without suffering any great losses.

Bishop Rade was opposed to the rebellion at Grabalj, though he did not look upon it too severely. He was afraid that the discontent there might invite Italian influence. Earlier, in a proclamation of May 20, he had issued a sharp threat to the people of the Bay of

Kotor and Dubrovnik if they "showed themselves to be unfaithful to their governor and accepted foreign rule." But he also understood and supported the justified complaints of the people of Grabalj. In February, 1849, he wrote a letter to Austrian Minister of the Interior Stadion * cautioning him that "if these same burdens continue to hang on their necks," he could not influence them, "for I would then be acting against my honor." He wrote in similar terms about the people of Grabalj to Governor Jelačić.† His stand was clear and forthright: the people had a right to complain, and if the causes of their discontent were not removed, the Sovereign of Montenegro would not and could not do anything to bring peace. The Bishop's uncle Captain Lazo, conscious of the importance of the moment, was to send a proclamation to those very same men of Dobrota whom he had pillaged but a month before: "We are brothers, kith and kin, and should not give joy to the enemy with our mutual feuding, but let us live in brotherly love, as the children of one mother." Vengeance and booty were one thing, but the struggle against foreign rule was quite another.

The Croatians had already—on March 25, 1848—proclaimed the Triune Kingdom of Croatia, Slavonia, and Dalmatia, and elected Jelačić, an Austrian general, their governor. Bishop Rade had hopes and expectations that Jelačić would gain in strength and become independent of Austria as well as of Hungary. The decisions of the Diet in Zagreb were democratic and promised more than an end to serfdom. Jelačić himself wrote at the time, "Nationalism, freedom, equality and the union of our brethren of one people under the crown of our Yugoslav King Ferdinand, there is our greatness, our welfare, our glory, this is to be the proud achievement of our Dalmatian patriots." That "under the crown of . . . Ferdinand" seemed conventional and incidental beside the unification of the Yugoslavs, whose nationality was threatened by the Magyars and the Italians. Though they were the bearers of revolution and civil liberties, the Magyars and the Italians were no less intolerant of the Slavs in their nationalism.

Bishop Rade was not forced to make any concessions to the Hapsburg monarchy, and he made none. On the other hand, he

* Count Franz Stadion (1806–53).

† Count Josip Jelačić (1801–59), Austrian general and Governor of Croatia who led an army against the Hungarians in 1848.

felt an obligation, especially at such a time, to help the Yugoslav cause regardless of who was behind it. Even had he been able, he did not dare support the revolution that came out of Italy, for that would have meant the Italianization of Dalmatia. In the previously mentioned proclamation he barely referred to "the Imperial Crown," but his real intention was to encourage the people of Kotor and Dubrovnik to remain faithful to their own nationality. Griez, however dense, saw through this slight to the Hapsburg court and Austria and demanded an explanation from the Bishop. The Bishop afforded him indirect satisfaction by pointing to the places in his proclamation in which he insisted that Dalmatia be faithful to Jelačić, and "is not Jelačić the Emperor's man?" That game of sophistry ended without any outcome; events took a turn different from what the Montenegrin Sovereign expected.

In those days the popular leaders of the people of the Bay of Kotor demonstrated both wisdom and patriotism. From their assembly at Prčanj, on June 1, 1848, they addressed themselves to both Zagreb and Cetinje. They confirmed receipt of the Bishop's letter, "in which you urge us to make common cause with the Governor of the Triune Kingdom." But they rejected unconditional annexation. "We have nothing against uniting with all Slavo-Serbian states when they become independent and are free of foreign influence under the Imperial Crown. As for your promise to lend us a helping hand against every foreign attack, we do thank you for this in the name of the entire people and we hope firmly and resolutely that, in your patriotism, which is so well known to us, you will spring to our aid as a brother whenever the need may arise." As for the Croatian Diet, they gave it to understand that they were not Dalmatians, but Bocchesi, and they presented it with their conditions for unification:

Without doubt were events to take such a turn that the Slavo-Serbian, that is, the Yugoslav lands were to unite under the aegis of the Empire free of the influence of any foreign nationality such as, for example, the Italian, the Magyar, the German, or other, the Bay of Kotor would doubtless not be against fulfilling your desire as far as unification is concerned. However, today's conditions, and especially those which involve the Hungarian Crown, do not permit us to sacrifice to unification the independence of our own nationality, which has been guaranteed to us in the new constitution of the Austrian Empire. When every

Yugoslav state becomes rightfully independent of all foreign influence, when that occurs which we all desire, that is, the foundation of a Slavic empire under the Kaiser's aegis, when finally equal rights shall be freely established between said states, the region of the Bay of Kotor shall joyfully unite itself to such a union.

Thus the people of the Bay of Kotor stressed from the start the principle of a federation of South Slavs—"equal rights . . . freely established between said states"—and the separation of Croatia from Hungary. The emphasis on "the Kaiser's aegis" signified nothing other than the acceptance of the monarchy, which in the Europe of that time was but a realistic and still-customary outlook, due to the predominance of conservative forces. Unification with Montenegro was unrealistic except with the dissolution of the Austrian Empire, and the people of the Bay of Kotor had reduced their relations with Montenegro to accepting aid in the event of Italian pressure. The constitution to which they referred was ratified only to be abrogated later as being too democratic, and it was not put into force until 1859. Yet how far the people of the Bay of Kotor looked ahead in 1848 may be seen from the fact that until 1918—and the creation of Yugoslavia—the Bay of Kotor remained an entity unto itself, outside of Croatia, as a component province of the Austro-Hungarian Empire.

Bishop Rade was not opposed to these views of the leaders of the Bocchesi, even though they did not lead to unification with Montenegro. The Bocchesi insisted on the preservation and strengthening of their own nationality; this was basic from their point of view, and they were doing what they believed to be the only possible thing—favoring Zagreb and Jelačić, but with reserve.

Firm in their stand, the Bocchesi waited.

Bishop Rade did the same for reasons of his own.

Waiting is also a policy, sometimes as realistic as any other.

3.

Bishop Rade expected the course of events to take two directions: a Serbian, anti-Turkish one, which was the closer to him emotionally, and a Yugoslav one, that is, the unification of the South Slavs, which agreed with his political ideas. He did not strictly differentiate between these two courses. The Serbs and the Croats were not as different from one another in their political consciousness as they were later to become, and they were even less hostile to one another. They were an ethnic mass of great affinity, divided by religion and mentality, but not yet by various feelings of nationalism. Yugoslavism and the Yugoslav Idea meant the association of the Serbian lands with the Croatian lands, which were still under Austria; thus Bishop Rade knew that he had to proceed gradually and carefully. Not only was Russia against the partition of the Hapsburg monarchy, but Montenegro and Serbia were not able to lend open support to the Croatian movement for independence and unification, much less sacrifice their own existence as states to the Viennese crown. A spontaneous and irrepressible aspiration of long standing, Yugoslavism was just taking shape as an ideology and a program, and was still a long way from practical realization. Bishop Rade acted accordingly in dealing with Yugoslav unification: he yearned for it and propagated it, but he sought first to obtain the prerequisites for a South Slavic union—to win independence for the Serbian lands, to unite the Serbs through the struggle to oust the Turks and to put an end to their rule.

This is what seemed the most possible to him. His view proved to be correct and his policy justified, though only much, much later, and after him.

The Serbian effort against Turkey seemed all the more possible in that Austria, which was embroiled in its own internal troubles, was not able to hinder it. But the Balkan raia were torpid—caught in a momentary calm, so frequent in that clime, between desire and possibility, idea and realization, or, as Njegoš himself put it, "A big head and weak legs."

The movement of the Serbs and the Croats in Austria, and later of the Serbs in Serbia, turned against the Magyars, against the revolution, and not against the reactionaries in Austria. Bishop Rade could in no way contribute to the revolution without coming into conflict not only with Austria, but also with the Serbian and Croatian leaders, and ultimately with himself and his own nationalist political line.

Then, too, Bishop Rade had his own internal troubles, as always arising from the recalcitrance of the Montenegrins. Sensing the instability of the government in the Bay of Kotor and conditions there, they systematically went on with their looting, which actually assumed the proportions of minor campaigns. At the end of July the people of Risan complained to the Bishop that the men of Krivošije and his Cuce clansmen "are attacking the state at Novi, and are barbarically slaughtering and cutting down not only the men but also the women, they are laying desolate the houses with fire and plundering the animals both small and large." Montenegro presented the picture of a disjointed, lawless land in which clan differences and the craving for plunder were still very powerful. Even Jelačić turned to the Bishop to have him stop these Montenegrin raids. Griez threatened to end all commerce with Montenegro. The Bishop did what he could to restrain the Montenegrins.

As for political activity in Austria, he could do nothing other than express his Yugoslav sympathies to Jelačić and—wait.

Toward Turkey his hands were free. He could get around Russian disapproval somehow. But there was no popular movement in Turkey, and his own Montenegrin forces were too meager. Everything was just getting started and still unorganized.

The initiative came from Serbia, from Garašanin, whose view had not only the greatest breadth but also the most realism—until the coming of the Radicals and Nikola Pašić—with respect to the national problems of both Serbs and South Slavs. Garašanin was a completely harmonious combination of a modern European statesman and a Balkan conspirator. The time of great uprisings against the Turks was on the wane, and the role of opposition to the Turks was assumed by the recently created Balkan states. Yet Serbia was not up to this task, being headed by Prince Miloš, who was incapable of fully subordinating his own princely interests to national and state interests. During the collapse of the First Insurrection in 1813, when not only were the gains of nine years of the most destructive fighting being obliterated by the Turkish assault, but when it seemed as though the Serbs of Serbia would disappear root and branch, Miloš alone among the rebel leaders perceived, with the vision of a genius, that all was not lost and that though the Turks were militarily able to suppress the uprising, they were powerless to re-establish the old state of affairs, let alone accomplish their intentions. A peasant but also a genius, Miloš struck a compromise between the rebellious peasants and Istanbul in the form of internal autonomy for Serbia. But once that compromise had outlived its usefulness and Serbia had gained from it all that it could gain, he himself became superfluous and an obstacle to the further free internal development of the new state and to its more substantial pan-Serbian, Yugoslav, and Balkan role. The clash took on an incongruous aspect: the defenders of the constitution—the *hatti-sherif* granted by Istanbul—against Prince Miloš's arbitrary rule turned out to be the adversaries of the Turks in the course of that struggle. The absurdity was all the more complete, as is usually the case with everything new in the beginning, in that parliamentary Britain supported the Prince's despotism in Serbia, while despotic Russia supported constitutionalism. Meanwhile peasant Serbia had no developed class which could act as a unifying and leading force; there was only the Prince and his servitors. Garašanin perceived that such a role could be assumed by a modern bureaucratic administration—modern for Serbia and for the Balkans, for it was harsh, arbitrary, and rapacious. It was a matter of superimposing a European model on the chaotic orient and on but recently liberated and still-self-willed and defiant Balkan peasants. But the model was a suitable one in that it did unite and ensure some measure of order. Serbia was to spend half a century, if not longer, in that mold, until new forces and new tasks came along to undo it.

It was with this new bureaucratic Serbia of Garašanin's that Bishop Rade had to co-operate.

He immediately perceived Garašanin's significance; though the latter was neither a writer nor an orator, the effective scope of his activities extended beyond the Serbian border and opened a way to the future. One felt in Garašanin the irrepressible pulsation of the but recently pacified uprisings, but also a sober program for an effective administration and free trade. Garašanin's strength was all the more apparent in the light of Prince Alexander's impotence, for the Prince merely reflected the glory of his great father Karadjordje. "You best see the state of affairs, you are the greatest friend of the Serbian people, and everything else is but trifling and trivial," Njegoš wrote to Garašanin toward the close of 1850. Njegoš also had a personal, intimate feeling for Garašanin, engendered by the force of the spontaneous attraction great men have for one another. Though they never met, and the only real contact they had centered around the year 1848, Njegoš felt close enough to Garašanin to confide to him even his personal troubles, which the latter would understand were also obstacles to their common aims. Njegoš thus wrote to him on July 5, 1850:

Thanks be to the Illustrious Prince and Sovereign and to you, his councillors, for whatever thought you may from time to time lend this bloody Serbian crag. This will win you the honor of posterity when our people are raised up in spirit. . . . I have been very ill. . . . I have been in Italy . . . got steadily worse . . . was completely worn out, and so necessity and counsel prevailed and I returned to our native clime after a month. I feel rather better, but I am still weak. . . . My dear and esteemed Mr. Garašanin, as backward as our Serbian state of affairs is in our century, it is no wonder that I have been exhausted by this bloody cathedra to which I ascended lo these twenty years ago. Everyone is mortal and must die. I would be sorry for nothing now save for not seeing some progress among our whole people and for not being able in some way to establish the internal government of Montenegro on a firm foundation, and thus I fear that after me there will come back to Montenegro all those woes which existed before me, and that this small folk of ours, uneducated but militant and strong in spirit, will remain in perpetual misery. There is not a Serb who does more and thinks more for the Serbs than you, there is not a Serb whom Serbdom loves more sincerely and respects more than you, and there is not a Serb who loves and respects you more than I.

Njegoš never wrote in this way to anyone else, giving expression to so much and such love. And truly Garašanin, like Njegoš in another way, was unique in Serbdom and Yugoslavdom.

Four of Njegoš's letters to Garašanin have been preserved: two are rather long and brim full of content and political problems—while to Prince Alexander he sent only empty tirades; a third is a request for more concern over Montenegrin settlers in Serbia; while a fourth is a militant call, consisting of two short, very short, sentences, written at the beginning of a great and unrealized project, on May 2, 1848: "If there is anyone at all, here we are; if there is no one, I cannot but be ashamed that I am your brother."

Words are deeds.

And the great are drawn forward by an irresistible force—by the future.

4.

MATIJA BAN arrived in Cetinje by the middle of April, 1848, in his capacity as a confidential Serbian emissary. Before that, he had visited Karlovci—the center of the Vojvodina Serbs—and Zagreb—the Croatian center.

Bishop Rade greeted Ban with open arms, even ceremoniously. Ban immediately recognized Njegoš among the chieftains, by his bearing and handsomeness. He was to visit Njegoš twice again. He left some fine notes, which, though all too brief, are compactly full of observations, and provide the gist of the conversations and negotiations between the Montenegrin Sovereign and Belgrade's emissary. They also reveal more clearly than any other source Njegoš's political image, and even his personality—"a fiery nature beneath a rather cold exterior." From sentence to sentence Njegoš's ideas come through, to reveal the vast range of his vision beyond daily cares, though these also elicited his deep concern. Njegoš is obviously troubled by the existing state of affairs—the reality; he suffers in it, and at every prospect of a way out of it, he is seized by transports of delirious joy. Whatever he does, his sights are always on great goals, and behind him is the measureless tragedy of Kosovo.

Today, especially after the researches of Durković-Jakšić, the import of Ban's secret missions to the hermit at Cetinje has been completely elucidated.

The subject of their negotiations was the raising of a rebellion in Turkey—in Old Serbia, Macedonia, and Bosnia—with the aid of the two Serbian states. Garašanin was anxious not to lose any opportunity the revolution in Europe might present him in the event of any change in the balance of power that could affect Turkey adversely, and he wished also to keep up the spirits of the raia. Just in case, he began to establish ties with the raia in Turkey and to organize them. By its very proximity, Cetinje was expected to carry out especially important tasks in Bosnia, Hercegovina, and Old Serbia.

Yet despite the harmony of aims between Belgrade and Cetinje, as before and certainly after, there were differences in their approach, even with respect to the most immediate tasks. Bishop

Rade maintained that the main effort should be devoted to Bosnia, while Belgrade was more inclined to action in the south, in Old Serbia. The differences were not insuperable. The Sovereign of Montenegro did not conceal his magnanimous willingness to renounce his rights as a ruler in the future Serbian state. It was anticipated that he would become the first patriarch of modern Serbia; Bishop Rade was still occupied with his ecclesiastical duties, and the idea itself has been ascribed to Sarajlija. Njegoš stressed that the capital of the new state should be Prizren, as it had been in the medieval Serbian Empire, which still lived in his breast with all its grievous devastation. In his enthusiasm, he broke into the midst of Ban's exposition in favor of Belgrade's view and pointed out how it had occurred to him to march across the Turkish zone between Montenegro and Serbia—the Sandjak of today—with five thousand Montenegrins and thus force the Serbian government into action. Perhaps Njegoš did not express himself in quite that way, but his mind worked furiously to bridge the gap between him and the cold and infallible Garašanin. Both, each in his own way, undertook what was necessary to keep from being caught off guard by the events.

There was in all of this a romantic nationalism full of the unreal and intransigent hopes of the long and mercilessly oppressed. Yet along with it there was a great deal of organizational work, financed generously out of Belgrade. Bishop Rade also received financial aid from that quarter. Belgrade reached as far as the Albanian leaders. The Bishop was quite pleased when Ban informed him that the Albanian chieftain Bib Doda would make contact with him to offer his co-operation, all the more so inasmuch as this was a valiant clan which had shed much blood in fighting with the Montenegrins. In Turkey, especially in Bosnia, agents were recruited, revolutionary committees were formed, and a network stretched out on all sides. An air of conspiracy and rebellion spread with an intoxicating contagion which the Turkish authorities found terrifying and impervious. It began to appear as though the ancient vows, those for which Njegoš lived, were beginning to gain muscle and sinew and to be transformed into reality.

Matija Ban was generally a very suitable choice as intermediary between Belgrade and Zagreb and as a collaborator with Bishop Rade in the organization of a conspiratorial network in the south, spreading from Hercegovina. A Serb from Dubrovnik, he did not need to acclimate himself to conditions and the situation in that quarter. He was a man of vast and refined culture, and having grown up in a Croatian milieu, he knew its mentality and found working with Croatians quite natural. He was a poet—and has been remembered and appreciated as such—but his was not a great talent, despite his sincerely patriotic ideas. This facilitated his contact with Njegoš and turned their political collaboration into friendship and understanding. He was of a reflective, rational nature—such was needed in that time and for that task. He enjoyed the confidence of Belgrade and of Prince Alexander himself, whose children he tutored. Overesteemed as a poet, he has been forgotten in that area where his true worth really lay, as an inspirer and inventor of a new political program—Yugoslavism. This activity of his has remained overshadowed by that of more significant politicians—Garašanin—and ideologists—Njegoš. Yet he was one of those who formulated the program about which the struggle of nearly a century was to revolve. The native of a city that breathed "Slavism," that is, Yugoslavism, even before Yugoslavism was a word, Ban was a Yugoslav both ideologically and emotionally, and capable of overlooking inherited provincial and religious differences and of striding into the future. He was in his element. But it was not the right time.

Reality—the one yet to come—always begins as a dream and a hope.

5.

FROM THE VERY BEGINNING the course of events took a turn different from what the Serbian and Croatian leaders wished.

It was the misfortune of the revolution, especially the one in Hungary, that it was what it had to be; national and democratic in the face of Vienna and feudalism, it was also to a lesser degree nationalistic and oppressive toward the Slavic peoples, particularly toward the Serbs and Croats. Nor was it any different in Italy, in Venice: Tommaseo issued a proclamation to the Croats, but, being Italianized himself, he did not give them a word of hope concerning even the right to their own language, let alone all the rest. In

Hungary, where there existed the possibility of doing something practical, what took place instead—the closing of their schools and an outbreak of persecution and massacres stemming from chauvinism—could only embitter the Slavic peoples. The middling gentry, with Lajos Kossuth at their head, into whose hands the leadership of the revolution had fallen, were themselves unstable and inconstant, having combined an inherited Hungarian medieval imperialism with an undeveloped bourgeois nationalism. The Magyars aroused the admiration of the world by their endeavors and sacrifices in the name of their national and universal ideals, but it was also true that their leaders were petty and intolerant on domestic questions, especially concerning the rights of other peoples.

Not only the reactionary and feudal classes of the Serbs and Croats, but also the people themselves were caught between the hammer and the anvil: the revolution threatened their extinction as nations, while the reaction in Vienna and St. Petersburg closed to them any prospect of democracy. There were democratic and peasant movements among them as well. Great spirits, such as Jakov Ignjatović, sensed the ugly and shameful future that lay in store for the Serbs and Croats who rose up against the Magyars under reactionary leaders. Yet their own democratic current was choked off by the oppressive and chauvinistic intolerance of the Magyar leaders and unrestrained mobs. While these leaders could have been democrats as well as nationalists, in our situation only the nationalists came to the fore—and the reins of the nation fell into the hands of nationalist bishops and rich landowners. What happened was what inevitably happens whenever the question becomes one of survival—one and all cling to the possible, regardless of whether or not it agrees with the most desired ends and ideals. Don Quixotes inspire, but they do not create. Theoreticians who approached revolution as an absolute ideal were not capable of understanding—as they are not capable of understanding today—the inevitability of such a, shall we say, counterrevolutionary role of the Serbs and Croats. This is why such theoreticians are all the more prepared to burden the Serbs and Croats with the blame and responsibility for the defeat of the revolution.

The history of 1848 took place contrary to the desires and projects of its own executors. With the suppression of revolution and democracy in central Europe, the Serbs and Croats resorted to other forces and to their own means to achieve what the Germans, Italians, and Magyars had done under the leadership of revolutionaries; they joined forces as nations and became conscious of their identity. Eighteen forty-eight did not happen in vain even for us, despite the undemocratic role imposed upon us, as much by the bourgeois nationalist character of the revolution as by domestic forces of despotism. Our reactionaries were able to maintain their leadership over the people only by recognizing, as did the reactionaries of Vienna, that the revolution had broken out in the name of nationalism and to end feudal relations. It was not by chance that Jelačić proclaimed the abolition of serfdom before the Magyar revolutionaries did. The reactionaries were strong enough to wrest control out of the hands of the revolutionaries, but not to re-establish (which no one has ever been able to do) the old order, both ideological and social, which the revolution had destroyed.

Marx and Engels, who were then but young men and themselves engaged in the revolution, not only knew very little about our peoples, but did not comprehend the complexity of the relations between ourselves and the Magyars and the Germans. As revolutionaries, and still Hegelians in many respects, they comprehended the revolution, the one in their own country, as an absolute ideal and the highest form of social movement; moreover, in Engels one also feels a Great German spirit, however revolutionary it might also be. In their writings of that period they, like many European revolutionaries and incurable progressivists, went so far as to prophesy that those barbarian Balkan Slavs would never achieve a state organization—at a time when we already had our own states—and that it would be a most noble historic role for the Germans to wipe them out as nations.

Yes, we were against those neighboring revolutions, but they were also against us, against our political and national survival. Still in a precapitalist social order, we could not have commanded the forces necessary to lead us into a democratic revolution. Yet except for the one in France, the revolutions did not attract other peoples; on the contrary, they provoked their opposition by their denationalizing policies and practices.

And just what does it mean to be a barbarian? Among men and

nations there exist only differences in way of life and outlook and the level of technical development achieved. Those who believe in progress as a universal law and maintain on this basis that they are also able to alter human nature usually find it easy to ignore the fact that civilization in itself does not decrease violence and evil but merely affords them different means and forms, inasmuch as these depend on the totality of existing conditions, and primarily on the social relations in which a given human society must operate and exist. The technically backward can be and frequently are more humane than the highly civilized.

It is true that at that time the Montenegrins took pride in cutting off heads and lived in the same room with cattle, while the men of Banija and Lika dipped their bread in the blood of Moslems from the Krajina, as though they were taking a form of communion, and took fetuses out of bottles in Viennese museums in order to drink the alcohol, and in Hungary they were notorious for their antics and vices. But how did civilized Europe behave toward its own proletariat, and what did its reactionaries do to the democrats? The Russian Emperor Nicholas I, known as the Stick, envied Emperor Francis Joseph I of Austria because God had given him a general such as Jelačić, to balance Windisch-Graetz and De Galifen, who were not Slavs. The Prince in Belgrade, Karadjordje's son and still a semivassal of the Turks, with his councilors and all that brotherhood of monks who were still fighting Vuk's linguistic reforms out of ignorance and stupidity—all these did indeed slavishly oppose Hungarian freedom while forgetting their own brethren under the Turkish heel. But the Hungarian revolutionaries also flirted with Turkey. All of that could have happened even had we been civilized and among the most civilized. Was it not that most civilized people, those same Germans, who almost one hundred years later permitted all of Europe to be transformed in their name into a camp of planned and mechanized death in comparison with which our sins and barbarities in 1848 and 1849 look like the naïve bloody exploits of simple-minded savages? All of this is too ghastly and bloody and too involved with ideological schemes and all kinds of political necessities to enable anyone to lay the blame on this or that nation.

The duality of the 1848 Revolution—which was democratic in the face of absolutism, and yet oppressive toward other peoples—

gave our own struggle a dual aspect: reactionary in the face of revolution, and yet justified in the defense of our nationality. The duality lay in the objective historical course of events.

And why seek to justify? We, too, had to survive.

The Montenegrin Bishop and Sovereign was not against all revolution. After all, he and Belgrade together were planning a rebellion in Turkey, in connection with a campaign of liberation by Serbia and Montenegro. He was prepared to help, and offered his help to the Croats and the Serbs against the Italians and the Magyars. But he was also deeply dissatisfied with the results of our role in those struggles. In fact, he was more consistent than all the rest in following the line of national liberation, and when our conflict with the Magyars did not yield the expected results, but turned out to benefit largely Vienna and St. Petersburg, Njegoš withdrew, pointing out it had amounted to nothing more than toiling and shedding blood for another's profit by Slavic slaves who did not yet deserve to be anything else.

Bishop Rade was prepared to help his Serbo-Croatian brethren, and later the Russians as well, against the Magyars, that is, against the revolution.

Prince Alexander first informed him in a letter of May 29, 1848, brought by Ban, "And so in order to prevent this dangerous union between the Magyars and the enemies of the Serbs, and in order to strengthen Serbdom, I have found it necessary to help the Serbs in Austria to lift themselves sufficiently to gain recognition for our nationality and to permit both their moral and their physical forces to develop." Though there were deliberations with Ban concerning the unification of the South Slavs through a rebellion in Turkey, in practice Serbia acted only against Hungary. Hoping that the struggle against the Magyars would develop into a separate movement leading to South Slavic independence, Njegoš offered Jelačić, at the close of 1848, a force of two thousand Montenegrins, but the latter, in his headquarters in Vienna, refused the offer in the hope that it would not be necessary, though he was also apprehensive over possible difficulties with the self-willed Montenegrins. Yet Jelačić could have and must have known that the aspirations of Montenegro's Sovereign went beyond conflict with the Magyars—toward the unification of the South Slavs and severance from Austria, something that never would have entered Jelačić's mind even in his dreams, even if he had not been governor of Croatia and an Austrian general. In 1849 the Bishop offered the Russians a force of four to five thousand Montenegrins to fight in Hungary. He knew himself that the Montenegrins were an irregular army, good only for mountain fighting. "Northern Hungary is a mountainous region, and our army consists only of experienced mountaineers," he wrote on June 2 to General Aleksei Fëdorovich Orlov, chief of the Imperial secret police. But not even the Russians accepted his help; there was a transportation problem involving Trieste, and there was certainly the thought that it might be best to keep these refractory mountaineers and their sovereign at a distance from European politics, as the exclusive wards of Russia. Bishop Rade was likewise conscious of Austria's irrepressible intolerance, and pointed this out to the Austrian Minister of the interior, in a letter of February, 1849, expressing the polite hope that in the future Austria would nurture "generous sympathies for the Montenegrins."

In those revolutionary years the Bishop knocked on all doors in the hope of furthering his consistent program of national liberation. Yet he remained isolated with his ideas and desires. Belgrade gave priority to action in the Vojvodina, that is, against the Magyars, while Zagreb was far removed from the thought of any action against Turkey, and especially against the Apostolic Monarchy.

There was nothing left for him to do but to wail over the Serbian and Yugoslav destiny and plight, something he had learned in his cradle.

The future is a reality for those who see far.

6.

THERE WERE MANY REASONS why Njegoš was able to see farther than his contemporaries in the other Serbian and Yugoslav lands. He was not under the pressure of the immediate reality—Magyar anti-Slavism—to the degree that Zagreb and Belgrade were. Thus his nationalistic ideas—Serbianism and Yugoslavism—could manifest themselves not only in almost absolute purity but also in full consistency. After all, Montenegro was already the national idea realized in miniature, being independent in all aspects. Njegoš could afford to be consistent because his starting point was the Montenegrin reality and the Montenegrin spirit, and Montenegro was at that time the crystal-clear quintessence of the Serbian spirit.

Yet he himself also possessed certain qualities that permitted him to perceive clearly and to see far during those times of Serbian and Yugoslav confusion. He derived his nationalistic idea from myths, from the conditions of the life of our people, which were bequeathed to him and which he regarded as a higher law and destiny. He had within himself lasting and ineradicable foundations for his political ideas, those that one also finds in his poetry. He was not alone in this, but he was the most profound, the most categorical. Garašanin was more enterprising in his politics and had a more realistic view of the near future. But the ideas—those that transcend this workaday world and inspire and lead generation upon generation—were more crystallized in Njegoš, though of unattainable purity. The great poet of the destiny of the Serbian people, and in many ways of the Balkan peoples as well, Njegoš was also the ideologist of the Serbian and Yugoslav future.

Even by the close of 1848 he perceived that our participation on behalf of the reactionaries in Vienna and St. Petersburg could not lead to any essential change in our national destiny—to unification and political independence. As early as October he expressed this in a letter to Vraz: "Will our people show to the world . . . that it is worthy of independence, or will it forever worship alien chains which have for so many centuries galled their necks and oppressed their nationality?" At the same time he observed the hopelessness of the situation: "I see terrible mistakes. It seems to me that a great departure has been made from the main goal. God grant that I may be mistaken." As anything Serbian and Yugoslav always did, so this evoked from him tones of tragic helplessness and personal unhappiness: "At night I pray to dream of something good, and at day that the newspapers might bring me good news. It is a hundred times easier for him who fights than for him who sits and waits at home."

This attitude is significant not only as a trait of the man and the poet, but also as a reflection of the clash between idea and reality which is inescapable in a man who sees far and knows something for certain, but is not in a position to undertake anything to check the undesirable course of events.

Njegoš was to adhere to the nationalist cause to the end and to offer help on all sides. But he was to see with increasing clarity the cracks and the inconsistencies, the selfishness and the squalor that accompanied the realization of our national program. Apparently this is the fate of all causes. He was to bestow the Obilić Medal on Serbian commanders who fought the Magyars, and at the same time point out that our people and the Slavs would not shake off their own yoke through these struggles. His private inclination was to take advantage of all the disorder in Europe and go our own way—to complete national liberation. But he was alone in these aspirations, tragically isolated and powerless, and torn between the desire to help the Serbian and Yugoslav cause such as it was and the awareness that it was not what it ought to be. A month following the words quoted above, in November, 1848, when no one had yet perceived the senselessness of our role, he wrote to someone in Trieste with an unsparing finality which did not even leave any ashes:

> O wretched Slavs, what would Europe do without such slaves. Were it not for them, *mein Herr* would have to take off his gloves and *effendim benim* put aside his pipe, and they would be compelled to become blood brothers, had not their good fortune given them the Slavs. Yes, our race is owned like any other cattle by other nations, and whoever has the largest herd is the richest. Whoever has the slightest doubt that the Slavs are born to be slaves, let him look upon their actions today. Can there be anything more loathsome in the world than their blindness? I am always amazed, and can never get over my astonishment, how shameful slavery can be so dear to some men. They are like dogs, for a dog tugs to gain his freedom, but once he gains it, he runs back to the leash to be tied.

At the time he was writing this in disgust, Jelačić had reached Vienna with his counterrevolutionary troops, and a triumphant intoxication had seized the strategists of the Croatian and Serbian policy. A month later he was to write to Jelačić, in the hope of stopping him short and influencing him:

> A mysterious destiny has placed you at the head of the South Slavs . . . but your prospects are all being dimmed. You have saved the throne, the dynasty and all of its servitors; you have done them a favor such as no one has done them since their inception, and yet just a few days later, instead of being grateful, your debtors impose the old iron

yoke on Dalmatia. . . . Why are we given to servility? Why do we not know our own strength? Why does a blind force direct the Slavs so as to make them take on alien chains of their own free will? It is true that I and this handful of my people are rid of the anathema of tyranny and spying, but what good does it do me when I must watch millions of my brethren as they groan in alien fetters? . . . Whatever cannot be held by the strength of one's arm is as good as nothing.

This awareness grew more intense and the tone became sharper, to the point where relations with Jelačić cooled and died out. The Governor of the Triune Kingdom of Croatia did not for a moment cease to be an Austrian general, and his Yugoslavism was not capable of emerging from the shadow of the black double-headed Austrian eagle.

Bishop Rade had the same attitude toward the Serbian policy in the Vojvodina, which defended the Serbs against the Magyars at the price of turning them into Austrian hirelings. "The Duchy is standing on weak legs," he wrote Prince Alexander on April 14, 1849, "and even were it to become entirely free of the Magyars, there would be in it no advantage whatever for Serbdom inasmuch as the Serbs are not fighting for themselves but for someone else." In his letter of April 23, 1849, to Medo Pucić,* he summed up the situation in the Vojvodina and Croatia as well as the entire Yugoslav problem in a single passage: "In the beginning I had some hope, but today I see that Yugoslavism is for the present simply an idealistic word whose emptiness has a beautiful ring to it. What are the Banate and the Duchy [Croatia and the Vojvodina]? They are dead historical words—nothing else."

Njegoš was in fact what would be known today as a nationalist revolutionary. And a very consistent one at that. He wished to turn the conflict with the Magyars and the Italians to their advantage and his own—for himself and his people, and no one else. But Montenegro was small and too weak, while the forces in Serbia and Croatia were not capable of seeing beyond their own personal and class interests.

True to the Montenegrin cause as well as to the Serbian reality, he believed that it was first necessary to settle age-old accounts with Turkey. This is why he waited so enthusiastically for Matija Ban to bring him news and concrete plans. Ban appeared before

* (1821–82). A poet, scholar, and politician from Dubrovnik.

him in the spring of 1849. "What a happy thing it would have been," Njegoš wrote to Prince Alexander on April 14, 1849, "had we marched on Bosnia instead of in the Vojvodina. Today we would have in our hands something that could not be easily lost." In his enthusiasm he wished to believe that his relations with Belgrade were now firmer and more indissoluble, and on taking leave of Ban, he fixed as their next meeting place Prizren, the capital of the Serbian Empire in days of yore.

But the collapse of the revolution meant an end to these plans as well, which Njegoš suspected all along. The ancient Viennese monarchy rose from the ruins for the last time, while Russian Cossacks stomped across the heart of Europe. What Belgrade and Cetinje hoped to undertake no longer depended on them; the Great Powers were well disposed toward Turkey. Even those gains that had been achieved were dissipated and slowly vanished—all too quickly and painfully for Njegoš. Ban came to Cetinje to inform the ailing Bishop that the insurgent forces had been dissolved.

Hopes in a different reality waned. His life also waned. Without enthusiasm he distributed medals for Serbian heroism—to Knićanin, to Jovan Ristić.*

There remained only the idea, the one he drew out of the course of national history—out of the human and the cosmic destiny. Though disappointed, he did not despair. He never despaired. That ethical and Serbian core always remained intact in him.

After all was done, he wrote to Knićanin on January 20, 1850, "Deception alone is ruinous for men and nations. . . . I look every misfortune straight in the eye."

One triumphs over the reality by not making peace with it.

7.

BY HIS EMOTIONAL MAKE-UP and expression, as well as by political experience, Njegoš was necessarily a Montenegrin. In ideas, traditions, and goals, he was a Serb.

He always differentiated between the Serbs of Serbia and the Montenegrins. Yet this distinction was not ethnic or, as one would

* (1831–99). Serbian statesman and historian.

say today, national. For him, as for Prince Danilo and even King Nikola later, these were differences that existed within the same people.

The idea of the Montenegrins as a separate nationality appeared for the first time during the First World War, as an attempt to find some more profound, supposedly national reasons for justifying the retention of the Petrović dynasty and the Montenegrin state. Conceived by the camarilla, the thesis of the Montenegrins as a separate nationality appeared and gained strength later, after the unification with Serbia in 1918, as an expression of the dissatisfaction of the popular peasant masses with the new state of affairs. Later the Communists also took it up, as a means of weakening Belgrade's hegemony and of associating themselves with the unextinguished tradition of Montenegrin statehood. They, too, of course, justified their practical needs and particular interests with idealistic and, in this concrete case, with allegedly scholarly arguments which seemed all the more convincing at the time because they could be made to fit the theories of Stalin, and not just his alone, concerning nations as exclusively the product of capitalism, though it cannot be denied that capitalism does in the final analysis give a political national form to groups which have ethnic and territorial ties. Having accepted the thesis that a nation is the product of capitalism, as though the nation had no preconditions of its own, it was not difficult to make Montenegro out to be a nation, in view of the fact that capitalism developed there later and more slowly than in Serbia. Besides, the dissatisfaction with Belgrade's centralism and hegemony, as well as with even worse evils, gained a Montenegrin cast of its own. It could hardly be otherwise in view of the differences in mentality, in social structure, and in political traditions. Because of my own position in the realm of ideology and government, I was particularly involved in advancing untenable theoretical explanations concerning the Montenegrin nation. Yet not even then did I maintain that the Montenegrins were not Serbs—a variant of the Serbian nationality—just as I maintain still today that their administrative separateness is justified.

An examination of Njegoš can convince any unbiased person, wherever there are such, that there is no separate Montenegrin nationality.

Montenegro was for Njegoš Serbia's "very own sister"—the closest possible kin, but yet not the same. This differentiation was political rather than ethnic. Later it was to play a much greater role, in the interests of the dynasty. He spoke of "my consanguine Serbia," which in his language denoted the utmost closeness—a community of blood and spirit.

In common action with Serbia Njegoš visualized the realization of a sacred cause and the requisite for Serbian survival in the future. In his case it was also a family tradition; Karadjordje wrote to Bishop Petar as Njegoš did to Garašanin, "However, if . . . you make haste with your army to unite with us so that we can give each other all the necessary support, we shall accomplish something for which the Serbs will bless us for a thousand years to come."

Njegoš felt something more for Serbia—a moral obligation. "There is not a bandit," he wrote on March 5, 1845, "who could commit a crime in Serbia, which is so dear to my heart, and be able to find refuge here with me, for he knows full well that if I were to apprehend him, he would pay with nothing less than his head."

One people, one land, and one state—but a different way of fighting and of expressing the same essences.

In Njegoš's view—and in actual fact—the Montenegrins were a local variety of the larger Serbian people. The Montenegrins had, and still have, peculiar mental traits. Of special significance to Njegoš was their implacable hostility toward the Turks. That attitude was reflected in the living memories of the medieval state, and in the desire for national independence. This is why Njegoš regarded the Montenegrins as the most Serbian of the Serbs—the essence of Serbdom. "The bloody Serbian rock"—this was Montenegro for Njegoš. Montenegro was not the core of Serbdom—there could be no such core. But it was the essence, in a given time and in a special way. And for Njegoš this was the most important, the most exalted, the purest and most ultimate reality. He maintained that after the catastrophe at Kosovo, the Serbian nobility took refuge in the ravines of Montenegro and there preserved the kernel of national independence. He inherited this as a myth, only in his case, as with so many other things, he believed in it as a historic fact. The essence was indeed true: the idea of Serbian freedom had become a reality in Montenegro—the spiritual condition of its existence. "Let Serbian blood run like a river, let come what suffering may," Njegoš wrote to Prince Alexander Karadjordjević on May 2, 1848.

Matija Ban was something more than an intermediary between Belgrade, Cetinje, and Zagreb. He was the first to use the word *Yugoslavia,* in a poem entitled "Karadjordje," written in 1844; it was published in his work *Prizren* in the *Zora Dalmatinska (The Dalmatian Dawn)* on October 23, 1848. That name hardly appeared by chance at a time that bridged the past and the future of the South Slavic peoples, and from a man whose origin was in a city that was first to write poetry in the Croatian, or Serbian, language of the people. That name arose in the atmosphere of new and concrete ideas and after a long awakening and mortal struggle out of Turkish, Austrian, and Venetian slavery. The quarrel over that name was to last a long time—and it is still going on, and will until the South Slavs win the right to determine their own fate and their own place in Europe and in the world. The name *Yugoslavia* sprang from Njegoš's flaming thoughts and heroic sufferings.

Njegoš differentiated between Serbs and Croats, mostly because of the difference in their religion and historic past. He was for "the religion of the people," that is, for union on the basis of ethnic affinities, ignoring religious differences. Njegoš was for the unification of the South Slavs.

It is interesting and extremely significant that the very idea of a federative Yugoslav state, which was to be called Yugoslavia, originated with him and the project he and Garašanin were preparing. Durković-Jakšić has given documentary proof of this—in an unpublished work on this subject which he was kind enough to lend me. That state was to expand via Serbia and Montenegro across Bosnia to include the Croats, and probably others, too. Somewhere in that period Njegoš placed at the head of his *Stephen the Small* the well-known verses:

> Do not ask how one doth cross himself,
> Rather ask which blood doth warm his breast,
> Whose the milk upon which he was fed.

They have no connection with the work itself, but through them he wished, at that very time, to stress the vital idea of the unification of the South Slavs. The title page of that work, published in Trieste in 1851, reads "In Yugoslavia." That name came out of the secret negotiations and reflected Njegoš's perseverance and uncompromising will—for the sake of future generations.

Yugoslavism was for Njegoš something higher and deeper than a political goal; it was the union of peoples ordained to share the same destiny, nurtured with the same milk, and warmed by the same blood, as he put it. Yet that idea, which waned so quickly and tragically after 1848, did not develop in him fully—in a pure and passionate artistic expression.

This was no step-by-step progression—from Montenegro to Serbia and thence to Yugoslavia—but an appreciation for the differences and possibilities involved in realizing the idea of national freedom, which he regarded also as the concrete aspect of good.

Slavism, or, to be more exact, Pan-Slavism, was for him a purely practical necessity—without inner content and distant prospects. He was against the struggle of the Poles—and they were against him—for Russia was thus being weakened, and Russia was the protector of the enslaved Serbs; this despite the fact that he stood for ideas very similar to those of the Polish revolutionaries against Russian imperialism.

In Serbdom, and especially in Montenegro, there did not exist the requisites for any Pan-Slavic idea, least of all a Great Russian and Orthodox one. However, there did indeed exist a political—even vital—necessity for leaning on Russia. In a country and a people and a poet all of whom derived their ideas and passions from their own centuries-old existence, Pan-Slavism as an idea based on practical hegemonistic needs could find no response except in a passing moment of political necessity. And even in these matters, regarding these practical interests, there were various goals and starting points. Pan-Slavism was for the tsarist government a most convenient way of penetrating and of gaining recruits among the subjugated Slavic peoples, and for these peoples it was an outside support in the struggle for liberation. That was in fact the bad side of that struggle—that in the fight for freedom we had to look for support to the darkest and most despotic power in Europe.

That, too, was a myth, that belief in the common primeval origin of the Slavic peoples. But that myth was long since dead, if indeed it had ever been alive since our separation into the various Slavic peoples and our migration into the Balkans, as early as the seventh century.

There is nothing uglier and falser than a dead myth, that is, a myth that ceases to be true and a living human reality.

8.

YET COMBAT unites the combatants, regardless of their differences. Though they relied on the despotic powers of Europe in their thoughts and aspirations, the South Slavs were for democracy and freedom. So it was with Njegoš, especially with him. He held it against England, precisely because it was democratic, that it was led by its imperialistic interests to keep the dead Turkish hand at our throat—"a knot on a healthy offshoot." This national libertarian looked to the center of Serbdom—Belgrade—but also to the democratic United States of America. "I have long wished to visit Serbia, and then the United States of America," he said to Ban. "For the present, political considerations prevent me from carrying out my first desire, but as for the second, do not be surprised to hear that I have set out on the Atlantic Ocean and that I am sailing to New York. . . . It is proper for free Montenegro to receive aid only from a free country such as America, seeing that it cannot get along without aid. . . . I like Russia, but I do not like having to bear the price of its aid on every occasion. I am tired of it and wish to throw off that yoke." Ljuba Nenadović managed to catch the invisible vibrations that passed between the Montenegrin sovereign and the unaffected Americans during Njegoš's visit to an American ship in the harbor at Naples—a certain cordiality without high-sounding words and a certain affinity in unspoken thoughts. They understood each other without words: the spirit of the Montenegrin crag and of the unconstrained men and space of America.

It is not at all important what America was really like. For Njegoš it was free—and indeed it was, and in many ways the freest; while the Americans saw Montenegro and its Sovereign in the same way—unextinguishable human aspirations in different aspects.

Man is indestructible in his yearning for freedom, for humaneness. Freedom and humanity are indestructible in man. They bring men together despite the various forms in which they manifest themselves. They are one and the same, and the spiritual essence and inner meaning of man's existence. Njegoš's struggle against evil—this was a struggle for freedom. The very antithesis of evil is freedom. The evil is always different and the freedom new. "My heart is always pure and cleansed toward men, but one is forced to deal inhumanly with inhuman men," he vainly argued with Osman Pasha in a letter of October 5, 1847.

A poet out of evil, Njegoš is in fact the poet of human freedom —human in its Serbian, national form. "We are a poor people, but rich in proud courage and human freedom, which is the finest gift of humanity . . . the only and most sacred sign of Serbian pride and glory," he states in a letter of January 6, 1849.

His Serbian and Yugoslav political ideas were only a reflection of his understanding of human destiny—the necessity of the struggle against evil—which he derived from the sufferings, strife, and misfortunes of the Serbian people.

It is risky to prophesy the fate of these ideas, which were not Njegoš's alone, but shared by the majority of leading Serbian and Yugoslav spirits. Yet as poetry and philosophy they belonged largely to him. Serbianism and Yugoslavism were joined, though much later and, of course, in a manner different from what he could have imagined. They endure and shall endure, becoming a part of European and world unity. The unification of mankind is inevitable, inasmuch as that is the requisite for the expansion and perfection of production, that is, of man's livelihood. This, too, was Njegoš's thought, in essence.

For him the national was identical with the human.

Freedom is identical with the struggle against evil. That is the essence of Njegoš. And Serbianism is a concrete form of the human desire for good, for freedom. The light-giving powers of man's reason are boundless. Through them he shall ensure the immortality of his kind and with his seed plant the cosmos from which he gained this power. The poet-sage was free before the law—and Njegoš was not a slave even to God, knowing that man is not only the product of the law, but that he also possesses its power. That is what endures forever—for it is universal. And that is what is in his political ideas, and what will unite every true fighter for human freedom, for this world, with national and human destiny.

That was a turning point in our national existence—from the Middle Ages into modern times. Only such a moment could have produced a Njegoš. But only a Njegoš was capable of lending that moment permanence, as a work of art, and of binding together with it both our past and our future.

He was a flash of our lightning in the world, in the cosmos.

IN SICKNESS

1.

THERE WAS apparently in Njegoš's physical constitution a susceptibility to tuberculosis: height without a strong muscularity, a conspicuous caving in of the chest, and a long protruding neck. His secretary Milaković noted his "proneness to the dry sickness" as early as 1847. This susceptibility was heightened by an unbroken chain of troubles as a ruler and the tribulations of his people, which kept him, overly sensitive as he was, in a state of constant turmoil. He was a being who was tragically doomed from the outset and forced to suffer laceration: alien to asceticism, he was doomed to monkhood, and he was driven by duty to burn himself out, though he was given to the joy of living. He was burdened at conception, so to speak, with Montenegro's ills and Serbian misfortunes. As a ruler he bore them heroically, but the poet, the man, reacted to them through all the pores of his being with the most acute, most absolute pain.

The Montenegrins, like all mountaineers, were easily and incurably infected by tuberculosis. So, too, was Njegoš, who may have been exposed while abroad, although that disease was no longer rare in Montenegro either. The unfortunate ruler was to take a long time to die, and in full awareness—thus linking our greatest spirit with the tragic destiny of the nation. He felt this parallel, and he accepted his dying as the triumph of human and Serbian ills over him.

And yet he fought back, especially in spirit, to his last breath. It was dying in the style of Njegoš—looking death straight in the eye, with boundless courage, with pain, and with a tranquil conscience.

Njegoš's dying began with the collapse of our and his national hopes, which 1848 had aroused and dashed.

Sickness fell upon him suddenly, in spring, as is frequently the case with tuberculosis, with the first damp days of 1850. Up to that time he had never been ill, but that winter he was beset by colds and a cough. Novica Cerović recalled that while the Bishop was playing billiards, he suddenly became sick, retired, and began to cough up blood from the depths of his chest. Having been concealed for so long, the disease advanced rapidly. Njegoš wrote on March 12 to Franc Miklošič,* "It is now four months that I have not been quite well." And by March 24 he wrote to Gagić, "I have gone down to Kotor, for my chest gives me much trouble, and the change of air has done me good, while even the doctors promise that my health will improve. The trip was a very hard one, but a drowning man does not choose boats." The paths were still covered with snow, and he had to go on foot.

His illness, the sense of impending death, was not to leave him for a moment after that. Death was to pervade all he did—all that he spoke and wrote—wherever he went and whatever he thought about—including the already shattered prospects of the Serbs.

It was an illness without great pain, with its little fevers, dull pressure, and tiring cough, which kept him tense and reminded him even in his sleep, as its momentary absence aroused hopes in him of a quick recovery. Among the people there was a superstitious fear of this disease which slowly drained and wasted away its victims, which had no cure, and which, once it imbedded itself, cut down whole families. To comfort themselves as well as Njegoš, his entourage spoke of a neglected cold. There were also tales that he had strained himself in a fall from his horse, and that he was being slowly poisoned. In the foreign press, on the other hand, there was speculation, when he left Montenegro in search of a cure, that he had fled before a rebellion.

Njegoš remained in Kotor, or, rather, in nearby Prčanj, a rather long time—from March 23 to the end of May. He felt considerable pain on the right side of his neck—a reaction to his diseased right lung. He was in the care of Petar Marinković, a well-known physician in Kotor; Cetinje did not yet have a doctor. However, Marin-

* (1813–91). Slovenian Slavic scholar, linguist, grammarian, philologist, and professor at the University of Vienna.

ković was no lung specialist. Njegoš established with him an air and relationship of sober cordiality, which was so typical of him. His illness was noised abroad, and the people came in a stream to bring him gifts: meat, honey, lambs—the fruits of the earth and of their own hands—which he then distributed to the poor. The espionage became livelier, while the Orthodox priests of Kotor were beset by the same problems as when he had been consecrated bishop, namely, what do to if the Bishop of Montenegro should suddenly show up in church. Were they to seat him on the episcopal throne? But Njegoš freed them of all such ecclesiastical and political problems simply by not visiting a single church. Having withdrawn to a little room in Prčanj, he wasted away, left to search inside himself in ever-deeper isolation.

His illness grew increasingly insistent, and he finally decided to go to an Italian physician.

But he was faced first by a serious and most pressing duty—his will.

He wrote his will in Prčanj on May 20, 1850, and sent it to Gagić for safekeeping on May 27, from the harbor of Dubrovnik, where his ship made a stop on its way to Trieste.

One can already sense the exhaustion of a sick and tortured man. On May 4 he informed Gagić from Trieste that he had left his brother Pero, the President of the Senate, to represent him in Montenegro, though he could have done this at the time he sent his will.

The disquiet of a mortally ill human being intruded on his national cares and cosmic encounters. But he never forgot his duty. That disquiet also brought it to mind, and only now did duty appear to him in its final form. Even his illness and the search for a cure now became a duty for him.

Duty is above and beyond everything. There is nothing that remains after it.

2.

HAD HE WRITTEN nothing else, Njegoš would have been famous for his will.

He wrote the "Testament" at one sitting, without even copying it, left it with all its deletions and additions, exactly as he set it to paper, straight from the inspiration of the most moving pure thought. These corrections, so typical of Njegoš, are only in the first, so to speak, spiritual section. The selection of a successor and material questions, the second section, are set down simply and without deletions or corrections; here was a man who was not troubled over material things and whose conscience was clear.

That first section of the Testament is short—just a few sentences. Yet in them is the whole Njegoš—in all his poetic thought, and with something else, something, if we may so put it, higher and more beautiful than that: a view of eternity, of death and life, of man's destiny and the cosmos. Here is human existence and Njegoš, the land and people, and our history before absolute laws—in this case before God, before the cosmos and other peoples and cultures.

Is there anything as profound in its simplicity, as moving in its directness, and as plastic in its human contact and bond with eternity and man's existence? And yet it was not Njegoš's aim—least of all at such a time—to make poetry. Poetry and wisdom issued from him as soon as he opened his mouth or took pen in hand. So it was with him also in the hour of his confrontation with death, perhaps more earnestly and profoundly than ever before. Everything fell into place—his personal life and experience, the nation's past and the destiny of the human race—and found expression in a passionate yet thoughtful acclamation of man's lasting and changeless existence in the cosmos.

Ivo Andrić was the first to recognize the marvelous beauty of Njegoš's Testament, while Isidora Sekulić based a study on it, a chapter in her inspired book about Njegoš.

That first section of the Testament is short enough to be cited fully in even brief studies; it is too beautiful and too rare to be passed over. It reads:

> Thanks be to Thee, O Lord, for having deigned to bring me to the shore of this world of Thine and for having been pleased to nourish me in the rays of this wondrous sun of Thine. Thanks be to Thee, O Lord, for having favored me above millions on earth in soul and body. From my childhood up, as often as Thine unattainable majesty has moved me to hymns of divine rapture and awe before Thy great beauty, so often have I beheld in horror and bewailed man's wretched lot. Thy word has created all from nothing. To Thy law are all things subject. Man is mortal and must die.

With hope I come before Thy sacred altar whose radiant glory I glimpsed even from the shore which my mortal steps have measured. I go calmly at Thy call, either to abide in eternal sleep in Thy bosom or to glorify Thee forever in deathless choirs.

After this comes the practical part. That is how testaments were generally done: first thanks to God, and then the ordering of mundane affairs. Njegoš designated as his successor Danilo, Stanko's son and his nephew, while he left his money to "the unfortunate Montenegrin people," "to the wretched and yet chivalrous Montenegrin people"—"that it might serve them in need," "that they may buy powder to defend their freedom."

And finally a curse, as in other testaments, but grave and vivid in the Njegoš manner: "Whoever changes any of this, may his face be black before men and may the dread judgment of God be brought down upon him for the terrible wrong which he has committed in the sight of heaven and earth."

Njegoš was to live longer. He took almost another year and a half in dying. But he did not touch his Testament which was final in every sense. He was yet to write a few sentences in letters and two or three poems, which are his in thought and point of view, but not in expression. The Testament was in fact his last literary work and among his greatest achievements.

It would seem that here we have predominantly the Njegoš of *The Ray of the Microcosm*—in view of its religious tone, and even language. The only allusion to Serbian misfortunes is in the words "the unfortunate Montenegrin people." Yet it is not quite so. Njegoš adhered to tradition, and he composed his Testament as others did. But the attitude is different. And even the Serbian destiny is expressed in this very attitude—pride before absolute laws, the light of reason in the midst of evil, the interlacing of the joys and beauties of life with human tragedy. It is expressed, finally, in what he left his people, so chivalrous in their destined woes.

Such is the Njegoš of *The Ray of the Microcosm*—joyfully grateful for being nourished by the light of creation in one of the worlds, conscious of himself and the world. He stands upright, cognizant of his human exceptionality before the very laws. Njegoš is aware of his own fairness and power—"above millions on earth in soul and body." One of the Psalms—and if Njegoš knew it, he did not give it a thought at that moment—reads: "Lord! . . . I thank thee that I am so wondrously made. . . ." Yet the coincidence is not accidental; the relation between man and eternity is not transitory. Both in the Testament and in the Psalms a man speaks of laws: I am subject to you, but I also apprehend you—for I, too, am a creator. Njegoš is convinced that he as a mortal has apprehended the laws—"whose radiant glory I glimpsed." He stands before God as peer before peer.

Yet this is not the attitude of a single strong individual only, but of a people with all of its history and its obstinate defiance of evil and misfortune, even though these might come by a higher dispensation. This is the outlook, too, of the ruler of a people—a people which has remained unbroken, which became a nation unto themselves through evil, and which turned slavery and struggle into their greatest, most rapturous glory. Njegoš is the Serbian people.

In the Testament every sentence is an abrupt transition—so typical for Njegoš—to something new and apparently without any connection with what comes before. This is how a testament ought to be written—like a covenant.

The first passage ends with the avowal that all is subject to laws and that man is mortal—the core of an earthly and cosmic conception. The following passage ends with a reconciliation which is even more absolute—the return to an original state, into eternal slumber and light. Yet that is the reconciliation of a man who has come to know the truth, the reconciliation of a poet whose work is already done. Then comes the identification with God, with the laws themselves, in that man knows them and that his final fate is identical with them.

But the Testament has hardly any of Njegoš's language and imagery, or better to say, they are indirectly implied—in the attitude, the meaning—as is the human and Serbian destiny.

The poet grasped at a moment of man's indissoluble bond with eternity even as national misfortunes beset the ruler. The poet of terrible vengeance is become the sage—in the realm of light and laws.

Before death, before eternity, everything was stripped bare down to the last.

The sage does not fight death, but the sap of life resists it, even when it is no longer young.

3.

NJEGOŠ did not remain long in Trieste and in Italy, for he returned suddenly from Padua. Traveling in the summer heat had a bad effect on him. Besides, his decision was prompted by his anxiety over the ever-more-rapid progress of his illness.

In Kotor he had been greeted by the wailing and keening of the Montenegrins. The men smote their heads, while his women relatives disfigured their faces. It was more terrible than a dark foreboding; it was mourning while he still lived. The Bishop was brought to tears on taking leave of his land and people—of his own life—as he shouted, "Be with God and live in peace!"

The land and people did not leave him for a moment, nor did he leave them. For in addition to his nephew Stevan Perović-Cuco, Novica Cerović was with him. Novica urged him onward, especially after his fainting spell in Padua: "Let us fly, for the Sovereign is dying!" The folk sage feared that the Sovereign of Montenegro might expire in a strange land. And the Bishop himself realized this: "Would that I had never moved from Cetinje!" The physicians also recommended that he return as soon as possible to his homeland and come back to Italy in the winter. He hurried back, this time not even tarrying in Dubrovnik; he simply informed Gagić, on June 26, of his return and complained of "the great Italian sultriness," which had so weakened him that he could hardly keep on his legs.

From Kotor—"in straitened life"—he immediately proceeded to Njeguši. Though exhausted by illness, worry, traveling, and the heat, he managed to stay on his horse.

Tuberculosis is deceptive—and sensitive to change. "I am fairly weak at present, but I hope for a speedy improvement in my health," he informed Gagić, convinced that he would feel better with the change in climate.

Judging by his letters, Njegoš spent most of the summer in Cetinje, and perhaps in Njeguši as well, with his own family, though the name of the capital was placed at the head of his letters. It is noteworthy that the only letters preserved from this period are those addressed to prominent persons. Apparently either there was no more of that petty and daily correspondence with Kotor or he had entrusted it to others for the time being.

Surrounded by the cares of his family and of the chieftains, Njegoš undertook a cure in the folk way by eating nourishing and light mountain food—honey, cream, and lamb—and by imbibing the sea and mountain air, fresh and thick. He was told not to lie on his back or to turn his eyes to young women. In this period he paid much heed to self-taught physicians. Even the cultured Ban recommended to him a certain Catholic priest in Dalmatia who was allegedly a great expert in the curing of consumption. At that time the medical profession knew very little about tuberculosis and was even less successful in combating it, so that the physicians gave Njegoš contradictory and erroneous advice—to go to the seaside, to eat little. He took medicines reluctantly. He used to say then, "While there's life, there's a cure."

And indeed, he did suddenly feel better—and his hopes were aroused. In July he informed Garašanin and Gagić that he was rather better, and on August 10 he wrote to the physician Marinković that he was "much improved." That letter breathes with the cheerfulness of a patient who is recovering and who not only speaks of death bravely but also speaks of it as something that has passed him by. The letter is noteworthy for its beauty of thought as well as for that brand of humor of his which sprang not from a situation or a certain character, but from the senselessness of something. The nearness of death made everything keener—not only his faith in the immortality of the soul but also his laughter at human folly. It put an edge on his bitterness, too. He says this in a letter to Garašanin, on July 5, and still more emphatically in a letter to Dean Nikolajević of Dubrovnik, on October 18: "Even blissful Eden would have been filled with evil and corrupted with evil had such a fate overtaken it."

Njegoš sensed that the improvement could be short-lived. His illness was marking time and gaining strength for a new attack. In September Djordje Stratimirović spent a night in Cetinje, and Njegoš complained to him that his illness weighed heavily on him and hindered him in carrying out his plans for the liberation of the Serbs. "Have a look, Djoko, here is death," he told him, pointing at his own chest. He presented Stratimirović with the dagger of Smaïl Aga Čengić, even though he was not terribly impressed by the visit of this prominent Serb and Austrian general.

Njegoš had decided earlier to spend the winter in Italy, in a gentler climate. At the end of autumn, probably in the beginning of November, he set out on his journey. Deacon Djurašković, who long served him, told of the sadness of this parting: "As he rode toward the coast, he kept looking back at his crag."

It was Njegoš's last journey. Perhaps he was afraid that it was his final parting with Montenegro. But no, he was to return even more quickly as soon as he felt that death might separate him from it.

This time, too, he did not tarry in Dubrovnik, and he went straight from Trieste to Vienna.

Vienna left no trace at all in Njegoš's poetry, or in his correspondence, though he sojourned there on several occasions—always for reasons of state. Vienna was uninviting by virtue of its politics, and especially, with respect to the person of the Montenegrin Sovereign, by its spying and condescension. It seems that Njegoš did not take to its cold orderliness, though he himself liked order. But his order and neatness were of a different kind, a yearning for spiritual and natural orderliness, not the administrative and artificial kind. He could experience only the outward side of Vienna—its administration and cold regularity. He liked colors and irregular shapes and he was attracted by the cities of Italy, which were warmer and more inviting not only in climate but in their way of life. But Vienna was a great center which could not be easily circumvented. It was also a center of Serbian and Slavic culture and politics. Even if the Vienna of the spirit, of culture and subtle naturalness, was not accessible to Njegoš, while official and bureaucratic Vienna repelled him, the Serbian and Slavic part had an irresistible attraction for him.

Nevertheless it is not clear why he went to Vienna, except that he did consult physicians. He did not stay long, but returned to Trieste.

He still felt rather well, though he was a sick man possessed by an insistent disease that never failed to remind him of its presence—with nightly outbreaks of sweat which suddenly became chill and which roused him from sleep or brought him tormenting dreams.

"My chest is still troubling me," he complained to Garašanin from Trieste just before leaving for Vienna. And on his way back, from Venice, he wrote to Vuk Karadžić, on December 25, that he nearly froze between Vienna and Ljubljana and from Trieste via

Furlania to Venice: "The snow was enough to make one lose one's eyesight, and neither the coach nor clothing helped, but it was shivering and more shivering the whole way."

He was ill. He was sensitive to all discomfort and took it hard. He had never before complained of physical privation, but now his body was very susceptible and demanded care. The letter to Vuk from Venice was unusually prolix for Njegoš and for the first time betrays a certain confusion of mind: he dwelled long on trifles—jumping from a description of the furniture in his hotel apartment to a quick reference by association to the Turks, and giving the ceaseless ringing of bells as the reason for his not writing about other things because they gave him no rest. And yet he added: "My health is fairly good." Not even his own confusion escaped him. In a long and characteristic letter to a teacher in Trieste, Dimitrije Vladisavljević, he remarked, "I am in writing as I am in traveling; I can never hold to one direction but wander all over." It was not so. He had a direction always and in everything he did, but Njegoš was conscious of his momentary failings, and even in this way revealed his true self—critical, self-aware.

A soul before the eternity to which it belongs, a human being powerless and alone before death, a warrior and a poet of his people.

Everything leads inevitably to its essence.

4.

IT WAS HIS ILLNESS that drove Njegoš to winter in Italy. But he had not come to Italy to sit out the winter in some quiet spot. Weak and sick as he was, he toured the most famous cities, especially Naples, and, though exhausted, he tirelessly gazed at the sights and studied them. This was a spiritual encounter with history, with deeds and wisdom universal by their very height of perfection and unbroken advancement.

From December, 1850, to May, 1851, Njegoš traversed a long and, for a sick man, a tiring way: Vienna-Trieste-Venice-Milan-Rome-Naples-Rome-Civitavecchia-Livorno-Florence-Genoa-Turin-Venice. And nowhere did he go as a sick man, but as one intent on seeing and learning as much as he could. Not once during his long illness did he falter or give in to it.

Had not Ljuba Nenadović, the writer from Serbia, met him in Naples, even this Italian journey of his, as well as many intimate sides of his personality, would have remained obscure. Nenadović was only twenty-five years old at the time, well-to-do, healthy, and happy-go-lucky, the son of Dean Matija, one of the leaders—perhaps the wisest—of the First Serbian Insurrection. Nenadović closed his eyes, without much effort, to all that was unpleasant in Serbdom, as did all the good Serbs of that romantic time, and he set out to see the European world and to enjoy it as much as to learn from it. The Montenegrin Sovereign, on the other hand, had come to take refuge from the winter, but also to learn. Nenadović was curious, while Njegoš gave thought to everything. Nenadović was just entering life and eagerly grasped at everything it offered; Njegoš had never been like that, and particularly not now, while fighting off death. Njegoš chose to see places of beauty and fame and made his own conclusions about them, mostly to himself. There were great physical differences as well: Nenadović was small and swaggering, a stocky lowlander, with widely separated green eyes and a stubby pert nose, while illness made Njegoš even more rawboned, nervously tense, and sunk in his own thoughts. It is unfortunate that Nenadović worked up his notes much later, when Njegoš had already been accorded a most exalted place in history, so that a certain obfuscation is inevitable.

Nevertheless Nenadović comprehended Njegoš more clearly and fully than others. It is of inestimable value that he, a cultured man of letters, found himself in the company of the Montenegrin Sovereign at the very time the inner personality of the latter was emerging most completely, and that he had both the love and the skill to take note of it and to preserve it. Nenadović's Njegoš is not only the one from Montenegro, but the one whose face was turned to the world abroad—and hence the image is more human and clear-cut. His Njegoš does not rule, but merely feels like a ruler, and he is not overshadowed by Serbian and Montenegrin daily woes, but clearly sees Serbdom and man as concepts—a poet and a sage directly engaged in experiences and conclusions.

What Nenadović portrays and presents is significant enough, but much less so than what one infers from that which he leaves unsaid. Nenadović was not especially gifted, but he knew how to generate enthusiasm when he found the right subject. Such a subject later proved to be the Montenegrins and Montenegro. This interest began in Italy with Bishop Rade, who was by his personal destiny and attitude and work a living essence of Serbdom. This was unlike the dark dynastic struggles that rent Serbia and the renowned Nenadović family itself until Ljuba's own brother paid with his head for his participation in the senseless and disgusting murder of Prince Michael. That Montenegrin motif, from which there emerged two books—one about the Montenegrins and the other about Njegoš—is certain to preserve Ljuba Nenadović the writer from oblivion.

Nenadović depicted the Montenegrin—the romantic poet and the Serbian patriot in Njegoš—but in the background there emerged the essential Njegoš—an individual to the last, even before death and while abroad. Nedić was right to reproach Nenadović for describing the ruler as he imagined he ought to be. But he failed to recognize that this was Njegoš just the same, through his words and deeds, which showed despite Nenadović's touching up. Though hidden, Njegoš was most completely revealed here.

Njegoš does not speak of illness or of death; indeed, he does not speak much at all. Yet he is very ill. That is apparent at every step. He is absorbed deep within himself, as though that were his only occupation besides his traveling and sight-seeing.

In Naples Nenadović found him pensively stoking the fire in the fireplace with a poker. It reminded Njegoš of his homeland; he liked fires, which inspired the telling of tales around him. He felt lonely, and would have even if he had not been abroad. The three Montenegrins who accompanied him were unlearned and had other interests. The major-domo Djuko Srdanović and the bodyguard Vukalo were there to serve him, while his brother-in-law Andrija had come so that he would have someone of his own kin about if death should strike him down abroad. Njegoš had never opened himself up to others before, and now, toward his suite, he was more reserved than ever and had no deep contact with them. Withdrawn into himself he meditated, observed, concluded. This is how he lived in the midst of the quiet of an urban life of receptions and invitations. This is why he was glad to be with Nenadović, a cultured Serb with whom he shared a broader and similar outlook. It was lonely and sad to be locked up inside oneself. Eager to converse, he would talk and talk, and then suddenly stop and grow pensive. What was he looking at? What was that world of his like? And he would remain withdrawn into whatever it was that made him silent.

Montenegro's heroism had become known in the world, and everywhere people were eager to greet its prince. But he was not interested in meeting people. He avoided wearing his Montenegrin dress in order to be inconspicuous, and went visiting only if it would have been discourteous or politically harmful not to go. He found visits tiring, and yet he wished to find out all that he could. He could never get over the restlessness of discerning truths. Now, before death, that thirst, that restlessness was heightened. Every page of Nenadović's *Letters from Italy* aches with the Montenegrin Sovereign and with the concern of his entourage about him, but it also throbs with Njegoš's longing for insights.

"I am traveling through Italy only for the sake of the dead," he explained as he refused invitations. He was interested in past civilizations. He was enlarging his thought concerning the transience of everything that human hands have built. Only ideas endure and are transmitted. There is no end to freedom and justice, and men will always fight for them, one way or another and regardless of how they live, so that they might live. In that most magnificent palace, the Church of St. Peter in Rome, he wrote verses about how trifling everything was in the sight of eternal laws. Pompeii was for him the image of the folly of man's obsession with material concerns. He looked at churches as he did any other buildings, and at relics as at museum rarities. He showed no interest in the Pope, only the pride of a mountain ruler. God did not exist for him outside of the spirit. Apparently he went even farther in his conception of God: there exist certain laws by which man lives and to which he is thereby subject—nothing else. For Rome has been, and is no more, despite its worldly power. There was once a primitive Christianity, and now there was papism. Before absolute laws, Montenegrin poverty was as great in its heroism as anything else.

He wrote in Italy, but about Italy hardly anything at all, two or three poems inspired by ruins, by the transience of human might. These poems are not finished pieces, but the reflection of first impressions and thoughts. He avoided nationalist poetic motifs; he lived with these all too painfully, and he had said what he had to say, what could be said. Rarely did he even speak of poetry, but he did remark to Nenadović that *The Mountain Wreath* was better than *Stephen the Small.* Nenadović noted that in Naples Njegoš dictated a history of Montenegro for a Frenchman named Stanislas Bellanger. But Vuksan has shown that Njegoš wrote a reply to Bellanger's inaccuracies. Even there he was carrying out his duty.

In Italy Njegoš spent his time learning, more than anything else. The wise man learns everywhere and always, even while dying.

5.

ITALY was his last acquisition of knowledge, his last book—with its history unfolded and its art on display, and, over it all, human destiny. Njegoš was constantly hungry for knowledge, even now. Yet he was more eager to penetrate truths.

This is less evident in his few writings from that journey than it is from his attitude and the way he lived. He returned to Rome, faithful to its ruins. The deterioration of material things, which first strikes one about Italy, and especially Rome, was for Njegoš the ultimate proof of the immutability and might of the law. This motif and thought were hardly new to him; they appeared, so to speak, with his first verse and conception of the world. What was new was his experience before this deterioration, so tragic and beautiful in its revelation and irreversibility. Still, it was not this in itself—the scene—that attracted him, but, rather, its expression of an idea. He was experiencing ideas, laws, distilling essence from substance. For the reality, including even that endurance through deterioration, did not exist for him outside the law. Moreover, reality was the materialization, the actualization of the law, the idea. He did not buy antiques, not so much because he was frugal with money, but because of his attitude: these things were like any other, more or less vivid images of the deterioration of man's works and the impermanence of the forms of matter. "In Rome, an Italian broke off a beautiful marble decoration from Caesar's palace and brought it to him, asking three thalers," Nenadović relates. "When the Bishop saw it, he smiled and said, 'What good is that stone? In Montenegro all our stone is millions of years old; come and take shiploads of it, and you will pay nothing.' "

For this reason Njegoš did not look at everything, but chose only the most beautiful and renowned—that which was the absolute expression and brought absolutes to mind. He had neither the time, the strength, nor the desire to go into details and minutiae, though it is precisely these from which the beauty of Venice, Rome, and Italy is woven, but he went straight to the famous places, those that could be taken in at a glance. He was especially interested in whatever was huge in size. Again it was not the achievement of the human mind and hands that impressed him, but the experiencing of a deterioration all the more total because it involved objects constructed and fortified to last for eternity. At times it seemed to him that not even heaven and God himself were immune to deterioration, to change. He would ride slowly in a coach and gaze, getting out only when he could not see otherwise, and take in everything at a glance, and then he would look and look—he would look at the whole and ponder. Even in this he was Njegoš—the poet of myths and ideas, and not of details. This is what he got from Rome, as stated in a letter of January 31, 1851: "Majestic Rome! Those ruins of great Rome! When a man comes into it, he does not know which grips him more, the amazement and excitement, or a soul-smiling sadness over the tomb of worldly greatness. Truly these two elements fought within me like a bad mother-in-law with a good daughter-in-law when they take to pulling each other by the hair and fighting for supremacy. . . . Time is mighty, and it has terrible teeth. It is a terror even to almighty heaven, let alone to the wretched earth, where all is easily crushed, where all stands on a weak foundation." Of course, this was not Rome. But it was Njegoš in Rome.

In Italy, through Nenadović's travel account, Njegoš is revealed to the last—freed of daily cares and trifles. That was his, and our, confrontation with Europe, with its civilization and history. We, too, are Europe, but in our own way, and perhaps most expressively through Njegoš in Italy—a small young race with a world of its own coming into an ancient and high civilization.

In Italy he did not reveal truths but experienced them, those he already bore within himself. Here he clarified, polished, and refined them. Even Kosovo made him sadder here than in Montenegro. "My verses are all sad, I no longer write any," he replied to an Englishman who asked him to write two or three verses below his picture. He had cried himself out over the Serbian destiny, and his tears had turned to stone—had been transformed into perceptions. To a man from the Vojvodina, a simple man who complained to him that he had not been home in eight years, Njegoš replied, "We have no home anywhere; it perished at Kosovo."

In Italy Njegoš became utterly spiritualized even by his way of life. He ate very little, being most content with a slice or two of fruit. He seemed to be awake all the time, as though afraid that he might miss something important and new. Sick and worried over Turkish designs on Montenegro—and news of this kept coming constantly—still he was spiritually calm and composed. He said, "The Kingdom of heaven, the Kingdom of light, will come, but not one of us who is now living will see it. Mankind moves forward slowly. It matures together with the planet which it inhabits."

Everywhere, even in Italy, at all times, he remained the Montenegrin—and with all the Montenegrin primitiveness under those layers of culture and civilization. His outlook, his reactions were Montenegrin. He was to ask his bodyguard for a small rifle so that he could fire it into the maw of Vesuvius, though he was ill and tired and choked by the sulphur fumes. Here was the Montenegrin challenging the might of a volcano, defying it and thereby establishing a bond with it. He was a Christian bishop, but he refused to kiss the chains of Saint Peter: "A Montenegrin does not kiss chains," he replied curtly. He paused for a long time before Raphael's "Transfiguration." What was it about that painting that possessed him? The consummate calm of the man—Christ—who had fulfilled his duty? Njegoš was also a man of duty. Perhaps he asked himself, "Have I done my duty?" There is nothing greater and more important for a man. The victory of duty is a victory of the mind, of light, the transfiguration of a man into his spirit. This is what he saw in that painting and what he pointed out in that letter of January 21, 1851: "Above all there stands and shines Raphael's painting of The Transfiguration, as the enchanting Morning Star shines with its joyous face on the forbidding and somber crags which have been rent by terrible lightning." And before the sculpture of "The Laocoön"—a masterpiece of antiquity, whose meaning and expression penetrate all ages—Njegoš was horrified: "That," said he, "is something Omer Pasha or one of the Turkish sultans would keep in his dining room to give zest to his meals." Such observation might seem to betray a terrible primitiveness and a worse misunderstanding. There is some of that, but also a certain fidelity to oneself and to something more profound and significant: for Njegoš neither art nor anything else of value existed unless it contained the idea of humanity. "The Laocoön" with all of its horrible pathos, however human and most human, had to remain closed to a poet who was open only to what was expressly humane as such. Njegoš was so much his own man—and accordingly a Montenegrin—that he quickly rejected and excluded all that with which he had no affinity and which jarred with his world. He and his land had more than their fill of horror and so rejected it even in a work of art. The poet could not separate the deed and the idea, the expression and the thought, when these two were the same for him, as for the earliest tellers of tales. Even in Roman galleries he had to avoid Montenegrin affliction. He did not wish to look when they lowered dogs into a certain cave and brought them out unconscious. The ethical view prevailed over the aesthetic, the humane over the scientific. Njegoš also wanted the world to be good, and it was bad, alas, in Italy, too.

In his last hours he was engaged in establishing truths, in settling accounts with himself and before himself—in measuring the world against Montenegro, for Montenegro, too, was a measure with a dimension all its own.

Not even here did it leave him—they were married to each other forever. And even if it did not mean what it did to him, news of it got into the press, and letters came to him, all about trouble, domestic and Turkish.

And those three Montenegrins who were with him, they, too, were Montenegro, living and present. Serdar Andrija, the Bishop's brother-in-law, was an elderly man, taciturn and remote from everything not Montenegrin in him. He always smoked a long pipe and sat on the balcony, in wonder at the city's hustle and bustle. Perhaps he also wondered to himself why the Bishop did not stay in one place. Vukalo was a simple man, with no knowledge of a foreign tongue, but he had a penetrating sense of humor, untamed and jocund. Once when they found themselves on board a ship next to some Turks, he could not get over the fact that here he was sitting next to a Turk and yet was not permitted to cut him down or even to push him into the water. Djuko was different—

bright, quick in speech, witty, literate. He brought with him *The Mountain Wreath* and books printed in Cetinje. He was always completely transparent. He, too, wondered at the strange world and how it measured up against his Montenegro. His master also wondered a bit, always yearning for his homeland. Nowhere was there a Serb to be seen or heard, he complained to Nenadović. So, too, Djuko never left Montenegro, whose beauties and truths were irreplaceable, and in all his cheerfulness there was sadness for it.

It was with greater bitterness than ever that Njegoš received news from the homeland. Misfortunes and woes seem magnified from afar, in a strange land, and as though he were to blame for them. On their account he easily became angry and caustic—he was ill. And every effort took its heavy toll, though it seemed to him in Italy that he was getting better. The newspapers carried accounts of Turkish reforms in Bosnia. But Njegoš was not deceived; he knew what Turkey wanted and what it was capable of doing. He also received a coded message bearing the news of the death of Ali Pasha Stočević, his last and only friend in Turkey. His brother Pero had already written about these events in Bosnia and Hercegovina.

From a supporter of Istanbul, Ali Pasha had become a foe of its administrative centralism and reforms. As soon as Omer Pasha Latas, an Austrian petty officer deserter from Otočac, in Lika, who had become a Moslem, became Vizir of Bosnia, thanks to his zeal in suppressing rebellions in the vast and heterogeneous empire, it was clear to Ali Pasha that his independence and overlordship were threatened. Sensing danger, the wily Vizir of Hercegovina sent his own son Hafiz Pasha and Bishop Josif to greet Omer Pasha. They met Omer Pasha in Nova Varoš, excusing Ali Pasha on account of his lameness and age for not having come himself, and offering, in roundabout fashion, a bride as well as some recruits. But bribery did not work with Omer Pasha, while the gathering of recruits was a main part of his reform program. He issued an order that Ali Pasha come to Sarajevo without fail. At an assembly of notables in Sarajevo, Omer Pasha read a firman which Ali Pasha cautiously opposed: it was not favorable to Hercegovina. As soon as he returned to Mostar, open resistance to Omer Pasha broke out, at first in Konjic, and then elsewhere. Possessed with a relentless, quick, and deceptive energy, Omer Pasha already had rich experience in suppressing rebellions, especially by the beys. At Borce his lieutenant Skender Beg, the former Polish Count Jan Iliński, defeated Muyaga Pamuk, who had replaced Kavas Piyuliya when the latter went off to get help from the beys of the Drina and Zagorje. Ali Pasha himself withdrew, from old habit, to Stolac, and, encountering no resistance, Skender Beg descended on Mostar on January 29, 1851. Without any prospect of a successful resistance, Ali Pasha permitted himself to be enticed, together with his sons, into surrender. Omer Pasha arrived in Mostar and ordered Ali Pasha to be led through town on a donkey, facing the tail. Thither came also Ali Pasha's rival from Trebinje, Hasan Beg Resulbegović, to make his obeisance to the new vizir and to make life even bitterer for his enemy. On February 21 Omer Pasha set out from Mostar via Duvno to the Krajina, to pacify some rebellious beys and restless raia, and he took Ali Pasha with him as his prisoner. The once glorious and mighty Vizir of Hercegovina, now fallen and humiliated, rode a mangy mule led by his son Hafiz. According to a report, one night he was strangled in Dobrun, near Banja Luka. "He died shamefully," Bishop Rade's brother Pero informed him on April 5, 1851.

The news of Ali Pasha's death troubled the Bishop greatly. Not even he, Ali Pasha, was able to escape his environment and his time and to rejoin his Serbian kin. Istanbul was gaining strength. The prospects of a rebellion in Bosnia vanished, while Omer Pasha overcame obstacle after obstacle and was making ready to march on Montenegro. Omer Pasha—another countryman of ours, a Turkish renegade.

The Bishop suspected and expected an attack and cursed Omer Pasha by the milk that had nurtured him. "That dog," he exclaimed, "will not leave me to my illness or let me die in peace."

Evil struck Bishop Rade from every side.

The sage is more tragic than the poet.

6.

NENADOVIĆ AND NJEGOŠ parted ways in May, 1851, in Florence, after two months of travel through Italy. Njegoš was accorded a formal farewell—delegations from the city and its educational institutions, tourists, Russians with flowers, and a man from the

Vojvodina, a sergeant, and a wandering Serb. There reigned an atmosphere of quiet respect, as much for the sick man as for the ruler, and Njegoš felt that he was taking his leave of all beauty and joy—and so it really was.

He hurried to Vienna—hoping to anticipate Omer Pasha's invasion of Montenegro. He wished to go to the Russian Tsar. However, he was refused on this occasion as well, even though Nicholas I was taking a cure at the time in the Austrian spa of Olmütz. The Russians made the excuse that the trip would be strenuous in view of his health—a transparently insulting affront to the sick Sovereign of Montenegro. The Bishop sensed that Omer Pasha was not one of those vizirs who comes to power thanks to bribery in order to get rich on bribes, only to fall in disfavor and to make way for an even more listless successor. Omer Pasha exuded a fresh vigor and a brutality which penetrated anything he undertook to accomplish. The Bishop did not live to see his invasion of Montenegro in 1853, the dread year of Omer Pasha, but he foresaw as early as 1851 all the horror that it held in store for a hungry, poor, unprepared land. Montenegro was to be saved from destruction by the intervention of the Great Powers, an intervention that did not come too late thanks only to the heroic resistance of the Montenegrins and Prince Danilo.

Bishop Rade failed to accomplish anything in Vienna. While waiting for the inane and ambiguous replies of the slow Russian bureaucracy and the inconsiderate consideration of Vienna, he was overtaken by the sultry summer and a rapid worsening of his illness.

Milica Stojadinović, the poetess, noted—"in remembrance of May 16, 1851"—her meeting with Njegoš in Vienna. He remained in Vienna nearly two months after that, and also met Branko Radičević (the first dew of Serbian poetry in the folk language of Vuk Karadžić) himself ill with tuberculosis (he was to outlive Njegoš by one year). Also in Vienna were Vuk Karadžić, Anastas Jovanović, and the physician Joseph Škoda. The ailing Njegoš attracted now more than ever the numerous Slavic public figures in Vienna; they sent him medicines, physicians, gifts. And the press, particularly the Serbian press, gave him a good deal of attention—and from their reports one sees that at times he felt better, and at other times worse, as with other consumptives.

Those were difficult and painful days for Njegoš. From the reports of that time concerning his illness, the only fairly complete ones, one can see that his bronchial glands had swollen, that his aorta was distended, and that the tuberculosis had invaded the region of the lungs along the spinal column and both lungs. To preserve quiet they spread straw in front of his house. Even had they known what to do, the doctors were no longer able to help him. As it was, good Dr. Škoda recommended that he bathe in the sea in the summer and next spring, that he avoid pork and beef but take fowl, clear water, milk, and Bordeaux wine with water. As for medicines, he was given a hydroiodate, four grams of salicin, and five grams of bicarbonate of soda daily.

The disease broke down all resistance—all save Njegoš's spirit. One more Serbian misfortune since Kosovo was inevitable: the premature death of the greatest poet in the spirit of Kosovo and a ruler whose task was not done—a myth in himself and a never-to-be-forgotten votary to the future.

He frequently admitted to himself the nearness of death. Yet no one has noted that he had any fear of it. And how could he—a man who believed so steadfastly, and now more than ever, in the might of the human spirit? That spirit did not permit him to lose hope. Courage and hope. He told Stratimirović about Dr. Škoda, "Tell him, Djoko, that I am Bishop of Montenegro, that I do not fear death. He has told you the truth; you tell me."

And they told him, finally, that his condition was grave, and that one could expect his death at any moment.

It had been different in Italy, where the disease ate away quietly, where there was something at every step to arouse joyous thought, and where only the echo of Montenegrin woes could reach. Here, in Vienna, he fell into a vortex of political intrigue, deception, and cross-purposes over Montenegro arising from the selfish interests of the European chanceries. The coughing choked him all night long, so that he took to sitting up in an armchair, in the Goldenes Lamm Hotel. In April he moved to a villa in Hitzing which had been rented for him. Now even he spoke of death and dreamed of improving just enough to be able to get back to Montenegro. After all, it was his concern over its fate that had brought him to this.

He met death, as he did everything, looking it straight in the eye, and he also looked back at his own life. He felt that he could have done more—for Serbdom and for poetry. This is how he spoke to Stratimirović: he did not fear death, but he regretted not having succeeded in writing still another, perhaps immortal, poem. He also told this to Ban: "I am not sad to die, but I am sad that I have done nothing notable in my life—such has been my evil fate, which has been terrible from beginning to end. . . . Let posterity at least know our intentions, inasmuch as I could not leave it my deeds."

Before death, before eternity, every human accomplishment seems trivial—to a man of Njegoš's conscientiousness.

In three, in two, weeks, Njegoš was transformed from a worried patient in Italy to a dying man in Vienna. He could not even move about, and went nowhere, in an alien land, alone with death —more isolated than ever.

The Italian Francesco Carrara, who had met Njegoš in Split in 1846 with the Englishman A. A. Paton and described in all its splendor the beauty of Njegoš's physical form and poetic speech, visited him now in Hitzing and was stunned by his appearance: "He has become transformed. The pale cast of his emaciated face was even more pronounced within the frame of his long hair and black beard. His eyes were dull and burned out, his voice hoarse, his breathing hard. When he sat up, he was a burden to himself." Njegoš talked to him about Italy: Naples was a dream of beauty—he had still been only a patient there, breathing in the perfumed azure where he could forget about himself as he gazed into a benign infinity, constantly delighted at the restless movement of the colors and shapes and at peace with the obviousness of the irrevocable decay of all things human.

It seems as though the ruler and the poet had withdrawn or just faded away before the human being fighting for his bare life. But it was not so; rather, it was as though all of his qualities were finally converging in death. Faith in Serbdom and in the spirit as well as his sense of duty never left him for a moment. His yearning for Montenegro was stronger than all else. The physicians opposed his traveling to Montenegro. But he paid no attention to their counsels. As soon as he was, as soon as he thought that he was, feeling better, he set out for his homeland, in the middle of July. He reached his decision without assuming any pose, without a word that would be remembered. Back—to the rock, into the wilderness from which he had sprung, even though there were no physicians there, no nurses, or anyone who would know what the patient required.

What compelled him to do this? He had to go back to a land threatened by invasion, and besides, it was his duty as its sovereign to lay his bones to rest there and thus return what he had taken away from it. Perhaps, too, he was acting on instinct; birds of passage always return to their home. And might not the fresh air of the Montenegrin hills act as balm for his torn breast?

Even this—his irrepressible yearning for the homeland—involved his sense of duty and obligation. When Stratimirović admitted to him that he might live longer, but that he might also die at any time, he seemed to make peace with death, but not with Vienna. He would not die there, but only in his Montenegro. To be ailing abroad made sense only while there was hope of a cure. Now he had to decide, according to his own conscience, without regard for the opinions of the physicians. And what if he died in an alien land, he, the Sovereign of Montenegro? He was to remain true to the end to the idea, to himself—to misfortune and sacrifice.

His only thought was not to remain abroad. "I am ill and have been wandering the earth for the sake of my health," he complained from Trieste on July 21, 1851, to the Czech Slavophile Václav Hanka, "but were I in better health and at home, I would have my fill of grieving over my foolish and blind brother Slavs." A cry—arising from the last throes and a final realization.

As though taking his leave, he sojourned briefly in Zara, then in Dubrovnik, with Gagić. They were now to forgive each other and forget each other's harsh words and suspicions as something humanly inevitable.

And when the steamer sailed into the Bay of Kotor, Njegoš would not leave the deck, but waited for something the rest knew nothing about and that only he sensed inside himself, knowing that it must appear. And then it did appear, suddenly, behind a rocky cape imbedded in the sea and the sky—Mount Lovćen, looming proud and high above the blue calm of the bay. "Never again shall we two part," Njegoš cried out to Lovćen—and to himself.

On Lovćen there had already been built a chapel of unhewn stone and lime which was to receive what remained of his body.

From here, from the sea, it was not visible. There are two peaks on Lovćen—Štirovnik, which faces the sea, and Jezerski Vrh, toward Montenegro. Njegoš decided to be buried on the lower peak, for it faced Montenegro and could be seen from it. Once, when he had climbed Jezerski Vrh, he tapped with his cane and said, "When I die, you shall bury me here." They did not believe him, they did not understand, and he had to repeat it, but he did not move to get the building of the chapel under way. Then on one occasion, long before his death, he suddenly turned to Deacon Djurašković and asked whether he had ordered master builders to come from Herceg Novi. The Deacon replied that there was time for that. "Call them as soon as possible," the Bishop said, and repeated once again for him, "I wish to be buried there." The chapel and the crypt in it were built by 1844, at a time when he had not yet published a single famous work, having just written *The Ray of the Microcosm*. But he knew what he bore within himself.

To be buried on Lovćen was in itself a stroke of artistic genius. What greater awareness of beauty could there be than to abide through eternity amid the thunder and the sunlight, in view of one's land—a guard against evil and misfortune.

Now, on returning, he had an intimate feeling for Lovćen, the dwelling in which he would finally rest. The poet and his mountain finally came together.

He arrived in Kotor around August 10. He could not stay on a horse, and yet he did not wish to be carried on a stretcher, like a corpse. And so something had to be done: they attached an armchair to the poles of a stretcher, he sat in it, and they bore him sitting thus to Cetinje. As they climbed into the heights, he could gaze upon his dear sea and the happily scattered settlements along it and his raw, unruly highlands.

Such a mode of travel was inconvenient and more tiring than had he been lying down. But he wished to remain upright—to watch and to meditate as he watched.

Nothing is harder for a mountaineer to bear than not to be able to keep on his own two feet; his horizons become shut off and the paths break off, a dungeon without walls. Njegoš probably did not even know about Bishop Danilo—though everything about Njegoš began with him—how bitterly he complained over his infirm legs: "Why, when the rest of the body is whole though unprofitable, have the legs given out and collapsed, why do they not bear the entire body as well as this rocky land which they serve most, for without them all is in vain, and we eat our bread for nothing." Now Njegoš, too, was traveling through his land as a paralytic, but he kept in touch with it through his eyes—with all its horrible reality and stark but unequaled beauty, and with this thoughts on heaven, on boundless eternity, just as he always lived.

Upright, toward Montenegro and truth, he would remain to the end, and would lie down only to die. Such had been his life. This was he—on guard before Serbdom and the cosmos.

In Cetinje he was greeted by silence and the wilderness, which closed in on the dying man even more inexorably and impenetrably. He was too intelligent not to see it all clearly. But that is what he wished. This accursed land of his had bound him to itself in suffering, evil, and courage and intoxicated him with its bitter and pure poetry.

He hastened to its last stony embrace.

"There where the seed did first begin to sprout . . ."

DEATH AND LASTINGNESS

1.

AND AGAIN he felt somewhat better, as soon as he reached his native climate. Like all living things, he fought off death to the end and did not lose hope, but his diseased body never failed to remind him of its painful deterioration.

He sent his first letter following his return to Knićanin, on August 17, regarding a strange encounter: the Albanian Mirditë chieftain Mark Prekljesh had been awaiting the Montenegrin Sovereign at Cetinje for four months out of a desire to see him. The letter, in which Njegoš recommended Prekljesh, was short and businesslike. Yet it radiated the undimmed luster of a friendship such as can arise only between two mountain heroes. The Albanian clan of Mirditës had feuded with the Montenegrin clans from time immemorial, and now the time had come for one of their standard-bearers to wait and to wait in the midst of Montenegro for the renowned Bishop. Njegoš was obviously gladdened by this selfless perseverance and heroic friendship.

He tried from the very first day to get back into the swing of daily affairs—of both living and ruling. His concern led him to note that there had been a good harvest that year, and he tried to resell the wheat he had bought in Trieste in case of an emergency. He took up again that petty but tense and tiresome correspondence with Rešetar, the Commandant at Kotor. He got back into domestic affairs and troubles.

But he could not take up the old life again. That concern with details was too much for him. He was in a hurry to settle all material problems and had a horror of doing anyone a wrong.

"Forgive me for troubling you for every little problem of mine," he excused himself to Gagić in a letter of September 6, "but to whom can I turn if not to a true brother Serb and to the trusted confidant (in these parts) of my exalted protector." There is tenderness in his tone, and even more of forgiveness and oblivion. He signed himself "Yours now and ever."

The idea of death, the feeling of dying penetrated all of him. It grew irresistibly, filling his every moment, casting a shadow over every intention. "Should it happen that I die," he begins an order to the Trieste merchant Bajović, on September 15, 1851, that he pay his uncle Lazo Proroković fifteen hundred lire. There has also been transmitted an excerpt from a letter to Nesselrode, two days later: "I am still suffering from a lung disease and have almost completely lost my voice." On October 5 he replied to Vuk Karadžić that he had received Frankl's *Gusle* and Branko Radičević's *Poems* with "your dear letter," and then suddenly he added, "I would write a fine answer to your letter if death would let me, but in view of the condition I am in, even this much is enough, for when the body suffers and groans, the soul is tempest-tossed."

It was as though the very idea of death was being realized in him, through him. He was testing the truth of his own belief: the body is a prison, the torture chamber of the soul, and it was capable, alas, of disturbing and muddling it.

There was the consciousness of impending death, grasping at the threads of life, and conscientiousness to the very last breath.

As late as October 10 he took up in a letter to the inexorable Rešetar the question of some quarrels between the Montenegrins and the Littoral, and then on October 12 there came a sudden and unimpeded final flight into the purest heights, in a letter to the writer Frankl, who had presented him with his translation of the *Gusle* and thus moved him. In that letter Njegoš summed up his entire conception of his own existence, his outlook, in a few sentences, with all of the terseness and lucidness of a dying man:

The poet is a mortal calling out from our storm-swept shore. The poet is a voice crying in the wilderness. He dreams of immortality, calls after it and yearns for it. He sees open a great page of the book of life. . . . Through the power of imagination he lifts a germ of heavenly life out of the mud and deifies the corruptible. . . . I am outside the pale of the enlightened world. Over my narrow patch the thunder of tyranny constantly resounds. Thus my little land has been disfigured by the darkness of savagery. For the right-thinking man there is neither dreariness nor enjoyment in this world, for all human delights are mixed with gall, and all woes offer some satisfaction. When his time comes, a man is quite as ready to weep as to sing. This is how I understand our poetry. The world is God's garden, and so in its every cranny are visible the works of a great master. I would rather observe the diligence and art of the ant and the bee, and the orderly flight of the cranes than all the parades of the European capitals. Goodbye, Mr. Frankl, be kind enough to keep me in your precious memory.

Was this the spirit finally prevailing over the body and breaking loose from its bonds?

The same day that he sent that letter to Frankl, Njegoš's condition, which had been bad enough till then, suddenly grew worse. In the clear face of death his spiritual powers seemed to have rallied and gained strength. True to himself even in death, despite the terrible and inexorable dying—such was Njegoš! Even that "goodbye" and "keep me in your precious memory," at the end of the letter to Frankl, coming after sentences in which he confirmed his truths, even as he gasped for breath and his every nerve and muscle strained—all this came from a man who was impassively going to the hour of his death, taking leave of his acquaintances without pathos and without fuss.

The next day, October 13, he informed Gagić, "Concerning my health, about which you may wish to know as my friend, I cannot say anything good to you, especially since yesterday, when it became rather worse." And that is all. Friendship prompted him to complain. He had not complained much before then, truly as though he was not part of an earth where men moan over the slightest hurt—and even at the very thought of death.

Njegoš had little opportunity to demonstrate his bravery on the field of battle. His heroism of the highest kind was revealed and confirmed by his devotion to duty, to the idea, in those few letters and few sentences of those days, by a man worn out by sleeplessness, exhausted in strength, and broken in body, but untouched in spirit.

He was prepared long ago.

Heroic wisdom is above death itself.

2.

IT HAS still not been explained why he sent his nephew Danilo, whom he designated in his will as his successor, to school in Russia at the last moment. Danilo was the son of that Stanko Stijepov who had played such a prominent part at his inaugural and at the beginning of his reign. Danilo had spent several years in Cetinje at Bishop Rade's side. Yet nowhere in the Bishop's letters, and not even in oral tradition, is there any trace of Danilo. Danilo was the closest relative—a brother's son—and as such the closest heir. Njegoš upheld this order of succession; nor is there any record of Danilo's dissatisfaction. In the face of his own death, Njegoš must have realized that Danilo was too young and that it would be a good thing to have his brother Pero hold power until Danilo was educated. Besides, he knew better than anyone the inevitable conflicts and troubles that attend any take-over of power. Certainly intrigues and ambitions played a part. Brother Pero yearned for power more than anything, nor could cousin Djordjije get over not gaining the first place, which he himself had lost. Be that as it may, Bishop Rade never in any way denied Danilo's right, already traditional in the family and established by his Testament; yet he did not think that the time was right to have power come into his hands immediately. He thus obviously wished to avoid complaints and opposition, whose bitterness and woe he had himself experienced. Again a youth would be tonsured and consecrated as prince-bishop of Montenegro. He wished to avoid trouble and dissension among the Petrovići.

Montenegrin ills did not even let him die in peace. In the very days when he was dying, two clans took to fighting each other—before his eyes. That disturbed and embittered him and caused him to wonder what would become of his labors, his bringing law to Montenegro. But the tension of doubt did not grip him for long. His faith in the spirit and in the triumph over the country's misfortunes returned.

He died in the midst of affliction, but never losing courage.

The Austrian authorities watched vigilantly and far too obtrusively at what was going on around the dying Montenegrin Sovereign. The Sovereign's entourage concealed the state of his health, but Commandant Rešetar found a convenient way to learn the true state of the Bishop's health—through his physician, probably that same Marinković with whom the ailing Njegoš had first come into contact. Rešetar kept the Governor of Dalmatia, in Zara, informed, and so reliable data concerning Bishop Rade's last days have been preserved. The physician spent three days in Cetinje and returned to Kotor on October 16. Rešetar reported:

> Judging by what this physician says, I am convinced that the condition of the Bishop's health is desperate. For several days now he has been suffering from a constant high fever and serious dysentery, his breathing is difficult and hard, and he is troubled by a cough which forces the patient to sit up. He has neither appetite nor rest day or night. A swelling has appeared on his hands and the patient feels a general weakening throughout his entire body. In accordance with the physician's orders, the patient was bled and after that he felt better, so that he could sleep for half an hour. In a word, the physician assures me that never has the Bishop been in such a desperate state, and he declares that the patient might still prolong his life for a short time, but that he might also die very shortly.

But the interest of the Austrian authorities did not stop there. They also tried to help the sovereign of a neighboring backward and wild country. General Mamula,* a Croat by origin, went down to Kotor personally, taking along the well-known Dubrovnik physician Novotný, while the latter bore a letter for the Bishop's brother Pero to dispel any suspicions about himself. But Novotný arrived too late—on the very day of the Bishop's death or the next day.

Njegoš's dying lasted for days. Ljuba Nenadović arrived to record whatever he could from the eyewitnesses and to save it from oblivion. Some of it was noted down by that priest-spy from Kotor, and some by others. It is known how Njegoš expired. There was constant suffering and boundless pain, and a struggle between thought and death, the body and conviction.

He had intended earlier to spend the winter in the valley of the Crnojevići River; he did not wish to go abroad. But inasmuch as he grew worse rapidly, he decided to go to the Littoral, which was not alien to him, and besides, there was a doctor there.

By some inexplicable urge, men flee in the face of death to some

* Baron Lazar Mamula (1795–1878), Austrian general and administrator.

other place, finding excuses and deceiving themselves and others in various ways. It seems that not even the physician, who visited Njegoš by order of the Austrian officials, opposed this journey. On October 16, the same day that the physician returned to Kotor, the Bishop informed Rešetar, "The unfavorable state of my health forces me to depart hence for Kotor, in the hope of gaining improvement there or elsewhere with the help of physicians, about which I will inform you, remaining respectfully and with esteem Your Excellency's humb. servant, Bishop of Montenegro P. P. Njegoš." These were the last words to come from Njegoš's pen—informing a foreign government of an intended journey. Just one sentence, whose starkness tells of his relation with the Austrian authorities and the efforts of a human being—one who is conscious of the inevitability of death—to deny death to the end.

The rest was also without embellishment, without postscripts, without witnesses. Njegoš and death were alone, facing one another in the wilderness of Cetinje.

Man and death are inseparable.

3.

OCTOBER 17 came and went, but Njegoš did not set out for Kotor, though he had everything in readiness—bearers and stretcher.

A cold rain began to fall, one of those that in these dry regions comes down for days, weeks, enshrouding the shrunken horizon in wet fogs and laying bare the rock, lending it an even starker somberness. There is no escape from its downpour save under a solid roof, while from its murky melancholy there is no refuge even there. The damp permeates everything, while the smoke lingers and sinks with a heavy bitterness over men and their conversations. The autumn begins joyfully here—filled with unfurled silk and beaten gold and the eagle's cry and the shouts of shepherds—but it is changed in a moment into an unfinished refrain and impenetrable languor.

Around the Bishop and his chambers it was quiet, and ever more quiet, except for the water dripping from the eaves. At night there was a rushing sound, as if of underground streams. The chieftains came calling, but not on business—he was no longer fit for that—but just to inquire about his health. Not one of them looked him in the eye, only darted a fleeting glance, as though by chance, and everyone was careful not to offend him in any way. Both men and things became imperceptible. Njegoš knew what that meant. He kept silent, suffered and pondered.

The same day that Njegoš had intended to depart on his journey, his octogenarian father, Tomo, came through the downpour. His son Rade greeted him: "Welcome, Tomo! I am glad that you have come. You never used to see me off, but now you want to."

All understood the meaning of Njegoš's words, fought back their tears, and turned misfortune into jest. In roundabout fashion they got to talking about the journey to Kotor—discouraging the Sovereign, though not too energetically. They were afraid he would die on the way. Not even the Bishop was as determined as before. He reflected—whether to go or not to go. Then the son turned to the father: "If you tell me to go, I shall go, and if you tell me to stay—I shall stay." The father replied without hesitation, "Stay until tomorrow; let us see if the weather will take a turn for the better."

Apparently the son could hardly wait for just this reply. The Sovereign ordered the journey to be postponed.

But he did not depart the following day either. The weather was still worse, and he himself no longer even mentioned the trip.

That day—October 18—was an extremely long one for Njegoš. The sky poured a leaden rain over the windows and the tile, and he felt more choked than ever. The pain and his thoughts gave him not a moment of peace. He would sit, then get up, take a few steps around the room, then sit again in his armchair. Just before evening he remarked sadly, "God be praised, if my day has been like this, what will the night bring me!" He seemed to have forgotten about the journey and to have reconciled himself to staying, or with the inevitable, as never before. It was in these very hours that he thought, more insistently than ever, about his intention to bind himself to Lovćen—an idea as sculpturally plastic as it was symbolically poetic. At dusk he called Pero and Djordjije to him and implored them to bury him on Lovćen. They promised. But it seemed to him that they were lukewarm about it, and he demanded an oath of them. They swore to it.

That, too, was done. He would be alone even after death, but beyond daily cares, watching over the land he had transformed into a state and a poem. Lovćen is neither the highest nor the fairest Montenegrin mountain, but at that time it was the most Montenegrin of all, because of what had taken place around it. Now, with Njegoš on its peak, Lovćen would become the symbol of a people and of an idea—of the inexorable, terrible, and evil and frantic human struggle for goodness and light, for reason and beauty.

Through the rain and the fog came the night—maddeningly long, though the last. Not even Njegoš knew what to do with himself, and no one was able to tell him what to do. He wished to walk—but he was too weak. He wished to talk—but could not—or to listen—but it was no use. Yet thought did not dim; it radiated, out of his large and suffering but wise eyes, and lit up his forehead. What was he thinking? Was he reviewing his life and weighing his truths for the last time?

He managed to get through, to suffer his way through that night as well. He was greeted by a dull dawn, which barely broke away from the night and the fog—October 19. Njegoš's sufferings did not diminish. The day was not different from the night. He no longer even remembered the trip; he had got over that long ago.

With the break of day his pains subsided. But that did not deceive him. "I would like to live," he said, "just two more years." What did he have in mind? Perhaps he hoped that in that time Serbdom would set out on the path it had to take. Perhaps there lay within him another great poem, which remained unuttered. And perhaps it was human self-deception concerning the final realization of the goal. Whatever it was, it was not just a bare desire to live: he referred to a definite period—some unfinished task.

The chieftains gathered around him. They were silent. Yet they had to speak. They saw that the Sovereign would die soon, and it behooved him—he was a man, and one with greater responsibilities than others—to declare his last will. But the Sovereign kept silent. He had already done all there was to do. At one point he got up. He wanted to cheer them up and to jest with them, with himself, with death. In his breast all was mangled and laid waste, but he still felt strength in his limbs. He wished, he would have liked, to live longer. Being fond of Serdar Filip Djurašković, he embraced him and shook him saying, "See Filip, I am still alive and my strength has not left me." The Serdar could not contain himself, and the tears began to flow thickly. According to an agreement with the chieftains, Secretary Milaković was to ask Njegoš for final instructions. But he choked up with tears.

Finally Novica Cerović, who was collected even in carrying out this direst and most painful duty, declared, "Sire, your life is coming to an end!"

Njegoš agreed, "It is indeed."

The chieftains declared in a single voice, "Forgive us, sire, thy bread and salt."

By a last effort Njegoš lifted his head and in the silence said distinctly, "May ye be forgiven! And may God bless you and every Montenegrin and Serb, wherever he may be, and increase every good work." He paused, and then added, "Do not forget my words! Love Montenegro and render justice to the poor!"

He also told them that his Testament was with Gagić, and to Filip's query as to what was to be done if the people did not wish Danilo, he replied simply, "Let the people choose another."

After all this he took communion, but he took the cup himself and did not wish to confess—a sovereign with a clear conscience.

All was said and done that needed to be. There was still a final prayer—without kneeling and crossing himself—alone with the highest law. Even this prayer was not for himself, but for Montenegro. Njegoš lifted his cap and again said distinctly, "O great Self-Creator, help the poor but heroic Montenegrin people, keep them in unity and knightly honor!"

The chieftains wept throughout. Rough faces, heavy fists, unkempt whiskers, bodies covered with the scars of Turkish sabers and bullets, souls hardened with woe and misfortune—the people and the land.

Njegoš arose, took a few steps, and lay down in bed. He was long silent, his eyelids closed. What was he pondering? What else would he tell them? He opened his eyes, as though to look about, and—breathed his last.

The Sovereign of Montenegro, the greatest poet of Serbian misfortune, Balkan evil, and the Yugoslav dream was dead. He was acquainted with grief and struggle, and neither surrendered nor escaped. And his message remained unfinished, but lasting.

This took place at ten o'clock in the morning on October 19, 1851, on the same day on which, twenty-one years earlier, he had been forced to don the black cassock and to govern Montenegro, and twelve days before he would have completed his thirty-eighth year.

"Much of living in this time of troubles."

4.

HIS MOTHER, Ivana, did not find him alive.

On being told that her son was on his deathbed, the old woman hastened through the bad weather to hear his final wish. Within sight of the Billiard and the monastery she heard the keening and the wailing and felt her misfortune.

That woman, whom no misfortune could even for a moment deprive of her senses, kept crying, "He is not dead, no! He is alive for me!" She approached her dead son—they had already bathed and dressed him in the episcopal vestments he neither liked nor wore—and her first words were directed at his handsomeness, crushed as she was: "How God has made you fair above all others, O my glory!" She fell over him, kissed him, and covered him with tears, then she straightened up with composure and declared, "Thanks be to God!" Whereupon she turned calmly to her son Pero, saying, "Don't you get killed, but let your mother look at you, let your sisters swear by you that they may not be brotherless!"

Njegoš was indeed her very own child—by the unextinguishable force of his intellect and feeling. None remembers a Montenegrin woman with such self-possession, such a blend of suffering and equanimity. There has come down an unusual and puzzling anecdote concerning this. After Njegoš's funeral, his parents, Ivana and Tomo, returned to Njeguši—lonely old people in a house of mourning. She caught sight of some corn that was needed for fodder for the livestock and told Tomo that it had to be gathered. Lost in grief, Tomo marveled at her, saying, "We buried the Bishop but yesterday, and you are thinking of corn."

She replied without hesitation, "One can live without someone, but not without something." This could have been uttered only by Njegoš's mother—the one being who was the most bereaved by his death, and yet the one most in possession of her senses.

The death of the young and unfortunate Sovereign was marked by a long mourning, such as none could remember.

Djordjije and Pero kept Njegoš in the monastery four days, hoping that the bad weather would subside and that they could bury him on Lovćen. With his unclosed eyes and bristling beard, Njegoš's enormous length took up most of the cramped stone nave of the church. The candles burned; the clergy chanted ceaselessly. And the rain and cold did not cease. However, the Petrovići were in no haste with the funeral; let Montenegro gather to bid farewell to its Sovereign. The brotherhoods kept coming in groups, even those from the most remote hills and across the border. The keening women wailed in unbroken shifts in ever-more-mournful dirge while the lamentation of the men echoed across the rocky cliffs as they smote their heads with their fists and cast away their weapons in despair. The young womenfolk of the Petrovići scratched their faces with their nails and cut off their plaits of hair. Their men also disfigured their own faces.

By the fourth day, around noon, there gathered around the monastery a multitude of some four thousand Montenegrins. The priests alone numbered around a hundred. There was already a crypt of lime and rock, and they lowered the coffin into it without any parting eulogies or volleys in his honor, just the wail of some poor little bells choked with the damp, and the keening and the moaning. That is how one is buried in Montenegro.

Pero officially informed Kotor of the Bishop's death only on November 1. The news had spread earlier—there is a dispatch of October 29 from Zara—that Montenegro was in mourning. Prince Michael, then still in exile, informed Prince Miloš in Bucharest about the event. The *Srpske Novine (Serbian News)* in Belgrade published the news on November 1.

Bishop Rade's death did not surprise anyone. Yet only now—so it is always after the death of anyone—was the emptiness felt; no other man of the Serbian people could fill his place. Garašanin wrote to Knićanin in Kragujevac on November 1, "Montenegro has lost its Sovereign, and Serbdom a worthy pillar." Yugoslav Croatian Zagreb also lifted its voice. But it was Gagić who found the fairest word for him, "a noble genius," thereby proving that he had understood him, despite all their disagreements.

As for the poet, hardly anyone said anything about him, or else only incidentally, without lending it much significance. The only exception was Jovan Subotić, at a memorial service which Prince Michael held in Vienna on November 11. Subotić spoke at fair length about Njegoš's poetry, but without any profound comprehension of its significance. Nor were much greater spirits—Vuk Karadžić, Ivan Mažuranić, Branko Radičević—able at the time to evaluate Njegoš's poetic greatness.

All mourned the Serb, the Yugoslav, and the ruler, who had obvious merit as such.

The poet began to rise in the estimation of educated men only a full thirty years later, when the ruler was no longer mourned or remembered in the already established routine life of the state.

After his death all kinds of reports concerning disorders and rebellions spread in the outside world, but peace reigned in Montenegro. Russian Consul Gagić arrived in Cetinje on November 27—to examine what was necessary and to confirm the execution of the Testament. The successor, Danilo, whom the news of the Bishop's death found in Vienna, did not continue on his way to St. Petersburg, but hurried back.

He reached Kotor by December 1 and set out for Cetinje without delay.

Pero, the Bishop's brother, with Djordjije's support, was trying to limit the power of the new Sovereign to ecclesiastical affairs, even though the latter had not even been tonsured as yet. Pero wrote to Gagić that Danilo should be sent to a theological school, while he informed both Kotor and Belgrade that the Senate had recognized himself as the sovereign. The Russian Tsar commanded Danilo to go to Cetinje and to assume power, and then to come to St. Petersburg for his consecration as bishop. The old rivalry between *guvernadur* and bishop was now continued in a new form, within the narrow confines of the Petrović family. A struggle for power as well as for material survival, and frequently over an idea, rarely knows scruples or limits.

Danilo managed somehow to settle the matter in Cetinje, to go to Russia, and there to convince the Russians that it was high time to secularize the throne of Montenegro, and so he proclaimed himself a prince. He first obtained the formal consent of the Senate, and then of the Russians, who sponsored the whole affair. Bishop Rade had not shared power either, but the episcopal calling constrained both the personality and the ruler. Danilo abolished that institution, and returned in 1852 to assume complete power, to put an end to all haggling with the clans, and to give ultimate control to the authority of the state, but under a personal despotism.

With this the institutions that marked Bishop Rade's reign vanished, and its personalities gave way to new ones.

But Njegoš's spirit and poetry were irreplaceable.

Yet truly there is no one without whom the life of any human society could not go on.

5.

EVERYTHING that pertained to Njegoš and had contact with him waned rapidly and inexorably vanished.

His parents endured the most complete misfortune.

Prince Danilo first crushed all resistance to his power in his own brotherhood. Pero and Djordjije were forced to flee the country. Pero took refuge in Kotor, where a male child was born to him. He gave him the name of Rade, hoping to preserve the line and the living memory of his brother. But the infant died after two months, while Pero died in 1854. Thus the male line of Tomo and Ivana was extinguished.

Abandoned and forgotten, Tomo and Ivana languished in Njeguši for years. By 1858 Ivana was no longer alive, but Tomo was, having passed ninety.

Prince Danilo decided in the fall of 1855 to transfer Njegoš's remains to Lovćen and thus realize his uncle's last wish. They opened the crypt, and he expressed the wish to see what remained of his predecessor. Horrified, he later repented having done so: nothing but bones amid the decay—"mire," as Njegoš would have said—was left of all that fairness which had radiated such intellect and strength. Only one of the Bishop's hands was preserved, and the unhappy father, Tomo, struggled to kiss it, calling his son by endearing names and wetting it with his tears. He, too, accompanied his son to the mountain, and then fell into a still-greater loneliness. His memories never left him, while his enormous physical strength forced him to live through every evil and misfortune without being drowned in them. He lived to see it all—his brothers and sons at their zenith, battles with the Turks and massacres among the Montenegrins—and he remained in the end without comfort or aid. He lived beyond his time—a stony monument to misfortune.

Njegoš's closest collaborators hardly fared better. Stevan Perkov was forced out and discarded, while tradition has it that the stormy Prince Danilo ordered his son Petar—later Prince Nikola's father-in-law—to be shot, but some chieftains gained him a reprieve. Filip Djurašković was no longer to be a serdar, and there is a report that his son was killed. As for Novica Cerović, he had to flee to Kotor for having, with Miljan Vukov, attacked and demolished Kolašin, against the will of the Prince, even after peace had been concluded with the Turks. Miljan himself was imprisoned. Milaković also had to leave Cetinje. Even Radovan Piper, the Bishop's confidant, had to flee to Turkey. He remained there many years, until, in 1880, amnestied by oblivion, he returned to Montenegro to die. They say that on his deathbed he asked to have someone come so that he could tell him something important. But no one came, and he took his secret to the grave. The son of Njegoš's sister, Stevan Perović-Cuco, a young man with a flair for poetry, the son of that Serdar Andrija who had accompanied the sick Bishop to Italy, was struck down by the relentless hand—a hireling killed him abroad for having opposed the inexorable Sovereign Danilo. It was even said that he had had pretensions to the throne. And finally, Njegoš's successor, Prince Danilo, was killed in Kotor, in 1860; a Montenegrin was found, Todor Kadić, whose hand did not flinch from vengeance even before a prince's majesty.

Njegoš's belongings went to ruin and were irretrievably lost. Contributing to this were changes in the government, wars, the expansion of Cetinje, and, most of all, indifference, a lack of understanding of his significance, and a manner of looking at things merely as useful until they are worn out, like their owner. Njegoš, on the other hand, had preserved every slip of paper, every little thing.

There is not a trace of his clothing, weapons, pens, and pipes. Books containing his marginal notes lay around in Cetinje schools and gradually disappeared. Of all the furniture, the paintings in his rooms, and personal articles, there has remained only a single

armchair, presumably his because its legs had been lengthened. Several of his portraits have survived—all outside Montenegro. The billiard table at which he whiled away the loneliness of Cetinje ended up first in a Podgorica coffeehouse, and then in a Nikšić coffeehouse, and finally in a hotel on Mount Durmitor, which burned down when the Partisans razed Žabljak in 1942. Of the Billiard itself nothing much remained either. Its towers and outside walls were demolished, but it was rebuilt, and finally restored after the last war. The elm beside the Billiard, beneath which the Montenegrin chieftains palavered and dealt justice, was cut down to make room for a monument, also destroyed in the last war, to the assassinated King Alexander Karadjordjević. Njegoš's cannon, which his heroes captured from the surrounding fortresses and which he inscribed with his own verses, were dragged away by Austrian occupation forces to their smelting furnaces. His manuscripts also disappeared, including *The Ray of the Microcosm* and *Stephen the Small.* The first half of *The Mountain Wreath* was discovered in Vienna; it came into the possession of King Alexander Karadjordjević, only to vanish from the Dedinje Palace during the struggle for the liberation of Belgrade in 1944. Luckily a good photocopy edition has been preserved.

Not even Njegoš's bones were allowed to rest. Prince Danilo carried out the pledge made by the Bishop's brothers and collaborators, and he transferred his uncle's remains to Lovćen in 1855. But storms and thunderbolts demolished the little chapel, and it was only after his military victories that Prince Nikola remembered, in 1879, to repair it and to give it the protection of a lightning rod.

The Austrians were disturbed by this symbol of national sentiment and resistance, which was rapidly aroused by their occupation of Montenegro. Governor General von Weber ordered Njegoš's remains to be taken to Cetinje, which was done on August 12, 1916. Soldiers carried out the digging, with all the carelessness of aliens and conquerors. Bishop Dožić, later Serbian Patriarch, reported that many bones had been lost. And indeed, an Austrian soldier, a Serb, found three little bones which had not been collected, took them, kept them during the war, and sent them to Cetinje. A woman, Jelena Lazarević, during a climb to Lovćen, found the bone of a hand and sent it to Bishop Dožić. On Septem-

ber 23, 1925—fifty years after Njegoš's burial on Lovćen—King Alexander Karadjordjević carried out the ceremonial transfer of Njegoš's remains to a newly built chapel and a marble sarcophagus.

That chapel, all of cut stone, whose color and form are in keeping with Lovćen's gray crags, is a small masterpiece in its purity and quiet harmony.

But King Alexander, as ruler of a united Yugoslav state, wished to join in himself both dynasties—the Karadjordjević and the Petrović—all the more so since his conscience could not rest for having appropriated the crown of his maternal grandfather, King Nikola. The inscription on the chapel stressed that tie between Alexander and Njegoš. The King also left his sword overnight in the sarcophagus. And as the sarcophagus was being sealed, he was moved to tear from his breast the Albanian Memorial Medal and to fling it inside. That was a great gesture, which linked two tragedies—the Kosovo of Njegoš and of the Serbian army which retreated across Albania in the First World War.

In touch with the great, even the small can be great in moments of greatness.

6.

WHAT HAPPENED, and is happening, to Njegoš is what happens to all great spirits who have been able to grasp a piece of eternity: the more time separates them from men, the more everything about them takes on a greater, purer, and more abstract meaning. Circumstances may change—new classes and parties come to the fore, new states and governments, generations with different conceptions and goals—but every new social force seeks to justify its own existence and aspirations by linking itself with past greatness and truth—in this case with Njegoš. There is some good in this: everyone thus adds some new interpretation of the past—of Njegoš, the human destiny—thereby saying something about themselves as well. All is transitory, but life and thought go on building and there remains something that is by its very nature imperishable and inscrutable—the act, Njegoš.

At this very moment two epochs, two social systems, confront each other, and sometimes even join with one another, around

Njegoš, out of their own particular and inevitable interests. Also involved in this process has been the great sculptor Ivan Meštrović, who has managed to reveal many truths—both his own and those of Njegoš. By his political and social ideas, Meštrović belongs to a time gone by, but as an artist, whose roots are in the depths of ancient myths, he cuts across any given period of time. He, too, is building Njegoš a monument on Lovćen. Perhaps he wishes to lend that monument the vision and the outlook of his own time—his own Njegoš. Yet he in fact creates like Njegoš—for all time, an imperishable work.

According to models I have seen, Meštrović's monument to Njegoš expresses more than either the transitory or the lasting world of the sculptor. It is, first of all, an extension of Lovćen's peak—the poet is joined to the mountain—and, what is most significant and best of all, the carving of Njegoš's poetry into the sculpture. The monument is Meštrović's lifework—all of pure and clean and simple lines, like Njegoš's poetry. The monument is unparalleled in its strength and harmony and expressiveness, but also in its portrayal of the essence of Njegoš. Is it not so because Meštrović has been carved from the same block and springs from the same sources?

And it is all of granite, capable of lasting as long as Lovćen itself throughout the distant ages, when nothing will remain of our own age save pure thought, shape, and color. Truly it took the most durable stone, in a manner never before seen on earth, to carve out Njegoš's poetry—so that the world could always keep it in sight, in mind, that it might thus become a part of the culture of mankind and of the implacable, inevitable, and always different struggle for freedom.

One must not give in to evil.

In prison, in Sremska Mitrovica, 1957–1959

THE PETROVIĆ-NJEGOŠ DYNASTY OF MONTENEGRO

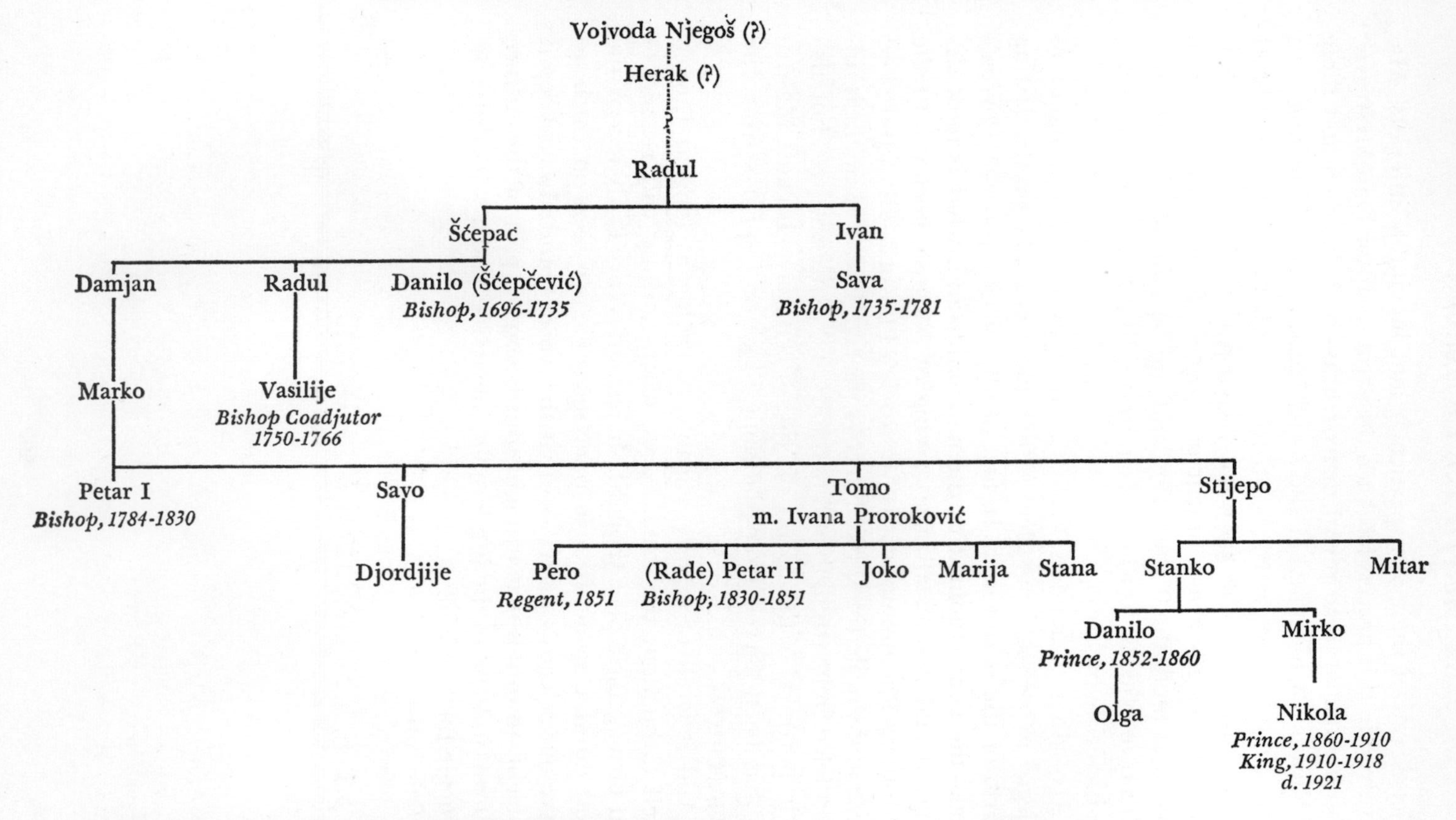

Based on the Djilas text and supplemented by Dušan D. Vuksan, *Petar I Petrović Njegoš i njegovo doba* (Cetinje, 1951), p. 5.

Bibliography

There is a vast amount of literature, not only about Montenegro but about Njegoš himself. By far the most complete list of books and articles about Njegoš is that by the Montenegrin historian Ljubomir Durković-Jakšić, *Bibliografija o Njegošu* (Belgrade: Prosveta, 1951), which contains 3085 items, and much has been written in the fifteen years since that bibliography appeared. Some more recent literature is listed in the bibliography *Ten Years of Yugoslav Historiography 1945–1955* (Belgrade: National Committee for Historical Studies, 1955), especially in the chapter "Le Monténégro du XVIe au XXe siècles," pp. 335–384, which is in both French and English. The most extensive bibliography listing works on Montenegro in languages other than Serbo-Croatian is that by Pero Šoć, *Ogled bibliografije o Crnoj Gori na stranim jezicima; Essai de la bibliographie sur le Monténégro en langues étrangères* (Belgrade: Serbian Academy of Sciences, 1948) ; it contains 4128 items many of which deal with Njegoš and his times.

It is not the aim of the list which follows to offer a comprehensive or even a selected general bibliography of Njegoš and his Montenegro. Rather it is to list those authors which Djilas mentions specifically in his text and the works which he cites or which one may presume that he used on the basis of the context. However extensive this list may appear, Djilas's text leaves no doubt that his acquaintance with the scholarly literature on Njegoš goes well beyond these works.

Ivo Andrić, *Njegoš kao tragični junak kosovske misli* (Belgrade: Biblioteka Kolarčevog narodnog univerziteta, Book 12, 1935). A study of Njegoš's outlook by the Nobel Prize winner.

Ksenija Atanasijević, "Jedan pogled na Njegoševo mislilaštvo," *Srpski književni glasnik,* XLII (1934), 18–25. An analysis of Njegoš's philosophical thought by a leading Serbian scholar.

Ljub. A. Bakić, "O pravosudju u Crnoj Gori," *Arhiv za pravne i društvene nauke,* VI (1923), 161–176. A historical study of Montenegrin legal institutions.

Matija Ban, "Podaci o Petru P. Njegošu," *Preodnica* (1884), 107–109, 125–126, 141–143, 171–173; also in *Zapisi,* XX (1938), 336–348.

Nikola Banašević, "Bifon i Njegoš," *Zbornik u čast Bogdana Popovića* (Belgrade, 1929), 121–137. The author relates the significance of Buffon's *Histoire naturelle,* a copy of which he discovered in Njegoš's library, to Njegoš's ideas.

——, "Njegoševo učenje stranih jezika," *Zapisi,* V (1929), 193–202. Deals with the question of Njegoš's knowledge of foreign languages.

——, "Oko Njegoševe Luče mikrokozma," *Godišnjak Skopskog Filozofskog Fakulteta,* I (1930), 39–48. An analysis of Njegoš's *Ray of the Microcosm.*

Bartolomeo Biasoletto, *Viaggio del re Federico Augusto di Sassonia nell'Istria, Dalmazia e Montenegro, fatto nella primavera 1838* (Trieste, 1841). Account of the visit to Montenegro in 1838 of King Friedrich August of Saxony. A Serbian translation in *Glas Crnogoraca,* Nos. 4–5 (1897) was done from a German translation by E. von Gutschmied in Dresden in 1842.

Francesco Carrara, *Il vladica di Montenegro; ritratto da' suoi colloqui,* in his *Letture di Famiglia,* I (Trieste, 1852). Impressions of Njegoš by an Italian writer.

Vladimir Ćorović, "Njegošev deseterac," *Misao,* XIX (1925), 1371–1379. An analysis of Njegoš's decasyllabic line.

Jovan Cvijić, *La Péninsule balcanique; géographie humaine* (Paris, 1918). A capital work on the human geography of the Balkan Peninsula by the leading Serbian geographer. There is an expanded Serbian translation entitled *Balkansko Poluostrvo i južnoslovenske zemlje—Osnove antropogeografije* (Belgrade, 1922).

Branislav Djurdjev, *Turska vlast u Crnoj Gori u XVI i XVII veku* (Sarajevo, 1953). An important monograph dealing with Montenegro's relations with the Ottoman Empire in the 16th and 17th centuries.

Risto J. Dragićević, "Godina Njegoševog rodjenja," *Istoriski zapisi,* II, Nos. 5–6 (1948), 259–268. Deals with the problem of the date of Njegoš's birth.

——, *Članci o Njegošu* (Cetinje, 1949). A collection of articles on such subjects as the date of Njegoš's birth, his family, his education, the Billiard, the historical characters in *The Mountain Wreath,* his illness and death, and the removal of his remains to Mount Lovćen.

——. "Guvernaduri u Crnoj Gori," *Zapisi,* XXIII (1940), 14–27, 75–95, 144–159. A study of the institution of the Governor in Montenegro.

——, "Njegoševi roditelji i braća," *Istoriski zapisi,* II, Nos. 1–2 (1948), 9–38. This study describes Njegoš's family, especially his parents and brothers.

——, "Njegoševo ukidanje guvernadurstva," *Istoriski zapisi,* III, Nos. 1–2 (1949), 1–22, 134–155. Based on previously unpublished documents, this article describes how the Venetian-imposed office of Governor of Montenegro was abolished by Njegoš.

——, "Testament mitropolita Petra I," *Istoriski zapisi,* III, Nos. 5–6 (1949), 233–247. Deals with the problem of the authenticity of the last will and testament of Bishop Petar I, which brought Njegoš to the throne.

Sekula Drljević, "Organizacija crnogorskih redovnih gradjanskih sudova u svome istoriskom razvitku," *Arhiv za pravne i društvene nauke,* IX (1910), 386–412. A historical survey of the organization of civil courts in Montenegro.

Nićifor Dučić, *Crna Gora* (Belgrade, 1874; also in *Književni radovi,* Vol. III, 1894). A history of Montenegro by a Serbian archimandrite of Hercegovina, a warrior-priest and littérateur.

Ljubomir Durković-Jakšić, "Njegošev lik," *Glasnik,* Official Journal of the Serbian Orthodox Church (1947), 108–115. A description of Njegoš's portraits. Also in *Stogodišnjica Gorskog vijenca* (Belgrade, 1947), published by the Serbian Patriarchate.

——, "Njegošev veliki san," *Glasnik Srpske pravoslavne crkve* (1946), 154–157. This study sheds light on Njegoš's "great dream" to become the Patriarch of the entire Serbian Orthodox Church.

——, "Njegoševa država i Vojvodina," *Glasnik Srpske pravoslavne crkve* (1948), 131–138. This study tells of Njegoš's enthusiasm for the movement of the Serbs in Austria in 1848 and of his desire to intervene actively

——, "Njegoševe slike," *Glasnik,* Official Journal of the Serbian Orthodox Church (1947), 129–130. Portraits of Njegoš. Also in *Stogodišnjica Gorskog vijenca* (Belgrade, 1947).

—— (Lubomir Durkowicz), *Petar II Petrović-Njegoš 1813–1851* (Warsaw, 1938). Written by a leading Montenegrin scholar, this monograph is in Polish.

——, *Srbijanska štampa o Njegošu i Crnoj Gori 1833–1851* (Belgrade:

Serbian Academy of Sciences, 1951). Valuable excerpts from the press of Serbia 1833 to 1851 regarding Montenegro and Njegoš. See p. 207, No. 300, for the telegram announcing Njegoš's death, to which Djilas refers.

Jovan Erdeljanović, "Stara Crna Gora; etnička prošlost i formiranje crnogorskih plemena," *Srpski Etnografski Zbornik,* XXXIX (1926), 1–891. A study of the origins of the Montenegrin population and tribal organization by a leading Serbian ethnographer.

Andra Gavrilović, "Godina Njegoševa rodjenja," *Godišnjica Nikole Čupića,* XXIX (1910), 171–176.

Gerhard Gesemann, *Die Serbo-kroatische Literatur* (Leipzig, 1930). The Serbian translation is entitled *Srpsko-hrvatska književnost* (Belgrade, 1934).

——, *Heroische Lebensform zur Literatur und Wesenskunde der Balkanischen Patriarchalität* (Berlin, 1943). A study of heroism in literature within the framework of Balkan patriarchal society.

Julius Heidenreich, "Sima Milutinović i Njegoševa 'Luča Mikrokozma,' " *Prilozi,* XVIII (1938), 122–139. A Czech scholar analyzes the similarities between Milutinović's themes and Njegoš's *Ray of the Microcosm.*

Josef Holeček, *Za svobodu; kresby z bojů černohorských a hercegovských proti Turkům* (Prague: Part I, 1878; Part II, 1879; Part III, 1880; 2nd edition, 1883). Translated into Serbo-Croatian by K. Dančin, *Za slobodu–slike i crte iz crnogorskih i hercegovačkih bojeva protiv Turske* (Novi Sad: Vol. I, 1880; Vol. II, 1881).

Ilija Jelić, "Staro crnogorsko pravosudje," *Cetinje i Crna Gora* (Belgrade, 1927), 267–277. A study of old legal institutions among the Montenegrins.

Konstantin Jireček, *Istorija Srba,* translated by Jovan Radonić, Vols. I–IV (Belgrade, 1922–23).

Jagoš Jovanović, "Crna Gora u revolucionarnoj 1848 godini," *Istoriski zapisi* (1948), 3–11. Deals with Montenegro and Njegoš's attitude toward the 1848 Revolution.

Vuk Stefanović Karadžić, *Crna Gora i Boka Kotorska* (Belgrade: Srpska Književna Zadruga, 1922; also Novo Pokolenje, 1953). Translated from the German.

——, *Montenegro und die Montenegriner; ein Beitrag zur Kentniss des europäischen Türkei und des serbischen Volkes* (Stuttgart and Tübingen, 1837).

——, *Vukova prepiska,* 7 vols. (Belgrade, 1907–1913). This is the most complete collection of Karadžić's letters. Vol. VI is especially useful on Montenegrin matters.

J. G. Kohl, *Reisen nach Istrien, Dalmatien und Montenegro* (Dresden: Part I, 1851; Part II, 1856). A German travel account which deals with Montenegro in Part II, pages 269–369.

Petar Kolendić, "Njegoš u Državnom arhivu u Veneciji," *Zbornik radova Instituta za proučavanje književnosti SAN,* II (1952), 269–283. This study deals with the concern of Austrian authorities over Njegoš's researches in the State Archives of Venice.

——, "Njegoš u Dubrovniku," *Glasnik Skopskog Naučnog Društva,* XXI (1940), 83–93. A study of Njegoš's sojourn in Dubrovnik based on the archives of that city.

——, "Njegošev 'Glas kamenštaka' u talijanskom prevodu Petra Sentića," *Spomenik Srpske kraljevske akademije,* XCIV (73), 1–49.

Egor P. Kovalevskii, *Chernogoriia i slavianskie zemli* (St. Petersburg, 1872).

——, *Chetyre mesiatsa v Chernogorii* (St. Petersburg, 1841). A Russian officer and geologist describes his four months' stay in Montenegro during Njegoš's reign.

——, *Putevyia zapiski o slavianskikh zemliakh* (St. Petersburg, 1859). A travel account of Montenegro.

Risto Kovijanić, "P. P. Njegoš, Gorski Vijenac. Osmo izdanje M. Rešetara . . . ," *Prilozi,* III (1923), 254–261. A review of *The Mountain Wreath.*

Charles Lamb, "A Ramble in Montenegro," *Blackwood's Magazine* (1845), 33–51. A travel account by an Englishman who, with his wife, visited Montenegro in late 1843.

Pëtr Alekseevich Lavrov, *Pëtr II Petrovich Negosh, vladyka Chernogorii i ego literaturnaia deiatel'nost'* (Moscow, 1887). A standard Russian work on Njegoš's literary activity.

A. Henry Layard, *Autobiography and Letters* (London, Vols. I–II, 1903). The section on Montenegro and Njegoš is in Volume I, pp. 39–49.

François Lenorman (also Lenormant), "Description et histoire du Monténégro," *Revue Orientale et Américaine* (1849), and, separately, in Paris.

——, *Turcs et Monténégrins* (Paris, 1866).

Mladen Leskovac, "O prevodima Njegoševa Gorskoga vijenca," *Letopis Matice Srpske,* CCCLXI (1947), 28–36. Also in his *Članci i eseji* (Novi Sad, 1949), 53–63. A critique of the translations of *The Mountain Wreath.*

Pierre Loti, *Voyage en Monténégro* (Paris, 1899). An account by the French writer of his trip to Montenegro in October and November of 1889.

Ivan Lovrić (G. Lovrich), *Osservazioni sopra diversi pezzi del "Viaggio in Dalmatia" dell'Abate Fortis* (Venice, 1776).

Sima Matavulj, *Iz Crne Gore i Primorja* (Zagreb: Matica Hrvatska, Vol. I, 1888; Vol. II, 1889). A rich gallery of Montenegrin types by a well-known Dalmatian writer who spent some time in Montenegro.

Ivan Mažuranić, *Smrt Smail-age Čengijića* first appeared in the almanac *Iskra* (1846). It has been published in many editions in Serbo-Croatian, and there are translations in German, Hungarian, Russian, French, Italian, Swedish, Polish, and Czech. The English translation, *The Death of Smail Aga,* was published by James W. Wiles (London, 1925).

Milorad Medaković, *Povijestnica Crnegore* (Zemun, 1850). A pioneer history of Montenegro by one of Njegoš's secretaries and closest collaborators.

Dimitrije Milaković, *Istorija Crne Gore* (Zadar, 1856).

Marko Miljanov, *Primjeri čojstva i junaštva* (1901). This recital of Montenegrin "manliness and heroism" by the chieftain of the Kuči has become a classic of Serbian literature.

Jevto Milović, "Austrijski izvještaji o posjeti Crnoj Gori ruskog rudarskog kapetana Jegora Kovaljevskog," *Istoriski zapisi,* III, Nos. 5–6 (1948), 248–259. This describes the mission of a Russian officer, Kovalevsky, to Montenegro in 1838, based on Austrian reports.

——, "Boravak Jakova Ozereckovskog u Crnoj Gori," *Istoriski zapisi,* IX, No. 1 (1953), 114–123. This description of an official Russian mission to Njegoš is based on the archives of Zadar (Zara).

——, "Dnevnik Eduarda Grija od 7 aprila 1842 g.," *Istoriski zapisi,* VII, Nos. 1–3 (1951), 68–72. Eduard Griez de Ronse, Austrian official involved in border negotiations with Montenegro, left an account, in French, of the four days he spent in Montenegro and with Njegoš in 1842. The original is in the Archives of Zadar (Zara).

——, *Memoari o ispravljanju granice izmedju Dalmacije i Crna Gore od kapetana Fridriha Oreškovća iz 1838 god.* (Cetinje: Historical Institute of Montenegro, 1949). This study of the attempts to rectify the Austrian-Montenegrin border in 1838 is based on the reports of an Austrian officer which furnish a detailed picture of Njegoš.

——, "Neki arhivski podaci o Njegoševom učitelju Josifu Tripoviću," *Stvaranje,* VII–VIII (1952), 472–473. Some facts about Njegoš's teacher Tropović or Tripović.

——, "O kovanju medalja u doba vladike Rada," *Istoriski zapisi,* V, Nos.1–3 (1950), 69–74. This study describes the visit to Kotor in 1839 of the Russian emissary A. V. Chevkin.

——, "O podizanju Njegoševe kapele na Lovćenu," *Istoriski zapisi,* VII, Nos. 1–3 (1951), 117–119. On the erection of Njegoš's tomb on Mount Lovćen.

——, "Pokušaj Austrije da otme Njegošu Podmaine i Stanojeviće," *Istoriski zapisi,* VII, Nos. 7–9 (1951), 311–319. This study deals with Austria's attempt to deprive Montenegro of two monasteries along the border.

——, "Posjeta kralja saksonskoga Fridriha Augusta vladici Radu 1838 g.," *Istoriski zapisi,* III, Nos. 1–2 (1949), 50–61. This is a description of the visit to Montenegro in 1838 by King Frederick August of Saxony.

Ljubomir Nenadović, *Pisma iz Italije* (Belgrade, 1907; also 1946 and 1950). A collection of "Letters from Italy" by a well-known Serbian writer who was at Njegoš's side during the latter's last days in Italy and who left a description of Njegoš which has become a classic of Serbian literature.

Petar Petrović Njegoš, *Cjelokupna djela,* edited by Danilo Vušović, 2nd edition (Belgrade, 1936). In addition to Njegoš's literary works, this volume contains a collection of 71 letters by Njegoš.

——, *Njegoševa bilježnica* (Cetinje: Historical Institute, 1956). This volume contains a facsimile copy of Njegoš's *Notebook,* photographed from the original, the gift of Xenia Petrović, the daughter of King Nicholas I of Montenegro. There is also a printed transcription in the second part of the volume.

A. A. Paton, *Highlands and Islands of the Adriatic* (London, 1848), Vols. I–II.

Vuko Pavićević, "Sadržaj i pjesnička snaga 'Gorskog vijenca,'" *Omladinski pokret* (Cetinje), June 12, 1947. A critique of the poetic inspiration in *The Mountain Wreath.*

Milivoje Pavlović, "Struktura Gorskog vijenca," *Glasnik, Službeni list Srpske Pravoslavne Crkve* (1947), 50–55; also in *Stogodišnjica Gorskog vijenca* (Belgrade: Serbian Orthodox Patriarchate, 1947). An analysis of the structure of *The Mountain Wreath.*

Branislav Petronijević, "Filozofija u 'Luči mikrokozma,'" introduction to *Luča mikrokozma* (Belgrade, 1923), iv–xvi. An analysis of Njegoš's philosophy in *The Ray of the Microcosm.*

Rastko Petrović, "Sa Gorskim vijencem," *Srpski književni glasnik,* XVI (1925), 531–533. A critique of *The Mountain Wreath* by a leading Serbian littérateur.

Svetislav Petrović, "Znepoljac–prvi učitelj velikog Njegoša. Misail Cvetković-Bajkuš," *Republika* (Belgrade), February 28, 1950.

Vasilije Petrović, *Istoriia o Chernoi Gory* (Moscow, 1754). This is the first published history of Montenegro, by a predecessor of Njegoš's who was Bishop of Montenegro 1744–1766. The author published it during his mission to Russia, in order to impress the Russian government.

Aleksandr N. Popov, "Ocherk istorii Chernogorii," *Zhurnal Ministerstva Narodnogo Prosveshcheniia,* XLIX (1846), otd. II, 17–118. An early history of Montenegro, by a Russian historian.

——, *Puteshestvie v Chernogoriiu* (St. Petersburg, 1847). A travel account of Montenegro.

Pavle Popović, "Jedno izgubljeno delo Njegoševo," *Srpski književni glasnik,* IV (1901), 317–320. Deals with the History of Montenegro that Nenadović mentions in his *Letters from Italy* as having been dictated by Njegoš for the French writer Stanislas Bellanger.

——, *O Gorskom vijencu* (Mostar, 1900; second, revised edition, Belgrade, 1923). An analysis of *The Mountain Wreath* by a distinguished Serbian historian of literature.

Petar I. Popović, *Crna Gora u doba Petra I i Petra II* (Belgrade: Srpska Književna Zadruga, 1951). Until the appearance of Djilas's work, the second half of this monograph was the only historical work devoted entirely to a survey of the reign of Njegoš in its political aspects.

Jaša Prodanović, "Petar II Petrović Njegoš," introduction to Njegoš's *Lažni car Šćepan Mali* (Belgrade, 1902), 1–56.

Milan Rešetar, "Zur Erklärung des Gorski Vijenac," *Archiv für slavische Philologie,* XI (1888), 289–297. The first of many articles by this Serbian literary critic and historian on the subject of Njegoš's literary works.

Alexander Reutz, "Die freien Landgemeinden von Zernagora (Montenegro), Poglizza und Andere," *Dorpater Jahrbücher,* Nos. 2, 4, 5 (1933). Djilas probably came to know of this work by the Russian professor in the article by Ljubomir Vlačić, "Ruski profesor Aleksandar Reutz u Crnoj Gori 1832," *Prilozi za književnost, jezik, istoriju i folklor,* XV, Nos. 1–2 (1935), 156–165.

Pavel Apollonovich Rovinskii, *Chernogoriia v eia proshlom i nastoiashchem* (St. Petersburg: Vol. I, 1888; Vol. II, Part 1, 1897; Vol. II, Part 2, 1901; Vol. II, Part 3, 1909; Vol. II, Part 4, 1909; Vol. III, 1915). The major Russian work on Montenegro before the 1917 Revolution.

Ilarion Ruvarac, *Montenegrina* (Sremski Karlovci, 1897). A classic by the father of the Critical School of Serbian historiography, who enjoyed exploding myths.

Alois Schmaus, "Njegoš i Milton," *Misao,* XIX (1925), 1128–1142. A comparison of Milton's *Paradise Lost* and Njegoš's *Ray of the Microcosm* by the leading German expert on Njegoš as a writer.

——, *Njegoševa Luča mikrokozma* (Belgrade, 1927). A study of Njegoš's *Ray of the Microcosm.*

Isidora Sekulić, *Njegošu, knjiga duboke odanosti* (Belgrade: Srpska Književna Zadruga, 1951). Until the appearance of Djilas's work, this study of Njegoš's life and works by a leading Serbian literary critic was the standard work on Njegoš as a writer. It is particularly known for its literary qualities and philosophical insight.

M. T. Selesković, "Poseta Gustava ritera fon Frankla Njegošu," *Letopis Matice Srpske,* CCCVI (1925), 84–35. On the visit of Ludwig August Frankl to Njegoš.

Serbian Patriarchate, *Stogodišnjica Gorskog vijenca* (Belgrade, 1947). A volume published to commemorate the hundredth anniversary of *The Mountain Wreath.* It reprints many articles from the *Glasnik,* or Official Journal, of the Serbian Orthodox Church, many of which Djilas has obviously used.

Jovan Skerlić, *Istorija nove srpske književnosti* (Belgrade, 1912). Pages 109–116 of this standard survey of modern Serbian literature deal with Njegoš's literary works. There are several later editions of this work, for example, 1914 and 1921.

Pero Slijepčević, "Gorski vijenac i pozornica," *Srpski književni glasnik,* XLIV (1935), 447–454. A study of the attempts to perform *The Mountain Wreath* on the stage.

Pero Šoć, "O posveti 'Gorskog vijenca,'" *Glasnik Srpske Akademije Nauka,* I, Nos. 1–2 (1949), 181–182. Deals with problems connected with Njegoš's Dedication in *The Mountain Wreath.*

——, "Pohod vladike Rada na Podgoricu," *Istoriski zapisi,* VI, Nos. 7–9 (1950), 293–295. This contains two previously unknown Austrian documents dealing with Njegoš's campaign against Podgorica in 1832.

L. O. Vialla de Sommières, *Travels in Montenegro, containing a topographical, picturesque and statistical account of that hitherto undescribed country* (London, 1820). An English translation of the work below.

——, *Voyage historique et politique au Monténégro, Contenant l'origine des Monténégrins, peuple autochtone ou aborigène et très peu connu* etc. Vols. I–II (Paris, 1820). A sweeping account of Montenegrin ethnography, ethnology, geography, etc. by a French colonel who was Napoleon's commandant and governor in Kotor during the French occupation, from 1807 to 1813.

Dušan Stojanović, "Milton i Njegoš," *Hrišćansko Delo* (1939), 339–351, and separately. Also published in 1940 as Volume 41 of the Luč series. This is a detailed comparison of Milton's *Paradise Lost* and Njegoš's *Ray of the Microcosm.*

Dragoslav Stranjaković, "Njegoš i Djordje Stratimirović," *Glasnik Srpske pravoslavne crkve* (1951), 130–133. Deals with Njegoš's relations with a leader of the Serbs in Austrian Vojvodina.

——, "Njegoš i Srbija," *Glasnik Srpske pravoslavne crkve* (1947), 75–85. Discusses Njegoš's contacts with the Principality of Serbia.

Djordje Stratimirović, *Was ich erlebte* (Vienna, 1911). An account by an Austrian general of Serbian origin who met Njegoš. Vladimir Ćorović translated it into Serbo-Croatian under the title *Uspomene Djenerala Stratimirovića* (Vienna, 1912).

Imbro Ignjatijević Tkalac, "De visu et auditu," *Vijenac* (1893), 304–306.

Laza Tomanović, "Dogadjaj na Bašinoj Vodi," *Brankovo Kolo* (1896), 1203–1208.

Jovan N. Tomić, *Crna Gora za morejskog rata 1684–1699* (Belgrade: Posebna izdanja of the Royal Serbian Academy, Vol. XXV, 1907). A historical study of Montenegro during the Morean War, 1684–1699.

——, "Kako se Šćepan Mali dokopao vlasti u Crnoj Gori," *Cetinje i Crna Gora* (1927), 67–95. A historical study on how Stephen the Small came to power.

Emile Vandervelde, "Au Monténégro," *Revue de Belgique,* VII, No. 2 (1893).

Nikola Vasojević, "Notice abregée sur les tribus de la Haute-Albanie, et notamment sur les montagnes indépendantes, tirée de l'histoire, des chansons nationales, des lettres patentes et des anciens manuscrits qui se trouvent dans les différentes tribus," *Bulletin de la Société de Géographie* (March, 1841). This is the article by Nikola "Consul" to which Djilas refers. For more about Nikola Vasojević see Dušan D. Vuksan, "Knez Nikola Radonjić-Vasojević," *Zapisi,* XXIII (1940), 213–224; for his letters, see *op. cit.,* 228–233, 301–304.

Nikolaj Velimirović, *Religija Njegoševa* (Belgrade: 1911, 2nd edition 1921). First published as a series of articles in the Belgrade journal *Delo,* this is a famous study of Njegoš's peculiar religious outlook by a well-known bishop of the Serbian Orthodox Church.

Ljubo Vlačić, "Učitelj Njegošev Mršić-Tropović," *Prilozi,* XVII (1937), 245–248. Some facts about Njegoš's teacher Tropović or Tripović.

Vuk Vrčević, *Život Petra II Petrovića Njegoša* (Novi Sad: Matica srpska, 1914). A biography of Njegoš written in 1870 by a collaborator of Karadžić and Bogišić, and who served as secretary to Njegoš's successor Prince Danilo 1852–1855.

R. Vrhovac, "Ideja o borbi za život u Njegoša," *Letopis Matice Srpske,* CCCVI (1925), 23–32. An analysis of the idea of the struggle for life in Njegoš's works.

——, "Petar Petrović Njegoš," *Letopis Matice Srpske,* CCCV (1925), 147–154.

Dušan D. Vuksan, "Da li je vladika Rade pisao istoriju Crne Gore?" *Zapisi,* XV (1936), 194–201. Deals with the History of Montenegro that, Nenadović reports in his *Letters from Italy,* Njegoš dictated for the use of the French writer Stanislas Bellanger.

——, "Gagićeva misija u Crnoj Gori 1832 godine," *Zapisi,* XIX (1938), 129–138. The mission to Montenegro in 1832 by Gagić, Russian consul in Dubrovnik.

——, "Govori uz članak Frankla 'Knez Pesnik' o vezama Frankla i vladike Rada," *Zapisi,* XX (1938), 34–35. On the connections between Frankl and Njegoš.

——, "Nekoliko dokumenata iz kotorskih arhiva," *Zapisi,* XIX (1938), 117–118, 172–177, 241–248, 308–312, 372–378; XX, 45–51. A collection of documents from the archives of Kotor.

——, *Njegoševa pisma,* I (Belgrade, 1940).

Svetislav Vulović, "Petar Petrović Njegoš, pesnik srpski," *Godišnjica Nikole Čupića,* I (1877), 310–347. A pioneer work on the significance of Njegoš's poetry. Also in Vulović's Collected Works, *Celokupna dela* (Belgrade: Biblioteka srpskih pisaca), Vol. I, 79–119.

J. Gardner Wilkinson, *Dalmatia and Montenegro, with a journey to Mostar in Hercegovina and remarks on the Slavonic nations; the history of Dalmatia and Ragusa; the uscocs* (London: Vol. I, 1848; Vol. II, 1863). One of the more famous and useful travel accounts of Montenegro, by an Englishman.

Radovan Zogović, "Predgovor," in P. P. Njegoš, *Gorski vijenac* (Belgrade, 1948). The preface to *The Mountain Wreath* by a contemporary Montenegrin writer and critic.

Index

Ahmet Pasha, 315
Albania, 8, 17, 19, 36, 76, 77, 96, 198, 215, 251, 410, 453, 468; rebellion in, 62, 92, 94
Albigenses, 269
Aleksić, Mirko, 180, 184
Alexander (Karadjordjević), Prince, 4n, 160, 407, 408, 411, 415, 419, 420, 423, 467, 468
Alexander, Tsar, 147
Alexis, Deacon, 45
Ali Aga, *see* Čengić, Ali Aga
Ali Pasha, *see* Rizvanbegović, Ali Pasha
Allgemeine Zeitung, 234
Anacreon, 280
Ananija, Archbishop of Raška and Prizren, 74
Andrić, Ivo, 335, 339, 431
Andrija, Father (character in *Stephen the Small*), 376, 389
Arad, 40
Aristotle, 280
Arslan Aga (character in *The Mountain Wreath*), 362
Austria, 17, 25, 73, 88, 89, 101, 103, 104, 134, 145, 147, 264; annexes Bay of Kotor, 51, 52; border question in, 25, 112, 130, 136, 162–66, 209, 224; dissolution of empire of, 404; emperor of, 414; interest of, in Montenegro, 53; occupies Montenegro, 467; political background of, 106; relations of, with Montenegro, 56–57, 81–83, 85, 118, 126, 142, 163–68, 170, 192, 196, 249, 256–58, 379, 400–06, 423; South Slavs' severance from, 415–16; spies of, 257–58; territorial claims of, 105
Austria-Hungary, 101, 404
Avvakum, 374

Bacon, Roger, 293
Bajica, Bishop Vissarion, 251, 311
Bajović, 454
Bakić, Ljubomir A., 73
Balerini, Giabasto, 208
Balkans, 8, 36, 150, 170, 198, 217, 254, 318, 319, 331, 341, 342, 372, 405, 406, 407, 425
Ban, Matija, 270, 322–23, 409, 410–11, 415, 419–20, 423, 425, 435
Banašević, Nikola, 45, 47, 267, 270, 280
Banija, 414
Banja Luka, 446
Banjani, the, 90
Banović Strahinja, 330
Basil the Great, 280
Bašine Vode, 190–91
Batrić, sister (characters in *The Mountain Wreath*), 241, 325, 328, 356–60, 363, 369
Bauk, Büyükbasha Ahmet, 178–80
Bayazid (Ilderim), 199
Begovići, the, 202
Belgrade, 40, 188, 397, 409, 420, 423, 425, 463, 464, 467
Bellanger, Stanislas, 441
Belomov, Gigoje, 199
Bembo, Doge, 21
Besac, 226
Bešina, Božo, 223
Biasoletto, Bartolomeo, 154

Bib Doda, 411
Bible, the, 47; as influence on Njegoš's poetry, 267, 269, 281, 282, 285, 287. *See also* Njegoš: religious philosophy of
Bijela Monastery, 180
Billiard, the, 155–57, 159, 233, 462, 467
Bjelica, 67
Bjelopavlić, Mirčeta, 137
Bjelopavlić, Vido, 137, 152
Bjelopavlići, the, 15, 55, 56, 60, 67, 133, 134, 136, 137, 141, 152, 180, 222; rebellion of, 251
Blood feuds, 135, 211–13, 227
Bocchesi, the, 403, 404
Bogišić, Professor Valtazar, 210
Bogomils, 269, 318
Bojović, Vojvoda Laza, 77–78
Boka, 34–36
Boljevići, village of, 226
Borčanin, Murat, 192
Borce, 446
Bosnia, 56, 75, 99, 100, 102, 138, 142, 169, 173, 184, 199, 409, 410, 420, 423, 445, 446; rebellion in, 62, 92–97, 100–02; Vizir of, *see* Mahmud Hamdi Pasha; Omer Pasha Latas
Bosporus, 109
Božović, Marko, 223
Božović, Rade, 192
Božović, Senator Todor Mušikin, 152, 222, 226–27, 228, 238
Božović brotherhood, 227
Brady, General Thomas, 207
Branković, Despot Djuradj, 14, 14n
Branković, Vuk, 14n, 336, 337
Brda (the Highlands), 15, 95
Brdjani (Highlanders), 30
Brkić, Patriarch (character in *Stephen the Small*), 387
Brockhaus Encyclopedia, 52
Bucharest, 463
Budapest, 40, 397
Budva, 36, 154, 164, 234
Buffon, Georges, 280
Bulgaria, 145
Buljubaša, Zeko, 40
Bushati (Crnojević), 200
Bushati, Kara-Mahmud Pasha, Vizir of Scutari, 51, 54–56, 57, 72–74, 99, 155, 169
Bushati, Mustafa Pasha, Vizir of Scutari, 93, 96, 98–99
Bushati, Tahir Pasha, 315
Bushatis, the, 198
Byron, Lord, 157
Byzantium, 318

Caboga, Count, 118–19, 165
Čajkanović, Veselin, 267
Candian War, 11
Carev Laz, Battle of, 315
Carrara, Francesco, 449
Cathedral of the Transfiguration of the Saviour (St. Petersburg), 116
Catherine the Great, 146, 251
Cek, Jakov, 33
Čekliće, 42
Ceklin, 66, 68, 141, 223
Čelikov Potok, 142
Čengić, Ali Aga, elder of Taslica, 180
Čengić, Smaïl Aga, Lord of Gacko, 101, 142–43, 175–84, 189, 198, 200, 214, 435
Čengići, the, 175
Cerović, Milutin, 177
Cerović, Novica, 157, 177–81, 183–84, 186, 391, 429, 434, 461, 466
Cetina River, 123–24
Cetinje, 6, 15, 16, 30, 32, 33, 37, 38, 40, 45, 48, 52, 54–56, 62, 64, 70, 82, 84, 90, 93, 103, 105, 108, 109, 119–22, 123, 124, 127, 132, 138–40, 149, 151, 154, 155, 164, 165, 168, 171–73, 180–82, 192, 194, 198, 213–17, 221, 223–27, 229, 233–35, 241, 242, 244–46, 249, 252, 257, 280, 310, 313, 320, 403, 409, 420, 423, 429, 434, 435, 445, 451, 452, 453, 456, 457, 464, 466, 467
Cetinje Library, 44
Čevo, 16, 67, 338
Chevkin, Russian official, 166
Church, the, *see* Orthodox Church
Church of the Vlahs (Cetinje), 124
Čipur, 124
Civitavecchia, 437
Clans and tribes, 8, 18–20, 23–24, 25, 35–36, 76, 89, 90, 160, 163, 171, 274; blood tie, 312; chieftains, 26, 160, 161, 164, 187, 203, 212, 213, 218, 219, 248; dissolution of, 207–09; internecine warfare of, 134, 142, 370, 388, 456; justice in, 210; law of, 84; unification of, 54, 58, 78–79, 202, 251–56; vs. state, 54, 122, 133–35, 203–05, 211–13, 215, 218–28, 248, 313. *See also* Blood feuds
Congress of Berlin (1878), 254
Constantine the Philosopher, 319
Cornaro, Doge, 22

Ćorović, Vladimir, 330
Courts, 57, 73, 91, 210. *See also* Law
Crmnica, 10, 51, 90, 141, 163, 166, 167, 194, 219, 222–24, 226, 321, 327, 397; rebellion in, 225–28
Crmnica River, 193
Crnojević, Ivan, 88, 314
Crnojević, Staniša (Stefan), 314
Crnojevići, the, 70, 102, 157, 255, 321, 328, 401
Crnojevići River, 16, 193, 199, 457
Croatia, 402, 403, 404, 405, 409, 411, 412, 413, 415, 419, 423
Čubro, *see* Sarajlija, Sima
Cuce, the, 6, 125, 137, 176, 406
Current Journal, 89, 100
Cvetković-Bajkuš, Mihail, 33
Cvijić, Jovan, 207
Czartoryski, Prince Adam, 217

Dabović, Inokentije, 34
Daković, Vojvoda Anto, 176
Daković, Jakov, Vojvoda of Grahovo, 138, 142, 143, 173, 174, 176–77
Dalmatia, 40, 45, 104, 185, 402, 403, 419, 435; Bishop of, 139; Governor of, 47, 82, 118, 208, 400, 401, 457
Danilo, Bishop, 9, 11, 17, 21–22, 30, 31, 36, 37–38, 49, 50, 53, 54, 59, 66, 87, 112, 123, 145–49, 159, 163, 164, 212, 222, 223, 230, 251, 255, 299, 310, 311, 313–17, 320, 321, 325, 327, 340–46, 348, 350–51, 352, 362, 363, 365, 366, 384, 451
Danilo II (Petrović), Prince, 5n, 6n, 53, 59, 70, 82, 133, 156, 205–06, 210, 212, 213n, 215, 217, 245, 252–56, 259, 421, 432, 447, 456, 461, 464–65, 466, 467
Dante Alighieri, 267, 286
Danube River, 109
Dapčevići, the, 125
Davidović, Father Tomo, 100, 243, 244
Death of Smaïl Aga Čengić (Mažuranić), 182–83
Decembrists, the, 115
Ded Aga, 176
Dedijer, Jevto, 102
Dedinje Palace, 467
Delgos, General, 53
Der Montenegrinische Mensch (Gesemann), 13n
Dioclea, 314
Dirge or Sad Memorial on the Death of My Ten-Year-Old Nephew Pavle Petrović Njegoš (Njegoš), 128
Divine Comedy, The (Dante), 267
Djaković, Joakim, 257
Djeknin, Stevan, 191
Djelal-ud-Din Pasha, Vizir of Travnik, 100
Djordjije (Savov Petrović Njegoš, cousin of Njegoš), 32, 63, 65, 109, 141, 142, 144, 158, 164, 186, 187, 226, 258, 456, 459, 463, 464, 465
Djovanin, Ivo, 125
Djurašković, Bogdan (character in *The Mountain Wreath*), 355
Djurašković, Deacon, 436, 451
Djurašković, Filip Nikolin, Serdar of Rijeka, 6, 66–67, 70, 71, 96, 97, 234, 460–61, 466
Djurdjev, Professor Branislav, 19, 19n, 160
Djuro, Knez, 125
Dnieper River, 318
Dobrnjac, Petar Todorović, 104
Dobrota, 209, 400, 402
Dobrun, 446
Dodoš, 194
Dolac, 156
Dolci de Visković, Francesco, 146, 146n, 147
Dolgorukov, Prince Yuri Vladimirovich (character in *Stephen the Small*), 148, 386, 387, 392–93, 394
Don River, 318
Dožić, Bishop, 467
Dragalji, 173
Dragičević, Risto, 22, 32, 33, 314, 315
Drago, Vojvoda (character in *The Mountain Wreath*), 385
Dragon of Bosnia, 92
Draško, Vojvoda (character in *The Mountain Wreath*), 321, 325–26, 350, 353–54
Drina, Bey of, 446
Drljević, Sekula, 91
Drobnjaci, the, 138, 175, 177–81, 198
Drobnjak, 177, 179, 180
Dubrovnik, 3, 4n, 51, 74, 89, 104, 106–08, 146n, 185–89, 196, 224, 402, 403, 411, 419n, 430, 434, 435, 436, 450
Dučić, Nićifor, 88, 89, 164
Dukljan, Tsar (character in fable), 268
Dumont d'Urville, Jules, 270
Durković-Jakšić, Dr. Ljubomir, 127, 230, 409, 423
Durmitor, Mount, 178
Duvno, 446

Eagle and the Swine, The (Njegoš), 228
Egypt, 93, 97
Elizabeth Petrovna, Empress, 146
Engels, Friedrich, 413
England, 53, 196, 217, 425
Erdeljanović, Jovan, 14
Executions, 227

Fabri-Brettini (Fitz-James), Flora, 236
False Tsar Stephen the Small, The (Njegoš), 49, 130, 132, 148, 228, 232–33, 260, 287, 292, 306, 315, 324, 329, 373–96, 397, 423, 441, 467; analysis of, 261–64; as a social drama, 382–83, 384; characters in, 384, 389–96; comparison of, with *The Mountain Wreath*, 394–96; form of, 331–32, 382–83; kolos in, 331, 394; language in, 333; motif of, 381–96
Family life, 18
Fatima, 40
Ferat Začir (character in *The Mountain Wreath*), 355
Ferdinand, King of Yugoslavia, 402
Ferik Ahmet Pasha, 101, 170
Feudalism, 159–61, 312, 397, 411, 413
Filipović, 200
First World War, 254, 258, 468
Fitz-James, Flora, *see* Fabri-Brettini, Flora
Florence, 437, 446
Flow of Turkish Ire, The (Njegoš), 128, 131
Folklore, *see* Myths and folklore
Fortis, Alberto, 285
France, 51, 53, 145, 146, 147, 196, 207, 217, 246, 401, 413
Francis Joseph I, Emperor of Austria, 414
Franićević, Stijepo, 126
Frankl, Ritter Ludwig August, 234, 302, 302n, 454, 455
Friedrich August, King of Saxony, 154–55, 157
Furlania, 437

Gacko (Kolašin), 142, 175, 180, 183
Gagić, Consul Jeremija, 3, 3–4, 4n, 6, 33, 38, 74, 81, 83, 85, 89, 90, 93, 95, 97, 98, 103, 104–08, 117, 134, 136, 137, 139, 141, 143, 144, 148, 149, 150, 161, 164, 166, 167, 171, 181, 182, 185, 186, 190, 191, 193, 194, 195, 220, 222, 226, 429, 430, 434, 435, 450, 454, 455, 461, 463, 464
Gagović, Prior, 252
Galifen, De, 414
Garašanin, Ilija, 26, 218, 259, 406–11, 417, 423, 435, 436, 463
Gavrilović, Andra, 4, 39
Genoa, 437
Germany, 40, 403, 413
Gesemann, Gerhard, 13, 13n
Gladstone, William, 196, 396
Globari, the, 209
Gnostics, 269, 270
Goethe, 43, 270, 330, 368
Golgi, Dr., 258
Golitsyn, Prince, 146
Golović, 178
Golubovci, village of, 87, 96
Gorica Hill, 95
Grabalj, 401–02
Gradačac, 92
Gradaščević Rebellion, 169
Gradičević, 200
Graf, Elisabeth, 249
Grahovljani, the, 138
Grahovo, 40, 138, 141–43, 170–74, 176–77, 185, 188, 189, 192; Vojvoda of, *see* Daković, Jakov
Grahovo, Plain of, 171
Grand Vizir, *see* Reshid Pasha
Grblji, 126
Great War of 1876, *see* War of 1875–78
Griez de Ronse, Eduard, Captain of Kotor, 168, 243, 244, 401, 403, 406
Grimm, Jacob, 43
Grmožur, 226
Gruža, 104
Guard (Police), 88–89, 91, 134, 151, 203
Gusinje, 68, 69
Gusle (Frankl), 454
Guvernadurovići, the, 8, 67
Guvernadurovići-Radonjići, the, 63

Hadji Ali Bey, 102, 185
Hafis Pasha, Vizir of Scutari, 138
Hafiz Pasha (Rizvanbegović), 445, 446
Hajrović, Mustai Bey ("Hajro"), 189–90, 191
Hanka, Václav, 450
Hapsburg monarchy, 402, 403, 405
Has, 68
Hasan Beg, *see* Resulbegović, Hasan Beg
Hasan Pasha, 195

Hayil, 101
Head-hunting, 133, 136, 142, 143, 155, 174, 180, 215, 235, 244–47, 414
Hegel, Georg, 271, 293
Heidenreich, Julius, 270
Herak (Erak), 8, 9, 80
Herakovići, the, 8
Herceg Novi, 34, 451
Hercegovina, 7, 8, 101, 102, 136, 138, 139, 142, 169, 172, 173, 175, 176, 185, 188, 190–91, 192, 193, 197, 209, 237, 334, 409, 411, 445
Herder, Johann, 43
Hermit of Cetinje, The (Njegoš), 120, 123, 131
Herzen, Aleksandr Ivanovich, 115, 115n
Hexameron (Basil the Great), 280
Histoire naturelle (Buffon), 280
History of Montenegro (Bishop Vasilije), 8, 22, 50, 311
Hitzing, 448, 449
Holeček, Josef, 183
Homer, 110
Hoti, the, 95–96
House of Aleksići, The (Njegoš), 130, 331, 382
Hugo, Victor, 46, 48, 273
Humac, 171, 189, 248
Hume, David, 293
Hungary, 402, 403, 404, 411, 412, 414, 416
Husein, Kapetan, 92, 93–94, 95, 99–101, 102

Ignjatijević-Tkalac, Imbro, 231, 231n
Ignjatović, Jakov, 412
Ilderim, *see* Bayazid
Iliad, 46, 271, 324
Iliński, Count Jan, 446
"Illyrian" movement, 6n
Illyrians, 8, 35
Islam, *see* Moslems
Istanbul, 40, 75, 92–94, 97, 98, 101, 102, 196, 199, 259, 326
Italy, 249, 402, 403, 408, 411, 413, 415, 419, 434–51
Ivačić, Gabriel, 168
Ivanchik, 33, 45
Ivelić, Marko, 107

Jabučanin, Lazo, 124
Jadar, 94
Janizaries, 78, 92
Janko, Knez (character in *The Mountain Wreath*), 326
Janko, Serdar (character in *The Mountain Wreath*), 66
Janković, Kenjo Stanko, 137
Jelačić, Count Josip, 402, 402n, 403, 404, 406, 413–16, 418–19
Jelić, Ilija, 69
Jezeri, 178
Jezerski Vrh, 451
Jireček, Konstantin Josef, 8, 8n
Jome, Antide (Antid Žom or Jaume), 45, 151
Josif, Bishop, 445
Jovan, smith of Zemun, 338
Jovanović, Anastas, 150, 231, 447
Jovo, Serdar (character in *Stephen the Small*), 386

Kadić, Todor, 466
Kameni, Battle of, 370
Kant, Immanuel, 271, 286, 293
Karadjordje, 21, 26, 30, 40, 68, 70, 73–74, 96, 157, 175, 198, 207, 216, 224, 332, 338, 407, 414, 422
"Karadjordje" (Ban), 423
Karadjordjević, Prince Alexander, *see* Alexander, Prince
Karadžić, Šujo, 175–76, 178, 179
Karadžić, Vuk Stefanović, 16, 16n, 17, 21, 22, 53, 59, 112, 114, 131–32, 135, 139, 140, 201, 208, 229, 257, 258, 306, 359, 414, 436, 437, 447, 454, 464
Karlovci, 40, 409
Katuni, Nahi (district) of, 9, 12, 14, 15, 16–17, 23, 29, 30, 67, 122, 223, 321, 332, 333, 350
Katunjani, the (men of Katuni), 9–11, 11–13, 14, 19, 21, 22, 24, 26, 30, 54, 70, 138, 141, 225, 226, 251, 327
Kishinev, 40
Kiuprili, Vizir, 146
Klobuk, town of, 171
Klopstock, Friedrich Gottlieb, 269, 269n
Knežević (Mahmutbegović), Obren, 200
Knićanin, Stevan Petrović, 4, 4n, 218, 420, 453, 463
Kohl, Johann Georg, 110
Kolašin (Gacko), 175, 466
Kolendić, Professor Petar, 110, 126, 186, 187, 243, 379
Koljenovići, 203
Kolos, 320, 324, 360–61, 362, 363, 394
Komani, 223
Kom Kučki, 173
Konjic, 445

Kosjerača, Joka Krstov, 125
Kosovo, Battle of, 11, 14n, 98, 158, 183, 264, 294, 317, 321, 326, 328, 335–37, 339, 340, 349, 367, 369, 370, 409, 422, 442, 443, 468
Kossuth, Lajos, 412
Kostić, Laza, 253–54
Kotor, 16, 17, 25, 40, 72, 82–83, 84, 104, 117, 119, 125, 126, 139, 146, 146n, 148, 154, 165, 168, 196, 215, 225, 258, 259, 379, 400, 403, 429, 430, 434, 451, 457, 458, 459, 463, 464, 465, 466; Captain of, 127, 243, 244, 259, 357, 401
Kotor, Bay of, 21, 33, 34, 35–37, 51, 52, 85, 104, 118, 119, 135, 159, 163, 167, 400, 401, 403–04, 405, 450
Kovačević, Šćepan, 173, 174
Kovalevsky, Captain Egor N., 13, 172, 211
Kovijanić, Risto, 323
Kragujevac, 104, 463
Krajina, 414, 446
Krivošije, 406
Krnjic, 226
Krnovo, 178, 180
Kršikapa, Hajduk Petar, 214, 237–38
Krstac, 16
Krug, Wilhelm, 43
Krusi, 56
Kuči, the, 12n, 14, 15, 19, 69, 188, 205, 209, 215, 216, 223, 251; Vojvoda of, *see* Vukić, Popov
Kulinović, 200
Kuluk (*corvée*), 57, 73

Lamartine, Alphonse de, 46, 48, 273
Lamb, Mr. and Mrs. Charles, 194
Lavrov, Pëtr Alekseevich, 49, 82, 164, 266
Law, 18n, 57, 69, 79, 84, 90, 210–13. *See also* Courts
"Laws of the Fatherland" (Vukotić), 90
Layard, Sir A. Henry, 209
Lazar, Prince, 14n, 335, 343
Lazarević, Jelena, 467
Lazo (gypsy), 233
Leibniz, Gottfried, 293
Lekić, Mehmed Spahi, 185
Lekići, the, 312
Lenormant, François, 52
Lesendro Rock, 193, 194, 196, 197, 220, 226, 238, 250, 260
Leskovac, Mladen, 370
Letters from Italy (Nenadović), 182, 440
Lijeva River, 217
Lika, 414, 445
Lilienberg, Count Wendel V., Governor of Dalmatia, 208
Lim Valley, 68, 223
Littoral, the, 30, 84, 122, 125, 141, 161, 165, 214, 243, 244, 314, 454, 457
Livorno, 437
Lješani, Nahi of, 10, 193, 194, 223, 233, 321
Ljuba, wife of Radun (characters in *The Mountain Wreath*), 356
Ljubljana, 45, 436
Ljubostinje, 246
Ljubotinja, 125, 251
Ljubović, 200
Ljuce, the, 312
Locke, John, 271
Lola, 178
Loti, Pierre, 14
Louis Philippe, 145
Lovćen, Mount, 9, 13, 21, 29, 30, 70, 124, 157, 206, 320, 397, 450, 451, 459, 460, 463, 465, 467, 468, 469
Lovrich, G., 285
Lubarda, Petar, 14
Luka, Father, 205
Lumbardić, Conte, 119
Lumbardić, Dafina, 119

Macedonia, 19, 54, 409
Magic, *see* Myth and folklore
Magyars, 402, 403, 405, 412, 413, 415, 416, 418, 419
Mahmud Hamdi Pasha, Vizir of Bosnia, 100
Mahmud Pasha, *see* Bushati, Kara-Mahmud Pasha
Mahmutbegović, *see* Knežević, Obren
Majine, 105, 144, 145; Monastery of, 36, 163–66
Makarije (Šumadinac), 180
Mamula, Baron Lazar, 457, 457n
Mandušić, Vuk (character in *The Mountain Wreath*), 241, 314–15, 320, 321, 325, 340, 352–53, 356, 362, 363, 364, 368, 384
Mandušić, Vuk, sister-in-law of, 356
Manichaeism, 269
Manin, Daniele, 401
Marinković, Dr. Petar, 284, 429–30, 435, 457
Marko (character in *The Mountain Wreath*), 336

Markov, Savo, *see* Petrović Njegoš, Savo Markov
Marmont, General, 51
Martinići, the, 222, 223
Martinići, Battle of, 56
Martinović, Djuro, 259
Martinović brothers, 351
Marx, Karl, 271, 413
Matavulj, Sima, 213, 213n, 256, 357, 374
Matić, Svetozar, 270
Mazda (Sarajlija), 271
Mažuranić, Ivan, 182–83, 464
Mazurevsky, Aleksandr Josifovich, 146, 146n
Medaković, Milorad, 5, 5n, 24, 45, 127, 130, 157, 189, 204, 224, 229–31, 308, 338
Medović, Hadji Ali (character in *The Mountain Wreath*), 355
Medun, Duke of, 374
Mehemet Ali, 97
Meštrović, Ivan, 469
Metković, 186
Metternich, Prince, 112, 144–45, 162, 166, 196
Michael, Prince, 439, 463, 464
Mićić, Jovan, 175
Mickiewicz, Adam, 218
Mićo, Father (character in *The Mountain Wreath*), 325, 344
Mićunović, Vuk (character in *The Mountain Wreath*), 287, 320, 325, 327, 342, 350–52, 384
Mikići, the, 312
Miklošić, Franc, 429, 429n
Milaković, Dimitrije (secretary to Njegoš), 5, 6, 6n, 46, 87, 88, 104, 108–09, 124, 143, 156, 186, 189, 234, 247, 428, 461, 466
Milan, 437
Miljanov, Marko, 12, 12n, 14, 60, 183, 203, 205, 209, 213–16, 256, 272–73, 334, 386
Miljonić (character in *The Mountain Wreath*), 241, 321
Miljonić, daughter-in-law of (character in *The Mountain Wreath*), 356, 364
Miloradovich, Colonel Mikhail, 146, 148
Miloš (Obrenović), Prince, 4n, 26, 39, 40, 44, 86, 92, 93, 94, 100, 132, 153, 159, 175, 181, 195, 224, 255, 338, 406–07, 463
Miloš Obilić (Sarajlija), 38, 340
Milović, Jevto M., 82, 88
Milton, John, 266–67
Milutinović-Sarajlija, Sima, *see* Sarajlija, Sima
Mirac, village of, 154
Miriditës, 453
Mitrović brothers, 223
Mljetičak, 178, 179
Monasteries: Bijela (Drobnjak), 180; Mother of God, 33; of Cetinje, 54, 132; of Majine, 36, 163–66, 248; of Morača, 132; of Ostrog, 132; of Piva, 252; of Stanjevići, 32, 36, 163–166, 248; St. Alexander Nevsky, 113–14; Savina, 118
Montenegrin Captured by a Fairy, A (Njegoš), 120, 271
Montenegrin Pride, The (Sarajlija), 131
Montenegrin to Almighty God, A (Njegoš), 120, 128, 271
Montenegro, 9, 10, 13, 22, 35, 36, 37, 56, 68, 101, 102, 133, 180, 223; aid from Belgade to, 410; and freedom, 94; annexation of Plain of Zeta by, 145; Assembly of 1770, 73; attacks on, 18, 56, 97, 101, 193; attempt to Europeanize, 133; banishment from, 84; bishopric of, 80, 172–74; border question in, 25, 130, 136, 162–66, 173, 185, 188–89, 209, 224; bourgeois society in, 256; character of, 30, 31; coalition of, with Serbia, projected, 51; cult of the sister in, 240–41; decline of, 256; deprived of outlet to the sea, 52; development of, 126, 254; distinction between Serbs of Serbia and, 420–21; education, 132–33, 257, 300; emergence of, under Bishop Petar, 53; epic poetry of, 241; fall of, in World War I, 99; famine of 1847 in, 221; feudalism in, 18, 159–61, 205, 255; feuds with Hercegovina, 188; first book on, 53; first primer in, 257; first printing press in, 117, 120, 131–33, 155; first prison in, 84; first school in, 132–33; foreign interest in, 52, 53; formation of state of, 208–09, 318; gain in stature, 254; government of, 57, 73–75, 80, 88–89, 90–91, 131, 144, 251–56, 375, 376; governorship of, 8, 38, 72–73; heroic poems of, 76; historical role of, 117; history of, 8, 12, 18n, 22, 47, 50, 108, 254, 255, 311; illiteracy in, 131; independ-

ence of, 57, 98, 168–69, 256, 314; in poetry, 53; internal disorganization of, 86; internal stabilization of, 103–04; invasion of, 252, 447; isolation from Western Europe, 397; landscape of, 14, 122–23; land scarcity in, 76; lawlessness of, 209; migration from, 75; mourning custom in, 357; national costume of, 135, 158–59; nationhood of, 421; negotiations of, with Hercegovina, 185; no class distinction in, 207; occupation of, by Austrians, 467; occupation of Gacko by, 183; origin of name of, 14; orthography, 132, 414; overpopulation of, 75–76; participation of, in Bosnian rebellion, 93–97; peasants of, 5; penury of, 249; people of, 57, 77, 207, 208, 229, 232, 245, 263, 300; population of, 15; pretenders in, 374–75; rebellions in, 66, 70, 141–42, 219–28, 251, 260, 397; religious beliefs, 27–29, 76, 272, 347; reports on, 105; robber economy of, 75–76, 188; role of, in Candian War, 11; role of poetry in, 303; secularization of throne of, 464–65; similarity of, to classical Greece, 110; social differences in, 76; sovereignty of, 165, 166; struggle for survival as independent country, 225; territorial rights of, 105; trade in, 17; turning point in history of, 315, 377; unification of, 250; unification with Serbia, 421–26; uniforms in, 152; weakness of, 195, 419; women in, 84, 356–60. *See also* Austria, relations with; Blood feuds; Clans and tribes; Courts; Family life; Guard; Head-hunting; Law; Myths; Russia, relations with; Senate; Taxation; Turkey, relations with

Morača, 132, 177, 178, 182

Moračani, the, 138, 179

Morača River, 95, 172

Morea (Peloponnesus), 19, 54

Morean War, 22, 311

Morgunov, 114

Moslems, 20, 76–77, 92, 95, 97, 100, 101, 159, 175, 246, 259, 291, 312–13, 314, 337, 354, 394, 414, 445

Mostar, 101, 142, 169, 173, 174, 181, 187, 445, 446; Vizir of, *see* Rizvanbegović, Ali Pasha

Mountain Wreath, The (Njegoš), 36, 48, 66, 98, 101, 111–12, 121, 128–29, 130, 138, 148, 159, 168, 212, 220, 224, 228, 230, 232, 246, 254, 260, 261–64, 272, 280, 287–88, 292, 294–95, 297, 299–300, 305, 306, 308, 309, 310–72, 373, 374, 377, 378–79, 381, 382, 383, 388, 390, 391, 394, 441, 445, 467; analysis of, 261–64; characters in, 325–28, 340–61, 384; compared with classic Greek drama, 323–24; comparison of, with *Stephen the Small,* 394–96; dedication of, 332–33, 338; first theatrical presentation of, 329; form of, 320–22, 328–31; grammatical peculiarities in, 333; kolos in, 320, 324, 360–61, 362, 363; language of, 333–35; lyrical epic fusion in, 368; motifs of, 310–72; original title of, 314; origin of title of, 339–40; scenes in, 361–64; style of, 365–66; subtitle of, 328; translations of, 370; women in, 356–60

Mourning Dove (almanac), 131

Mrčarica, Radovan, *see* Piper, Radovan

Mrkojević, Teodosije (character in *Stephen the Small*), 49, 379–80, 386, 388, 389–91, 398

Mršulja, Marko, 126

Mula Hasan, 394

Mušicki, Lukijan, 112, 112n

Mušikin, Jovan, 223

Mušikin, Todor, *see* Božović, Todor Mušikin

Mušović, Muy Aga, Captain of Nikšić, 143, 176

Mušovići, the, 312

Mustafa Pasha, *see* Bushati, Mustafa Pasha

Mustaj Kadi (character in *The Mountain Wreath*), 326, 354–55

Muštići, 126

Myths and folklore, 11–12, 15, 16n, 19, 23, 27, 28, 42, 60, 80, 111, 140, 147, 148, 160, 161, 230, 232, 267–68, 271, 274, 283, 285, 294, 300, 302, 308, 310, 325, 329, 330, 357, 358, 359, 361, 365–69, 371, 374, 382, 384, 394, 395, 417, 422, 424

Namik, 101

Naples, 425, 437, 439, 441, 449

Napoleon Bonaparte, 53, 54, 56, 251

Napoleon III, 149

National Library, 44

Nedić, Ljubomir, 182, 439
Nemanja dynasty, 69, 70, 318
Nenadović, Ljuba, 5, 46, 102, 110, 140, 182–83, 249, 323, 353, 425, 438–46, 457
Nenadović, Dean Matija, 438
Nesselrode, Count, 149, 454
Newton, Isaac, 286
Nicholas I, Tsar, 115–16, 151, 414, 447
Night Gathers the Age, The (Njegoš), 36–37, 127, 130, 239–40, 241, 307
Nikac of Rovin, 158, 232, 351
Nikola, Knez (character in *The Mountain Wreath*), 327
Nikola, Prince (King), 26, 59, 85, 99, 183, 203, 205, 210, 212, 214, 225, 240, 243, 245, 252, 253–54, 421, 466, 467, 468
Nikola, King, daughter of, 240
Nikola Consul, Knez, *see* Vasojević, Prince Nikola
Nikolajević, Dean, 435
Nikolin, Vule, 223
Nikšić, 77, 143, 176, 178, 180, 187, 190, 191, 251, 467
Nikšići, the, 15
Nišava Valley, 33
Njegoš (Rade Petrović, Bishop Petar II), LIFE, 17, 20, 25, 28, 31, 53, 88, 93–94, 99, 105; and head-hunting, 247; as an absolute monarch, 204–06, 248, 259; as first patriarch of modern Serbia, 410; as a Petrović, 23–24; as poet of historic movements, 322; as a poet of myths, 383; as a revolutionary, 397; as a ruler, 98, 202, 250–60; as successor of Bishop Petar, 32–33, 63, 64–68, 70–71; as a young man, 109–10; attempts unification of Montenegro, 58; belief in pre-existence, 268–70, 283–85, 287, 301; birth of, 3; birth date of, 4–6; bitterness of, against Prince Miloš, 94; castle of, *see* Billiard, the; character of, 13, 38, 86, 95, 149, 161–62, 206–07, 208, 214, 216, 218–19, 228, 236–50, 259–60, 287; childhood of, 26; complaints against, 149; concern of, for his people, 259; consecration of, 7, 91–92, 112, 116, 118; correspondence of, 4, 75, 84, 89–90, 91, 108, 114, 126–27, 138, 143, 151, 152, 175, 189–90, 191, 195, 199–201, 209, 210, 217, 221, 259, 284, 297, 302–03, 328, 333–34, 357–58, 402, 407–08, 416, 417, 418–19, 423, 425, 426, 434, 435, 436, 437, 442–43, 453, 455, 458; correspondence of, with Gagić, 81, 83, 134, 136, 137, 138–39, 144, 164–65, 167, 171, 182, 190, 191, 194, 195, 226, 429, 454, 455; cult of heroism, 12–13, 23; daily life of, 125–27, 233–35; death of, 457–62; decline of powers of, as a poet, 382; dedication of, to cause, 202; descendants of, 99; designates successor, 456; desire of, to Europeanize Montenegro, 133; development of, as a poet, 127–31; domestic policy of, 202; dress of, 158–59, 162; dying words of, 305; early rule of, 85, 131, 134–35; education of, autodidactic, 32–61, 110; establishes first hostel, 16; establishes first prison, 84; establishes first school, 132–33, 300; family of, 6; firmly established as a sovereign, 228; first trip abroad, 104; funeral of, 463; house of, 90; inaugurates taxes, 91; influence of, in Senate, 98; installation of, as bishop, 177; installed as archimandrite, 74–75; interests and pastimes of, 231–33, 235–36; investiture of, 80; issues patents of nobility, 104–05; knowledge of sciences, 46–47; languages of, 45–46, 151; last illness of, 428–57; lays road, 16; leads attack on Podgorica, 95, 97; love life of, 239–44; love of beauty, 236; manuscripts of, 467; maturation of, 127; monument to, 469; name of, 6–7, 8; name of, changed, 75; neglects church duties, 161; orders murder of Smaïl Aga Čengić, 176–77, 180, 184; originates idea of Yugoslavian state, 423; pardons Vuko Radonjić, 82; parsimony of, 247–50; peak period of creativity of, 129, 260; personal fortune of, 247–48; personality of, 85; photographs of, 150, 231; physical description of, 150–51, 187, 228–31; poem mistakenly attributed to, 182–83; political ideas of, 398–400, 404–26; portraits of, 115, 150, 230, 231, 467; printing press of, 117, 120, 131–33, 155; reign of, 83; relations with Ali Pasha, 102, 174–75, 181, 184–93, 197, 204; relations with chieftains, 96; relations with Djurašković, 66–67; relations with Milaković, 108–

09; relations with Osman Pasha, 196–201; relations with Russia, 95, 98, 137, 147–52, 192, 218, 416; religious philosophy of, 140, 232, 272, 274–302, 347–50, 386–87, 440; role of, 89, 213; rumor of poisoning of, 119; sale of state and church property by, 164–66; seal of, 157–58, 159; secretary of, *see* Milaković, Dimitrije; Nenadović, Ljuba; Serbianism of, 399, 420; spends life in struggle for order, 118; stories of illegitimate son of, 244; struggle of, with the Turks, 122; successor of, 82; Testament of, 255, 297, 430–33, 456, 461, 464; titles of, 158, 159; travels of, to Italy, 201, 236–37, 249, 353, 379, 425, 434–51; travels of, to Russia, 45, 91–92, 103–04, 108, 109–10, 112, 113–17, 118, 127, 131, 134, 139, 145, 149–53, 161, 163, 170, 220, 225; travels of, to Trieste, 104, 109, 150, 151, 153, 196, 236, 243, 434, 436; travels of, to Vienna, 46, 104, 109, 112, 123, 144, 145, 159, 162, 170, 171, 196, 201, 222, 223, 224, 235, 242, 243; willing to renounce rights in new Serbia, 410

Njegoš (Rade Petrović, Bishop Petar II), WORKS: comparison of, with Shakespeare, 340–42; early poetry, 41–43, 92, 110–12, 271; first preserved example of, 34; humor in, 362; influences in, 12, 23, 47, 60, 97, 101, 110, 111, 148–49, 160, 266–396; language of, 305–08; motifs in, 120–23, 128, 241, 259–60, 264, 266–396; non-Christian aspect of, 47; ode to Sarajlija, 41; only love poem, 36–37, 127, 130; poem, 155; poetic language in, 333–35; poetry, 228, 250; social drama in, 382–83; translations, 46, 318, 324; verse form in, 110, 111, 307, 328–31; *Dirge or Sad Memorial on the Death of My Ten-Year-Old Nephew Pavle Petrović Njegoš,* 128; *The Eagle and the Swine,* 228; *The False Tsar Stephen the Small,* 49, 130, 132, 148, 228, 232–33, 260, 261–64, 287, 292, 306, 315, 324, 329, 331–32, 333, 373–96, 397, 423, 441, 467; *The Flow of Turkish Ire,* 128, 131; *The Hermit of Cetinje,* 120, 123, 131; *The House of Aleksići,* 130, 331, 382; *A Montenegrin Captured by a Fairy,* 120, 271; *A Montenegrin to Almighty God,* 120, 128, 271; *The Mountain Wreath,* 36, 48, 66, 98, 101, 111–12, 121, 128–29, 130, 138, 148, 159, 168, 212, 220, 224, 228, 230, 232, 246, 254, 260, 261–64, 272, 280, 287–88, 292, 294–95, 297, 299–300, 305, 306, 308, 309, 310–72, 373, 374, 377, 378–79, 381–84, 388, 390, 391, 394–96, 441, 445, 467; *The Night Gathers the Age,* 36–37, 127, 130, 239–40, 241, 307; *Notebook,* 46, 48, 242, 273, 278, 279, 286, 292; *Ode to Liberty,* 105, 110, 111–12, 163, 239, 311; *Ode to the Sun Written on a Moonless Night,* 128; *The Ray of the Microcosm,* 42, 47, 101, 121, 128–30, 228, 260, 261–309, 324, 332, 346, 349, 369, 373, 378, 382, 384, 386, 396, 432, 451, 467; *Thought,* 127, 130, 301, 307; *The Tower of the Djurišići,* 66, 130, 228, 331, 382; *A Voice from the Rocky Crag,* 110; *Who Is That on Yon High Mountain?,* 129

Njegoš, Mount, 7

Njegoš, Vojvoda, 7, 8

Njeguši, 16, 21, 25, 73, 83, 141, 155, 217, 434, 462, 465; Captain of, 400; Serdar of, 125

Njeguši, the, 6, 7–9, 21, 22–23, 29, 30, 209

Notebook (Njegoš), 46, 48, 242, 273, 278, 279, 286, 292

Nova Varoš, 251, 445

Novi Pazar, 217

Novi Sad, 108

Novotný, 457

Obilić, Miloš, 11, 327, 336, 337, 338, 343, 349, 350

Obilić Medal, 158, 159, 226, 230

Obradović, Dositej, 40, 40n, 132, 153, 318

Obrenović, Prince Miloš, *see* Miloš, Prince

Ode to Liberty (Njegoš), 105, 110, 111–12, 163, 239, 311

Ode to the Sun Written on a Moonless Night (Njegoš), 128

Olmütz, 447

Omer Pasha Latas, Vizir of Bosnia, 252, 443, 445–46, 447

Onogošt, fortress of, 77

Onogšt-Nikšić, 96

Oreškovič, Captain Friedrich, 155, 257–58, 286
Orfelin, Zaharija, 315
Origen, 269, 270, 283, 284
Orlov, General Aleksei Fëdorovich, 416
Orlova-Chesmenskaya, Countess, 116
Orthodox Church, 20, 21, 76–77, 79, 81, 100, 145, 147, 160, 251, 312, 313, 347, 349, 424, 430
Osijek, 101
Osman Aga, 189
Osman Kapetan, 100
Osman Pasha, *see* Skopljak, Osman Pasha
Osmanli, the, 192, 197
Oštra Kosa, 180
Ostrog, 125, 132, 190; Archimandrite of, *see* Pavičević, Josif
Otočac, 445
Ottoman Empire, *see* Turkey
Ozeretskovsky, Lieutenant Colonel Jakov, 152, 156

Padua, 434
Palamida, Pero Stankov, 126
Pamuk, Muyaga, 446
Pančevo, 40
Paradise Lost (Milton), 266–67
Paris, 149, 218
Pašić, Nikola, 26, 406
Paštrovići, the, 54, 125, 163, 166
Paštrovići Hill, 157, 167
Paton, A. A., 16, 449
Pavičević, Josif, Archimandrite of Ostrog, 66, 67, 68, 71, 144
Pavičević, Vuko, 303
Pavlović, Milvoje, 323, 340, 363
Pavlović, Perko, 256
Pejović, Andrija, Serdar of the Cuce, 6, 96, 125, 176, 439, 444, 466
Pelevići, the, 312
Perast, 146n
Perkov, Petar, 466
Perkov, Senator Stevan (Zvizdo), 67, 82, 158, 177, 181, 192, 241, 247, 259, 391, 466
Perović-Cuco, Stevan, 238, 434, 466
Pešter, 70
Petar (I), Bishop (uncle of Njegoš), 7, 10, 16, 26, 36, 42, 45, 54, 66, 67, 72, 73, 75, 77, 89, 93, 97, 107, 111, 112, 172, 177, 216, 224, 311, 316, 367, 379; administration of Bay of Kotor by, 52; and border question, 164, 165; and the Turkish renegades, 223; as an old man, 58–59, 92; as orator, 59, 60; as a teacher, 132; as writer, 59–60, 61; as a young monk, 374; attempts to unify Montenegro, 57–58; battles of, 110; builds mill in Cetinje, 124; character of, 38, 49, 51; death of, 62–64, 71, 74, 249, 258–59; declaration against, 147; difficulties of, with pretenders, 374; driven from the Littoral, 30; emergence of Montenegro under, 53; encyclicals of, 79–80; establishment of court and law by, 57; failure of, to take Onogšt-Nikšić, 96; influence of, on Njegoš, 49n; in Njegoš's *Stephen the Small,* 380, 381, 382; letter of, to the Bjelopavlići, 60–61; library of, 44; poverty of, 17; relations of, with Austria, 56–57; relations of, with Russia, 87, 146–47; relations of, with Sarajlija, 39; reunification under, 78–79; rule of, 254; sainthood of, 27, 28, 127, 139–40, 209; *Short History of Montenegro,* 12; stays at Majine, 163; struggle of, against the Turks, 30–31; successor of, 32–33, 63–68; testament of, 85; troubles of, with Russia, 146–47; work of, 55–56, 57–58
Petar (II), Bishop, *see* Njegoš
Petar of Ravni Laz, 223
Peter the Great, Tsar, 9, 53, 87, 123, 145, 146, 148
Peter III, Tsar, 375
Petronijević, Brana, 291
Petrović, Djuro, Serdar of Njeguši, 125
Petrović, Rastko, 365
Petrović, Svetislav, 33
Petrović dynasty, 421
Petrović Njegoš, Danilo, *see* Danilo, Prince
Petrović Njegoš, Djordjije Savov (cousin of Njegoš), *see* Djordjije
Petrović Njegoš, Serdar Ivan, 73
Petrović Njegoš, Joko ("Piljo") (brother of Njegoš), 6, 24, 142, 186
Petrović Njegoš, Marija (sister of Njegoš), 6, 24
Petrović Njegoš, Vojvoda Mirko, 205
Petrović Njegoš, Nikola, *see* Nikola, Prince
Petrović Njegoš, Pavle (nephew of Njegoš), 128
Petrović Njegoš, Pero (Petar) Tomov (brother of Njegoš), 6, 17, 24, 109,

124, 128, 141, 142, 157, 177, 223–25, 258, 430, 445, 446, 456, 457, 459, 462, 463, 464, 465
Petrović Njegoš, Radivoje (Bishop Rade), *see* Njegoš
Petrović Njegoš, Savo Markov (uncle of Njegoš), 17, 63
Petrović Njegoš, Stana (sister of Njegoš), 6
Petrović Njegoš, Stanko Stijepov (cousin of Njegoš), 39, 65, 67, 68, 70, 74, 80, 142, 151, 177, 215, 216, 432, 456
Petrović Njegoš, Stevan, 142
Petrović Njegoš, Stijepo (uncle of Njegoš), 17
Petrović Njegoš, Tomo Markov (father of Njegoš), 5, 6, 17, 24, 459, 462, 465–66
Petrovići, the, 8, 17, 22–26, 29, 31, 37, 50, 59, 62–64, 66, 67, 70–75, 80–86, 88, 89, 103, 104, 141–44, 147, 151, 166, 176, 177, 220, 224, 225, 237, 239, 240, 243, 244, 251, 255, 315, 380, 381, 463; origin of name, 9
Piedmont, 9, 253
Pijulija, Ibro, 192
Piletić, Jole, 203, 256
Piletići, the, 223
Piper, Radovan Mrčarica, 152–53, 173, 189, 466
Piperi, the, 15, 55, 152, 219, 222, 223, 227; rebellion of, 226–28, 251
Piva Monastery, 252
Pivljanin, Hajduk Bajo, 362
Piyuliya, Kavas, 446
Plamenac, Arsenije, 51
Plamenac, Father Ilija, 225
Plamenac, Father Jovo, 214, 224
Plamenac, Markiša, Captain of the Guard, 222, 224, 225, 226, 228
Plamenac, Sava, 224
Plamenac brotherhood, 224–25, 226
Plato, 269–70, 271, 283, 284
Plav, Beys of, 68
Plevlje (Taslica), 175
Plovdiv, 188
Podgorica, 97, 99, 136, 137, 185, 194, 215–16, 227, 467; Battle of, 94–97, 98
Podgoričanin, Ivan, 87
Poems (Radičević), 454
Poland, 145, 217, 218, 424; insurrection (1830) in, 115
Police, *see* Guard
Pompeii, 440
Pope Pius II, 222
Popov, Aleksandr N., 18, 18n, 90, 147, 186
Popov, Vukić, Vojvoda of the Kuči, 215–16
Popović, Father Jakov, 258
Popović, Pavle, 120, 314, 323, 360
Popović, Petar I., 73
Potëmkin, Prince, 146
Prague, 40
Prčanj, 36, 130, 403, 429, 430
Prekljesh, Mark, 453
Presjeci, village of, 34
Pride of the Montenegrins (Sarajlija), 314
Pripet River, 318
Prizren, 74, 410, 420
Prizren (Ban), 423
Prodanović, Jaša, 266
Proroković, Ivana (mother of Njegoš), 6, 24, 462, 465
Proroković, Lazo, Captain of Njeguši (uncle of Njegoš), 24–25, 209, 400, 402, 454
Prorokovići, the, 25, 71
Proverbs (Karadžić), 131
Prvulović, 296
Pskov, 149, 150, 151
Pucić, Medo, 419, 419n
Pushkin, Aleksander, 53, 115, 157

Rade, Bishop (Vladika), *see* Njegoš
Radičević, Branko, 307, 447, 454, 464
Radjevina, 94
Radimir, Captain Anton, 125
Radonjić, Djordje (Djuzo), 81, 83, 112, 117
Radonjić, Joko, 73
Radonjić, Governor Jovan, 72–73
Radonjić, Marko, 84, 144
Radonjić, Governor Vuko, 71, 73, 74, 80–84
Radonjići, the, 8, 9, 22, 63, 64, 67, 72, 73, 80, 81–86, 89, 141, 217
Radonjići-Guvernadurovići, 67
Radović, Blažo, 229
Radović, Ivo, 187
Radović, Vojvoda Mino, 138
Radivoje, Andrija, 125
Raičev, Vujo, 251
Rajačić, Bishop, 118
Rajić, Prince Mirčeta, 8, 69, 80
Rajičevići, the, 8
Rakeyev, 134
Rakić, Mita, 33
Raška, 68, 74, 251

Ravni Laz, 223
Ray of the Microcosm, The (Njegoš), 42, 47, 101, 121, 128–30, 228, 260, 346, 349, 369, 373, 378, 382, 384, 386, 396, 432, 451, 467; analysis of, 261–309; form of, 332; motifs in, 266–309, 324; poetic language in, 305–09; verse form of, 307
Rebellion Against the Dahis (Višnjić), 316–17
Rešetar, Milan, 168, 266, 310, 371
Rešetar (Reszetar), Paolo, 168, 453, 454, 457, 458
Reshid Pasha, Grand Vizir, 93–98, 103
Resulbegović, Hasan Beg, Kadi of Mostar, 101, 175, 176, 181, 187, 190, 191, 446
Reutz, Professor Alexander, 103
Revolution of 1848, 4n, 5n, 397–426
Ribnica River, 95
Rifat, 101
Rijeka, 6, 10, 67, 97, 141, 321; Serdar of, *see* Djurašković, Filip Nikolin
Risan, 159, 329, 406
"Rising Spark, The," *see Mountain Wreath, The*
Ristić, Jovan, 420, 420n
Rizvanbegović, Ali Pasha (Stočević), Vizir of Mostar (Hercegovina), 101–02, 105, 136, 138, 142, 143, 169–75, 180, 181, 184–93, 197, 198, 200, 204, 231, 245, 246, 248, 445, 446
Rizvanbegovići, the, 102
Rogan, Knez (character in *The Mountain Wreath*), 315, 326
Rome, 236, 437, 440, 441, 442
Rovčani, the, 138
Rovin, 158, 232, 351
Rovinsky, Pavel Apolonovich, 52, 72, 75, 81, 82, 89, 107, 141, 147, 152, 171, 202, 250
Rožanstvo, 39
Rucović, 82
Ruma, 104
Russia, 17, 40, 50, 63, 65, 81, 83, 88, 89, 92, 109, 111, 112, 117, 133, 138, 217, 252, 456; aid from, to Montenegro, 85, 86–87, 145–48, 224, 247, 248, 249, 251–52, 425; as protector of Serbs, 424; complaints to, against Njegoš, 141, 143–44; feudal government in, 160; influence of, in the Balkans, 150; interest of, in Montenegro, 53; migration to, 75; military successes of, in Europe, 420; Montenegrin children sent for schooling to, 32, 128, 132; relations of, with Montenegro, 56, 57, 74, 95, 103, 106–07, 108, 113, 126–27, 136, 137, 142, 162–64, 181–82, 192, 196, 253, 256–58, 259, 400; relations of, with Turkey, 93, 97–98, 102, 103. *See also* Njegoš, relations with and travels to
Rustem Beg, 176, 180–81
Ruvarac, Ilarion, 7–8, 255, 310, 311, 316
Ruža, wife of Kasan (character in *The Mountain Wreath*), 338, 356

St. Alexander Nevsky, Monastery of, 113–14
St. Ambrose, 280
St. Petar, *see* Petar, Bishop
St. Peter's (Rome), 440
St. Petersburg, 41, 74, 84, 103, 104, 113, 114–15, 123, 127, 128, 131, 145, 146n, 149, 151, 163, 220, 224, 225, 412, 417, 464
St. Sava, *see* Sava, Bishop
St. Vasilije of Ostrog, 27
Salkovina, 157, 315
Sarajevo, 39, 40, 100, 101, 188, 445
Sarajlija, Sima (Milutinović-), 6, 7, 33, 37, 38–44, 58, 65, 68, 70, 74, 85–86, 110, 131, 217, 249, 266, 270–71, 297, 306, 311, 314, 316, 323–24, 330, 332, 410
Sava, Bishop (Saint), 9, 20, 36, 50, 51, 59, 73, 146, 163, 318, 374, 380, 381, 385
Sava River, 101
Savina Monastery, 34, 118
Schmaus, Alois, 267, 268, 271, 293
Scutari, 53, 97, 101, 169, 170, 173, 194, 196, 198, 199, 213, 223, 225–28, 238, 251, 327; Vizirs of, 69, 70, 77, 127, 136–38, 169, 205, 223, 225–27, 251, 314, 380. *See also* Bushati, Kara-Mahmud Pasha; Bushati, Mustafa Pasha; Hafis Pasha; Skopljak, Osman Pasha
Scutari, Lake, 193, 231, 247
Šehović Pasha, 215
Sekulić, Isidora, 34, 48, 49, 120, 121, 241, 259, 267, 273, 291, 323, 329, 333, 335, 370, 373, 431
Selim Bey, 185
Senate, 16, 88–89, 90–91, 93, 95, 98, 108, 117, 125, 151, 156, 203, 210, 223, 232, 464; Clerk of, 223; salaries of Senators, 161

Sentić, Petar, 110
Serbia, 9, 11, 15, 19, 36, 39, 57, 68, 70, 94, 145, 175, 192, 217, 252, 411; and Turkey, 316; and unification of Triune Kingdom, 406; attempt to re-establish, 78; campaign of liberation in, 415; class differentiation in, 78; coalition of, with Montenegro projected, 51; creation of state of, 318; destiny of, 238, 255, 258, 263, 271, 280, 294–95, 297, 313, 317, 324, 333, 335, 338, 339, 341, 342, 348, 378, 384, 395, 396, 416, 417, 418, 422; development of parliament in, 161; distinction between Montenegro and, 420–21; distinction between Serbs and Croats, 423; empire of, 38, 98, 102, 245, 374, 376, 420; expansion of, 94; freedom of, 25; history of, 19n, 231; insurrections in, 21, 39, 40, 104, 132, 198, 207–08, 314, 338, 406, 409, 410, 412, 413, 438; internal autonomy of, 407; language of, 44–45, 334; lords of, 79; migration to, 75; pacification of, 102; people of, 310, 372, 399, 405; policy of, 419; religion of, 20, 76; resistance in, 56; restlessness of Christians in, 54; role of, 253; statehood of, 369; strength of, 195; ties of, with Montenegro, 257; turning point in history of, 377; unification, 256, 398, 405, 421–26
Serbian Maid, The (Sarajlija), 40, 340
Shaban Aga, 69
Shakespeare, William, 270, 340–42
Shqipetar tribes, 77
Short History of Montenegro (Bishop Petar), 12
Siberia, 146
Sima, *see* Sarajlija, Sima
Siniša (character in *The Mountain Wreath*), 362
Sirović, Serdar, 119
Sister, cult of, 240–41, 357–61. *See also* Montenegro, women in
Sjenica, 251
Skender Aga (character in *The Mountain Wreath*), 326, 355
Skender Beg, 446
Skerlić, Jovan, 266, 323
Škoda, Joseph, 447, 448
Skopljak, Osman Pasha, Vizir of Scutari, 101, 102, 169, 170, 175, 193–201, 220, 221, 228, 236, 328, 426
Skoplje, 101
Slavonia, 402
Slavs, 145, 147, 402; Pan-Slavism, 424; South, 8, 111, 118, 145, 398, 404, 405, 406, 415, 418, 423, 424, 425
Slijepčević, Pero, 274, 323, 327, 329
Smaïl Aga, *see* Čengić, Smaïl Aga
Šobajić, Maksim, 221
Šoć, Pero, 338
Sofrić, 267
Sommièrse, Colonel L. O. Vialla de, 52–53
Špilja, 125
Spinoza, Baruch, 293
Split, 206, 449
Spuž, 96, 97, 136, 137
Srbski narodni list (Serbian National Journal), 271
Srdanović, Djuko, 140, 353, 354, 439, 444–45
Srdić, Djordje, Clerk of the Senate, 223
Srpske Novine (Serbian News), 463
Stadion, Count Franz, 402n
Stalin, Josef, 421
Stana (character in *The Mountain Wreath*), 358
Stanjevići, 105; Monastery of, 32, 36, 163–66
Stanjevići, the, 152
Stanojević, Marija, 17
Starčević, 100
Stefan, Abbot (character in *The Mountain Wreath*), 321, 325, 342, 344, 346–50, 363, 369, 384, 389–90
Stephen the Small, 22, 37, 50–51, 73, 86, 374, 375–78
Stephen the Small (Njegoš), *see False Tsar Stephen the Small, The*
Stevo, Father, 191
Stijepov, Mitar, 32
Stijepov, Stanko, *see* Petrović Njegoš, Stanko Stijepov
Štirovnik, 451
Stočević, Ali Pasha, *see* Rizvanbegović, Ali Pasha
Stojadinović, Milica, 242, 447
Stojanović, Dušan, 266
Stojković, Milenko, 104
Stolac, 102, 181, 191, 446
Stratimirović, Djordje, 229, 243, 435, 448, 450
Strugar, 226
Subotić, Jovan, 271, 464
Suleiman Pasha, 102, 198
Šumadija, 9

Šumadinac, *see* Makarije, 180
Šuvalija, Pasha, 394

Tablja, 157, 174, 180, 234, 245
Tale of the Host of Igor, 46, 318
Tanzimat, the, 92
Taslica (Plevlje), 175, 177, 180
Tatishchev, Dimitri Pavlovich, 97, 171
Tatz, General, 82, 83
Taxation, 91, 134–35, 141, 144, 211, 247–48
Tennyson, Alfred Lord, 53
Teodosije, Prior (character in *Stephen the Small*), 232, 378
Thought (Njegoš), 127, 130, 301, 307
Tkalac, Imbro, *see* Ignjatijević-Tkalac, Imbro
Tolicin, 152
Tomanović, Lazar, 82, 190, 191, 226, 250
Tomanović, Vuk, 351–52
Tomašević, King Stevan, 222
Tomić, Jovan, 22, 379
Tominz, Giuseppe, 150
Tommaseo, Niccolò, 379, 401, 411
Tomo of Zeta, 214
Topla, 33, 34
Toroman brothers, 217
Tower of the Djurišići, The (Njegoš), 66, 130, 228, 331, 382
Travnik, Vizir of, 101. *See also* Djelal-ud-Din Pasha; Vegi Mehmed Pasha
Trebinje, 142, 175, 446
Trieste, 40, 104, 109, 150, 151, 153, 196, 236, 243, 416, 418, 424, 430, 434, 436, 437, 450, 453
Triune Kingdom of Croatia, Slavonia, and Dalmatia, 402, 403, 419
Trojica, 400
Tropović, Josif, 33, 34, 37
Turin, 437
Turkey, 76, 87, 111, 147, 217, 264; alliance of, with Montenegrin clans, 220–27; and feudal system, 312; as rulers of Serbia, 218; border question of, 163, 188–89; dissolution of empire, 92; rebellions in, 374, 409, 410, 415; reforms of, in Bosnia, 445; relations of, with Hungary, 414; relations of, with Montenegro, 126, 130–31, 136, 168–82, 184, 244, 379, 406; relations of, with Russia, 93, 97–98, 102, 103; struggle against, 9–11, 12n, 14n, 15, 19, 20–23, 25, 28–30, 33, 38, 39, 43, 50, 53–56, 60–61, 66, 68–70, 75, 77–79, 86, 92–99, 110, 111, 122, 126, 133–39, 142–43, 153, 159–60, 164, 193–204, 207, 209, 213, 214–16, 225–26, 247, 250, 252, 253, 256, 263, 274, 276, 310, 311–21, 350, 370, 375, 377, 398, 399, 405, 406, 422, 423, 466
Turkish renegades, 291, 310, 312–16, 326–27, 337, 345, 346, 350, 354, 355–56, 362, 366, 388, 446. *See also* Moslems
Tušina, 178

Uhland, Johann Ludwig, 43
Una River, 92
United States, 425
Uskoks, the, 138, 170, 171–72, 178, 179, 188
Užice, 15, 39, 175

Vandervelde, Émile, 16, 16n
Vardar River, 92
Vasilije, Bishop, 8, 22, 38, 50, 59, 132, 146, 311
Vasilije of Ostrog, Saint, 27
Vasojević, Prince Nikola (Knez Nikola Consul), 216–18, 237, 371
Vasojevići, the, 68, 69, 70, 215, 217, 218, 311
Vegi Mehmed Pasha, Vizir of Travnik, 173
Velikie Luki, 149, 151
Velimirović, Bishop Nikolaj, 266, 281, 289–90
Velje Guvno, 65, 66
Veljko, Hajduk, 21
Venice, 10–11, 14, 19, 21–22, 50, 52, 53, 72, 103, 105, 111, 145–47, 163, 164, 196, 201, 225, 251, 311, 318, 353–54, 375, 379, 397, 401, 411, 423, 437, 442
Vesuvius, 443
Vialla de Sommièrse, Colonel L. O., *see* Sommièrse, Colonel L. O. Vialla de
Vidajić, Pasha of Zvornik, 94, 200
Vidin, 40
Vienna, 40, 46, 73, 104, 108, 109, 112, 123, 144, 145, 146n, 159, 162, 170, 171, 196, 201, 220, 222, 224, 235, 242, 243, 397, 401, 411, 412, 417, 436, 437, 447, 448, 449, 450, 464
Vinicka, 70
Virpazar, 226
Višnjić, Filip, 160, 316–17
Vissarion, Bishop, *see* Bajica, Bishop Vissarion

Vizirov Most, 95
Vizirs: Grand Vizir, *see* Reshid Pasha; Kiuprili, 146; of Bosnia, *see* Omer Pasha Latas; of Hercegovina, *see* Rizvanbegović, Ali Pasha (Stočević); of Mostar, *see* Rizvanbegović, Ali Pasha; of Scutari, 69, 70, 77, 127, 136–38, 169, 205, 223, 225, 226, 227, 251, 314, 380; *see also* Bushati, Kara-Mahmud Pasha; Bushati, Mustafa Pasha; Hafis Pasha; Skopljak, Osman Pasha; of Travnik, 100; *see also* Djelal-ud-Din Pasha; Vegi Mehmed Pasha; Skender Aga (character in *The Mountain Wreath*), 355
Vlačić, Ljubomir, 34
Vladisavljević, Dimitrije, 437
Voice from the Rocky Crag, A (Njegoš), 110
Vojvodina, 91, 112n, 374, 409, 416, 419, 420, 443, 447
Vranjina, 74, 193, 194, 196, 220, 226, 238, 250
Vraz, Stanko, 6, 6n, 417
Vrčević, Vuk, 27, 34, 82, 142, 163, 177, 187, 190, 192, 249
Vrhovac, Radivoje, 267
Vučićević, Matija, 4, 74, 75, 87
Vujić, Count, 374
Vukale, Serdar (character in *Stephen the Small*), 376
Vukalo (Njegoš's bodyguard), 439, 444
Vukčevići, the, 209
Vukota, Serdar (character in *The Mountain Wreath*), 295, 326
Vukotić, Vojvoda Bogdan, 73
Vukotić, Ivan Ivanović, 6, 87–89, 90, 91, 93, 95, 96, 97, 103, 108, 117–18, 124
Vukotići, the, 67
Vukov, Bogdan, 56
Vukov, Vojvoda Miljan, 215, 300, 311, 466
Vuković, Filip, 187
Vuksan, Dušan, 6, 89, 97, 129, 248, 314, 315, 441
Vuk the Robber, 76
Vulović, Svetislav, 250, 250n, 266, 322, 323
Vušović, Danilo, 333

War of 1875–78, 12n, 183, 204, 205, 245, 254
Warsaw, 152
Weber, Governor General von, 467
Who Is That on Yon High Mountain? (Njegoš), 129
Wilkinson, John Gardner, 190, 191, 199, 229, 245
Windisch-Graetz, Prince Alfred Candidus Ferdinand zu, 20, 414
World War I, *see* First World War

Yugoslavia, federation of, originated by Njegoš, 423; first use of word, 423; unification of, 402–26

Žabljak, 96, 137, 193, 467
Zadar archives, 240, 243
Zagarač, 217
Zagorje, Bey of, 446
Zagreb, 397, 402, 403, 404, 409, 423, 463
Zalaz, village of, 400
Zalažani, the, 125
Zara, 47, 82, 224, 401, 450, 457, 463
Zarathustra, 269
Zečević, Prior Mojsije, 68–70, 93–95, 181, 216, 217, 391
Zemun, 40, 104, 338
Zeta, 18, 87, 94, 95, 97, 102, 148, 214, 255
Zeta, Plain of, 29, 145, 194
Zlatica River, 172
Zogović, Radovan, 323
Žom, Antid, *see* Jome, Antide
Zora Dalmatinska (The Dalmatian Dawn), 423
Župa, 138
Župljani, the, 138
Žutković, Grujo, 83
Zvornik, 189; Pasha of, 94

60865

PG
1418
.P4
Z59

Dilas, Milovan
Njegos: poet, prince, bishop

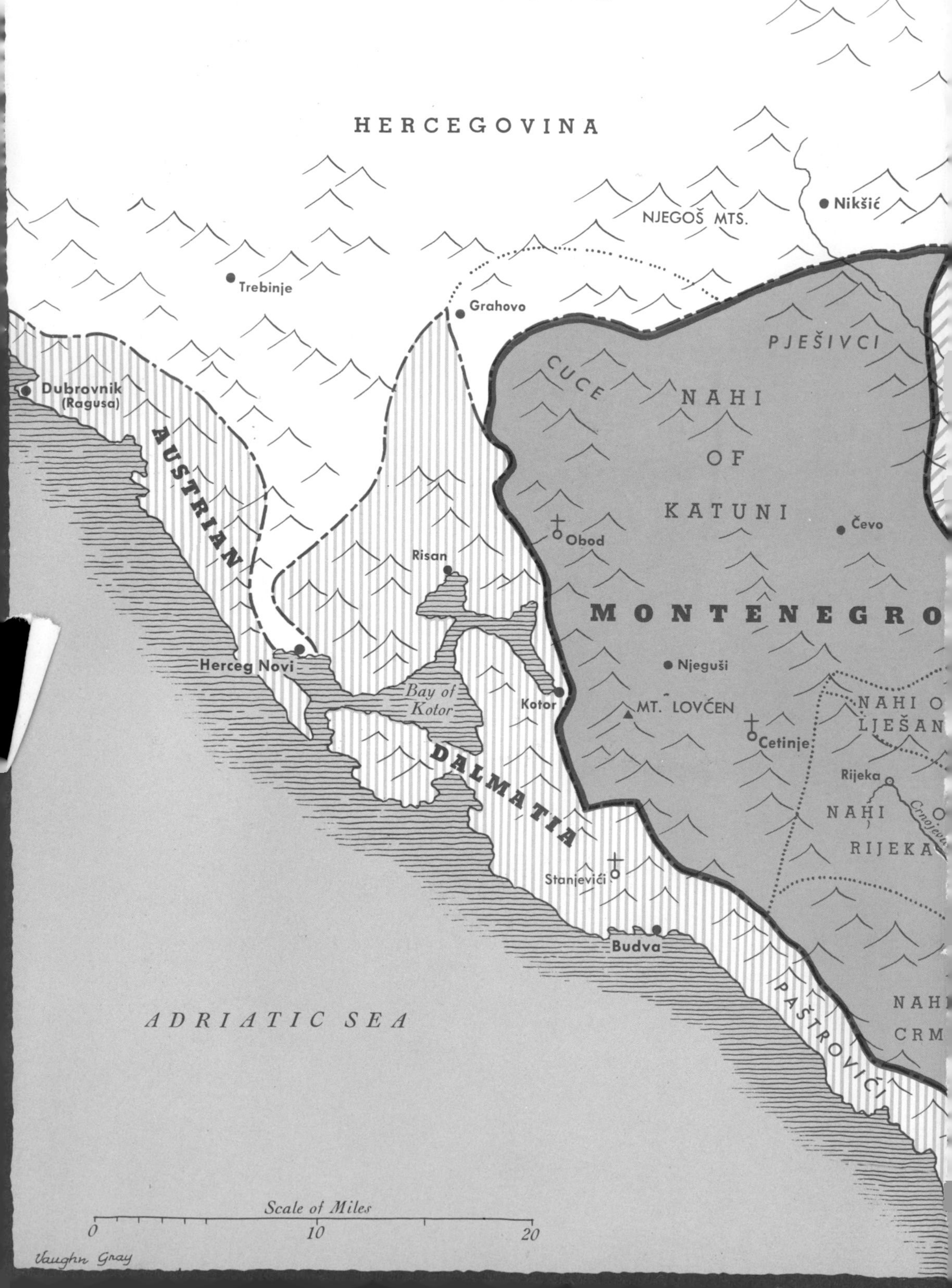
OTTOMAN EMPIRE
USKOCI
HERCEGOVINA
NJEGOŠ MTS.
Nikšić
Trebinje
Grahovo
PJEŠIVCI
CUCE
NAHI
OF
KATUNI
Dubrovnik
(Ragusa)
AUSTRIAN
Obod
Čevo
Risan
MONTENEGRO
Herceg Novi
Njeguši
Bay of
Kotor
Kotor
MT. LOVĆEN
NAHI O
LJEŠAN
Cetinje
DALMATIA
Rijeka
NAHI
RIJEKA
Stanjevići
Budva
PAŠTROVIĆI
NAH
CRM
ADRIATIC SEA
Scale of Miles
0
10
20
Vaughn Gray